JAM-PACKED FOXTROT

Other FoxTrot Books by Bill Amend

FoxTrot
Pass the Loot
Black Bart Says Draw
Eight Yards, Down and Out
Bury My Heart at Fun-Fun Mountain
Say Hello to Cactus Flats
May the Force Be with Us, Please
Take Us to Your Mall
The Return of the Lone Iguana
At Least This Place Sells T-shirts
Come Closer, Roger, There's a Mosquito on Your Nose
Welcome to Jasorassic Park
I'm Flying, Jack . . . I Mean, Roger
Think iFruity
Death by Field Trip
Encyclopedias Brown and White
His Code Name Was The Fox
Your Momma Thinks Square Roots Are Vegetables
Who's Up for Some Bonding?
Am I a Mutant, or What!
Orlando Bloom Has Ruined Everything
My Hot Dog Went Out, Can I Have Another?
How Come I'm Always Luigi?

Anthologies

FoxTrot: The Works
FoxTrot en masse
Enormously FoxTrot
Wildly FoxTrot
FoxTrot Beyond a Doubt
Camp FoxTrot
Assorted FoxTrot
FoxTrot: Assembled with Care
FoxTrotius Maximus

JAM-PACKED FOXTROT

by Bill Amend

**Andrews McMeel
Publishing, LLC**

Kansas City

FoxTrot is distributed internationally by Universal Press Syndicate.

Jam-Packed Foxtrot copyright © 2006 by Bill Amend. All rights reserved. Printed in the United States of America. No part of this book may be used or reproduced in any manner whatsoever without written permission except in the case of reprints in the context of reviews. For information, write Andrews McMeel Publishing, LLC, an Andrews McMeel Universal company, 4520 Main Street, Kansas City, Missouri 64111.

06 07 08 09 10 BAM 10 9 8 7 6 5 4 3 2 1

ISBN-13: 978-0-7407-6040-2
ISBN-10: 0-7407-6040-8

Library of Congress Control Number: 2006925698

www.andrewsmcmeel.com

www.foxtrot.com

─── **ATTENTION: SCHOOLS AND BUSINESSES** ───

Andrews McMeel books are available at quantity discounts with bulk purchase for educational, business, or sales promotional use. For information, please write to: Special Sales Department, Andrews McMeel Publishing, LLC, 4520 Main Street, Kansas City, Missouri 64111.

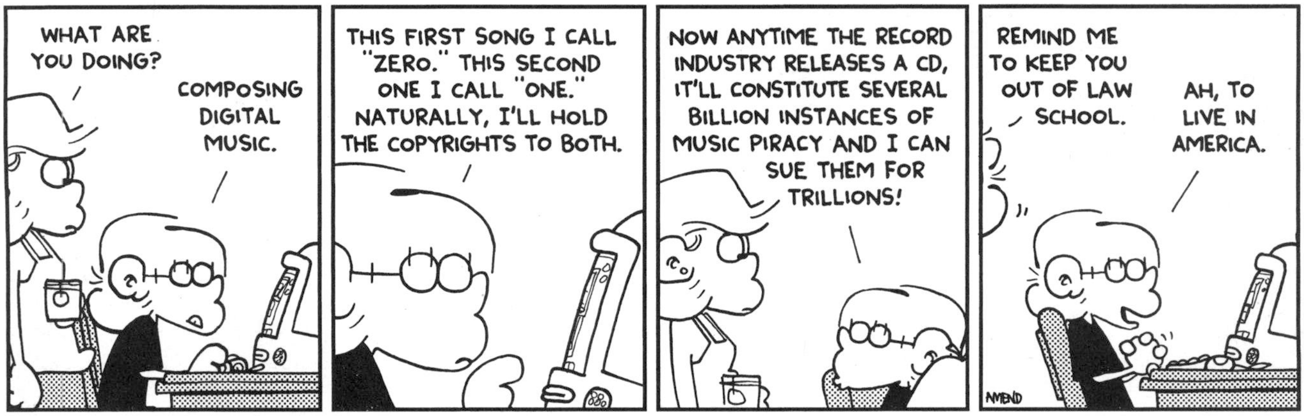
WHAT ARE YOU DOING?
COMPOSING DIGITAL MUSIC.
THIS FIRST SONG I CALL "ZERO." THIS SECOND ONE I CALL "ONE." NATURALLY, I'LL HOLD THE COPYRIGHTS TO BOTH.
NOW ANYTIME THE RECORD INDUSTRY RELEASES A CD, IT'LL CONSTITUTE SEVERAL BILLION INSTANCES OF MUSIC PIRACY AND I CAN SUE THEM FOR TRILLIONS!
REMIND ME TO KEEP YOU OUT OF LAW SCHOOL.
AH, TO LIVE IN AMERICA.

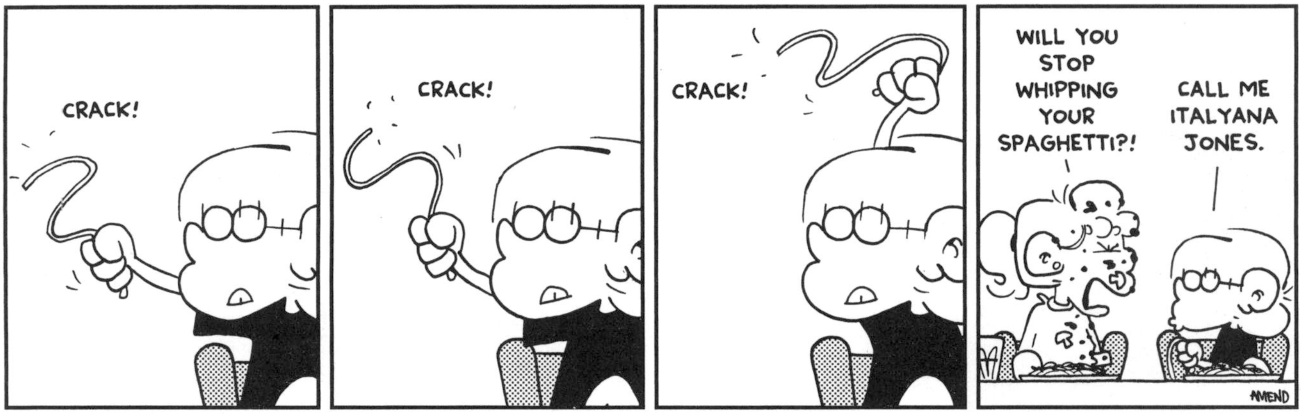
CRACK!
CRACK!
CRACK!
WILL YOU STOP WHIPPING YOUR SPAGHETTI?!
CALL ME ITALYANA JONES.

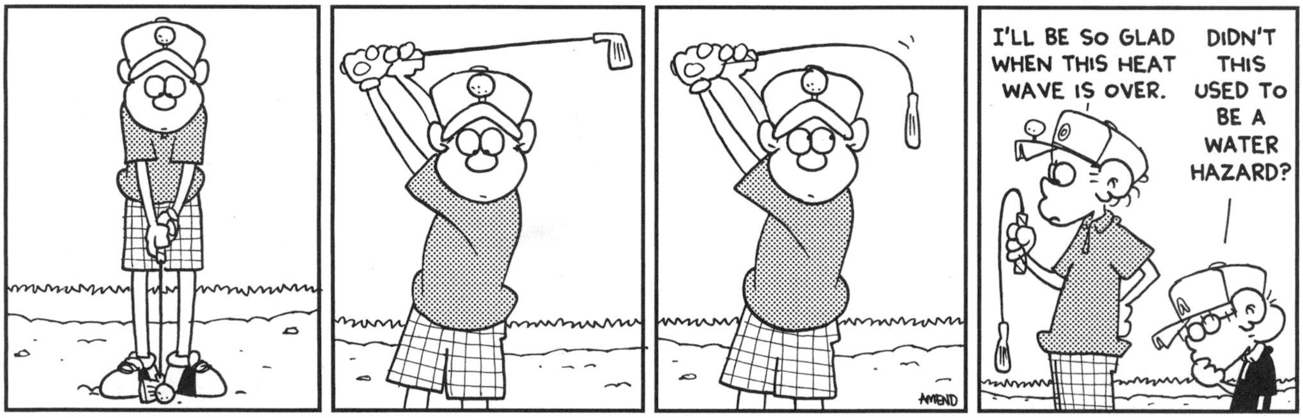
I'LL BE SO GLAD WHEN THIS HEAT WAVE IS OVER.
DIDN'T THIS USED TO BE A WATER HAZARD?

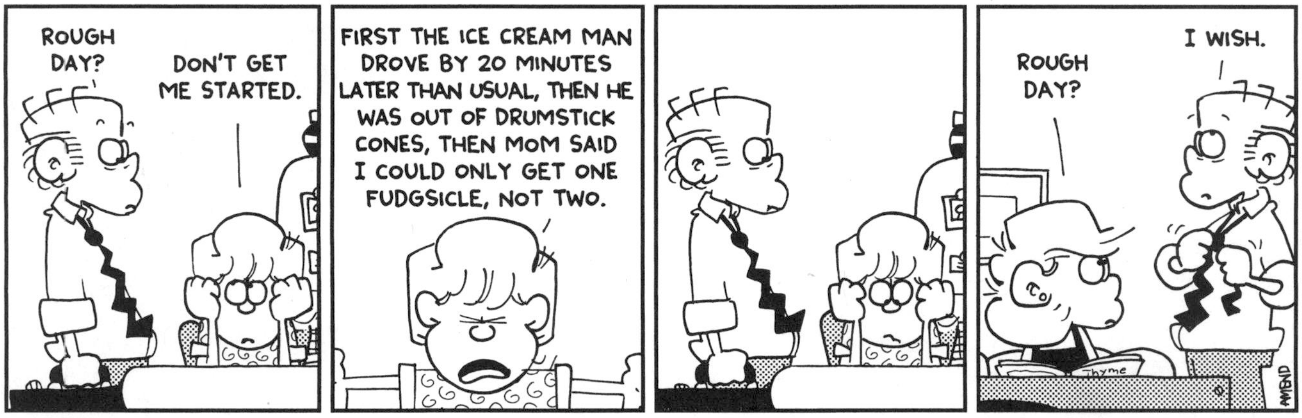
ROUGH DAY?
DON'T GET ME STARTED.
FIRST THE ICE CREAM MAN DROVE BY 20 MINUTES LATER THAN USUAL, THEN HE WAS OUT OF DRUMSTICK CONES, THEN MOM SAID I COULD ONLY GET ONE FUDGSICLE, NOT TWO.
ROUGH DAY?
I WISH.

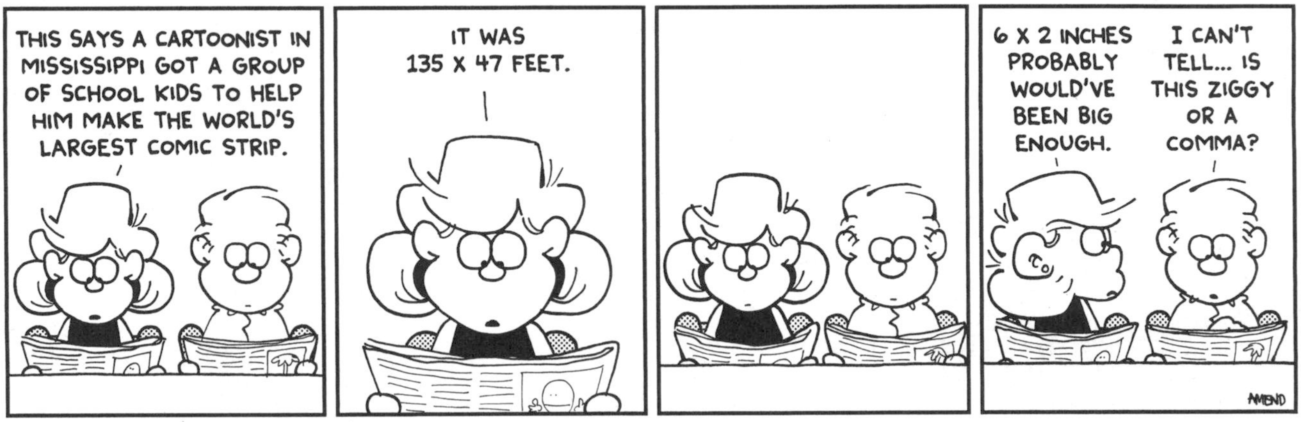
THIS SAYS A CARTOONIST IN MISSISSIPPI GOT A GROUP OF SCHOOL KIDS TO HELP HIM MAKE THE WORLD'S LARGEST COMIC STRIP.
IT WAS 135 X 47 FEET.
6 X 2 INCHES PROBABLY WOULD'VE BEEN BIG ENOUGH.
I CAN'T TELL... IS THIS ZIGGY OR A COMMA?
AMEND

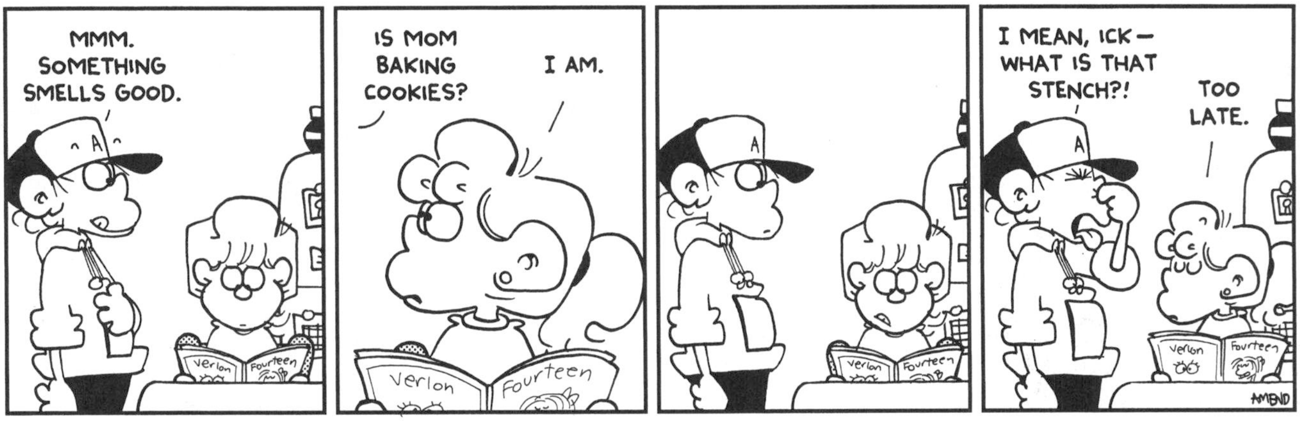
MMM. SOMETHING SMELLS GOOD.
IS MOM BAKING COOKIES?
I AM.
I MEAN, ICK— WHAT IS THAT STENCH?!
TOO LATE.
AMEND

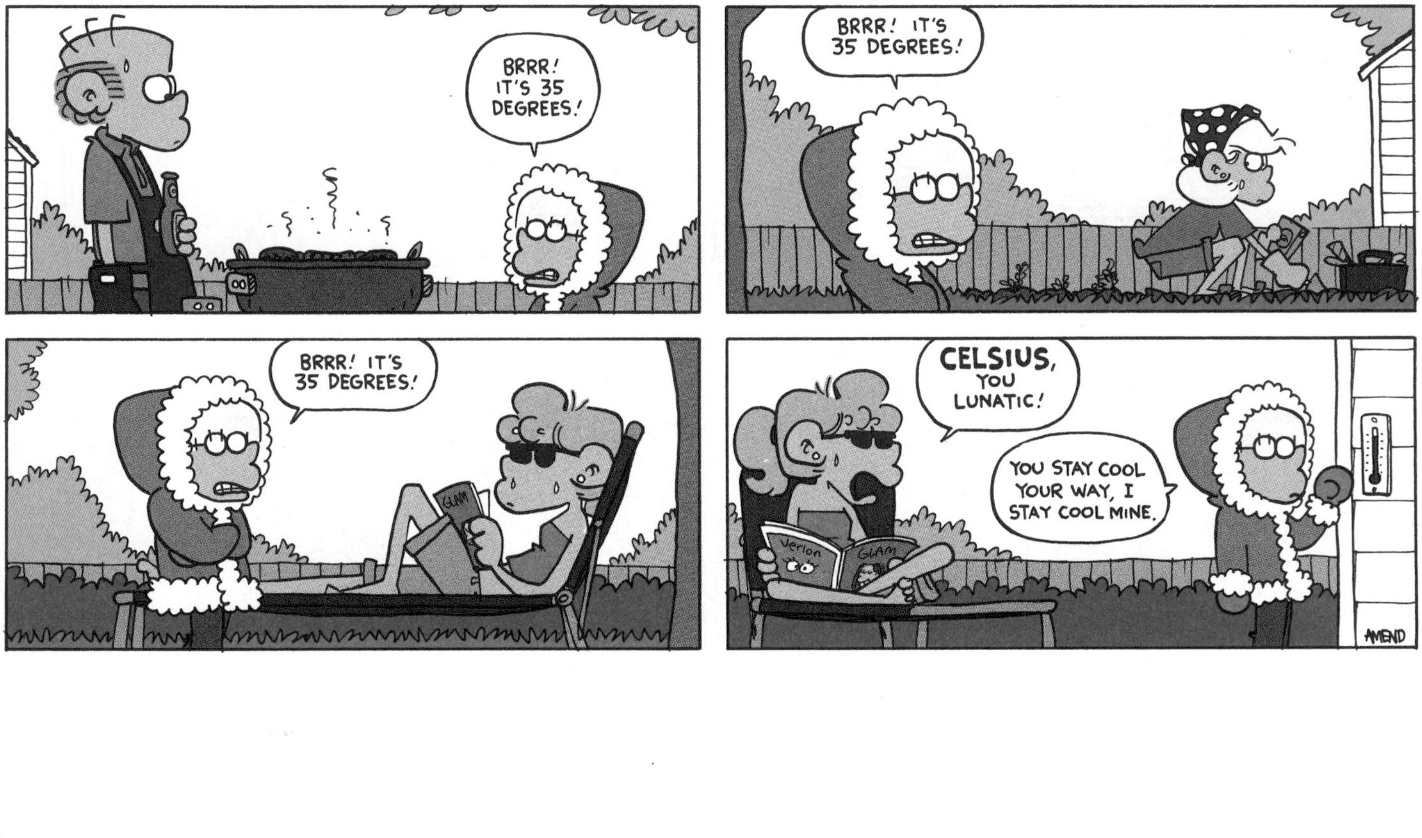
BRRR! IT'S 35 DEGREES!
BRRR! IT'S 35 DEGREES!
BRRR! IT'S 35 DEGREES!
CELSIUS, YOU LUNATIC!
YOU STAY COOL YOUR WAY, I STAY COOL MINE.
AMEND

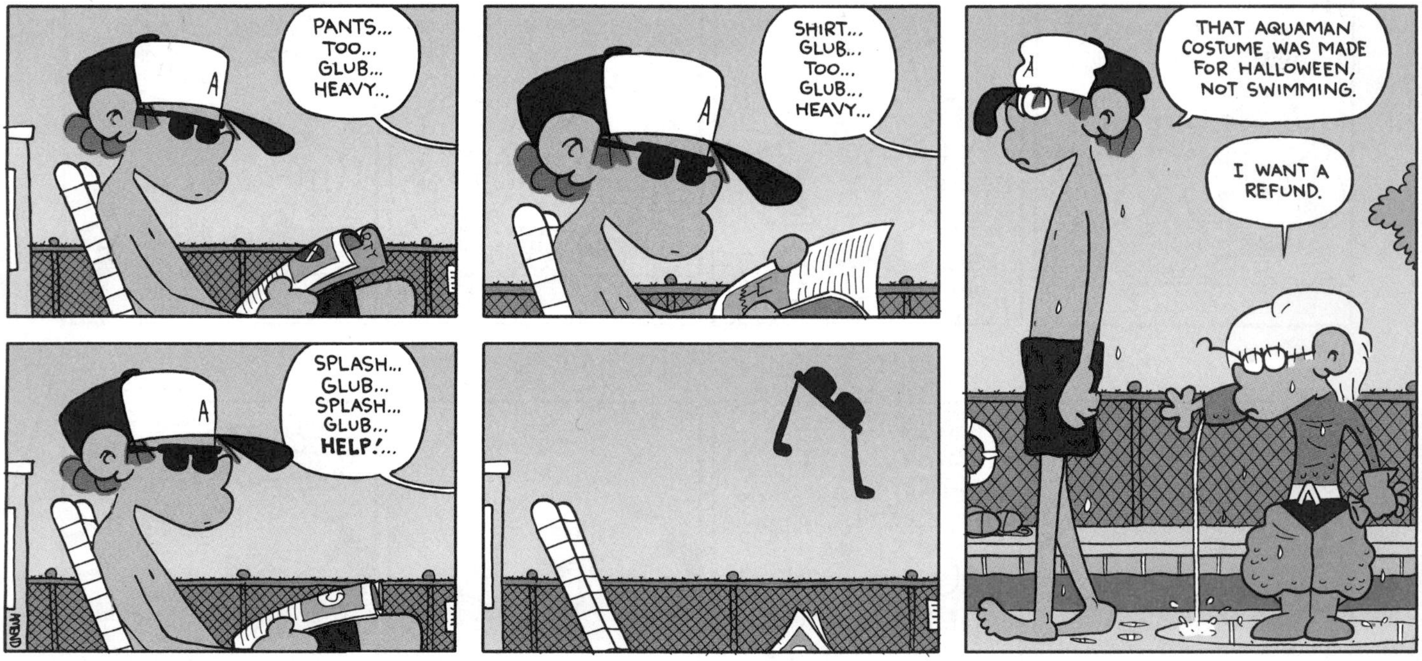
PANTS... TOO... GLUB... HEAVY...
SHIRT... GLUB... TOO... GLUB... HEAVY...
SPLASH... GLUB... SPLASH... GLUB... HELP!...
THAT AQUAMAN COSTUME WAS MADE FOR HALLOWEEN, NOT SWIMMING.
I WANT A REFUND.

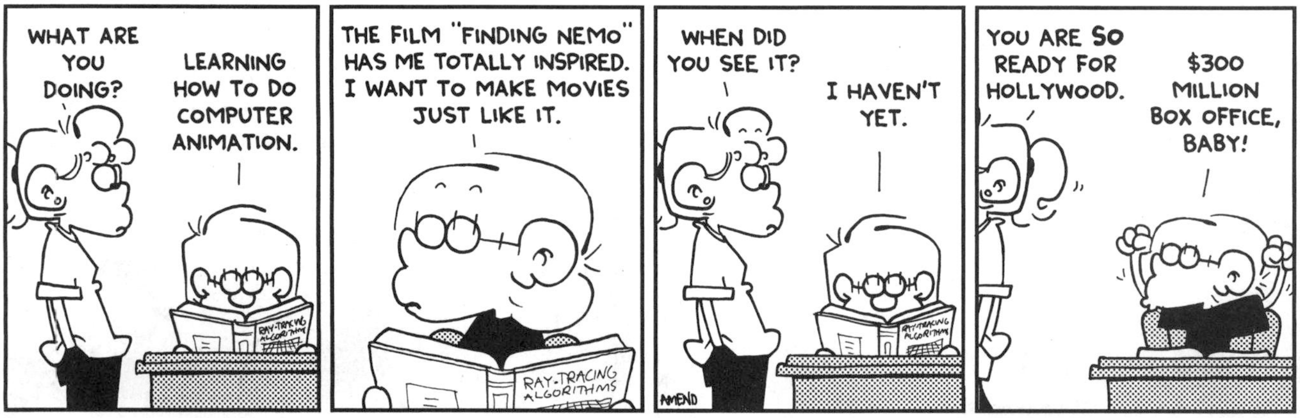
WHAT ARE YOU DOING?
LEARNING HOW TO DO COMPUTER ANIMATION.
RAY-TRACING ALGORITHMS
THE FILM "FINDING NEMO" HAS ME TOTALLY INSPIRED. I WANT TO MAKE MOVIES JUST LIKE IT.
RAY-TRACING ALGORITHMS
WHEN DID YOU SEE IT?
I HAVEN'T YET.
YOU ARE SO READY FOR HOLLYWOOD.
$300 MILLION BOX OFFICE, BABY!
AMEND

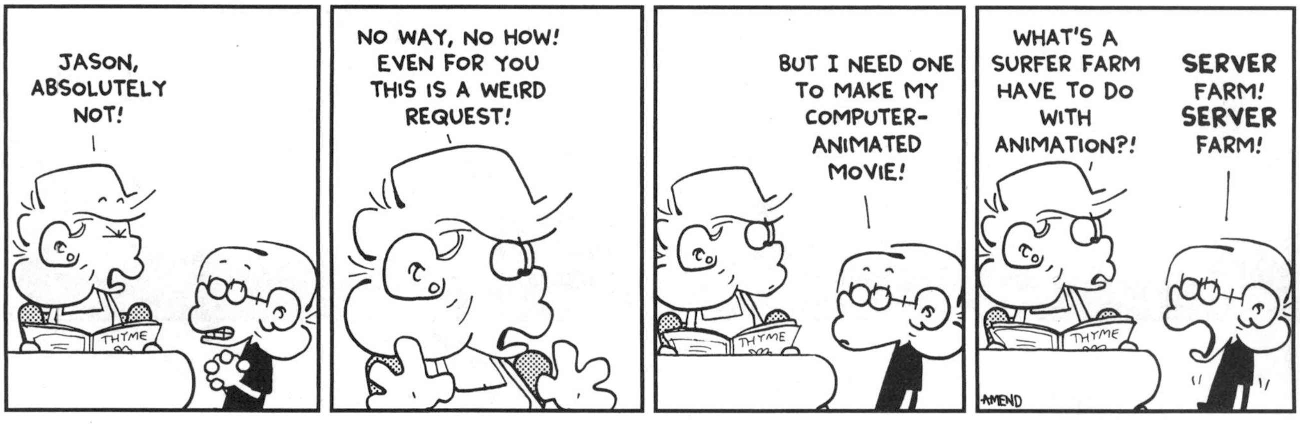
JASON, ABSOLUTELY NOT!
THYME
NO WAY, NO HOW! EVEN FOR YOU THIS IS A WEIRD REQUEST!
BUT I NEED ONE TO MAKE MY COMPUTER-ANIMATED MOVIE!
THYME
WHAT'S A SURFER FARM HAVE TO DO WITH ANIMATION?!
SERVER FARM! SERVER FARM!
THYME
AMEND

Panel 1:
I HEAR YOU'RE MAKING AN ANIMATED MOVIE.
YUP.

Panel 2:
IT'S THE TENDER STORY OF A LEECH'S SEARCH FOR HIS MISSING SON. I'M CALLING IT "FINDING HEMO."

Panel 3:
YOU CAN'T DO THAT! IT'S A TOTAL RIPOFF OF PIXAR!
SO?

Panel 4:
SO THAT'S DREAMWORKS' TURF.
GOOD POINT. I'D HATE TO MAKE THEM MAD.

Panel 5:
YOU'RE MAKING A MOVIE ABOUT LEECHES?! "FINDING HEMO." AND YOU KNOW WHAT'S THE BEST PART?

Panel 6:
IF A CRITIC SAYS IT SUCKS, PEOPLE WILL JUST ASSUME THEY ARE TALKING ABOUT MY ACCURATE PORTRAYAL OF THE LEAD CHARACTERS.
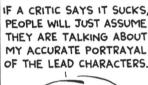

Panel 7:
AM I BRILLIANT, OR WHAT?

Panel 8:
I'LL GO WITH "WHAT."
I'VE ALSO GOT A SKUNK CAMEO, IN CASE THEY ALSO SAY IT STINKS.

Panel 9:
RENDERING ANIMATION... PLEASE WAIT...

Panel 10:
RENDERING ANIMATION... PLEASE WAIT...

Panel 11:
RENDERING ANIMATION... PLEASE WAIT...

Panel 12:
I SEE WHERE THEY GOT THE IDEA FOR "A BUG'S LIFE."
FRAME ONE COMPLETED.

Panel 13:
HOW GOES THE ANIMATION BUSINESS?
NOT SO GOOD. I'M THINKING OF THROWING IN THE TOWEL.

Panel 14:
I HAD NO IDEA PRODUCING A FAMILY-CLASSIC SUMMER BLOCKBUSTER TOOK SO MUCH WORK! STORYBOARDS! VOICES! RENDERING EVERY SINGLE FRAME! IF THIS IS WHAT IT TAKES TO MAKE $300 MILLION THESE DAYS, FORGET IT!

Panel 15:
JASON, YOU'VE BEEN AT IT FOR A DAY.
A DAY AND A HALF. DON'T REMIND ME.

Panel 16:
AH, GENERATION DOT-COM.
WHY, I REMEMBER WHEN A KID LIKE ME COULD MAKE A BILLION IN HIS SLEEP!

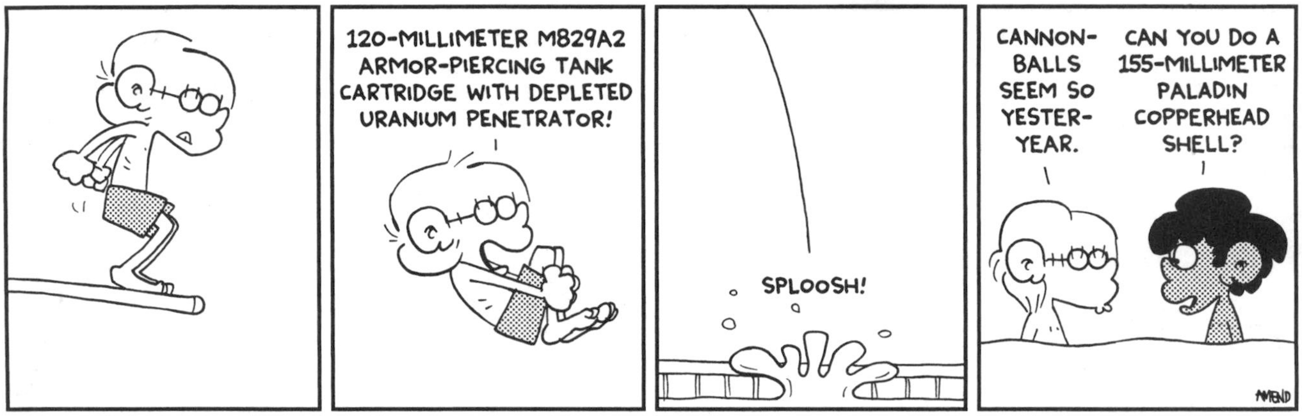
120-MILLIMETER M829A2 ARMOR-PIERCING TANK CARTRIDGE WITH DEPLETED URANIUM PENETRATOR!
SPLOOSH!
CANNON-BALLS SEEM SO YESTER-YEAR.
CAN YOU DO A 155-MILLIMETER PALADIN COPPERHEAD SHELL?
AMEND

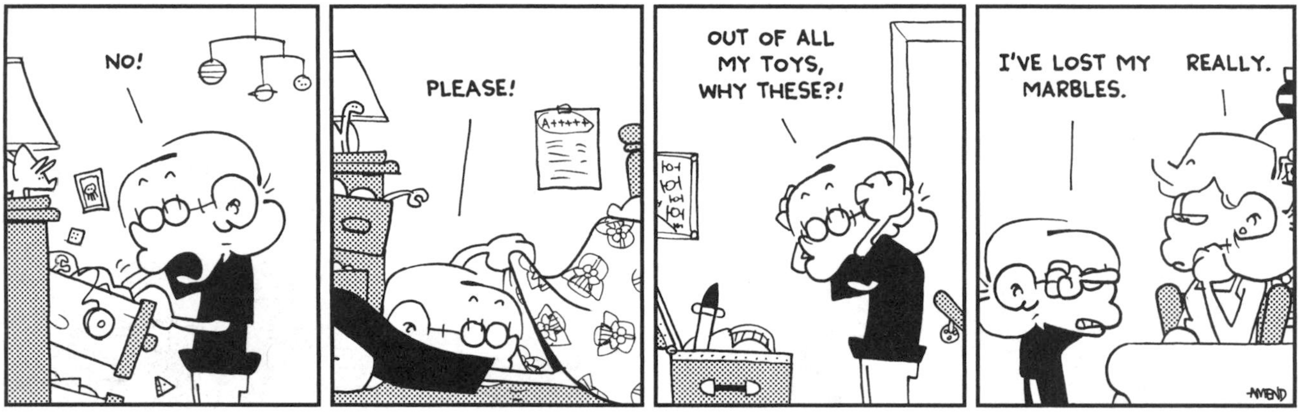
NO!
PLEASE!
OUT OF ALL MY TOYS, WHY THESE?!
I'VE LOST MY MARBLES.
REALLY.
AMEND

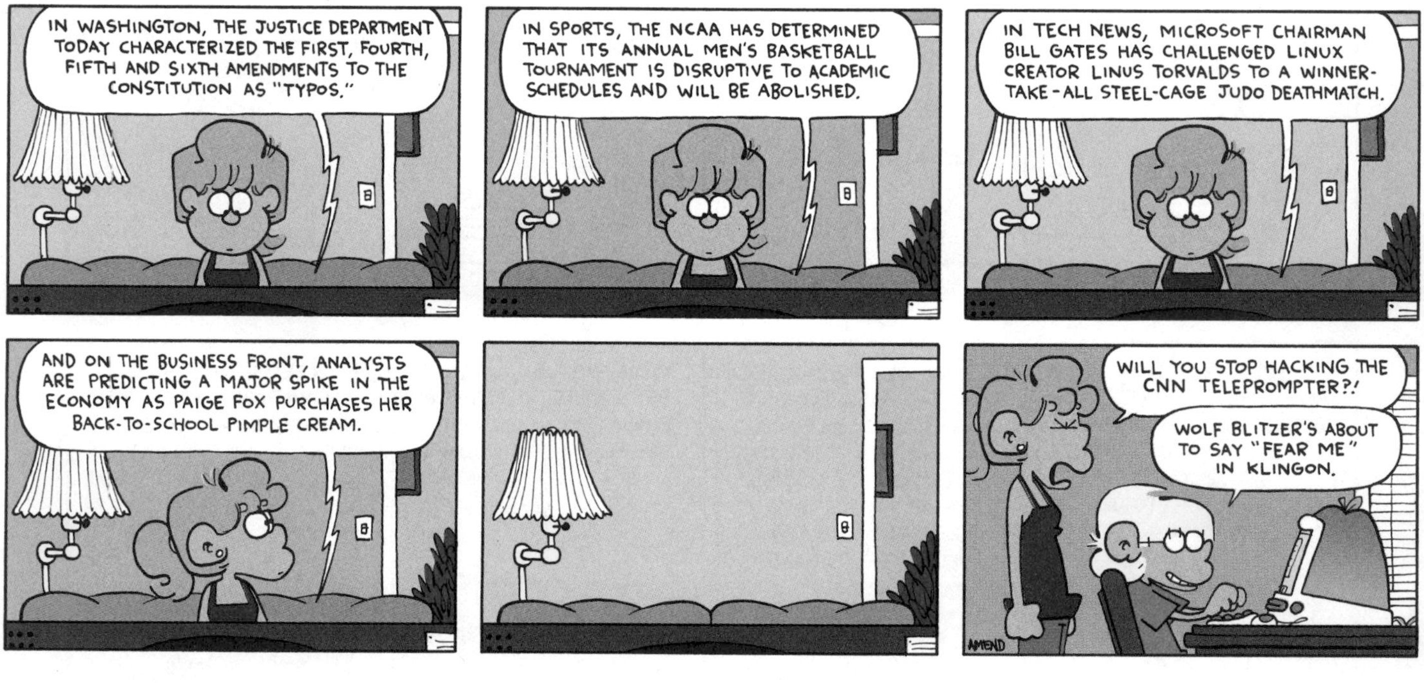
IN WASHINGTON, THE JUSTICE DEPARTMENT TODAY CHARACTERIZED THE FIRST, FOURTH, FIFTH AND SIXTH AMENDMENTS TO THE CONSTITUTION AS "TYPOS."
IN SPORTS, THE NCAA HAS DETERMINED THAT ITS ANNUAL MEN'S BASKETBALL TOURNAMENT IS DISRUPTIVE TO ACADEMIC SCHEDULES AND WILL BE ABOLISHED.
IN TECH NEWS, MICROSOFT CHAIRMAN BILL GATES HAS CHALLENGED LINUX CREATOR LINUS TORVALDS TO A WINNER-TAKE-ALL STEEL-CAGE JUDO DEATHMATCH.
AND ON THE BUSINESS FRONT, ANALYSTS ARE PREDICTING A MAJOR SPIKE IN THE ECONOMY AS PAIGE FOX PURCHASES HER BACK-TO-SCHOOL PIMPLE CREAM.
WILL YOU STOP HACKING THE CNN TELEPROMPTER?!
WOLF BLITZER'S ABOUT TO SAY "FEAR ME" IN KLINGON.
AMEND

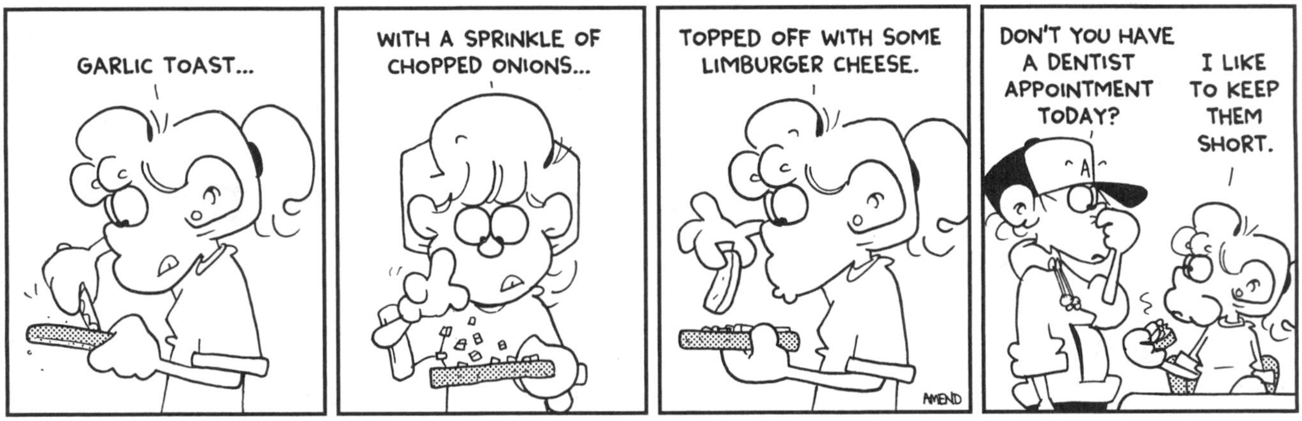
GARLIC TOAST...
WITH A SPRINKLE OF CHOPPED ONIONS...
TOPPED OFF WITH SOME LIMBURGER CHEESE.
DON'T YOU HAVE A DENTIST APPOINTMENT TODAY?
I LIKE TO KEEP THEM SHORT.
AMEND

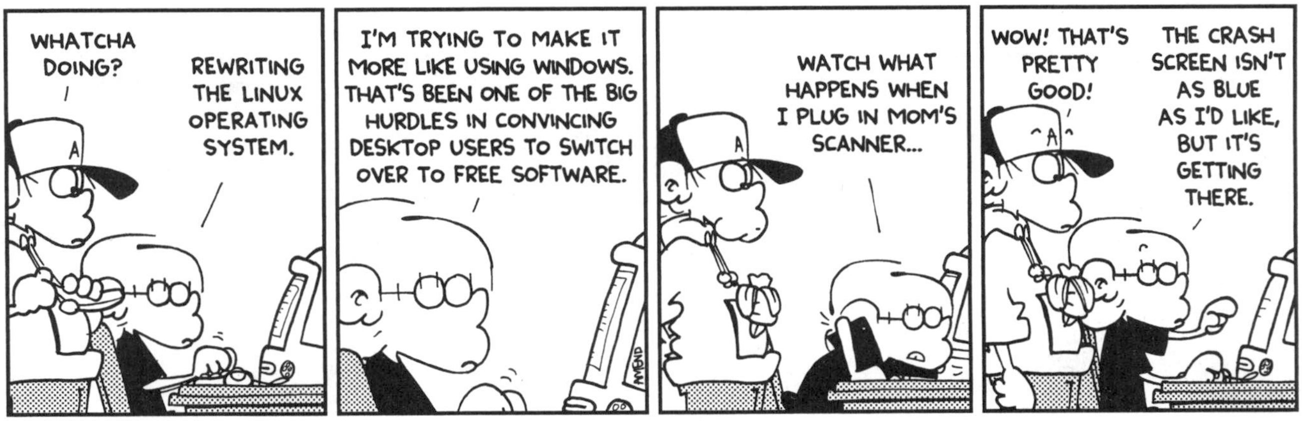
WHATCHA DOING?
REWRITING THE LINUX OPERATING SYSTEM.
I'M TRYING TO MAKE IT MORE LIKE USING WINDOWS. THAT'S BEEN ONE OF THE BIG HURDLES IN CONVINCING DESKTOP USERS TO SWITCH OVER TO FREE SOFTWARE.
WATCH WHAT HAPPENS WHEN I PLUG IN MOM'S SCANNER...
WOW! THAT'S PRETTY GOOD!
THE CRASH SCREEN ISN'T AS BLUE AS I'D LIKE, BUT IT'S GETTING THERE.
AMEND

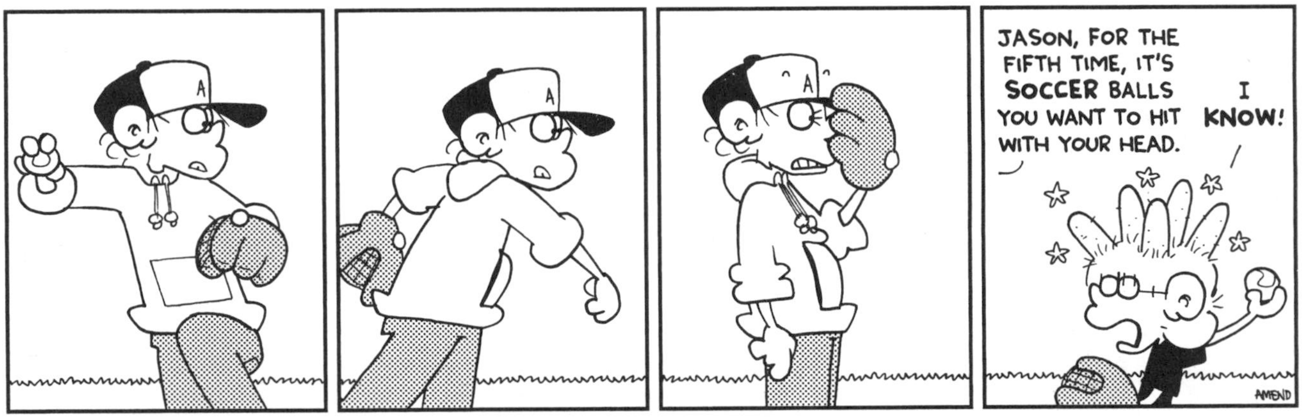
JASON, FOR THE FIFTH TIME, IT'S **SOCCER** BALLS YOU WANT TO HIT WITH YOUR HEAD.
I **KNOW**!
AMEND

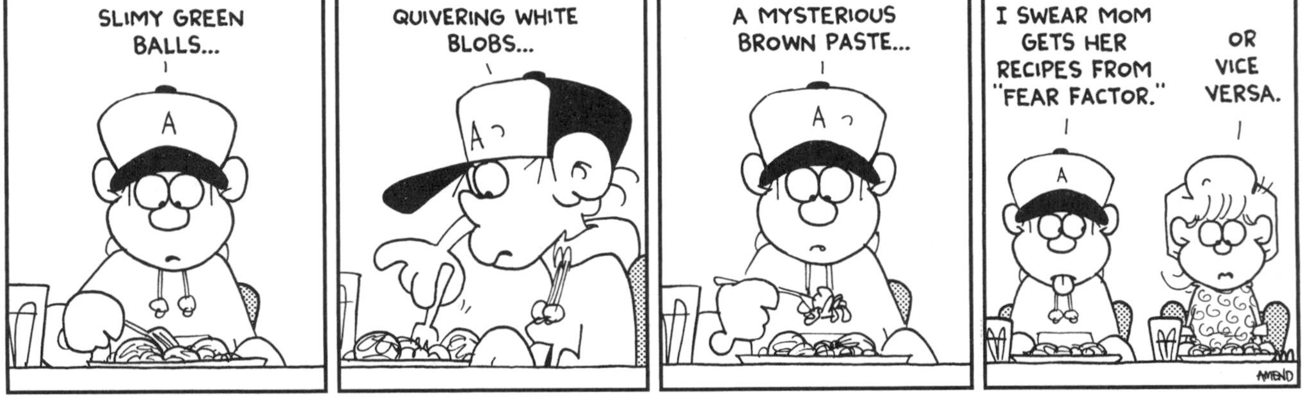
SLIMY GREEN BALLS...
QUIVERING WHITE BLOBS...
A MYSTERIOUS BROWN PASTE...
I SWEAR MOM GETS HER RECIPES FROM "FEAR FACTOR."
OR VICE VERSA.
AMEND

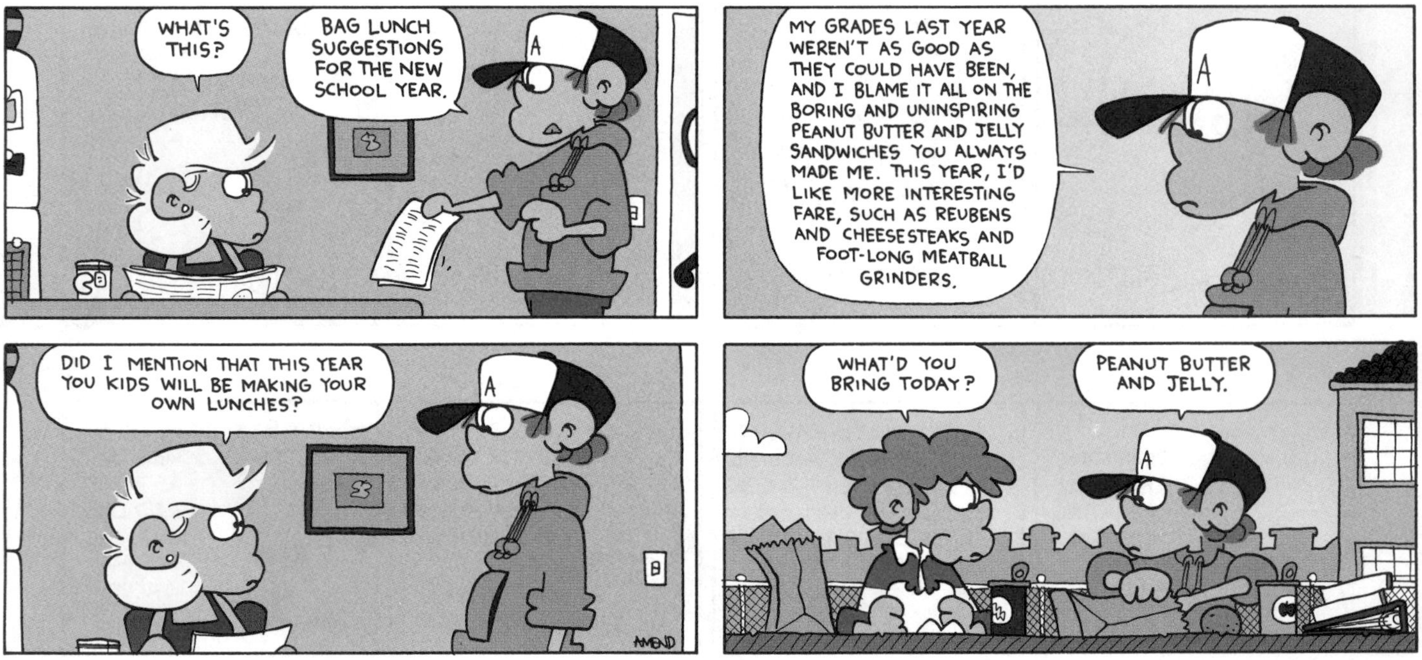
WHAT'S THIS?
BAG LUNCH SUGGESTIONS FOR THE NEW SCHOOL YEAR.
MY GRADES LAST YEAR WEREN'T AS GOOD AS THEY COULD HAVE BEEN, AND I BLAME IT ALL ON THE BORING AND UNINSPIRING PEANUT BUTTER AND JELLY SANDWICHES YOU ALWAYS MADE ME. THIS YEAR, I'D LIKE MORE INTERESTING FARE, SUCH AS REUBENS AND CHEESESTEAKS AND FOOT-LONG MEATBALL GRINDERS.
DID I MENTION THAT THIS YEAR YOU KIDS WILL BE MAKING YOUR OWN LUNCHES?
AMEND
WHAT'D YOU BRING TODAY?
PEANUT BUTTER AND JELLY.

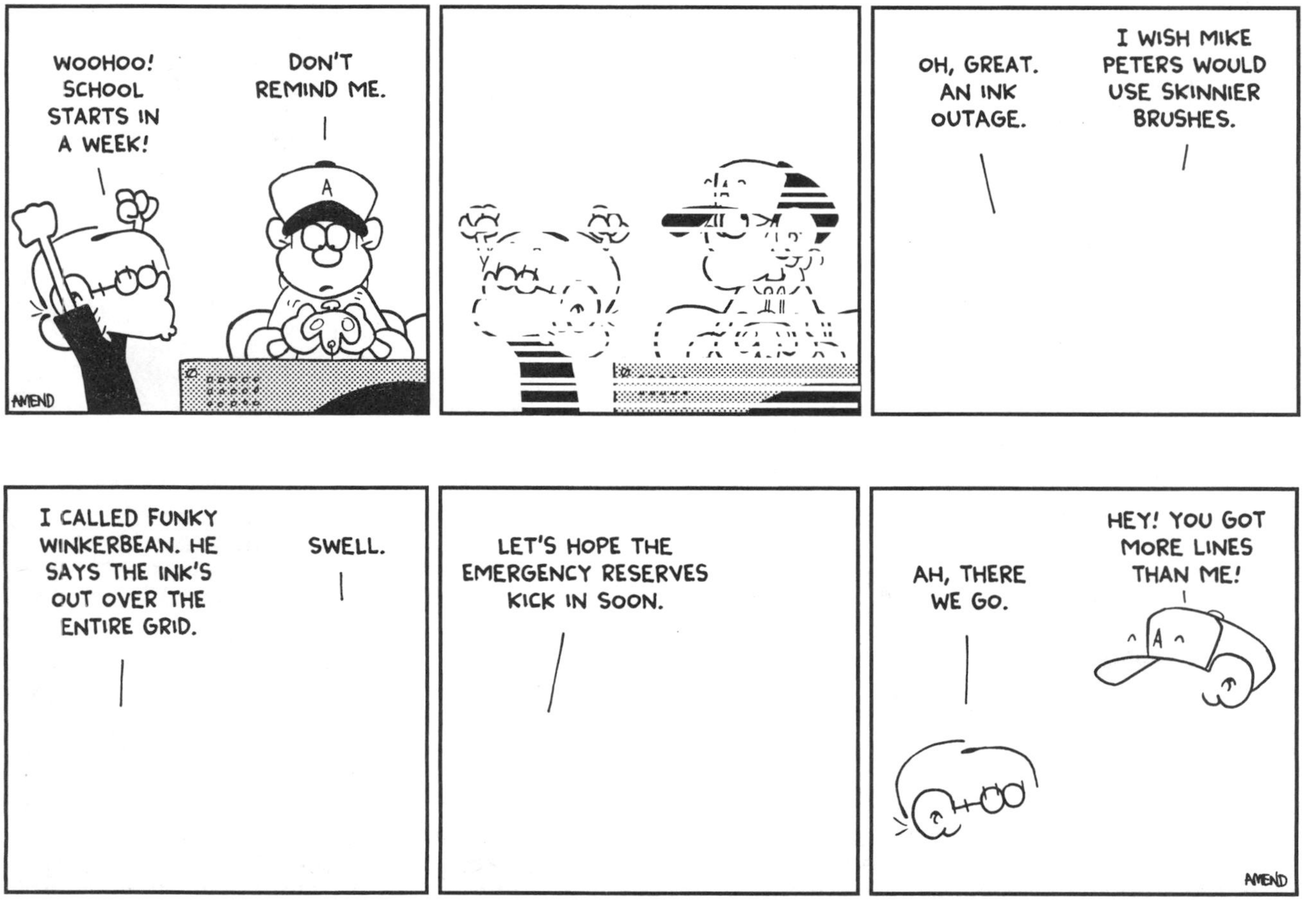
WOOHOO! SCHOOL STARTS IN A WEEK!
DON'T REMIND ME.
AMEND
OH, GREAT. AN INK OUTAGE.
I WISH MIKE PETERS WOULD USE SKINNIER BRUSHES.
I CALLED FUNKY WINKERBEAN. HE SAYS THE INK'S OUT OVER THE ENTIRE GRID.
SWELL.
LET'S HOPE THE EMERGENCY RESERVES KICK IN SOON.
AH, THERE WE GO.
HEY! YOU GOT MORE LINES THAN ME!
AMEND

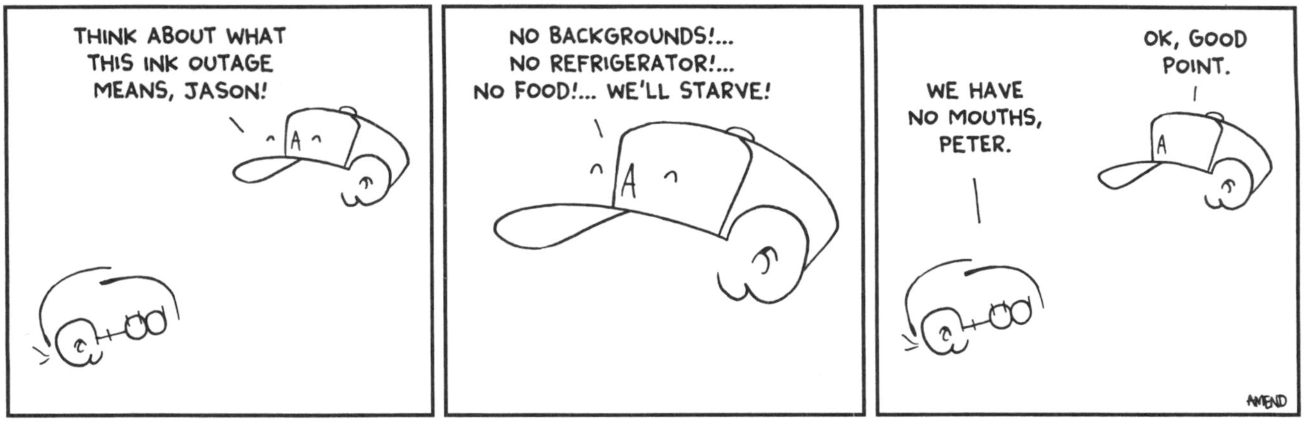
THINK ABOUT WHAT THIS INK OUTAGE MEANS, JASON!
NO BACKGROUNDS!... NO REFRIGERATOR!... NO FOOD!... WE'LL STARVE!
WE HAVE NO MOUTHS, PETER.
OK, GOOD POINT.
AMEND

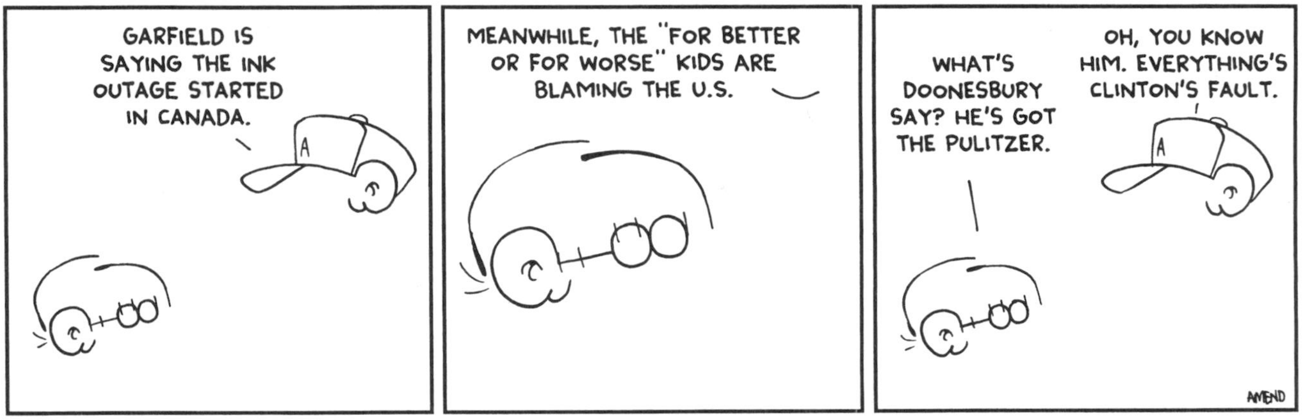
GARFIELD IS SAYING THE INK OUTAGE STARTED IN CANADA.
MEANWHILE, THE "FOR BETTER OR FOR WORSE" KIDS ARE BLAMING THE U.S.
WHAT'S DOONESBURY SAY? HE'S GOT THE PULITZER.
OH, YOU KNOW HIM. EVERYTHING'S CLINTON'S FAULT.
AMEND

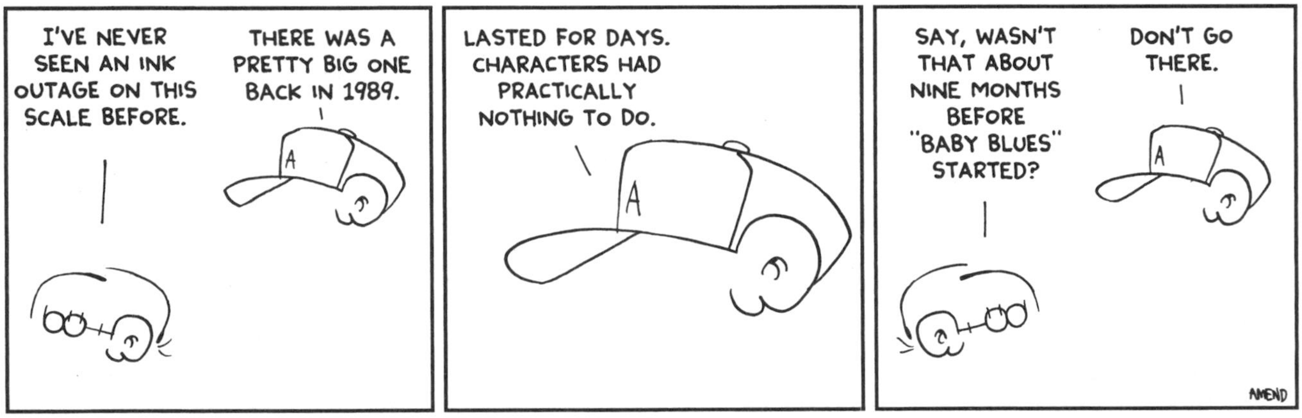
I'VE NEVER SEEN AN INK OUTAGE ON THIS SCALE BEFORE.
THERE WAS A PRETTY BIG ONE BACK IN 1989.
LASTED FOR DAYS. CHARACTERS HAD PRACTICALLY NOTHING TO DO.
SAY, WASN'T THAT ABOUT NINE MONTHS BEFORE "BABY BLUES" STARTED?
DON'T GO THERE.
AMEND

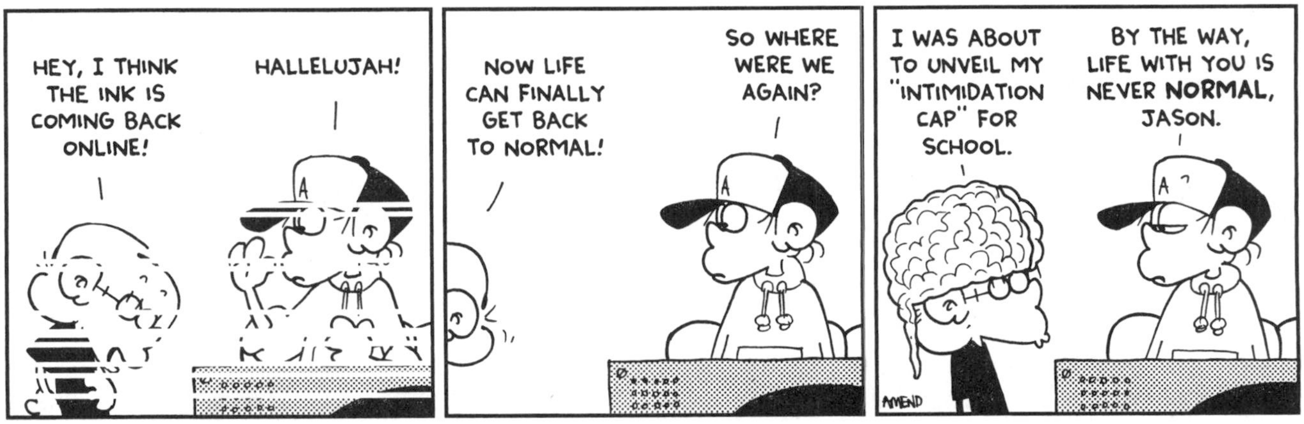
HEY, I THINK THE INK IS COMING BACK ONLINE!
HALLELUJAH!
NOW LIFE CAN FINALLY GET BACK TO NORMAL!
SO WHERE WERE WE AGAIN?
I WAS ABOUT TO UNVEIL MY "INTIMIDATION CAP" FOR SCHOOL.
BY THE WAY, LIFE WITH YOU IS NEVER NORMAL, JASON.
AMEND

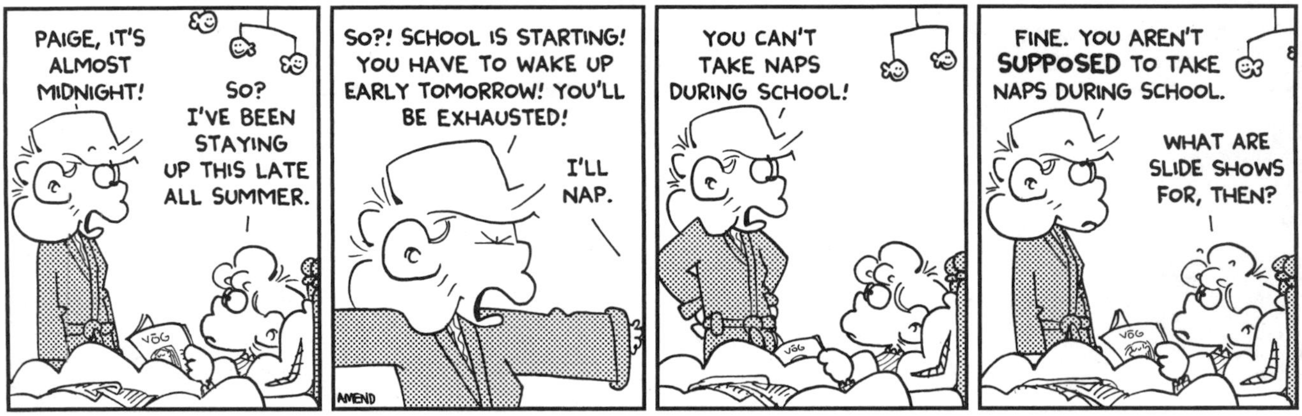
PAIGE, IT'S ALMOST MIDNIGHT!
SO? I'VE BEEN STAYING UP THIS LATE ALL SUMMER.
VÖG
SO?! SCHOOL IS STARTING! YOU HAVE TO WAKE UP EARLY TOMORROW! YOU'LL BE EXHAUSTED!
I'LL NAP.
AMEND
YOU CAN'T TAKE NAPS DURING SCHOOL!
VÖG
FINE. YOU AREN'T **SUPPOSED** TO TAKE NAPS DURING SCHOOL.
WHAT ARE SLIDE SHOWS FOR, THEN?
VÖG

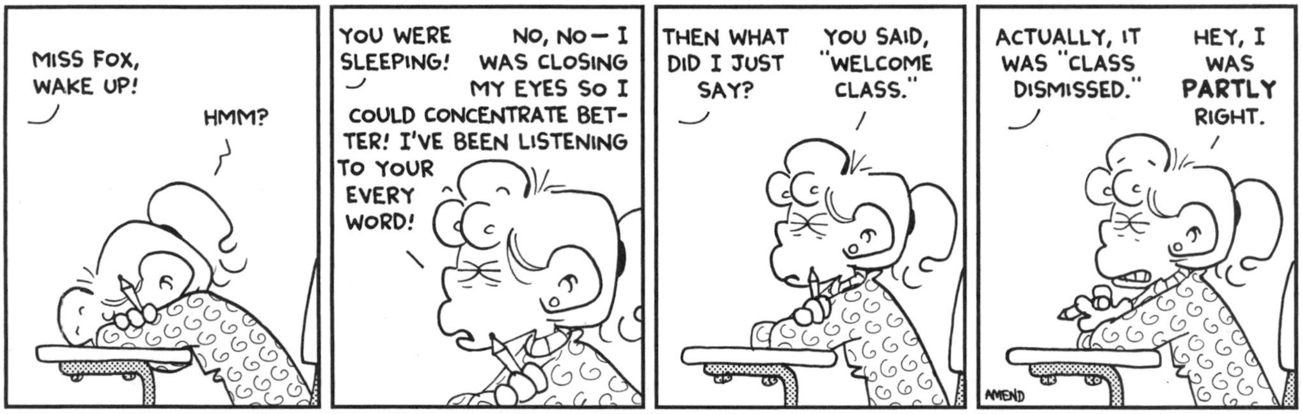
MISS FOX, WAKE UP!
HMM?
YOU WERE SLEEPING!
NO, NO— I WAS CLOSING MY EYES SO I COULD CONCENTRATE BETTER! I'VE BEEN LISTENING TO YOUR EVERY WORD!
THEN WHAT DID I JUST SAY?
YOU SAID, "WELCOME CLASS."
ACTUALLY, IT WAS "CLASS DISMISSED."
HEY, I WAS **PARTLY** RIGHT.
AMEND

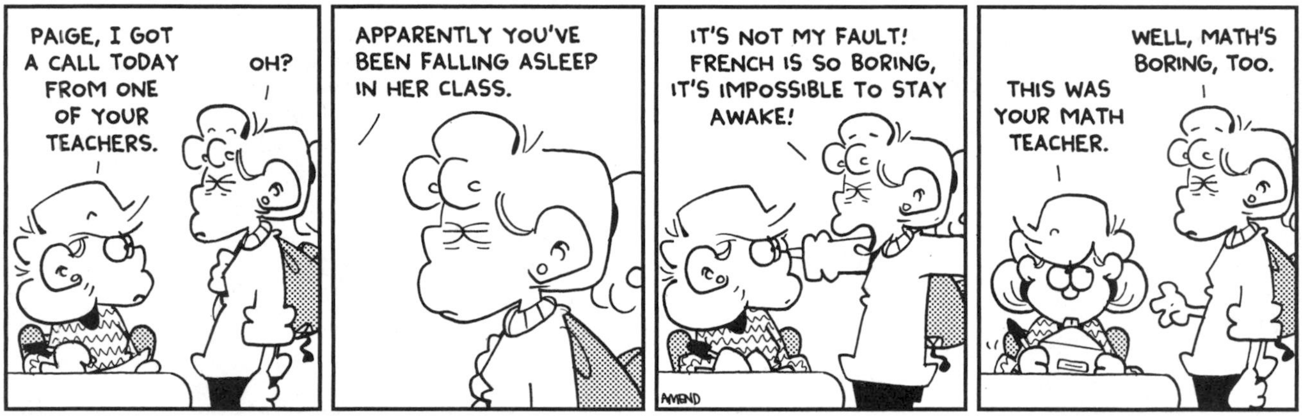
PAIGE, I GOT A CALL TODAY FROM ONE OF YOUR TEACHERS.
OH?
APPARENTLY YOU'VE BEEN FALLING ASLEEP IN HER CLASS.
IT'S NOT MY FAULT! FRENCH IS SO BORING, IT'S IMPOSSIBLE TO STAY AWAKE!
AMEND
THIS WAS YOUR MATH TEACHER.
WELL, MATH'S BORING, TOO.

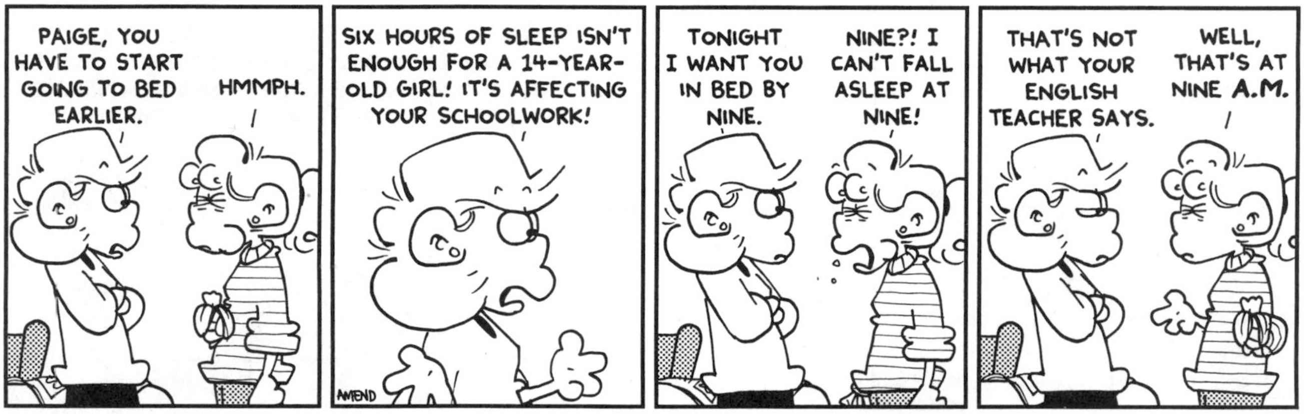
PAIGE, YOU HAVE TO START GOING TO BED EARLIER.
HMMPH.
SIX HOURS OF SLEEP ISN'T ENOUGH FOR A 14-YEAR-OLD GIRL! IT'S AFFECTING YOUR SCHOOLWORK!
AMEND
TONIGHT I WANT YOU IN BED BY NINE.
NINE?! I CAN'T FALL ASLEEP AT NINE!
THAT'S NOT WHAT YOUR ENGLISH TEACHER SAYS.
WELL, THAT'S AT NINE **A.M.**

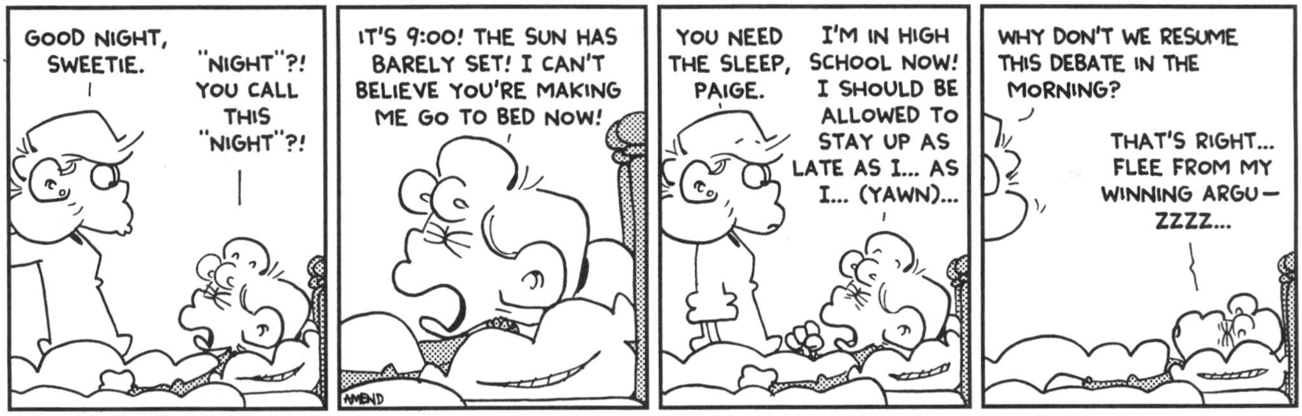
GOOD NIGHT, SWEETIE.
"NIGHT"?! YOU CALL THIS "NIGHT"?!
IT'S 9:00! THE SUN HAS BARELY SET! I CAN'T BELIEVE YOU'RE MAKING ME GO TO BED NOW!
YOU NEED THE SLEEP, PAIGE.
I'M IN HIGH SCHOOL NOW! I SHOULD BE ALLOWED TO STAY UP AS LATE AS I... AS I... (YAWN)...
WHY DON'T WE RESUME THIS DEBATE IN THE MORNING?
THAT'S RIGHT... FLEE FROM MY WINNING ARGU— ZZZZ...
AMEND

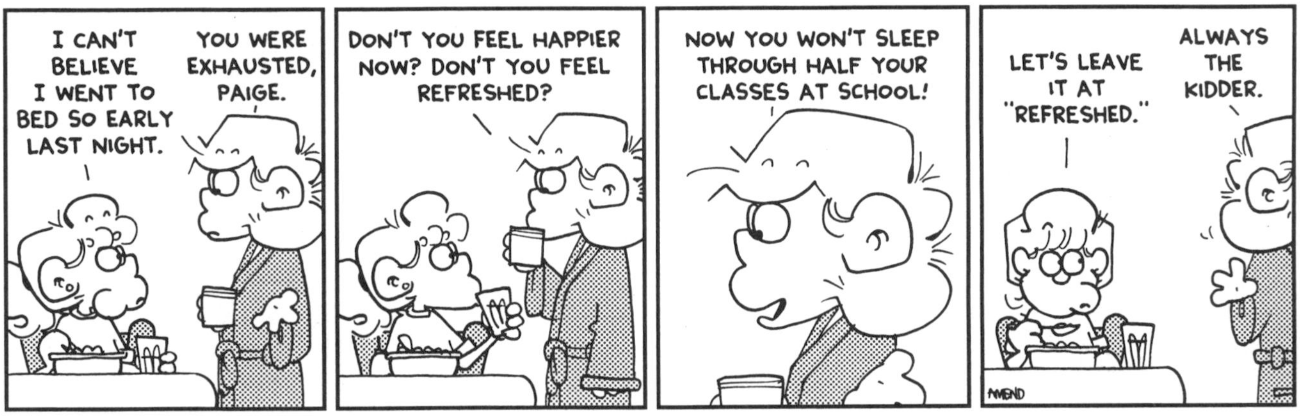
I CAN'T BELIEVE I WENT TO BED SO EARLY LAST NIGHT.
YOU WERE EXHAUSTED, PAIGE.
DON'T YOU FEEL HAPPIER NOW? DON'T YOU FEEL REFRESHED?
NOW YOU WON'T SLEEP THROUGH HALF YOUR CLASSES AT SCHOOL!
LET'S LEAVE IT AT "REFRESHED."
ALWAYS THE KIDDER.
AMEND

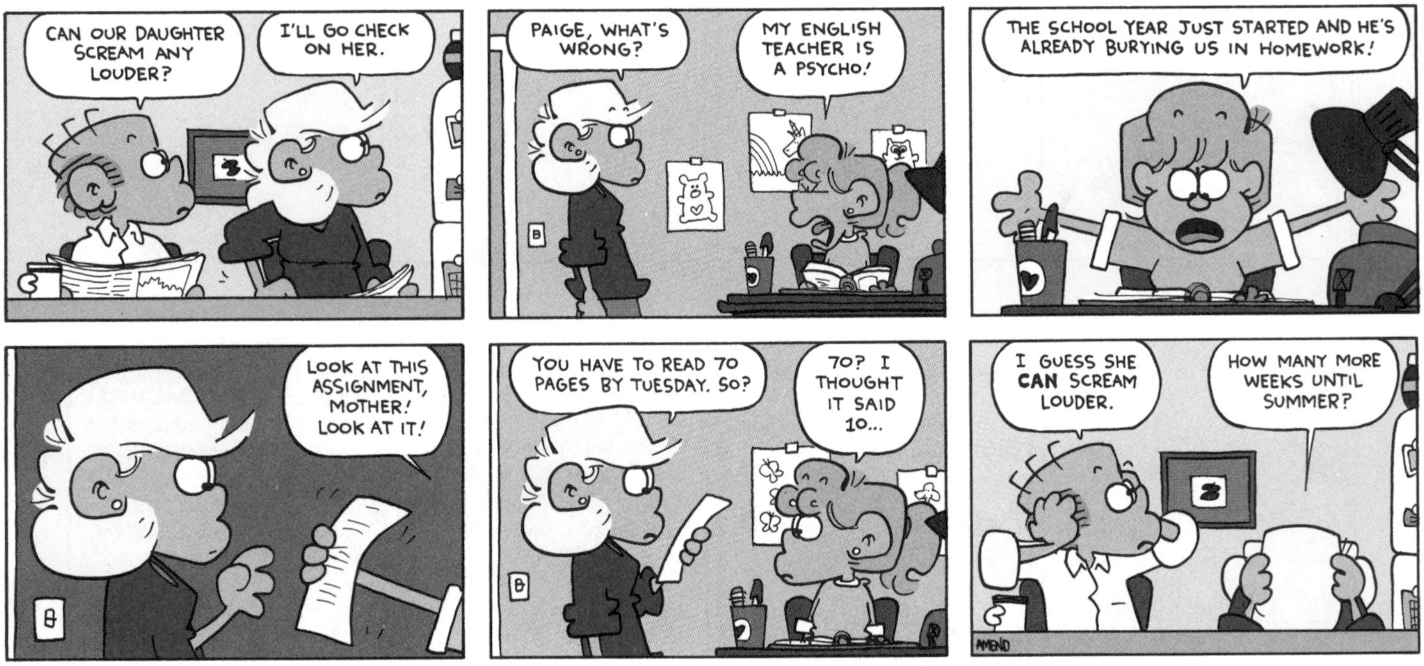
CAN OUR DAUGHTER SCREAM ANY LOUDER?
I'LL GO CHECK ON HER.
PAIGE, WHAT'S WRONG?
MY ENGLISH TEACHER IS A PSYCHO!
THE SCHOOL YEAR JUST STARTED AND HE'S ALREADY BURYING US IN HOMEWORK!
LOOK AT THIS ASSIGNMENT, MOTHER! LOOK AT IT!
YOU HAVE TO READ 70 PAGES BY TUESDAY. SO?
70? I THOUGHT IT SAID 10...
I GUESS SHE **CAN** SCREAM LOUDER.
HOW MANY MORE WEEKS UNTIL SUMMER?
AMEND

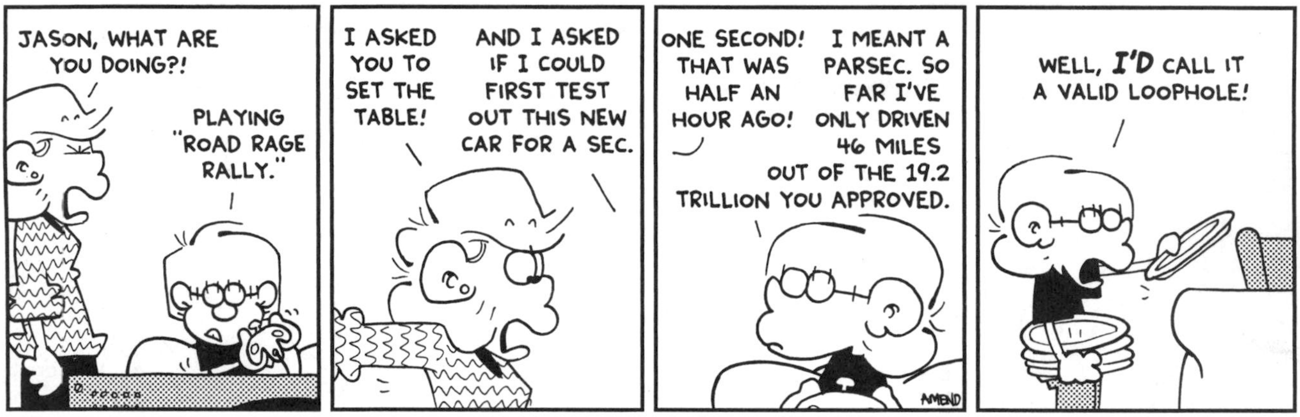
JASON, WHAT ARE YOU DOING?!
PLAYING "ROAD RAGE RALLY."
I ASKED YOU TO SET THE TABLE!
AND I ASKED IF I COULD FIRST TEST OUT THIS NEW CAR FOR A SEC.
ONE SECOND! THAT WAS HALF AN HOUR AGO!
I MEANT A PARSEC. SO FAR I'VE ONLY DRIVEN 46 MILES OUT OF THE 19.2 TRILLION YOU APPROVED.
WELL, I'D CALL IT A VALID LOOPHOLE!
AMEND

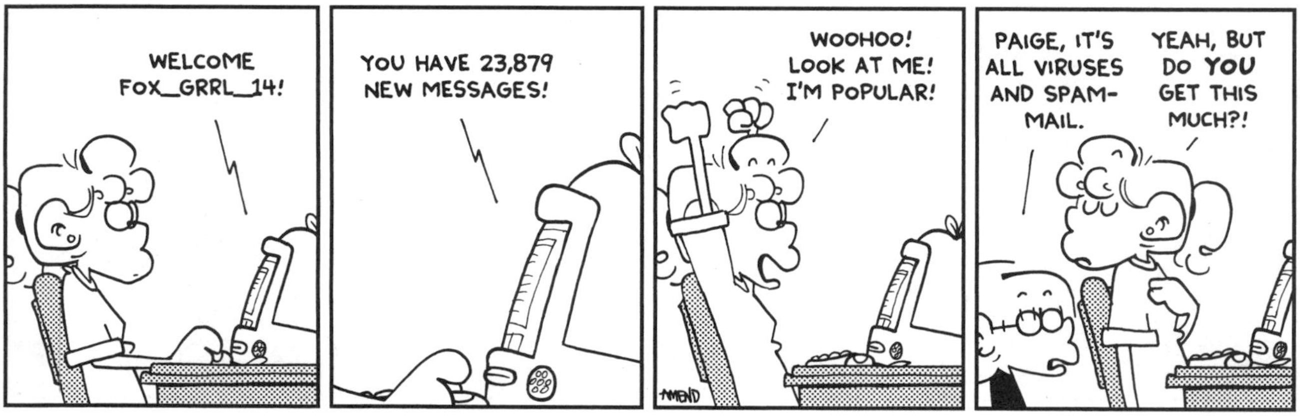
WELCOME FOX_GRRL_14!
YOU HAVE 23,879 NEW MESSAGES!
WOOHOO! LOOK AT ME! I'M POPULAR!
PAIGE, IT'S ALL VIRUSES AND SPAM-MAIL.
YEAH, BUT DO YOU GET THIS MUCH?!
AMEND

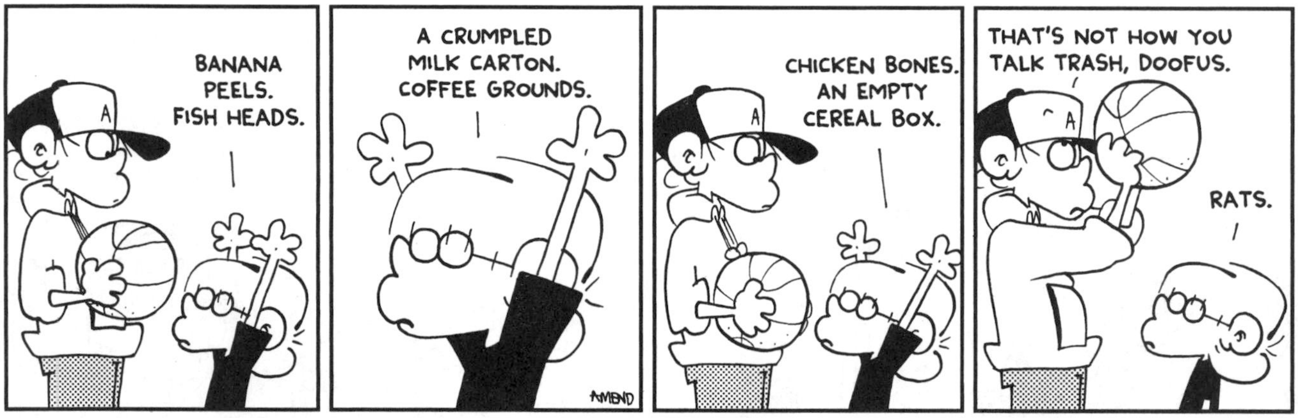
BANANA PEELS. FISH HEADS.
A CRUMPLED MILK CARTON. COFFEE GROUNDS.
CHICKEN BONES. AN EMPTY CEREAL BOX.
THAT'S NOT HOW YOU TALK TRASH, DOOFUS.
RATS.
AMEND

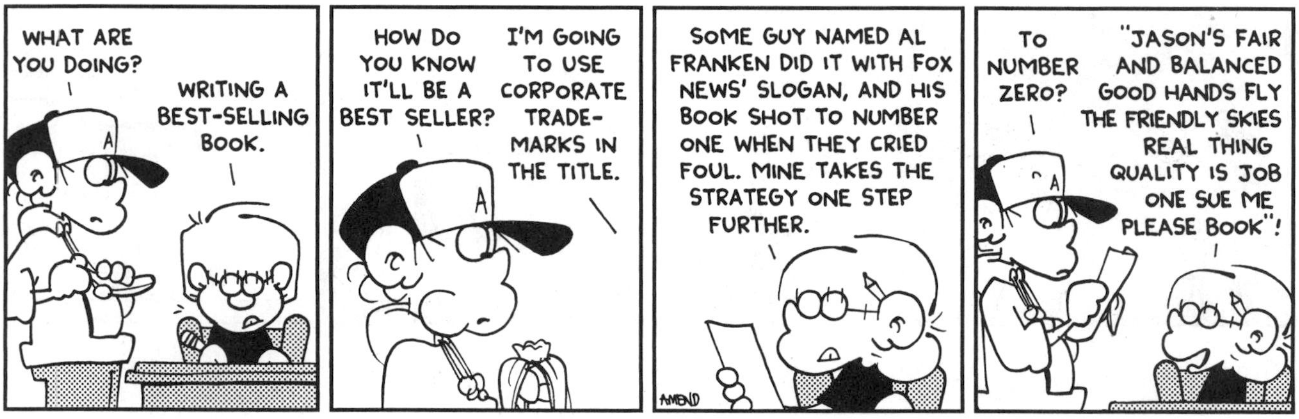
WHAT ARE YOU DOING?
WRITING A BEST-SELLING BOOK.
HOW DO YOU KNOW IT'LL BE A BEST SELLER?
I'M GOING TO USE CORPORATE TRADE-MARKS IN THE TITLE.
SOME GUY NAMED AL FRANKEN DID IT WITH FOX NEWS' SLOGAN, AND HIS BOOK SHOT TO NUMBER ONE WHEN THEY CRIED FOUL. MINE TAKES THE STRATEGY ONE STEP FURTHER.
TO NUMBER ZERO?
"JASON'S FAIR AND BALANCED GOOD HANDS FLY THE FRIENDLY SKIES REAL THING QUALITY IS JOB ONE SUE ME PLEASE BOOK"!
AMEND

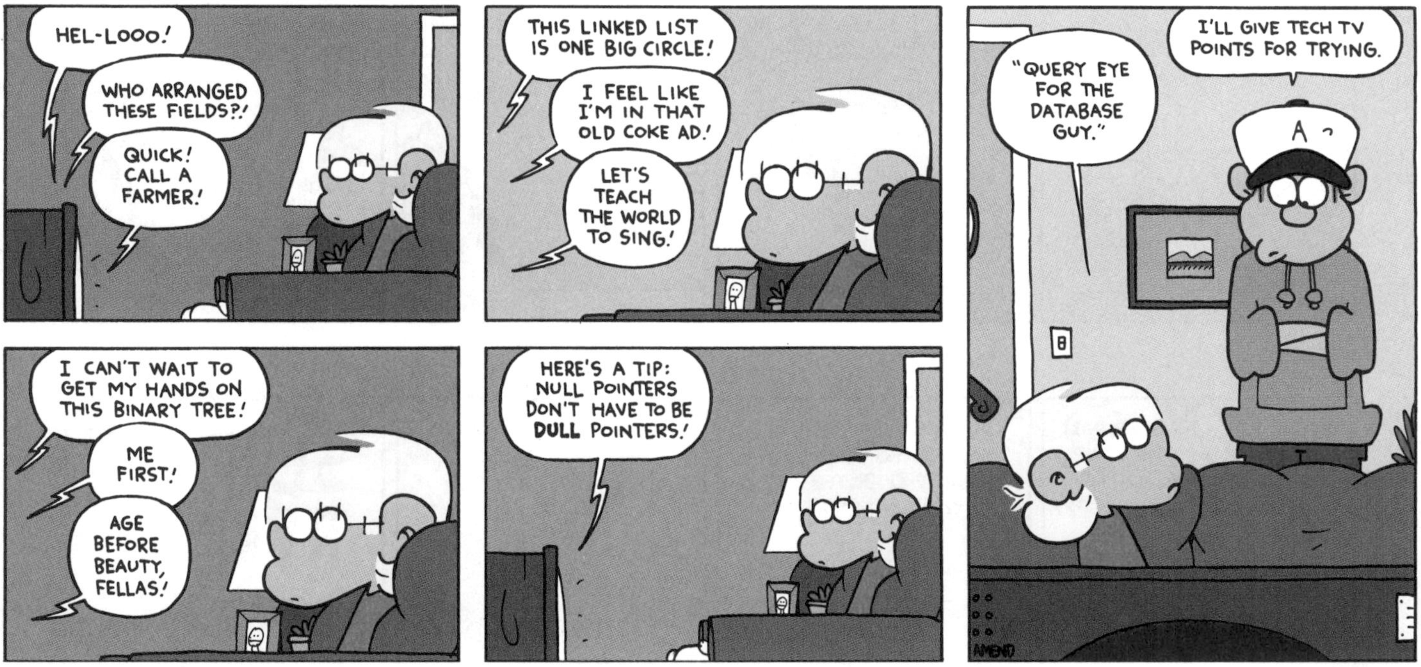
HEL-LOOO!
WHO ARRANGED THESE FIELDS?!
QUICK! CALL A FARMER!
THIS LINKED LIST IS ONE BIG CIRCLE!
I FEEL LIKE I'M IN THAT OLD COKE AD!
LET'S TEACH THE WORLD TO SING!
I CAN'T WAIT TO GET MY HANDS ON THIS BINARY TREE!
ME FIRST!
AGE BEFORE BEAUTY, FELLAS!
HERE'S A TIP: NULL POINTERS DON'T HAVE TO BE **DULL** POINTERS!
"QUERY EYE FOR THE DATABASE GUY."
I'LL GIVE TECH TV POINTS FOR TRYING.
AMEND

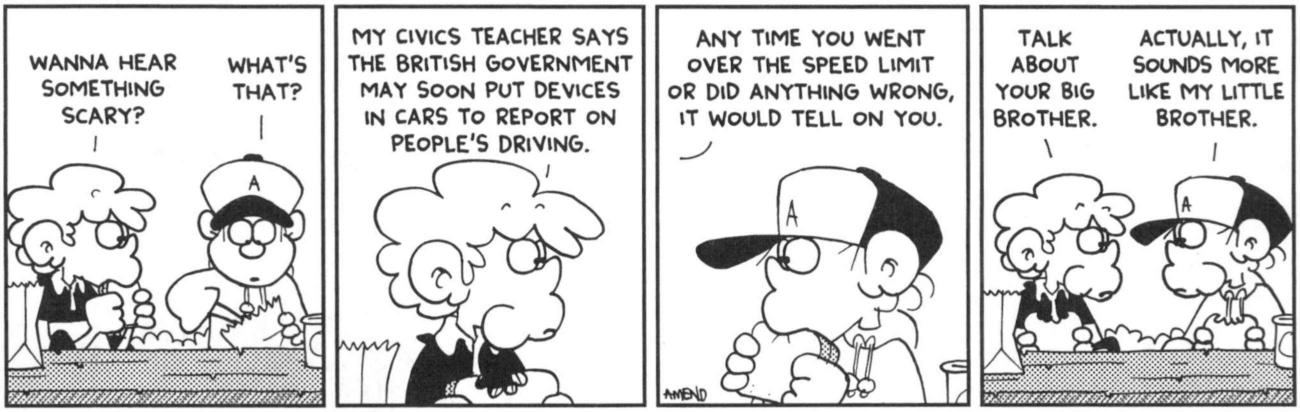
WANNA HEAR SOMETHING SCARY?
WHAT'S THAT?
MY CIVICS TEACHER SAYS THE BRITISH GOVERNMENT MAY SOON PUT DEVICES IN CARS TO REPORT ON PEOPLE'S DRIVING.
ANY TIME YOU WENT OVER THE SPEED LIMIT OR DID ANYTHING WRONG, IT WOULD TELL ON YOU.
AMEND
TALK ABOUT YOUR BIG BROTHER.
ACTUALLY, IT SOUNDS MORE LIKE MY LITTLE BROTHER.

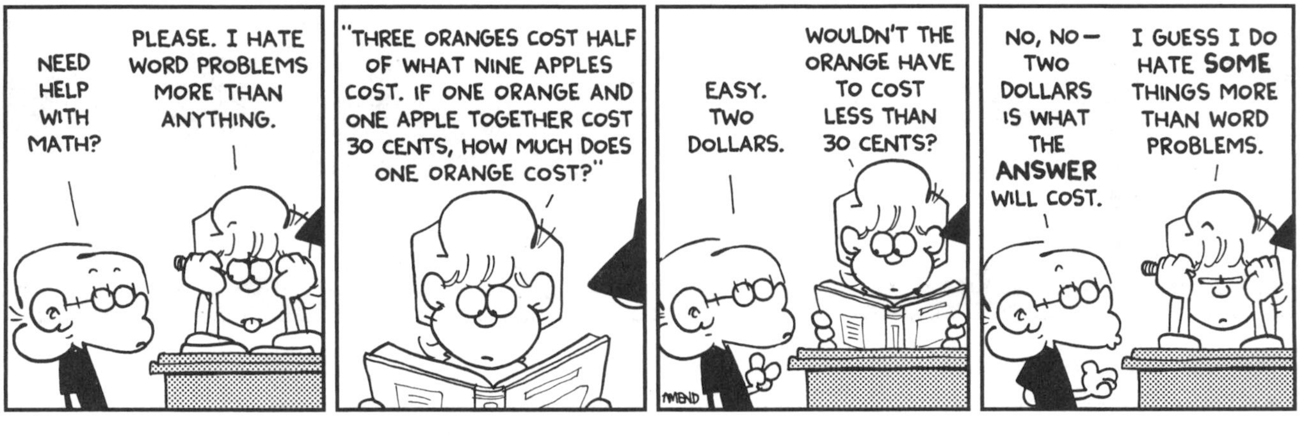
NEED HELP WITH MATH?
PLEASE. I HATE WORD PROBLEMS MORE THAN ANYTHING.
"THREE ORANGES COST HALF OF WHAT NINE APPLES COST. IF ONE ORANGE AND ONE APPLE TOGETHER COST 30 CENTS, HOW MUCH DOES ONE ORANGE COST?"
EASY. TWO DOLLARS.
WOULDN'T THE ORANGE HAVE TO COST LESS THAN 30 CENTS?
AMEND
NO, NO— TWO DOLLARS IS WHAT THE **ANSWER** WILL COST.
I GUESS I DO HATE **SOME** THINGS MORE THAN WORD PROBLEMS.

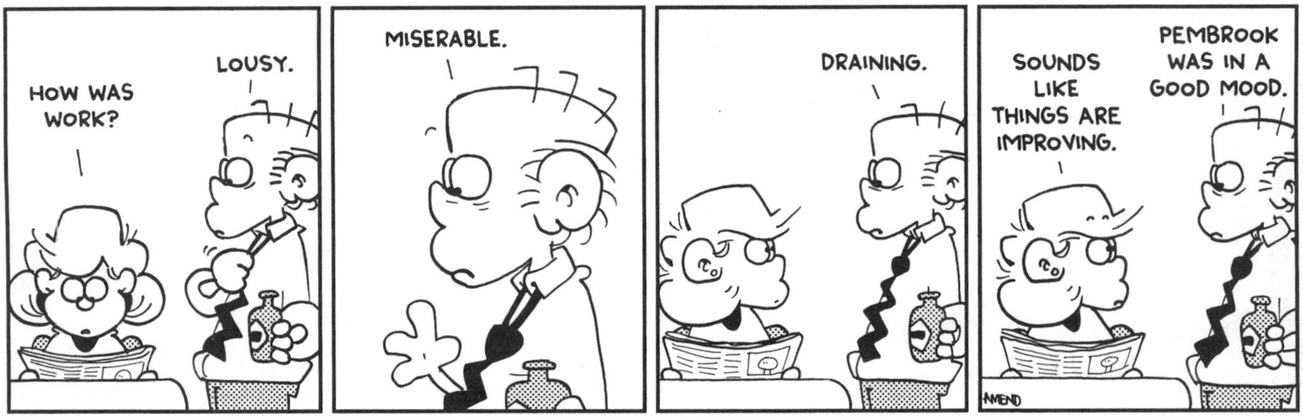
HOW WAS WORK?
LOUSY.
MISERABLE.
DRAINING.
SOUNDS LIKE THINGS ARE IMPROVING.
PEMBROOK WAS IN A GOOD MOOD.
AMEND

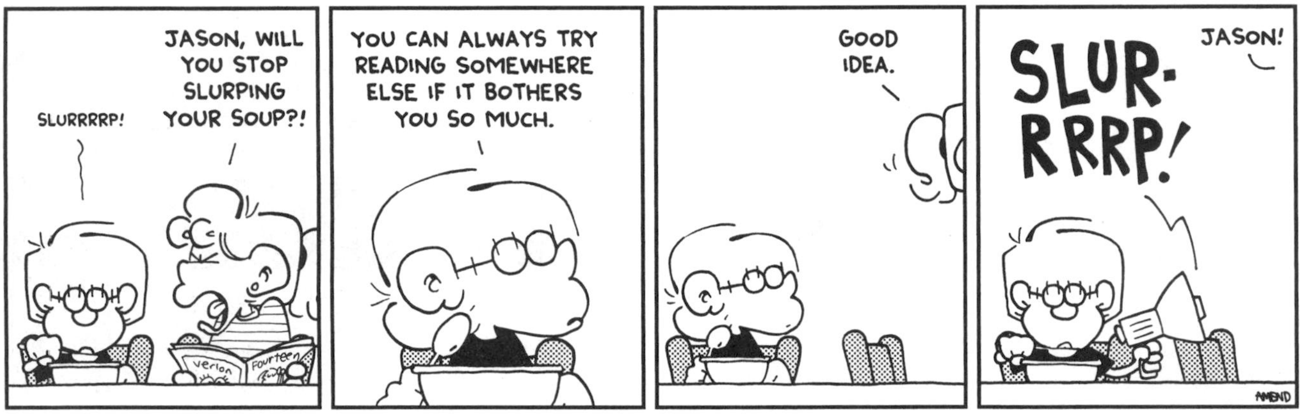
SLURRRRP!
JASON, WILL YOU STOP SLURPING YOUR SOUP?!
YOU CAN ALWAYS TRY READING SOMEWHERE ELSE IF IT BOTHERS YOU SO MUCH.
GOOD IDEA.
SLUR-RRRP!
JASON!
AMEND

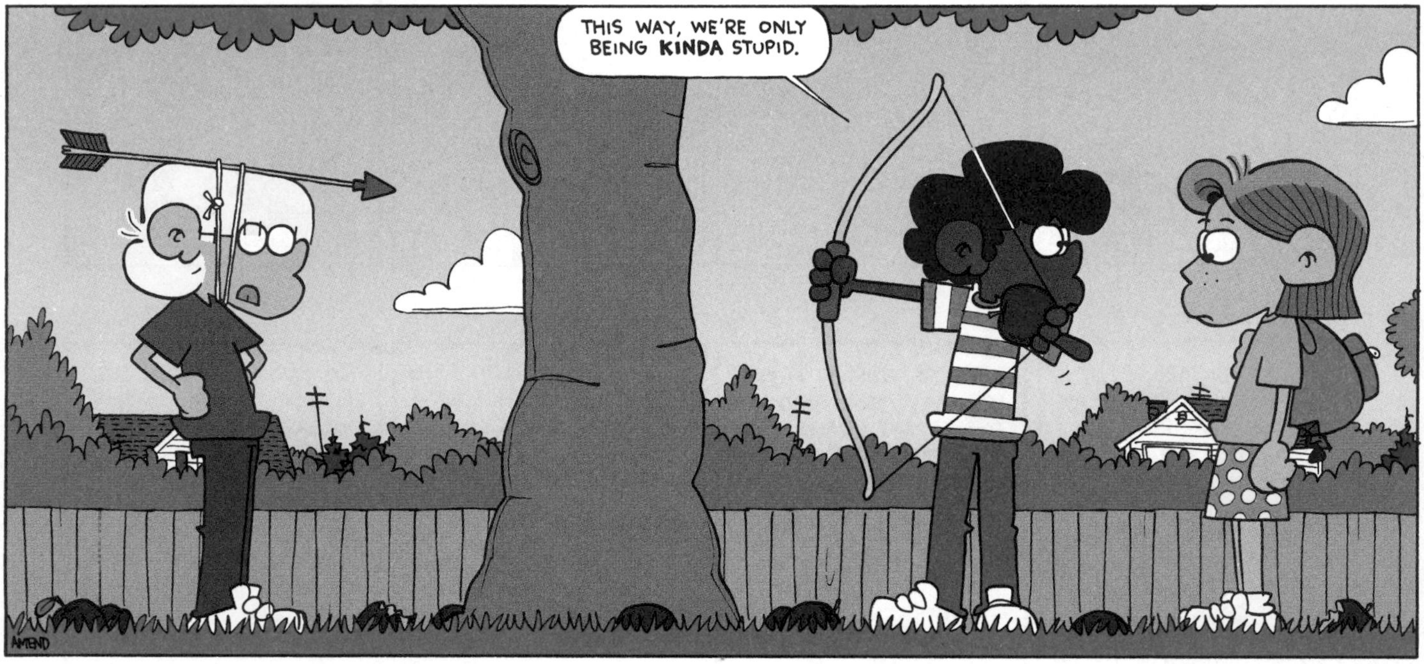
THIS WAY, WE'RE ONLY BEING **KINDA** STUPID.
AMEND

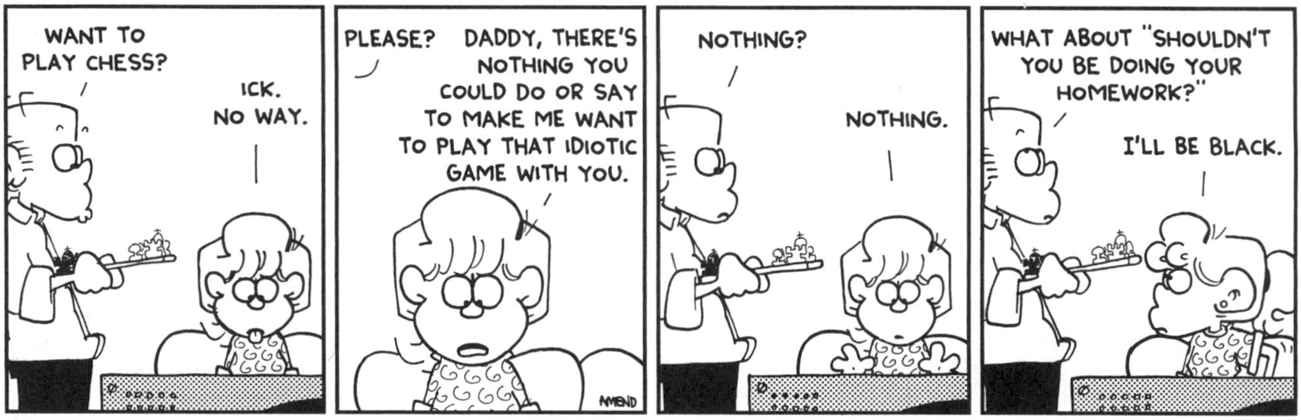
WANT TO PLAY CHESS?
ICK. NO WAY.
PLEASE?
DADDY, THERE'S NOTHING YOU COULD DO OR SAY TO MAKE ME WANT TO PLAY THAT IDIOTIC GAME WITH YOU.
AMEND
NOTHING?
NOTHING.
WHAT ABOUT "SHOULDN'T YOU BE DOING YOUR HOMEWORK?"
I'LL BE BLACK.

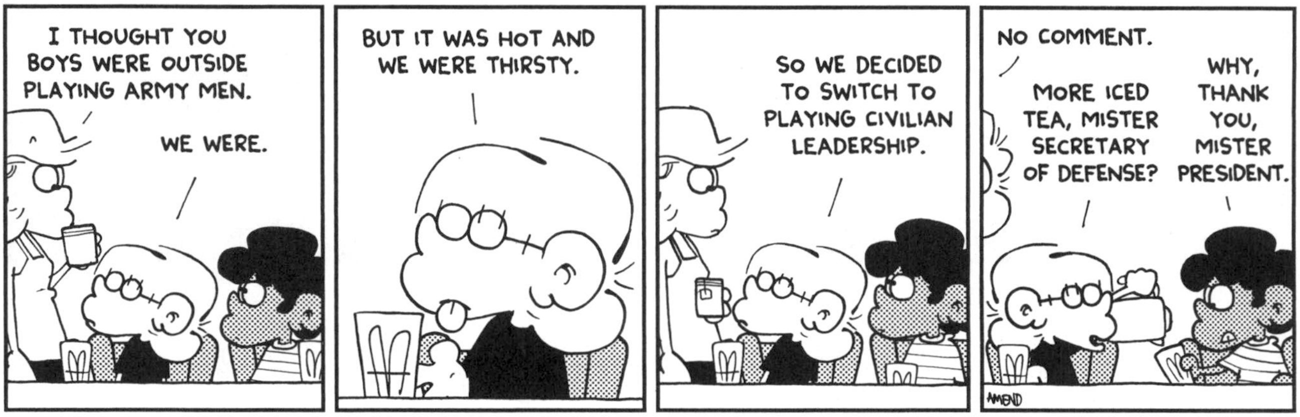
I THOUGHT YOU BOYS WERE OUTSIDE PLAYING ARMY MEN.
WE WERE.
BUT IT WAS HOT AND WE WERE THIRSTY.
SO WE DECIDED TO SWITCH TO PLAYING CIVILIAN LEADERSHIP.
NO COMMENT.
MORE ICED TEA, MISTER SECRETARY OF DEFENSE?
WHY, THANK YOU, MISTER PRESIDENT.
AMEND

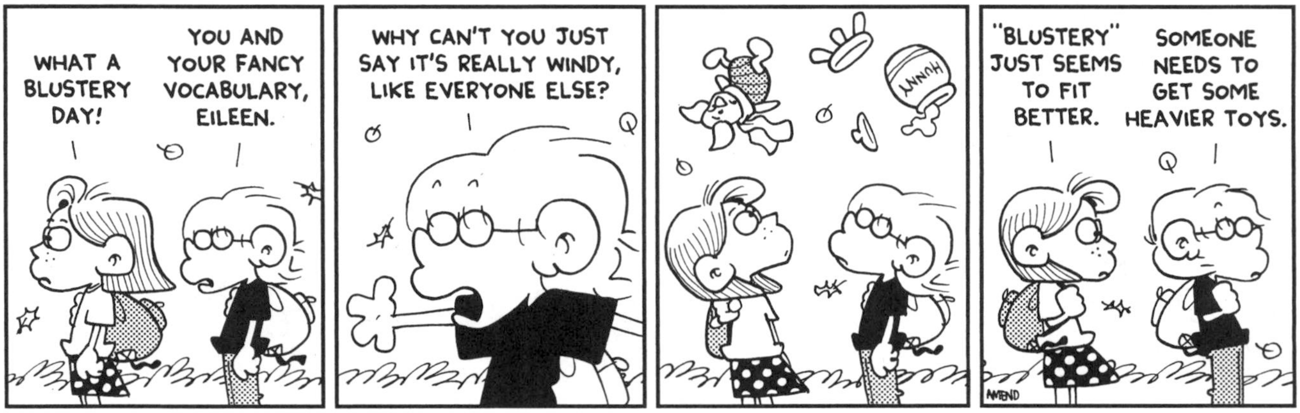
WHAT A BLUSTERY DAY!
YOU AND YOUR FANCY VOCABULARY, EILEEN.
WHY CAN'T YOU JUST SAY IT'S REALLY WINDY, LIKE EVERYONE ELSE?
"BLUSTERY" JUST SEEMS TO FIT BETTER.
SOMEONE NEEDS TO GET SOME HEAVIER TOYS.
AMEND

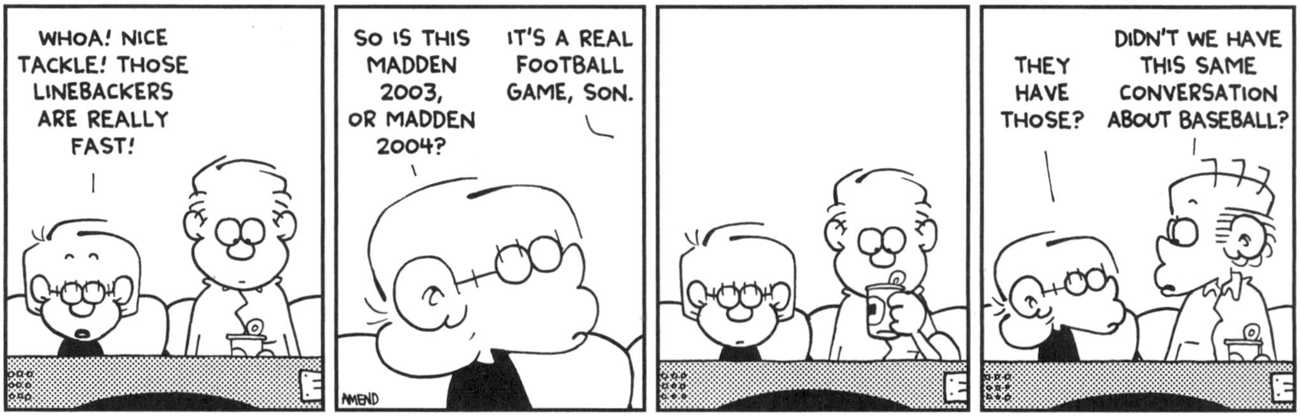
WHOA! NICE TACKLE! THOSE LINEBACKERS ARE REALLY FAST!
SO IS THIS MADDEN 2003, OR MADDEN 2004?
IT'S A REAL FOOTBALL GAME, SON.
AMEND
THEY HAVE THOSE?
DIDN'T WE HAVE THIS SAME CONVERSATION ABOUT BASEBALL?

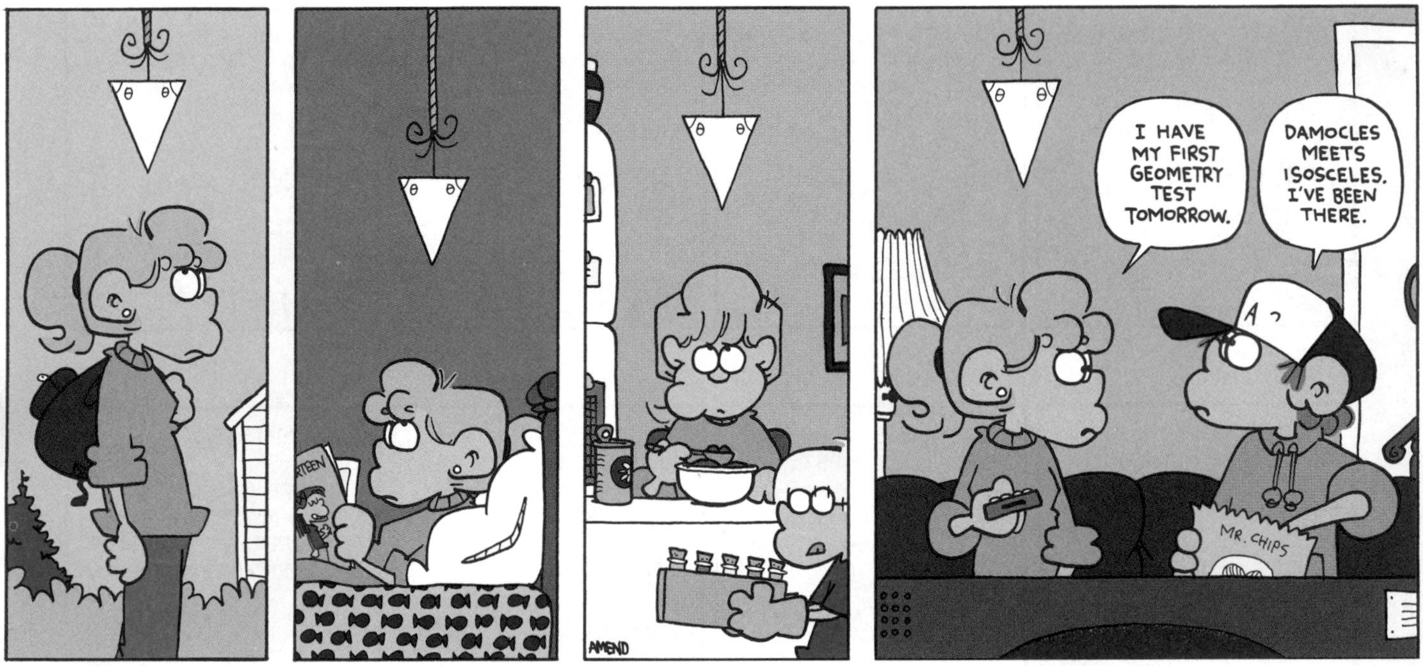
RTEEN
AMEND
I HAVE MY FIRST GEOMETRY TEST TOMORROW.
DAMOCLES MEETS ISOSCELES. I'VE BEEN THERE.
MR. CHIPS

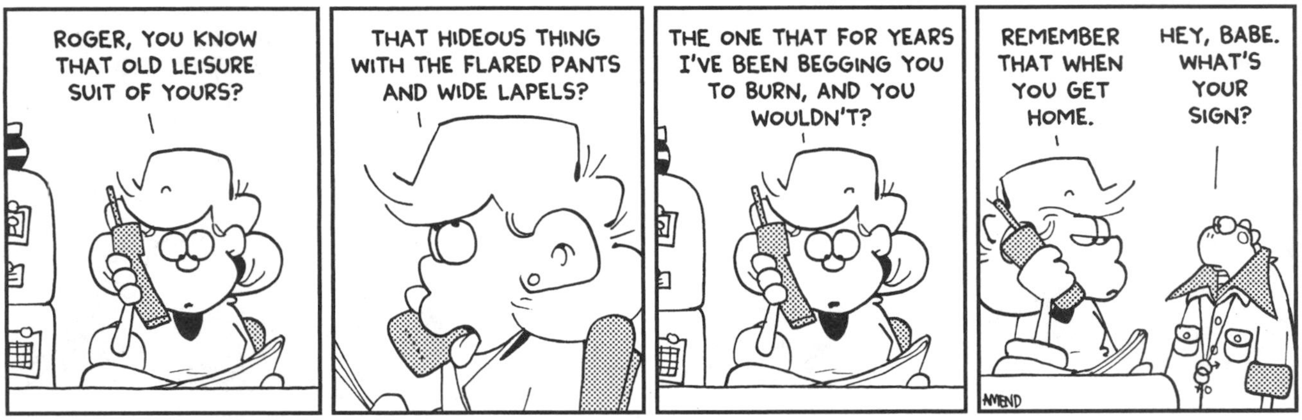
ROGER, YOU KNOW THAT OLD LEISURE SUIT OF YOURS?
THAT HIDEOUS THING WITH THE FLARED PANTS AND WIDE LAPELS?
THE ONE THAT FOR YEARS I'VE BEEN BEGGING YOU TO BURN, AND YOU WOULDN'T?
REMEMBER THAT WHEN YOU GET HOME.
HEY, BABE. WHAT'S YOUR SIGN?
AMEND

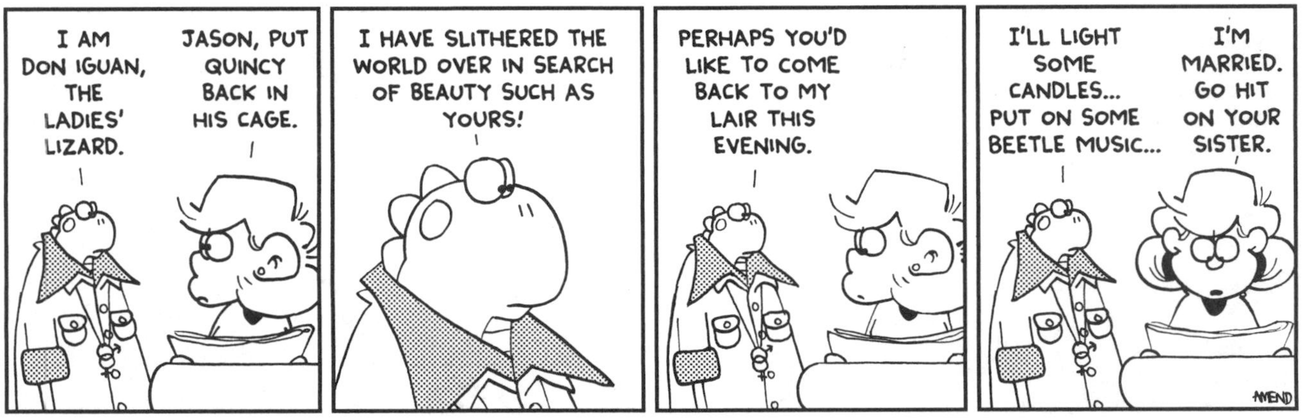
I AM DON IGUAN, THE LADIES' LIZARD.
JASON, PUT QUINCY BACK IN HIS CAGE.
I HAVE SLITHERED THE WORLD OVER IN SEARCH OF BEAUTY SUCH AS YOURS!
PERHAPS YOU'D LIKE TO COME BACK TO MY LAIR THIS EVENING.
I'LL LIGHT SOME CANDLES... PUT ON SOME BEETLE MUSIC...
I'M MARRIED. GO HIT ON YOUR SISTER.
AMEND

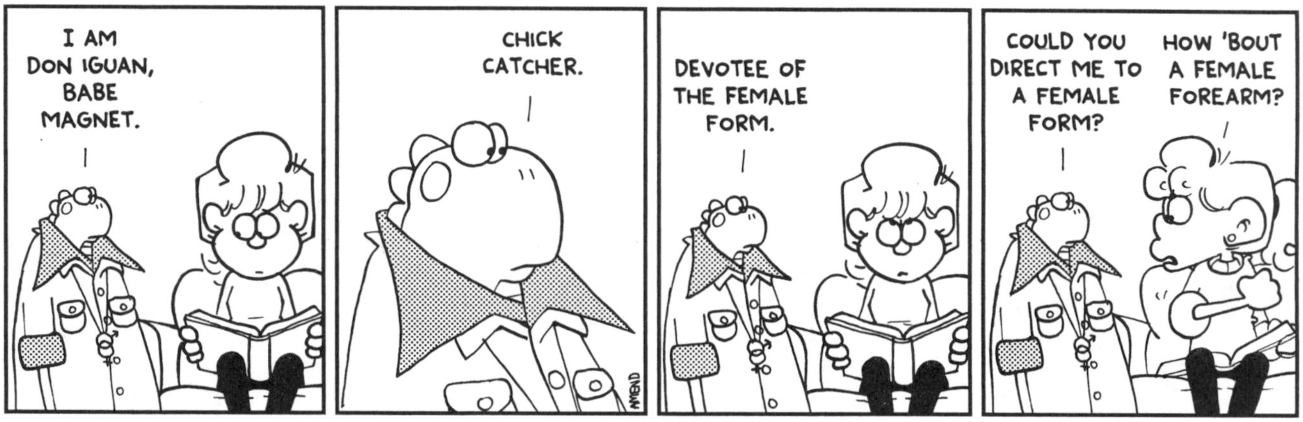
I AM DON IGUAN, BABE MAGNET.
CHICK CATCHER.
DEVOTEE OF THE FEMALE FORM.
COULD YOU DIRECT ME TO A FEMALE FORM?
HOW 'BOUT A FEMALE FOREARM?
AMEND

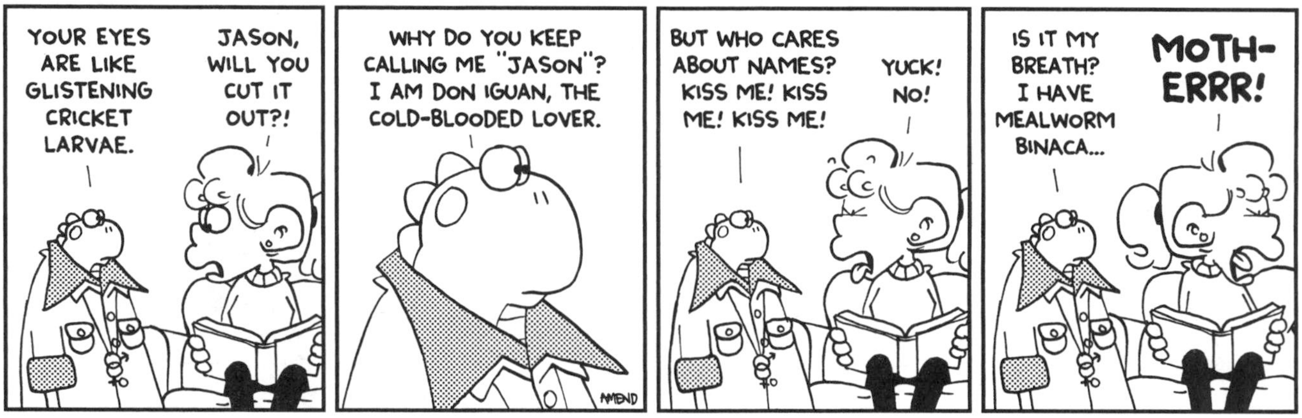
YOUR EYES ARE LIKE GLISTENING CRICKET LARVAE.
JASON, WILL YOU CUT IT OUT?!
WHY DO YOU KEEP CALLING ME "JASON"? I AM DON IGUAN, THE COLD-BLOODED LOVER.
BUT WHO CARES ABOUT NAMES? KISS ME! KISS ME! KISS ME!
YUCK! NO!
IS IT MY BREATH? I HAVE MEALWORM BINACA...
MOTH-ERRR!
AMEND

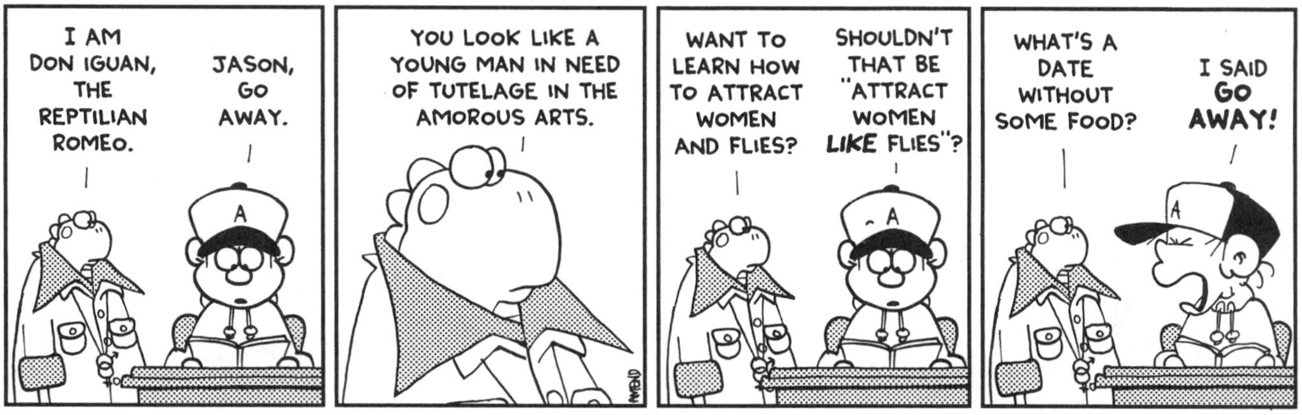
I AM DON IGUAN, THE REPTILIAN ROMEO.
JASON, GO AWAY.
YOU LOOK LIKE A YOUNG MAN IN NEED OF TUTELAGE IN THE AMOROUS ARTS.
WANT TO LEARN HOW TO ATTRACT WOMEN AND FLIES?
SHOULDN'T THAT BE "ATTRACT WOMEN LIKE FLIES"?
WHAT'S A DATE WITHOUT SOME FOOD?
I SAID GO AWAY!
AMEND

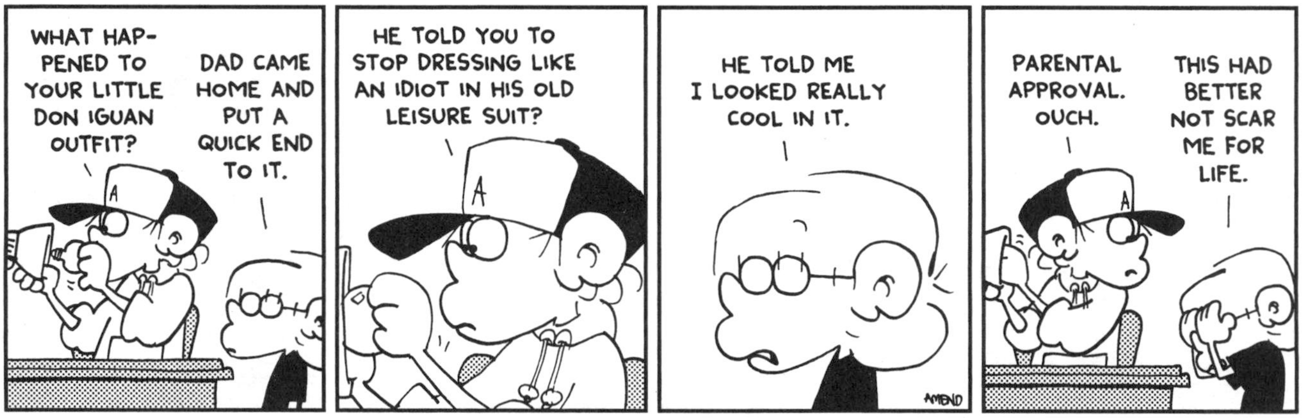
WHAT HAP-PENED TO YOUR LITTLE DON IGUAN OUTFIT?
DAD CAME HOME AND PUT A QUICK END TO IT.
HE TOLD YOU TO STOP DRESSING LIKE AN IDIOT IN HIS OLD LEISURE SUIT?
HE TOLD ME I LOOKED REALLY COOL IN IT.
PARENTAL APPROVAL. OUCH.
THIS HAD BETTER NOT SCAR ME FOR LIFE.
AMEND

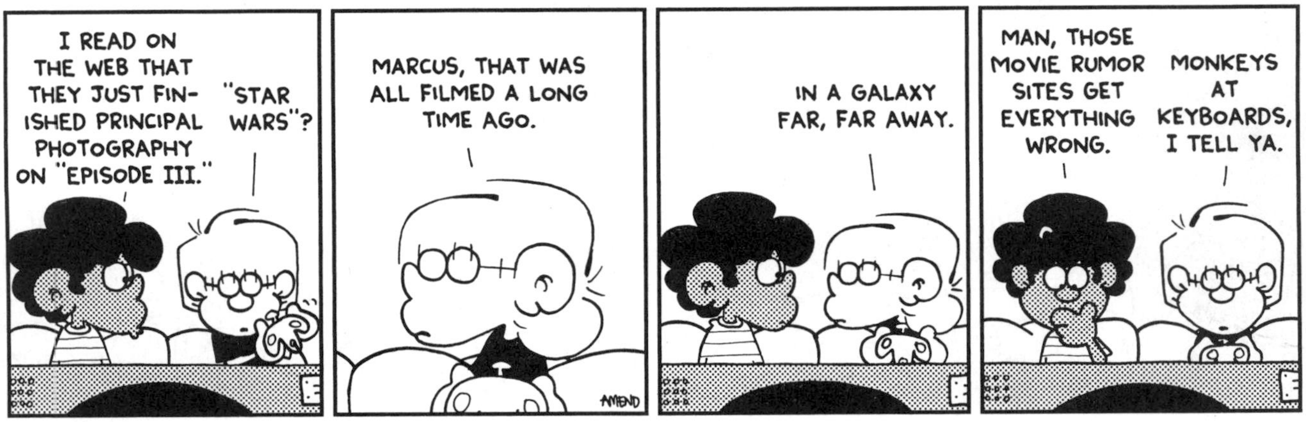
I READ ON THE WEB THAT THEY JUST FINISHED PRINCIPAL PHOTOGRAPHY ON "EPISODE III."
"STAR WARS"?
MARCUS, THAT WAS ALL FILMED A LONG TIME AGO.
IN A GALAXY FAR, FAR AWAY.
MAN, THOSE MOVIE RUMOR SITES GET EVERYTHING WRONG.
MONKEYS AT KEYBOARDS, I TELL YA.

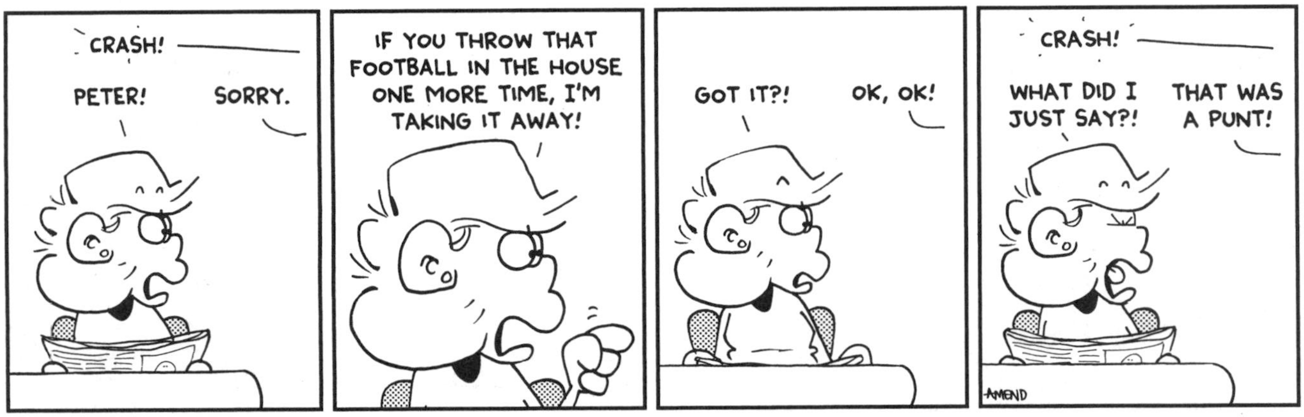
CRASH!
PETER!
SORRY.
IF YOU THROW THAT FOOTBALL IN THE HOUSE ONE MORE TIME, I'M TAKING IT AWAY!
GOT IT?!
OK, OK!
CRASH!
WHAT DID I JUST SAY?!
THAT WAS A PUNT!

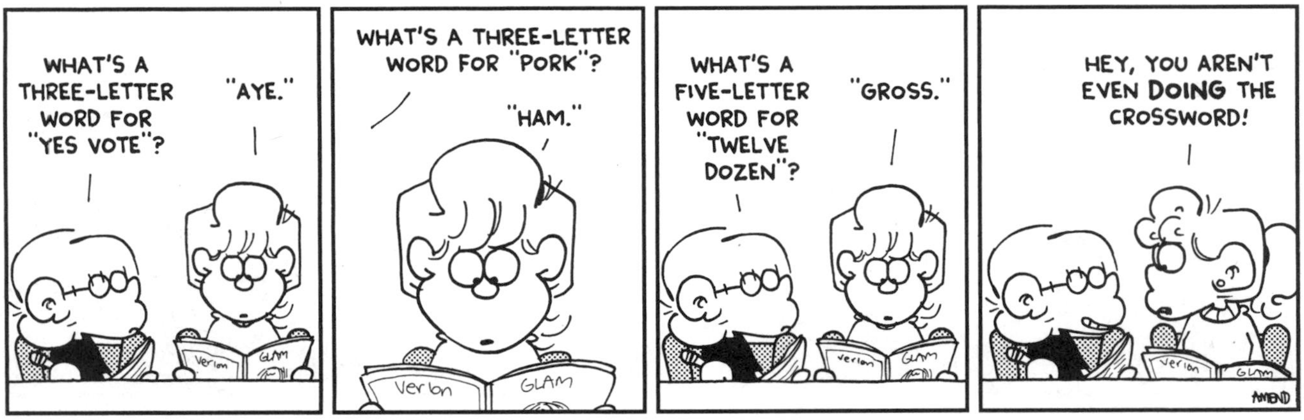
WHAT'S A THREE-LETTER WORD FOR "YES VOTE"?
"AYE."
WHAT'S A THREE-LETTER WORD FOR "PORK"?
"HAM."
WHAT'S A FIVE-LETTER WORD FOR "TWELVE DOZEN"?
"GROSS."
HEY, YOU AREN'T EVEN **DOING** THE CROSSWORD!

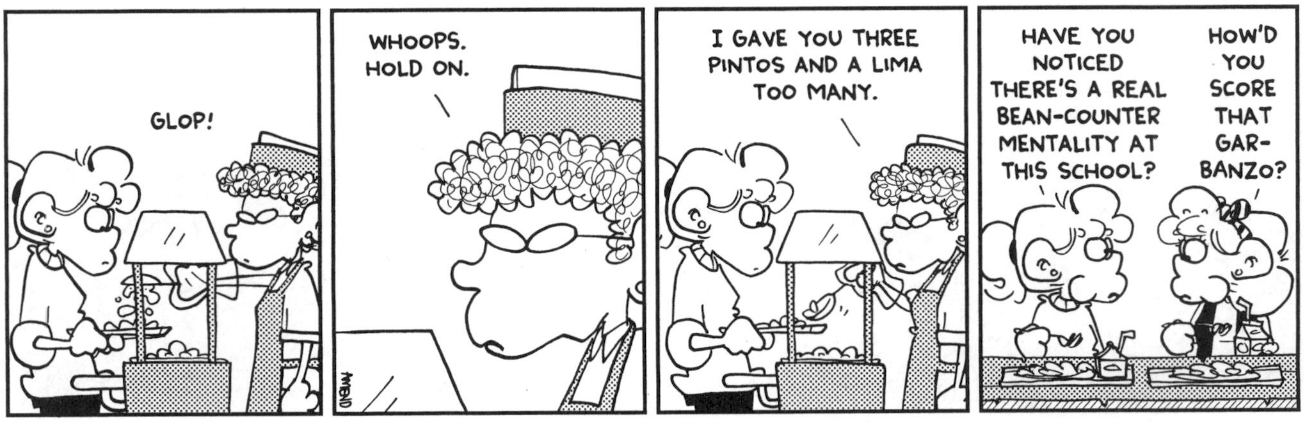
GLOP!
WHOOPS. HOLD ON.
I GAVE YOU THREE PINTOS AND A LIMA TOO MANY.
HAVE YOU NOTICED THERE'S A REAL BEAN-COUNTER MENTALITY AT THIS SCHOOL?
HOW'D YOU SCORE THAT GARBANZO?

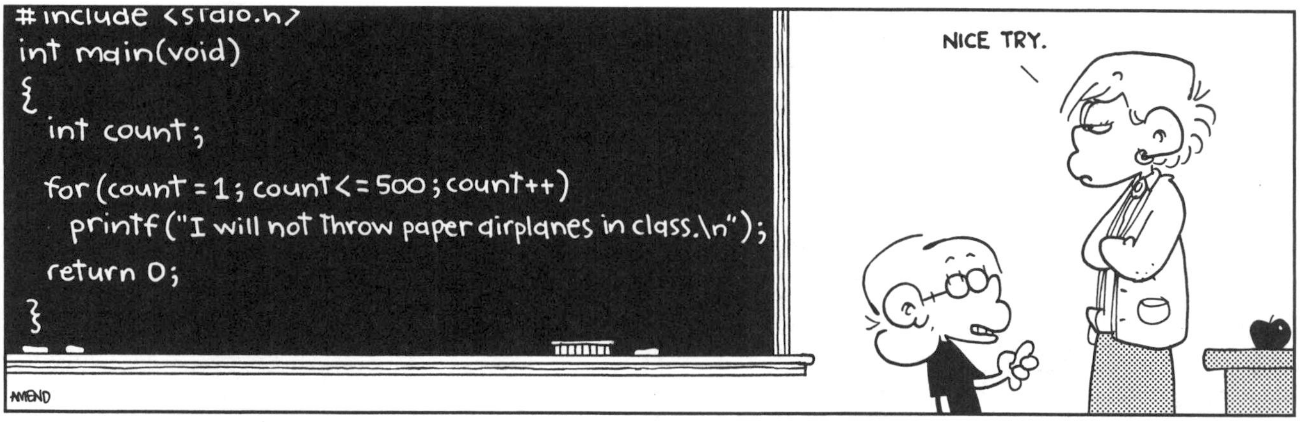
#include <stdio.h>
int main(void)
{
int count;
for(count = 1; count<= 500; count++)
printf("I will not throw paper airplanes in class.\n");
return 0;
}
NICE TRY.
AMEND

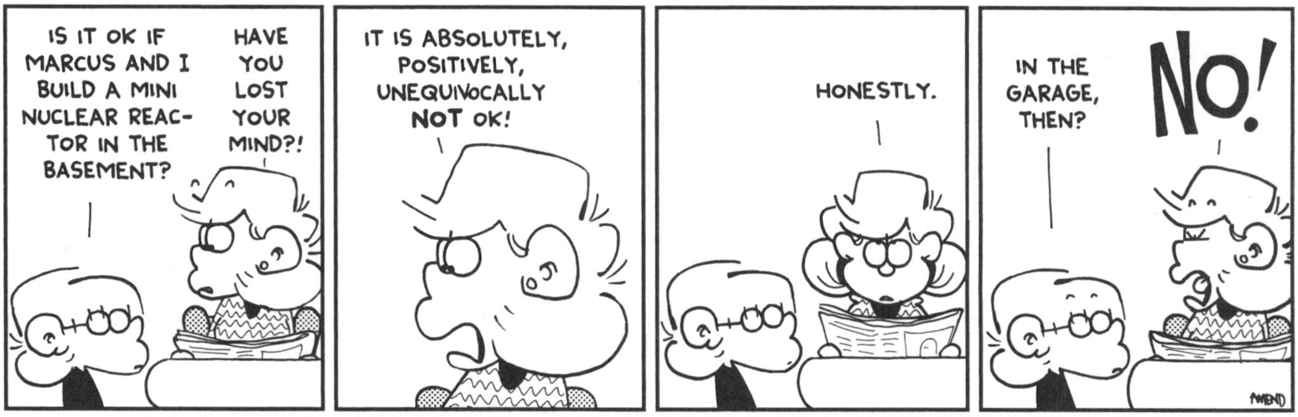
IS IT OK IF MARCUS AND I BUILD A MINI NUCLEAR REACTOR IN THE BASEMENT?
HAVE YOU LOST YOUR MIND?!
IT IS ABSOLUTELY, POSITIVELY, UNEQUIVOCALLY NOT OK!
HONESTLY.
IN THE GARAGE, THEN?
NO!
AMEND

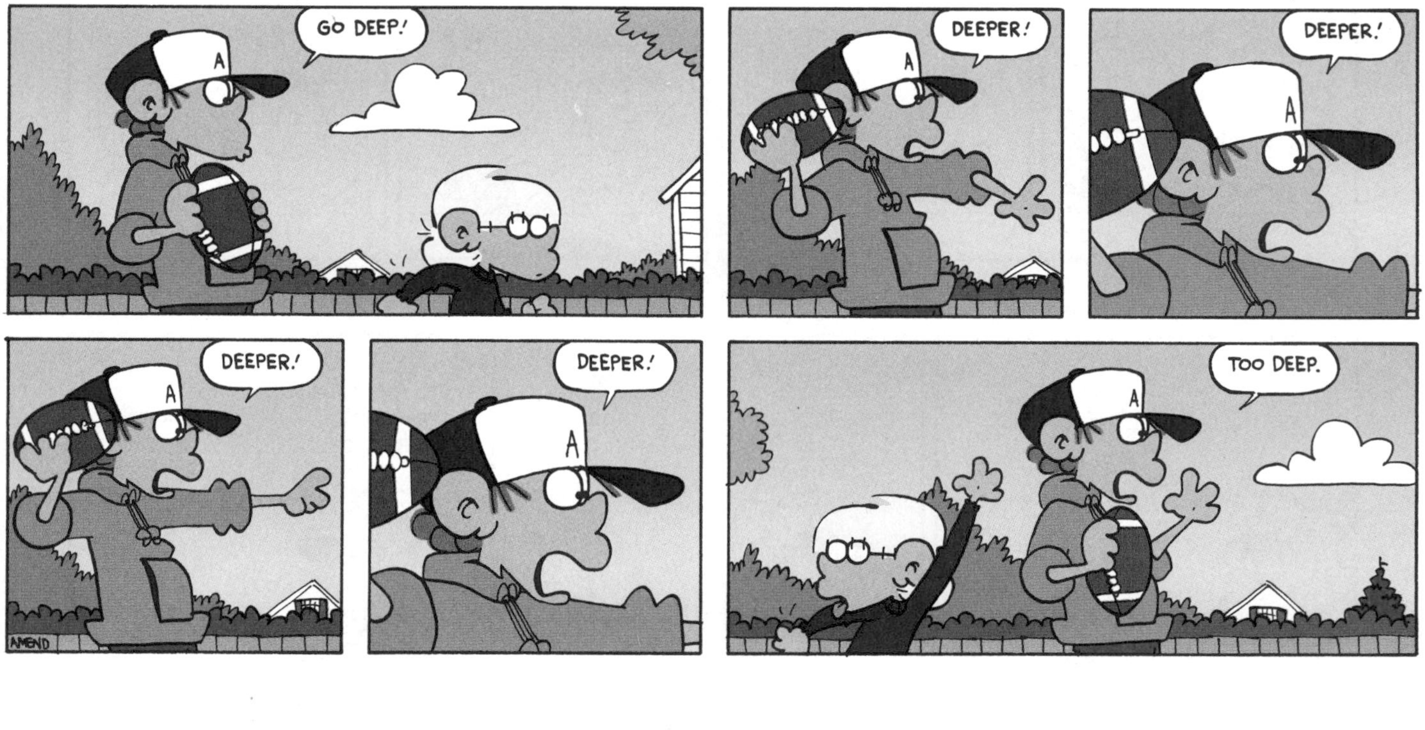
GO DEEP!
DEEPER!
DEEPER!
DEEPER!
DEEPER!
TOO DEEP.
AMEND

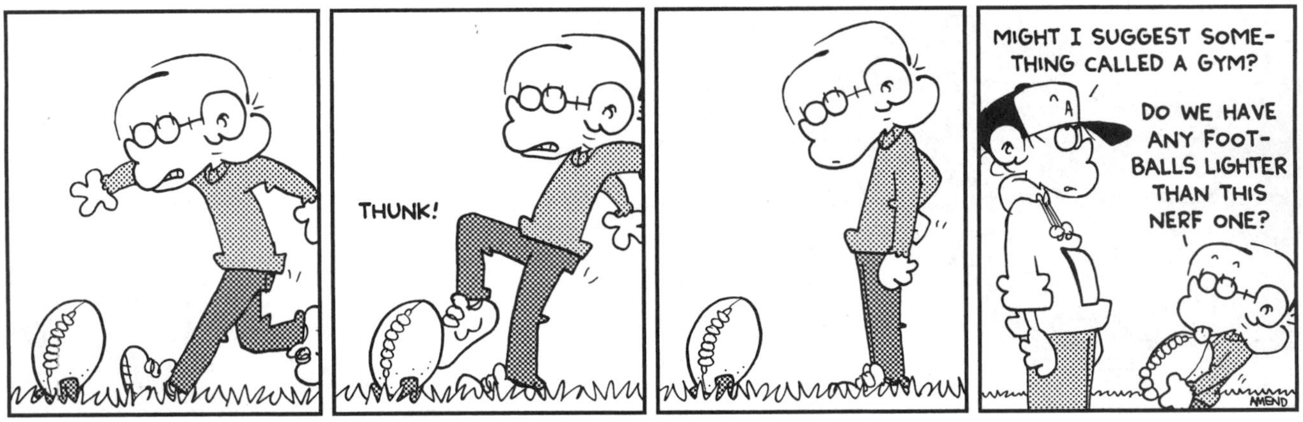
THUNK!
MIGHT I SUGGEST SOMETHING CALLED A GYM?
DO WE HAVE ANY FOOTBALLS LIGHTER THAN THIS NERF ONE?
AMEND

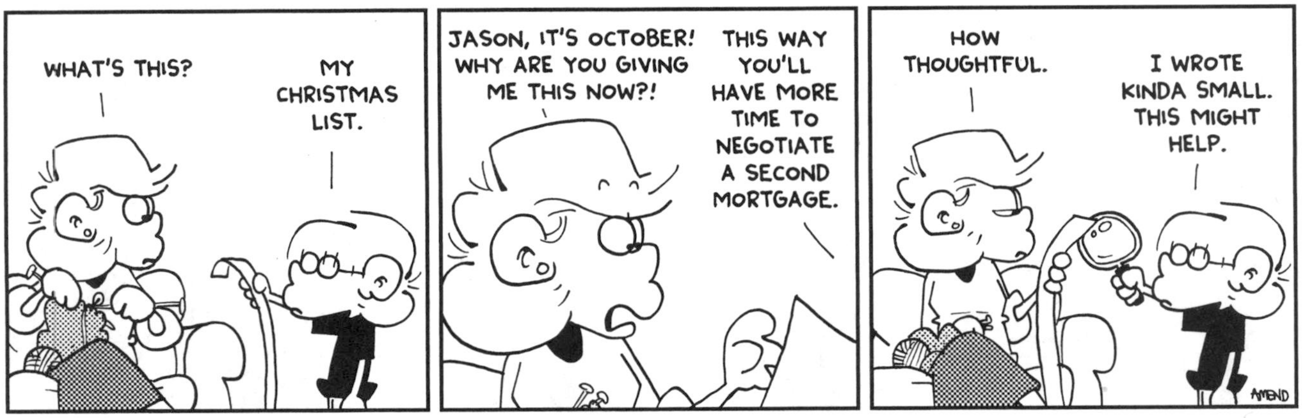
WHAT'S THIS?
MY CHRISTMAS LIST.
JASON, IT'S OCTOBER! WHY ARE YOU GIVING ME THIS NOW?!
THIS WAY YOU'LL HAVE MORE TIME TO NEGOTIATE A SECOND MORTGAGE.
HOW THOUGHTFUL.
I WROTE KINDA SMALL. THIS MIGHT HELP.
AMEND

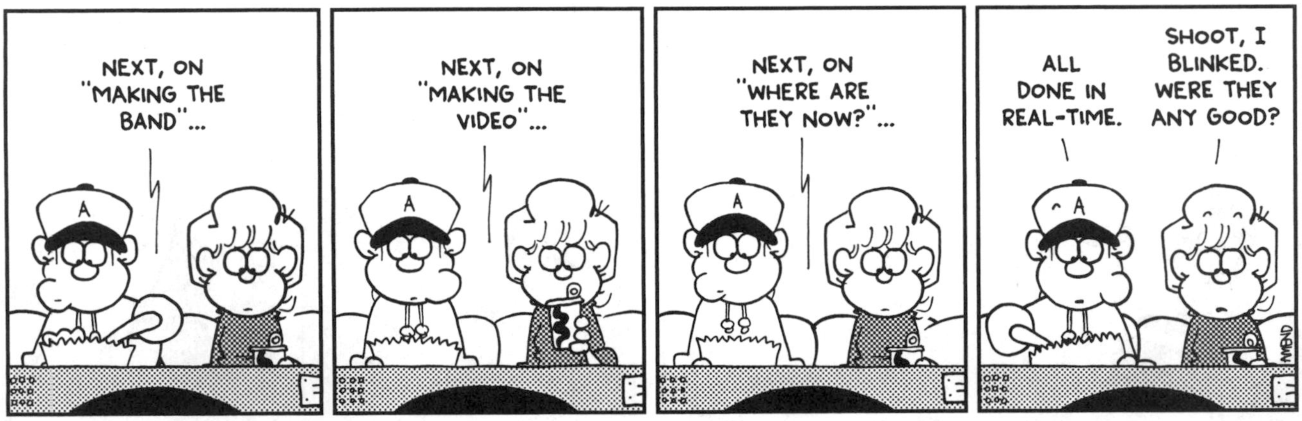
NEXT, ON "MAKING THE BAND"...
NEXT, ON "MAKING THE VIDEO"...
NEXT, ON "WHERE ARE THEY NOW?"...
ALL DONE IN REAL-TIME.
SHOOT, I BLINKED. WERE THEY ANY GOOD?
AMEND

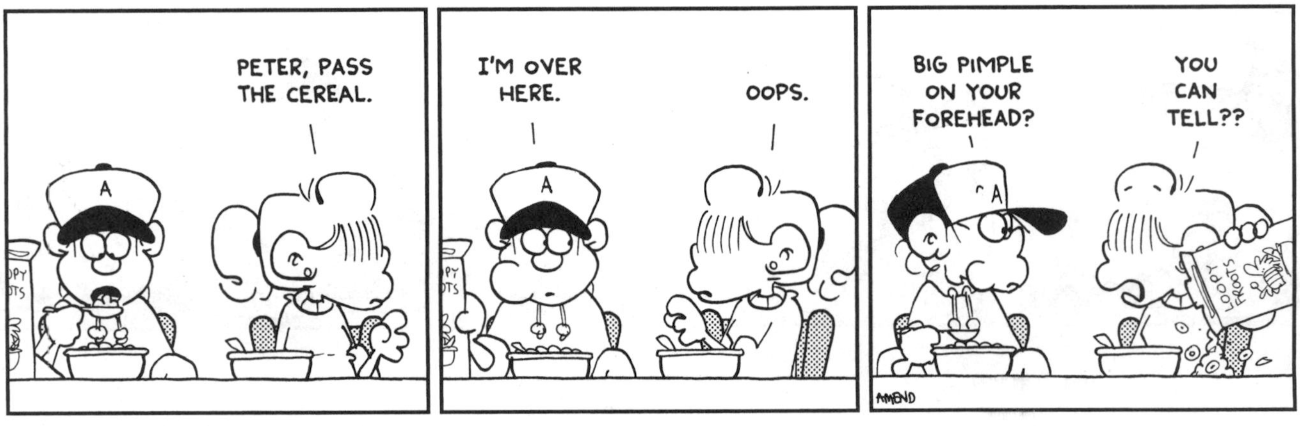
PETER, PASS THE CEREAL.
I'M OVER HERE.
OOPS.
BIG PIMPLE ON YOUR FOREHEAD?
YOU CAN TELL??
LOOPY FROOTS
AMEND

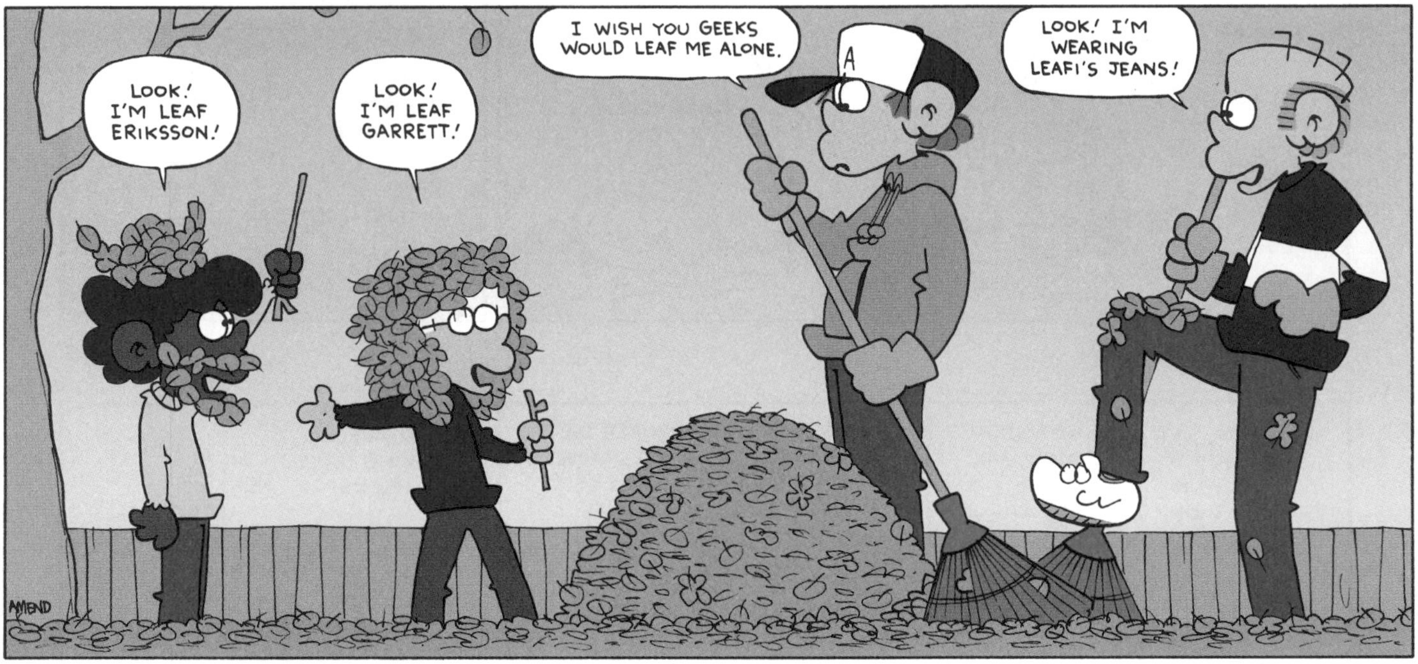
LOOK! I'M LEAF ERIKSSON!
LOOK! I'M LEAF GARRETT!
I WISH YOU GEEKS WOULD LEAF ME ALONE.
LOOK! I'M WEARING LEAFI'S JEANS!
AMEND

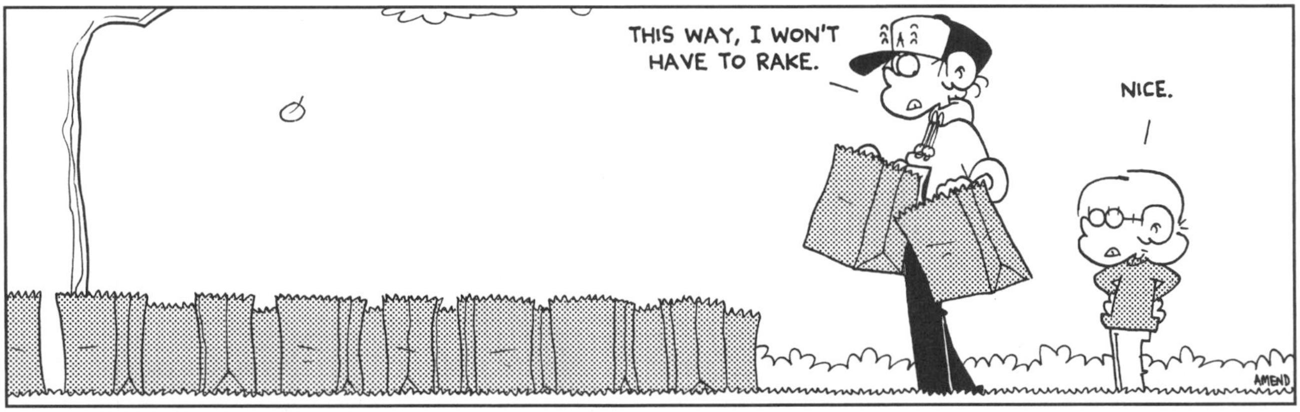
THIS WAY, I WON'T HAVE TO RAKE.
NICE.
AMEND

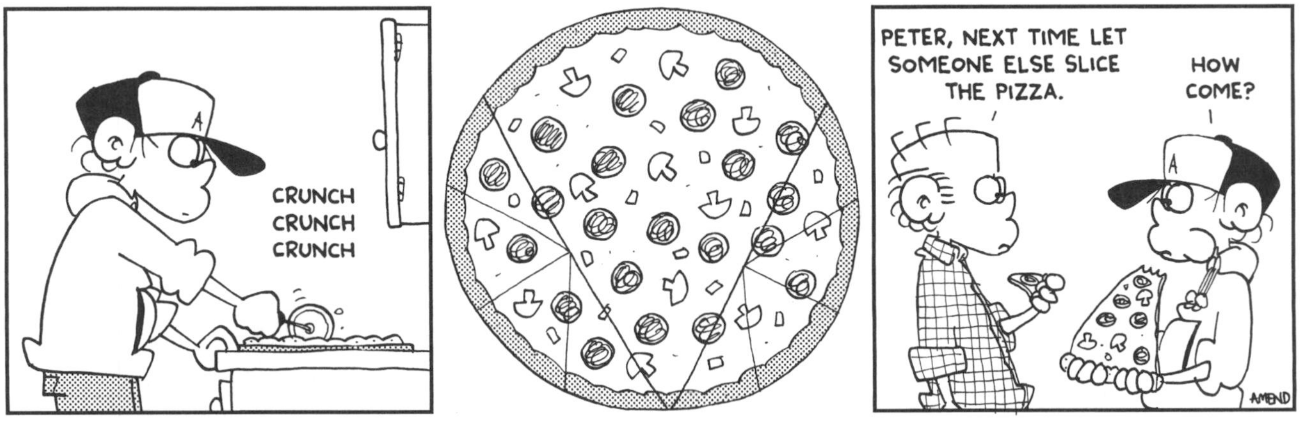
CRUNCH
CRUNCH
CRUNCH
PETER, NEXT TIME LET SOMEONE ELSE SLICE THE PIZZA.
HOW COME?
AMEND

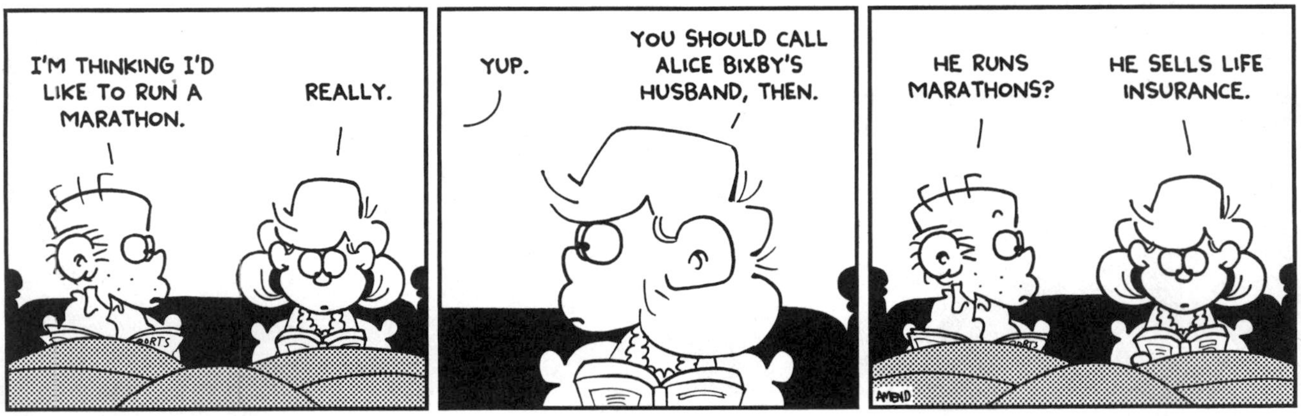
I'M THINKING I'D LIKE TO RUN A MARATHON.
REALLY.
YUP.
YOU SHOULD CALL ALICE BIXBY'S HUSBAND, THEN.
HE RUNS MARATHONS?
HE SELLS LIFE INSURANCE.

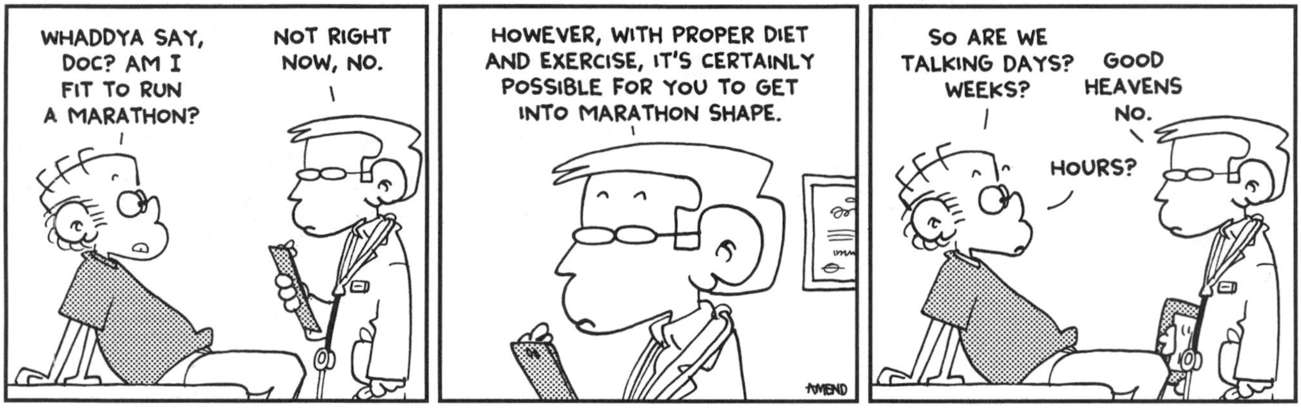
WHADDYA SAY, DOC? AM I FIT TO RUN A MARATHON?
NOT RIGHT NOW, NO.
HOWEVER, WITH PROPER DIET AND EXERCISE, IT'S CERTAINLY POSSIBLE FOR YOU TO GET INTO MARATHON SHAPE.
SO ARE WE TALKING DAYS? WEEKS?
GOOD HEAVENS NO.
HOURS?

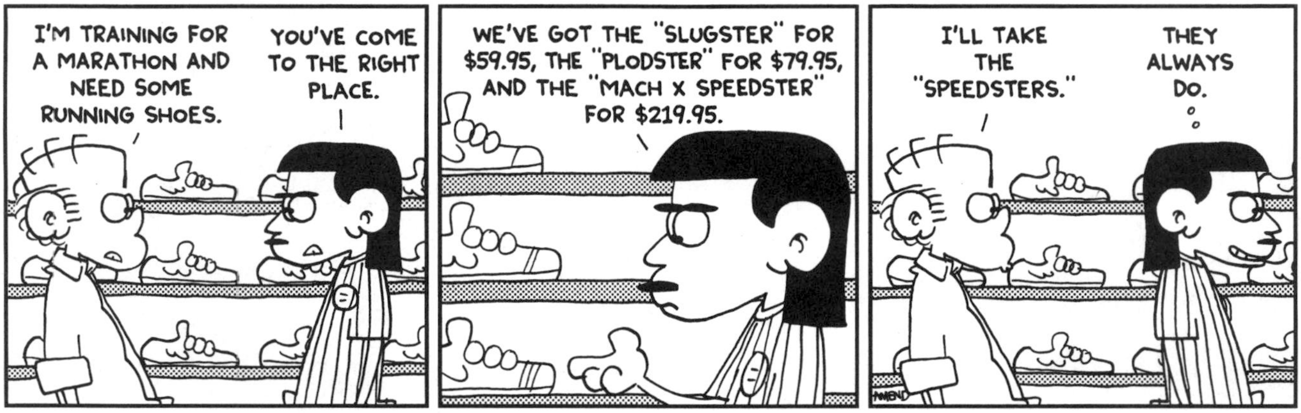
I'M TRAINING FOR A MARATHON AND NEED SOME RUNNING SHOES.
YOU'VE COME TO THE RIGHT PLACE.
WE'VE GOT THE "SLUGSTER" FOR $59.95, THE "PLODSTER" FOR $79.95, AND THE "MACH X SPEEDSTER" FOR $219.95.
I'LL TAKE THE "SPEEDSTERS."
THEY ALWAYS DO.

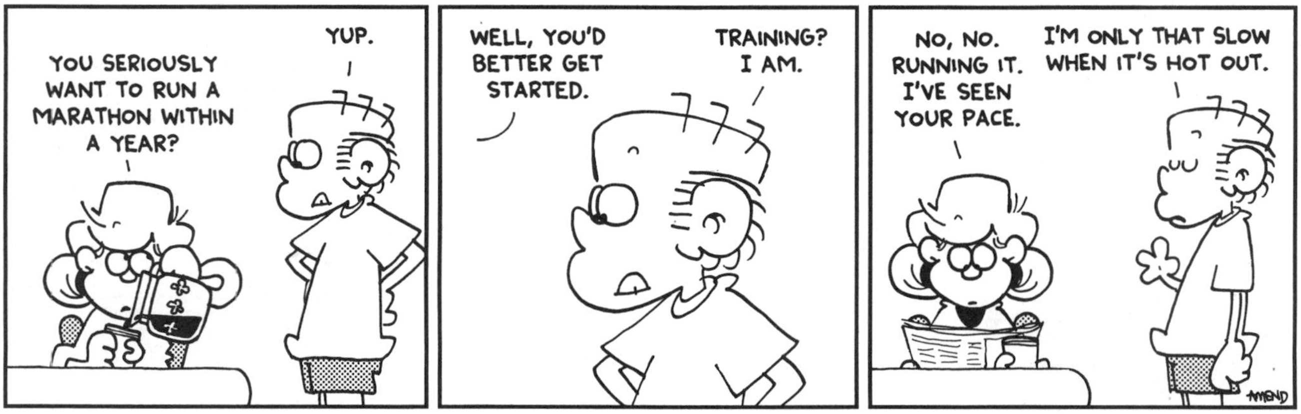
YOU SERIOUSLY WANT TO RUN A MARATHON WITHIN A YEAR?
YUP.
WELL, YOU'D BETTER GET STARTED.
TRAINING? I AM.
NO, NO. RUNNING IT. I'VE SEEN YOUR PACE.
I'M ONLY THAT SLOW WHEN IT'S HOT OUT.

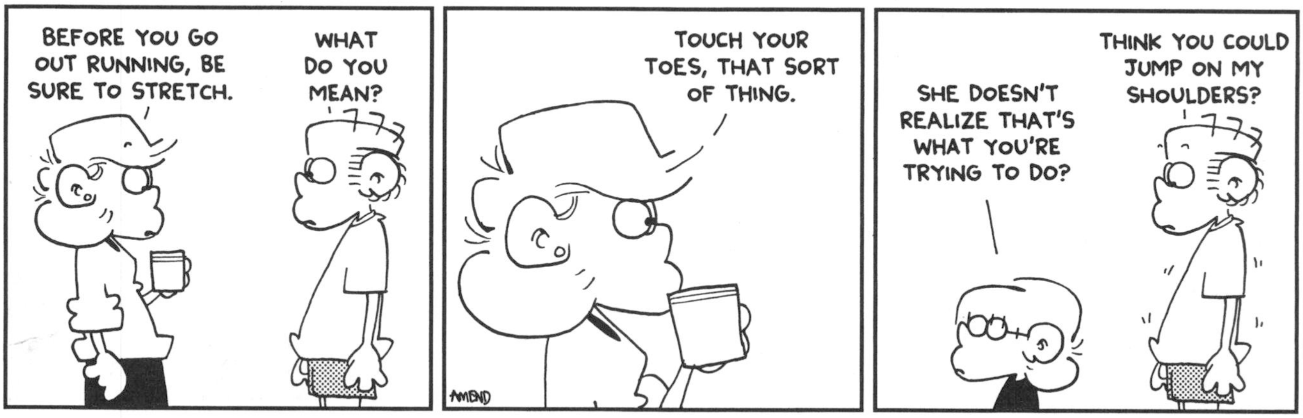
BEFORE YOU GO OUT RUNNING, BE SURE TO STRETCH.
WHAT DO YOU MEAN?
TOUCH YOUR TOES, THAT SORT OF THING.
AMEND
SHE DOESN'T REALIZE THAT'S WHAT YOU'RE TRYING TO DO?
THINK YOU COULD JUMP ON MY SHOULDERS?

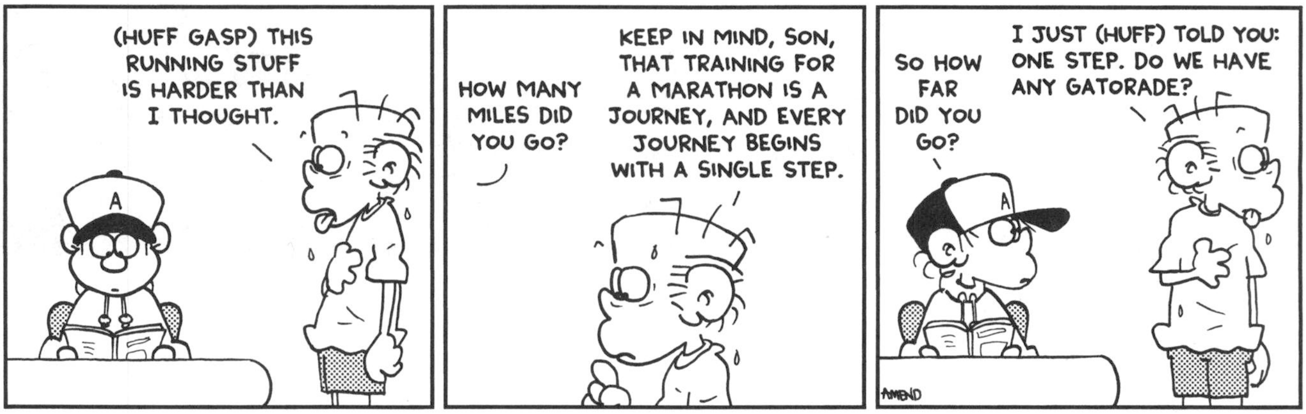
(HUFF GASP) THIS RUNNING STUFF IS HARDER THAN I THOUGHT.
A
HOW MANY MILES DID YOU GO?
KEEP IN MIND, SON, THAT TRAINING FOR A MARATHON IS A JOURNEY, AND EVERY JOURNEY BEGINS WITH A SINGLE STEP.
SO HOW FAR DID YOU GO?
I JUST (HUFF) TOLD YOU: ONE STEP. DO WE HAVE ANY GATORADE?
A
AMEND

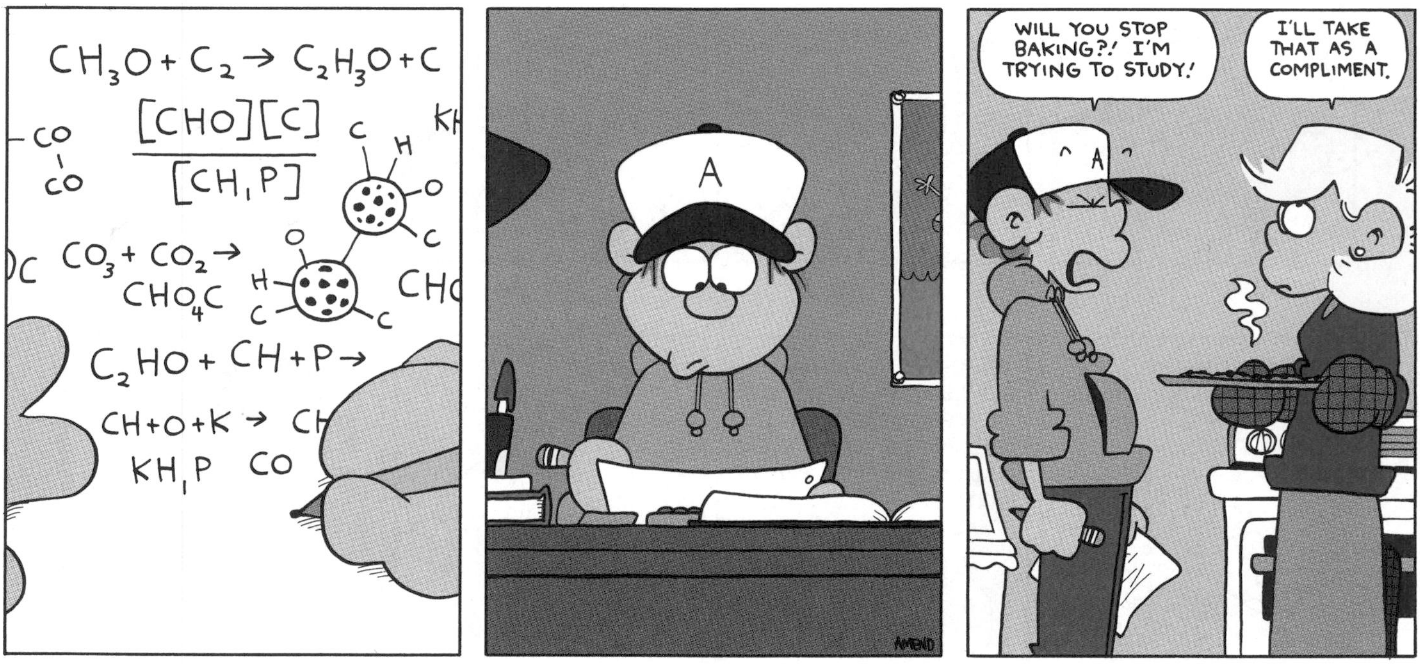
$CH_3O + C_2 \rightarrow C_2H_3O + C$
$\frac{[CHO][C]}{[CH_1P]}$
$CO_3 + CO_2 \rightarrow$
CHO_4C
$C_2HO + CH + P \rightarrow$
$CH + O + K \rightarrow$
KH_1P CO
A
AMEND
WILL YOU STOP BAKING?! I'M TRYING TO STUDY!
I'LL TAKE THAT AS A COMPLIMENT.
A

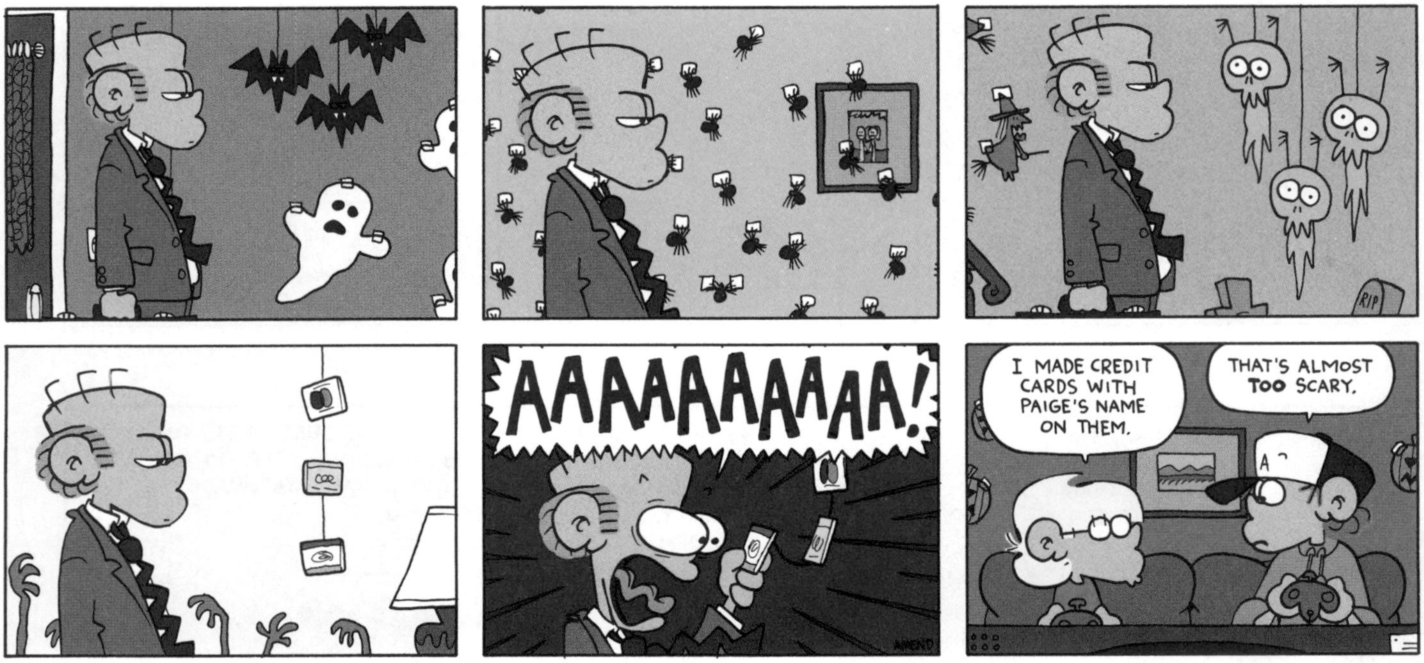
AAAAAAAAAA!
I MADE CREDIT CARDS WITH PAIGE'S NAME ON THEM.
THAT'S ALMOST **TOO** SCARY.

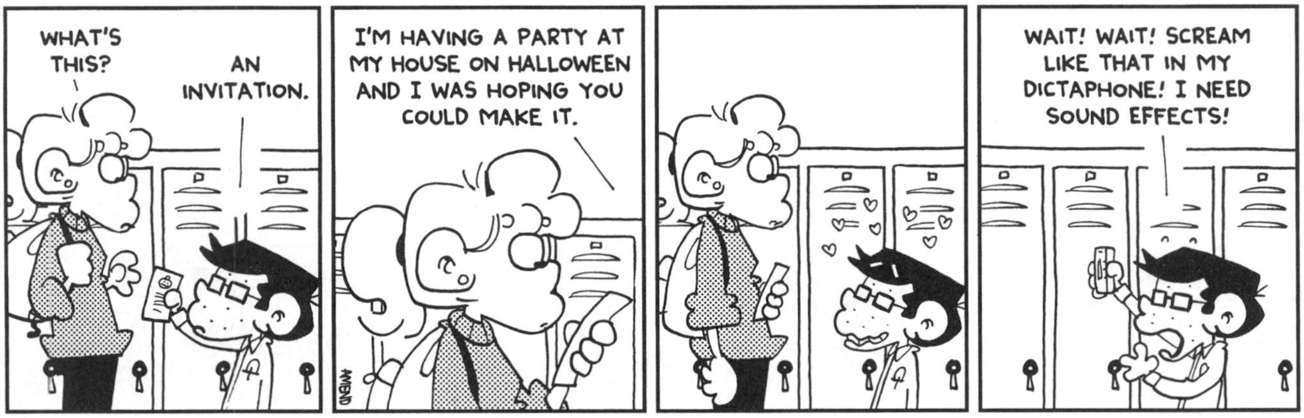
WHAT'S THIS?
AN INVITATION.
I'M HAVING A PARTY AT MY HOUSE ON HALLOWEEN AND I WAS HOPING YOU COULD MAKE IT.
WAIT! WAIT! SCREAM LIKE THAT IN MY DICTAPHONE! I NEED SOUND EFFECTS!

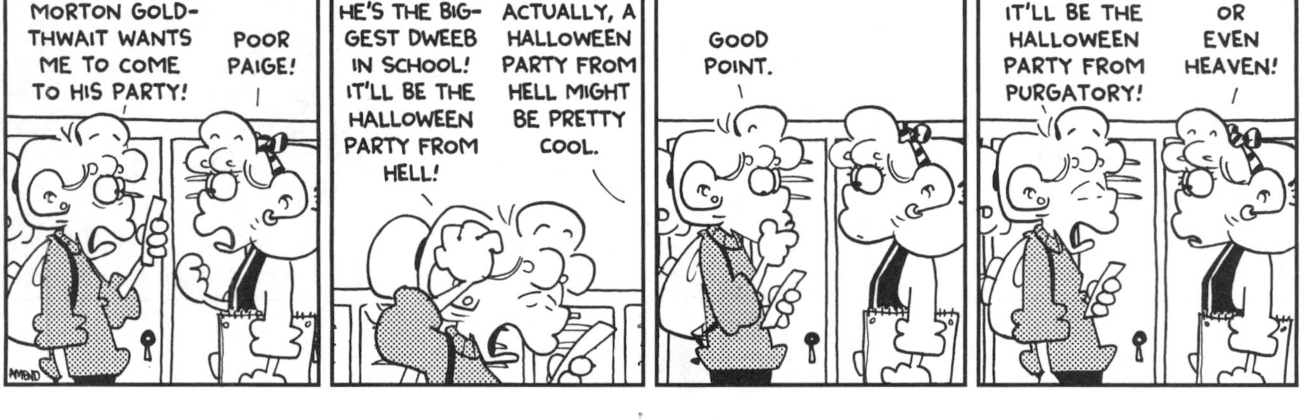
MORTON GOLD-THWAIT WANTS ME TO COME TO HIS PARTY!
POOR PAIGE!
HE'S THE BIG-GEST DWEEB IN SCHOOL! IT'LL BE THE HALLOWEEN PARTY FROM HELL!
ACTUALLY, A HALLOWEEN PARTY FROM HELL MIGHT BE PRETTY COOL.
GOOD POINT.
IT'LL BE THE HALLOWEEN PARTY FROM PURGATORY!
OR EVEN HEAVEN!

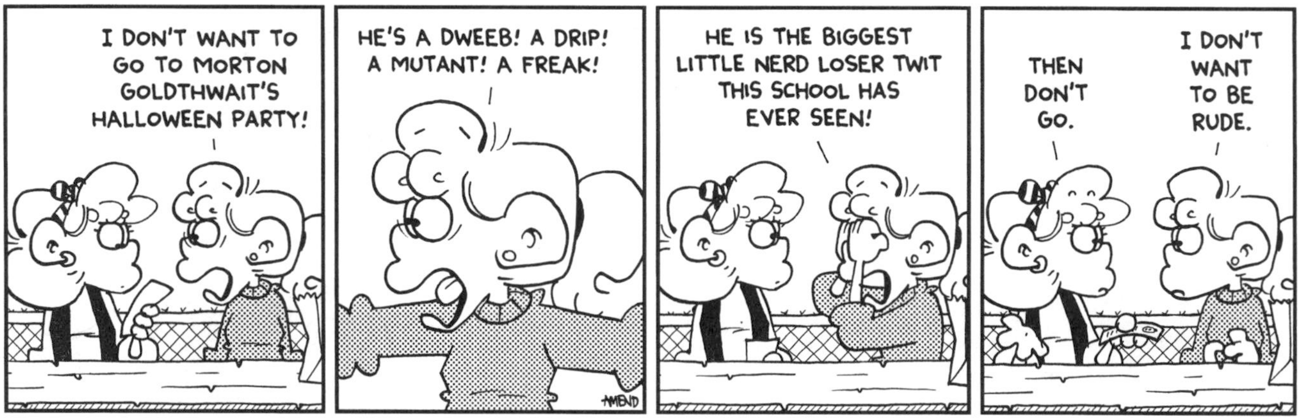
I DON'T WANT TO GO TO MORTON GOLDTHWAIT'S HALLOWEEN PARTY!
HE'S A DWEEB! A DRIP! A MUTANT! A FREAK!
HE IS THE BIGGEST LITTLE NERD LOSER TWIT THIS SCHOOL HAS EVER SEEN!
THEN DON'T GO.
I DON'T WANT TO BE RUDE.
AMEND

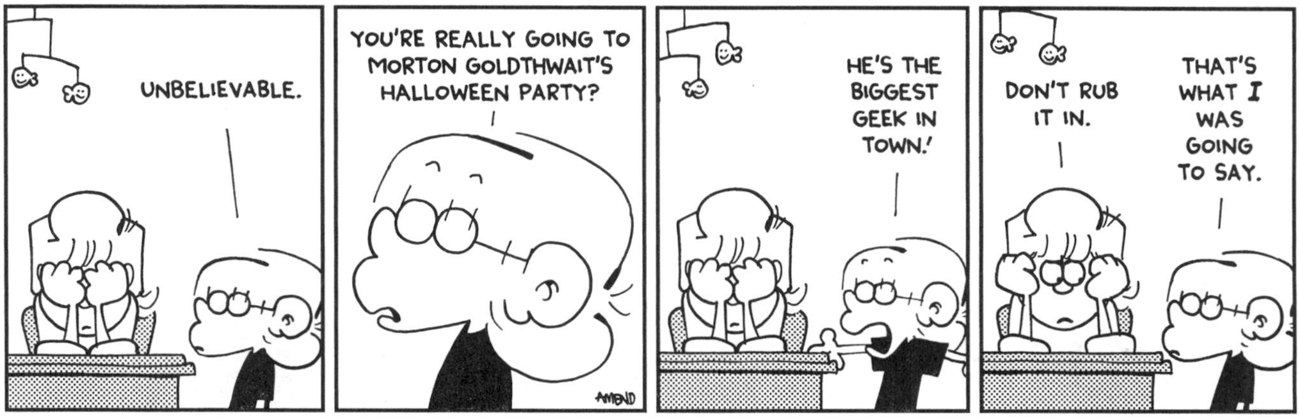
UNBELIEVABLE.
YOU'RE REALLY GOING TO MORTON GOLDTHWAIT'S HALLOWEEN PARTY?
HE'S THE BIGGEST GEEK IN TOWN!
DON'T RUB IT IN.
THAT'S WHAT I WAS GOING TO SAY.
AMEND

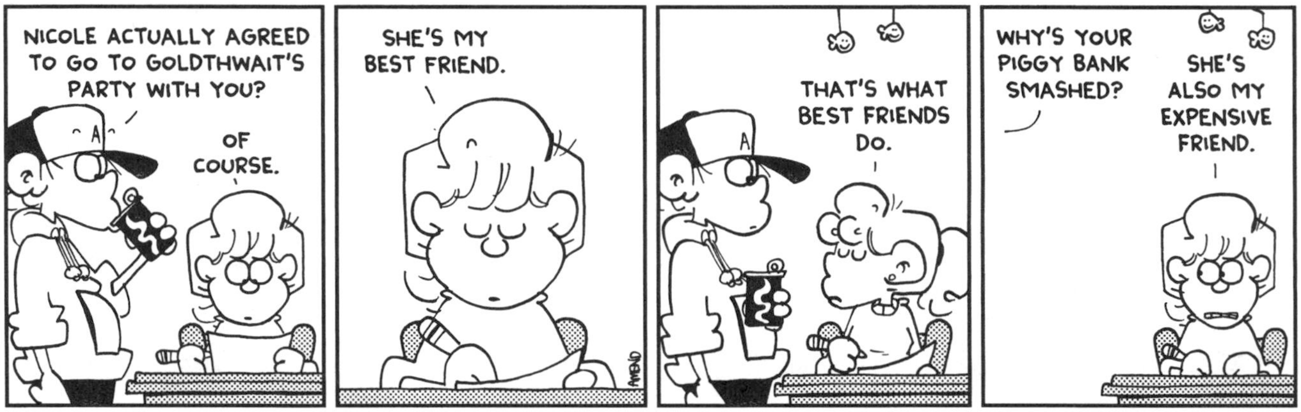
NICOLE ACTUALLY AGREED TO GO TO GOLDTHWAIT'S PARTY WITH YOU?
OF COURSE.
SHE'S MY BEST FRIEND.
THAT'S WHAT BEST FRIENDS DO.
WHY'S YOUR PIGGY BANK SMASHED?
SHE'S ALSO MY EXPENSIVE FRIEND.
AMEND

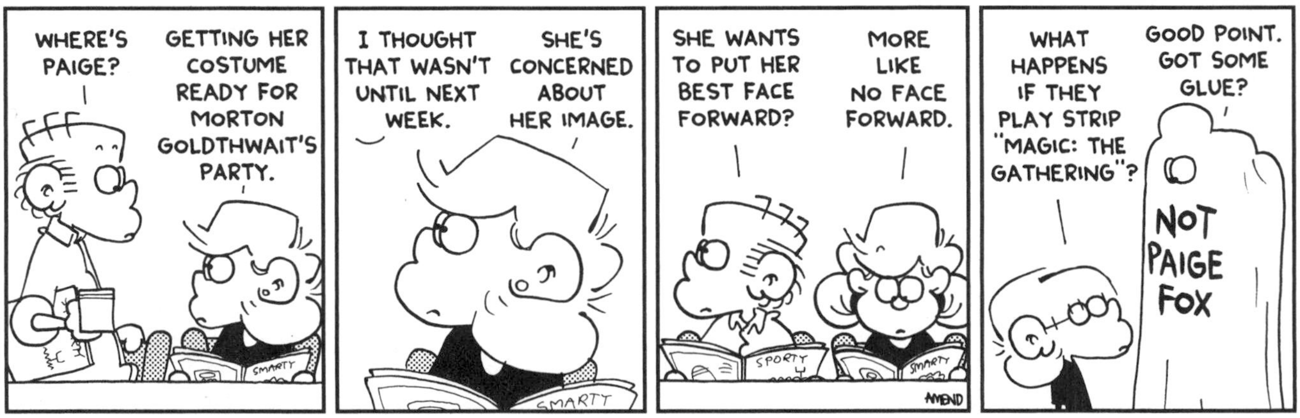
WHERE'S PAIGE?
GETTING HER COSTUME READY FOR MORTON GOLDTHWAIT'S PARTY.
SMARTY
I THOUGHT THAT WASN'T UNTIL NEXT WEEK.
SHE'S CONCERNED ABOUT HER IMAGE.
SMARTY
SHE WANTS TO PUT HER BEST FACE FORWARD?
MORE LIKE NO FACE FORWARD.
SPORTY
SMARTY
WHAT HAPPENS IF THEY PLAY STRIP "MAGIC: THE GATHERING"?
GOOD POINT. GOT SOME GLUE?
NOT PAIGE FOX
AMEND

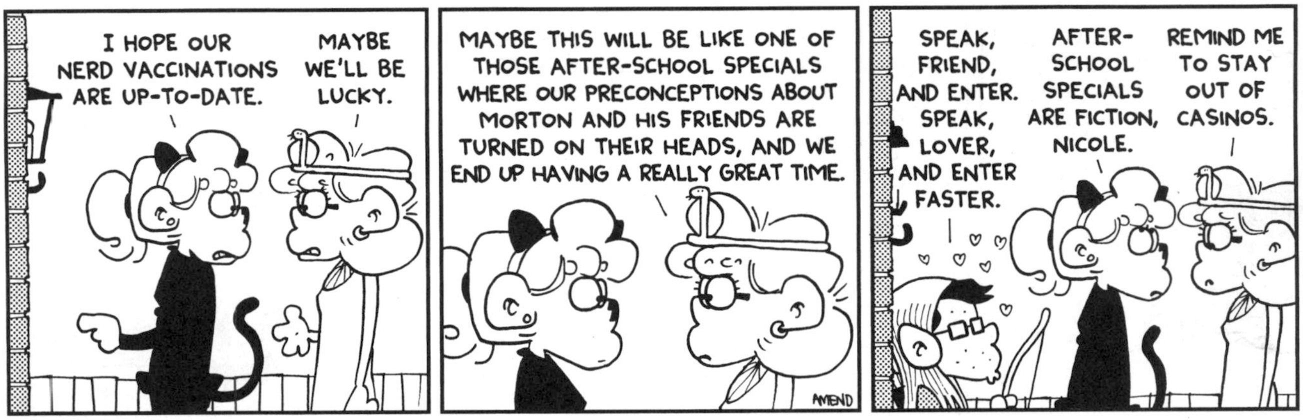
I HOPE OUR NERD VACCINATIONS ARE UP-TO-DATE.
MAYBE WE'LL BE LUCKY.
MAYBE THIS WILL BE LIKE ONE OF THOSE AFTER-SCHOOL SPECIALS WHERE OUR PRECONCEPTIONS ABOUT MORTON AND HIS FRIENDS ARE TURNED ON THEIR HEADS, AND WE END UP HAVING A REALLY GREAT TIME.
SPEAK, FRIEND, AND ENTER. SPEAK, LOVER, AND ENTER FASTER.
AFTER-SCHOOL SPECIALS ARE FICTION, NICOLE.
REMIND ME TO STAY OUT OF CASINOS.
AMEND

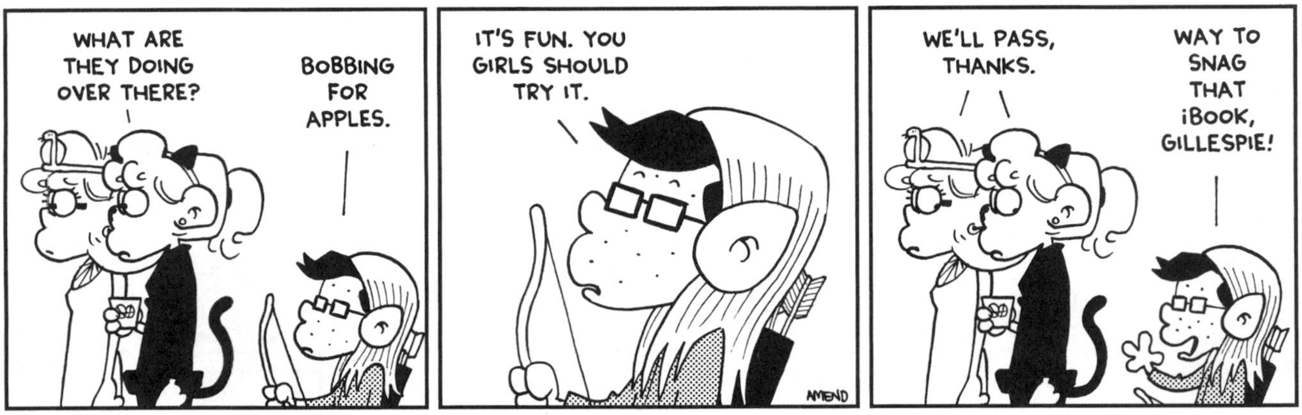
WHAT ARE THEY DOING OVER THERE?
BOBBING FOR APPLES.
IT'S FUN. YOU GIRLS SHOULD TRY IT.
WE'LL PASS, THANKS.
WAY TO SNAG THAT iBOOK, GILLESPIE!
AMEND

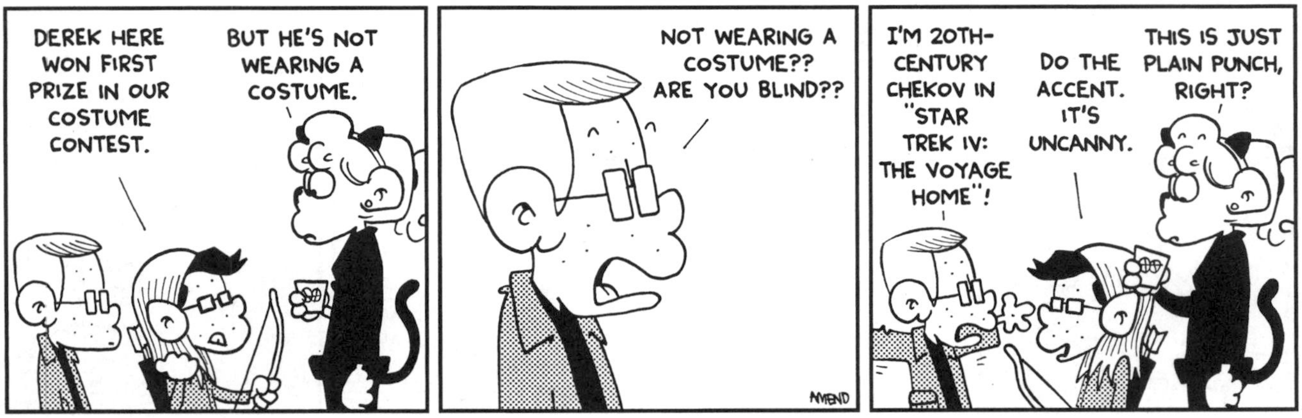
DEREK HERE WON FIRST PRIZE IN OUR COSTUME CONTEST.
BUT HE'S NOT WEARING A COSTUME.
NOT WEARING A COSTUME?? ARE YOU BLIND??
I'M 20TH-CENTURY CHEKOV IN "STAR TREK IV: THE VOYAGE HOME"!
DO THE ACCENT. IT'S UNCANNY.
THIS IS JUST PLAIN PUNCH, RIGHT?
AMEND

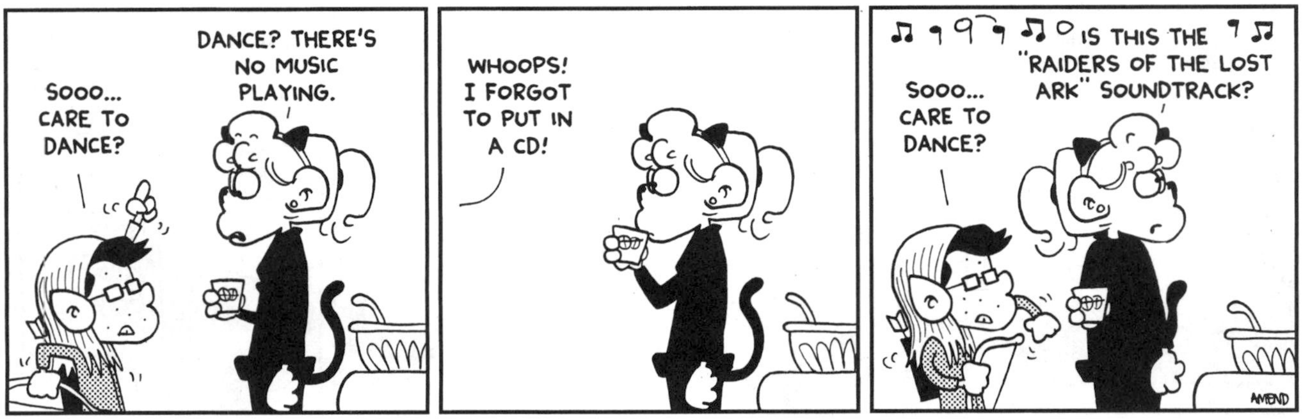
SOOO... CARE TO DANCE?
DANCE? THERE'S NO MUSIC PLAYING.
WHOOPS! I FORGOT TO PUT IN A CD!
SOOO... CARE TO DANCE?
IS THIS THE "RAIDERS OF THE LOST ARK" SOUNDTRACK?
AMEND

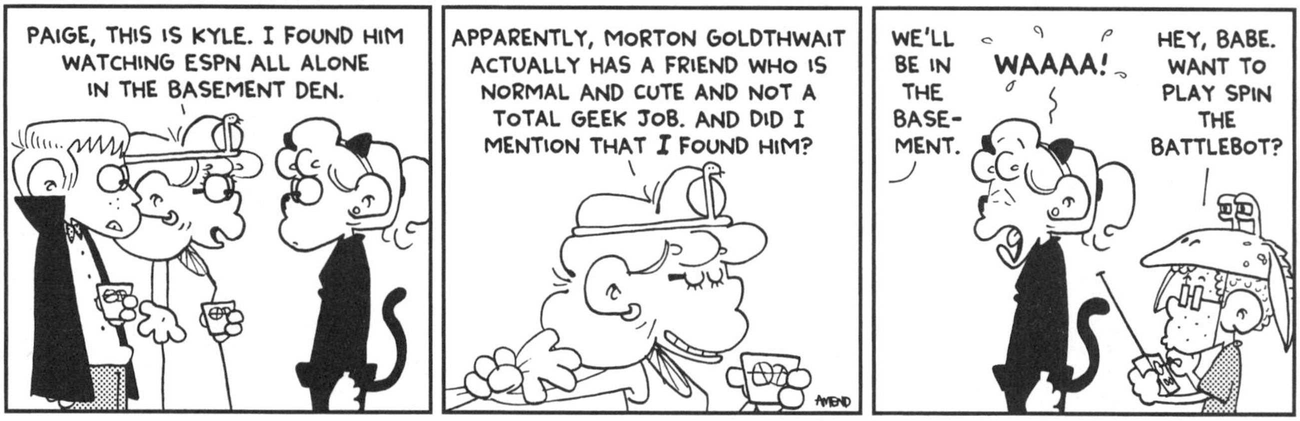
PAIGE, THIS IS KYLE. I FOUND HIM WATCHING ESPN ALL ALONE IN THE BASEMENT DEN.
APPARENTLY, MORTON GOLDTHWAIT ACTUALLY HAS A FRIEND WHO IS NORMAL AND CUTE AND NOT A TOTAL GEEK JOB. AND DID I MENTION THAT I FOUND HIM?
AMEND
WE'LL BE IN THE BASE- MENT.
WAAAA!
HEY, BABE. WANT TO PLAY SPIN THE BATTLEBOT?

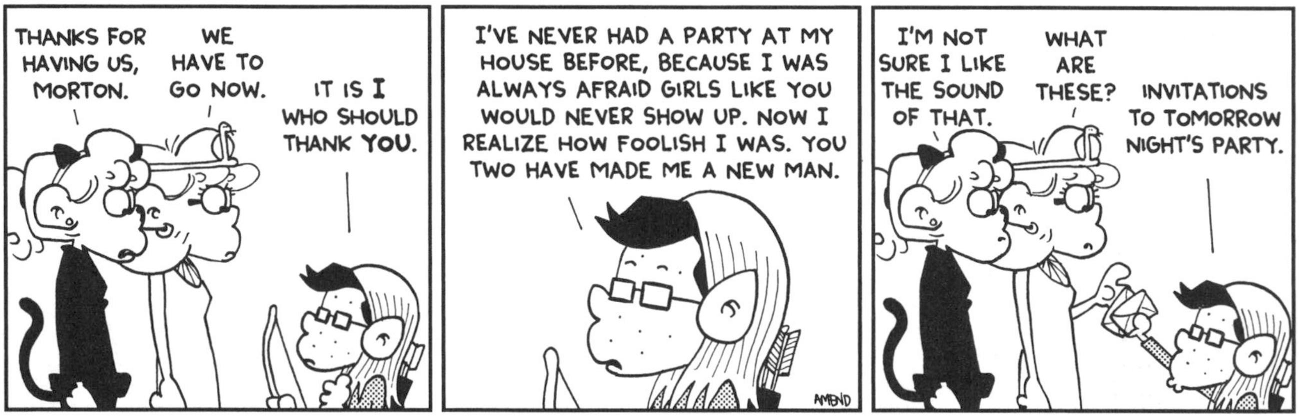
THANKS FOR HAVING US, MORTON.
WE HAVE TO GO NOW.
IT IS I WHO SHOULD THANK YOU.
I'VE NEVER HAD A PARTY AT MY HOUSE BEFORE, BECAUSE I WAS ALWAYS AFRAID GIRLS LIKE YOU WOULD NEVER SHOW UP. NOW I REALIZE HOW FOOLISH I WAS. YOU TWO HAVE MADE ME A NEW MAN.
AMEND
I'M NOT SURE I LIKE THE SOUND OF THAT.
WHAT ARE THESE?
INVITATIONS TO TOMORROW NIGHT'S PARTY.

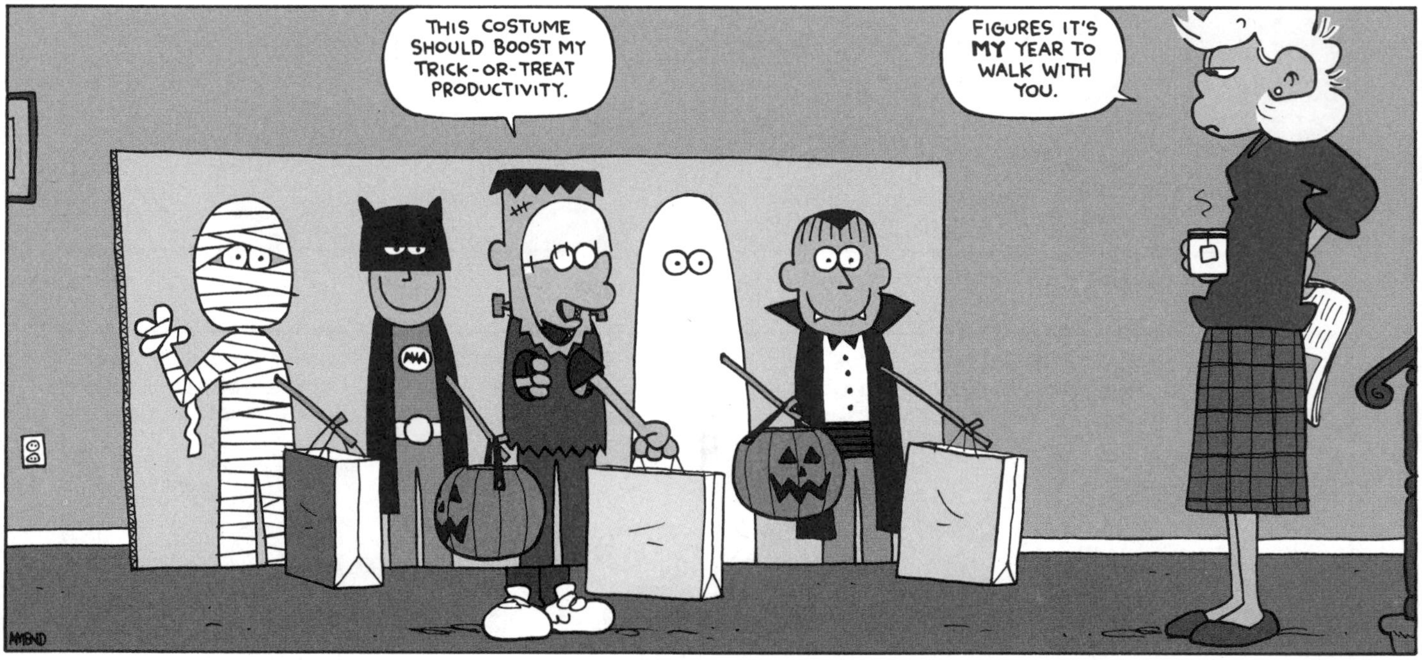
THIS COSTUME SHOULD BOOST MY TRICK-OR-TREAT PRODUCTIVITY.
FIGURES IT'S MY YEAR TO WALK WITH YOU.
AMEND

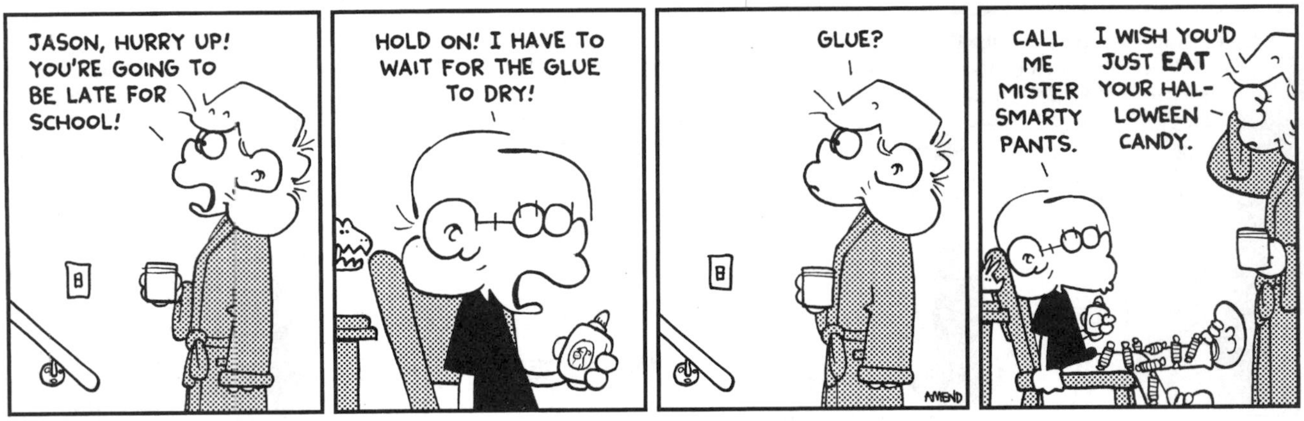
JASON, HURRY UP! YOU'RE GOING TO BE LATE FOR SCHOOL!
HOLD ON! I HAVE TO WAIT FOR THE GLUE TO DRY!
GLUE?
CALL ME MISTER SMARTY PANTS.
I WISH YOU'D JUST EAT YOUR HAL-LOWEEN CANDY.
AMEND

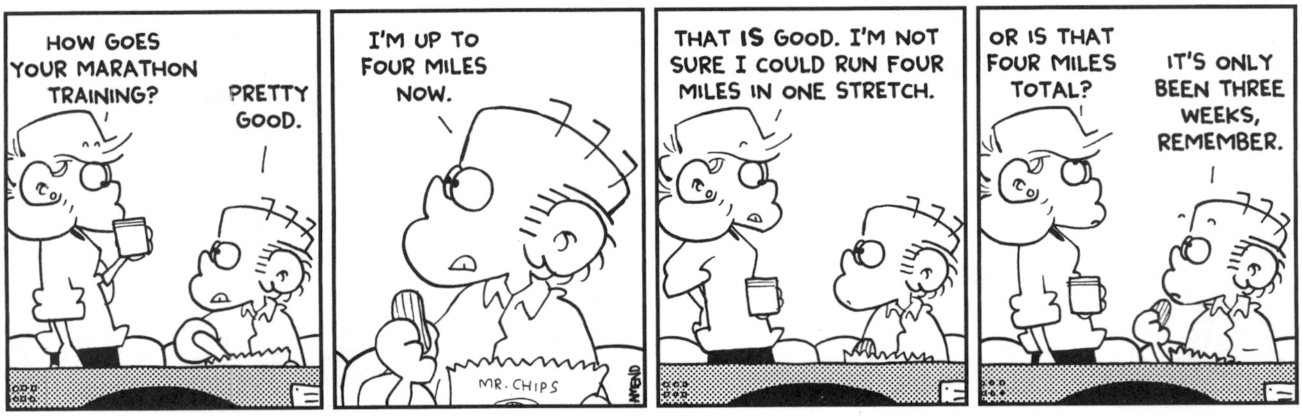
HOW GOES YOUR MARATHON TRAINING?
PRETTY GOOD.
I'M UP TO FOUR MILES NOW.
MR. CHIPS
AMEND
THAT IS GOOD. I'M NOT SURE I COULD RUN FOUR MILES IN ONE STRETCH.
OR IS THAT FOUR MILES TOTAL?
IT'S ONLY BEEN THREE WEEKS, REMEMBER.

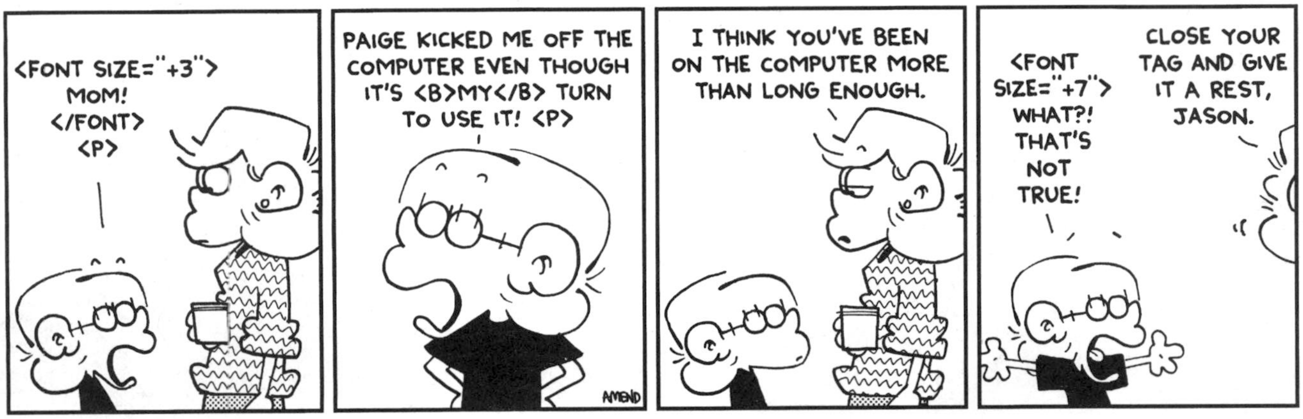
<FONT SIZE="+3"> MOM! </FONT> <P>
PAIGE KICKED ME OFF THE COMPUTER EVEN THOUGH IT'S <B>MY</B> TURN TO USE IT! <P>
AMEND
I THINK YOU'VE BEEN ON THE COMPUTER MORE THAN LONG ENOUGH.
<FONT SIZE="+7"> WHAT?! THAT'S NOT TRUE!
CLOSE YOUR TAG AND GIVE IT A REST, JASON.

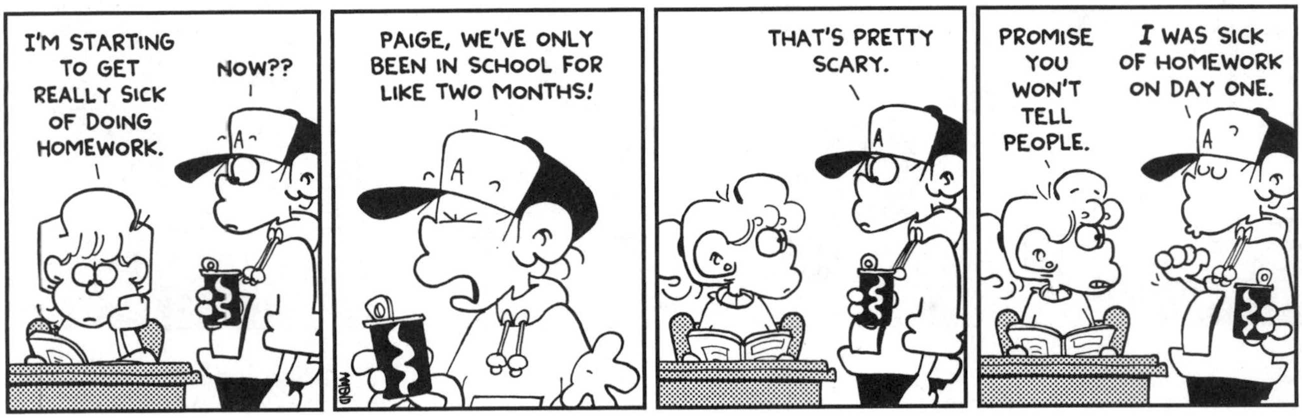
I'M STARTING TO GET REALLY SICK OF DOING HOMEWORK.
NOW??
PAIGE, WE'VE ONLY BEEN IN SCHOOL FOR LIKE TWO MONTHS!
THAT'S PRETTY SCARY.
PROMISE YOU WON'T TELL PEOPLE.
I WAS SICK OF HOMEWORK ON DAY ONE.

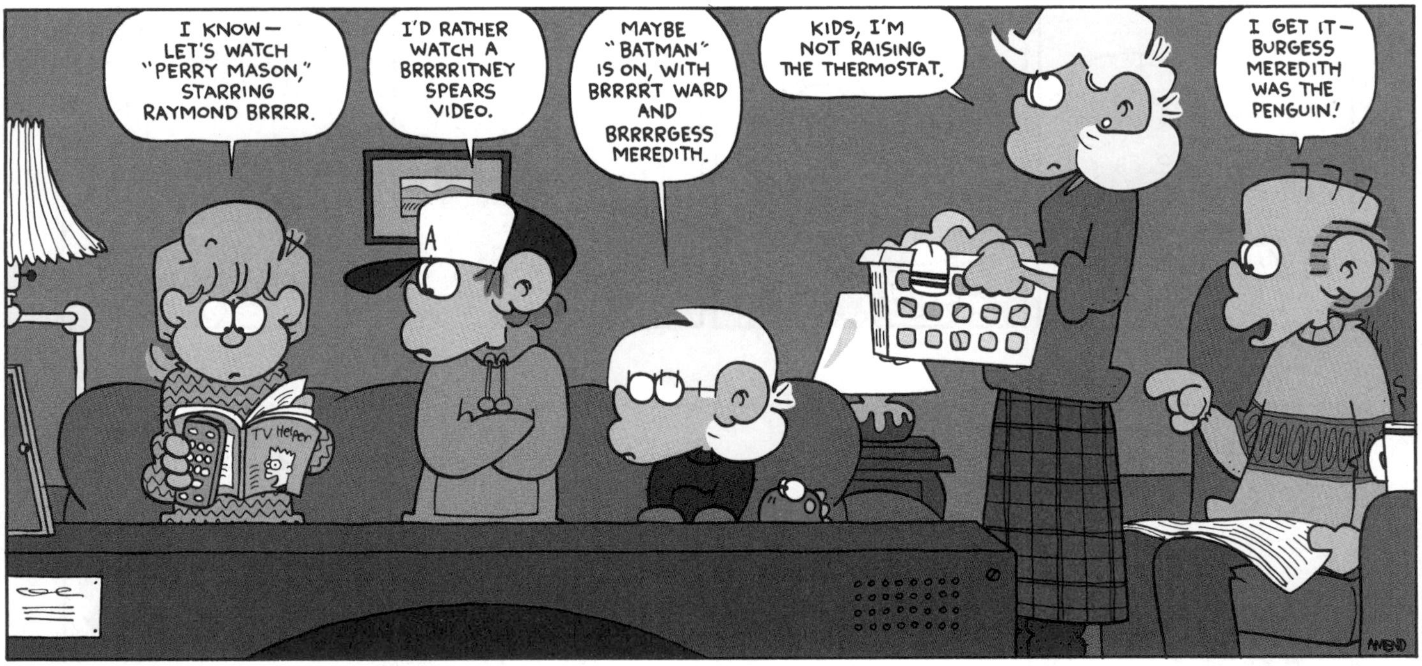
I KNOW— LET'S WATCH "PERRY MASON," STARRING RAYMOND BRRRR.
I'D RATHER WATCH A BRRRRITNEY SPEARS VIDEO.
MAYBE "BATMAN" IS ON, WITH BRRRRT WARD AND BRRRRGESS MEREDITH.
KIDS, I'M NOT RAISING THE THERMOSTAT.
I GET IT— BURGESS MEREDITH WAS THE PENGUIN!
TV Helper
AMEND

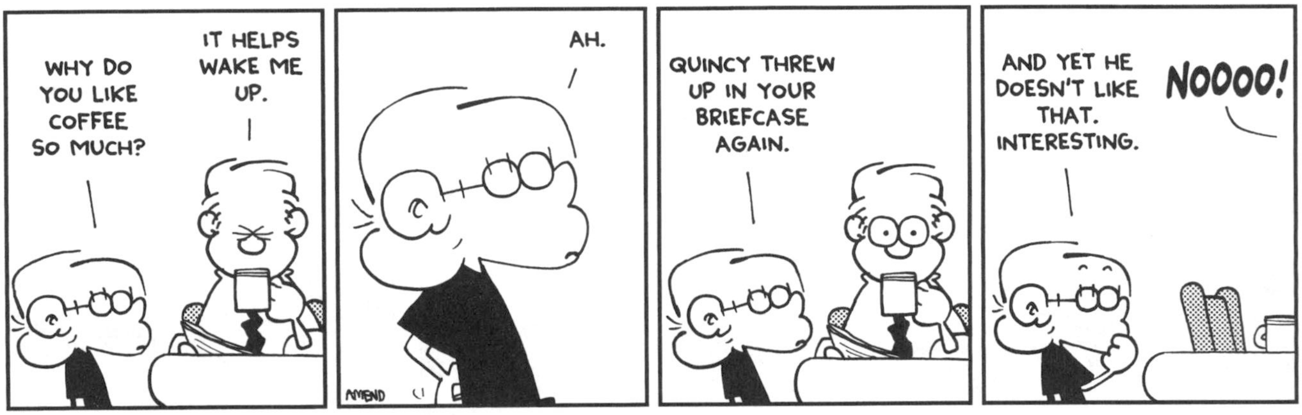
WHY DO YOU LIKE COFFEE SO MUCH?
IT HELPS WAKE ME UP.
AH.
AMEND
QUINCY THREW UP IN YOUR BRIEFCASE AGAIN.
AND YET HE DOESN'T LIKE THAT. INTERESTING.
NOOOO!

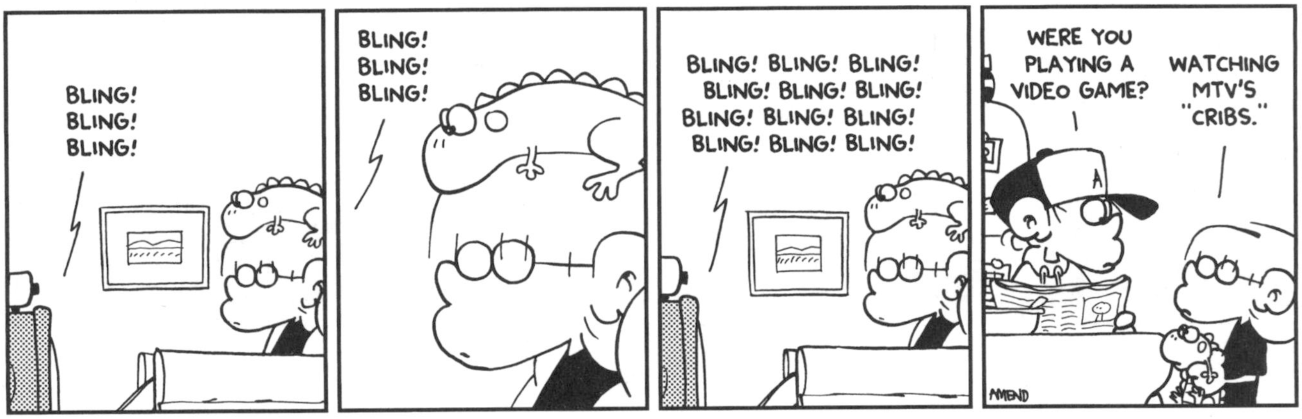
BLING! BLING! BLING!
BLING! BLING! BLING!
BLING! BLING! BLING! BLING! BLING! BLING! BLING! BLING! BLING! BLING! BLING! BLING!
WERE YOU PLAYING A VIDEO GAME?
WATCHING MTV'S "CRIBS."
AMEND

THE TEST WILL END IN TEN MINUTES, CLASS.

FIVE MINUTES.

TWO MINUTES.

FEEL FREE TO START ANYTIME NOW, JASON.

I LIKE A CHALLENGE.

GO DEEP.

HOW CAN FREE WILL COEXIST WITH DIVINE PREORDINATION?

TOO DEEP.

IF BATMAN DIED, WOULD THE JOKER BE HAPPY?

♫ ♩ ♪ ♪
IT'S THE EYE OF THE TIGER, IT'S THE THRILL OF THE FIGHT...

♪ ♫ ♩
MY EYES ADORED YOU...

EYETUNES?

I'M NOT SO SURE ABOUT THIS NEW MUSIC SERVICE.

♪ ♫♫ ♩
SHE'S GOT BETTY DAVIS EYES...

♫♫ ♩ ♩ ♪
YOU, MY BROWN-EYED GIRL...

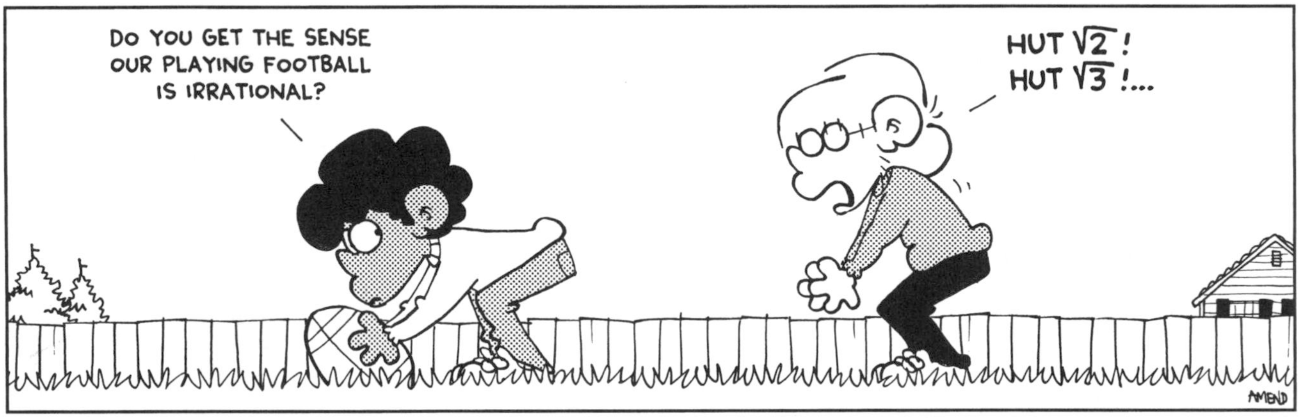
DO YOU GET THE SENSE OUR PLAYING FOOTBALL IS IRRATIONAL?
HUT $\sqrt{2}$! HUT $\sqrt{3}$!...
AMEND

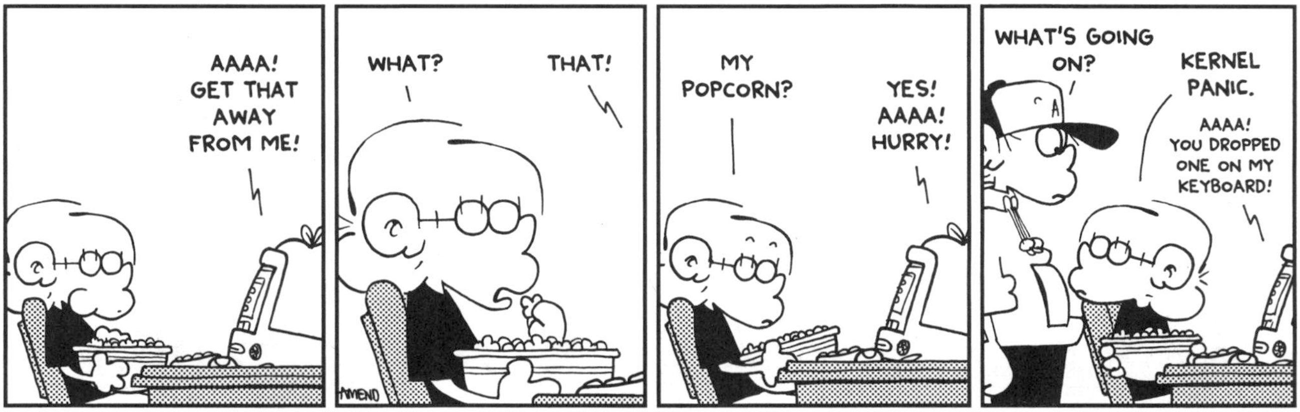
AAAA! GET THAT AWAY FROM ME!
WHAT?
THAT!
AMEND
MY POPCORN?
YES! AAAA! HURRY!
WHAT'S GOING ON?
KERNEL PANIC.
AAAA! YOU DROPPED ONE ON MY KEYBOARD!

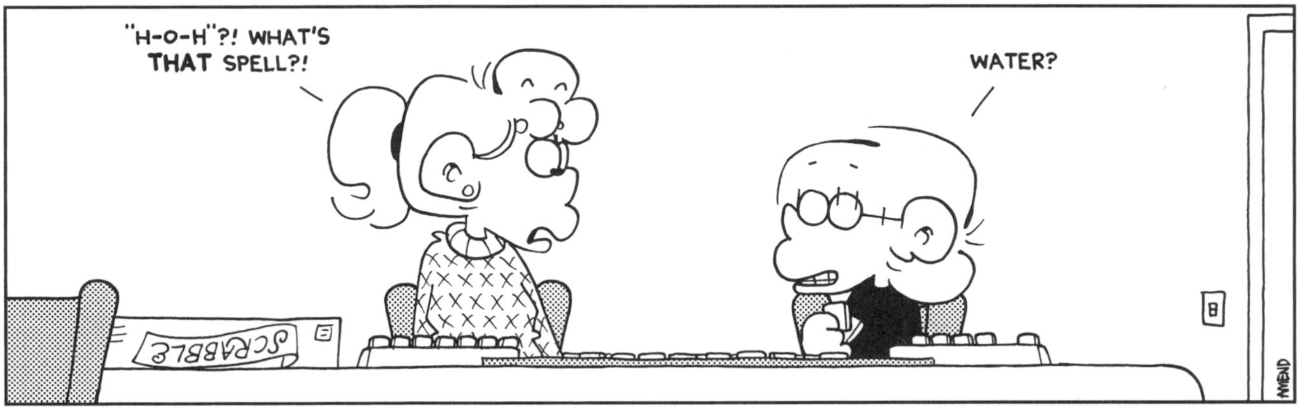
"H-O-H"?! WHAT'S **THAT** SPELL?!
WATER?
SCRABBLE
AMEND

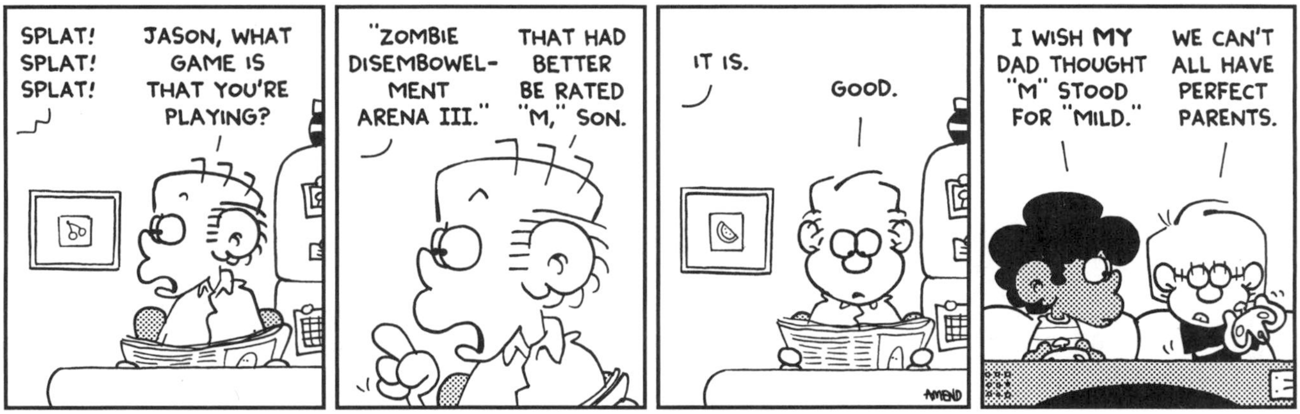
SPLAT! SPLAT! SPLAT!
JASON, WHAT GAME IS THAT YOU'RE PLAYING?
"ZOMBIE DISEMBOWEL-MENT ARENA III."
THAT HAD BETTER BE RATED "M," SON.
IT IS.
GOOD.
AMEND
I WISH **MY** DAD THOUGHT "M" STOOD FOR "MILD."
WE CAN'T ALL HAVE PERFECT PARENTS.

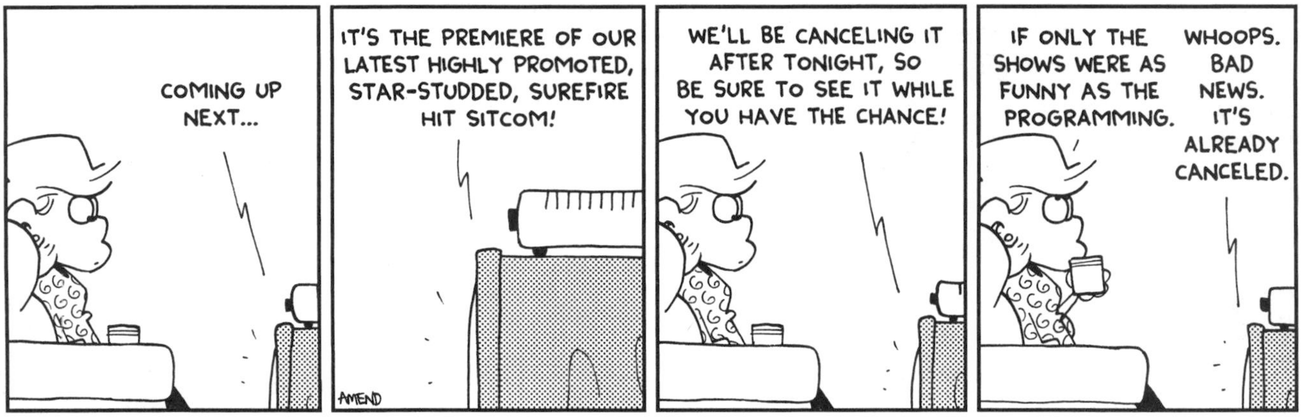
COMING UP NEXT...
IT'S THE PREMIERE OF OUR LATEST HIGHLY PROMOTED, STAR-STUDDED, SUREFIRE HIT SITCOM!
WE'LL BE CANCELING IT AFTER TONIGHT, SO BE SURE TO SEE IT WHILE YOU HAVE THE CHANCE!
IF ONLY THE SHOWS WERE AS FUNNY AS THE PROGRAMMING.
WHOOPS. BAD NEWS. IT'S ALREADY CANCELED.
AMEND

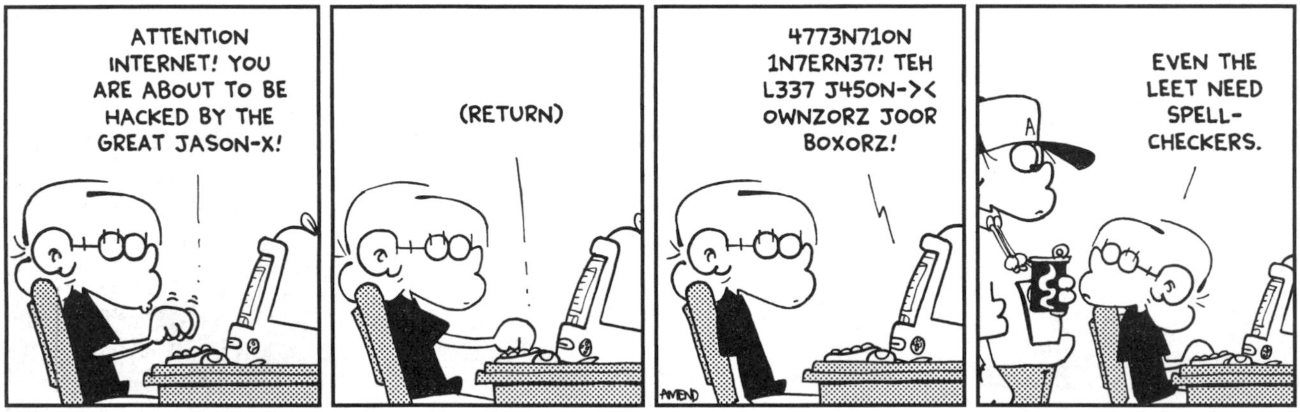
ATTENTION INTERNET! YOU ARE ABOUT TO BE HACKED BY THE GREAT JASON-X!
(RETURN)
4773N710N 1N7ERN37! TEH L337 J450N->< OWNZORZ JOOR BOXORZ!
EVEN THE LEET NEED SPELL-CHECKERS.
AMEND

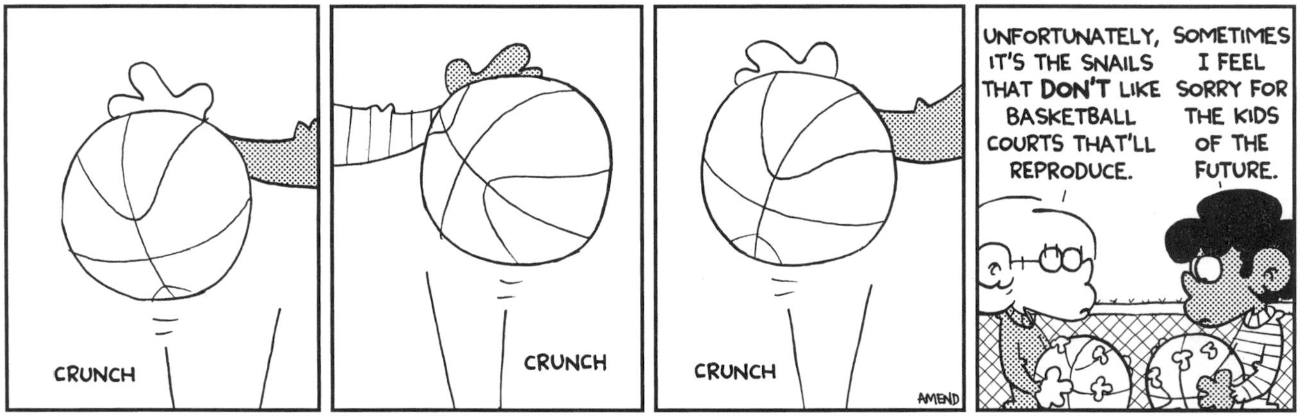
CRUNCH
CRUNCH
CRUNCH
UNFORTUNATELY, IT'S THE SNAILS THAT DON'T LIKE BASKETBALL COURTS THAT'LL REPRODUCE.
SOMETIMES I FEEL SORRY FOR THE KIDS OF THE FUTURE.
AMEND

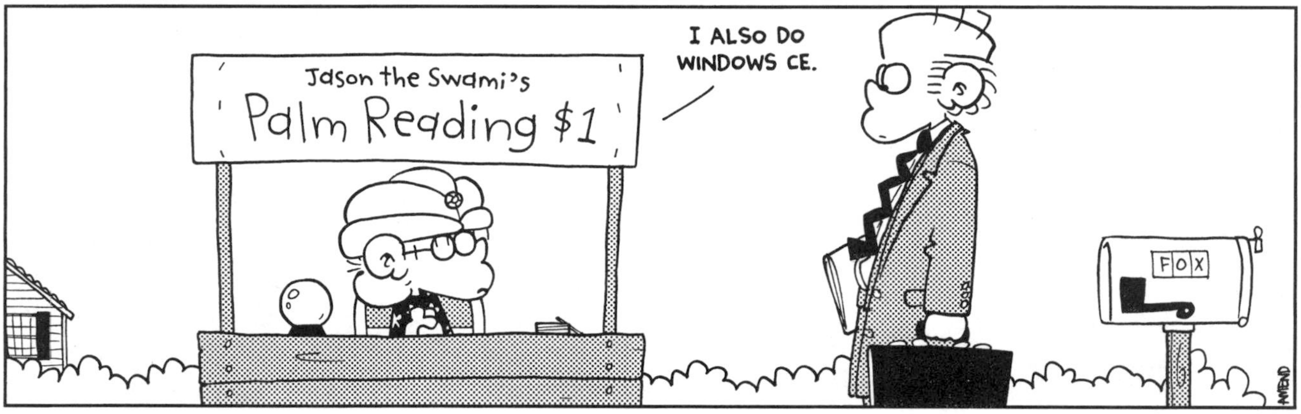
Jason the Swami's
Palm Reading $1
I ALSO DO WINDOWS CE.
FOX
AMEND

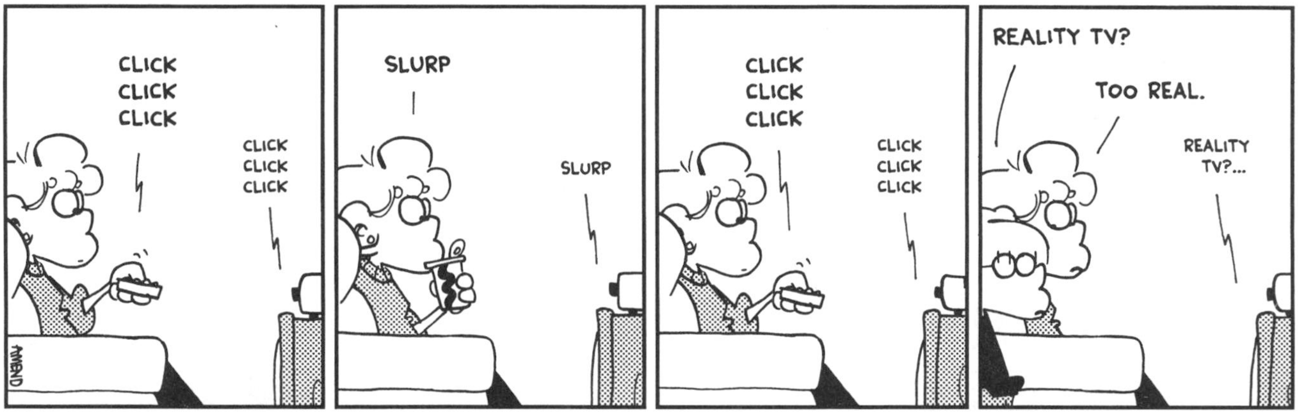
CLICK
CLICK
CLICK
CLICK
CLICK
CLICK
SLURP
SLURP
CLICK
CLICK
CLICK
CLICK
CLICK
CLICK
REALITY TV?
TOO REAL.
REALITY TV?...

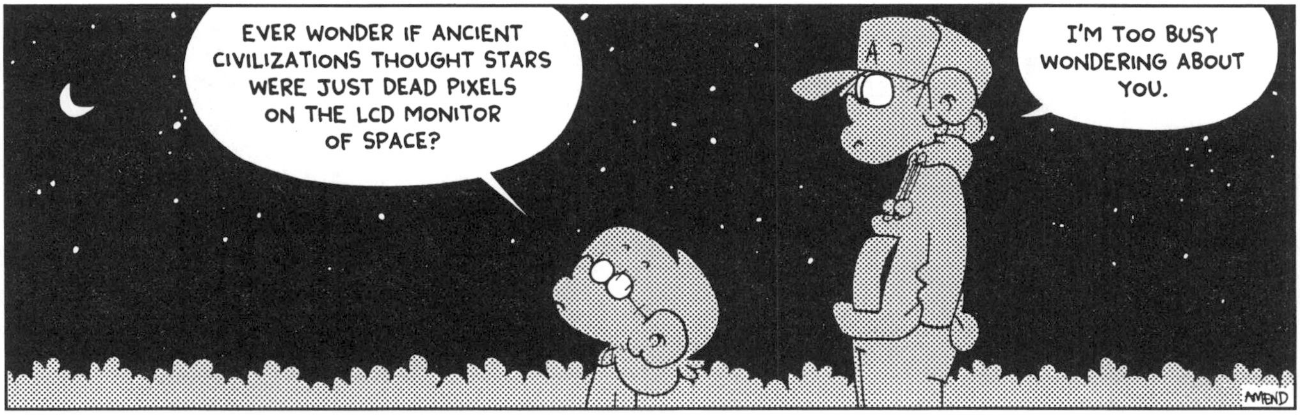
EVER WONDER IF ANCIENT CIVILIZATIONS THOUGHT STARS WERE JUST DEAD PIXELS ON THE LCD MONITOR OF SPACE?
I'M TOO BUSY WONDERING ABOUT YOU.

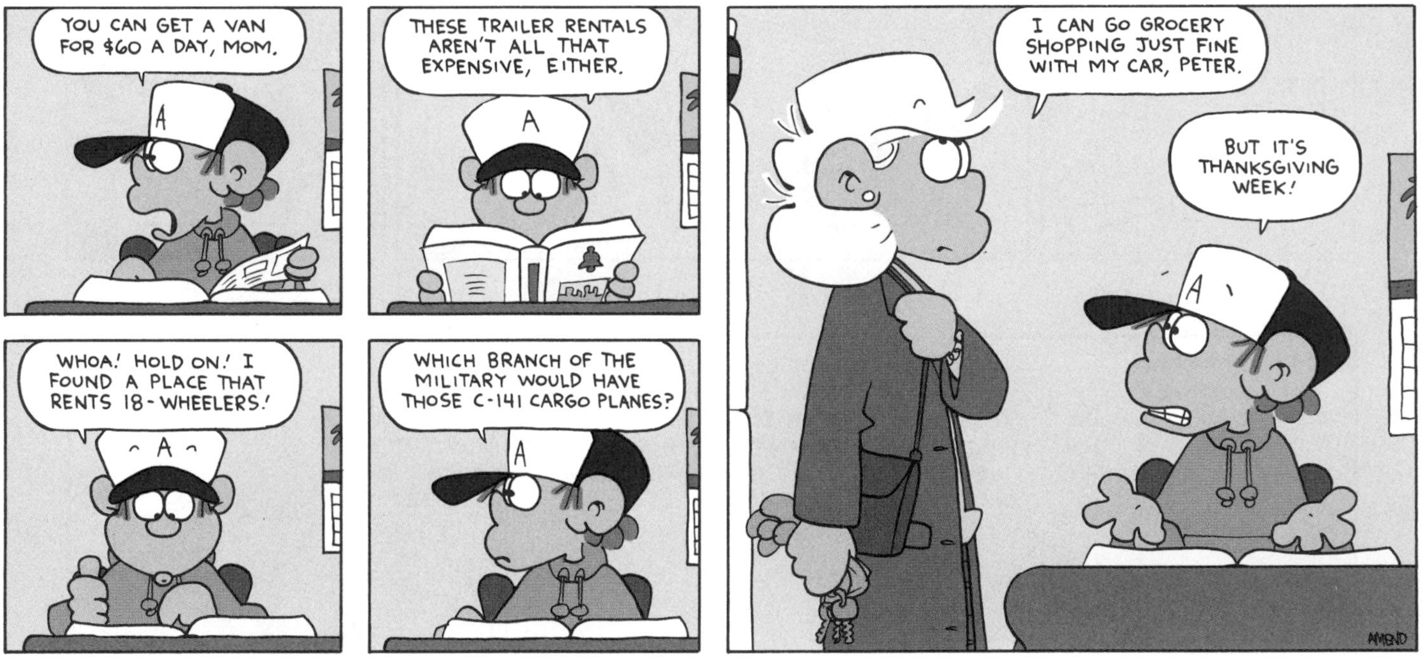
YOU CAN GET A VAN FOR $60 A DAY, MOM.
THESE TRAILER RENTALS AREN'T ALL THAT EXPENSIVE, EITHER.
WHOA! HOLD ON! I FOUND A PLACE THAT RENTS 18-WHEELERS!
WHICH BRANCH OF THE MILITARY WOULD HAVE THOSE C-141 CARGO PLANES?
I CAN GO GROCERY SHOPPING JUST FINE WITH MY CAR, PETER.
BUT IT'S THANKSGIVING WEEK!

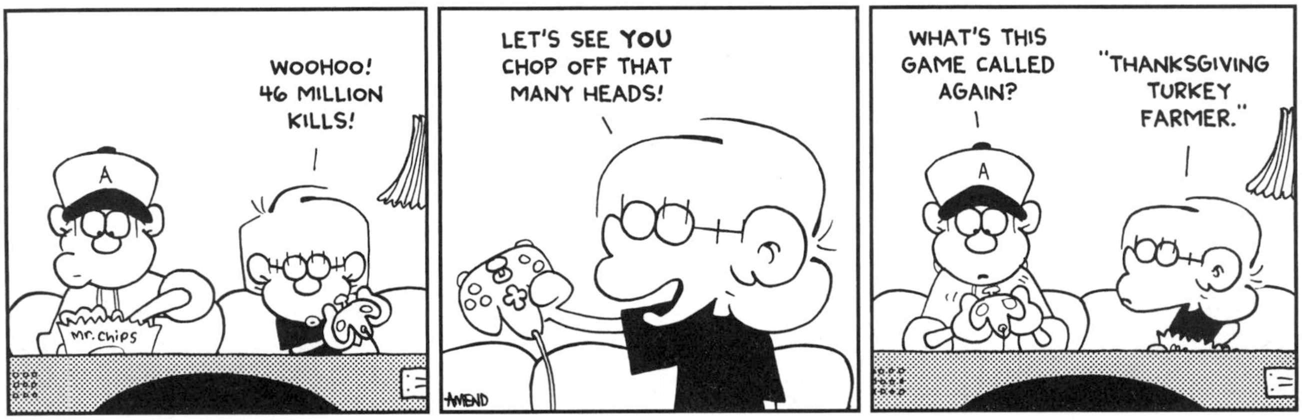
Mr. Chips
WOOHOO! 46 MILLION KILLS!
LET'S SEE **YOU** CHOP OFF THAT MANY HEADS!
AMEND
WHAT'S THIS GAME CALLED AGAIN?
"THANKSGIVING TURKEY FARMER."

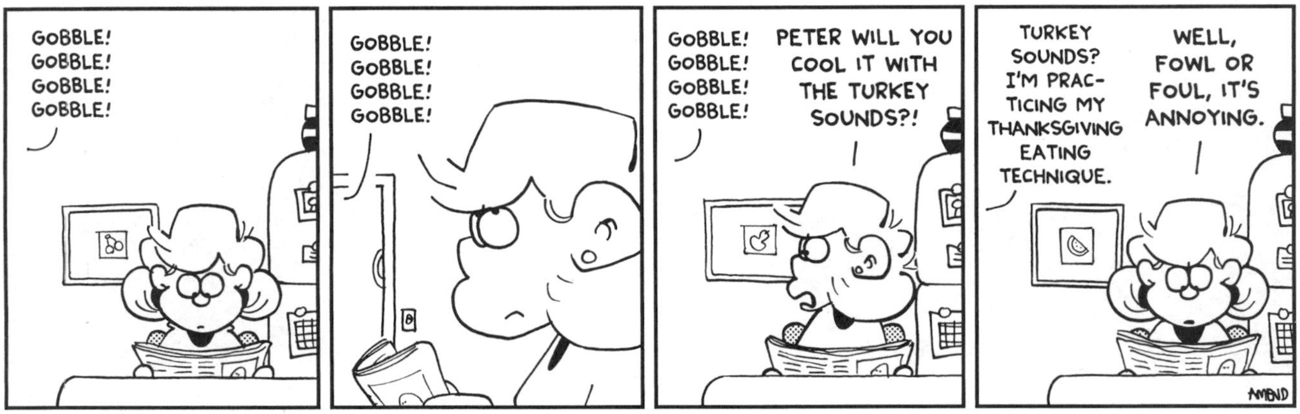
GOBBLE! GOBBLE! GOBBLE! GOBBLE!
GOBBLE! GOBBLE! GOBBLE! GOBBLE!
GOBBLE! GOBBLE! GOBBLE! GOBBLE!
PETER WILL YOU COOL IT WITH THE TURKEY SOUNDS?!
TURKEY SOUNDS? I'M PRACTICING MY THANKSGIVING EATING TECHNIQUE.
WELL, FOWL OR FOUL, IT'S ANNOYING.
AMEND

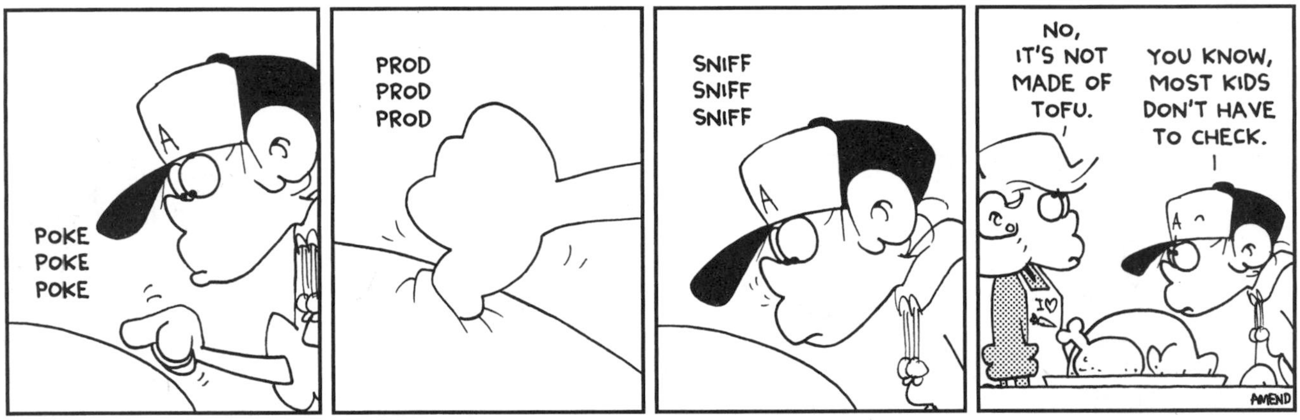
POKE POKE POKE
PROD PROD PROD
SNIFF SNIFF SNIFF
NO, IT'S NOT MADE OF TOFU.
YOU KNOW, MOST KIDS DON'T HAVE TO CHECK.
AMEND

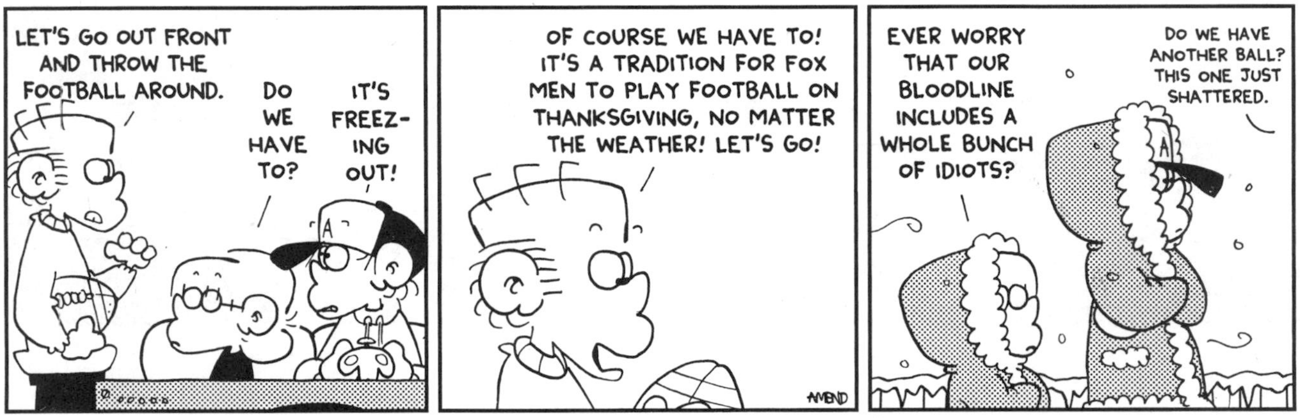
LET'S GO OUT FRONT AND THROW THE FOOTBALL AROUND.
DO WE HAVE TO?
IT'S FREEZING OUT!
OF COURSE WE HAVE TO! IT'S A TRADITION FOR FOX MEN TO PLAY FOOTBALL ON THANKSGIVING, NO MATTER THE WEATHER! LET'S GO!
AMEND
EVER WORRY THAT OUR BLOODLINE INCLUDES A WHOLE BUNCH OF IDIOTS?
DO WE HAVE ANOTHER BALL? THIS ONE JUST SHATTERED.

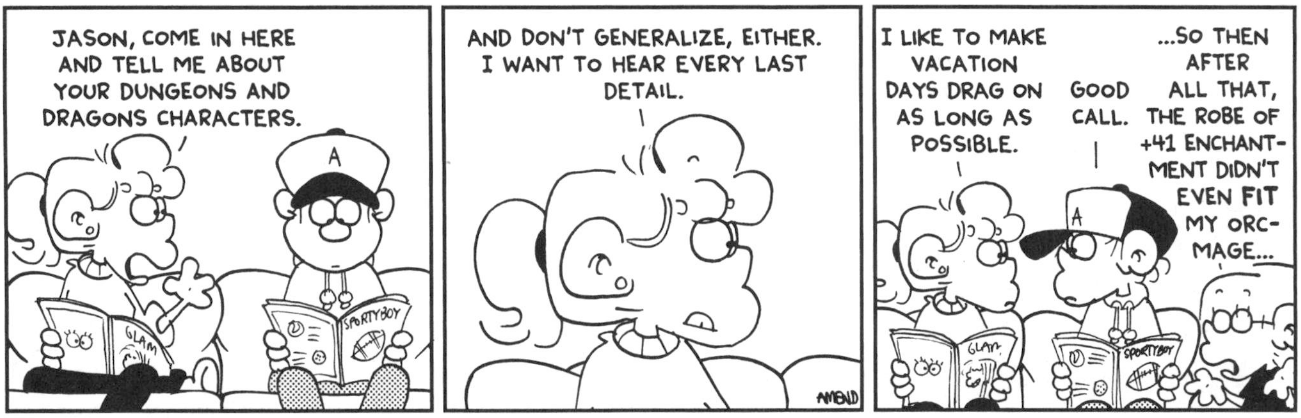
JASON, COME IN HERE AND TELL ME ABOUT YOUR DUNGEONS AND DRAGONS CHARACTERS.
AND DON'T GENERALIZE, EITHER. I WANT TO HEAR EVERY LAST DETAIL.
I LIKE TO MAKE VACATION DAYS DRAG ON AS LONG AS POSSIBLE.
GOOD CALL.
...SO THEN AFTER ALL THAT, THE ROBE OF +41 ENCHANTMENT DIDN'T EVEN FIT MY ORC-MAGE...
AMEND

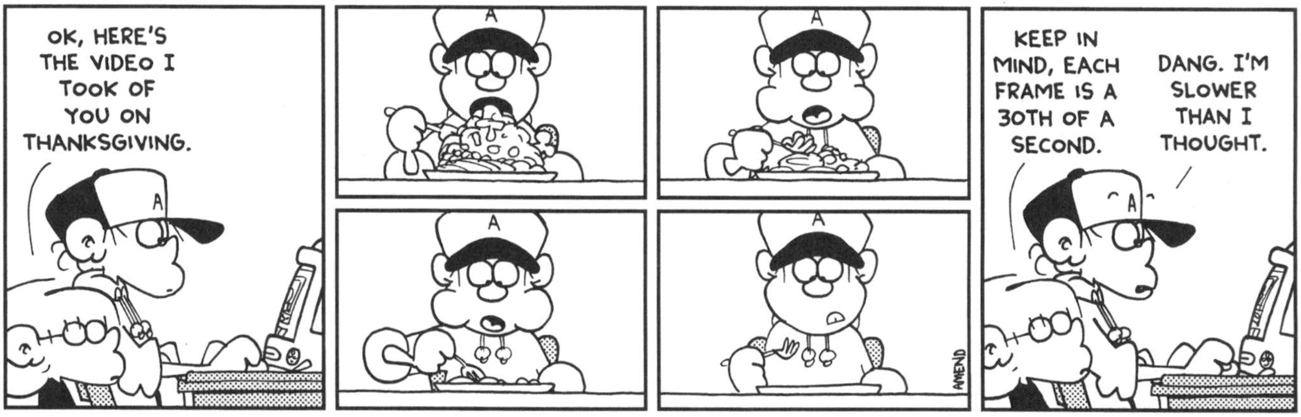
OK, HERE'S THE VIDEO I TOOK OF YOU ON THANKSGIVING.
KEEP IN MIND, EACH FRAME IS A 30TH OF A SECOND.
DANG. I'M SLOWER THAN I THOUGHT.
AMEND

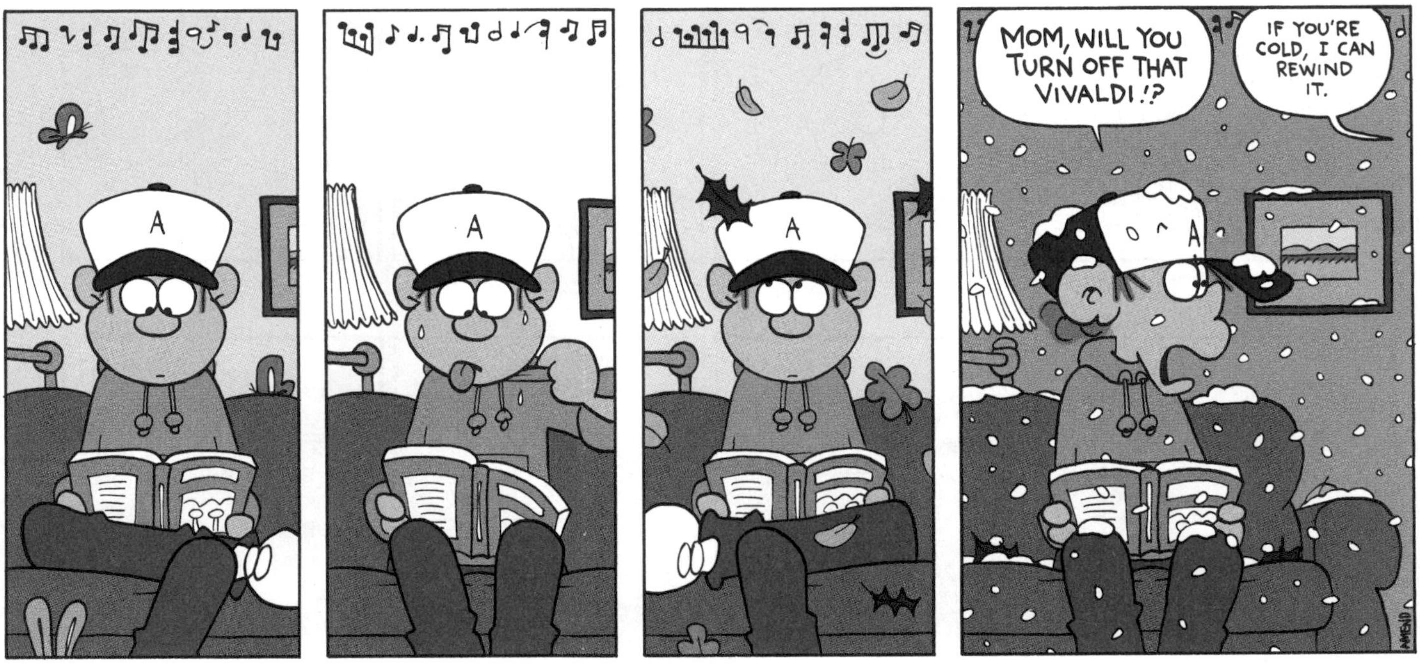
MOM, WILL YOU TURN OFF THAT VIVALDI!?
IF YOU'RE COLD, I CAN REWIND IT.
AMEND

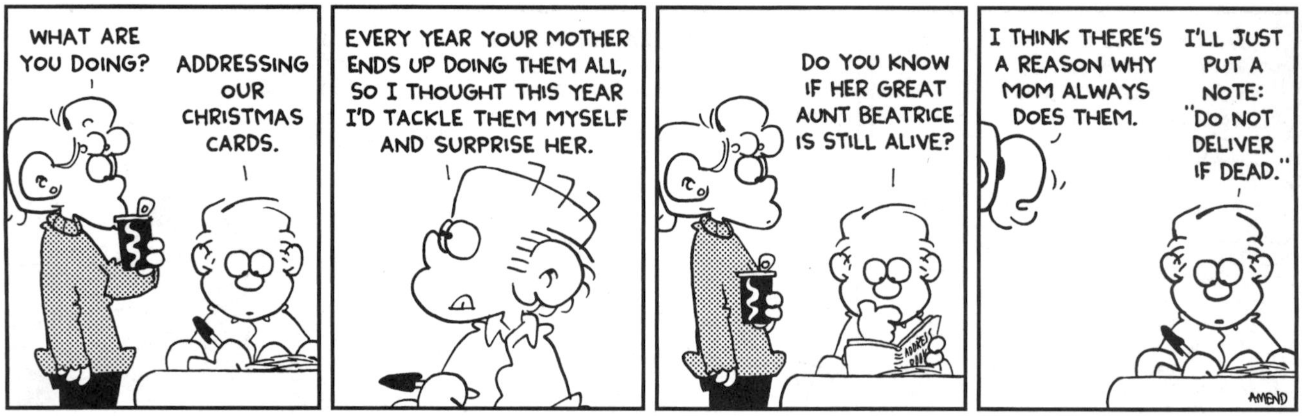
WHAT ARE YOU DOING?
ADDRESSING OUR CHRISTMAS CARDS.
EVERY YEAR YOUR MOTHER ENDS UP DOING THEM ALL, SO I THOUGHT THIS YEAR I'D TACKLE THEM MYSELF AND SURPRISE HER.
DO YOU KNOW IF HER GREAT AUNT BEATRICE IS STILL ALIVE?
I THINK THERE'S A REASON WHY MOM ALWAYS DOES THEM.
I'LL JUST PUT A NOTE: "DO NOT DELIVER IF DEAD."
AMEND

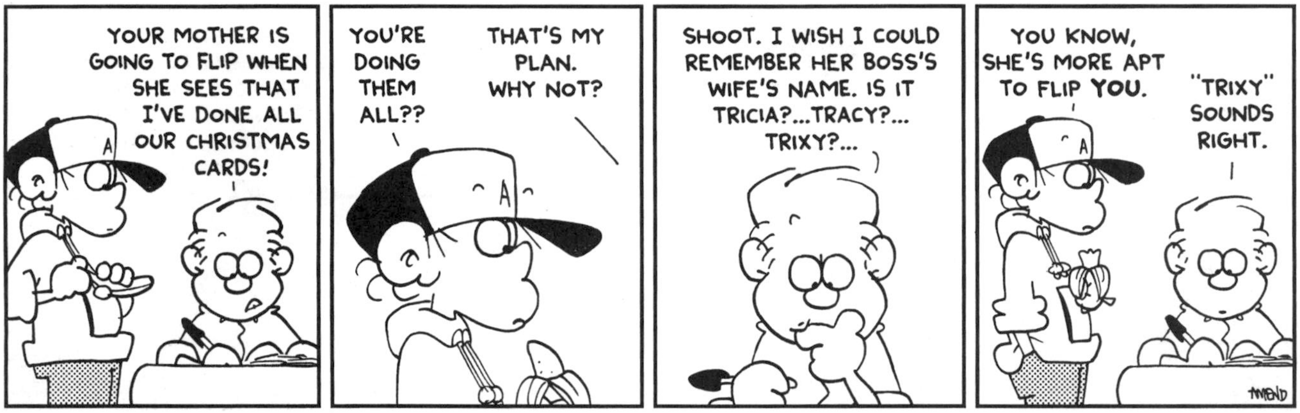
YOUR MOTHER IS GOING TO FLIP WHEN SHE SEES THAT I'VE DONE ALL OUR CHRISTMAS CARDS!
YOU'RE DOING THEM ALL??
THAT'S MY PLAN. WHY NOT?
SHOOT. I WISH I COULD REMEMBER HER BOSS'S WIFE'S NAME. IS IT TRICIA?...TRACY?... TRIXY?...
YOU KNOW, SHE'S MORE APT TO FLIP YOU.
"TRIXY" SOUNDS RIGHT.
AMEND

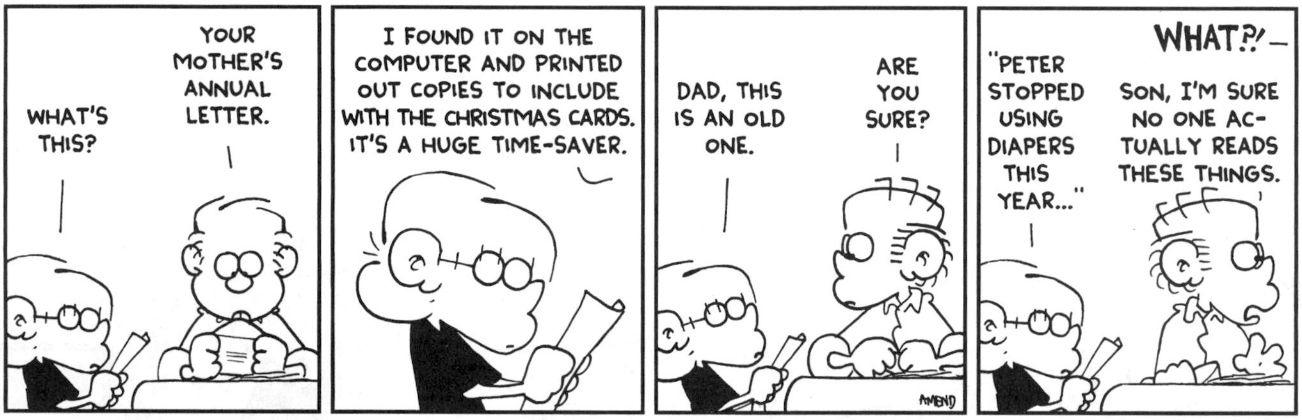
WHAT'S THIS?
YOUR MOTHER'S ANNUAL LETTER.
I FOUND IT ON THE COMPUTER AND PRINTED OUT COPIES TO INCLUDE WITH THE CHRISTMAS CARDS. IT'S A HUGE TIME-SAVER.
DAD, THIS IS AN OLD ONE.
ARE YOU SURE?
"PETER STOPPED USING DIAPERS THIS YEAR..."
WHAT?!
SON, I'M SURE NO ONE ACTUALLY READS THESE THINGS.
AMEND

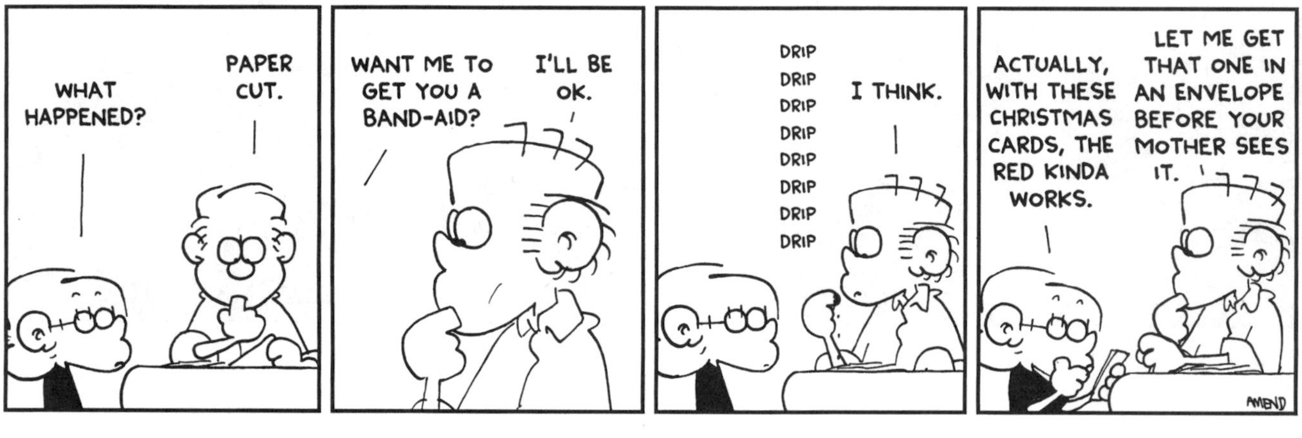
WHAT HAPPENED?
PAPER CUT.
WANT ME TO GET YOU A BAND-AID?
I'LL BE OK.
DRIP DRIP DRIP DRIP DRIP DRIP DRIP DRIP
I THINK.
ACTUALLY, WITH THESE CHRISTMAS CARDS, THE RED KINDA WORKS.
LET ME GET THAT ONE IN AN ENVELOPE BEFORE YOUR MOTHER SEES IT.
AMEND

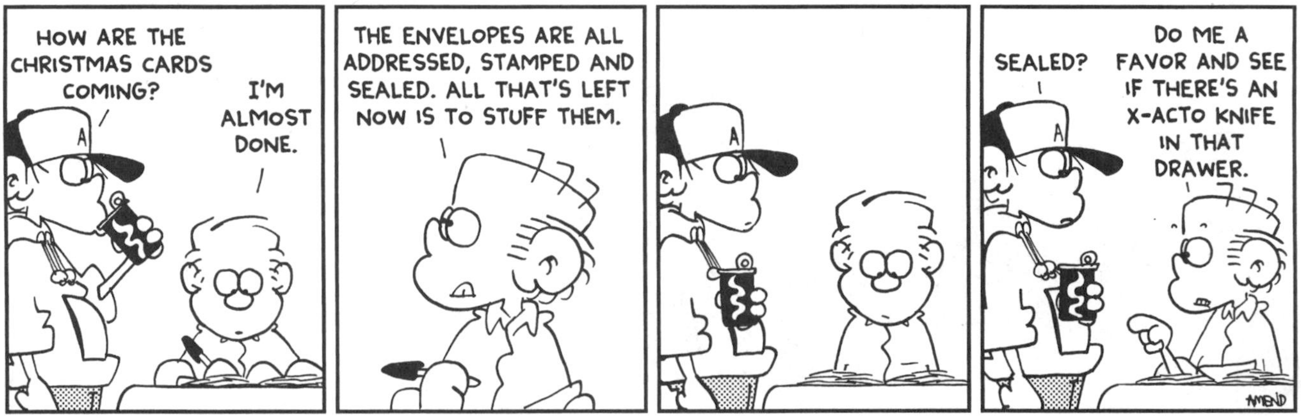
HOW ARE THE CHRISTMAS CARDS COMING?
I'M ALMOST DONE.
THE ENVELOPES ARE ALL ADDRESSED, STAMPED AND SEALED. ALL THAT'S LEFT NOW IS TO STUFF THEM.
SEALED?
DO ME A FAVOR AND SEE IF THERE'S AN X-ACTO KNIFE IN THAT DRAWER.
AMEND

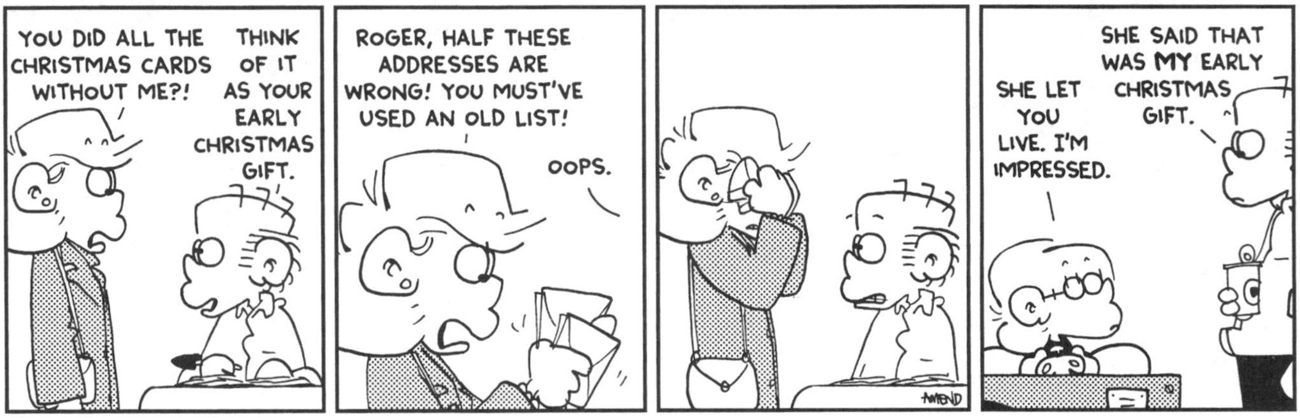
YOU DID ALL THE CHRISTMAS CARDS WITHOUT ME?!
THINK OF IT AS YOUR EARLY CHRISTMAS GIFT.
ROGER, HALF THESE ADDRESSES ARE WRONG! YOU MUST'VE USED AN OLD LIST!
OOPS.
AMEND
SHE LET YOU LIVE. I'M IMPRESSED.
SHE SAID THAT WAS MY EARLY CHRISTMAS GIFT.

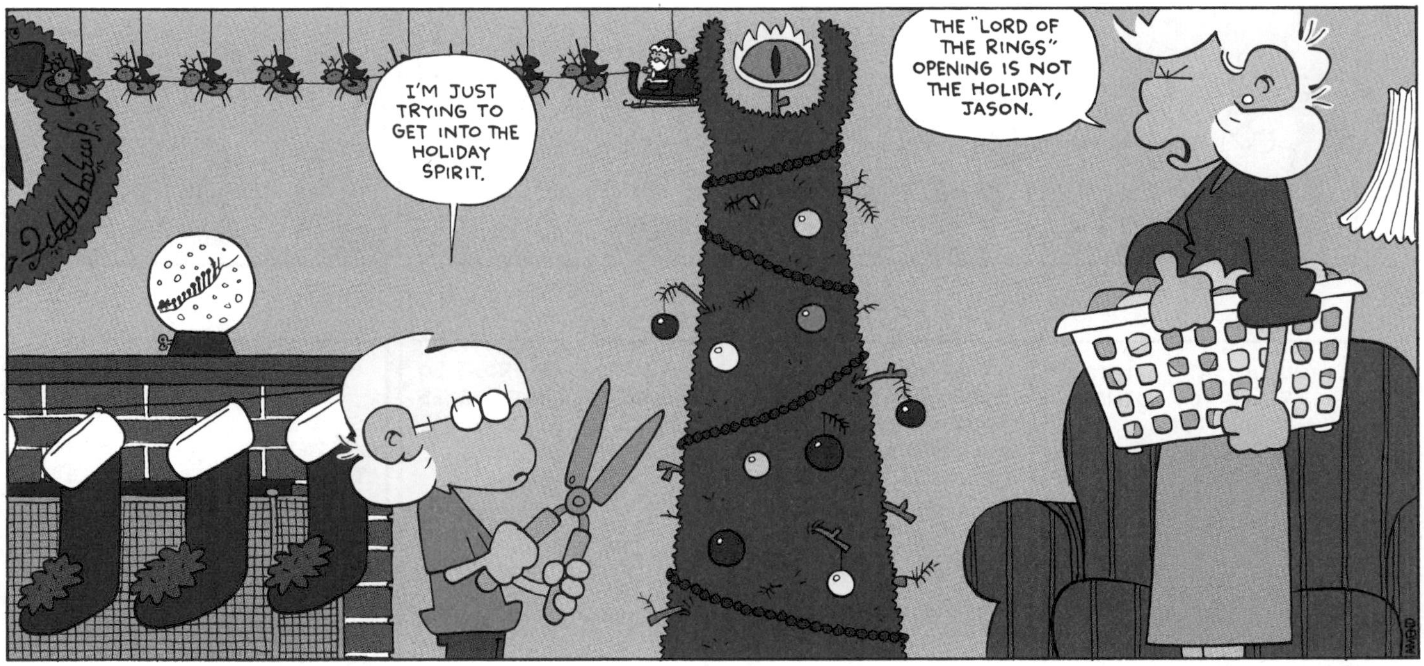
I'M JUST TRYING TO GET INTO THE HOLIDAY SPIRIT.
THE "LORD OF THE RINGS" OPENING IS NOT THE HOLIDAY, JASON.
AMEND

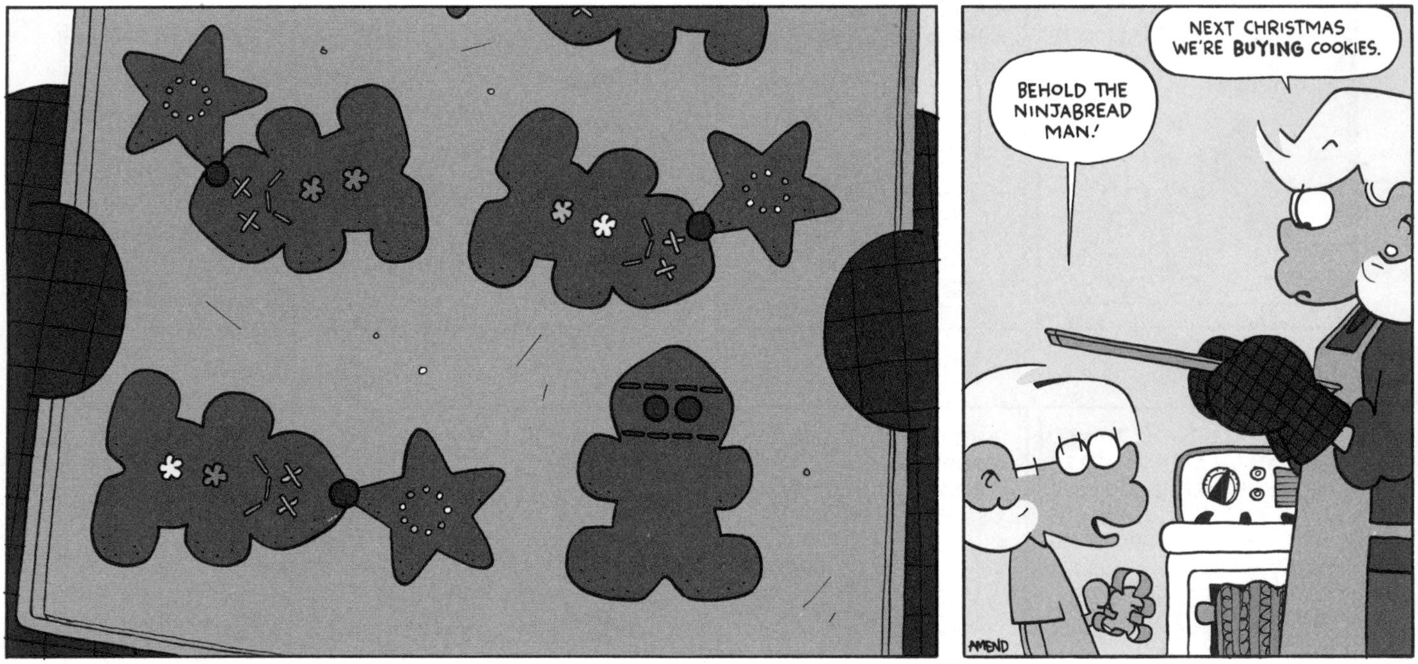

BEHOLD THE NINJABREAD MAN!
NEXT CHRISTMAS WE'RE **BUYING** COOKIES.
AMEND

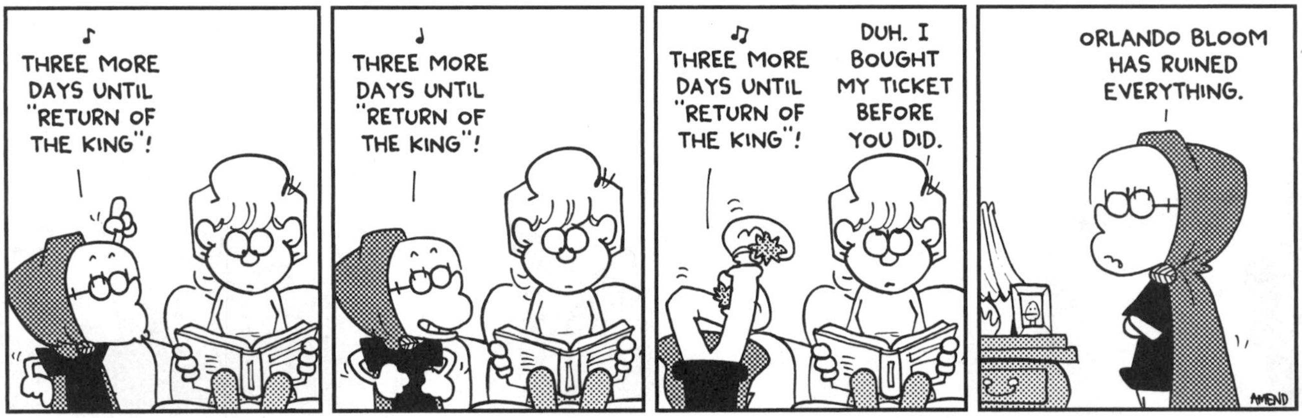

THREE MORE DAYS UNTIL "RETURN OF THE KING"!
THREE MORE DAYS UNTIL "RETURN OF THE KING"!
THREE MORE DAYS UNTIL "RETURN OF THE KING"!
DUH. I BOUGHT MY TICKET BEFORE YOU DID.
ORLANDO BLOOM HAS RUINED EVERYTHING.
AMEND

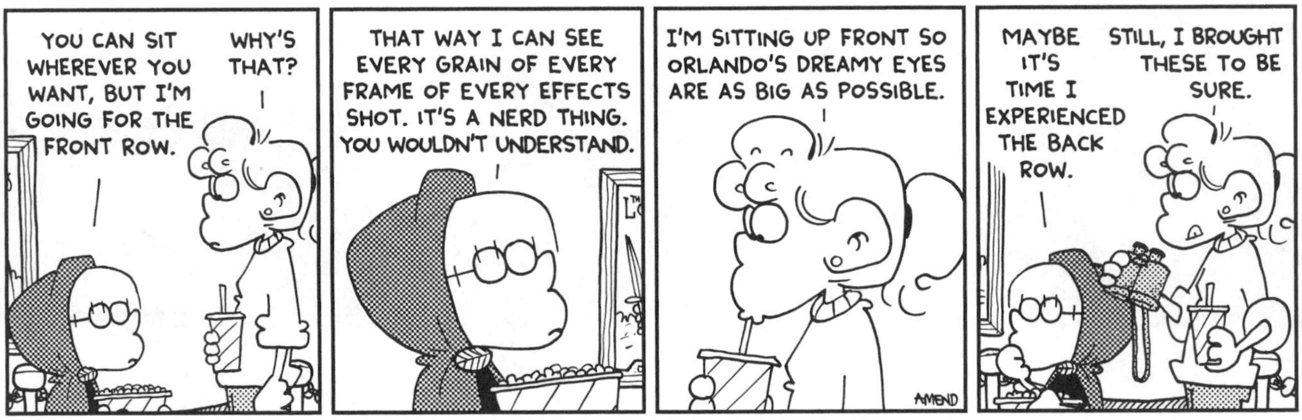

YOU CAN SIT WHEREVER YOU WANT, BUT I'M GOING FOR THE FRONT ROW.
WHY'S THAT?
THAT WAY I CAN SEE EVERY GRAIN OF EVERY FRAME OF EVERY EFFECTS SHOT. IT'S A NERD THING. YOU WOULDN'T UNDERSTAND.
I'M SITTING UP FRONT SO ORLANDO'S DREAMY EYES ARE AS BIG AS POSSIBLE.
MAYBE IT'S TIME I EXPERIENCED THE BACK ROW.
STILL, I BROUGHT THESE TO BE SURE.
AMEND

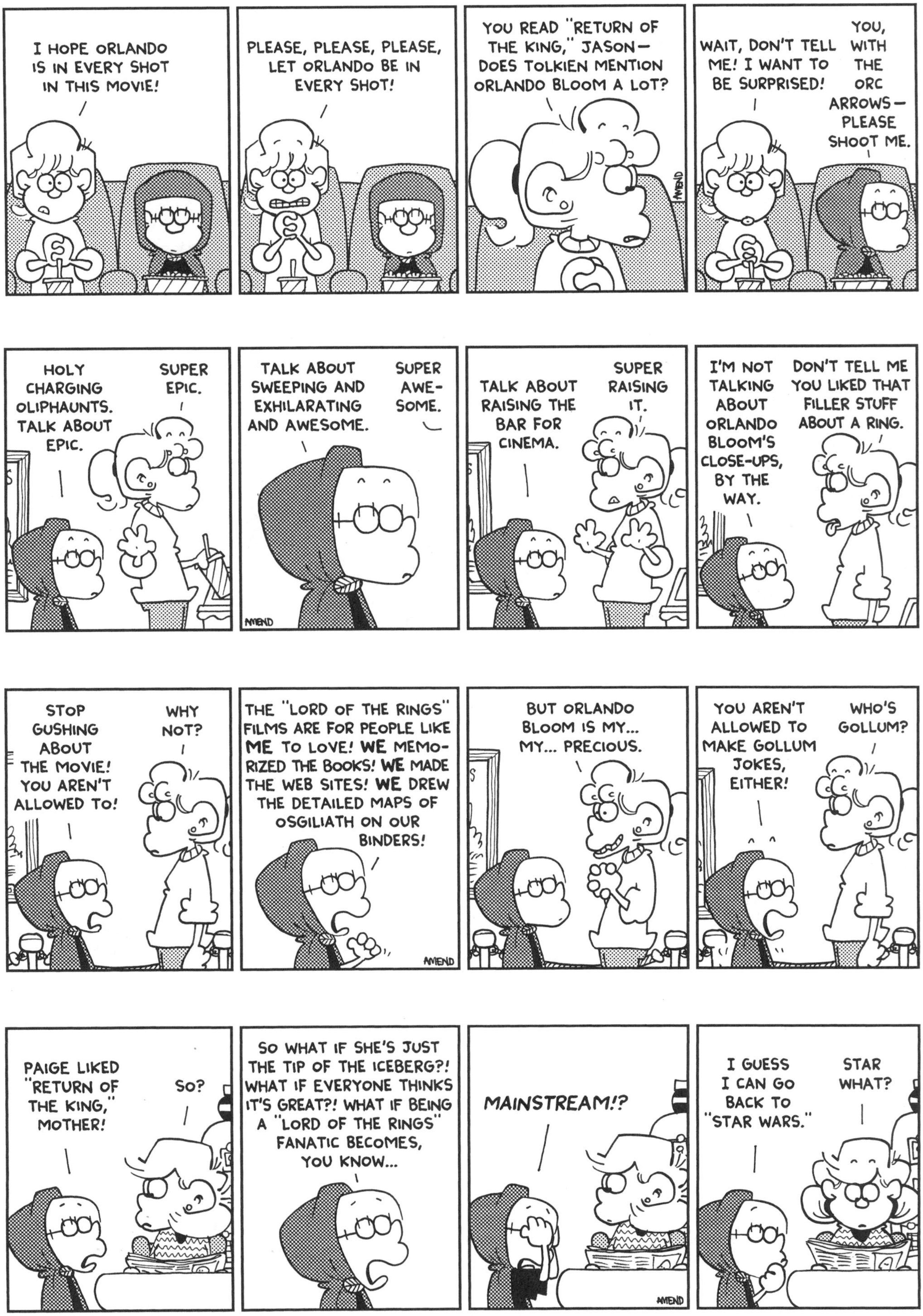

I HOPE ORLANDO IS IN EVERY SHOT IN THIS MOVIE!
PLEASE, PLEASE, PLEASE, LET ORLANDO BE IN EVERY SHOT!
YOU READ "RETURN OF THE KING," JASON— DOES TOLKIEN MENTION ORLANDO BLOOM A LOT?
WAIT, DON'T TELL ME! I WANT TO BE SURPRISED!
YOU, WITH THE ORC ARROWS— PLEASE SHOOT ME.
AMEND
HOLY CHARGING OLIPHAUNTS. TALK ABOUT EPIC.
SUPER EPIC.
TALK ABOUT SWEEPING AND EXHILARATING AND AWESOME.
SUPER AWE-SOME.
AMEND
TALK ABOUT RAISING THE BAR FOR CINEMA.
SUPER RAISING IT.
I'M NOT TALKING ABOUT ORLANDO BLOOM'S CLOSE-UPS, BY THE WAY.
DON'T TELL ME YOU LIKED THAT FILLER STUFF ABOUT A RING.
STOP GUSHING ABOUT THE MOVIE! YOU AREN'T ALLOWED TO!
WHY NOT?
THE "LORD OF THE RINGS" FILMS ARE FOR PEOPLE LIKE ME TO LOVE! WE MEMO-RIZED THE BOOKS! WE MADE THE WEB SITES! WE DREW THE DETAILED MAPS OF OSGILIATH ON OUR BINDERS!
AMEND
BUT ORLANDO BLOOM IS MY... MY... PRECIOUS.
YOU AREN'T ALLOWED TO MAKE GOLLUM JOKES, EITHER!
WHO'S GOLLUM?
PAIGE LIKED "RETURN OF THE KING," MOTHER!
SO?
SO WHAT IF SHE'S JUST THE TIP OF THE ICEBERG?! WHAT IF EVERYONE THINKS IT'S GREAT?! WHAT IF BEING A "LORD OF THE RINGS" FANATIC BECOMES, YOU KNOW...
MAINSTREAM!?
AMEND
I GUESS I CAN GO BACK TO "STAR WARS."
STAR WHAT?

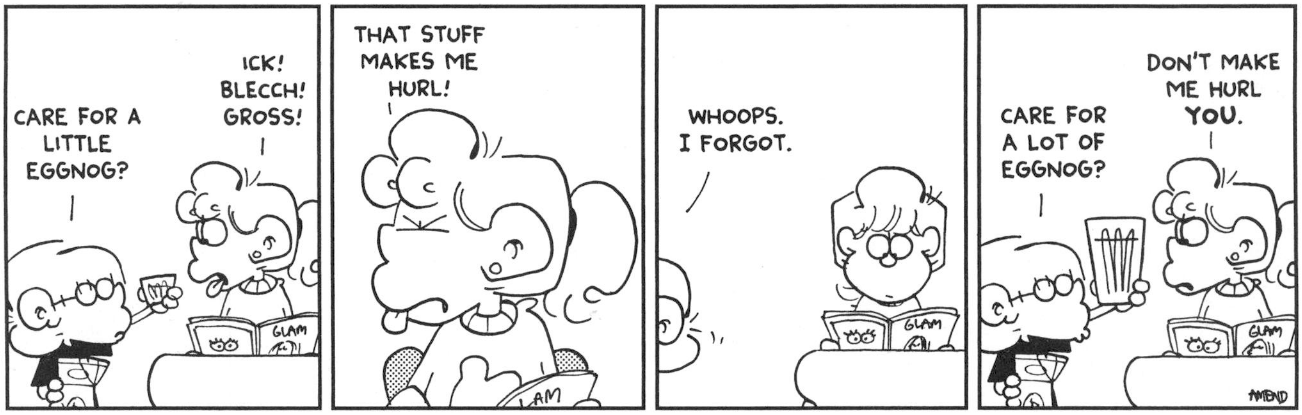
CARE FOR A LITTLE EGGNOG?
ICK! BLECCH! GROSS!
GLAM
THAT STUFF MAKES ME HURL!
WHOOPS. I FORGOT.
CARE FOR A LOT OF EGGNOG?
DON'T MAKE ME HURL **YOU**.
AMEND

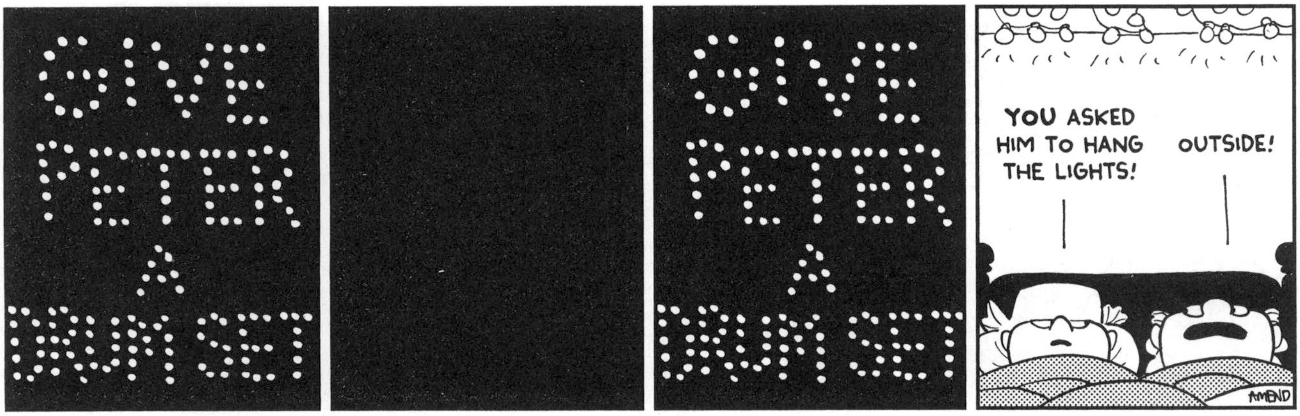
GIVE PETER A DRUM SET
GIVE PETER A DRUM SET
YOU ASKED HIM TO HANG THE LIGHTS!
OUTSIDE!
AMEND

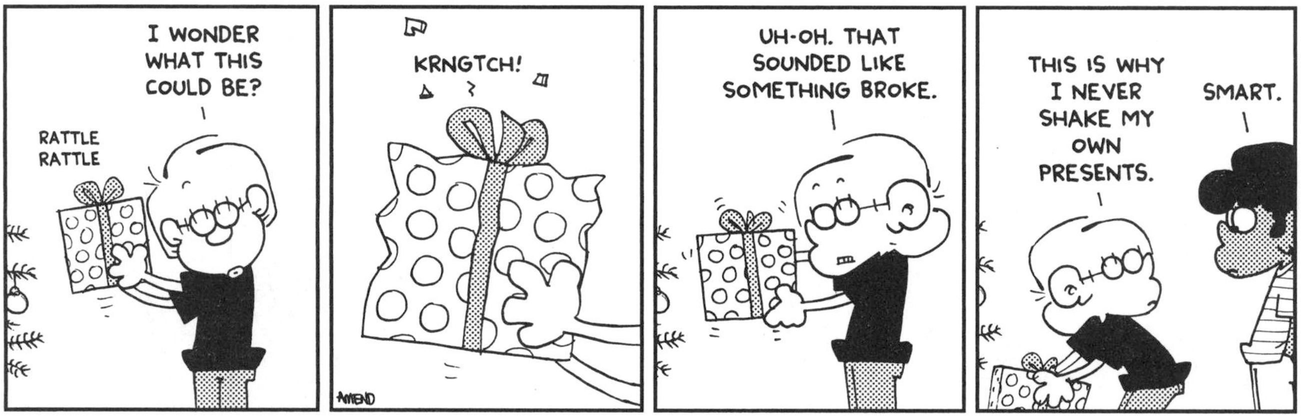
I WONDER WHAT THIS COULD BE?
RATTLE RATTLE
KRNGTCH!
AMEND
UH-OH. THAT SOUNDED LIKE SOMETHING BROKE.
THIS IS WHY I NEVER SHAKE MY OWN PRESENTS.
SMART.

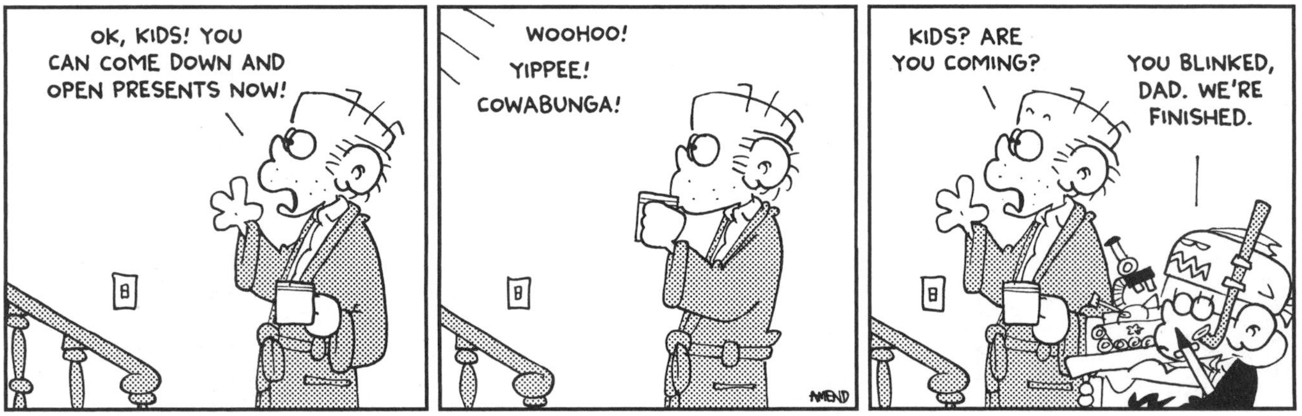
OK, KIDS! YOU CAN COME DOWN AND OPEN PRESENTS NOW!
WOOHOO!
YIPPEE!
COWABUNGA!
AMEND
KIDS? ARE YOU COMING?
YOU BLINKED, DAD. WE'RE FINISHED.

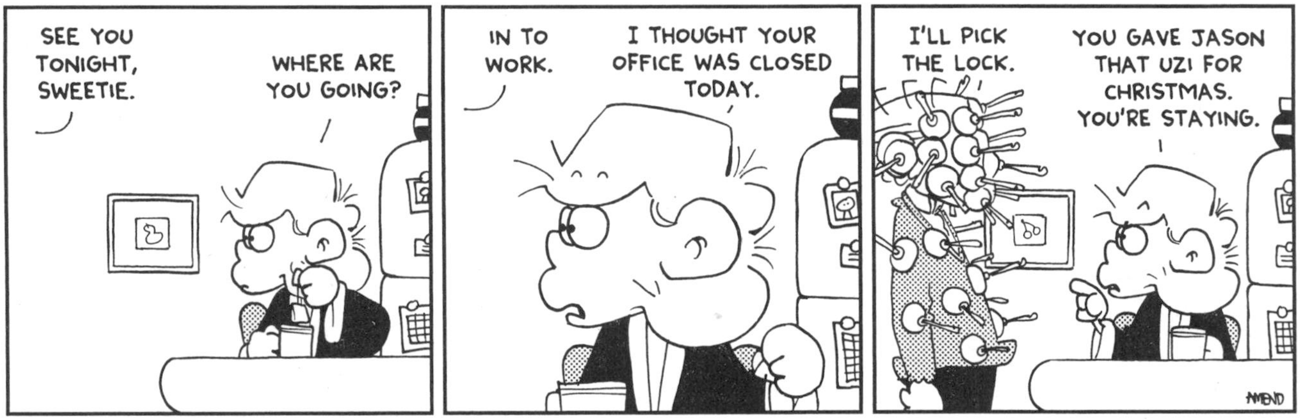
SEE YOU TONIGHT, SWEETIE.
WHERE ARE YOU GOING?
IN TO WORK.
I THOUGHT YOUR OFFICE WAS CLOSED TODAY.
I'LL PICK THE LOCK.
YOU GAVE JASON THAT UZI FOR CHRISTMAS. YOU'RE STAYING.
AMEND

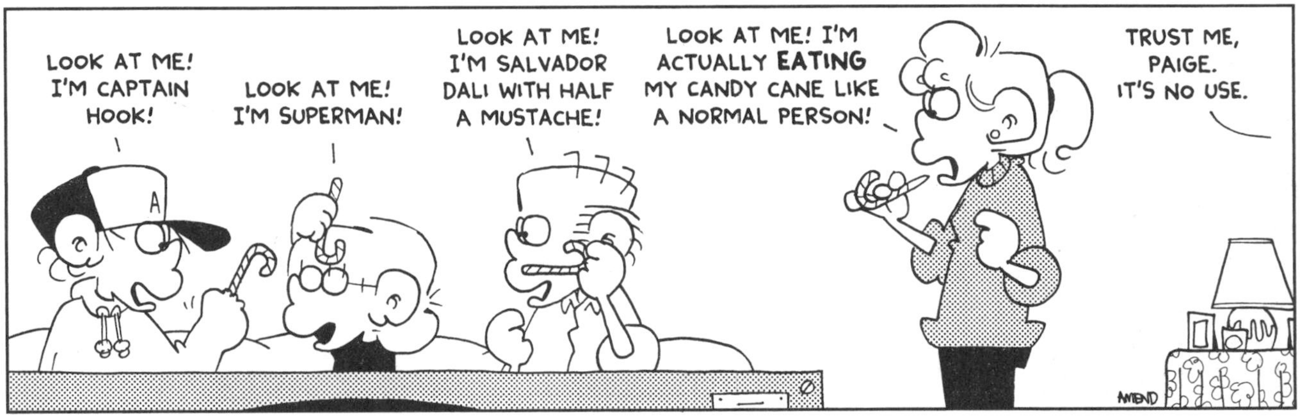
LOOK AT ME! I'M CAPTAIN HOOK!
LOOK AT ME! I'M SUPERMAN!
LOOK AT ME! I'M SALVADOR DALI WITH HALF A MUSTACHE!
LOOK AT ME! I'M ACTUALLY **EATING** MY CANDY CANE LIKE A NORMAL PERSON!
TRUST ME, PAIGE. IT'S NO USE.
AMEND

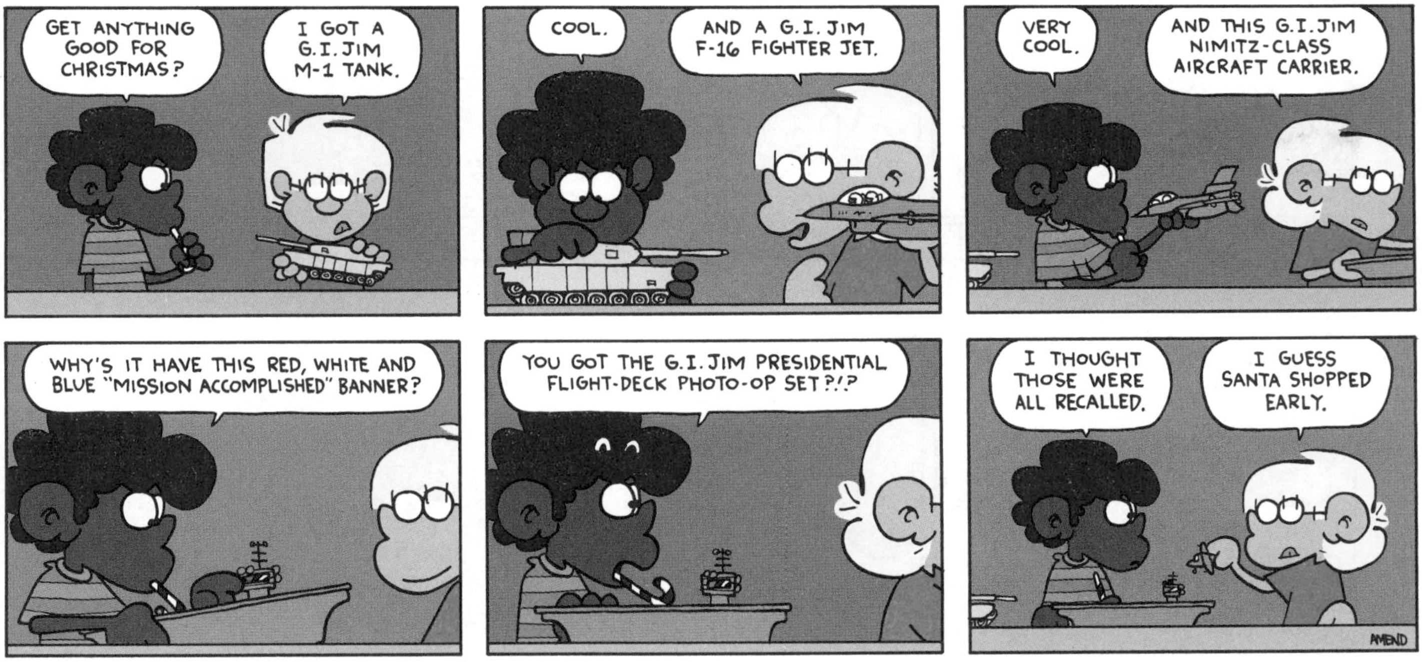
GET ANYTHING GOOD FOR CHRISTMAS?
I GOT A G.I. JIM M-1 TANK.
COOL.
AND A G.I. JIM F-16 FIGHTER JET.
VERY COOL.
AND THIS G.I. JIM NIMITZ-CLASS AIRCRAFT CARRIER.
WHY'S IT HAVE THIS RED, WHITE AND BLUE "MISSION ACCOMPLISHED" BANNER?
YOU GOT THE G.I. JIM PRESIDENTIAL FLIGHT-DECK PHOTO-OP SET?!?
I THOUGHT THOSE WERE ALL RECALLED.
I GUESS SANTA SHOPPED EARLY.
AMEND

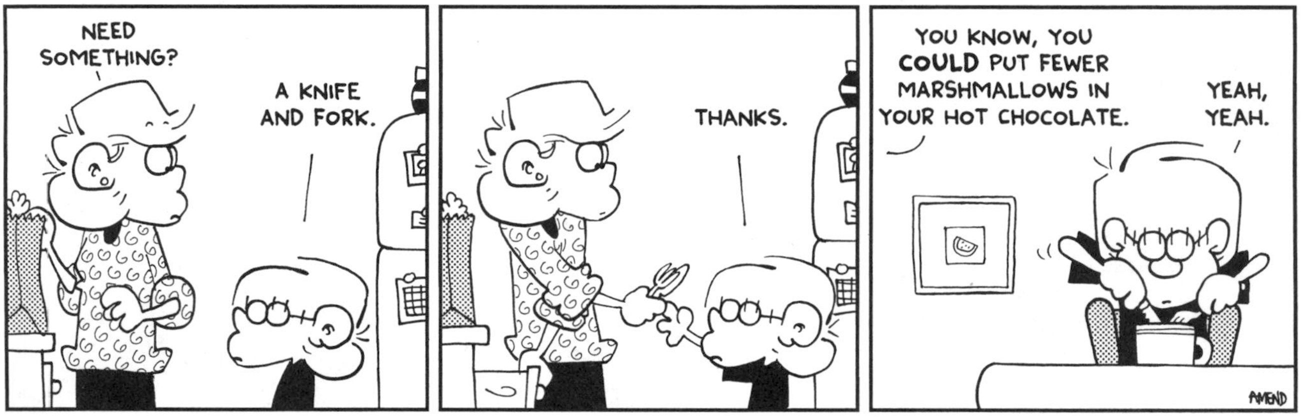
NEED SOMETHING?
A KNIFE AND FORK.
THANKS.
YOU KNOW, YOU **COULD** PUT FEWER MARSHMALLOWS IN YOUR HOT CHOCOLATE.
YEAH, YEAH.
AMEND

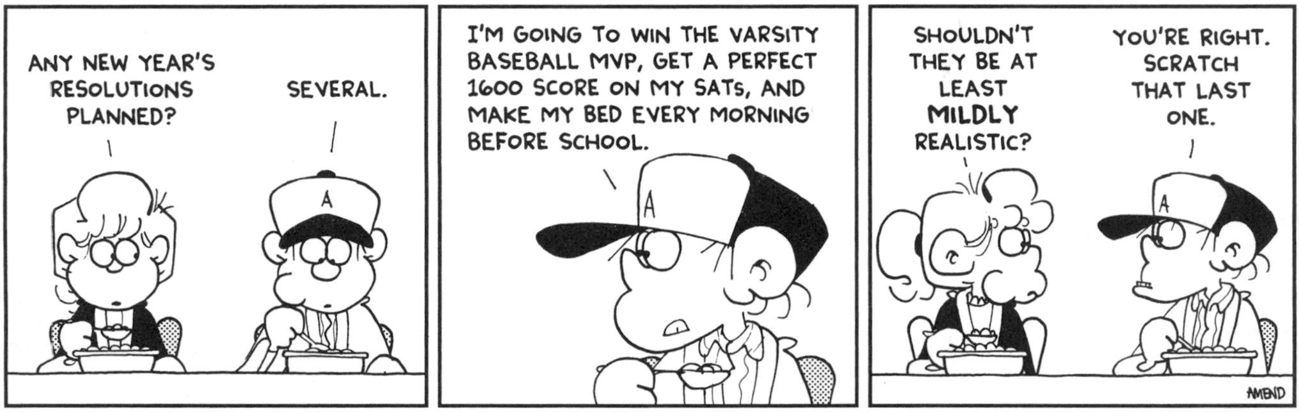
ANY NEW YEAR'S RESOLUTIONS PLANNED?
SEVERAL.
I'M GOING TO WIN THE VARSITY BASEBALL MVP, GET A PERFECT 1600 SCORE ON MY SATs, AND MAKE MY BED EVERY MORNING BEFORE SCHOOL.
SHOULDN'T THEY BE AT LEAST **MILDLY** REALISTIC?
YOU'RE RIGHT. SCRATCH THAT LAST ONE.
AMEND

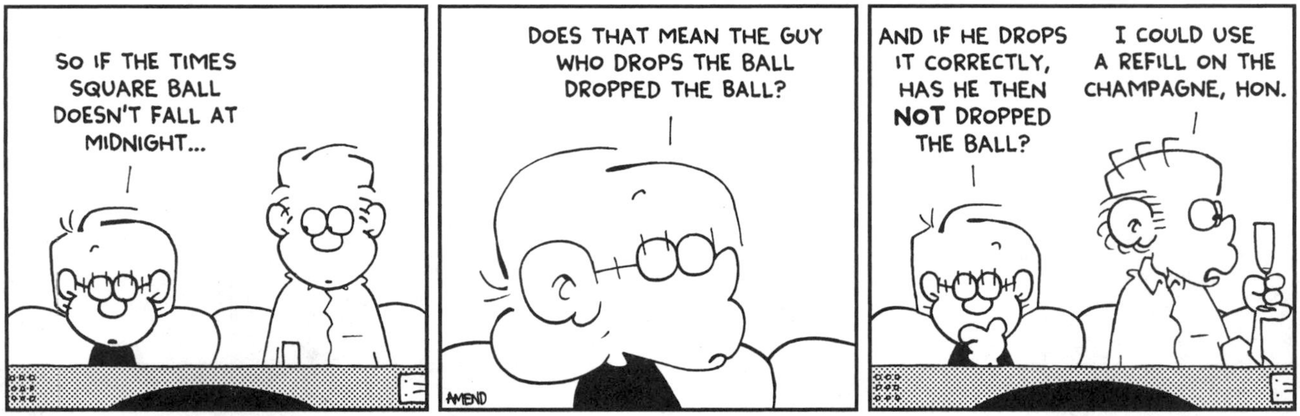
SO IF THE TIMES SQUARE BALL DOESN'T FALL AT MIDNIGHT...
DOES THAT MEAN THE GUY WHO DROPS THE BALL DROPPED THE BALL?
AMEND
AND IF HE DROPS IT CORRECTLY, HAS HE THEN **NOT** DROPPED THE BALL?
I COULD USE A REFILL ON THE CHAMPAGNE, HON.

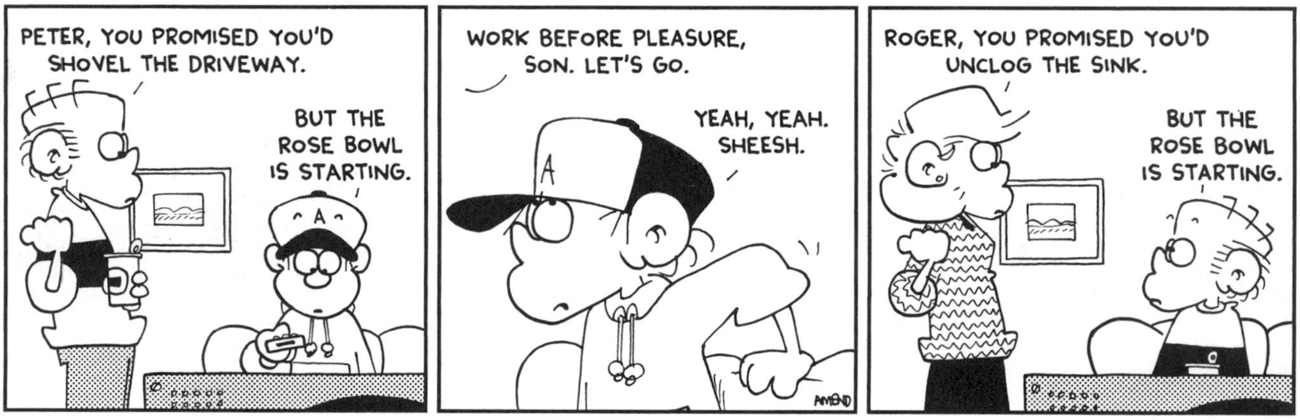
PETER, YOU PROMISED YOU'D SHOVEL THE DRIVEWAY.
BUT THE ROSE BOWL IS STARTING.
WORK BEFORE PLEASURE, SON. LET'S GO.
YEAH, YEAH. SHEESH.
AMEND
ROGER, YOU PROMISED YOU'D UNCLOG THE SINK.
BUT THE ROSE BOWL IS STARTING.

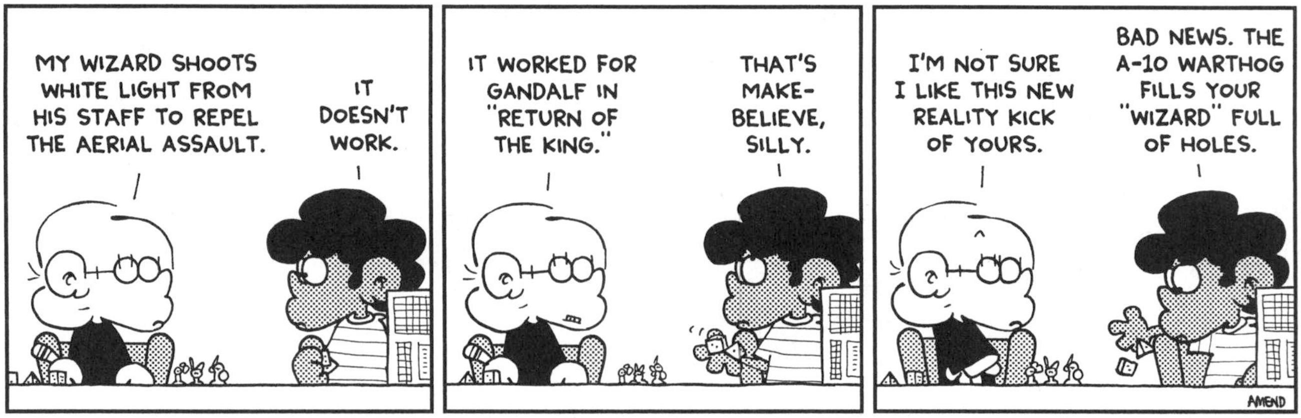
MY WIZARD SHOOTS WHITE LIGHT FROM HIS STAFF TO REPEL THE AERIAL ASSAULT.
IT DOESN'T WORK.
IT WORKED FOR GANDALF IN "RETURN OF THE KING."
THAT'S MAKE-BELIEVE, SILLY.
I'M NOT SURE I LIKE THIS NEW REALITY KICK OF YOURS.
BAD NEWS. THE A-10 WARTHOG FILLS YOUR "WIZARD" FULL OF HOLES.
AMEND

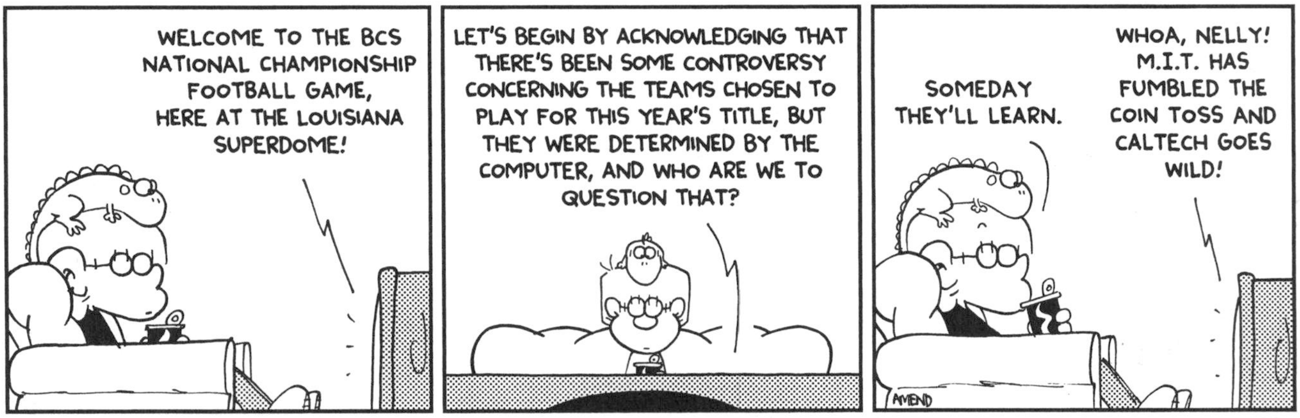
WELCOME TO THE BCS NATIONAL CHAMPIONSHIP FOOTBALL GAME, HERE AT THE LOUISIANA SUPERDOME!
LET'S BEGIN BY ACKNOWLEDGING THAT THERE'S BEEN SOME CONTROVERSY CONCERNING THE TEAMS CHOSEN TO PLAY FOR THIS YEAR'S TITLE, BUT THEY WERE DETERMINED BY THE COMPUTER, AND WHO ARE WE TO QUESTION THAT?
SOMEDAY THEY'LL LEARN.
WHOA, NELLY! M.I.T. HAS FUMBLED THE COIN TOSS AND CALTECH GOES WILD!
AMEND

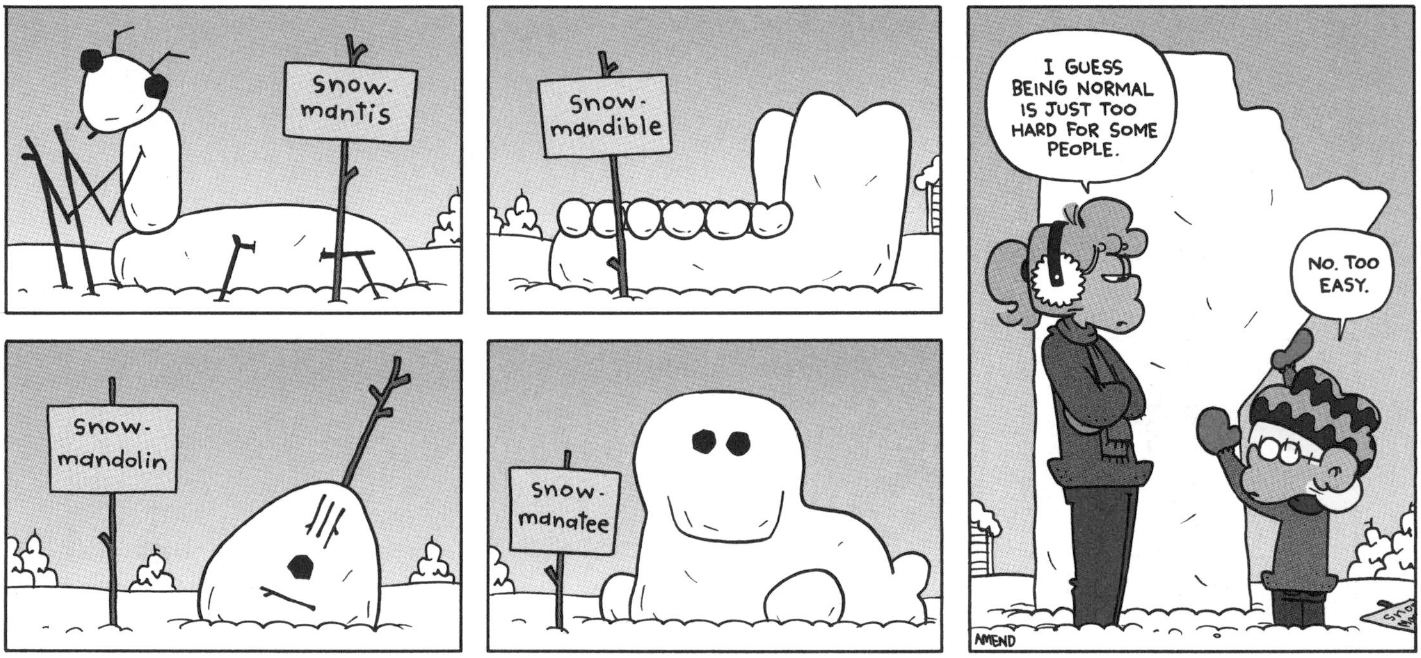
Snow-mantis
Snow-mandible
Snow-mandolin
Snow-manatee
I GUESS BEING NORMAL IS JUST TOO HARD FOR SOME PEOPLE.
NO. TOO EASY.
AMEND

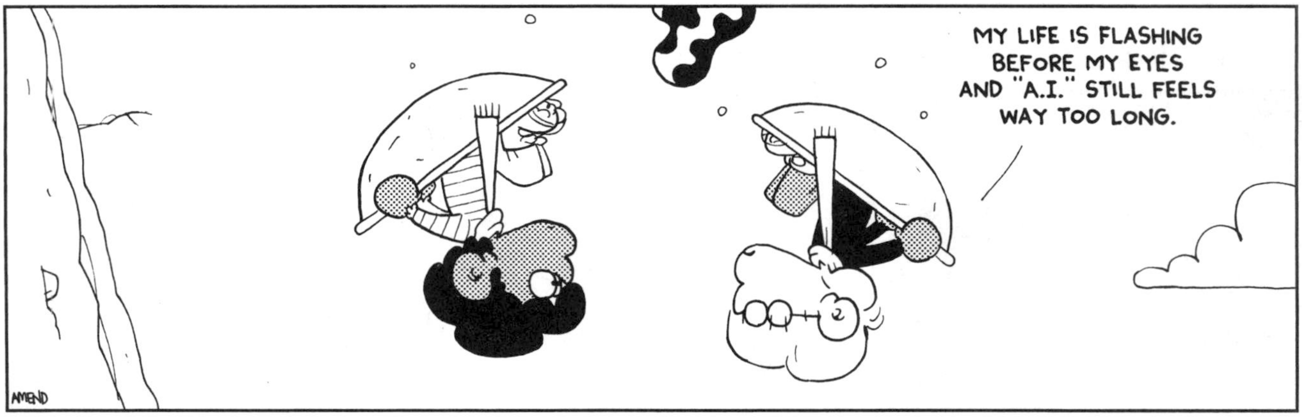
MY LIFE IS FLASHING BEFORE MY EYES AND "A.I." STILL FEELS WAY TOO LONG.
AMEND

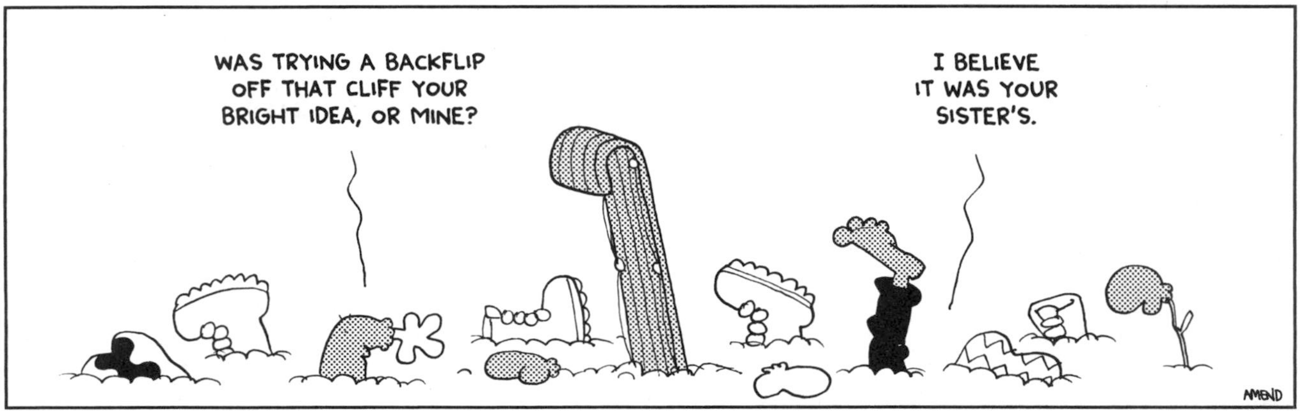
WAS TRYING A BACKFLIP OFF THAT CLIFF YOUR BRIGHT IDEA, OR MINE?
I BELIEVE IT WAS YOUR SISTER'S.
AMEND

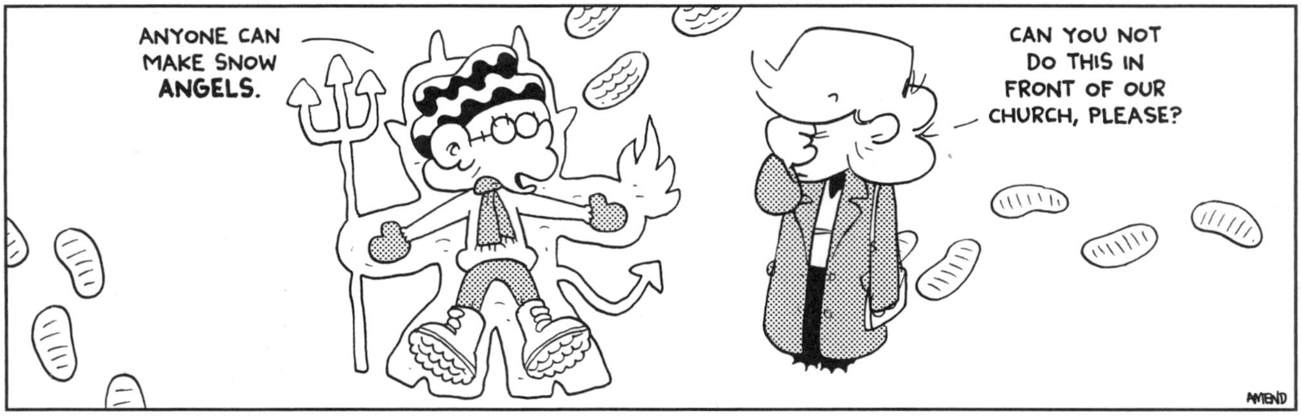
ANYONE CAN MAKE SNOW **ANGELS.**
CAN YOU NOT DO THIS IN FRONT OF OUR CHURCH, PLEASE?
AMEND

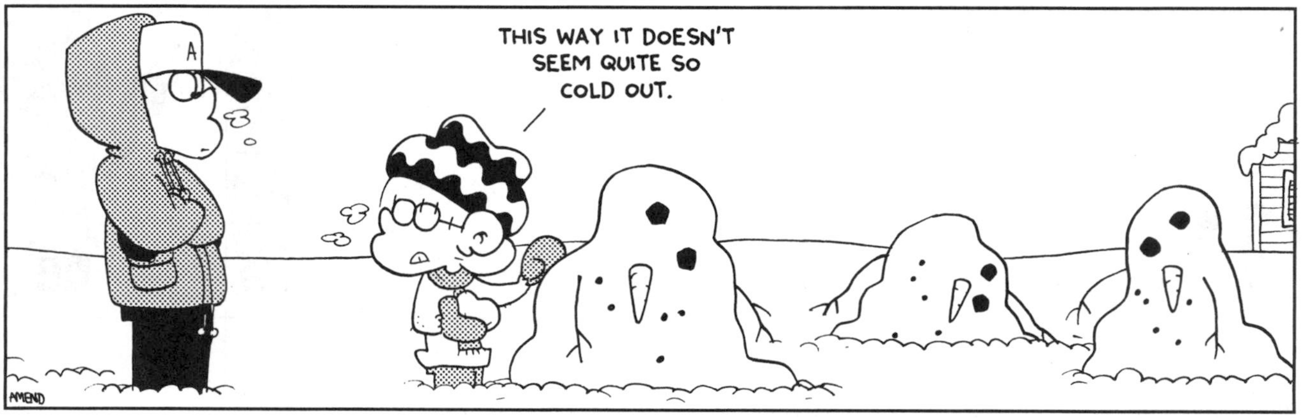
A
THIS WAY IT DOESN'T SEEM QUITE SO COLD OUT.
AMEND

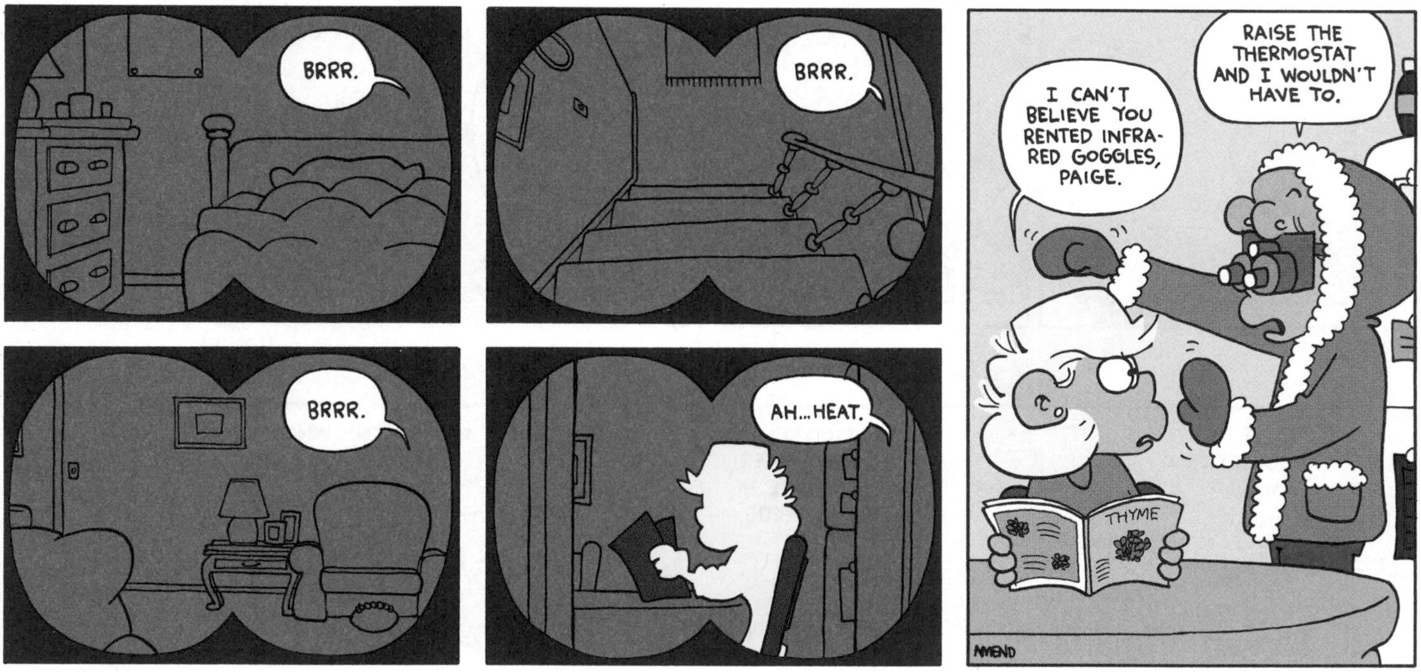
BRRR.
BRRR.
BRRR.
AH...HEAT.
I CAN'T BELIEVE YOU RENTED INFRA-RED GOGGLES, PAIGE.
RAISE THE THERMOSTAT AND I WOULDN'T HAVE TO.
THYME
AMEND

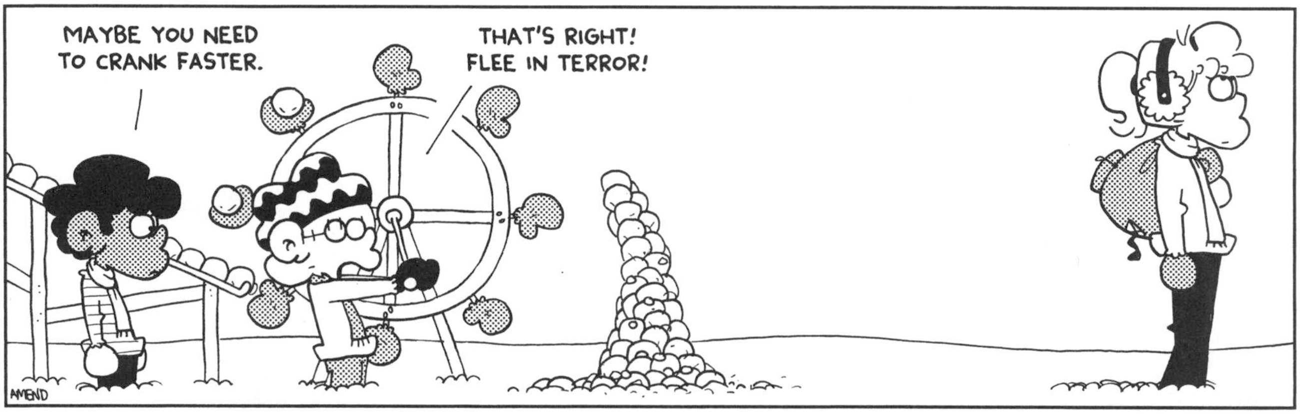
MAYBE YOU NEED TO CRANK FASTER.
THAT'S RIGHT! FLEE IN TERROR!
AMEND

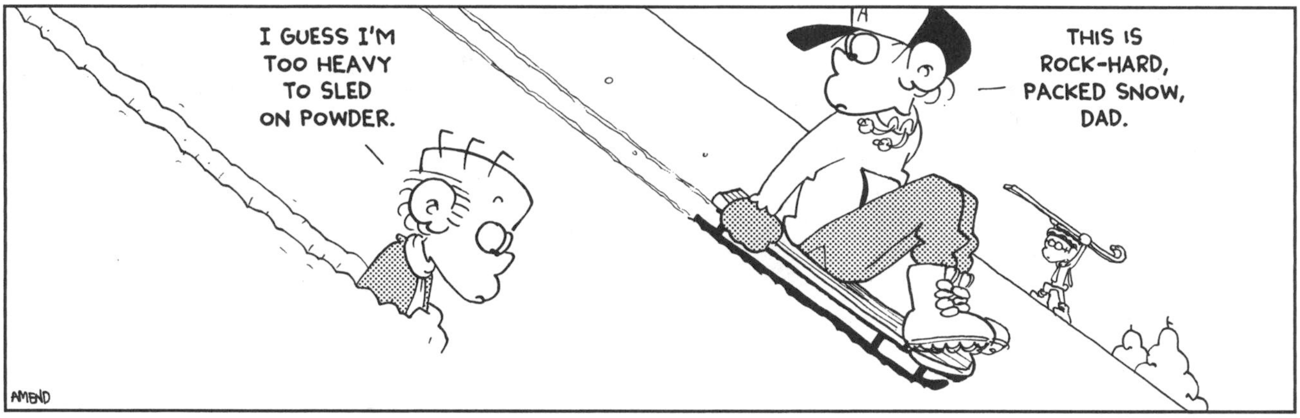
I GUESS I'M TOO HEAVY TO SLED ON POWDER.
THIS IS ROCK-HARD, PACKED SNOW, DAD.
AMEND

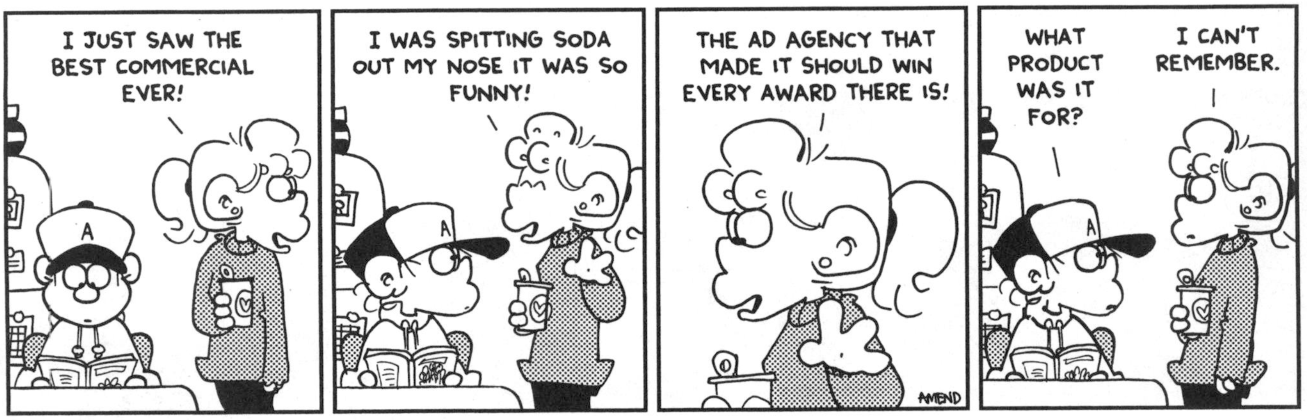
I JUST SAW THE BEST COMMERCIAL EVER!
I WAS SPITTING SODA OUT MY NOSE IT WAS SO FUNNY!
THE AD AGENCY THAT MADE IT SHOULD WIN EVERY AWARD THERE IS!
WHAT PRODUCT WAS IT FOR?
I CAN'T REMEMBER.
AMEND

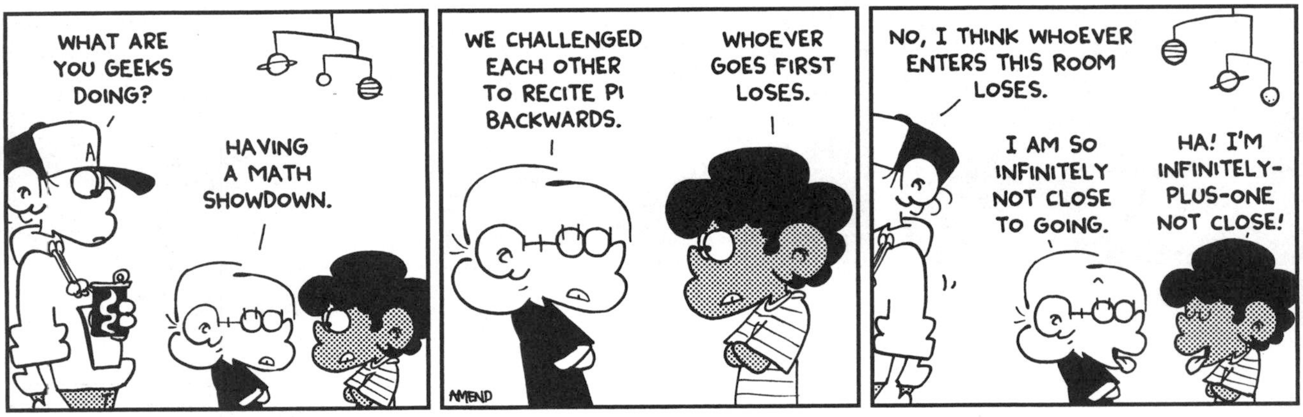
WHAT ARE YOU GEEKS DOING?
HAVING A MATH SHOWDOWN.
WE CHALLENGED EACH OTHER TO RECITE PI BACKWARDS.
WHOEVER GOES FIRST LOSES.
NO, I THINK WHOEVER ENTERS THIS ROOM LOSES.
I AM SO INFINITELY NOT CLOSE TO GOING.
HA! I'M INFINITELY-PLUS-ONE NOT CLOSE!
AMEND

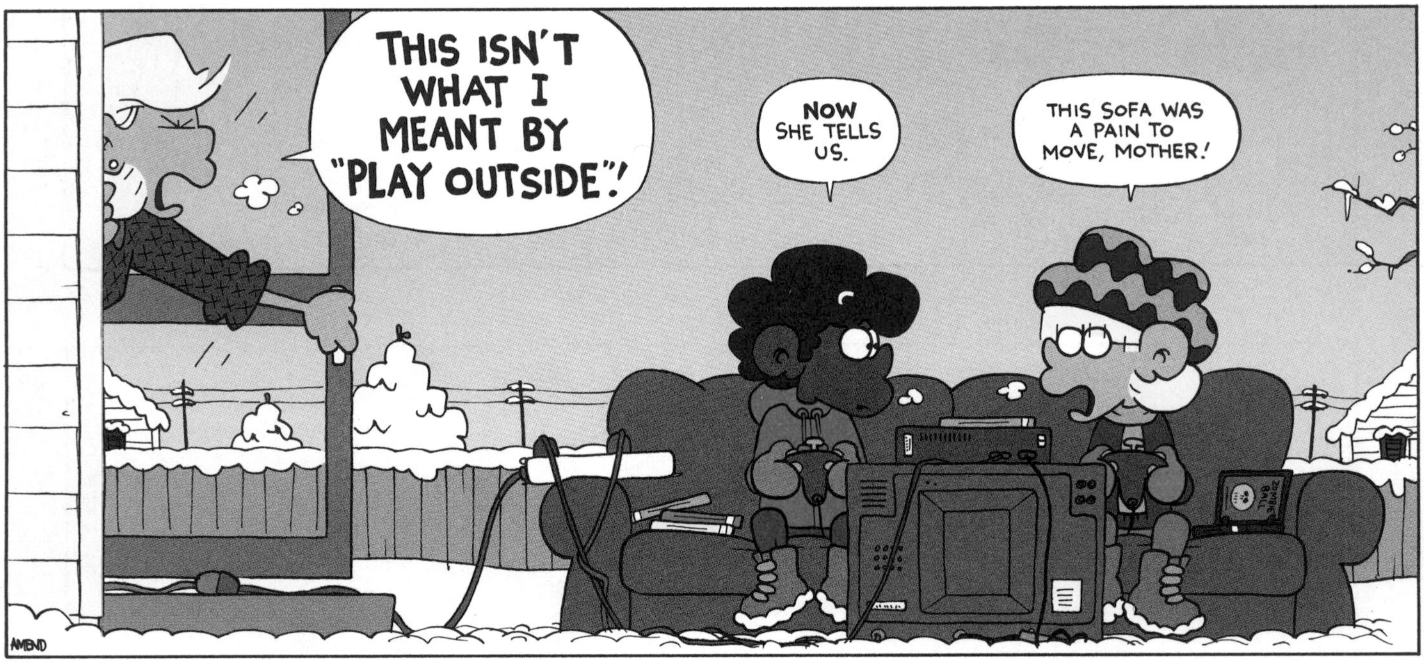
THIS ISN'T WHAT I MEANT BY "PLAY OUTSIDE"!
NOW SHE TELLS US.
THIS SOFA WAS A PAIN TO MOVE, MOTHER!
AMEND

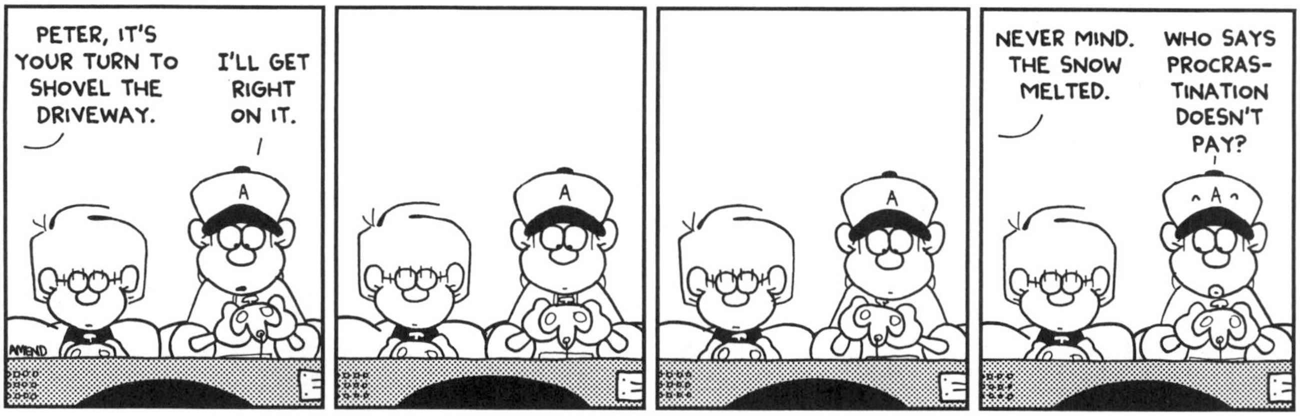
PETER, IT'S YOUR TURN TO SHOVEL THE DRIVEWAY.
I'LL GET RIGHT ON IT.
NEVER MIND. THE SNOW MELTED.
WHO SAYS PROCRAS-TINATION DOESN'T PAY?

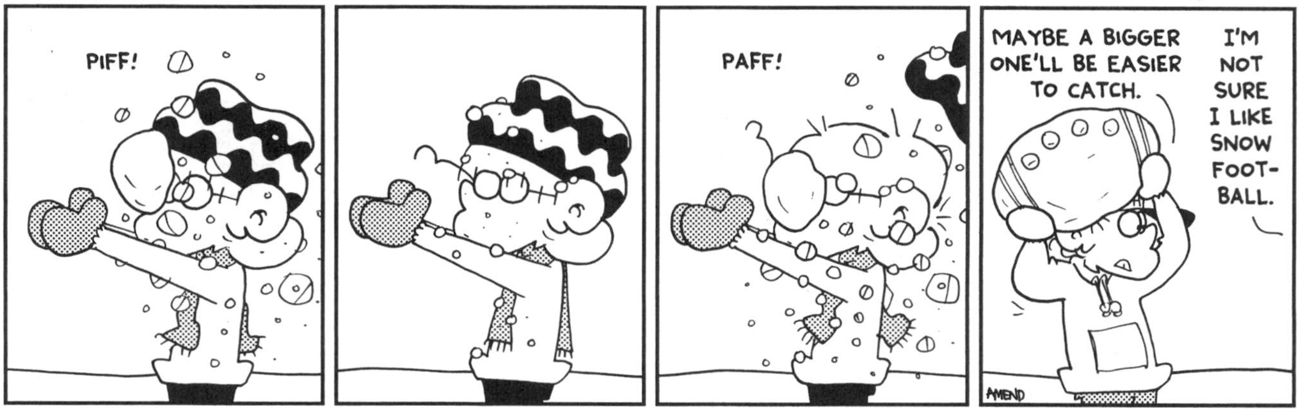
PIFF!
PAFF!
MAYBE A BIGGER ONE'LL BE EASIER TO CATCH.
I'M NOT SURE I LIKE SNOW FOOT-BALL.

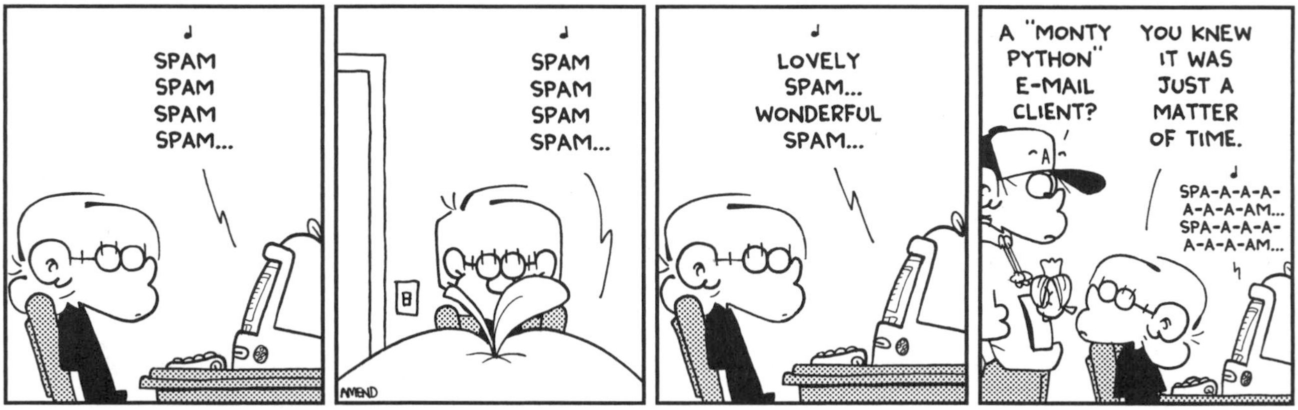
SPAM SPAM SPAM SPAM...
SPAM SPAM SPAM SPAM...
LOVELY SPAM... WONDERFUL SPAM...
A "MONTY PYTHON" E-MAIL CLIENT?
YOU KNEW IT WAS JUST A MATTER OF TIME.
SPA-A-A-A-A-A-A-AM... SPA-A-A-A-A-A-A-AM...

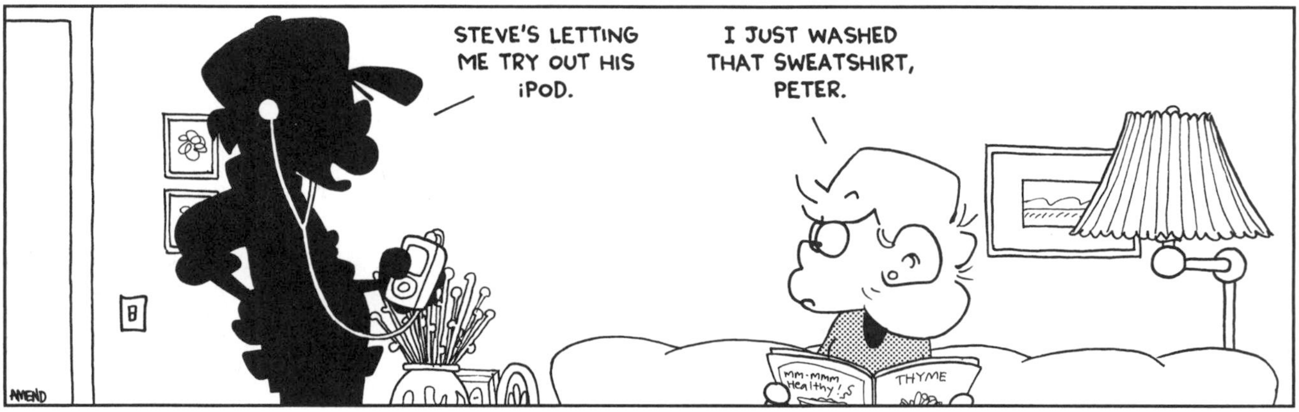
STEVE'S LETTING ME TRY OUT HIS iPOD.
I JUST WASHED THAT SWEATSHIRT, PETER.

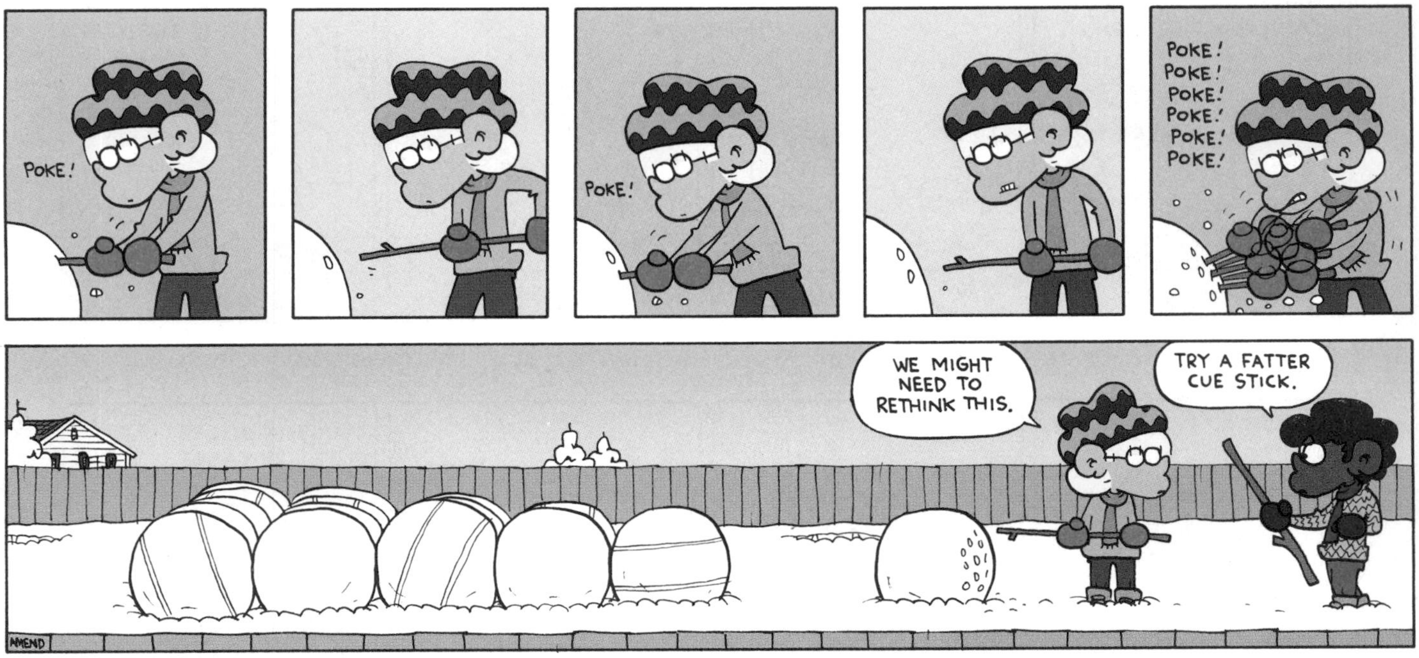
POKE!
POKE!
POKE! POKE! POKE! POKE! POKE! POKE!
WE MIGHT NEED TO RETHINK THIS.
TRY A FATTER CUE STICK.
AMEND

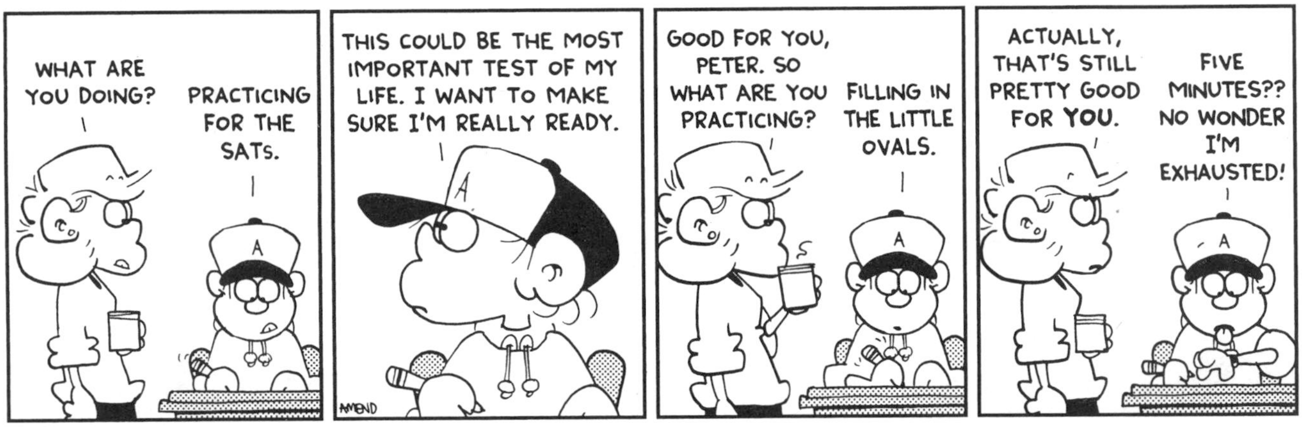
WHAT ARE YOU DOING?
PRACTICING FOR THE SATs.
THIS COULD BE THE MOST IMPORTANT TEST OF MY LIFE. I WANT TO MAKE SURE I'M REALLY READY.
AMEND
GOOD FOR YOU, PETER. SO WHAT ARE YOU PRACTICING?
FILLING IN THE LITTLE OVALS.
ACTUALLY, THAT'S STILL PRETTY GOOD FOR **YOU**.
FIVE MINUTES?? NO WONDER I'M EXHAUSTED!

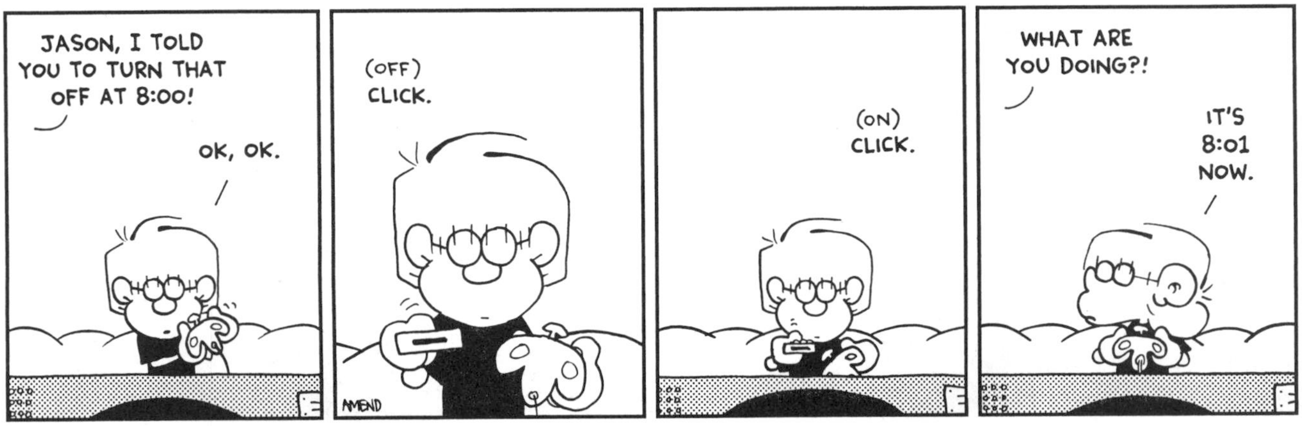
JASON, I TOLD YOU TO TURN THAT OFF AT 8:00!
OK, OK.
(OFF) CLICK.
AMEND
(ON) CLICK.
WHAT ARE YOU DOING?!
IT'S 8:01 NOW.

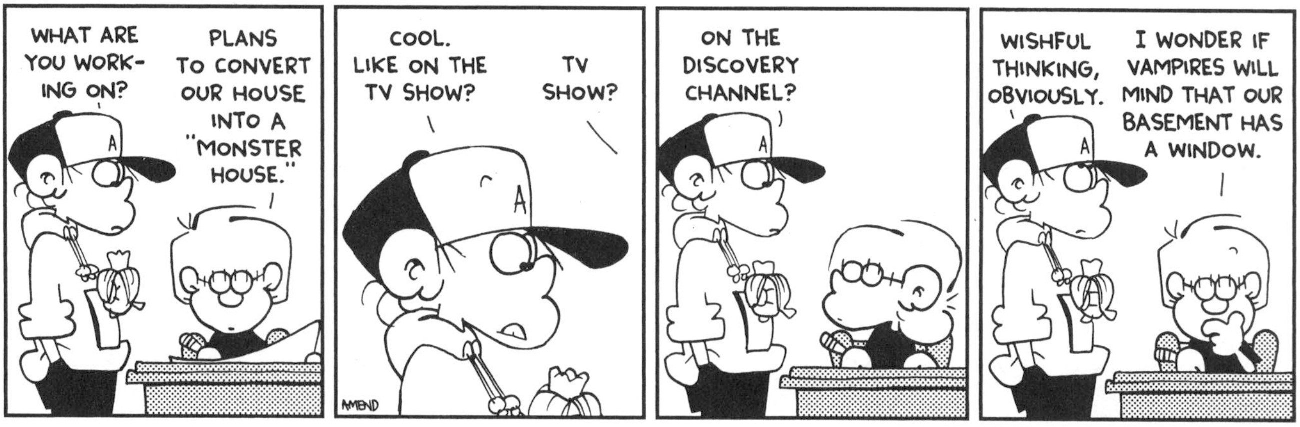
WHAT ARE YOU WORKING ON?
PLANS TO CONVERT OUR HOUSE INTO A "MONSTER HOUSE."
COOL. LIKE ON THE TV SHOW?
TV SHOW?
ON THE DISCOVERY CHANNEL?
WISHFUL THINKING, OBVIOUSLY.
I WONDER IF VAMPIRES WILL MIND THAT OUR BASEMENT HAS A WINDOW.
AMEND

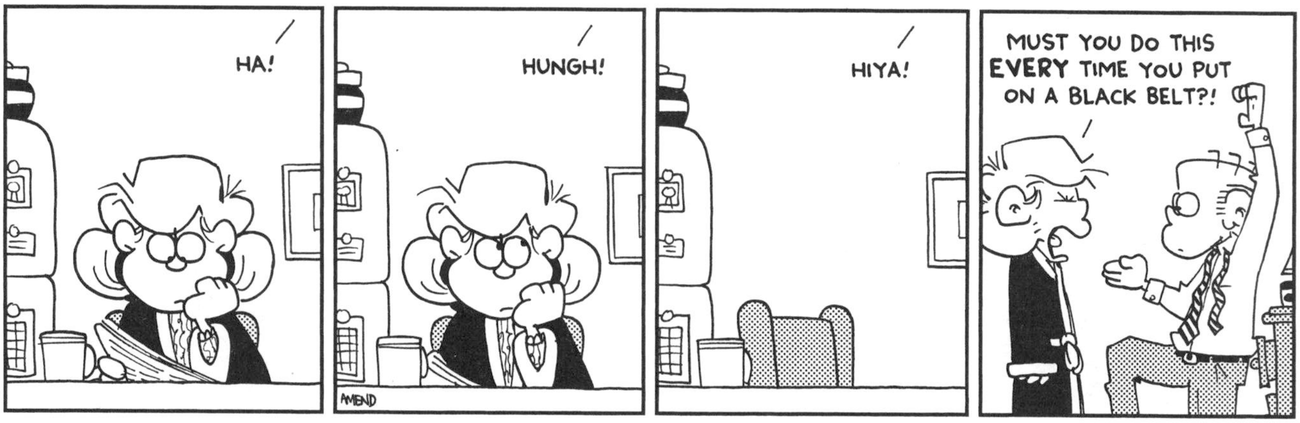
HA!
HUNGH!
AMEND
HIYA!
MUST YOU DO THIS **EVERY** TIME YOU PUT ON A BLACK BELT?!

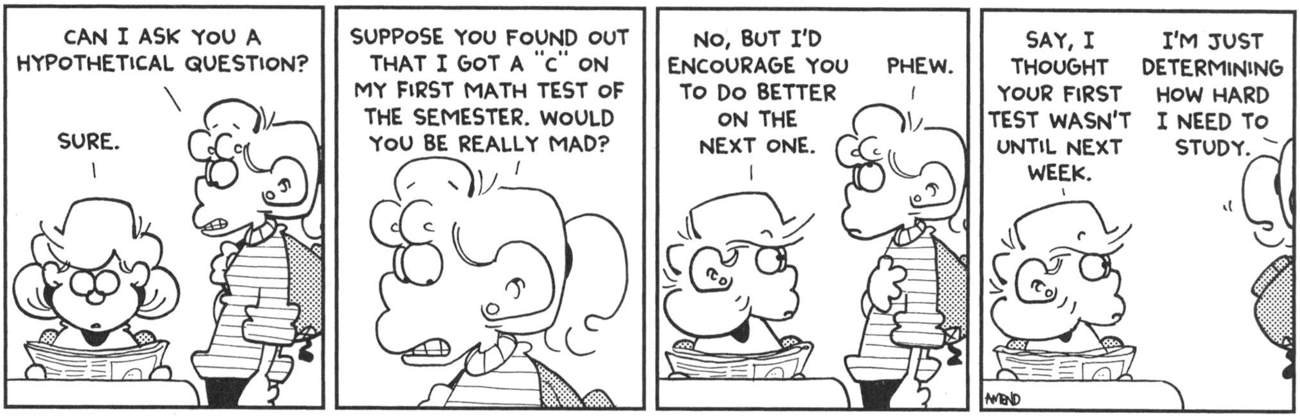
CAN I ASK YOU A HYPOTHETICAL QUESTION?
SURE.
SUPPOSE YOU FOUND OUT THAT I GOT A "C" ON MY FIRST MATH TEST OF THE SEMESTER. WOULD YOU BE REALLY MAD?
NO, BUT I'D ENCOURAGE YOU TO DO BETTER ON THE NEXT ONE.
PHEW.
SAY, I THOUGHT YOUR FIRST TEST WASN'T UNTIL NEXT WEEK.
I'M JUST DETERMINING HOW HARD I NEED TO STUDY.
AMEND

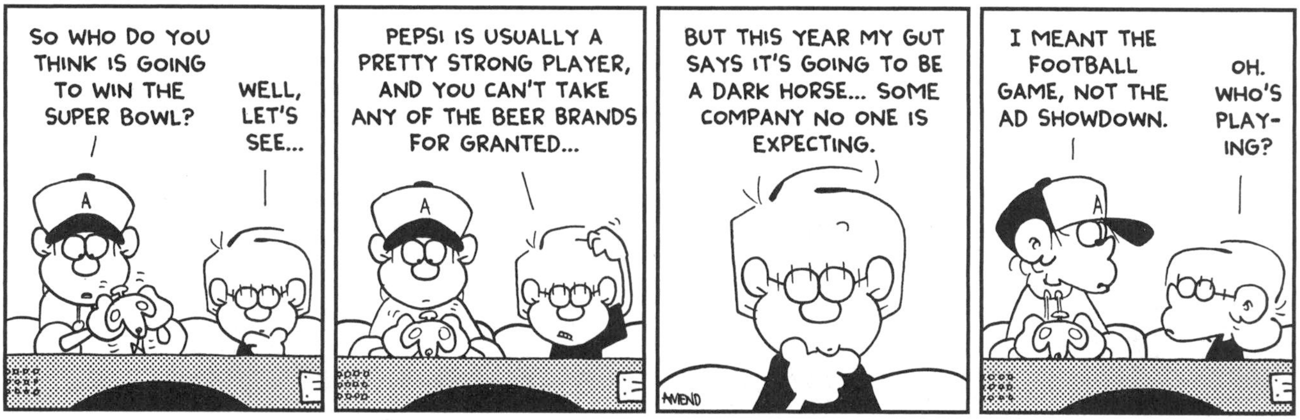
SO WHO DO YOU THINK IS GOING TO WIN THE SUPER BOWL?
WELL, LET'S SEE...
PEPSI IS USUALLY A PRETTY STRONG PLAYER, AND YOU CAN'T TAKE ANY OF THE BEER BRANDS FOR GRANTED...
BUT THIS YEAR MY GUT SAYS IT'S GOING TO BE A DARK HORSE... SOME COMPANY NO ONE IS EXPECTING.
AMEND
I MEANT THE FOOTBALL GAME, NOT THE AD SHOWDOWN.
OH. WHO'S PLAYING?

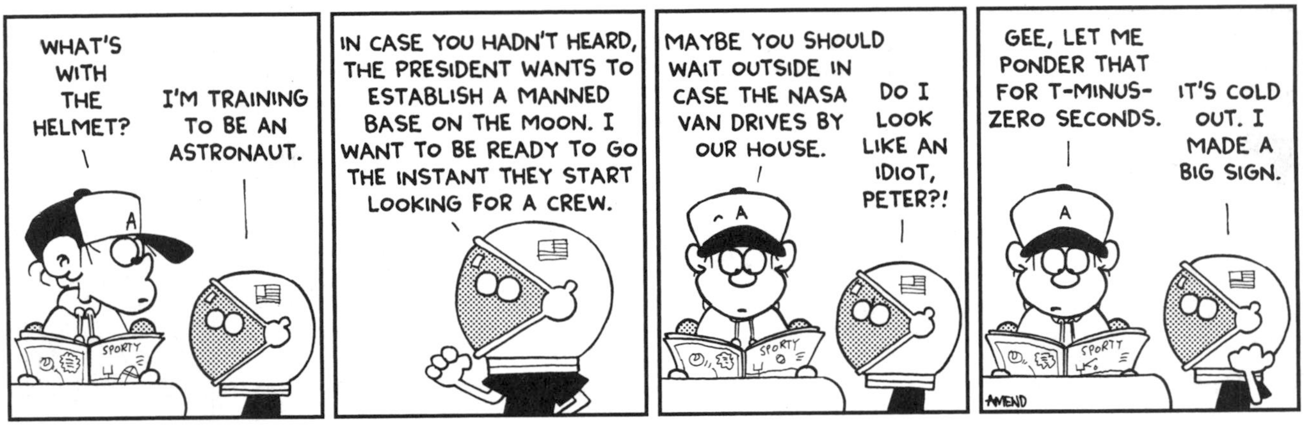
WHAT'S WITH THE HELMET?
I'M TRAINING TO BE AN ASTRONAUT.
IN CASE YOU HADN'T HEARD, THE PRESIDENT WANTS TO ESTABLISH A MANNED BASE ON THE MOON. I WANT TO BE READY TO GO THE INSTANT THEY START LOOKING FOR A CREW.
MAYBE YOU SHOULD WAIT OUTSIDE IN CASE THE NASA VAN DRIVES BY OUR HOUSE.
DO I LOOK LIKE AN IDIOT, PETER?!
GEE, LET ME PONDER THAT FOR T-MINUS-ZERO SECONDS.
IT'S COLD OUT. I MADE A BIG SIGN.
AMEND

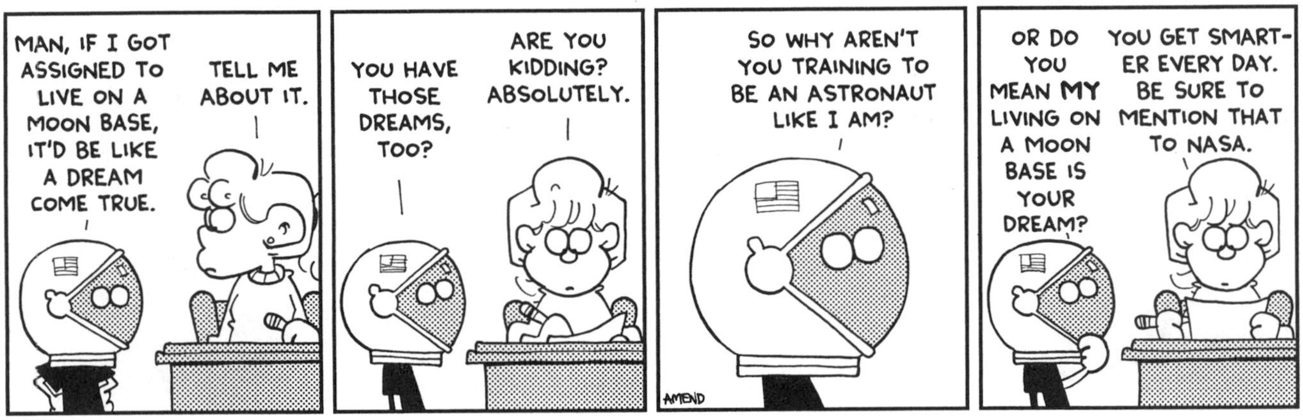
MAN, IF I GOT ASSIGNED TO LIVE ON A MOON BASE, IT'D BE LIKE A DREAM COME TRUE.
TELL ME ABOUT IT.
YOU HAVE THOSE DREAMS, TOO?
ARE YOU KIDDING? ABSOLUTELY.
SO WHY AREN'T YOU TRAINING TO BE AN ASTRONAUT LIKE I AM?
OR DO YOU MEAN MY LIVING ON A MOON BASE IS YOUR DREAM?
YOU GET SMARTER EVERY DAY. BE SURE TO MENTION THAT TO NASA.
AMEND

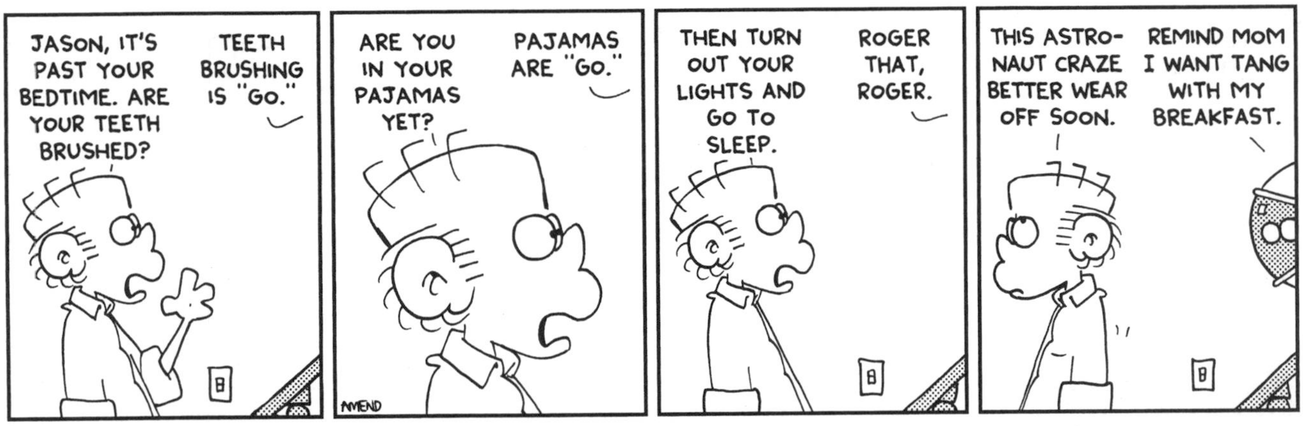
JASON, IT'S PAST YOUR BEDTIME. ARE YOUR TEETH BRUSHED?
TEETH BRUSHING IS "GO."
ARE YOU IN YOUR PAJAMAS YET?
PAJAMAS ARE "GO."
THEN TURN OUT YOUR LIGHTS AND GO TO SLEEP.
ROGER THAT, ROGER.
THIS ASTRONAUT CRAZE BETTER WEAR OFF SOON.
REMIND MOM I WANT TANG WITH MY BREAKFAST.
AMEND

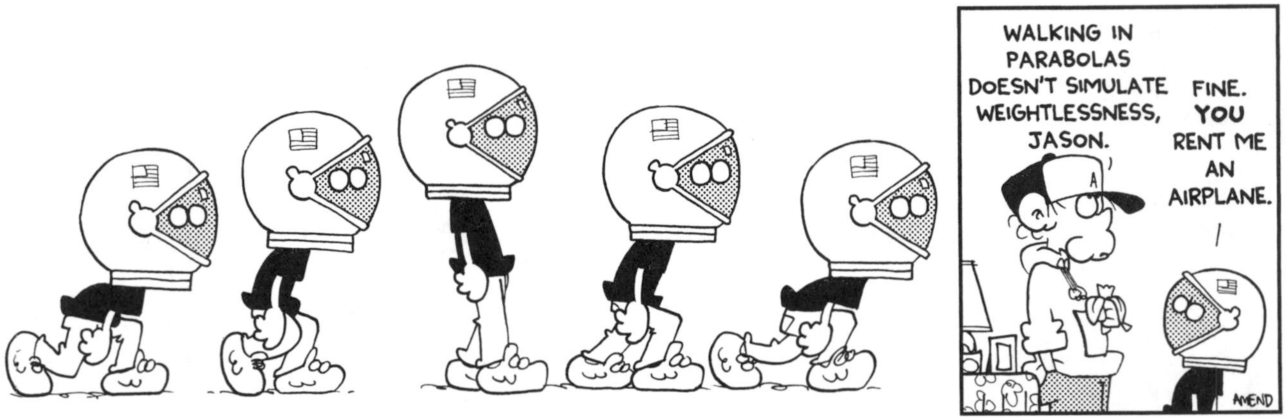
WALKING IN PARABOLAS DOESN'T SIMULATE WEIGHTLESSNESS, JASON.
FINE. YOU RENT ME AN AIRPLANE.
AMEND

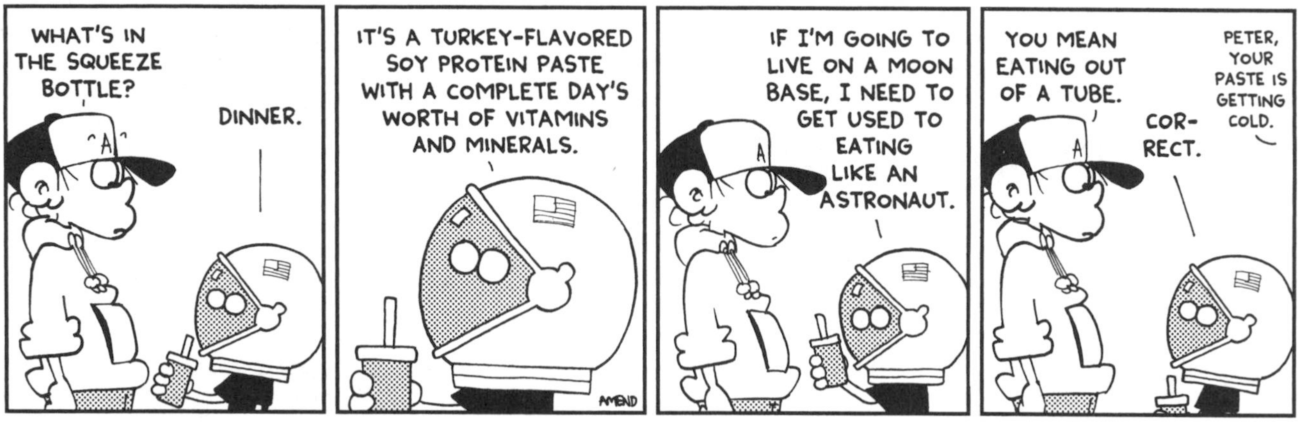
WHAT'S IN THE SQUEEZE BOTTLE?
DINNER.
IT'S A TURKEY-FLAVORED SOY PROTEIN PASTE WITH A COMPLETE DAY'S WORTH OF VITAMINS AND MINERALS.
IF I'M GOING TO LIVE ON A MOON BASE, I NEED TO GET USED TO EATING LIKE AN ASTRONAUT.
YOU MEAN EATING OUT OF A TUBE.
COR-RECT.
PETER, YOUR PASTE IS GETTING COLD.
AMEND

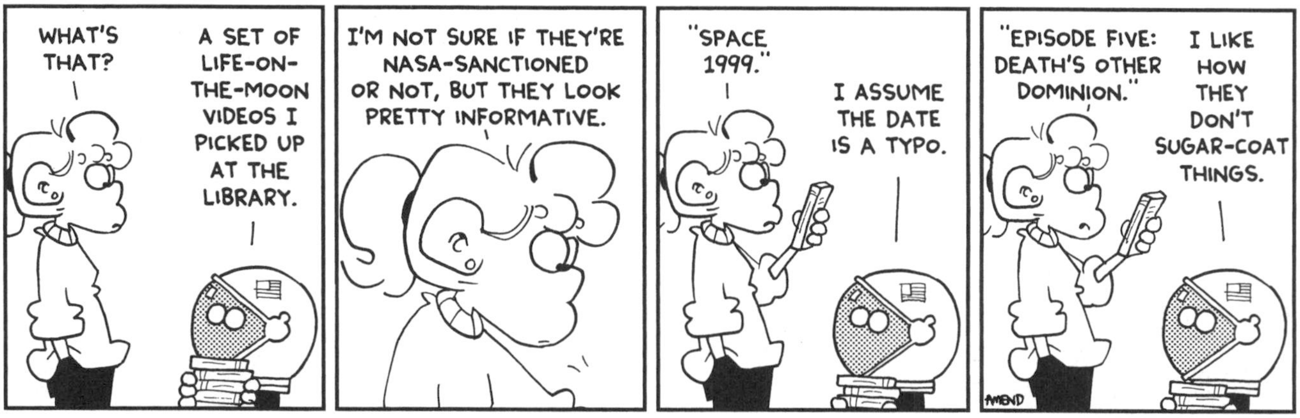
WHAT'S THAT?
A SET OF LIFE-ON-THE-MOON VIDEOS I PICKED UP AT THE LIBRARY.
I'M NOT SURE IF THEY'RE NASA-SANCTIONED OR NOT, BUT THEY LOOK PRETTY INFORMATIVE.
"SPACE 1999."
I ASSUME THE DATE IS A TYPO.
"EPISODE FIVE: DEATH'S OTHER DOMINION."
I LIKE HOW THEY DON'T SUGAR-COAT THINGS.
AMEND

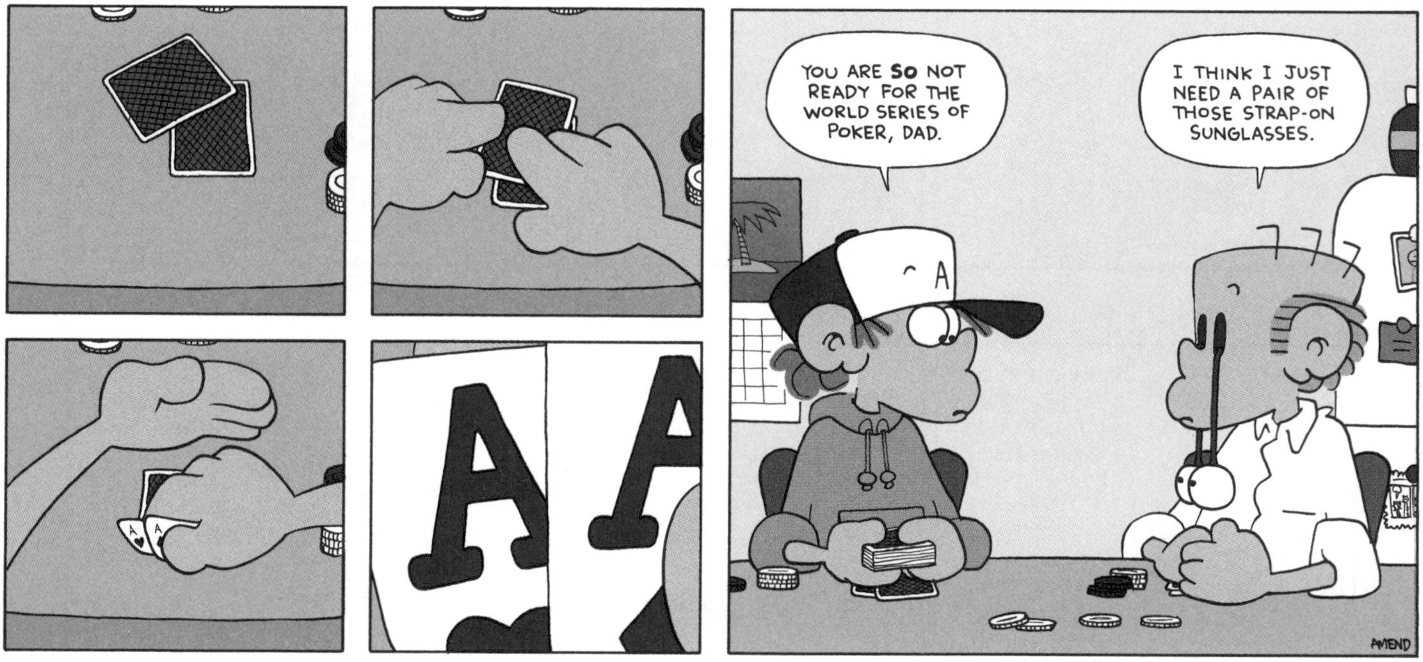
A
A
YOU ARE SO NOT READY FOR THE WORLD SERIES OF POKER, DAD.
I THINK I JUST NEED A PAIR OF THOSE STRAP-ON SUNGLASSES.
AMEND

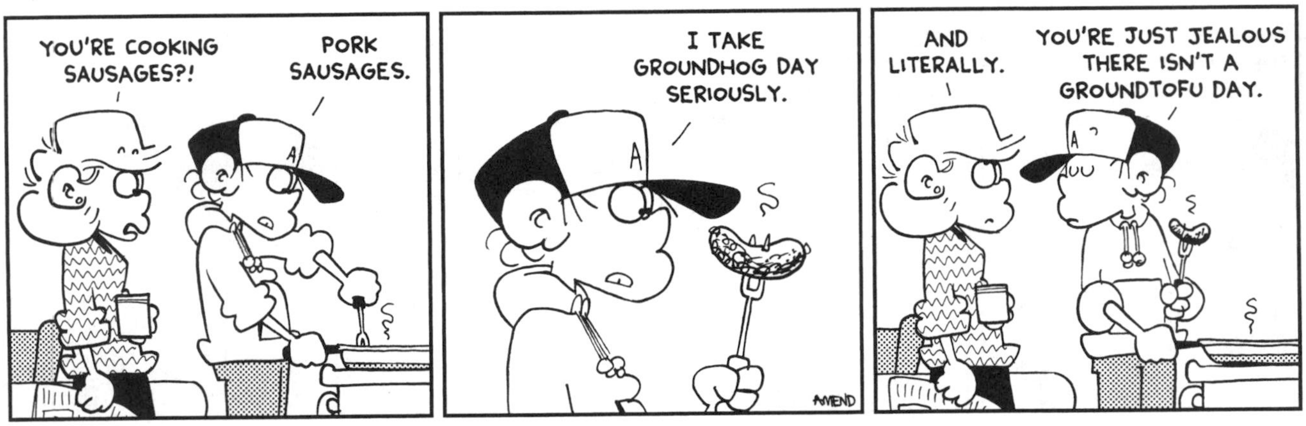
YOU'RE COOKING SAUSAGES?!
PORK SAUSAGES.
I TAKE GROUNDHOG DAY SERIOUSLY.
AMEND
AND LITERALLY.
YOU'RE JUST JEALOUS THERE ISN'T A GROUNDTOFU DAY.

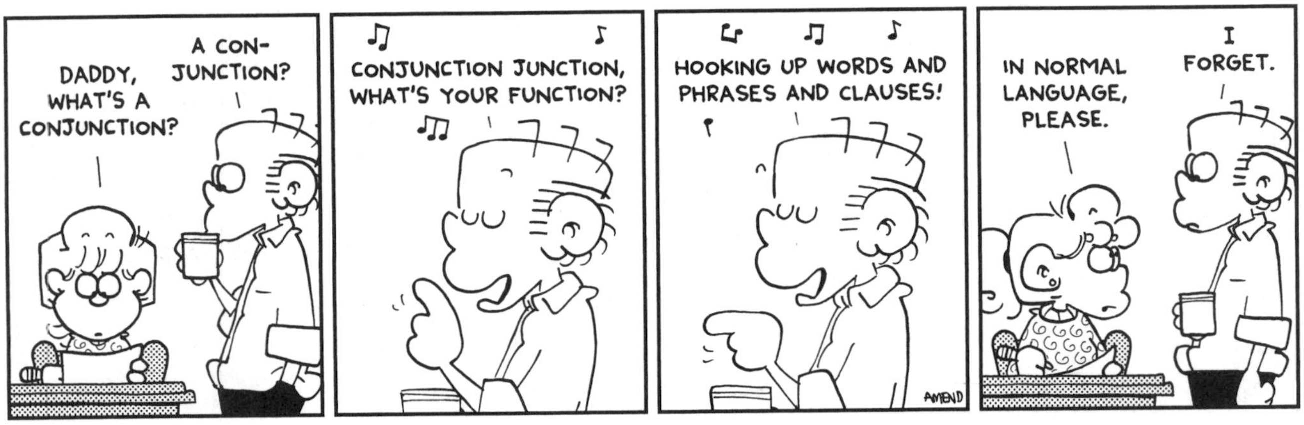
DADDY, WHAT'S A CONJUNCTION?
A CON-JUNCTION?
CONJUNCTION JUNCTION, WHAT'S YOUR FUNCTION?
HOOKING UP WORDS AND PHRASES AND CLAUSES!
AMEND
IN NORMAL LANGUAGE, PLEASE.
I FORGET.

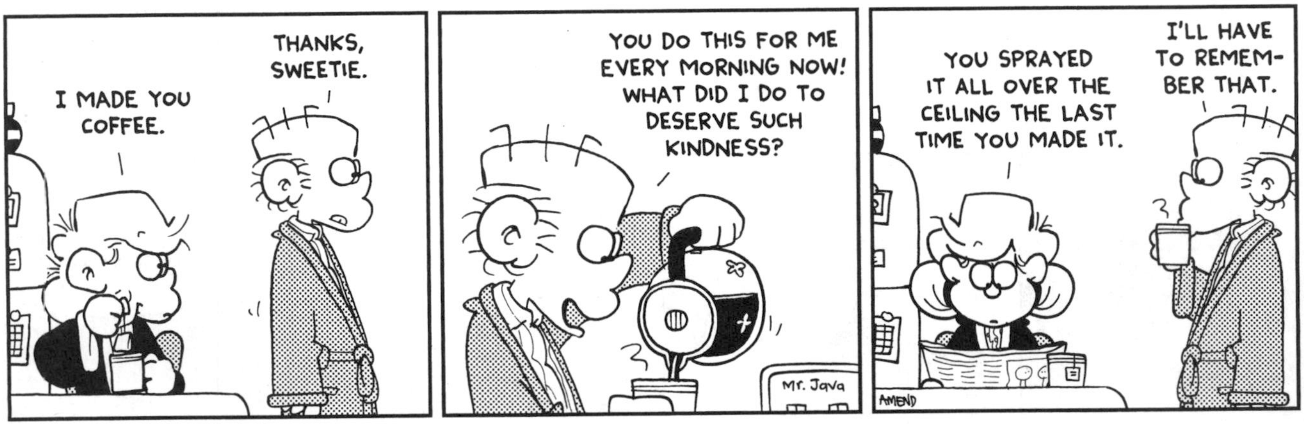
I MADE YOU COFFEE.
THANKS, SWEETIE.
YOU DO THIS FOR ME EVERY MORNING NOW! WHAT DID I DO TO DESERVE SUCH KINDNESS?
Mr. Java
YOU SPRAYED IT ALL OVER THE CEILING THE LAST TIME YOU MADE IT.
I'LL HAVE TO REMEMBER THAT.
AMEND

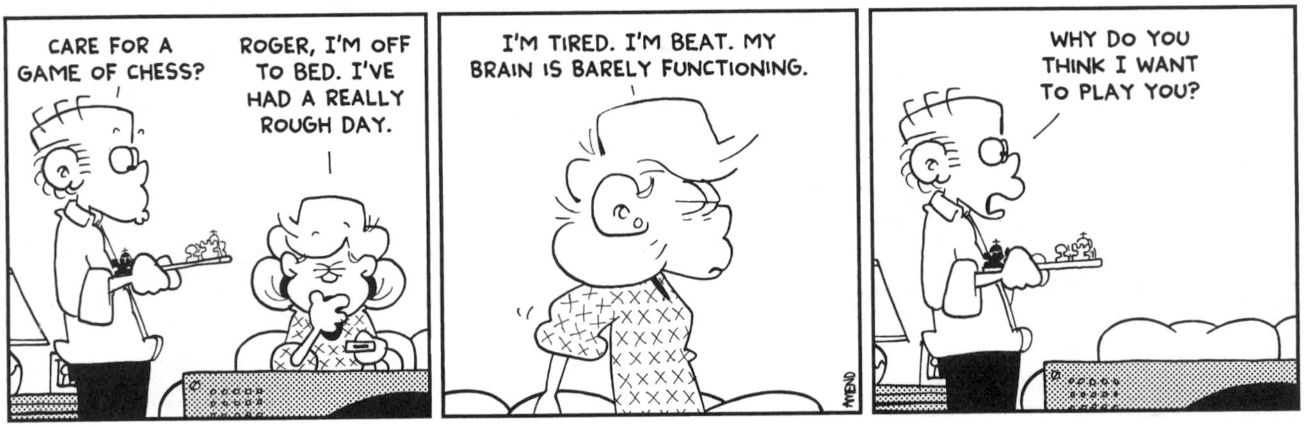
CARE FOR A GAME OF CHESS?
ROGER, I'M OFF TO BED. I'VE HAD A REALLY ROUGH DAY.
I'M TIRED. I'M BEAT. MY BRAIN IS BARELY FUNCTIONING.
AMEND
WHY DO YOU THINK I WANT TO PLAY YOU?

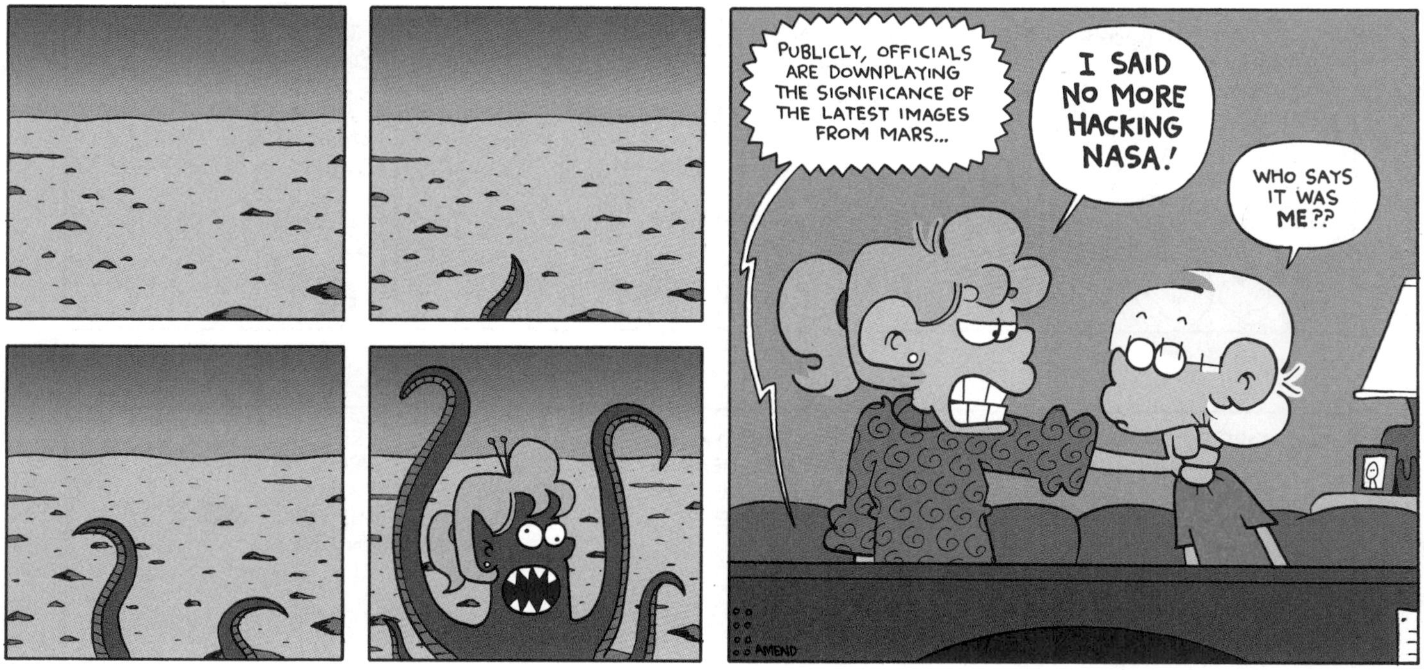
PUBLICLY, OFFICIALS ARE DOWNPLAYING THE SIGNIFICANCE OF THE LATEST IMAGES FROM MARS...
I SAID NO MORE HACKING NASA!
WHO SAYS IT WAS ME??
AMEND

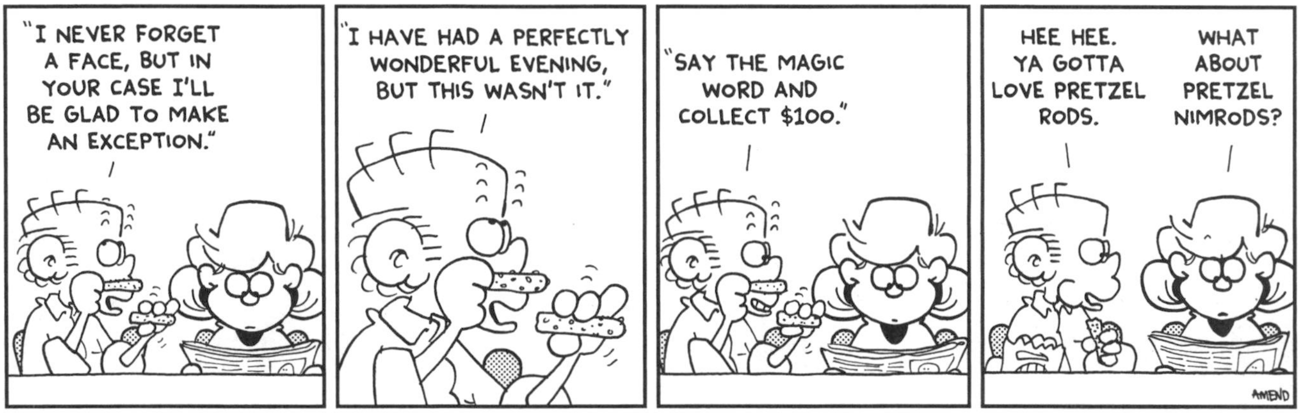
"I NEVER FORGET A FACE, BUT IN YOUR CASE I'LL BE GLAD TO MAKE AN EXCEPTION."
"I HAVE HAD A PERFECTLY WONDERFUL EVENING, BUT THIS WASN'T IT."
"SAY THE MAGIC WORD AND COLLECT $100."
HEE HEE. YA GOTTA LOVE PRETZEL RODS.
WHAT ABOUT PRETZEL NIMRODS?
AMEND

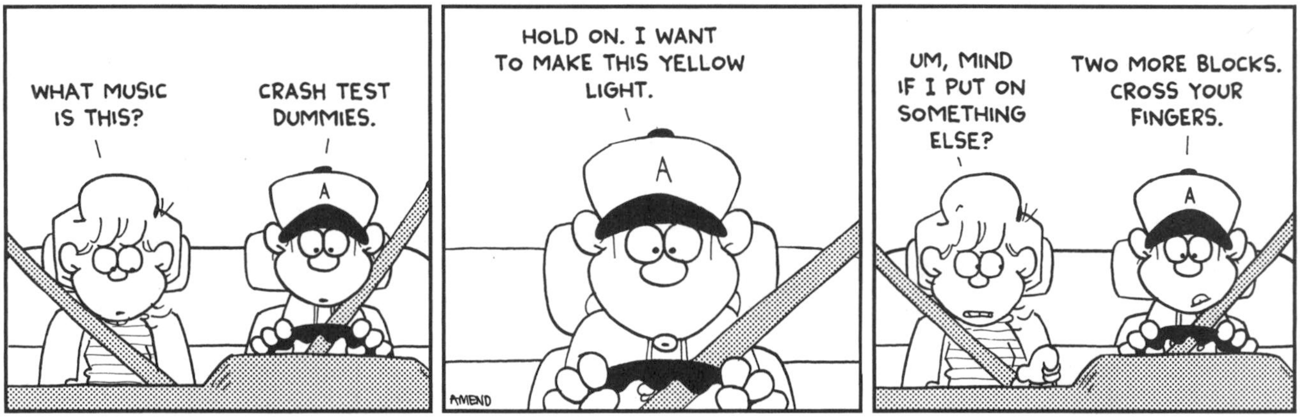
WHAT MUSIC IS THIS?
CRASH TEST DUMMIES.
HOLD ON. I WANT TO MAKE THIS YELLOW LIGHT.
AMEND
UM, MIND IF I PUT ON SOMETHING ELSE?
TWO MORE BLOCKS. CROSS YOUR FINGERS.

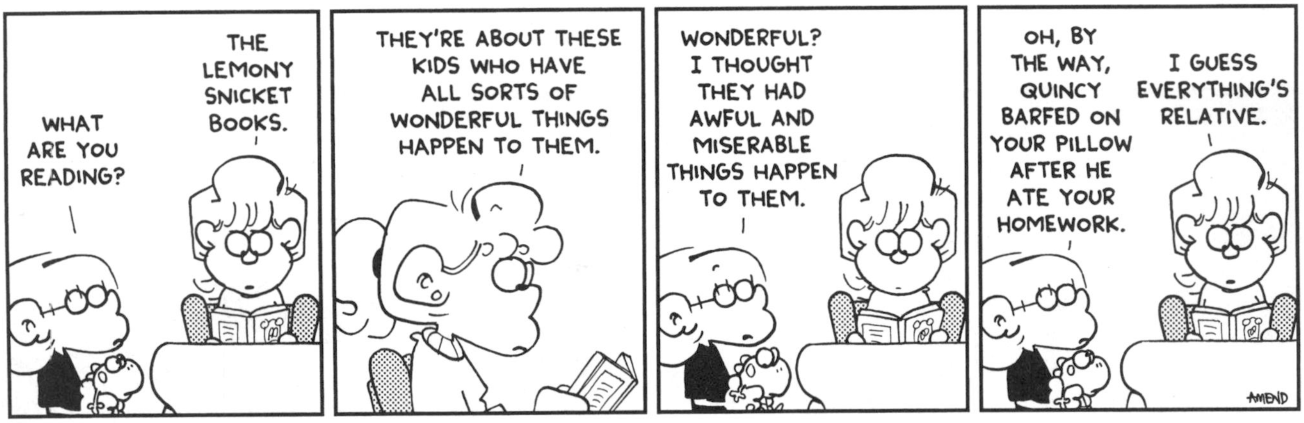
WHAT ARE YOU READING?
THE LEMONY SNICKET BOOKS.
THEY'RE ABOUT THESE KIDS WHO HAVE ALL SORTS OF WONDERFUL THINGS HAPPEN TO THEM.
WONDERFUL? I THOUGHT THEY HAD AWFUL AND MISERABLE THINGS HAPPEN TO THEM.
OH, BY THE WAY, QUINCY BARFED ON YOUR PILLOW AFTER HE ATE YOUR HOMEWORK.
I GUESS EVERYTHING'S RELATIVE.
AMEND

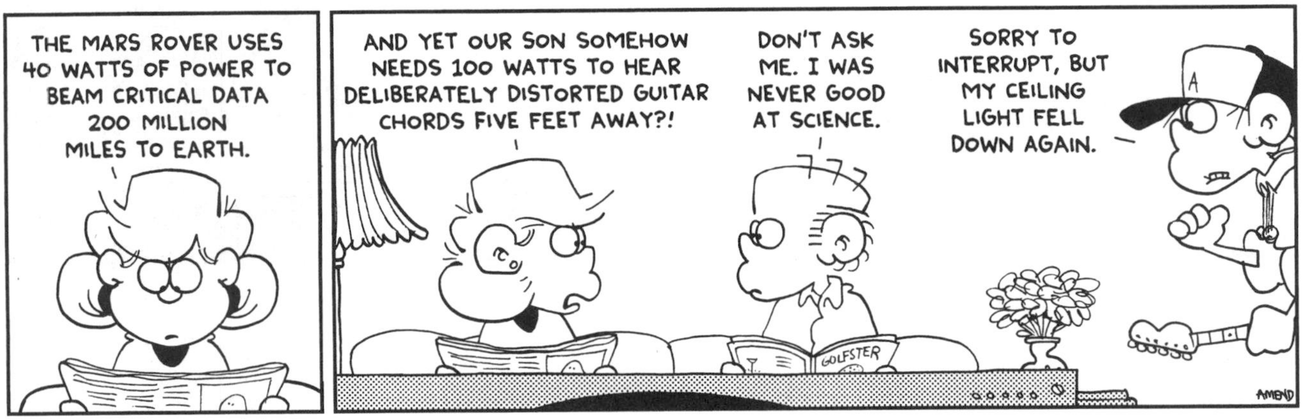
THE MARS ROVER USES 40 WATTS OF POWER TO BEAM CRITICAL DATA 200 MILLION MILES TO EARTH.
AND YET OUR SON SOMEHOW NEEDS 100 WATTS TO HEAR DELIBERATELY DISTORTED GUITAR CHORDS FIVE FEET AWAY?!
DON'T ASK ME. I WAS NEVER GOOD AT SCIENCE.
SORRY TO INTERRUPT, BUT MY CEILING LIGHT FELL DOWN AGAIN.
GOLFSTER
AMEND

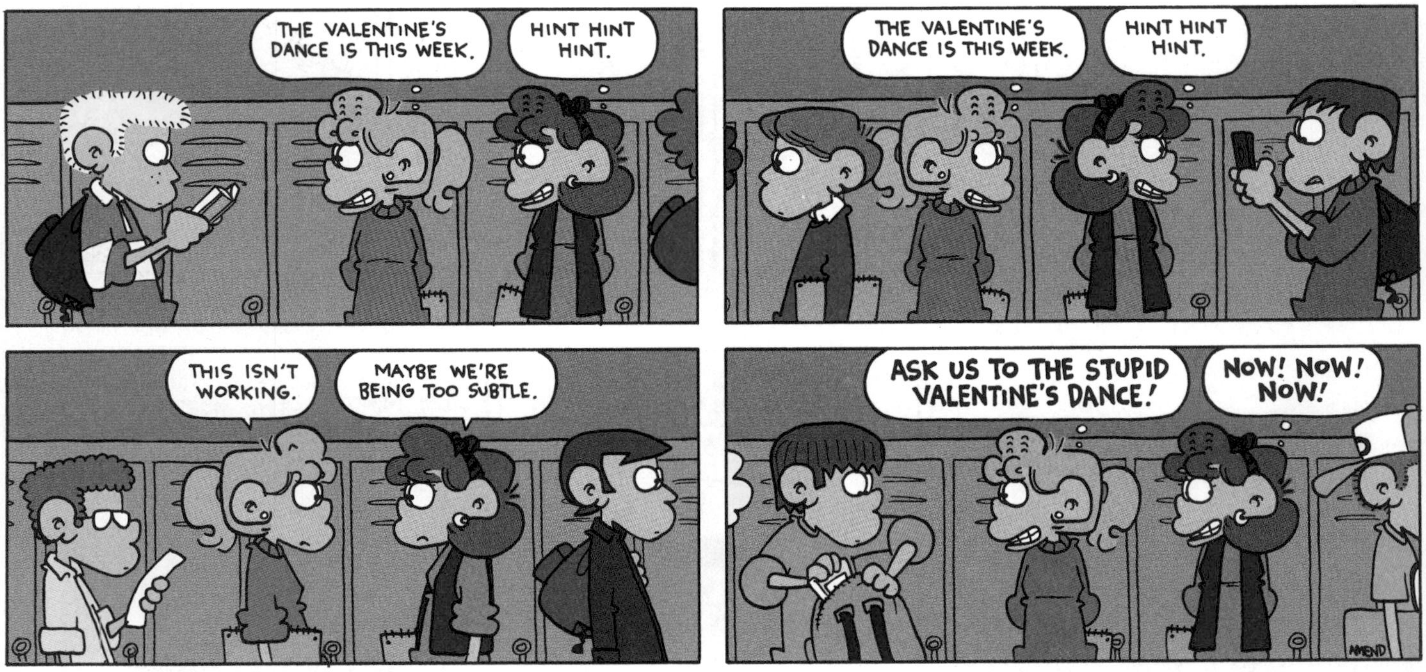
THE VALENTINE'S DANCE IS THIS WEEK.
HINT HINT HINT.
THE VALENTINE'S DANCE IS THIS WEEK.
HINT HINT HINT.
THIS ISN'T WORKING.
MAYBE WE'RE BEING TOO SUBTLE.
ASK US TO THE STUPID VALENTINE'S DANCE!
NOW! NOW! NOW!
AMEND

WHAT'D YOU GET MOM FOR VALENTINE'S DAY?

WHAT'D YOU GET MOM FOR VALENTINE'S DAY?

WHAT'D YOU GET MOM FOR VALENTINE'S DAY?

I WISH YOU'D CALL OFF YOUR SPIES.

KIDS, I SAID NO COSTUMES!

LET'S NOT GIVE YOUR MOTHER IDEAS, SON.

THIS **WAS** HER IDEA.

HEE HEE HEE...

WHAT'S SO FUNNY?

WE'RE SUPPOSED TO BRING A SHOEBOX TO SCHOOL FOR VALENTINE'S DAY, SO I GOT ONE OF PAIGE'S OLD BARBIE SHOEBOXES. LET'S SEE THE GIRLS TRY TO GET EVEN ONE OF THEIR GERMY CARDS INTO THIS BABY!

YOU KNOW, SOMETIMES PLAYING HARD-TO-GET ONLY MAKES GIRLS LIKE YOU MORE.

I'M GOING TO KILL MY BROTHER.

tention girls: lease give me lots of siny cards!

WHILE I WAS OUT, DID ANYONE CALL TO ASK ME TO THE VALENTINE'S DANCE?

NO, PAIGE.

ARE YOU SURE?! NO ONE CALLED TO ASK ME TO THE VALENTINE'S DANCE?!

NO, PAIGE.

YOU'RE TELLING ME NOT A SINGLE PERSON CALLED TO ASK ME TO THE VALENTINE'S DANCE?!

YES, PAIGE.

I THOUGHT THE VALENTINE'S DANCE WAS **LAST** NIGHT.

I'M GETTING A JUMP ON NEXT YEAR'S.

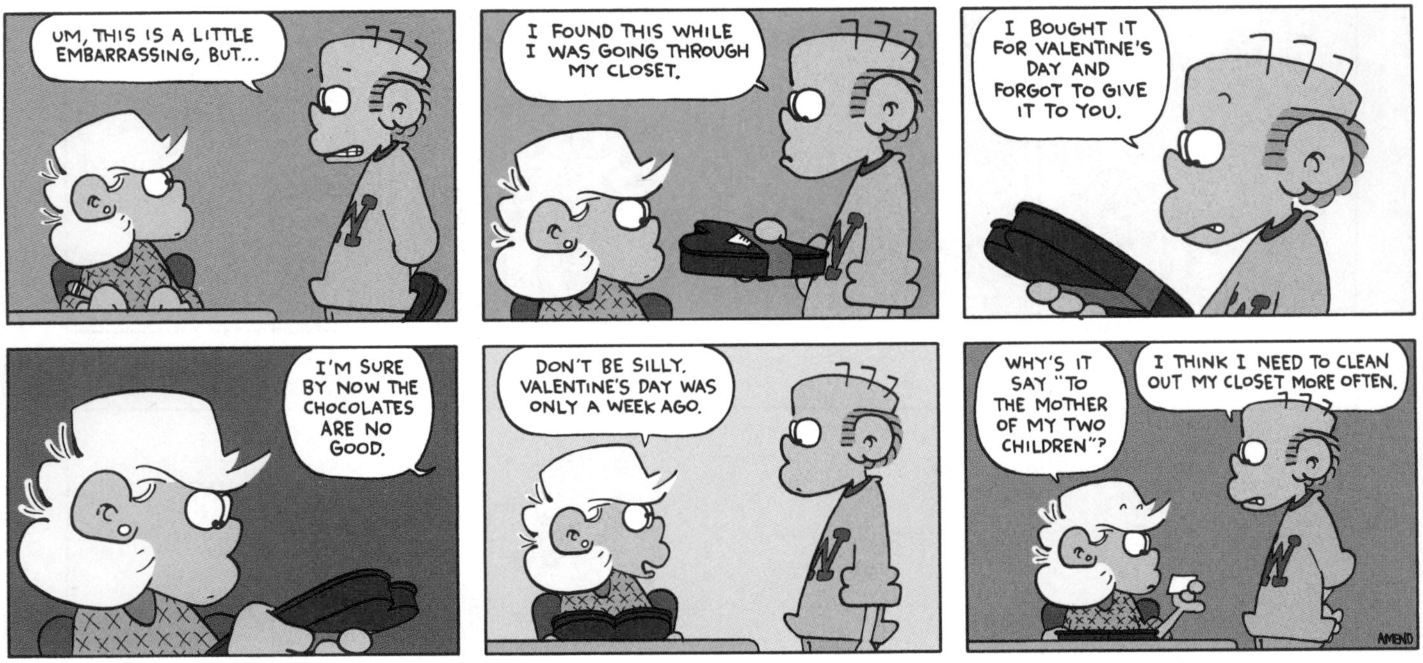
UM, THIS IS A LITTLE EMBARRASSING, BUT...
I FOUND THIS WHILE I WAS GOING THROUGH MY CLOSET.
I BOUGHT IT FOR VALENTINE'S DAY AND FORGOT TO GIVE IT TO YOU.
I'M SURE BY NOW THE CHOCOLATES ARE NO GOOD.
DON'T BE SILLY. VALENTINE'S DAY WAS ONLY A WEEK AGO.
WHY'S IT SAY "TO THE MOTHER OF MY TWO CHILDREN"?
I THINK I NEED TO CLEAN OUT MY CLOSET MORE OFTEN.
AMEND

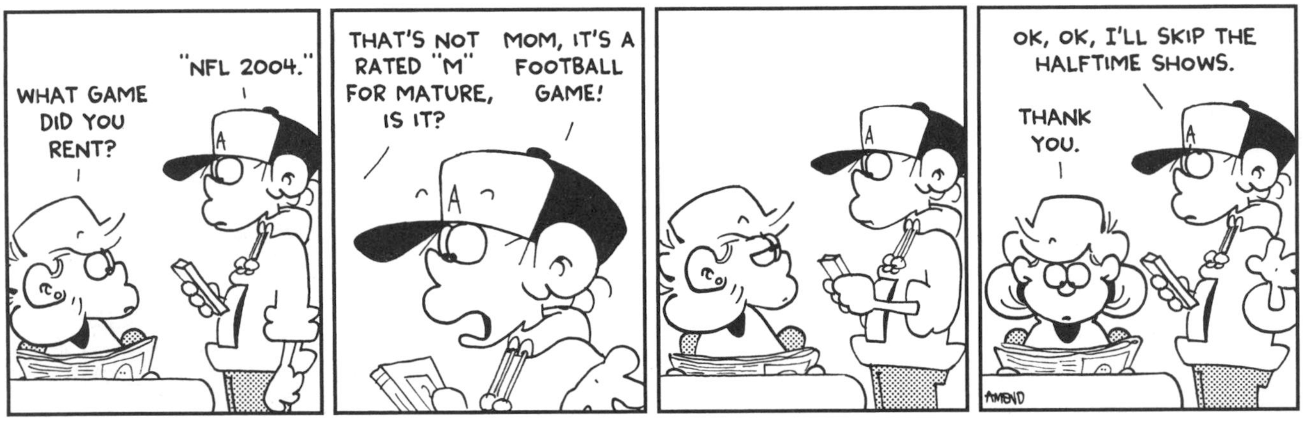
WHAT GAME DID YOU RENT?
"NFL 2004."
THAT'S NOT RATED "M" FOR MATURE, IS IT?
MOM, IT'S A FOOTBALL GAME!
OK, OK, I'LL SKIP THE HALFTIME SHOWS.
THANK YOU.
AMEND

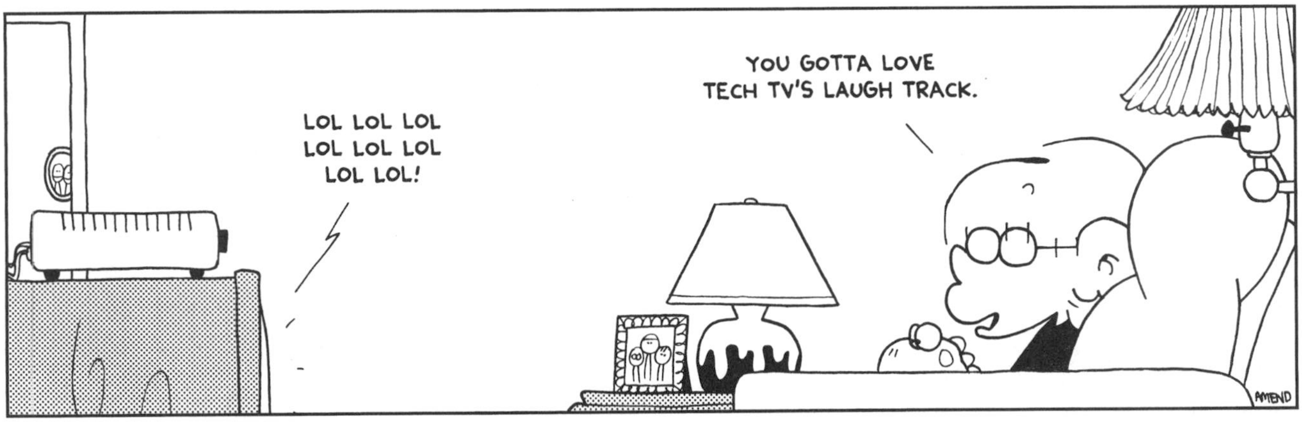
LOL LOL LOL LOL LOL LOL LOL LOL!
YOU GOTTA LOVE TECH TV'S LAUGH TRACK.
AMEND

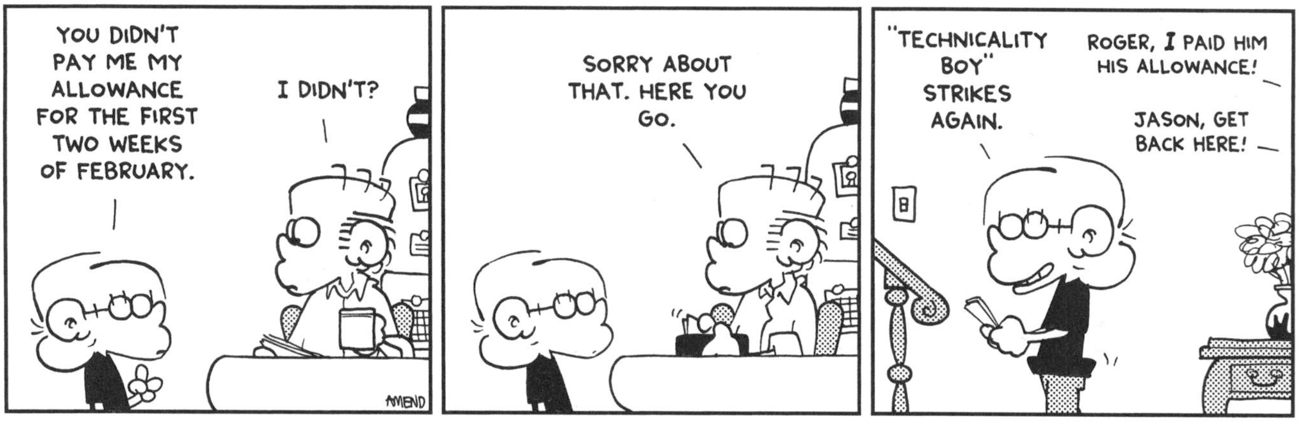
YOU DIDN'T PAY ME MY ALLOWANCE FOR THE FIRST TWO WEEKS OF FEBRUARY.
I DIDN'T?
SORRY ABOUT THAT. HERE YOU GO.
"TECHNICALITY BOY" STRIKES AGAIN.
ROGER, I PAID HIM HIS ALLOWANCE!
JASON, GET BACK HERE!
AMEND

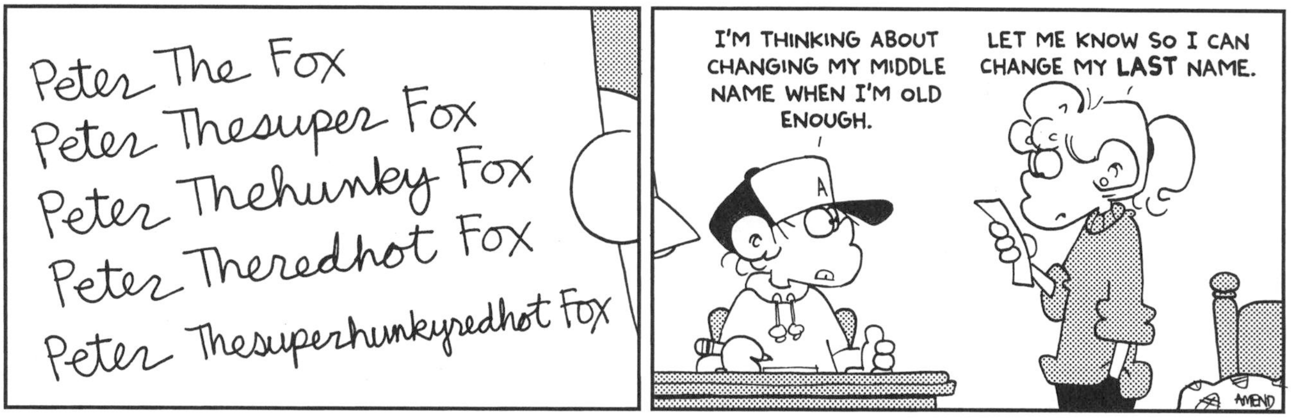
Peter The Fox
Peter Thesuper Fox
Peter Thehunky Fox
Peter Theredhot Fox
Peter Thesuperhunkyredhot Fox
I'M THINKING ABOUT CHANGING MY MIDDLE NAME WHEN I'M OLD ENOUGH.
LET ME KNOW SO I CAN CHANGE MY **LAST** NAME.
AMEND

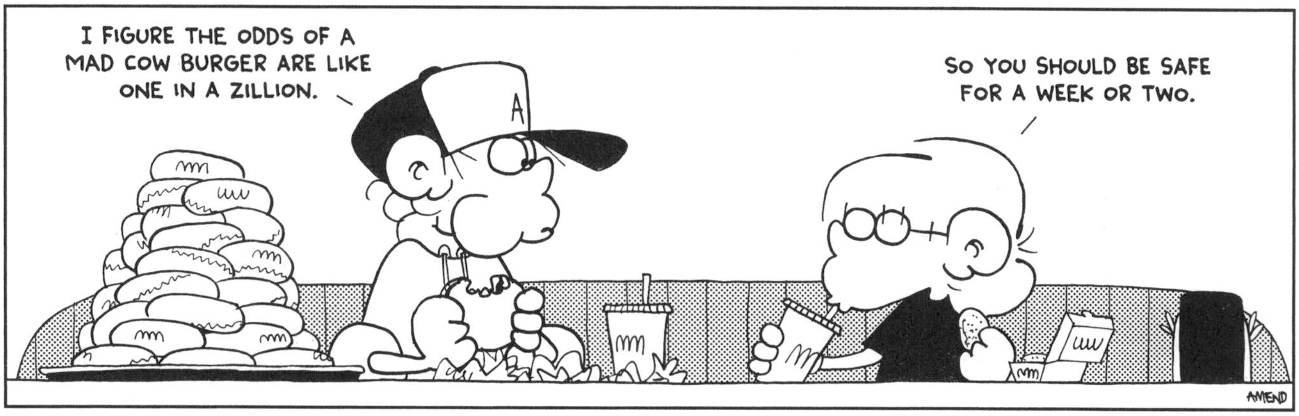
I FIGURE THE ODDS OF A MAD COW BURGER ARE LIKE ONE IN A ZILLION.
SO YOU SHOULD BE SAFE FOR A WEEK OR TWO.
AMEND

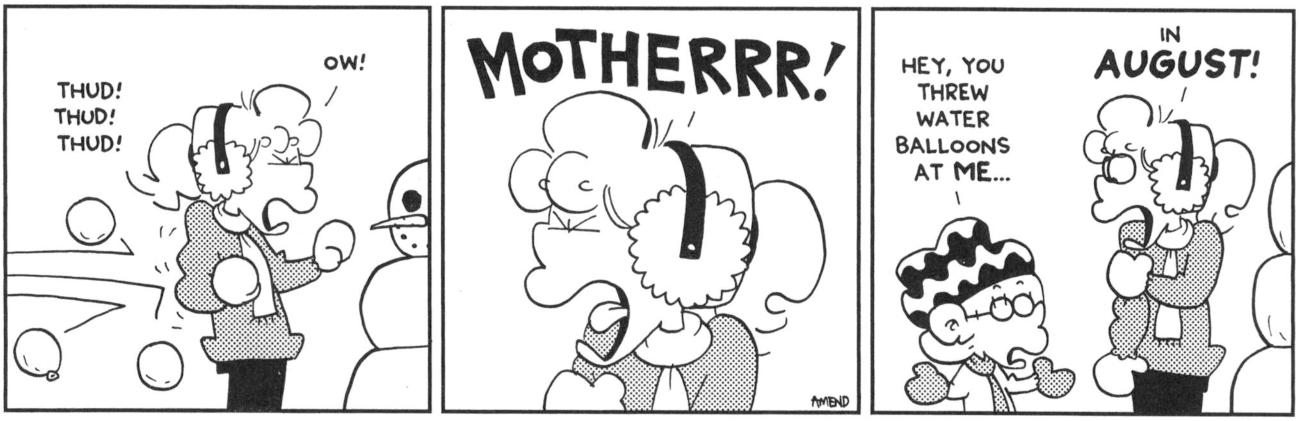
THUD! THUD! THUD!
OW!
MOTHERRR!
HEY, YOU THREW WATER BALLOONS AT **ME**...
IN **AUGUST!**
AMEND

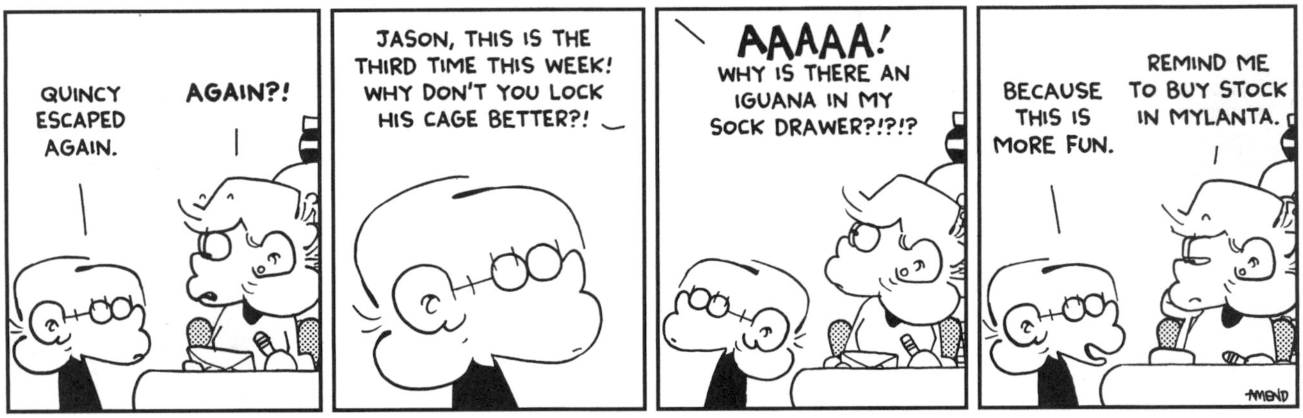
QUINCY ESCAPED AGAIN.
AGAIN?!
JASON, THIS IS THE THIRD TIME THIS WEEK! WHY DON'T YOU LOCK HIS CAGE BETTER?!
AAAAA! WHY IS THERE AN IGUANA IN MY SOCK DRAWER?!?!?
BECAUSE THIS IS MORE FUN.
REMIND ME TO BUY STOCK IN MYLANTA.

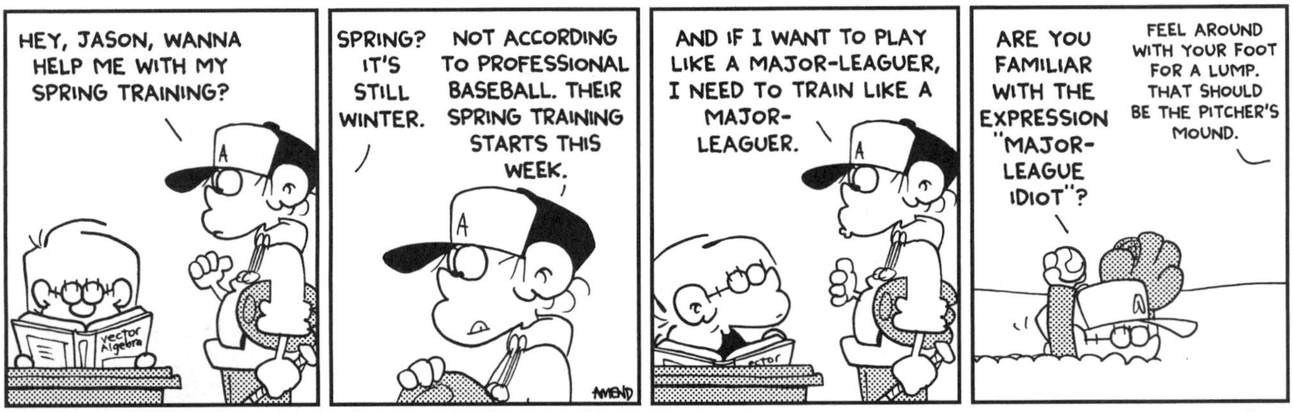
HEY, JASON, WANNA HELP ME WITH MY SPRING TRAINING?
SPRING? IT'S STILL WINTER.
NOT ACCORDING TO PROFESSIONAL BASEBALL. THEIR SPRING TRAINING STARTS THIS WEEK.
AND IF I WANT TO PLAY LIKE A MAJOR-LEAGUER, I NEED TO TRAIN LIKE A MAJOR-LEAGUER.
ARE YOU FAMILIAR WITH THE EXPRESSION "MAJOR-LEAGUE IDIOT"?
FEEL AROUND WITH YOUR FOOT FOR A LUMP. THAT SHOULD BE THE PITCHER'S MOUND.

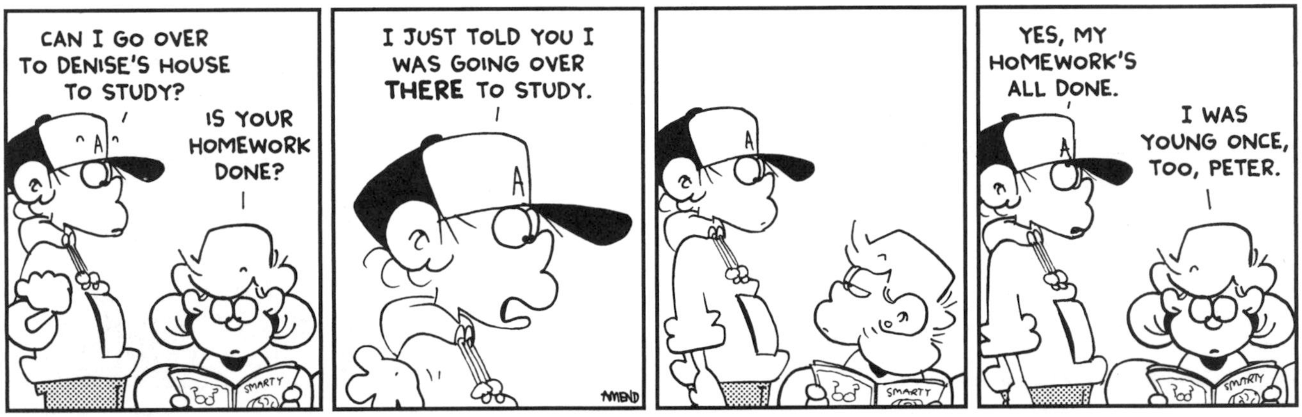
CAN I GO OVER TO DENISE'S HOUSE TO STUDY?
IS YOUR HOMEWORK DONE?
I JUST TOLD YOU I WAS GOING OVER THERE TO STUDY.
YES, MY HOMEWORK'S ALL DONE.
I WAS YOUNG ONCE, TOO, PETER.

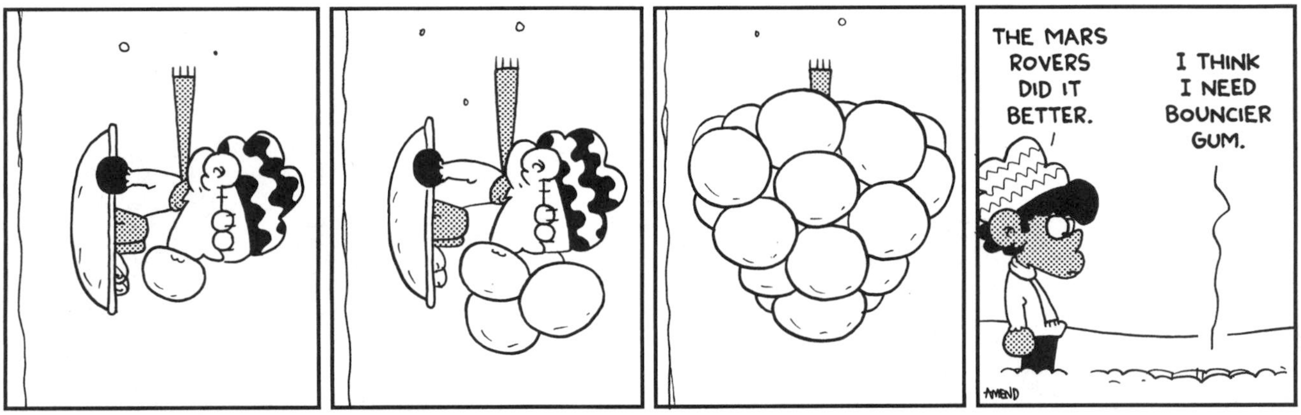
THE MARS ROVERS DID IT BETTER.
I THINK I NEED BOUNCIER GUM.

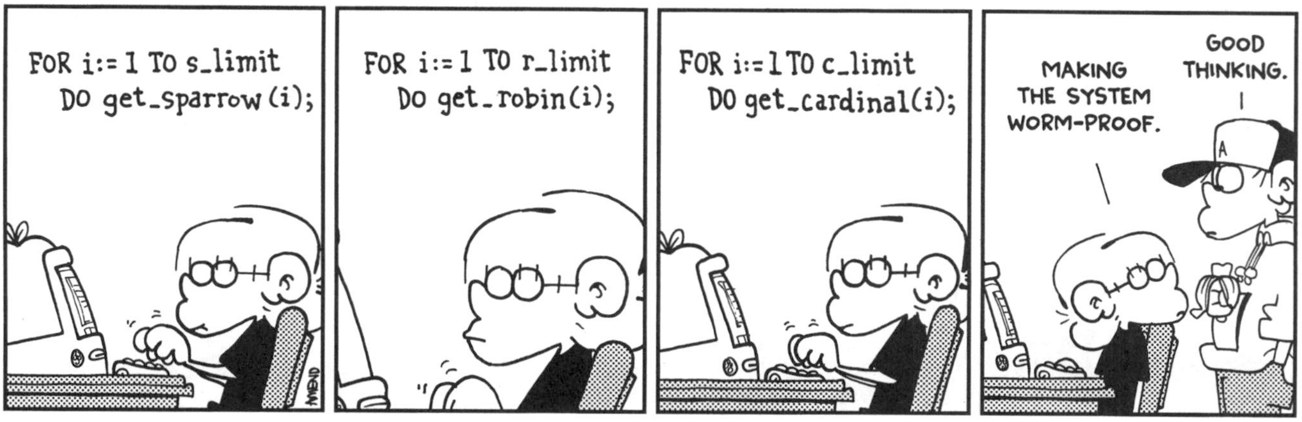
FOR i:= 1 TO s_limit
DO get_sparrow(i);
FOR i:= 1 TO r_limit
DO get_robin(i);
FOR i:=1 TO c_limit
DO get_cardinal(i);
MAKING THE SYSTEM WORM-PROOF.
GOOD THINKING.

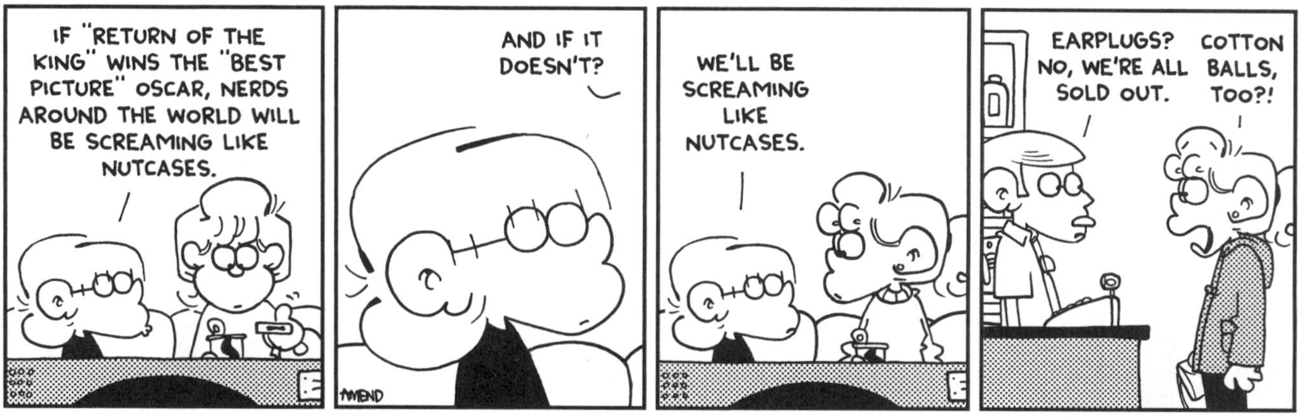
IF "RETURN OF THE KING" WINS THE "BEST PICTURE" OSCAR, NERDS AROUND THE WORLD WILL BE SCREAMING LIKE NUTCASES.
AND IF IT DOESN'T?
WE'LL BE SCREAMING LIKE NUTCASES.
EARPLUGS? NO, WE'RE ALL SOLD OUT.
COTTON BALLS, TOO?!

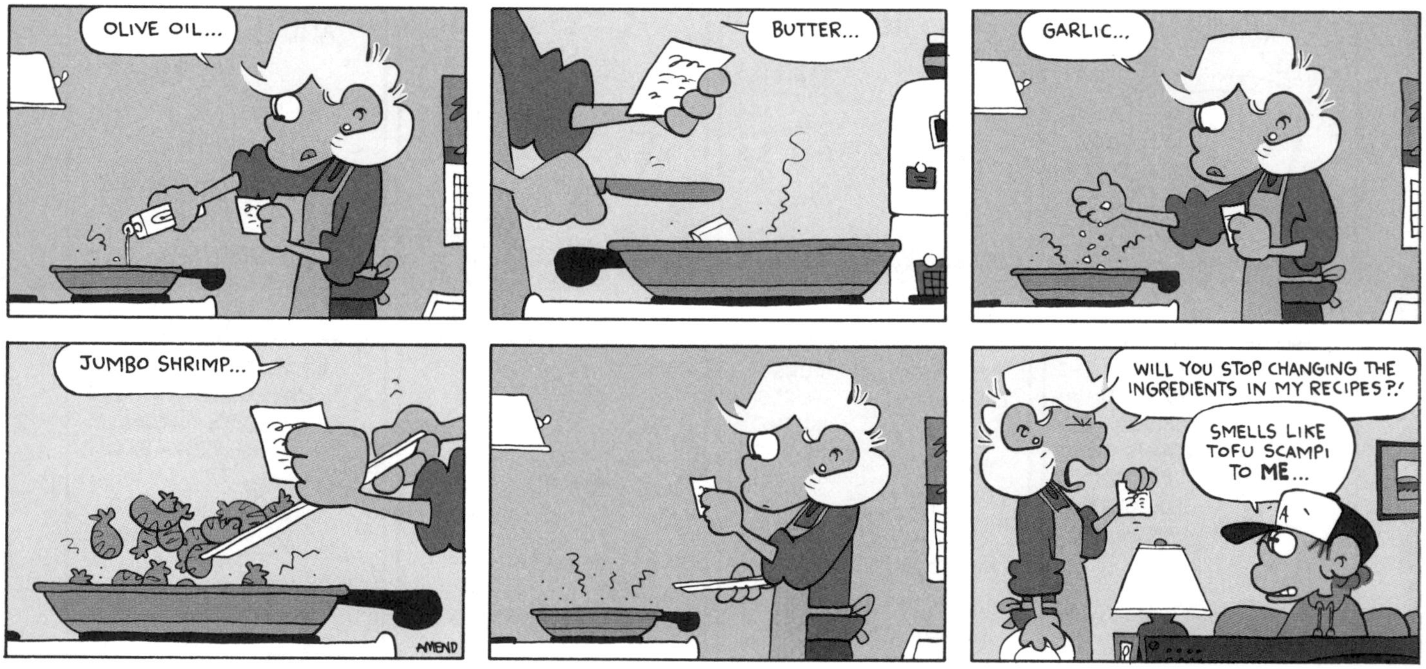
OLIVE OIL...
BUTTER...
GARLIC...
JUMBO SHRIMP...
WILL YOU STOP CHANGING THE INGREDIENTS IN MY RECIPES?!
SMELLS LIKE TOFU SCAMPI TO ME...

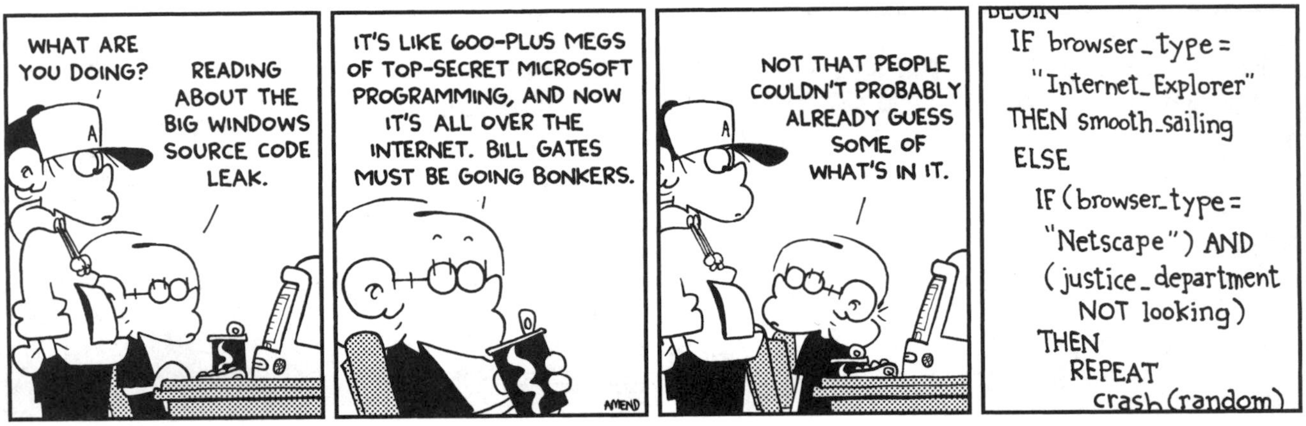
WHAT ARE YOU DOING?
READING ABOUT THE BIG WINDOWS SOURCE CODE LEAK.
IT'S LIKE 600-PLUS MEGS OF TOP-SECRET MICROSOFT PROGRAMMING, AND NOW IT'S ALL OVER THE INTERNET. BILL GATES MUST BE GOING BONKERS.
AMEND
NOT THAT PEOPLE COULDN'T PROBABLY ALREADY GUESS SOME OF WHAT'S IN IT.
IF browser_type =
"Internet_Explorer"
THEN smooth_sailing
ELSE
IF (browser_type =
"Netscape") AND
(justice_department
NOT looking)
THEN
REPEAT
crash(random)

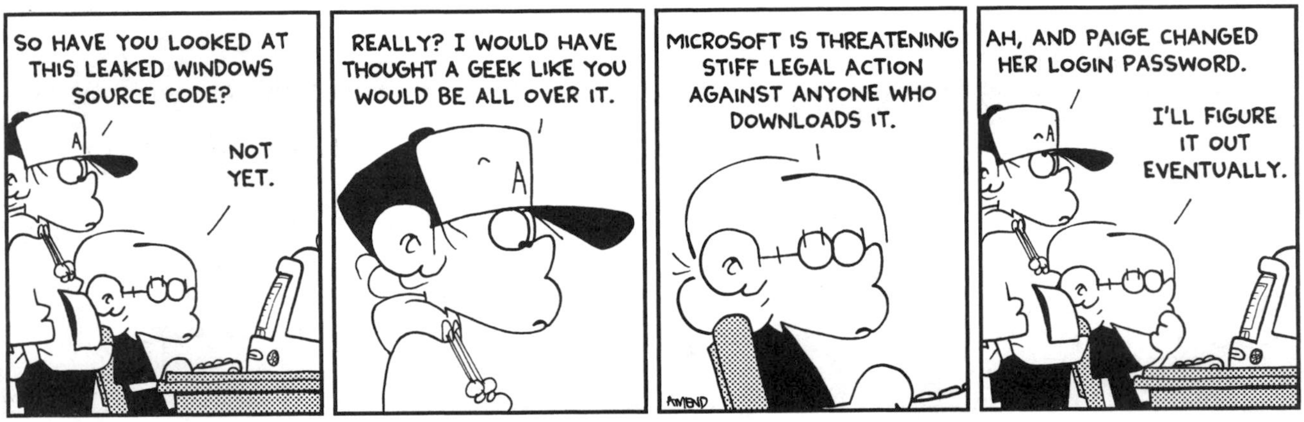
SO HAVE YOU LOOKED AT THIS LEAKED WINDOWS SOURCE CODE?
NOT YET.
REALLY? I WOULD HAVE THOUGHT A GEEK LIKE YOU WOULD BE ALL OVER IT.
MICROSOFT IS THREATENING STIFF LEGAL ACTION AGAINST ANYONE WHO DOWNLOADS IT.
AMEND
AH, AND PAIGE CHANGED HER LOGIN PASSWORD.
I'LL FIGURE IT OUT EVENTUALLY.

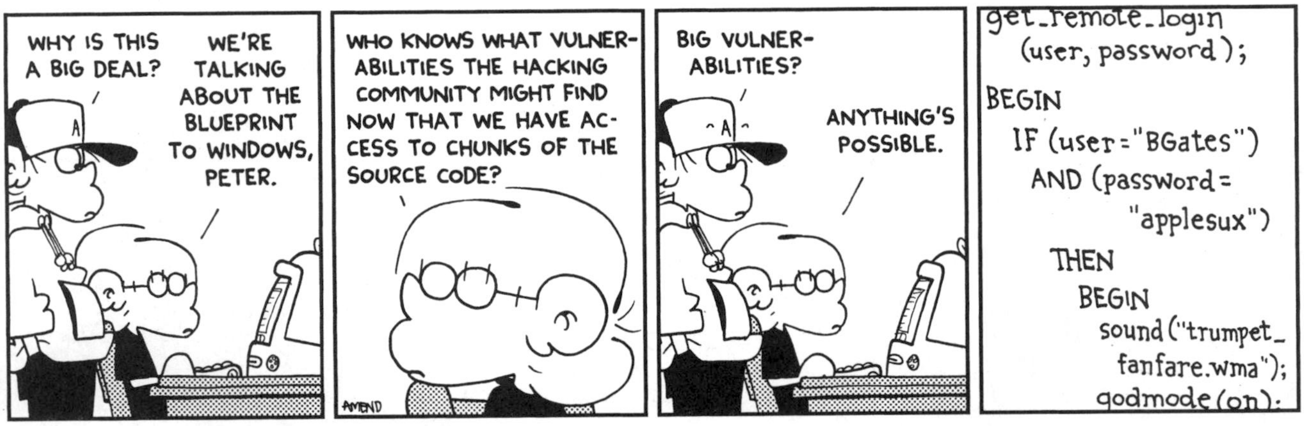
WHY IS THIS A BIG DEAL?
WE'RE TALKING ABOUT THE BLUEPRINT TO WINDOWS, PETER.
WHO KNOWS WHAT VULNERABILITIES THE HACKING COMMUNITY MIGHT FIND NOW THAT WE HAVE ACCESS TO CHUNKS OF THE SOURCE CODE?
AMEND
BIG VULNERABILITIES?
ANYTHING'S POSSIBLE.
get_remote_login
(user, password);
BEGIN
IF (user="BGates")
AND (password=
"applesux")
THEN
BEGIN
sound("trumpet_
fanfare.wma");
godmode(on);

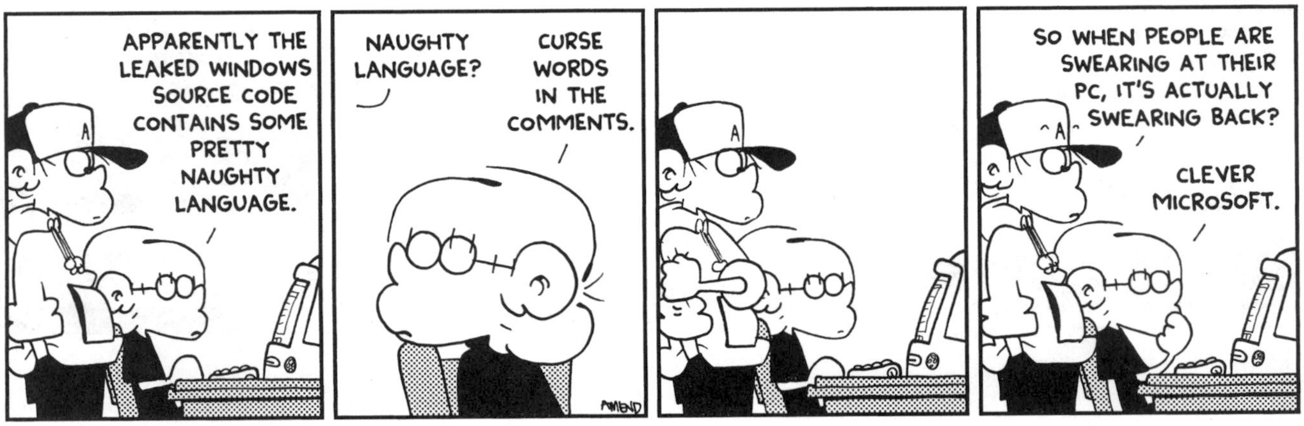
APPARENTLY THE LEAKED WINDOWS SOURCE CODE CONTAINS SOME PRETTY NAUGHTY LANGUAGE.
NAUGHTY LANGUAGE?
CURSE WORDS IN THE COMMENTS.
AMEND
SO WHEN PEOPLE ARE SWEARING AT THEIR PC, IT'S ACTUALLY SWEARING BACK?
CLEVER MICROSOFT.

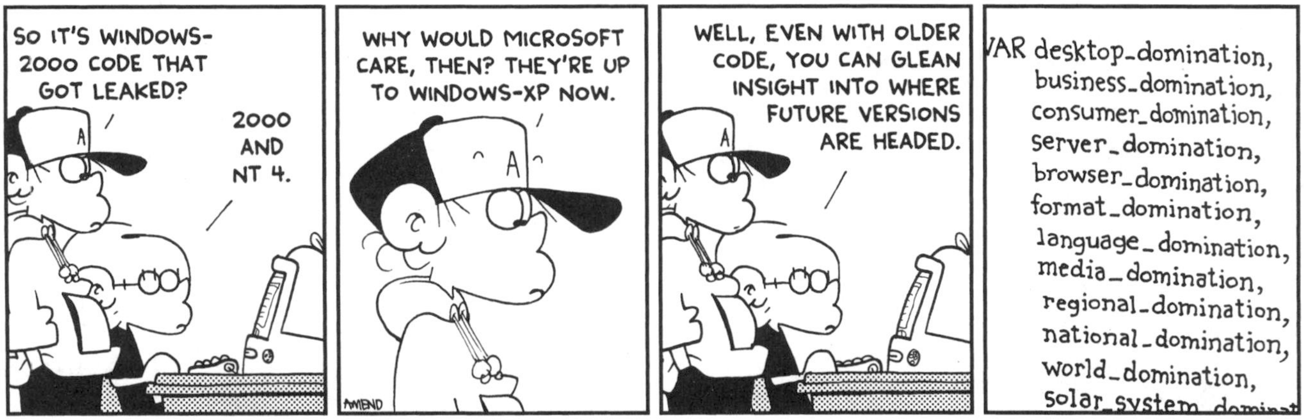
SO IT'S WINDOWS-2000 CODE THAT GOT LEAKED?
2000 AND NT 4.
WHY WOULD MICROSOFT CARE, THEN? THEY'RE UP TO WINDOWS-XP NOW.
WELL, EVEN WITH OLDER CODE, YOU CAN GLEAN INSIGHT INTO WHERE FUTURE VERSIONS ARE HEADED.
VAR desktop_domination,
business_domination,
consumer_domination,
server_domination,
browser_domination,
format_domination,
language_domination,
media_domination,
regional_domination,
national_domination,
world_domination,
solar_system_

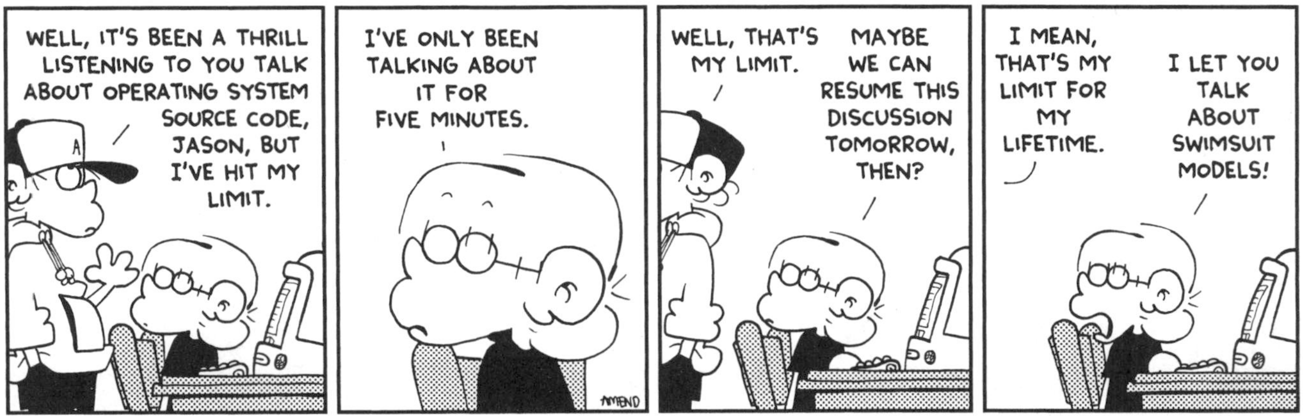
WELL, IT'S BEEN A THRILL LISTENING TO YOU TALK ABOUT OPERATING SYSTEM SOURCE CODE, JASON, BUT I'VE HIT MY LIMIT.
I'VE ONLY BEEN TALKING ABOUT IT FOR FIVE MINUTES.
WELL, THAT'S MY LIMIT.
MAYBE WE CAN RESUME THIS DISCUSSION TOMORROW, THEN?
I MEAN, THAT'S MY LIMIT FOR MY LIFETIME.
I LET YOU TALK ABOUT SWIMSUIT MODELS!

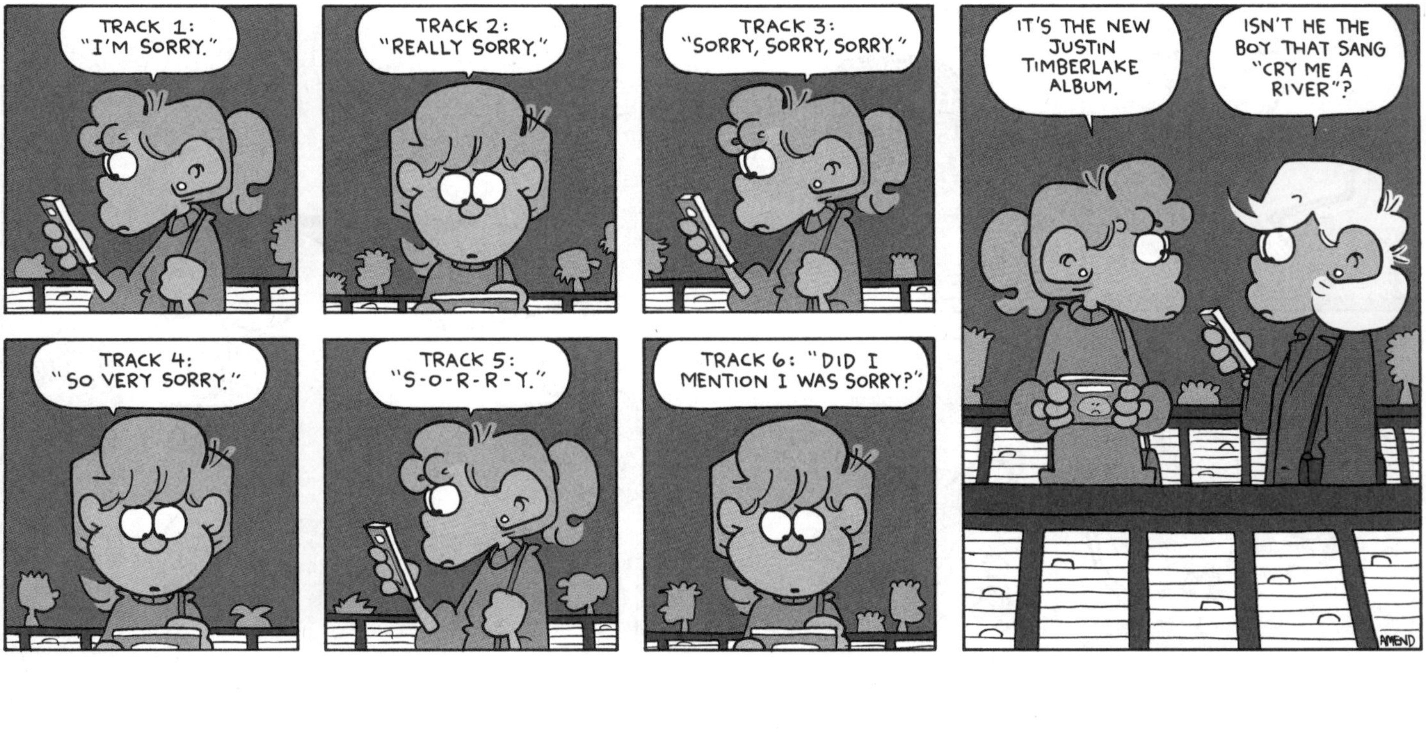
TRACK 1: "I'M SORRY."
TRACK 2: "REALLY SORRY."
TRACK 3: "SORRY, SORRY, SORRY."
TRACK 4: "SO VERY SORRY."
TRACK 5: "S-O-R-R-Y."
TRACK 6: "DID I MENTION I WAS SORRY?"
IT'S THE NEW JUSTIN TIMBERLAKE ALBUM.
ISN'T HE THE BOY THAT SANG "CRY ME A RIVER"?

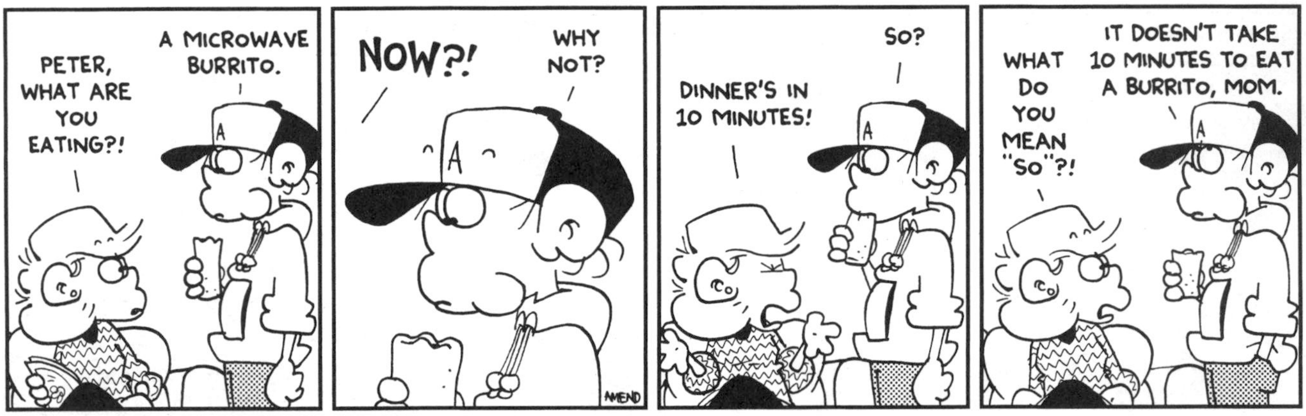
PETER, WHAT ARE YOU EATING?!
A MICROWAVE BURRITO.
NOW?!
WHY NOT?
DINNER'S IN 10 MINUTES!
SO?
WHAT DO YOU MEAN "SO"?!
IT DOESN'T TAKE 10 MINUTES TO EAT A BURRITO, MOM.
AMEND

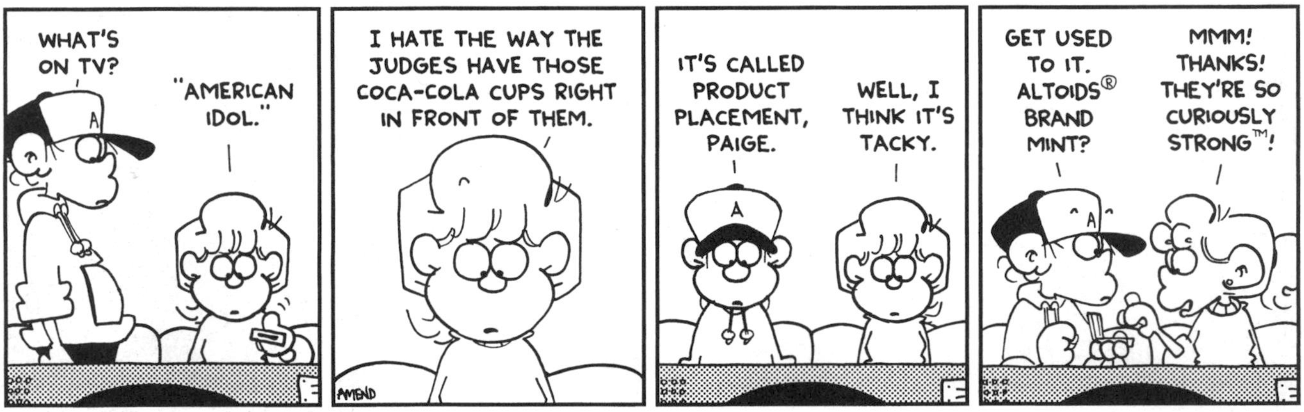
WHAT'S ON TV?
"AMERICAN IDOL."
I HATE THE WAY THE JUDGES HAVE THOSE COCA-COLA CUPS RIGHT IN FRONT OF THEM.
AMEND
IT'S CALLED PRODUCT PLACEMENT, PAIGE.
WELL, I THINK IT'S TACKY.
GET USED TO IT. ALTOIDS® BRAND MINT?
MMM! THANKS! THEY'RE SO CURIOUSLY STRONG™!

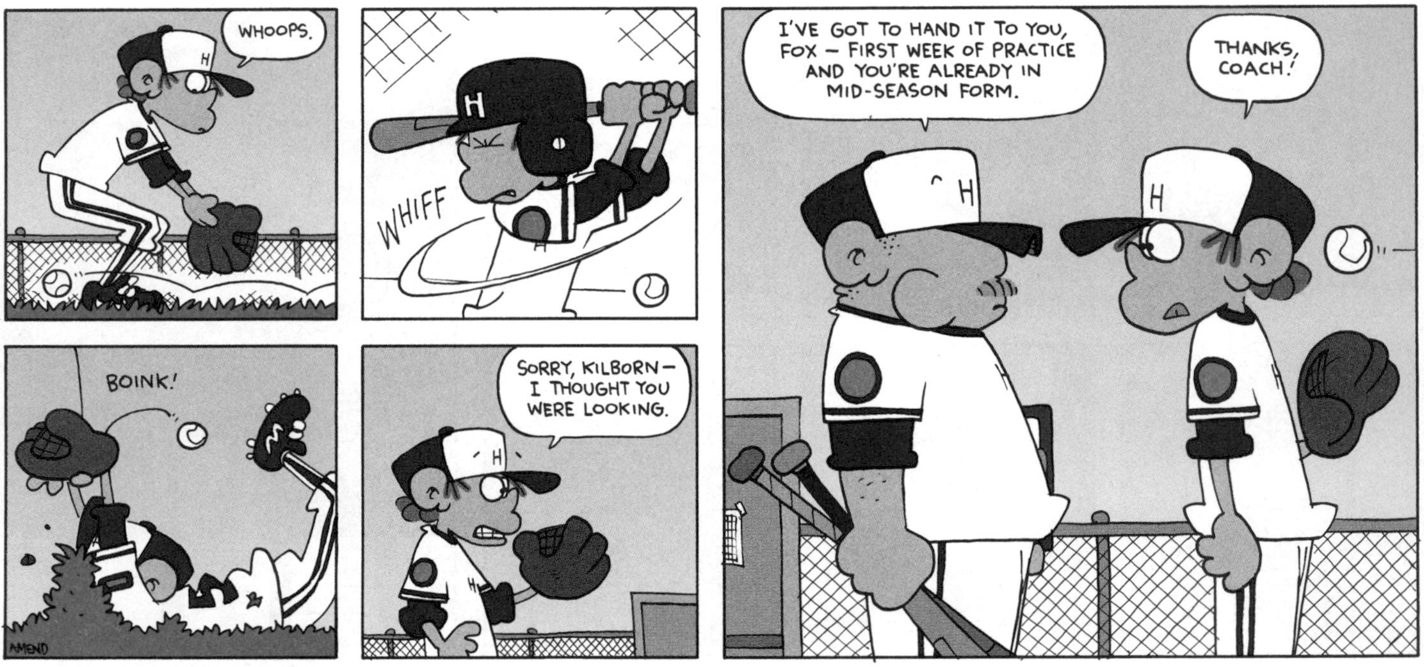
WHOOPS.
WHIFF
BOINK!
AMEND
SORRY, KILBORN— I THOUGHT YOU WERE LOOKING.
I'VE GOT TO HAND IT TO YOU, FOX — FIRST WEEK OF PRACTICE AND YOU'RE ALREADY IN MID-SEASON FORM.
THANKS, COACH!

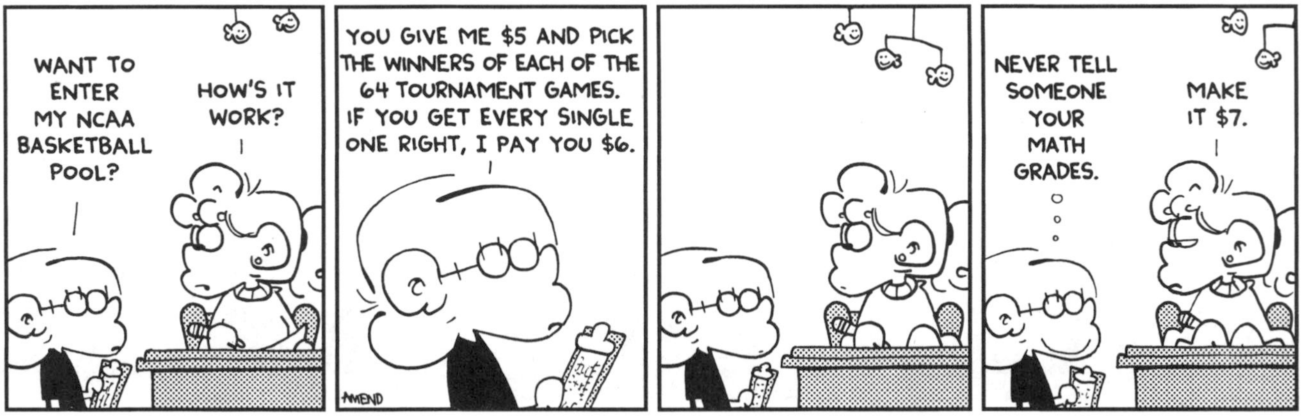
WANT TO ENTER MY NCAA BASKETBALL POOL?
HOW'S IT WORK?
YOU GIVE ME $5 AND PICK THE WINNERS OF EACH OF THE 64 TOURNAMENT GAMES. IF YOU GET EVERY SINGLE ONE RIGHT, I PAY YOU $6.
AMEND
NEVER TELL SOMEONE YOUR MATH GRADES.
MAKE IT $7.

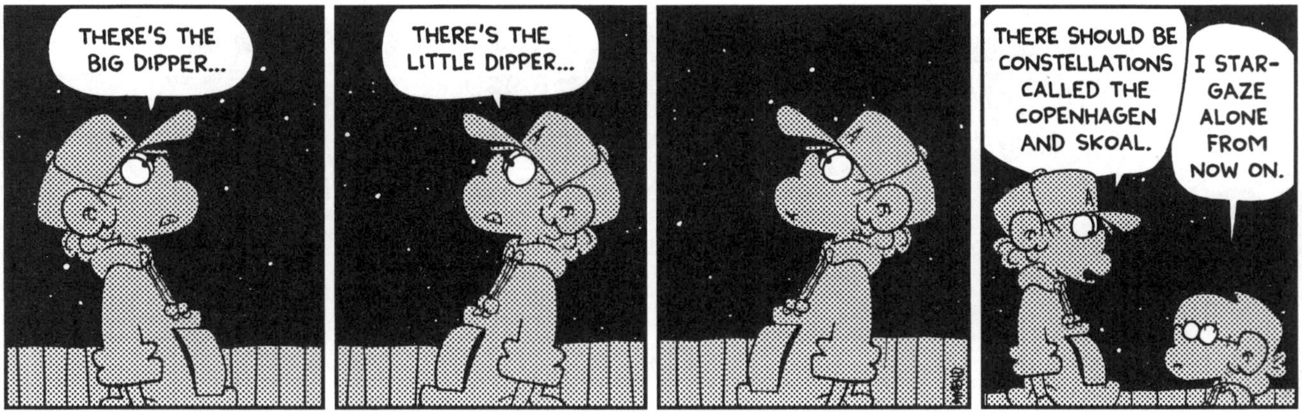
THERE'S THE BIG DIPPER...
THERE'S THE LITTLE DIPPER...
THERE SHOULD BE CONSTELLATIONS CALLED THE COPENHAGEN AND SKOAL.
I STAR-GAZE ALONE FROM NOW ON.

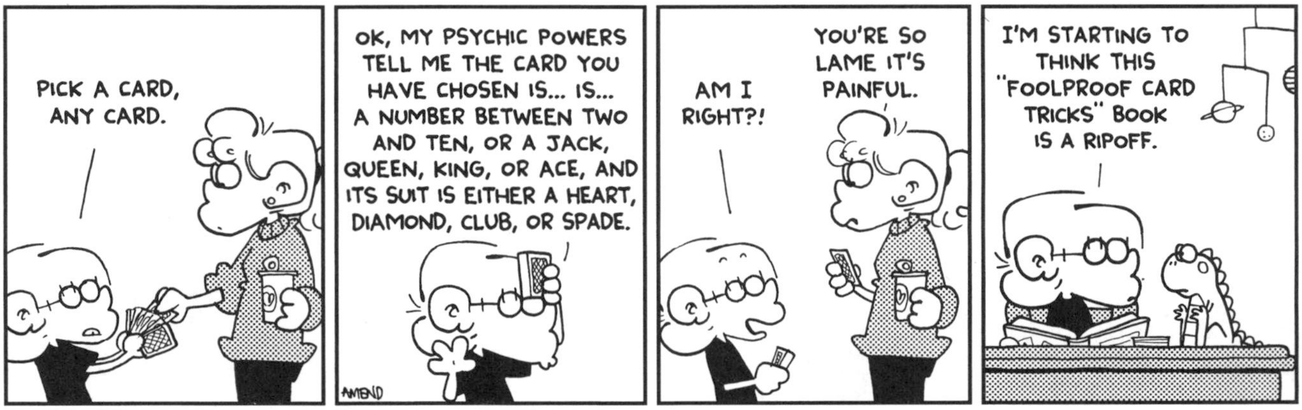
PICK A CARD, ANY CARD.
OK, MY PSYCHIC POWERS TELL ME THE CARD YOU HAVE CHOSEN IS... IS... A NUMBER BETWEEN TWO AND TEN, OR A JACK, QUEEN, KING, OR ACE, AND ITS SUIT IS EITHER A HEART, DIAMOND, CLUB, OR SPADE.
AMEND
AM I RIGHT?!
YOU'RE SO LAME IT'S PAINFUL.
I'M STARTING TO THINK THIS "FOOLPROOF CARD TRICKS" BOOK IS A RIPOFF.

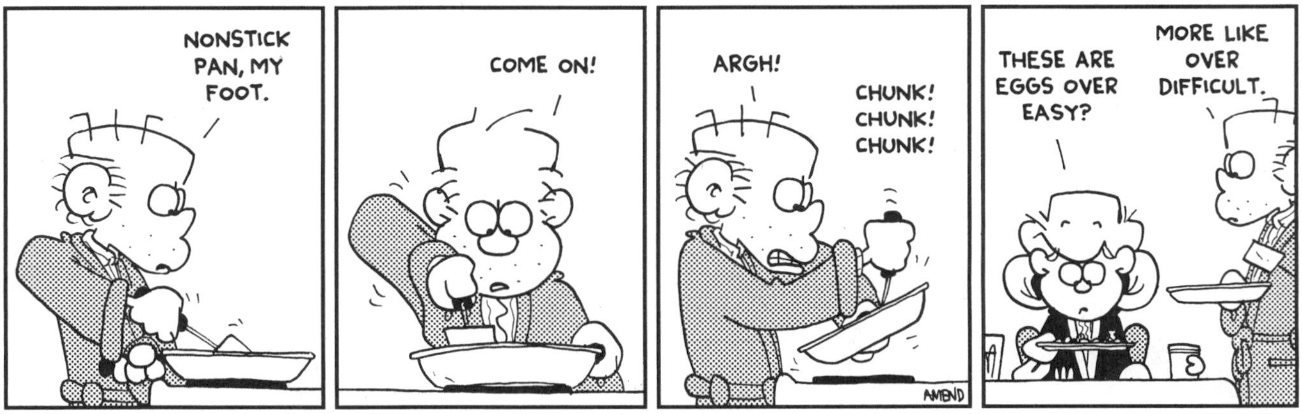
NONSTICK PAN, MY FOOT.
COME ON!
ARGH!
CHUNK! CHUNK! CHUNK!
AMEND
THESE ARE EGGS OVER EASY?
MORE LIKE OVER DIFFICULT.

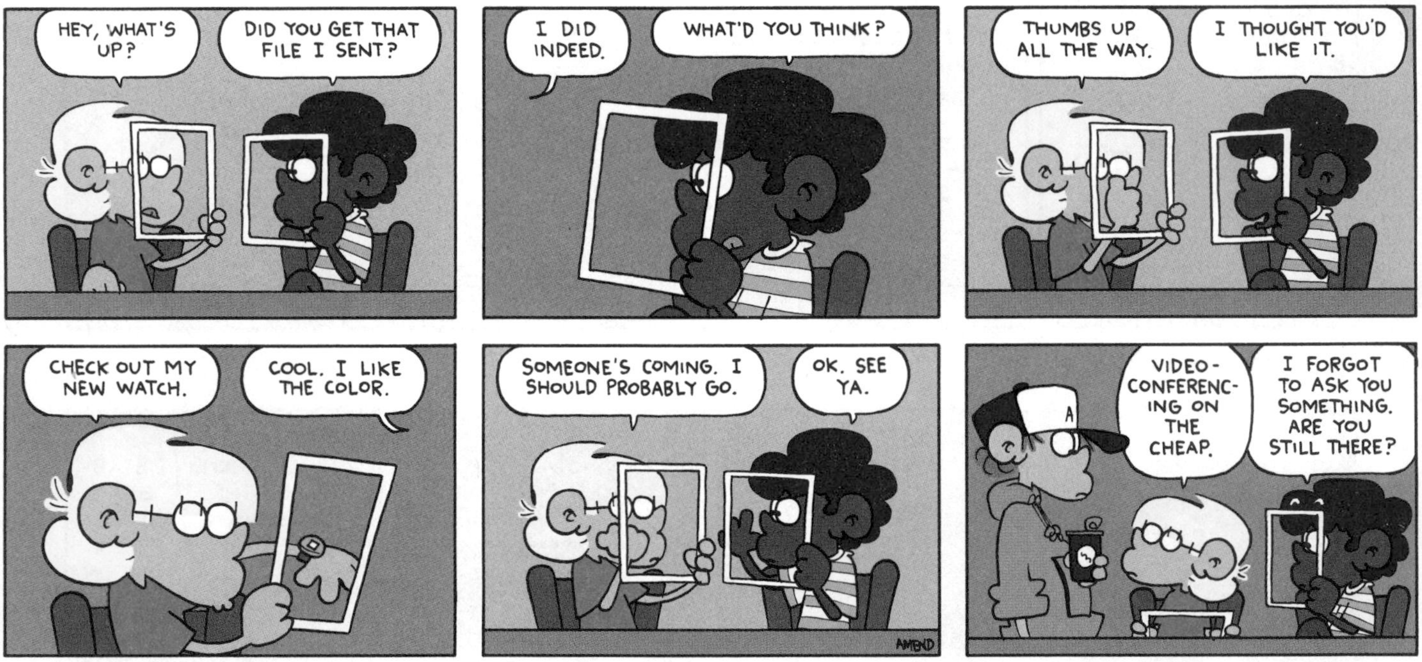
HEY, WHAT'S UP?
DID YOU GET THAT FILE I SENT?
I DID INDEED.
WHAT'D YOU THINK?
THUMBS UP ALL THE WAY.
I THOUGHT YOU'D LIKE IT.
CHECK OUT MY NEW WATCH.
COOL. I LIKE THE COLOR.
SOMEONE'S COMING. I SHOULD PROBABLY GO.
OK. SEE YA.
AMEND
VIDEO-CONFERENCING ON THE CHEAP.
I FORGOT TO ASK YOU SOMETHING. ARE YOU STILL THERE?

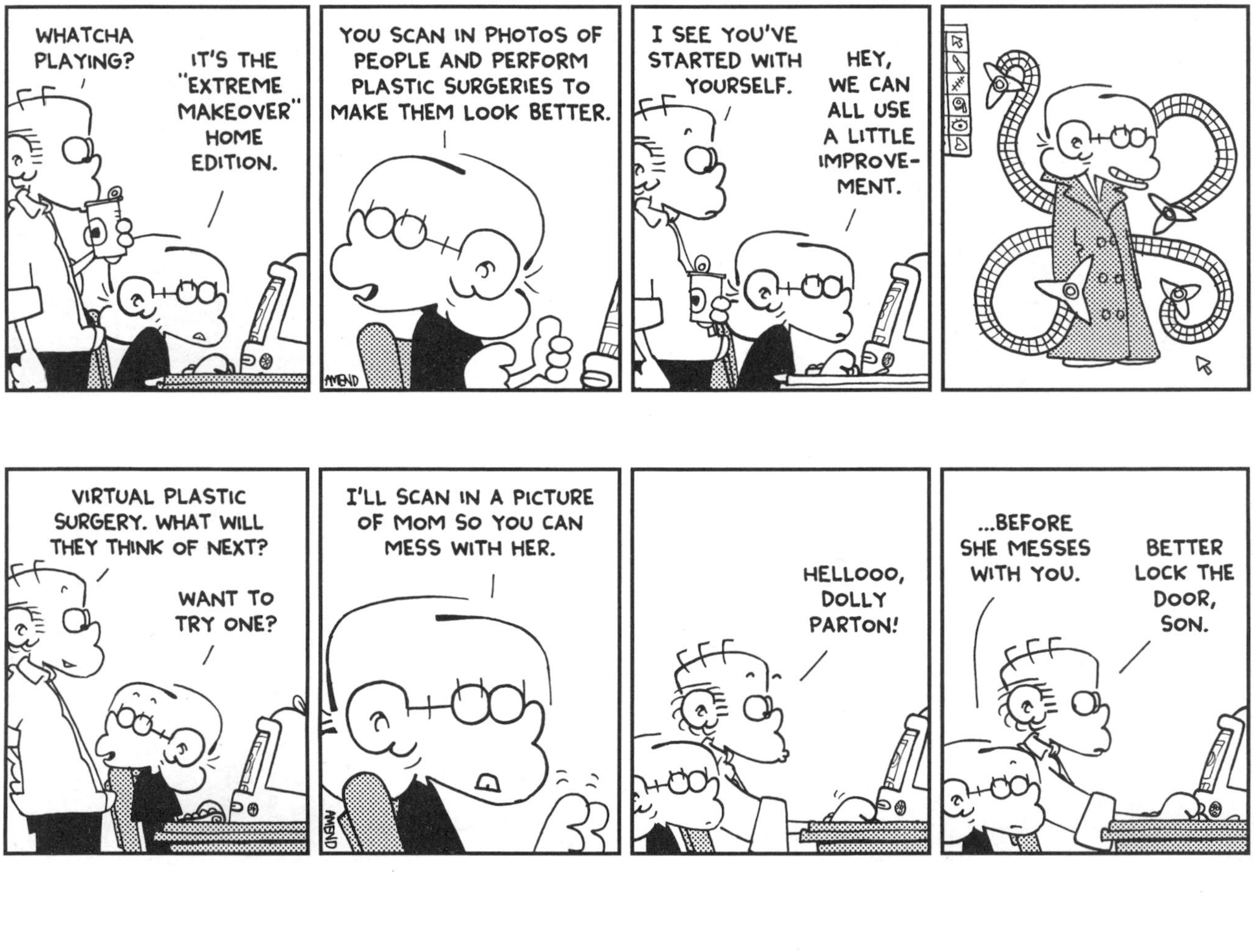
WHATCHA PLAYING?
IT'S THE "EXTREME MAKEOVER" HOME EDITION.
YOU SCAN IN PHOTOS OF PEOPLE AND PERFORM PLASTIC SURGERIES TO MAKE THEM LOOK BETTER.
AMEND
I SEE YOU'VE STARTED WITH YOURSELF.
HEY, WE CAN ALL USE A LITTLE IMPROVEMENT.
VIRTUAL PLASTIC SURGERY. WHAT WILL THEY THINK OF NEXT?
WANT TO TRY ONE?
I'LL SCAN IN A PICTURE OF MOM SO YOU CAN MESS WITH HER.
AMEND
HELLOOO, DOLLY PARTON!
...BEFORE SHE MESSES WITH YOU.
BETTER LOCK THE DOOR, SON.

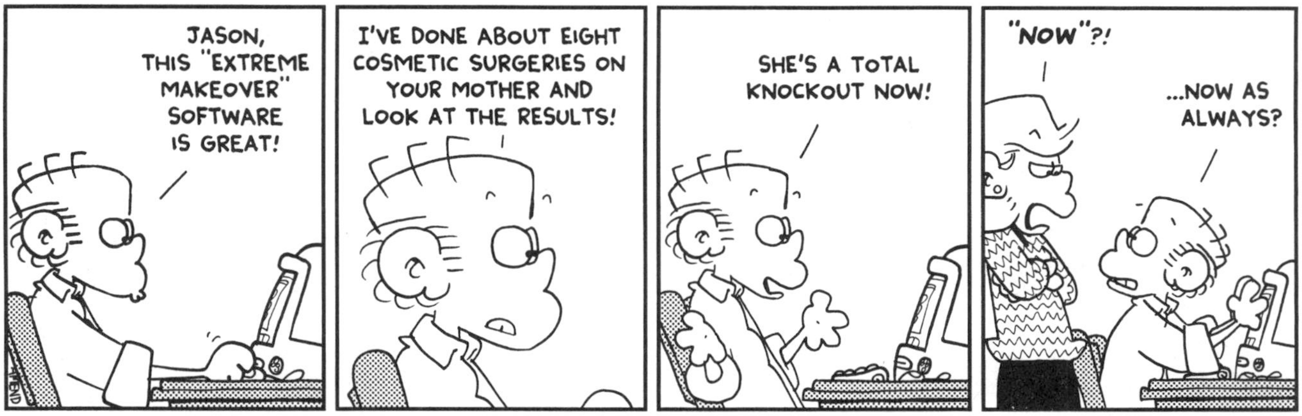
JASON, THIS "EXTREME MAKEOVER" SOFTWARE IS GREAT!
I'VE DONE ABOUT EIGHT COSMETIC SURGERIES ON YOUR MOTHER AND LOOK AT THE RESULTS!
SHE'S A TOTAL KNOCKOUT NOW!
"NOW"?!
...NOW AS ALWAYS?

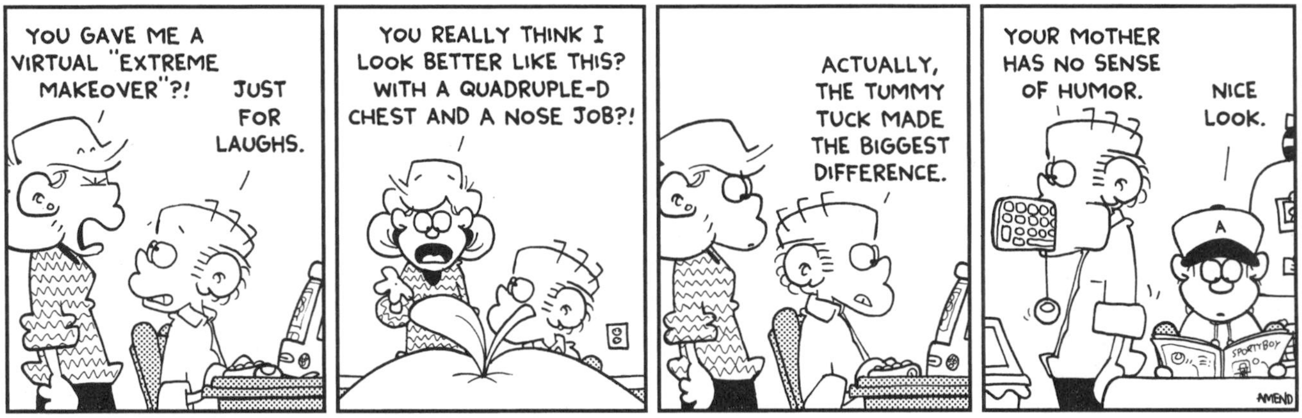
YOU GAVE ME A VIRTUAL "EXTREME MAKEOVER"?!
JUST FOR LAUGHS.
YOU REALLY THINK I LOOK BETTER LIKE THIS? WITH A QUADRUPLE-D CHEST AND A NOSE JOB?!
ACTUALLY, THE TUMMY TUCK MADE THE BIGGEST DIFFERENCE.
YOUR MOTHER HAS NO SENSE OF HUMOR.
NICE LOOK.

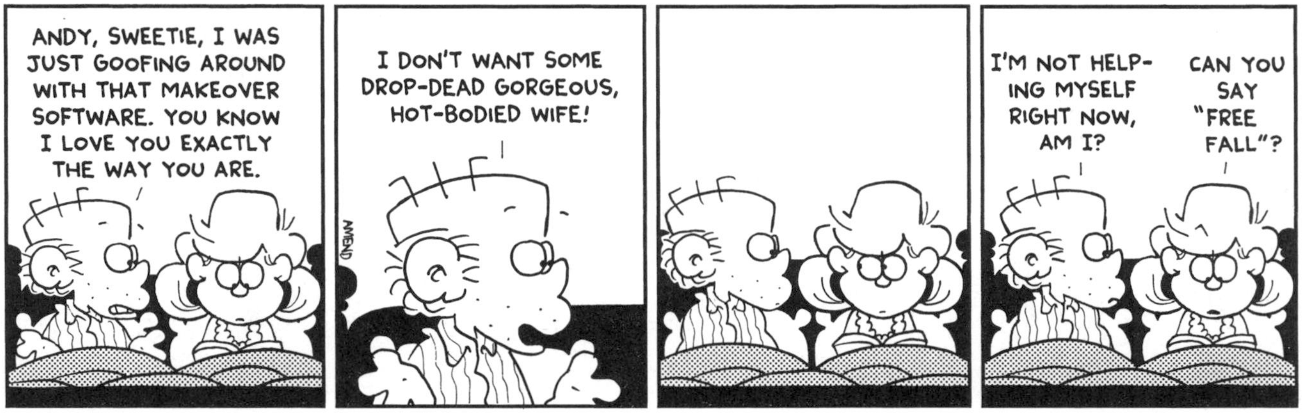
ANDY, SWEETIE, I WAS JUST GOOFING AROUND WITH THAT MAKEOVER SOFTWARE. YOU KNOW I LOVE YOU EXACTLY THE WAY YOU ARE.
I DON'T WANT SOME DROP-DEAD GORGEOUS, HOT-BODIED WIFE!
I'M NOT HELPING MYSELF RIGHT NOW, AM I?
CAN YOU SAY "FREE FALL"?

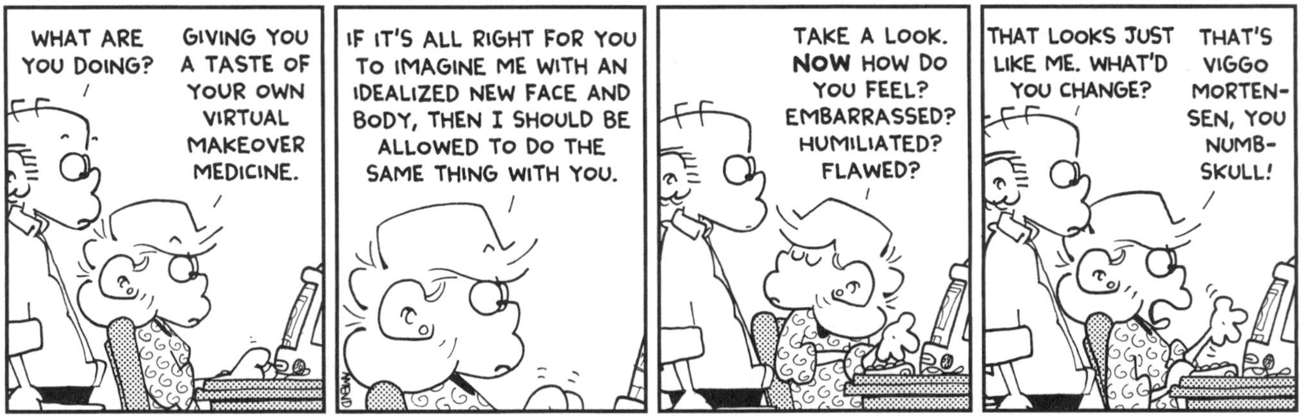
WHAT ARE YOU DOING?
GIVING YOU A TASTE OF YOUR OWN VIRTUAL MAKEOVER MEDICINE.
IF IT'S ALL RIGHT FOR YOU TO IMAGINE ME WITH AN IDEALIZED NEW FACE AND BODY, THEN I SHOULD BE ALLOWED TO DO THE SAME THING WITH YOU.
TAKE A LOOK. NOW HOW DO YOU FEEL? EMBARRASSED? HUMILIATED? FLAWED?
THAT LOOKS JUST LIKE ME. WHAT'D YOU CHANGE?
THAT'S VIGGO MORTENSEN, YOU NUMBSKULL!

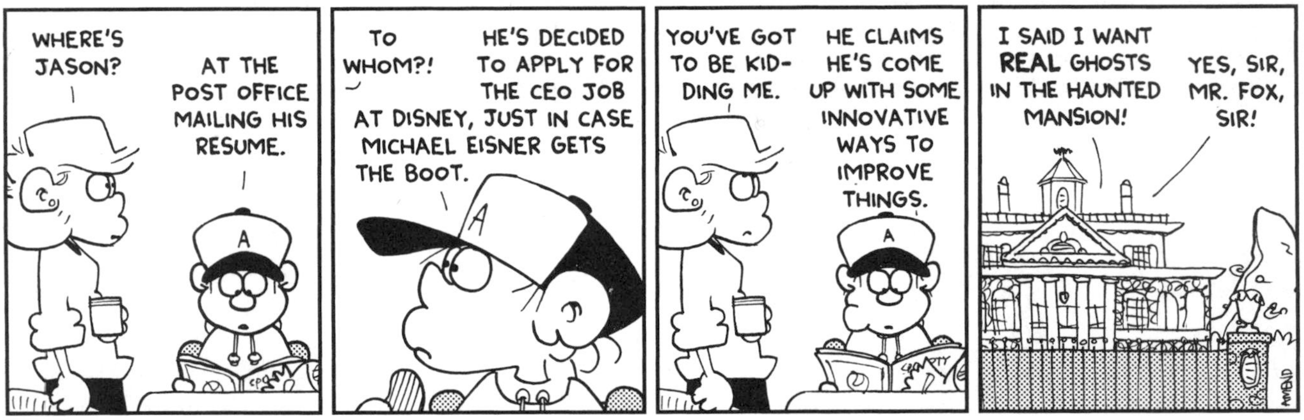
WHERE'S JASON?
AT THE POST OFFICE MAILING HIS RESUME.
TO WHOM?!
HE'S DECIDED TO APPLY FOR THE CEO JOB AT DISNEY, JUST IN CASE MICHAEL EISNER GETS THE BOOT.
YOU'VE GOT TO BE KIDDING ME.
HE CLAIMS HE'S COME UP WITH SOME INNOVATIVE WAYS TO IMPROVE THINGS.
I SAID I WANT REAL GHOSTS IN THE HAUNTED MANSION!
YES, SIR, MR. FOX, SIR!
AMEND

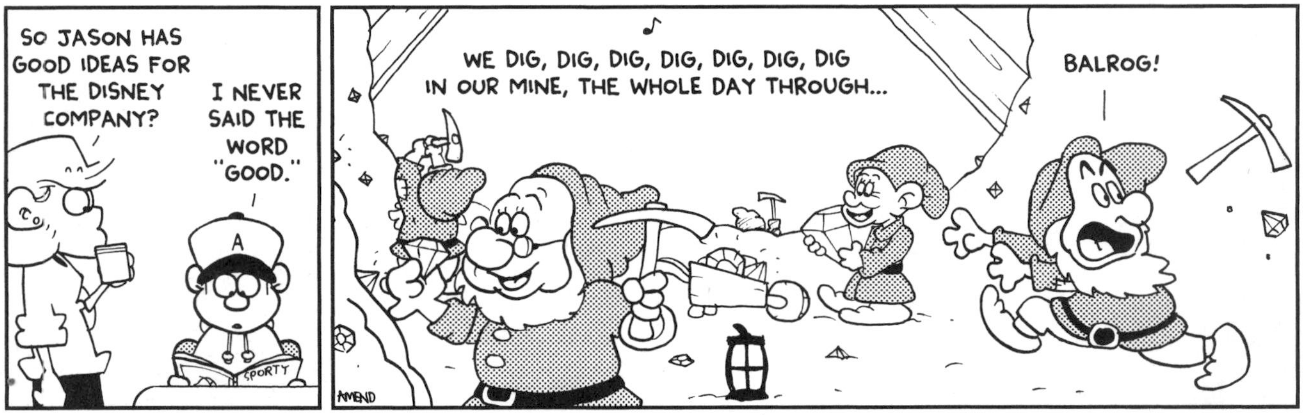
SO JASON HAS GOOD IDEAS FOR THE DISNEY COMPANY?
I NEVER SAID THE WORD "GOOD."
WE DIG, DIG, DIG, DIG, DIG, DIG, DIG IN OUR MINE, THE WHOLE DAY THROUGH...
BALROG!
AMEND

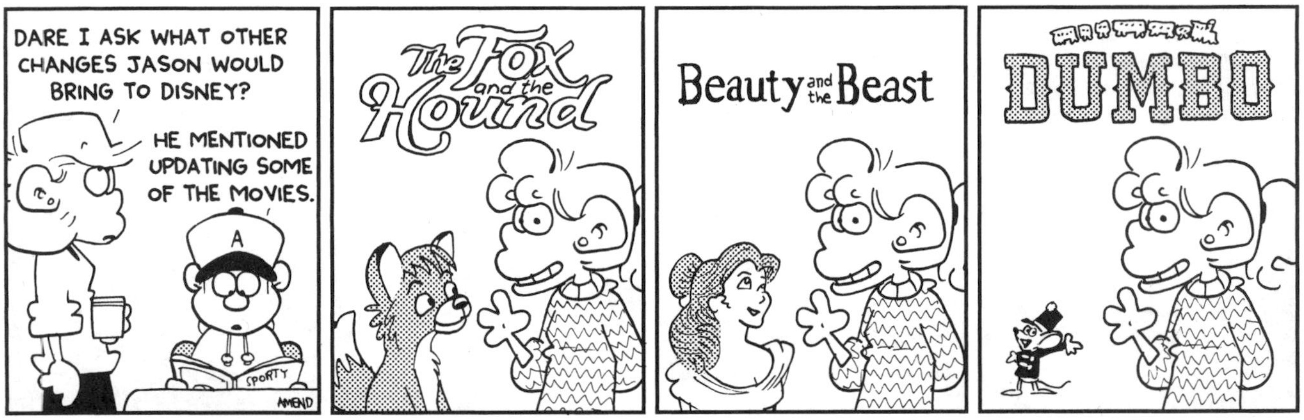
DARE I ASK WHAT OTHER CHANGES JASON WOULD BRING TO DISNEY?
HE MENTIONED UPDATING SOME OF THE MOVIES.
AMEND
The Fox and the Hound
Beauty and the Beast
DUMBO

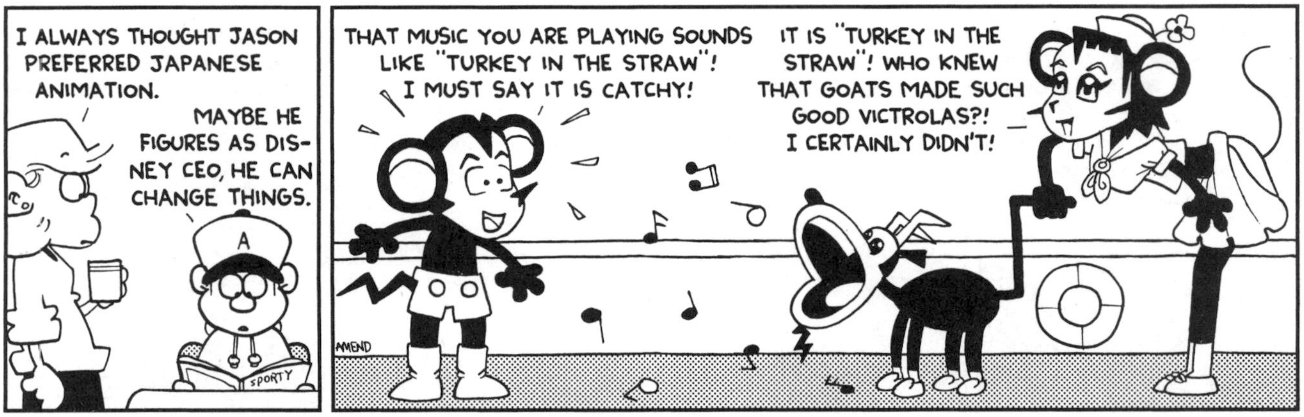
I ALWAYS THOUGHT JASON PREFERRED JAPANESE ANIMATION.
MAYBE HE FIGURES AS DISNEY CEO, HE CAN CHANGE THINGS.
THAT MUSIC YOU ARE PLAYING SOUNDS LIKE "TURKEY IN THE STRAW"! I MUST SAY IT IS CATCHY!
IT IS "TURKEY IN THE STRAW"! WHO KNEW THAT GOATS MADE SUCH GOOD VICTROLAS?! I CERTAINLY DIDN'T!
AMEND

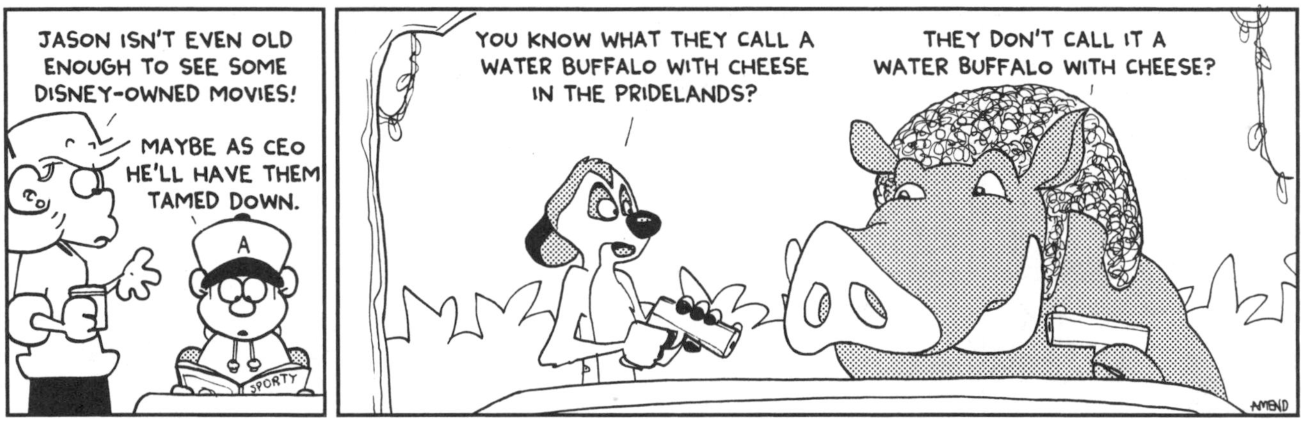
JASON ISN'T EVEN OLD ENOUGH TO SEE SOME DISNEY-OWNED MOVIES!
MAYBE AS CEO HE'LL HAVE THEM TAMED DOWN.
SPORTY
YOU KNOW WHAT THEY CALL A WATER BUFFALO WITH CHEESE IN THE PRIDELANDS?
THEY DON'T CALL IT A WATER BUFFALO WITH CHEESE?
AMEND

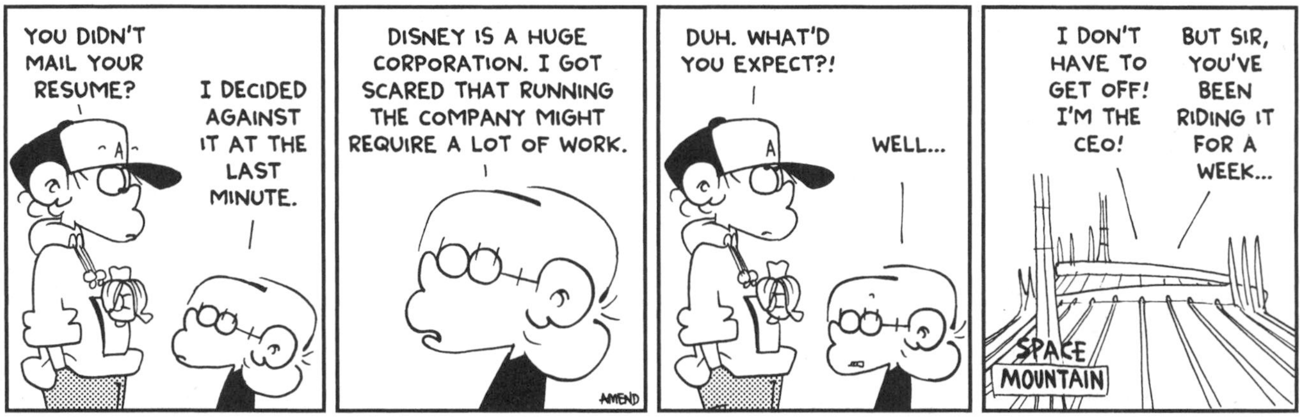
YOU DIDN'T MAIL YOUR RESUME?
I DECIDED AGAINST IT AT THE LAST MINUTE.
DISNEY IS A HUGE CORPORATION. I GOT SCARED THAT RUNNING THE COMPANY MIGHT REQUIRE A LOT OF WORK.
AMEND
DUH. WHAT'D YOU EXPECT?!
WELL...
I DON'T HAVE TO GET OFF! I'M THE CEO!
BUT SIR, YOU'VE BEEN RIDING IT FOR A WEEK...
SPACE MOUNTAIN

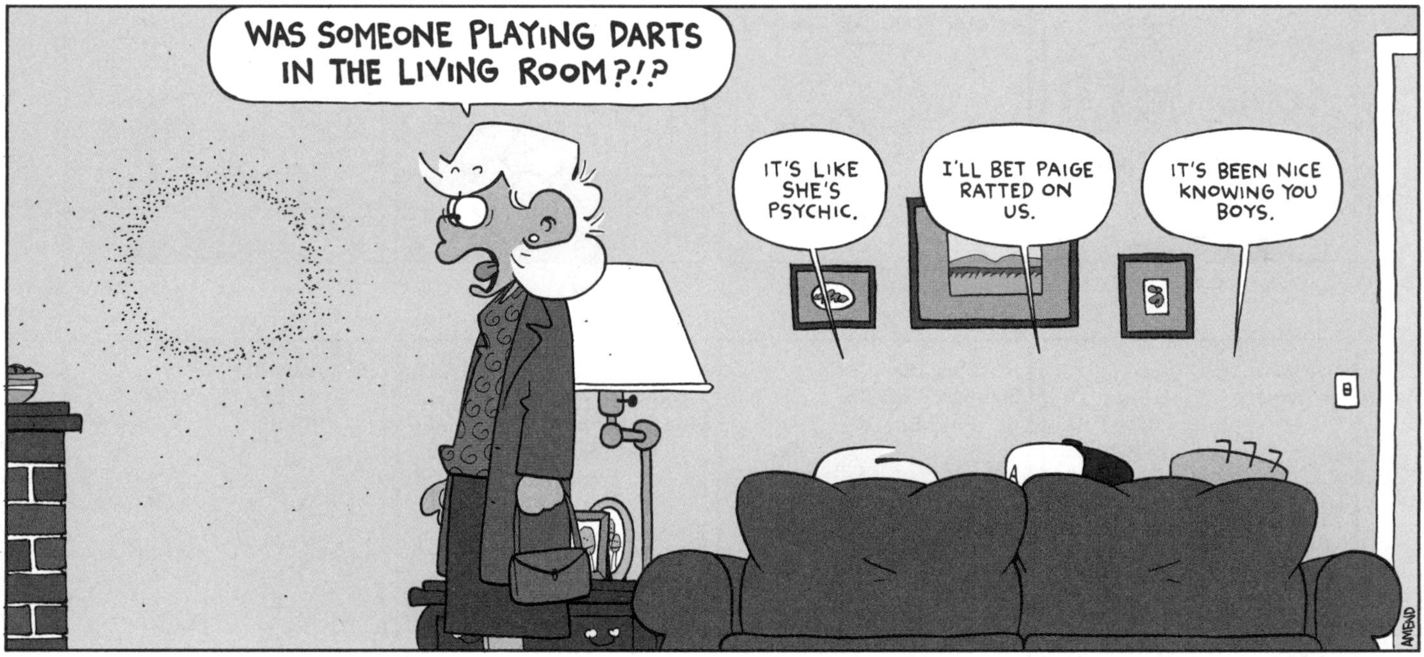
WAS SOMEONE PLAYING DARTS IN THE LIVING ROOM?!?
IT'S LIKE SHE'S PSYCHIC.
I'LL BET PAIGE RATTED ON US.
IT'S BEEN NICE KNOWING YOU BOYS.
AMEND

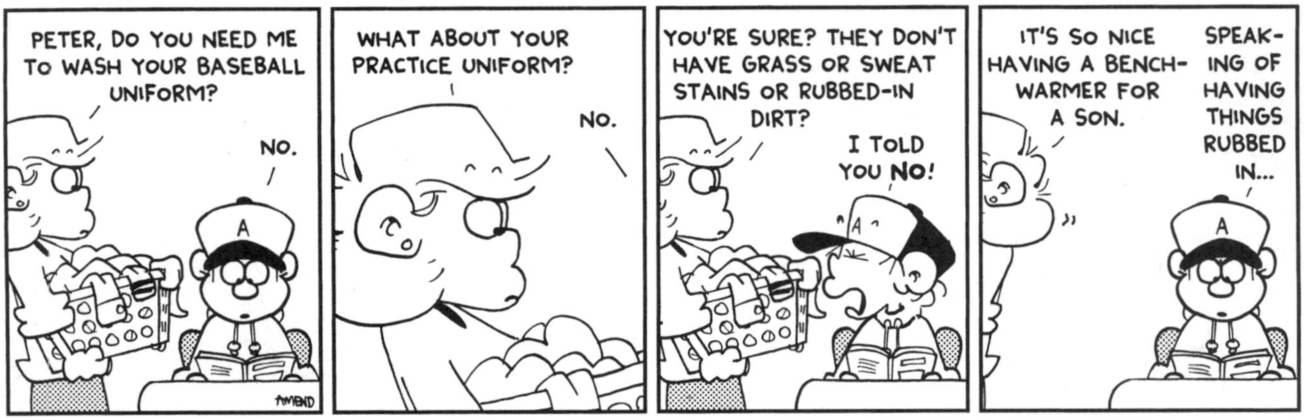
PETER, DO YOU NEED ME TO WASH YOUR BASEBALL UNIFORM?
NO.
WHAT ABOUT YOUR PRACTICE UNIFORM?
NO.
YOU'RE SURE? THEY DON'T HAVE GRASS OR SWEAT STAINS OR RUBBED-IN DIRT?
I TOLD YOU NO!
IT'S SO NICE HAVING A BENCH-WARMER FOR A SON.
SPEAK-ING OF HAVING THINGS RUBBED IN...
AMEND

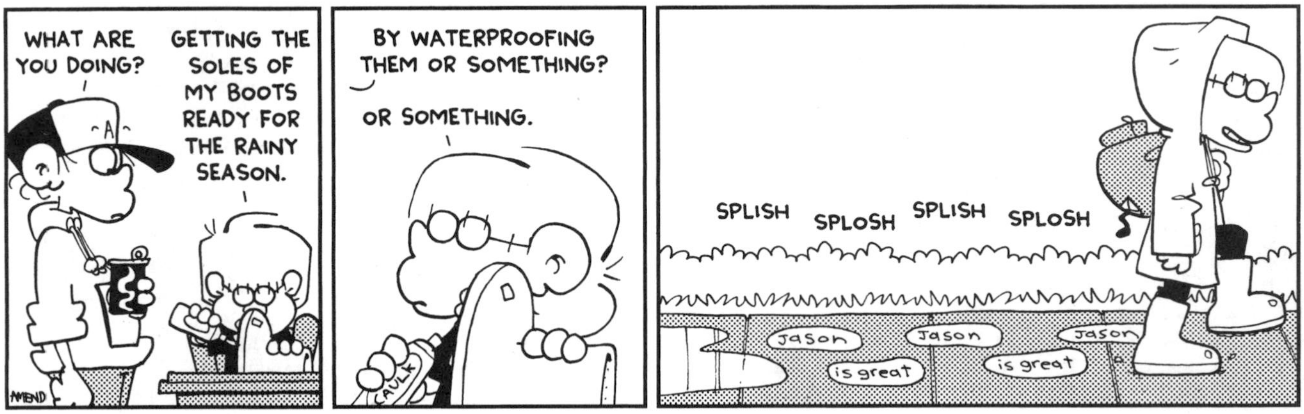
WHAT ARE YOU DOING?
GETTING THE SOLES OF MY BOOTS READY FOR THE RAINY SEASON.
AMEND
BY WATERPROOFING THEM OR SOMETHING?
OR SOMETHING.
CAULK
SPLISH
SPLOSH
SPLISH
SPLOSH
Jason
is great
Jason
is great
Jason

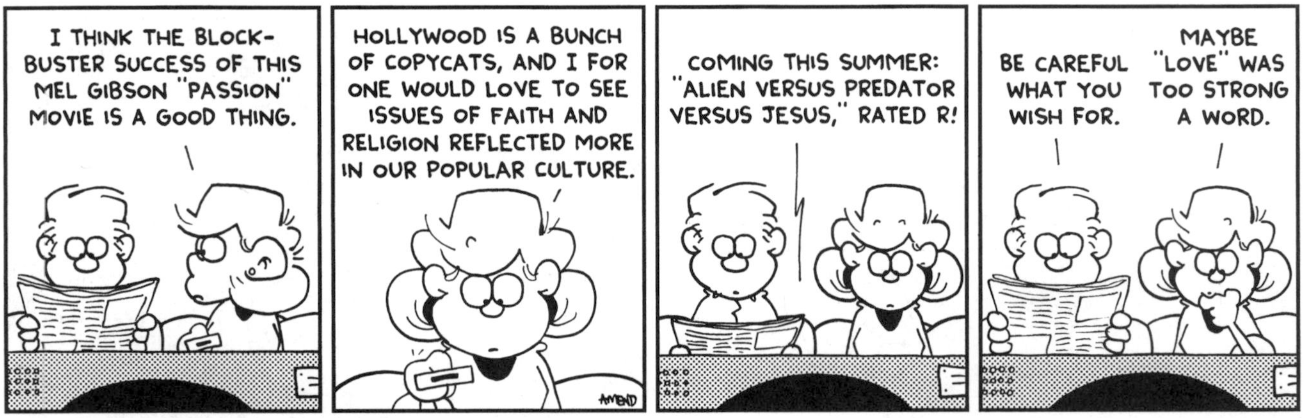
I THINK THE BLOCK-BUSTER SUCCESS OF THIS MEL GIBSON "PASSION" MOVIE IS A GOOD THING.
HOLLYWOOD IS A BUNCH OF COPYCATS, AND I FOR ONE WOULD LOVE TO SEE ISSUES OF FAITH AND RELIGION REFLECTED MORE IN OUR POPULAR CULTURE.
AMEND
COMING THIS SUMMER: "ALIEN VERSUS PREDATOR VERSUS JESUS," RATED R!
BE CAREFUL WHAT YOU WISH FOR.
MAYBE "LOVE" WAS TOO STRONG A WORD.

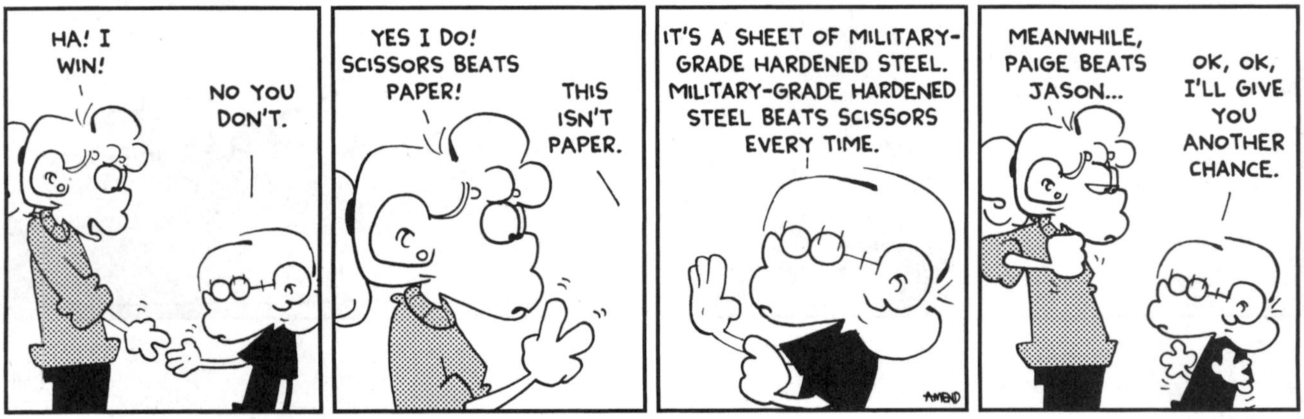
HA! I WIN!
NO YOU DON'T.
YES I DO! SCISSORS BEATS PAPER!
THIS ISN'T PAPER.
IT'S A SHEET OF MILITARY-GRADE HARDENED STEEL. MILITARY-GRADE HARDENED STEEL BEATS SCISSORS EVERY TIME.
AMEND
MEANWHILE, PAIGE BEATS JASON...
OK, OK, I'LL GIVE YOU ANOTHER CHANCE.

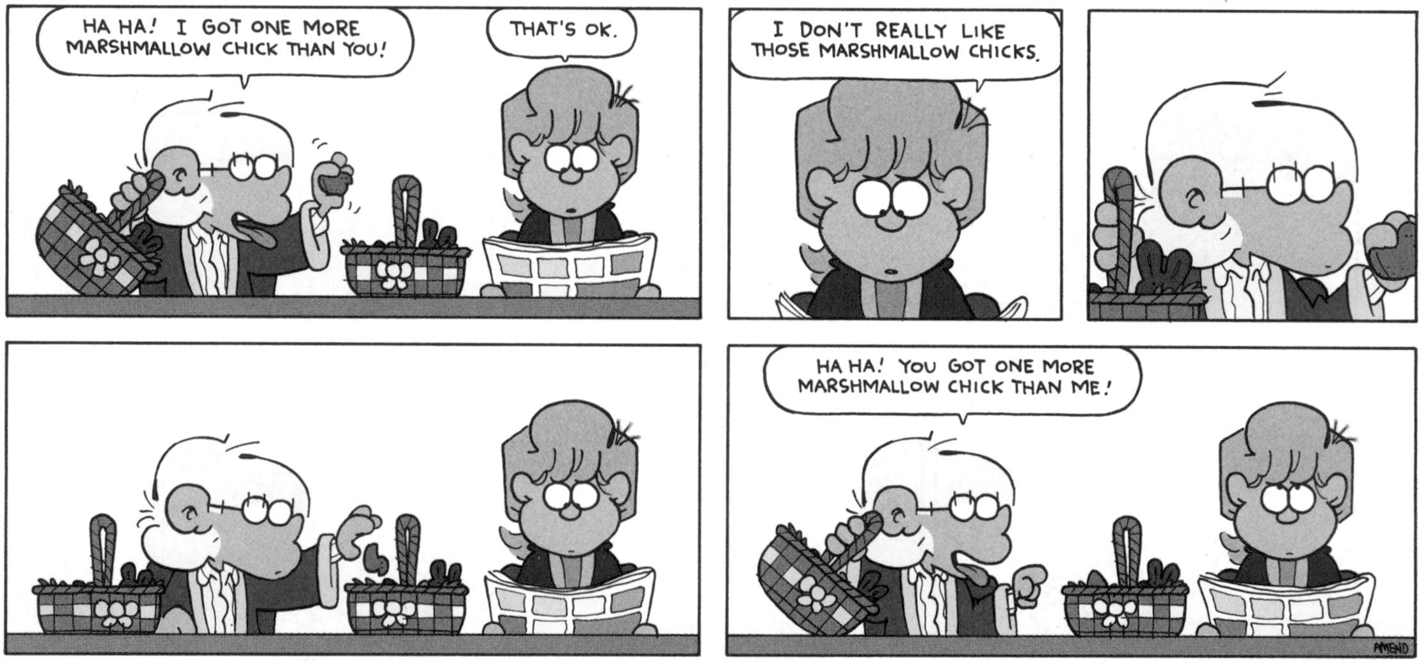
HA HA! I GOT ONE MORE MARSHMALLOW CHICK THAN YOU!
THAT'S OK.
I DON'T REALLY LIKE THOSE MARSHMALLOW CHICKS.
HA HA! YOU GOT ONE MORE MARSHMALLOW CHICK THAN ME!
AMEND

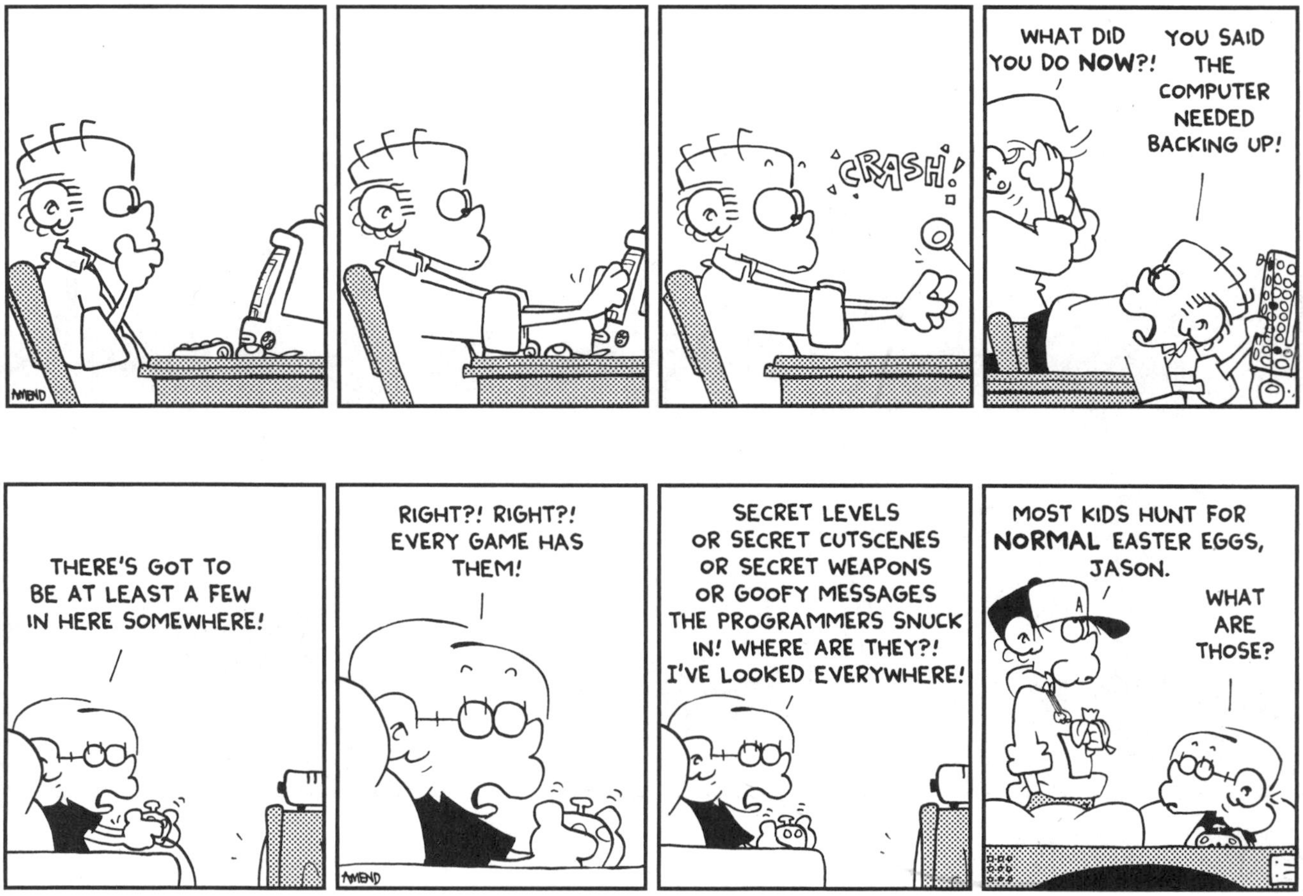
AMEND
CRASH!
WHAT DID YOU DO NOW?!
YOU SAID THE COMPUTER NEEDED BACKING UP!
THERE'S GOT TO BE AT LEAST A FEW IN HERE SOMEWHERE!
RIGHT?! RIGHT?! EVERY GAME HAS THEM!
AMEND
SECRET LEVELS OR SECRET CUTSCENES OR SECRET WEAPONS OR GOOFY MESSAGES THE PROGRAMMERS SNUCK IN! WHERE ARE THEY?! I'VE LOOKED EVERYWHERE!
MOST KIDS HUNT FOR NORMAL EASTER EGGS, JASON.
WHAT ARE THOSE?

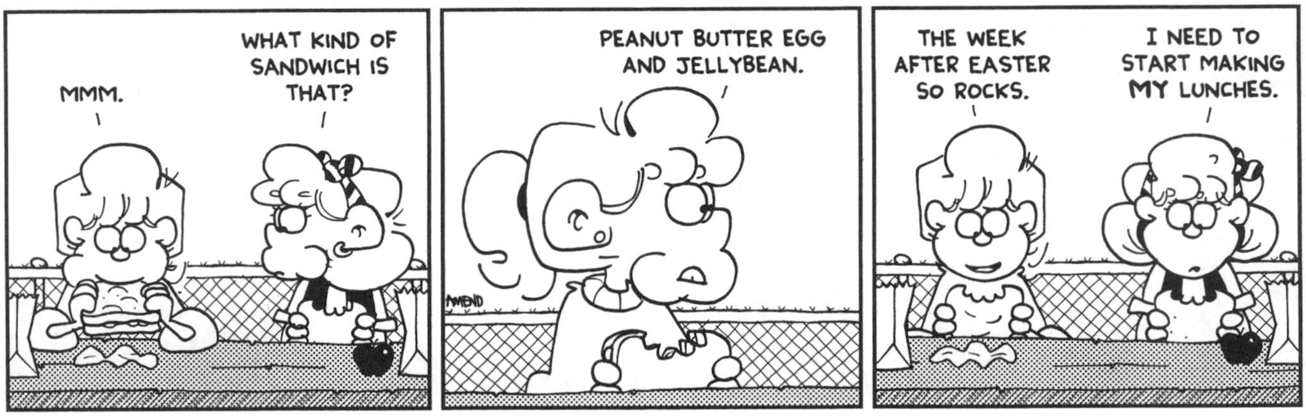
MMM.
WHAT KIND OF SANDWICH IS THAT?
PEANUT BUTTER EGG AND JELLYBEAN.
THE WEEK AFTER EASTER SO ROCKS.
I NEED TO START MAKING MY LUNCHES.

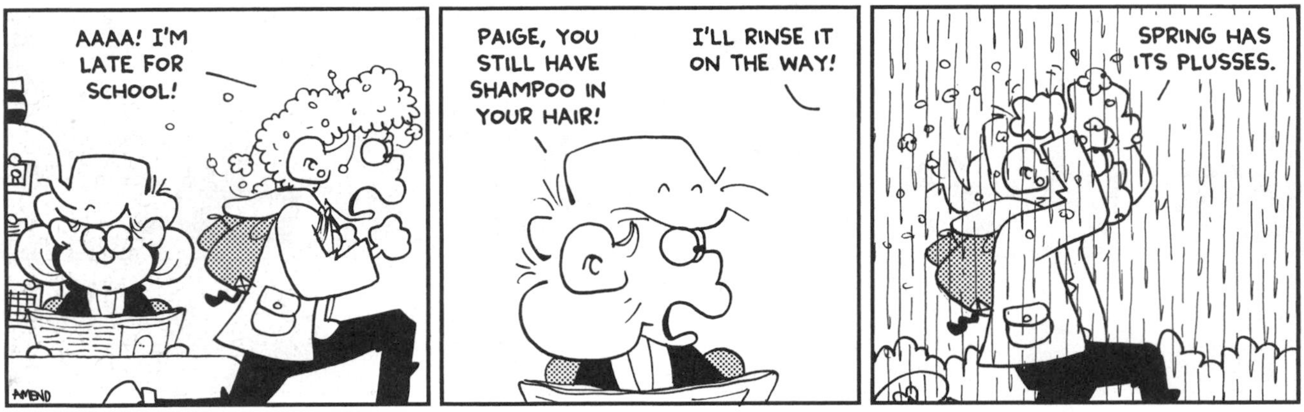
AAAA! I'M LATE FOR SCHOOL!
PAIGE, YOU STILL HAVE SHAMPOO IN YOUR HAIR!
I'LL RINSE IT ON THE WAY!
SPRING HAS ITS PLUSSES.

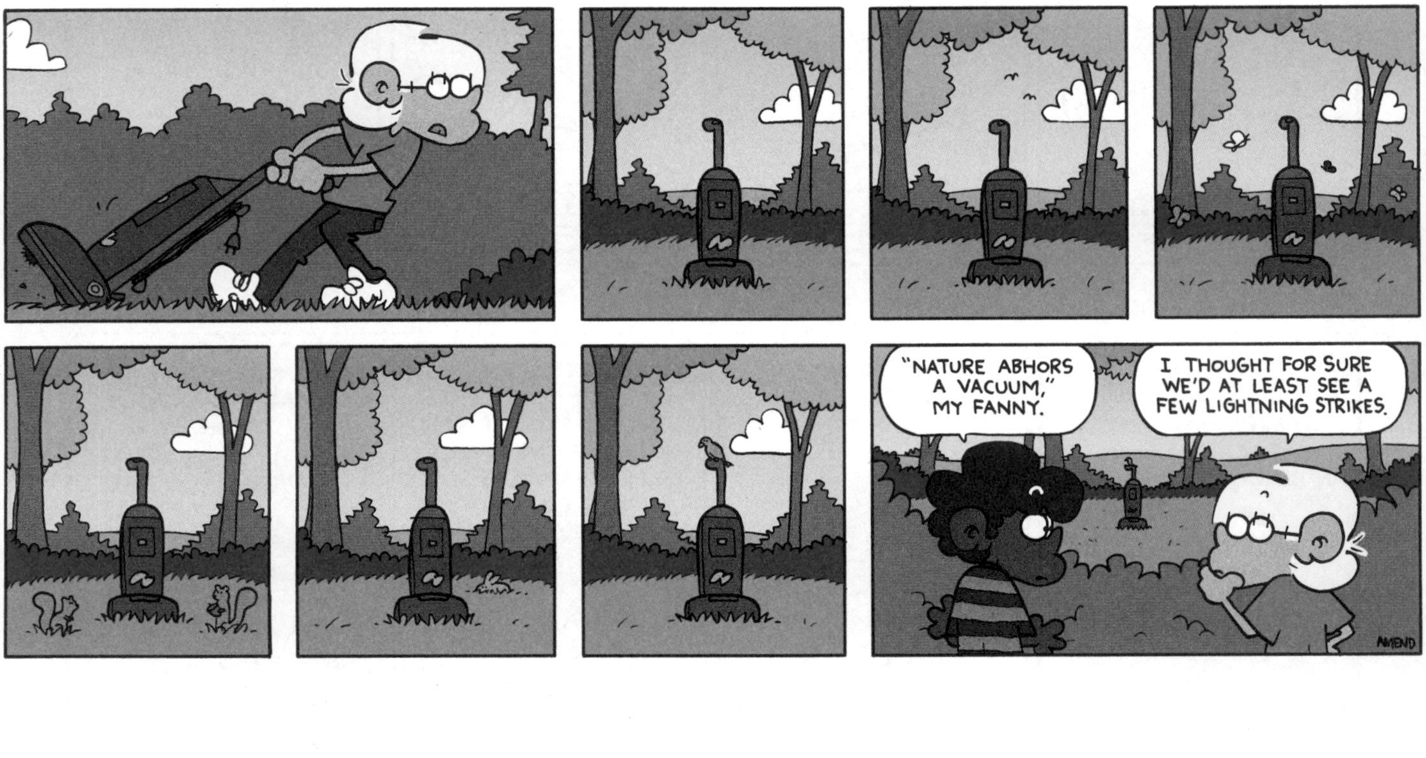
"NATURE ABHORS A VACUUM," MY FANNY.
I THOUGHT FOR SURE WE'D AT LEAST SEE A FEW LIGHTNING STRIKES.

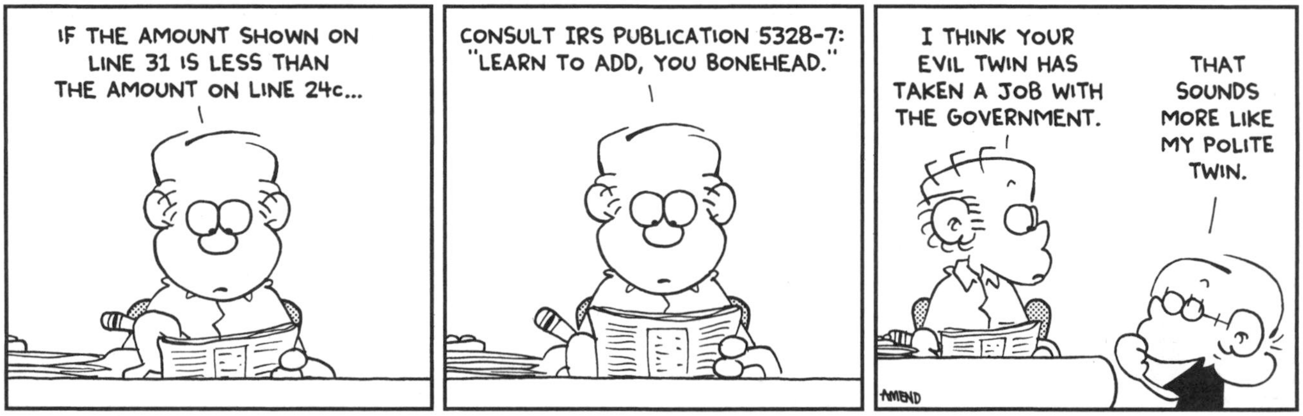
IF THE AMOUNT SHOWN ON LINE 31 IS LESS THAN THE AMOUNT ON LINE 24c...
CONSULT IRS PUBLICATION 5328-7: "LEARN TO ADD, YOU BONEHEAD."
I THINK YOUR EVIL TWIN HAS TAKEN A JOB WITH THE GOVERNMENT.
THAT SOUNDS MORE LIKE MY POLITE TWIN.
AMEND

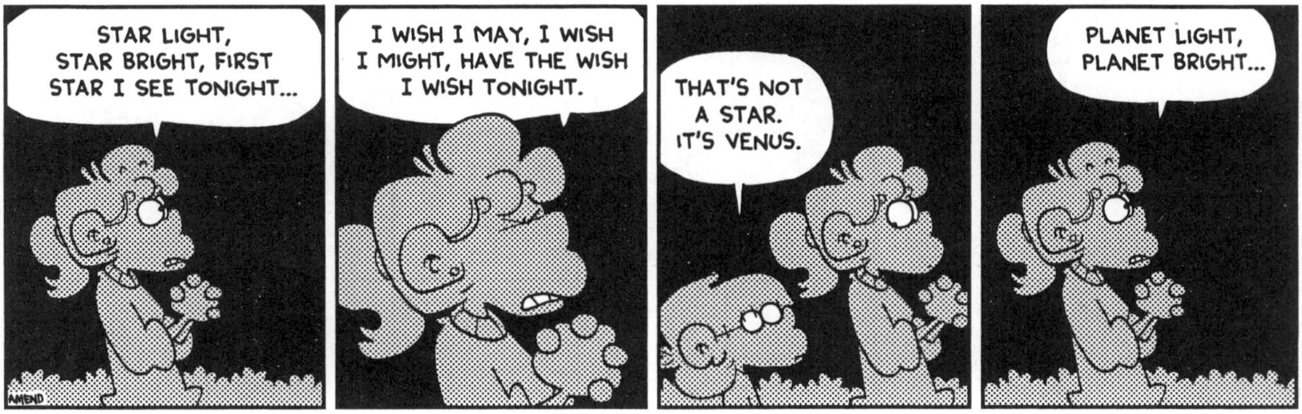
STAR LIGHT, STAR BRIGHT, FIRST STAR I SEE TONIGHT...
AMEND
I WISH I MAY, I WISH I MIGHT, HAVE THE WISH I WISH TONIGHT.
THAT'S NOT A STAR. IT'S VENUS.
PLANET LIGHT, PLANET BRIGHT...

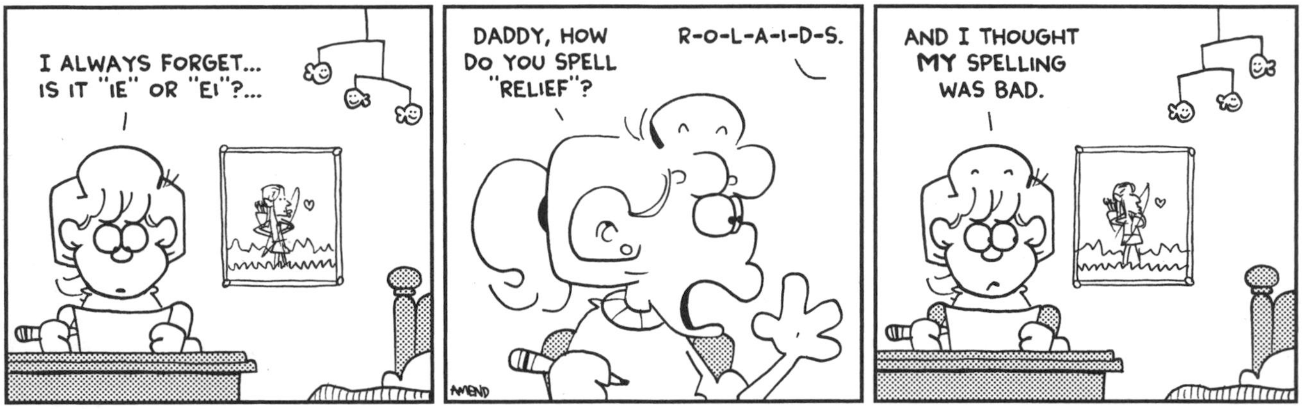
I ALWAYS FORGET... IS IT "IE" OR "EI"?...
DADDY, HOW DO YOU SPELL "RELIEF"?
R-O-L-A-I-D-S.
AMEND
AND I THOUGHT MY SPELLING WAS BAD.

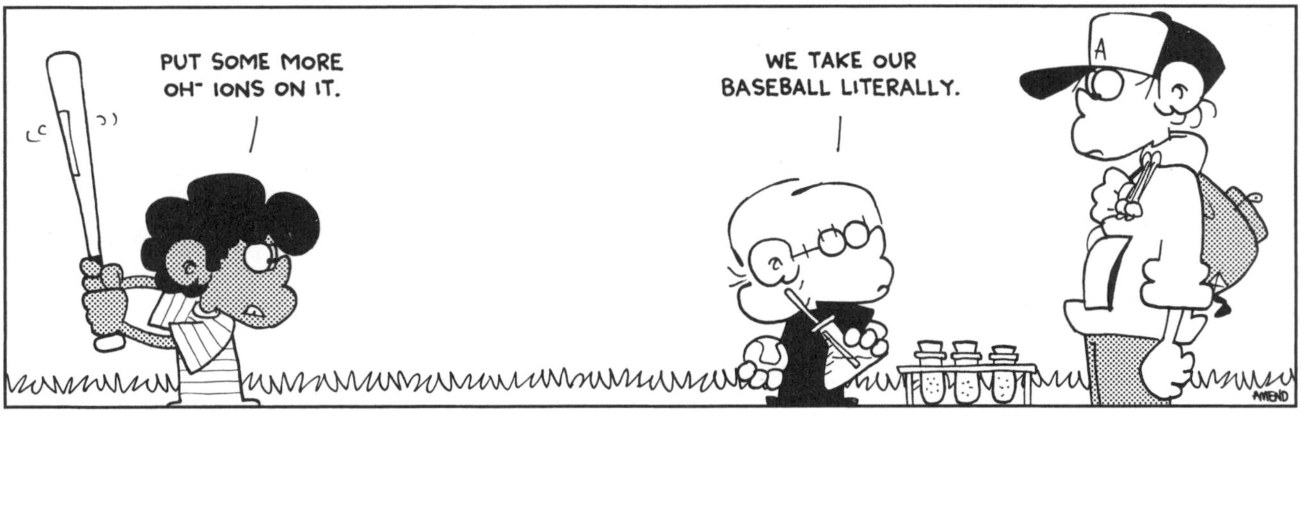
PUT SOME MORE OH- IONS ON IT.
WE TAKE OUR BASEBALL LITERALLY.
A
AMEND

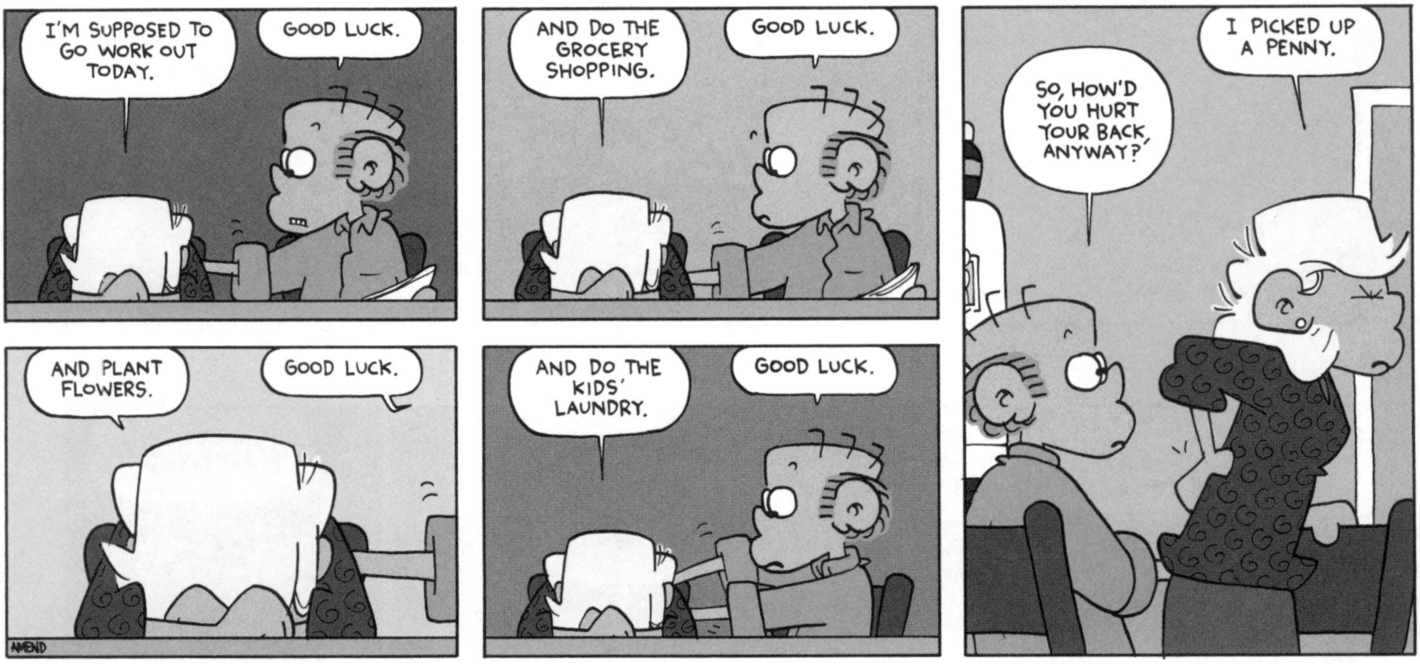
I'M SUPPOSED TO GO WORK OUT TODAY.
GOOD LUCK.
AND DO THE GROCERY SHOPPING.
GOOD LUCK.
AND PLANT FLOWERS.
GOOD LUCK.
AND DO THE KIDS' LAUNDRY.
GOOD LUCK.
SO, HOW'D YOU HURT YOUR BACK, ANYWAY?
I PICKED UP A PENNY.
AMEND

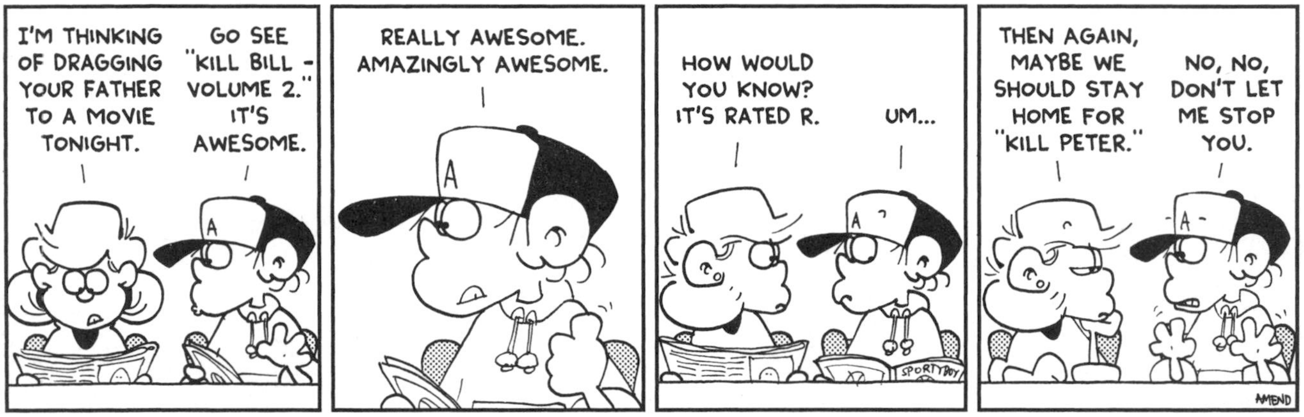
I'M THINKING OF DRAGGING YOUR FATHER TO A MOVIE TONIGHT.
GO SEE "KILL BILL - VOLUME 2." IT'S AWESOME.
REALLY AWESOME. AMAZINGLY AWESOME.
HOW WOULD YOU KNOW? IT'S RATED R.
UM...
SPORTY BOY
THEN AGAIN, MAYBE WE SHOULD STAY HOME FOR "KILL PETER."
NO, NO, DON'T LET ME STOP YOU.
AMEND

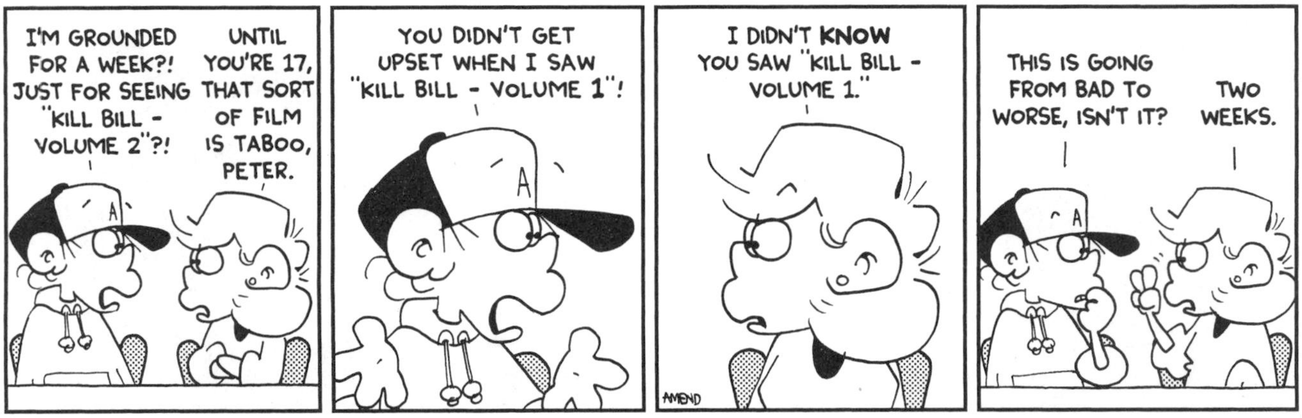
I'M GROUNDED FOR A WEEK?! JUST FOR SEEING "KILL BILL - VOLUME 2"?!
UNTIL YOU'RE 17, THAT SORT OF FILM IS TABOO, PETER.
YOU DIDN'T GET UPSET WHEN I SAW "KILL BILL - VOLUME 1"!
I DIDN'T **KNOW** YOU SAW "KILL BILL - VOLUME 1."
AMEND
THIS IS GOING FROM BAD TO WORSE, ISN'T IT?
TWO WEEKS.

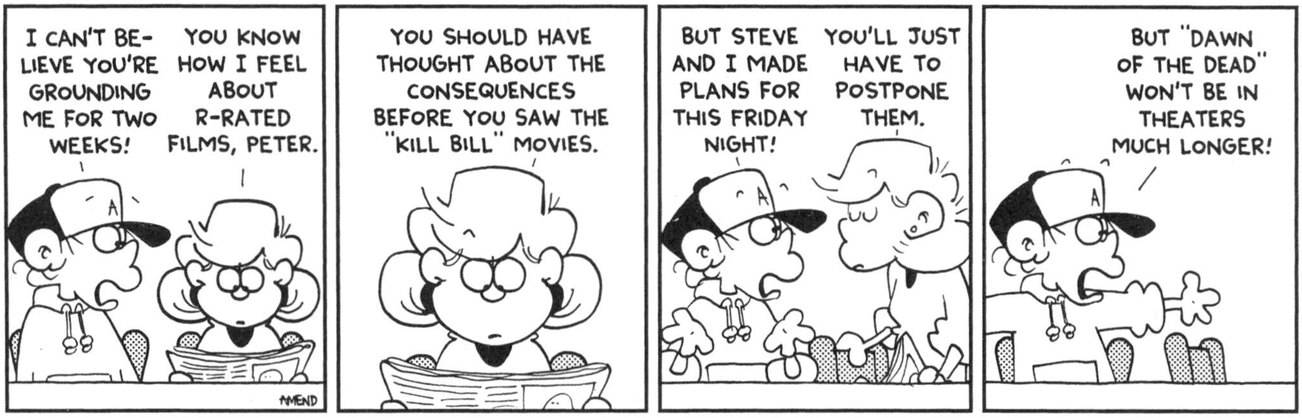
I CAN'T BE-LIEVE YOU'RE GROUNDING ME FOR TWO WEEKS!
YOU KNOW HOW I FEEL ABOUT R-RATED FILMS, PETER.
YOU SHOULD HAVE THOUGHT ABOUT THE CONSEQUENCES BEFORE YOU SAW THE "KILL BILL" MOVIES.
BUT STEVE AND I MADE PLANS FOR THIS FRIDAY NIGHT!
YOU'LL JUST HAVE TO POSTPONE THEM.
BUT "DAWN OF THE DEAD" WON'T BE IN THEATERS MUCH LONGER!

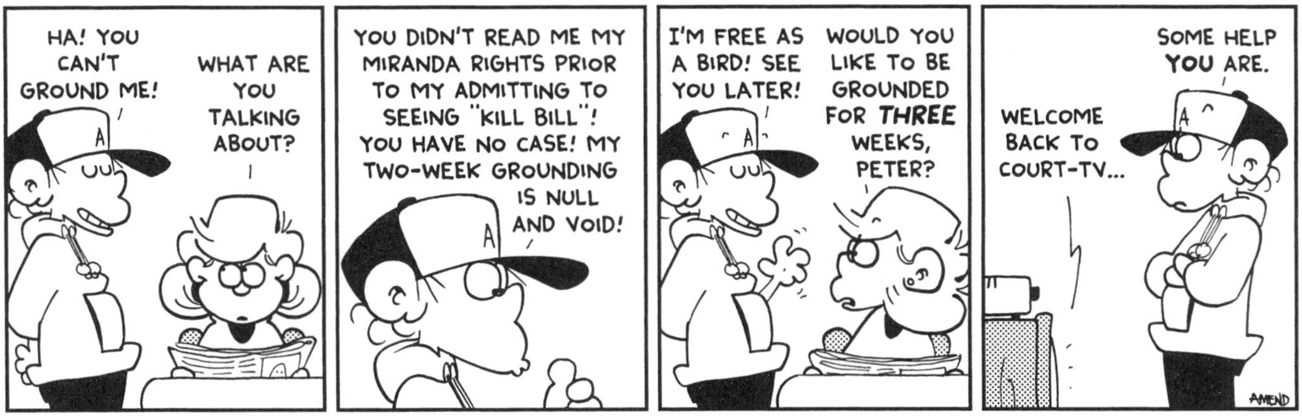
HA! YOU CAN'T GROUND ME!
WHAT ARE YOU TALKING ABOUT?
YOU DIDN'T READ ME MY MIRANDA RIGHTS PRIOR TO MY ADMITTING TO SEEING "KILL BILL"! YOU HAVE NO CASE! MY TWO-WEEK GROUNDING IS NULL AND VOID!
I'M FREE AS A BIRD! SEE YOU LATER!
WOULD YOU LIKE TO BE GROUNDED FOR **THREE** WEEKS, PETER?
WELCOME BACK TO COURT-TV...
SOME HELP **YOU** ARE.

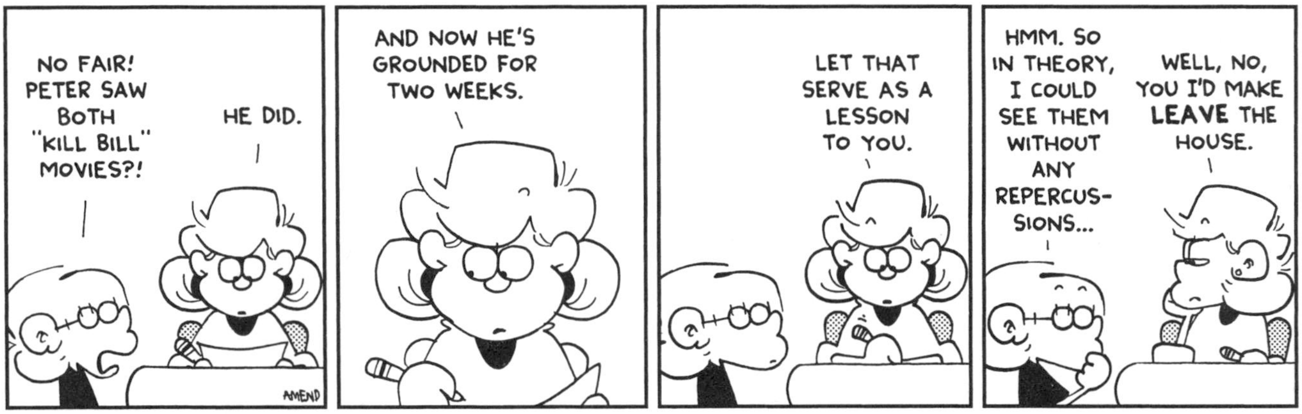
NO FAIR! PETER SAW BOTH "KILL BILL" MOVIES?!
HE DID.
AND NOW HE'S GROUNDED FOR TWO WEEKS.
LET THAT SERVE AS A LESSON TO YOU.
HMM. SO IN THEORY, I COULD SEE THEM WITHOUT ANY REPERCUS-SIONS...
WELL, NO, YOU I'D MAKE **LEAVE** THE HOUSE.

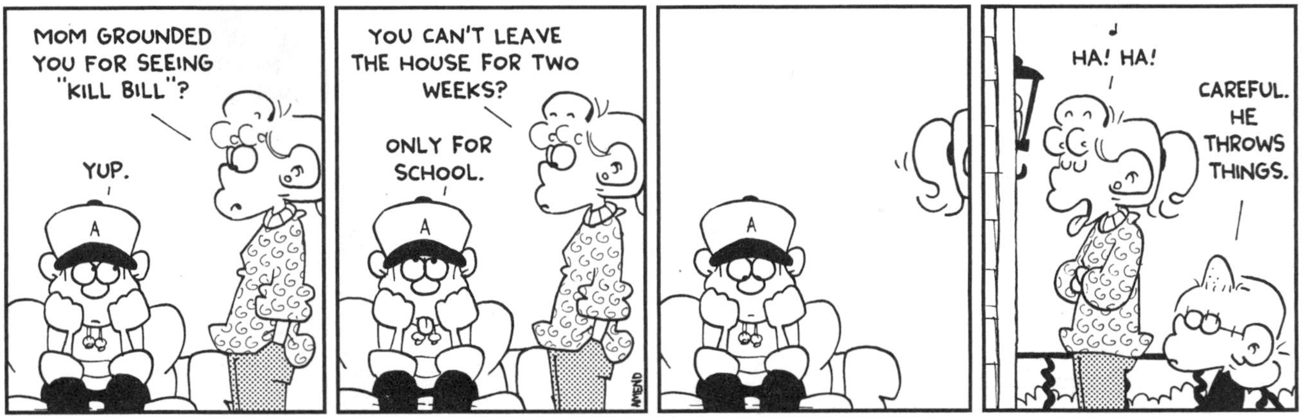
MOM GROUNDED YOU FOR SEEING "KILL BILL"?
YUP.
YOU CAN'T LEAVE THE HOUSE FOR TWO WEEKS?
ONLY FOR SCHOOL.
HA! HA!
CAREFUL. HE THROWS THINGS.

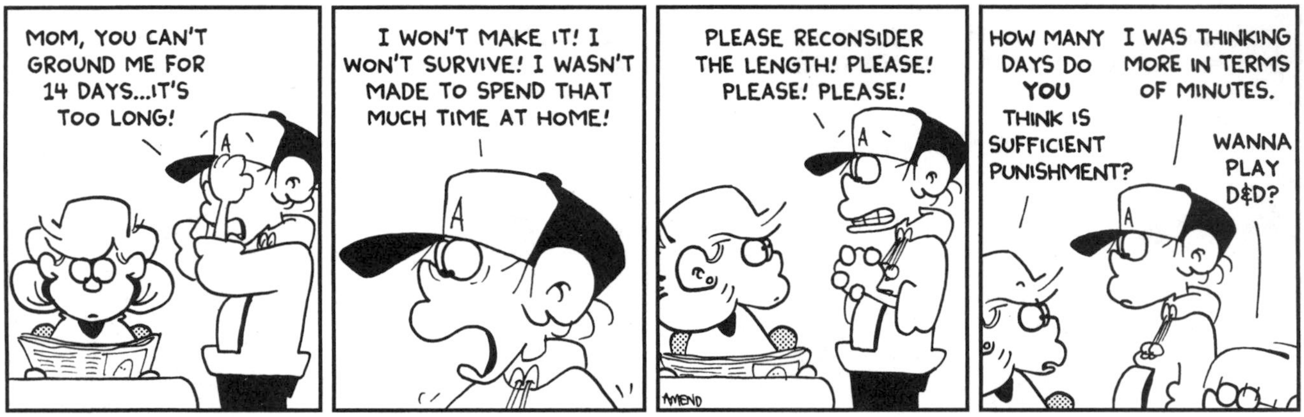
MOM, YOU CAN'T GROUND ME FOR 14 DAYS...IT'S TOO LONG!
I WON'T MAKE IT! I WON'T SURVIVE! I WASN'T MADE TO SPEND THAT MUCH TIME AT HOME!
PLEASE RECONSIDER THE LENGTH! PLEASE! PLEASE! PLEASE!
HOW MANY DAYS DO **YOU** THINK IS SUFFICIENT PUNISHMENT?
I WAS THINKING MORE IN TERMS OF MINUTES.
WANNA PLAY D&D?

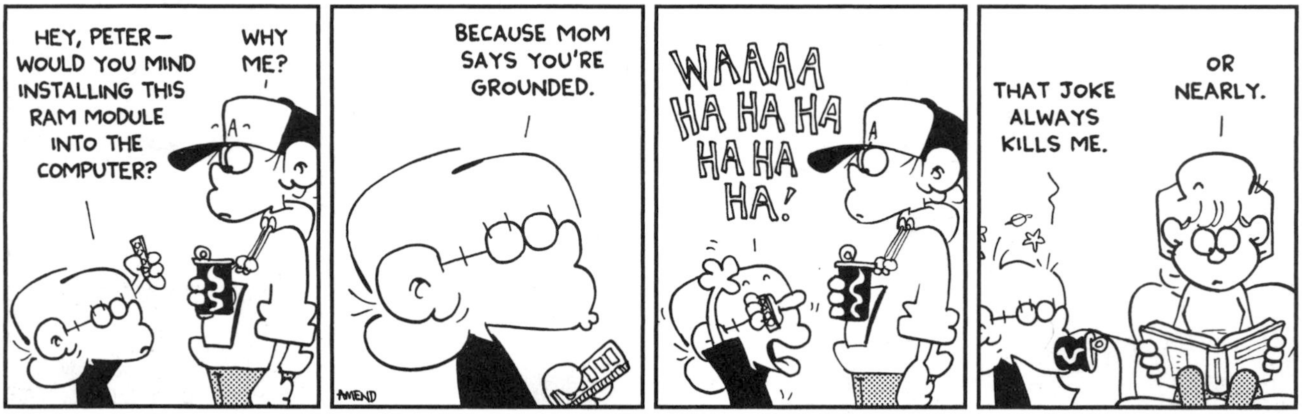
HEY, PETER— WOULD YOU MIND INSTALLING THIS RAM MODULE INTO THE COMPUTER?
WHY ME?
BECAUSE MOM SAYS YOU'RE GROUNDED.
WAAAA HA HA HA HA HA HA!
THAT JOKE ALWAYS KILLS ME.
OR NEARLY.

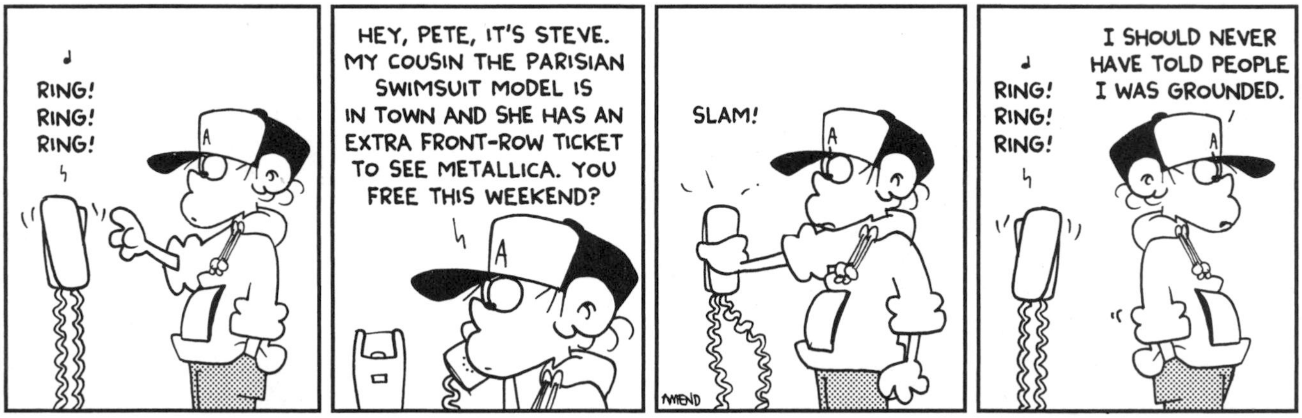
RING! RING! RING!
HEY, PETE, IT'S STEVE. MY COUSIN THE PARISIAN SWIMSUIT MODEL IS IN TOWN AND SHE HAS AN EXTRA FRONT-ROW TICKET TO SEE METALLICA. YOU FREE THIS WEEKEND?
SLAM!
RING! RING! RING!
I SHOULD NEVER HAVE TOLD PEOPLE I WAS GROUNDED.

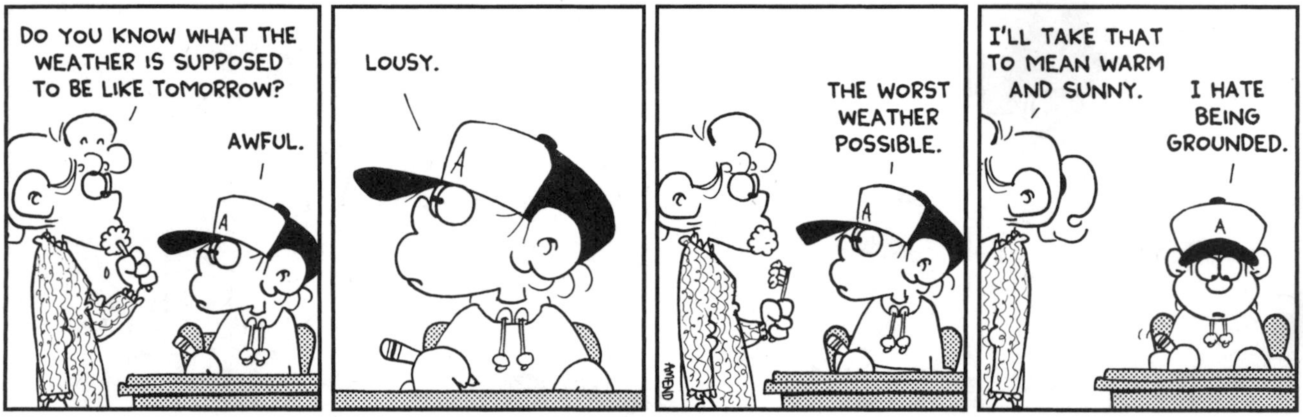
DO YOU KNOW WHAT THE WEATHER IS SUPPOSED TO BE LIKE TOMORROW?
AWFUL.
LOUSY.
THE WORST WEATHER POSSIBLE.
I'LL TAKE THAT TO MEAN WARM AND SUNNY.
I HATE BEING GROUNDED.

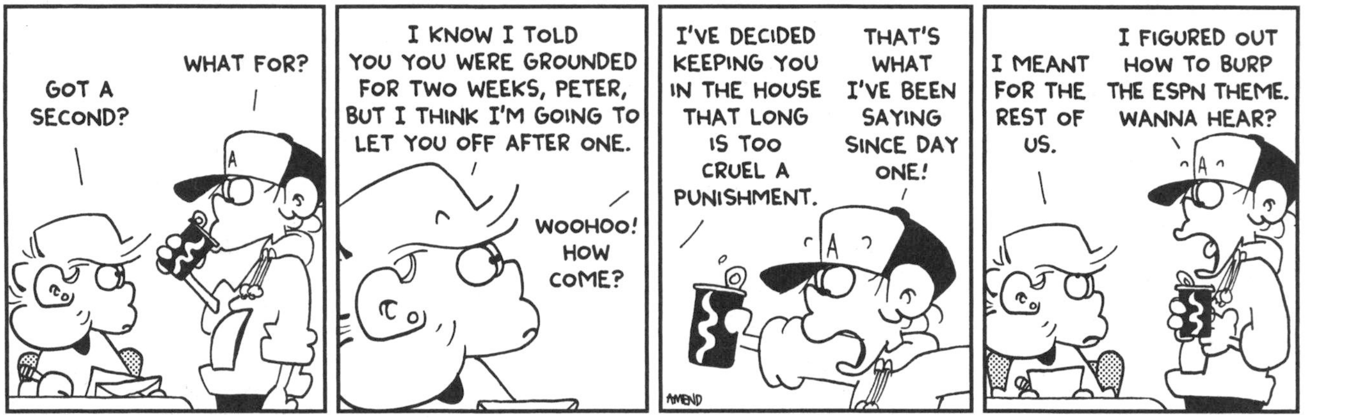
GOT A SECOND?
WHAT FOR?
I KNOW I TOLD YOU YOU WERE GROUNDED FOR TWO WEEKS, PETER, BUT I THINK I'M GOING TO LET YOU OFF AFTER ONE.
WOOHOO! HOW COME?
I'VE DECIDED KEEPING YOU IN THE HOUSE THAT LONG IS TOO CRUEL A PUNISHMENT.
THAT'S WHAT I'VE BEEN SAYING SINCE DAY ONE!
I MEANT FOR THE REST OF US.
I FIGURED OUT HOW TO BURP THE ESPN THEME. WANNA HEAR?
AMEND

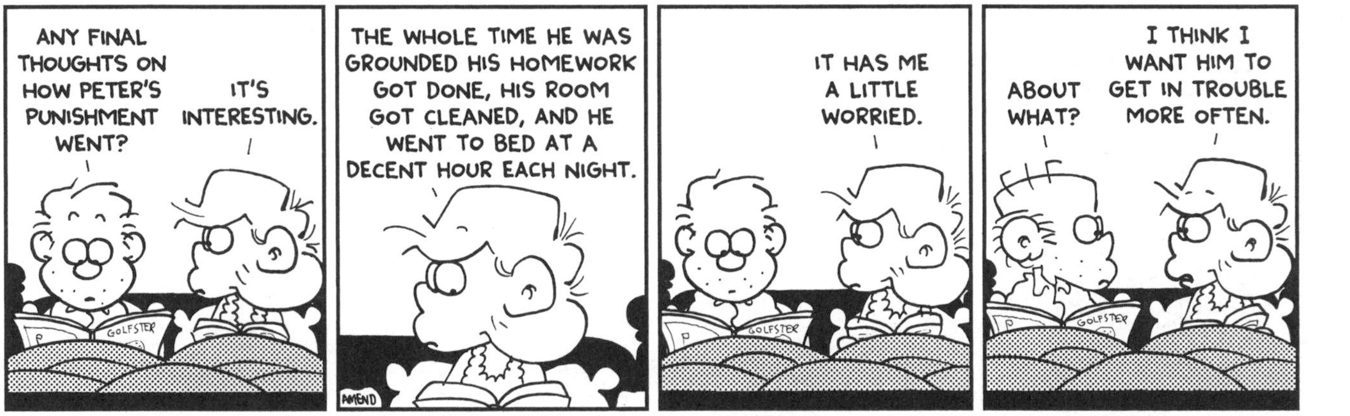
ANY FINAL THOUGHTS ON HOW PETER'S PUNISHMENT WENT?
IT'S INTERESTING.
THE WHOLE TIME HE WAS GROUNDED HIS HOMEWORK GOT DONE, HIS ROOM GOT CLEANED, AND HE WENT TO BED AT A DECENT HOUR EACH NIGHT.
IT HAS ME A LITTLE WORRIED.
ABOUT WHAT?
I THINK I WANT HIM TO GET IN TROUBLE MORE OFTEN.
GOLFSTER
AMEND

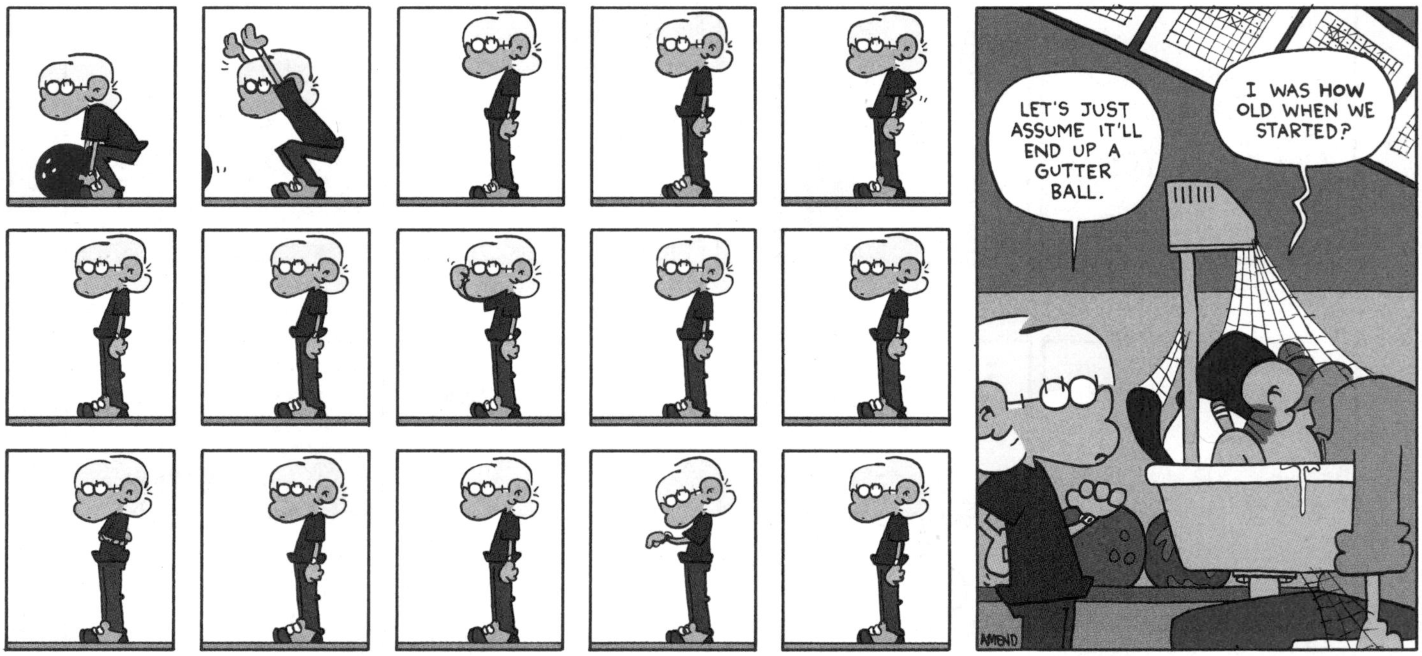
LET'S JUST ASSUME IT'LL END UP A GUTTER BALL.
I WAS HOW OLD WHEN WE STARTED?
AMEND

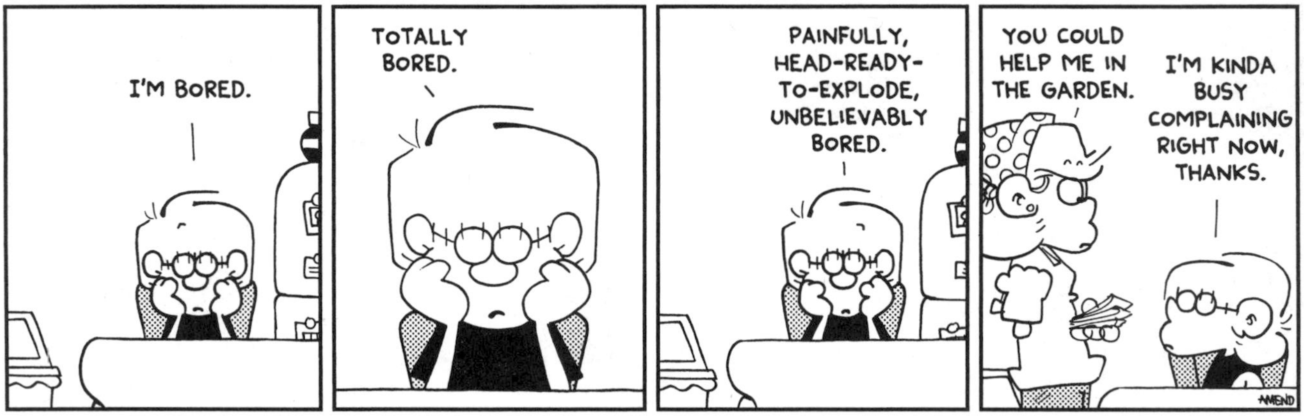
I'M BORED.
TOTALLY BORED.
PAINFULLY, HEAD-READY-TO-EXPLODE, UNBELIEVABLY BORED.
YOU COULD HELP ME IN THE GARDEN.
I'M KINDA BUSY COMPLAINING RIGHT NOW, THANKS.

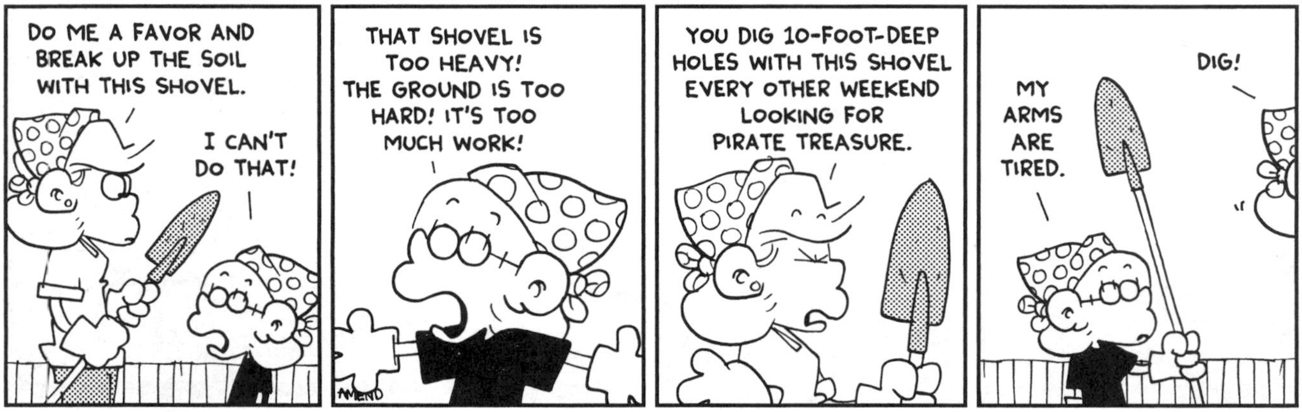
DO ME A FAVOR AND BREAK UP THE SOIL WITH THIS SHOVEL.
I CAN'T DO THAT!
THAT SHOVEL IS TOO HEAVY! THE GROUND IS TOO HARD! IT'S TOO MUCH WORK!
YOU DIG 10-FOOT-DEEP HOLES WITH THIS SHOVEL EVERY OTHER WEEKEND LOOKING FOR PIRATE TREASURE.
MY ARMS ARE TIRED.
DIG!

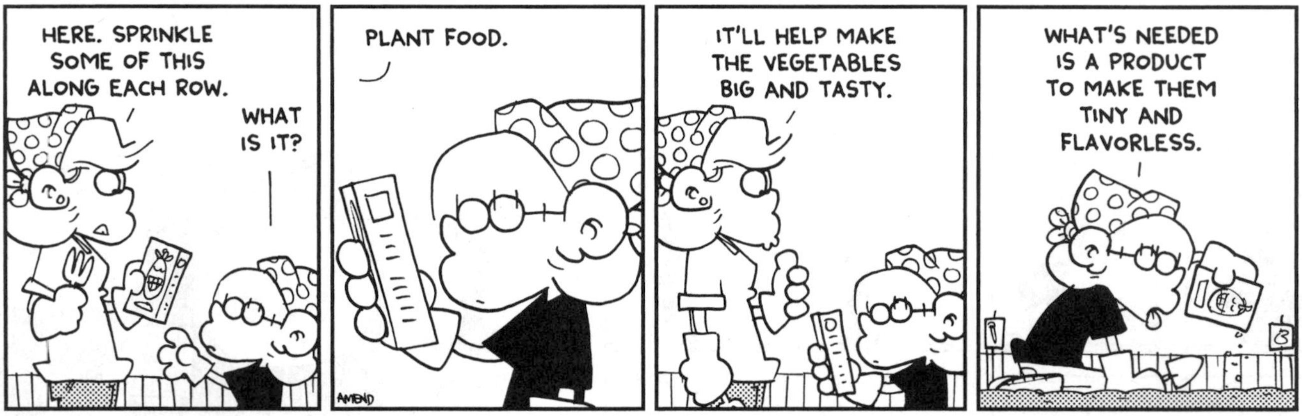
HERE. SPRINKLE SOME OF THIS ALONG EACH ROW.
WHAT IS IT?
PLANT FOOD.
IT'LL HELP MAKE THE VEGETABLES BIG AND TASTY.
WHAT'S NEEDED IS A PRODUCT TO MAKE THEM TINY AND FLAVORLESS.

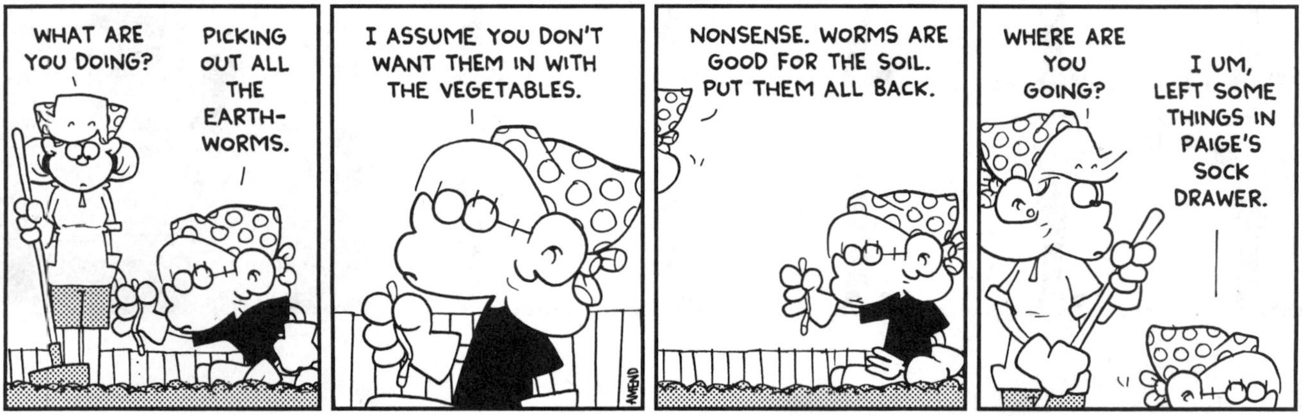
WHAT ARE YOU DOING?
PICKING OUT ALL THE EARTH-WORMS.
I ASSUME YOU DON'T WANT THEM IN WITH THE VEGETABLES.
NONSENSE. WORMS ARE GOOD FOR THE SOIL. PUT THEM ALL BACK.
WHERE ARE YOU GOING?
I UM, LEFT SOME THINGS IN PAIGE'S SOCK DRAWER.

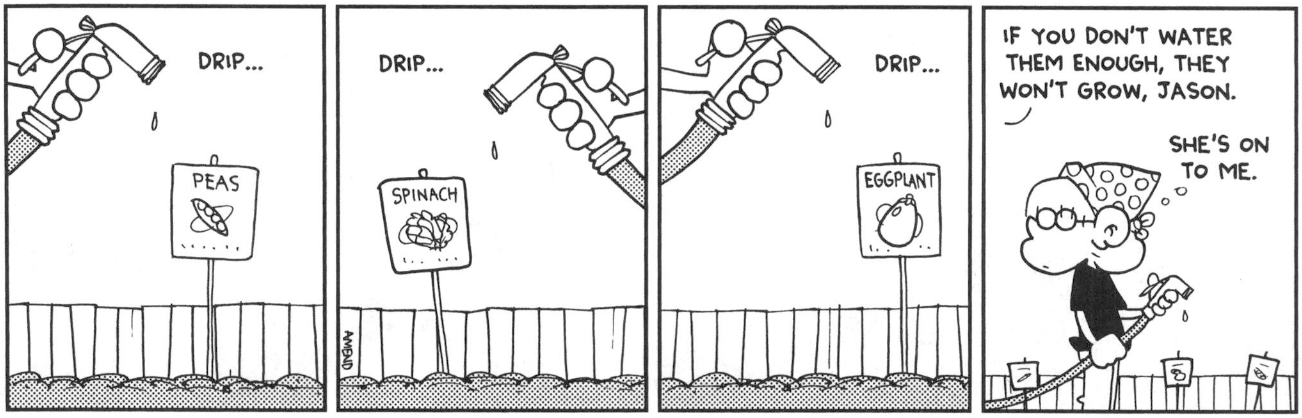

DRIP...
PEAS
DRIP...
SPINACH
AMEND
DRIP...
EGGPLANT
IF YOU DON'T WATER THEM ENOUGH, THEY WON'T GROW, JASON.
SHE'S ON TO ME.

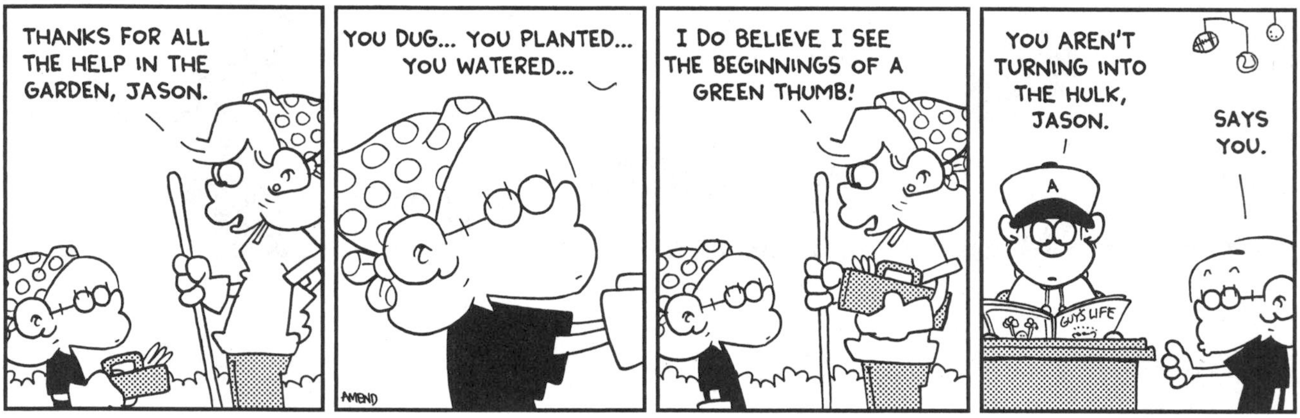

THANKS FOR ALL THE HELP IN THE GARDEN, JASON.
YOU DUG... YOU PLANTED... YOU WATERED...
AMEND
I DO BELIEVE I SEE THE BEGINNINGS OF A GREEN THUMB!
YOU AREN'T TURNING INTO THE HULK, JASON.
SAYS YOU.
A
GUY'S LIFE

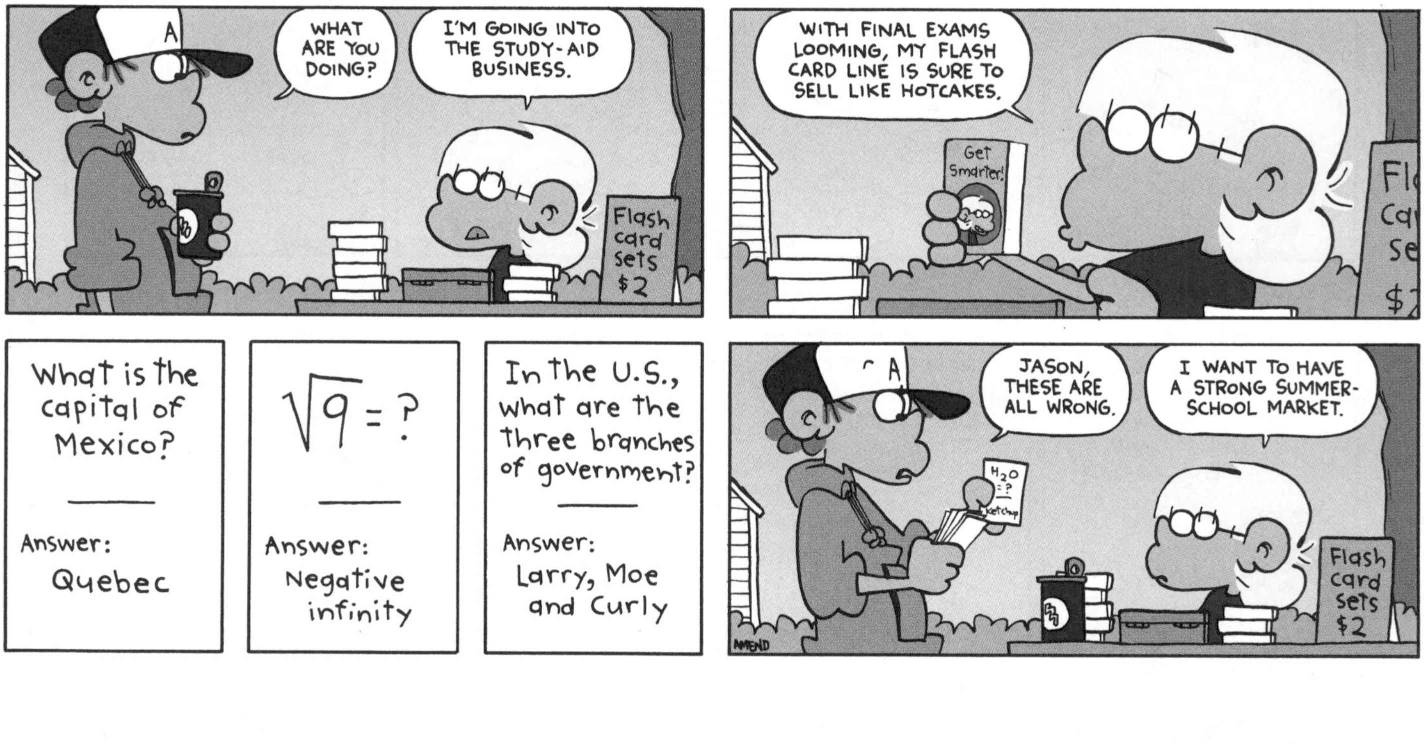

A
WHAT ARE YOU DOING?
I'M GOING INTO THE STUDY-AID BUSINESS.
Flash card sets $2
WITH FINAL EXAMS LOOMING, MY FLASH CARD LINE IS SURE TO SELL LIKE HOTCAKES.
Get Smarter!
What is the capital of Mexico?
Answer:
Quebec
√9 = ?
Answer:
Negative infinity
In the U.S., what are the three branches of government?
Answer:
Larry, Moe and Curly
JASON, THESE ARE ALL WRONG.
I WANT TO HAVE A STRONG SUMMER-SCHOOL MARKET.
Flash card sets $2
AMEND

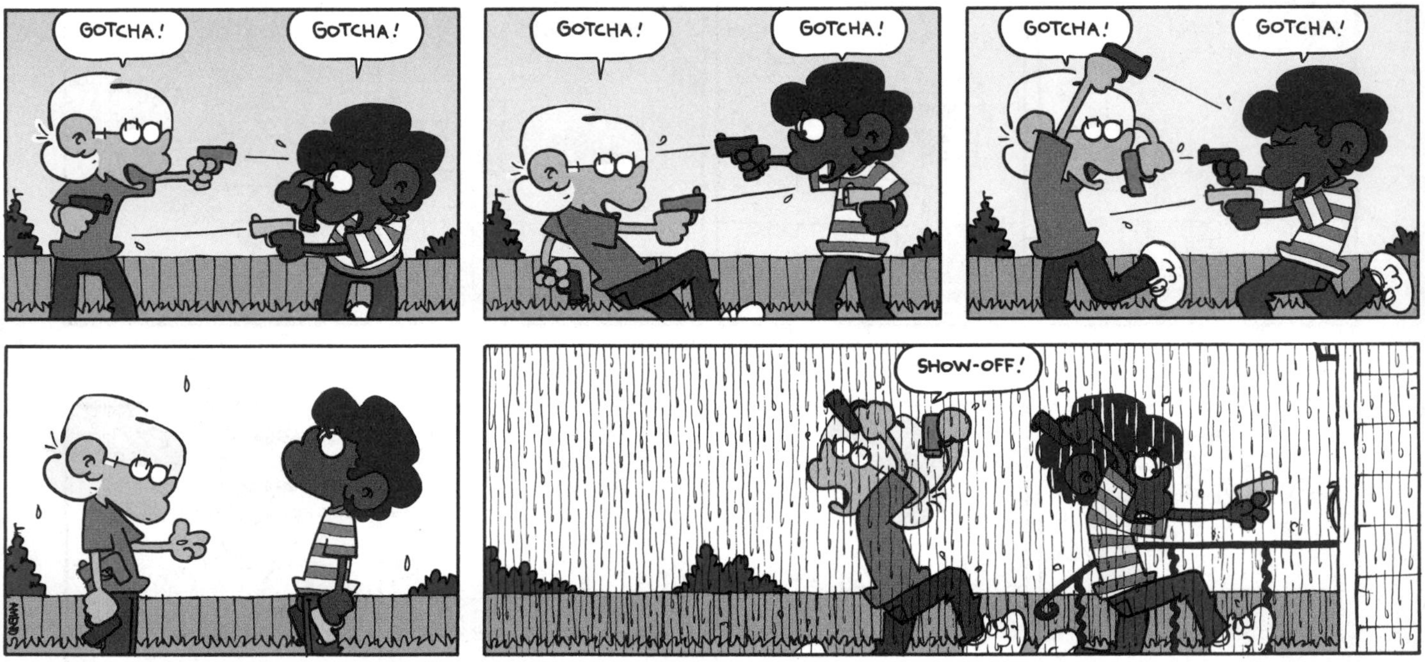
GOTCHA!
GOTCHA!
GOTCHA!
GOTCHA!
GOTCHA!
GOTCHA!
SHOW-OFF!

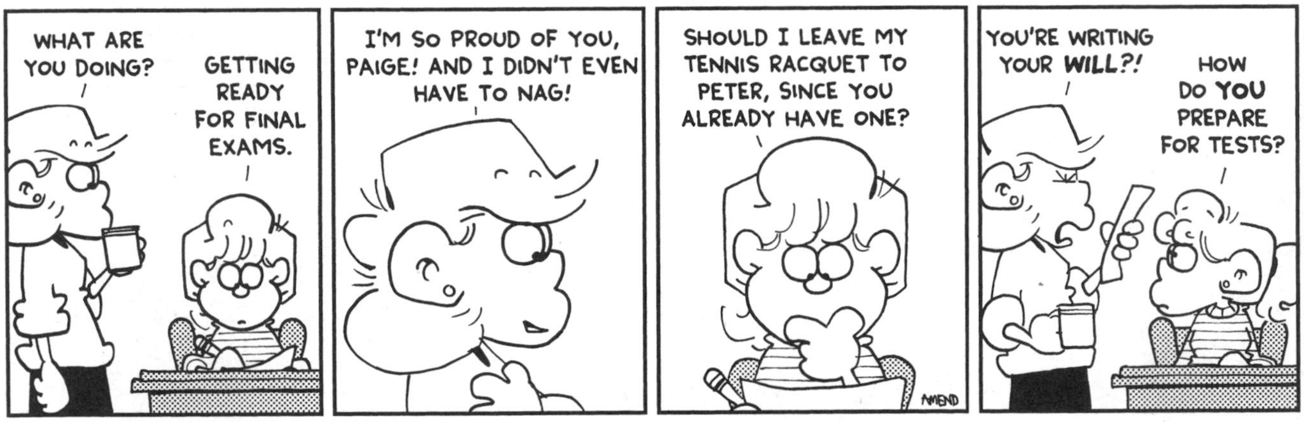
WHAT ARE YOU DOING?
GETTING READY FOR FINAL EXAMS.
I'M SO PROUD OF YOU, PAIGE! AND I DIDN'T EVEN HAVE TO NAG!
SHOULD I LEAVE MY TENNIS RACQUET TO PETER, SINCE YOU ALREADY HAVE ONE?
YOU'RE WRITING YOUR ***WILL?!***
HOW DO **YOU** PREPARE FOR TESTS?

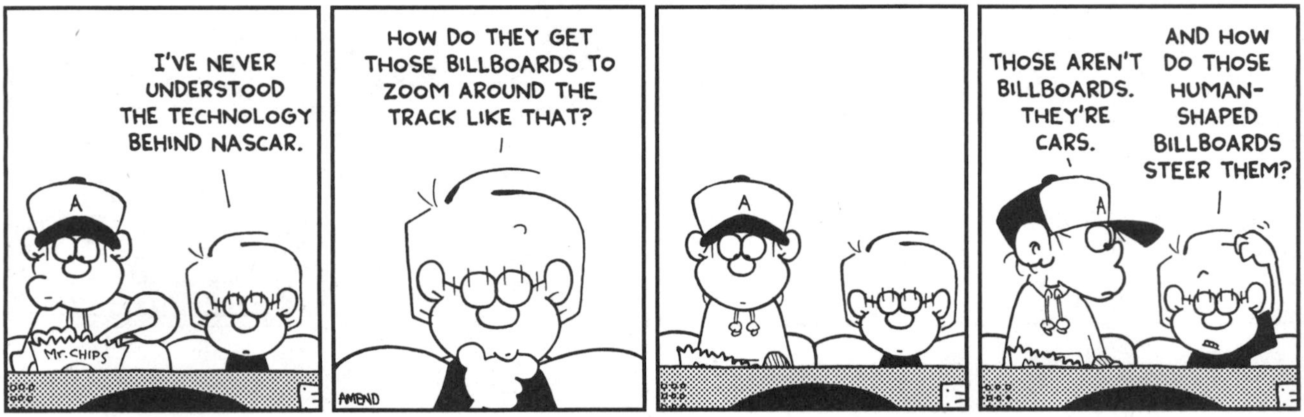
I'VE NEVER UNDERSTOOD THE TECHNOLOGY BEHIND NASCAR.
Mr. CHIPS
HOW DO THEY GET THOSE BILLBOARDS TO ZOOM AROUND THE TRACK LIKE THAT?
THOSE AREN'T BILLBOARDS. THEY'RE CARS.
AND HOW DO THOSE HUMAN-SHAPED BILLBOARDS STEER THEM?

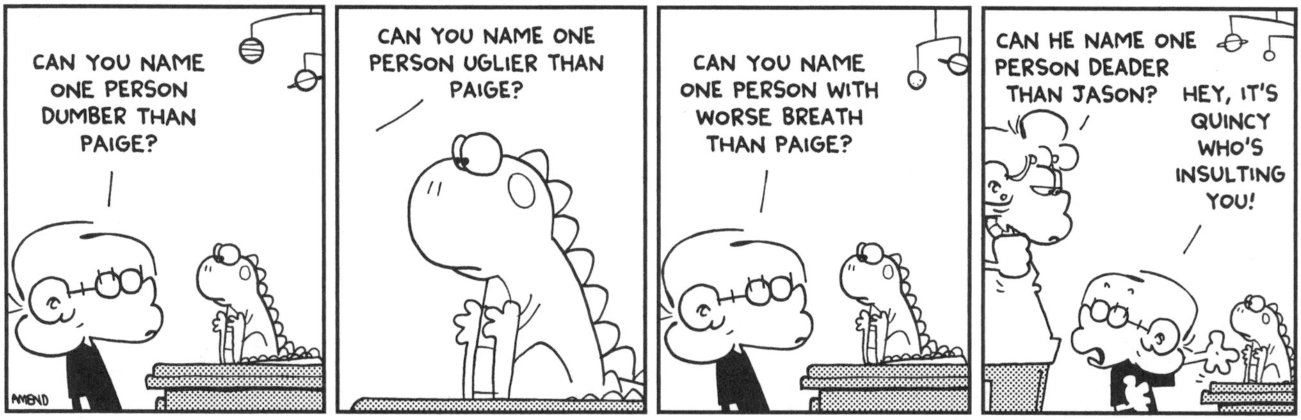
CAN YOU NAME ONE PERSON DUMBER THAN PAIGE?
CAN YOU NAME ONE PERSON UGLIER THAN PAIGE?
CAN YOU NAME ONE PERSON WITH WORSE BREATH THAN PAIGE?
CAN HE NAME ONE PERSON DEADER THAN JASON?
HEY, IT'S QUINCY WHO'S INSULTING YOU!

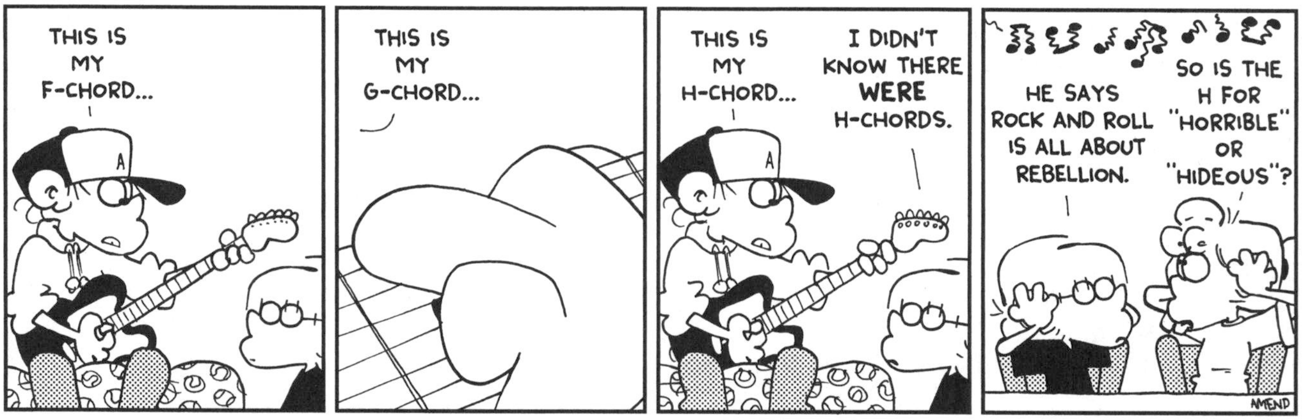
THIS IS MY F-CHORD...
THIS IS MY G-CHORD...
THIS IS MY H-CHORD...
I DIDN'T KNOW THERE **WERE** H-CHORDS.
HE SAYS ROCK AND ROLL IS ALL ABOUT REBELLION.
SO IS THE H FOR "HORRIBLE" OR "HIDEOUS"?

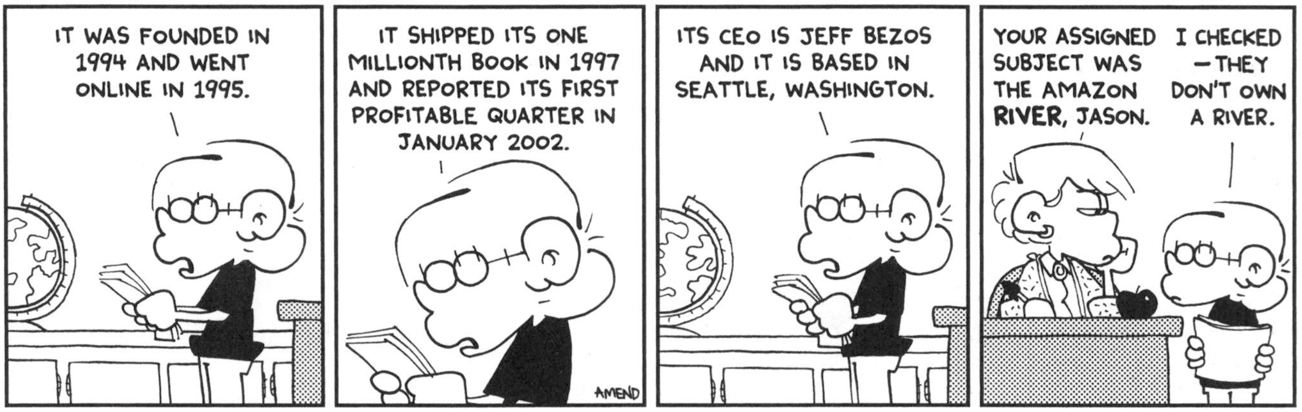
IT WAS FOUNDED IN 1994 AND WENT ONLINE IN 1995.
IT SHIPPED ITS ONE MILLIONTH BOOK IN 1997 AND REPORTED ITS FIRST PROFITABLE QUARTER IN JANUARY 2002.
ITS CEO IS JEFF BEZOS AND IT IS BASED IN SEATTLE, WASHINGTON.
YOUR ASSIGNED SUBJECT WAS THE AMAZON **RIVER**, JASON.
I CHECKED — THEY DON'T OWN A RIVER.

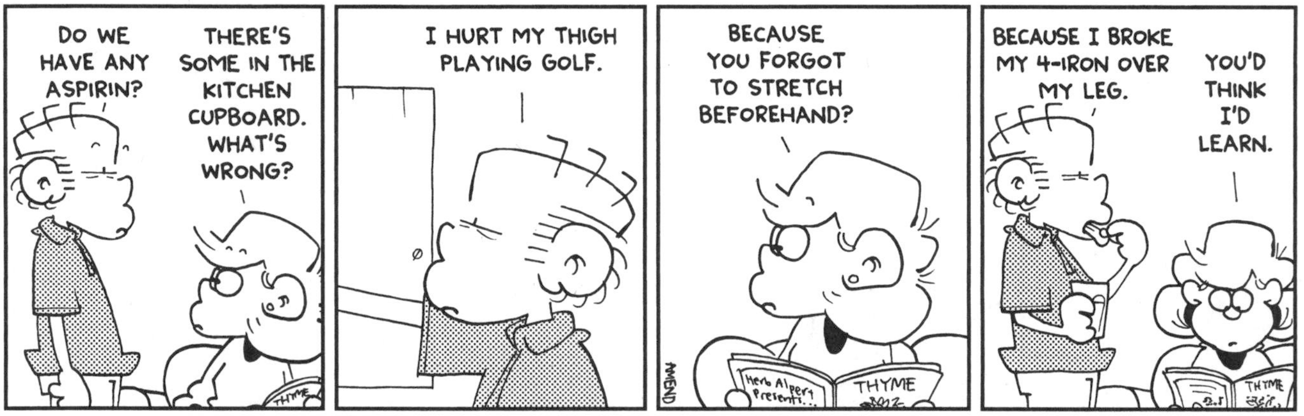
DO WE HAVE ANY ASPIRIN?
THERE'S SOME IN THE KITCHEN CUPBOARD. WHAT'S WRONG?
I HURT MY THIGH PLAYING GOLF.
BECAUSE YOU FORGOT TO STRETCH BEFOREHAND?
BECAUSE I BROKE MY 4-IRON OVER MY LEG.
YOU'D THINK I'D LEARN.

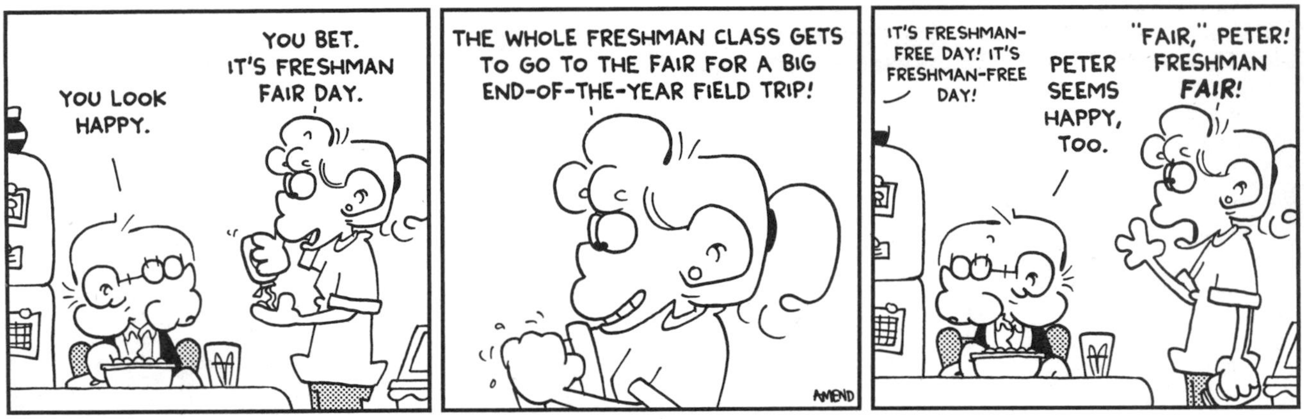
YOU LOOK HAPPY.
YOU BET. IT'S FRESHMAN FAIR DAY.
THE WHOLE FRESHMAN CLASS GETS TO GO TO THE FAIR FOR A BIG END-OF-THE-YEAR FIELD TRIP!
AMEND
IT'S FRESHMAN-FREE DAY! IT'S FRESHMAN-FREE DAY!
PETER SEEMS HAPPY, TOO.
"FAIR," PETER! FRESHMAN FAIR!

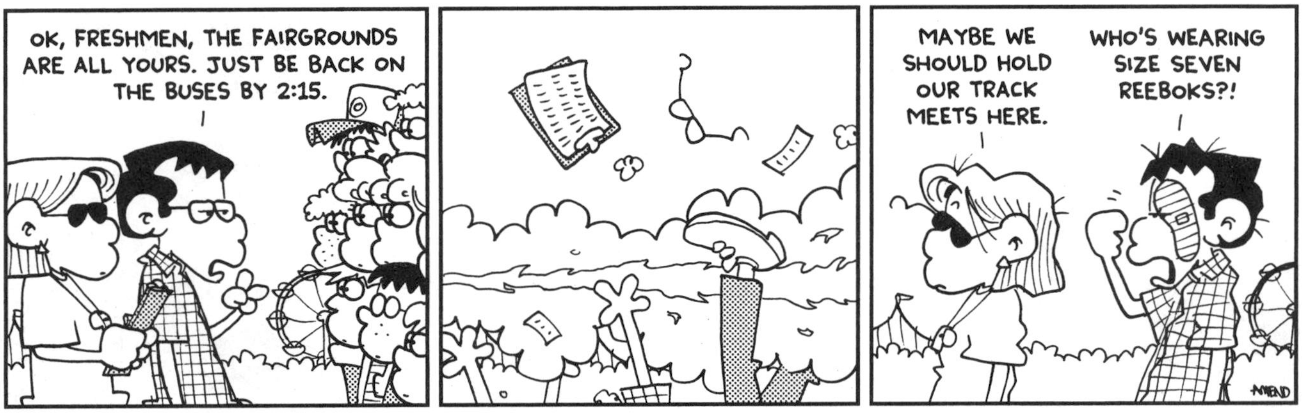
OK, FRESHMEN, THE FAIRGROUNDS ARE ALL YOURS. JUST BE BACK ON THE BUSES BY 2:15.
MAYBE WE SHOULD HOLD OUR TRACK MEETS HERE.
WHO'S WEARING SIZE SEVEN REEBOKS?!
AMEND

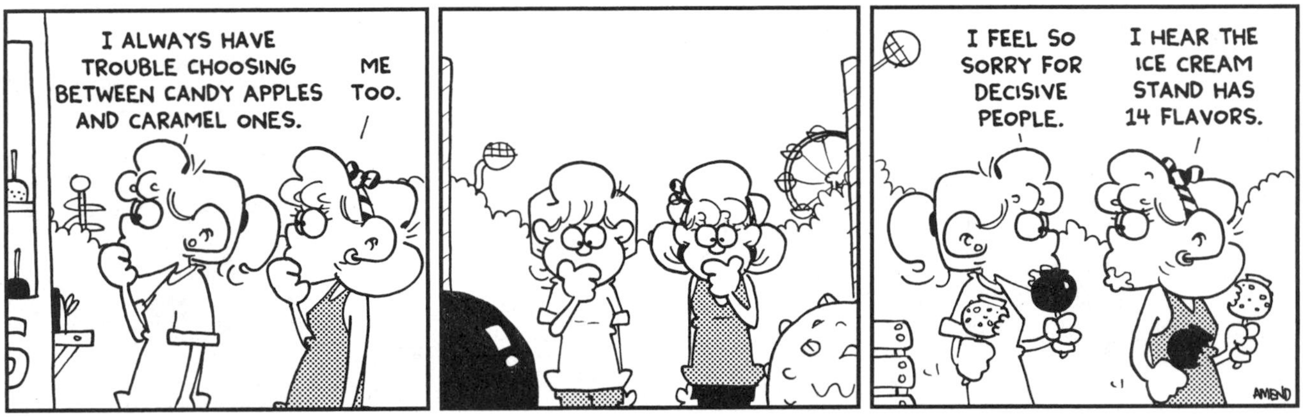
I ALWAYS HAVE TROUBLE CHOOSING BETWEEN CANDY APPLES AND CARAMEL ONES.
ME TOO.
I FEEL SO SORRY FOR DECISIVE PEOPLE.
I HEAR THE ICE CREAM STAND HAS 14 FLAVORS.
AMEND

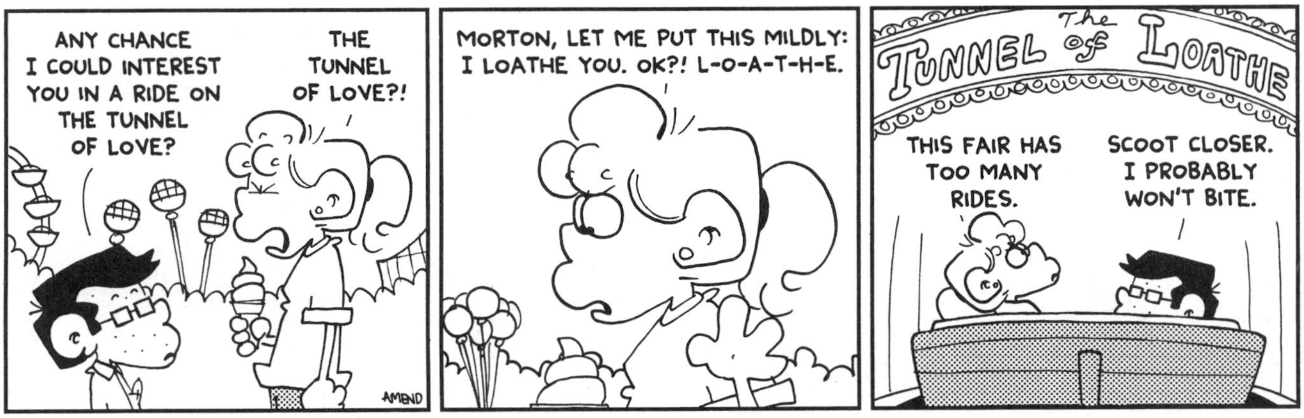
ANY CHANCE I COULD INTEREST YOU IN A RIDE ON THE TUNNEL OF LOVE?
THE TUNNEL OF LOVE?!
AMEND
MORTON, LET ME PUT THIS MILDLY: I LOATHE YOU. OK?! L-O-A-T-H-E.
The TUNNEL of LOATHE
THIS FAIR HAS TOO MANY RIDES.
SCOOT CLOSER. I PROBABLY WON'T BITE.

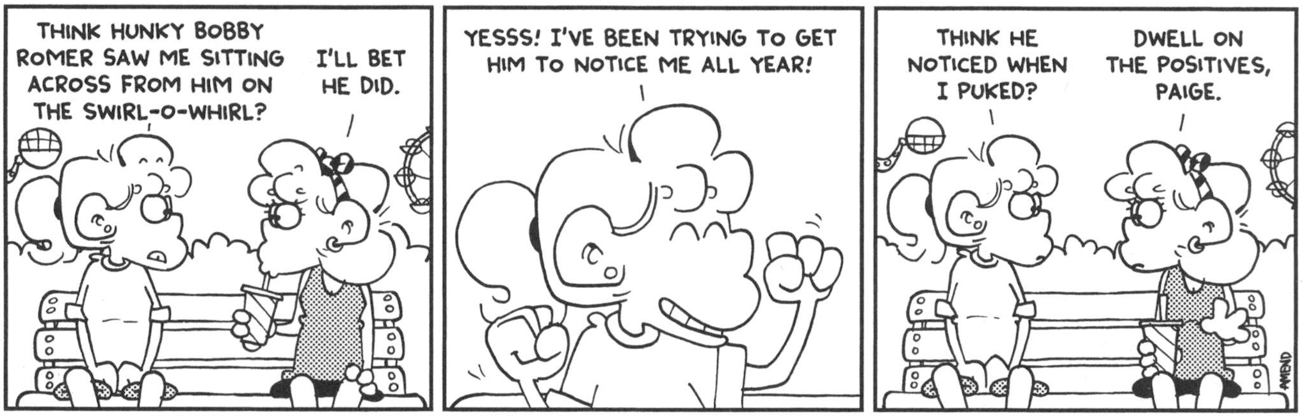
THINK HUNKY BOBBY ROMER SAW ME SITTING ACROSS FROM HIM ON THE SWIRL-O-WHIRL?
I'LL BET HE DID.
YESSS! I'VE BEEN TRYING TO GET HIM TO NOTICE ME ALL YEAR!
THINK HE NOTICED WHEN I PUKED?
DWELL ON THE POSITIVES, PAIGE.
AMEND

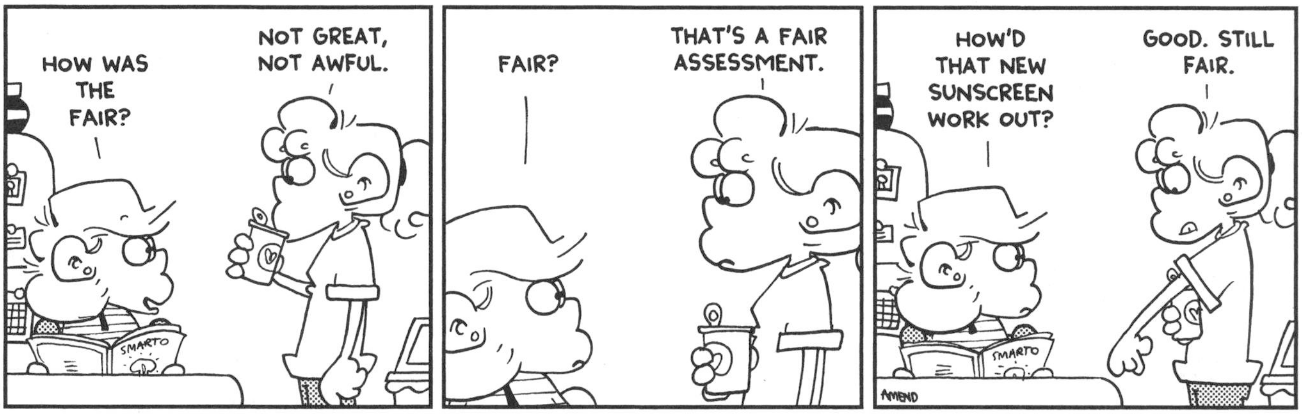
HOW WAS THE FAIR?
NOT GREAT, NOT AWFUL.
FAIR?
THAT'S A FAIR ASSESSMENT.
HOW'D THAT NEW SUNSCREEN WORK OUT?
GOOD. STILL FAIR.
SMARTO
AMEND

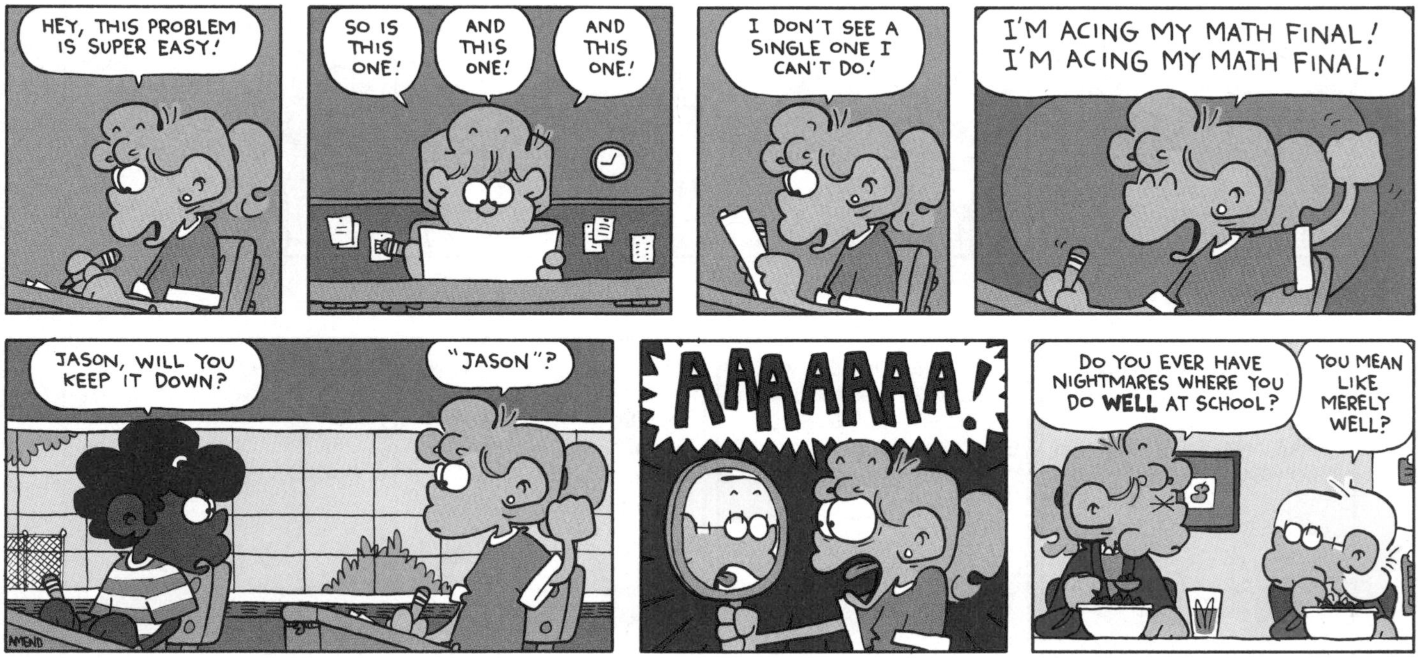
HEY, THIS PROBLEM IS SUPER EASY!
SO IS THIS ONE!
AND THIS ONE!
AND THIS ONE!
I DON'T SEE A SINGLE ONE I CAN'T DO!
I'M ACING MY MATH FINAL! I'M ACING MY MATH FINAL!
JASON, WILL YOU KEEP IT DOWN?
"JASON"?
AAAAAAA!
DO YOU EVER HAVE NIGHTMARES WHERE YOU DO **WELL** AT SCHOOL?
YOU MEAN LIKE MERELY WELL?
AMEND

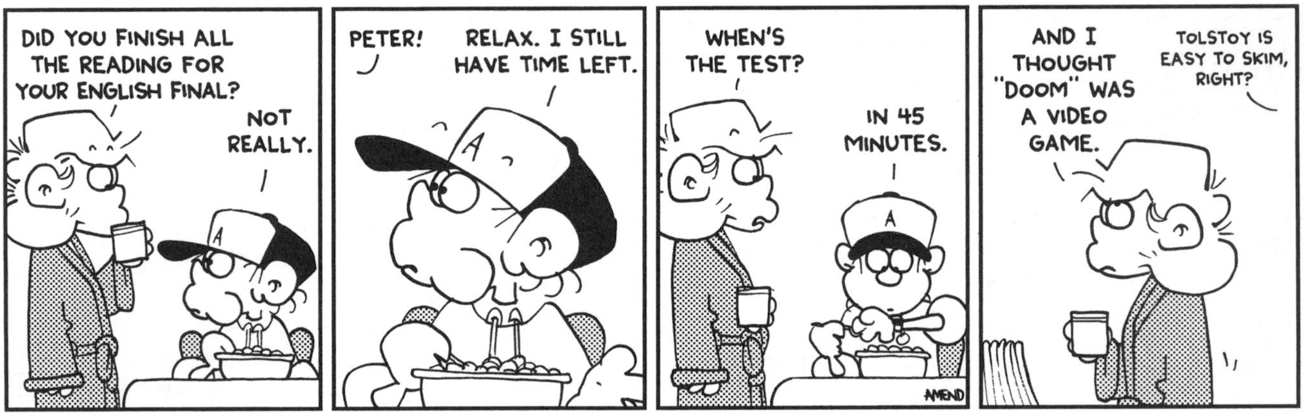
DID YOU FINISH ALL THE READING FOR YOUR ENGLISH FINAL?
NOT REALLY.
PETER!
RELAX. I STILL HAVE TIME LEFT.
WHEN'S THE TEST?
IN 45 MINUTES.
AND I THOUGHT "DOOM" WAS A VIDEO GAME.
TOLSTOY IS EASY TO SKIM, RIGHT?
AMEND

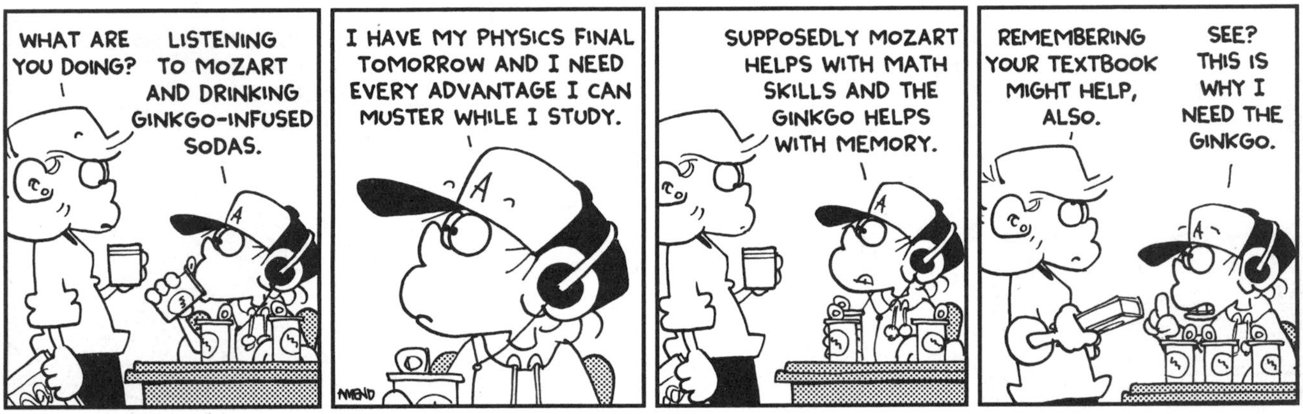
WHAT ARE YOU DOING?
LISTENING TO MOZART AND DRINKING GINKGO-INFUSED SODAS.
I HAVE MY PHYSICS FINAL TOMORROW AND I NEED EVERY ADVANTAGE I CAN MUSTER WHILE I STUDY.
SUPPOSEDLY MOZART HELPS WITH MATH SKILLS AND THE GINKGO HELPS WITH MEMORY.
REMEMBERING YOUR TEXTBOOK MIGHT HELP, ALSO.
SEE? THIS IS WHY I NEED THE GINKGO.
AMEND

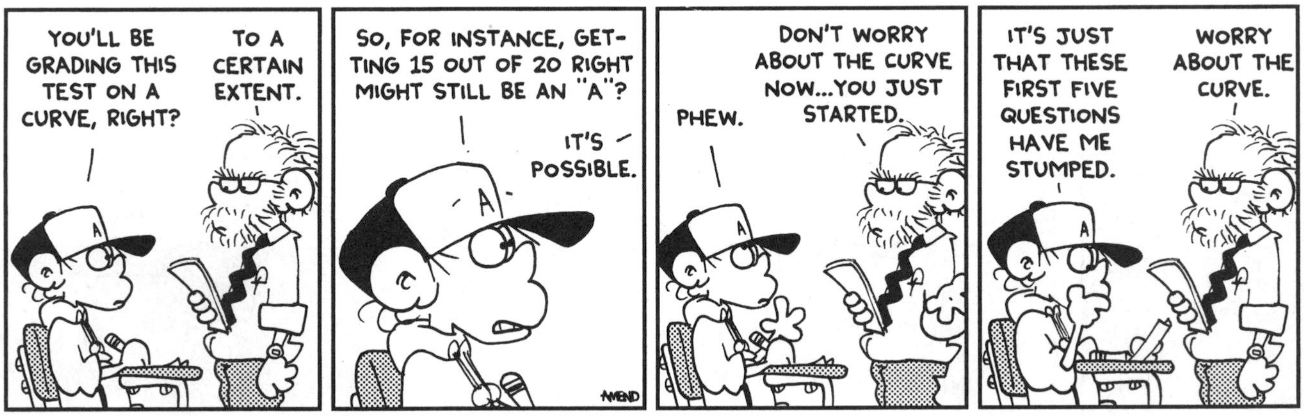
YOU'LL BE GRADING THIS TEST ON A CURVE, RIGHT?
TO A CERTAIN EXTENT.
SO, FOR INSTANCE, GETTING 15 OUT OF 20 RIGHT MIGHT STILL BE AN "A"?
IT'S POSSIBLE.
PHEW.
DON'T WORRY ABOUT THE CURVE NOW...YOU JUST STARTED.
IT'S JUST THAT THESE FIRST FIVE QUESTIONS HAVE ME STUMPED.
WORRY ABOUT THE CURVE.
AMEND

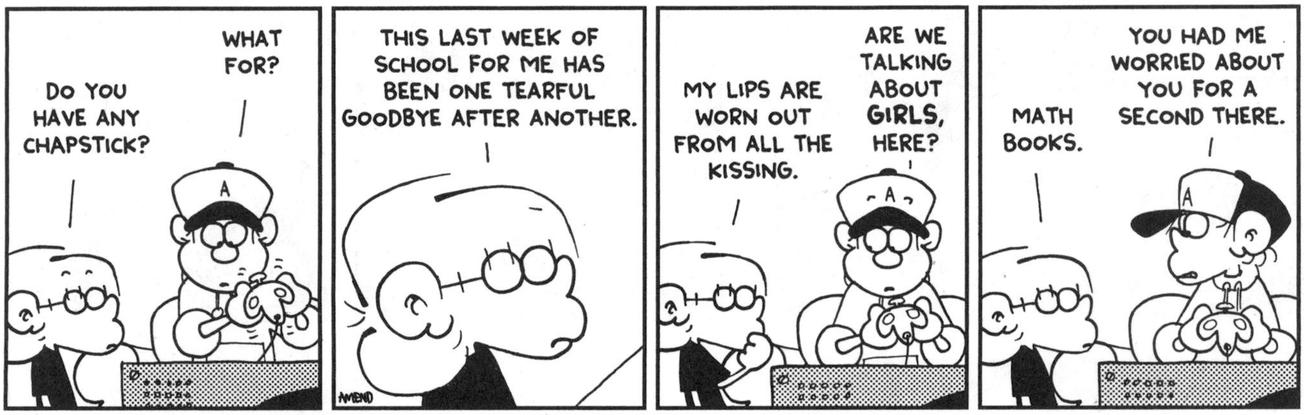
DO YOU HAVE ANY CHAPSTICK?
WHAT FOR?
THIS LAST WEEK OF SCHOOL FOR ME HAS BEEN ONE TEARFUL GOODBYE AFTER ANOTHER.
MY LIPS ARE WORN OUT FROM ALL THE KISSING.
ARE WE TALKING ABOUT GIRLS, HERE?
MATH BOOKS.
YOU HAD ME WORRIED ABOUT YOU FOR A SECOND THERE.
AMEND

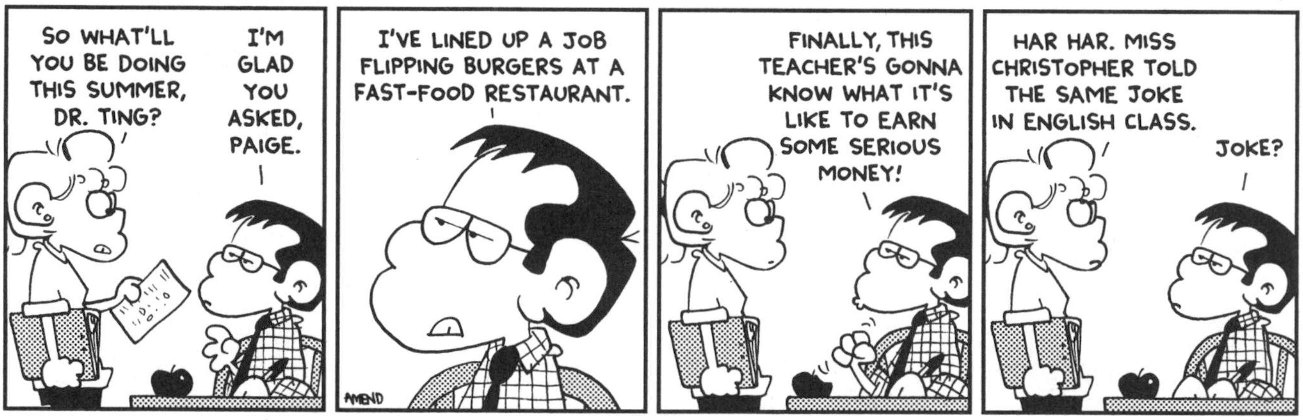
SO WHAT'LL YOU BE DOING THIS SUMMER, DR. TING?
I'M GLAD YOU ASKED, PAIGE.
I'VE LINED UP A JOB FLIPPING BURGERS AT A FAST-FOOD RESTAURANT.
FINALLY, THIS TEACHER'S GONNA KNOW WHAT IT'S LIKE TO EARN SOME SERIOUS MONEY!
HAR HAR. MISS CHRISTOPHER TOLD THE SAME JOKE IN ENGLISH CLASS.
JOKE?

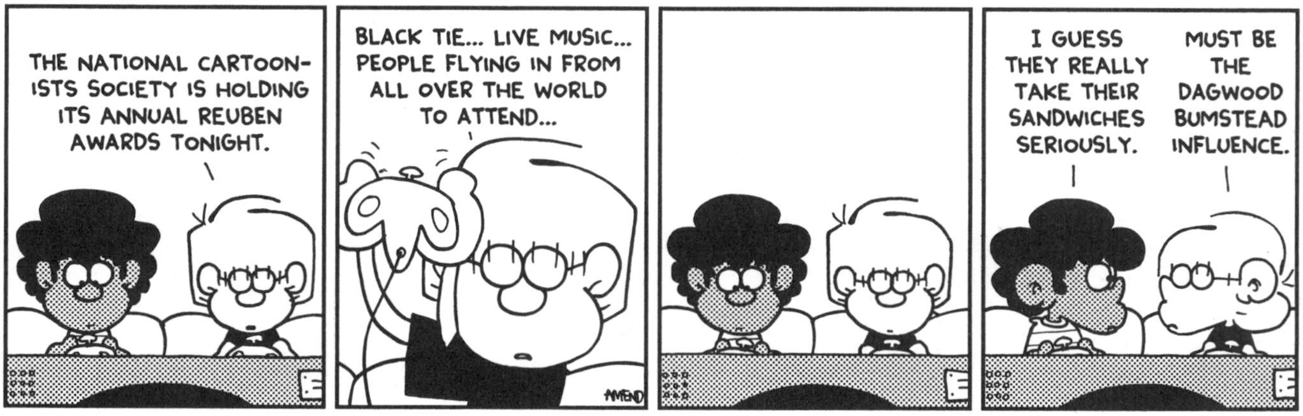
THE NATIONAL CARTOONISTS SOCIETY IS HOLDING ITS ANNUAL REUBEN AWARDS TONIGHT.
BLACK TIE... LIVE MUSIC... PEOPLE FLYING IN FROM ALL OVER THE WORLD TO ATTEND...
I GUESS THEY REALLY TAKE THEIR SANDWICHES SERIOUSLY.
MUST BE THE DAGWOOD BUMSTEAD INFLUENCE.

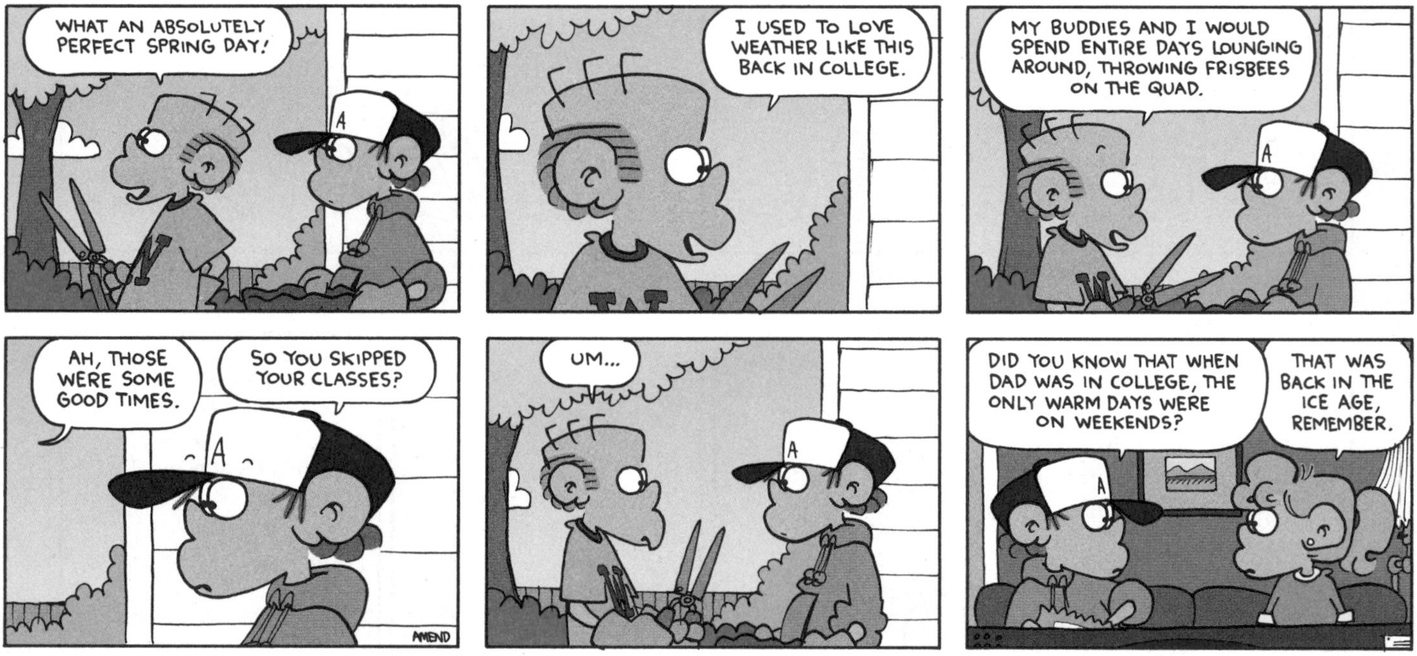
WHAT AN ABSOLUTELY PERFECT SPRING DAY!
I USED TO LOVE WEATHER LIKE THIS BACK IN COLLEGE.
MY BUDDIES AND I WOULD SPEND ENTIRE DAYS LOUNGING AROUND, THROWING FRISBEES ON THE QUAD.
AH, THOSE WERE SOME GOOD TIMES.
SO YOU SKIPPED YOUR CLASSES?
UM...
DID YOU KNOW THAT WHEN DAD WAS IN COLLEGE, THE ONLY WARM DAYS WERE ON WEEKENDS?
THAT WAS BACK IN THE ICE AGE, REMEMBER.

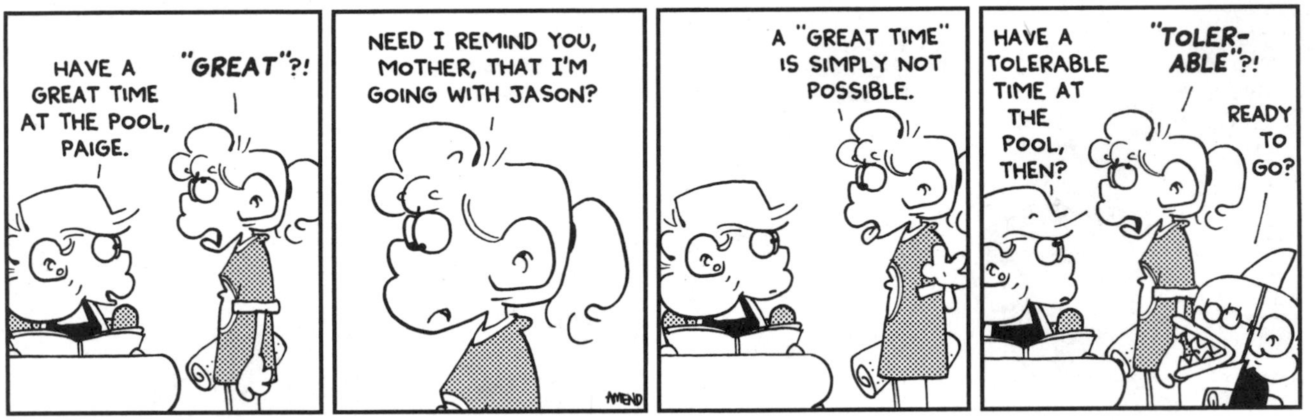
HAVE A GREAT TIME AT THE POOL, PAIGE.
"GREAT"?!
NEED I REMIND YOU, MOTHER, THAT I'M GOING WITH JASON?
A "GREAT TIME" IS SIMPLY NOT POSSIBLE.
HAVE A TOLERABLE TIME AT THE POOL, THEN?
"TOLERABLE"?!
READY TO GO?
AMEND

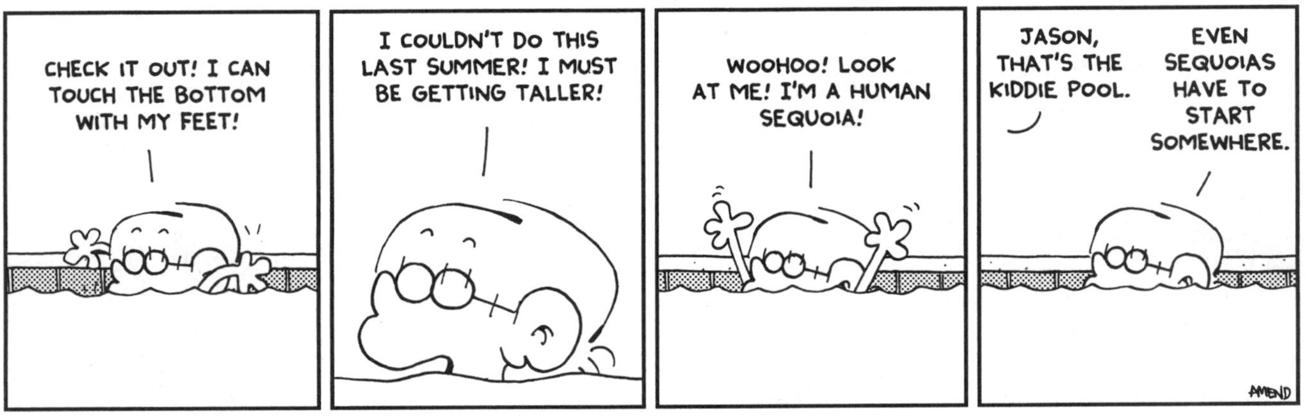
CHECK IT OUT! I CAN TOUCH THE BOTTOM WITH MY FEET!
I COULDN'T DO THIS LAST SUMMER! I MUST BE GETTING TALLER!
WOOHOO! LOOK AT ME! I'M A HUMAN SEQUOIA!
JASON, THAT'S THE KIDDIE POOL.
EVEN SEQUOIAS HAVE TO START SOMEWHERE.
AMEND

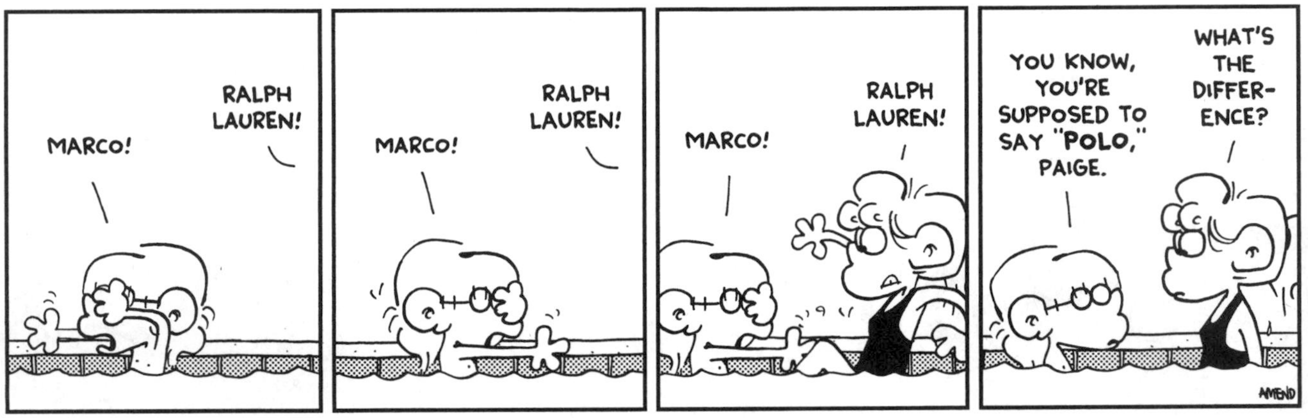
MARCO!
RALPH LAUREN!
MARCO!
RALPH LAUREN!
MARCO!
RALPH LAUREN!
YOU KNOW, YOU'RE SUPPOSED TO SAY "POLO," PAIGE.
WHAT'S THE DIFFERENCE?
AMEND

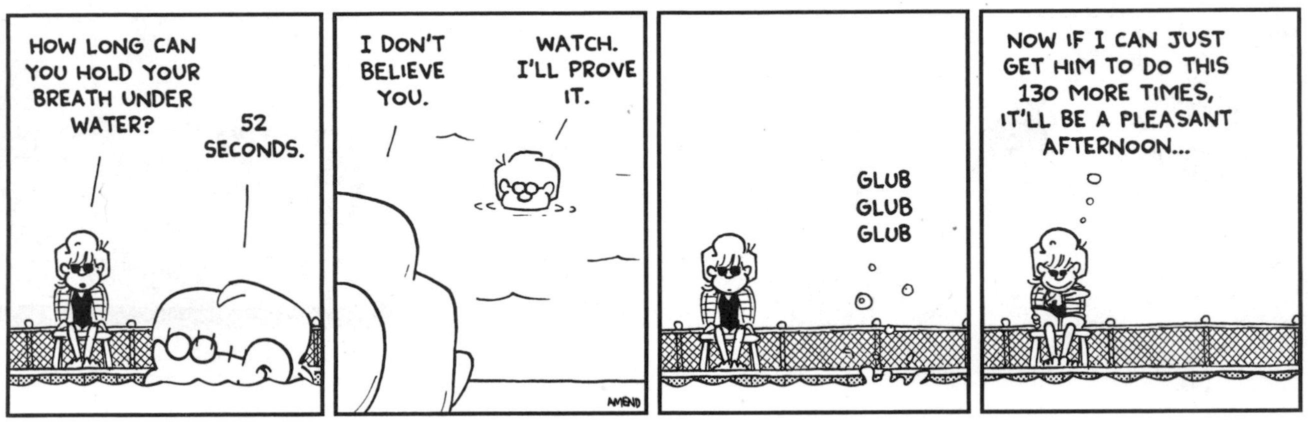
HOW LONG CAN YOU HOLD YOUR BREATH UNDER WATER?
52 SECONDS.
I DON'T BELIEVE YOU.
WATCH. I'LL PROVE IT.
AMEND
GLUB
GLUB
GLUB
NOW IF I CAN JUST GET HIM TO DO THIS 130 MORE TIMES, IT'LL BE A PLEASANT AFTERNOON...

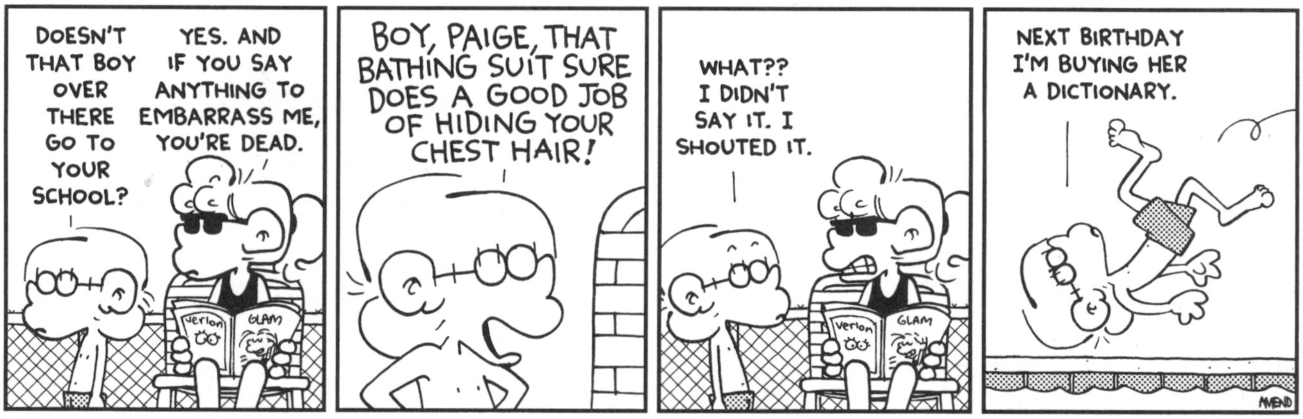
DOESN'T THAT BOY OVER THERE GO TO YOUR SCHOOL?
YES. AND IF YOU SAY ANYTHING TO EMBARRASS ME, YOU'RE DEAD.
BOY, PAIGE, THAT BATHING SUIT SURE DOES A GOOD JOB OF HIDING YOUR CHEST HAIR!
WHAT?? I DIDN'T SAY IT. I SHOUTED IT.
NEXT BIRTHDAY I'M BUYING HER A DICTIONARY.
AMEND

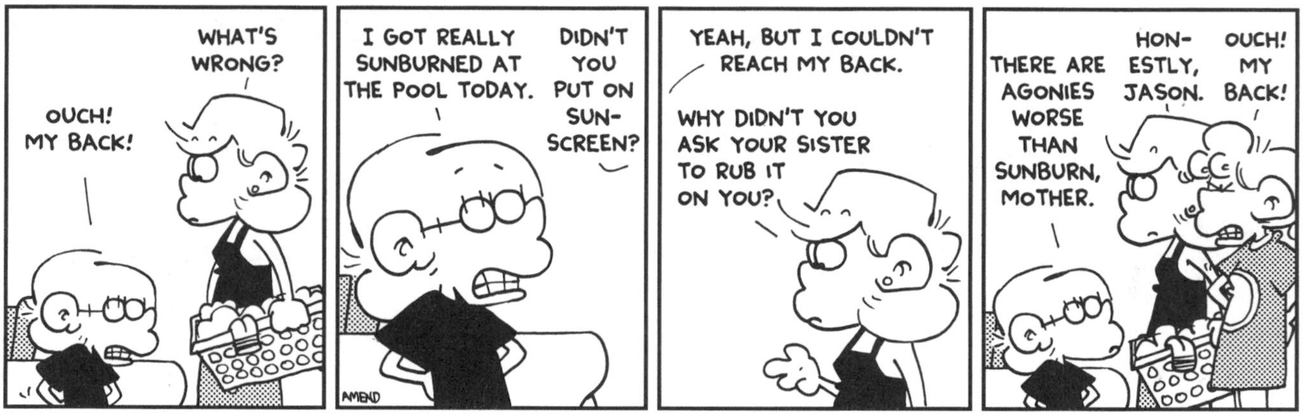
OUCH! MY BACK!
WHAT'S WRONG?
I GOT REALLY SUNBURNED AT THE POOL TODAY.
DIDN'T YOU PUT ON SUN-SCREEN?
AMEND
YEAH, BUT I COULDN'T REACH MY BACK.
WHY DIDN'T YOU ASK YOUR SISTER TO RUB IT ON YOU?
THERE ARE AGONIES WORSE THAN SUNBURN, MOTHER.
HON-ESTLY, JASON.
OUCH! MY BACK!

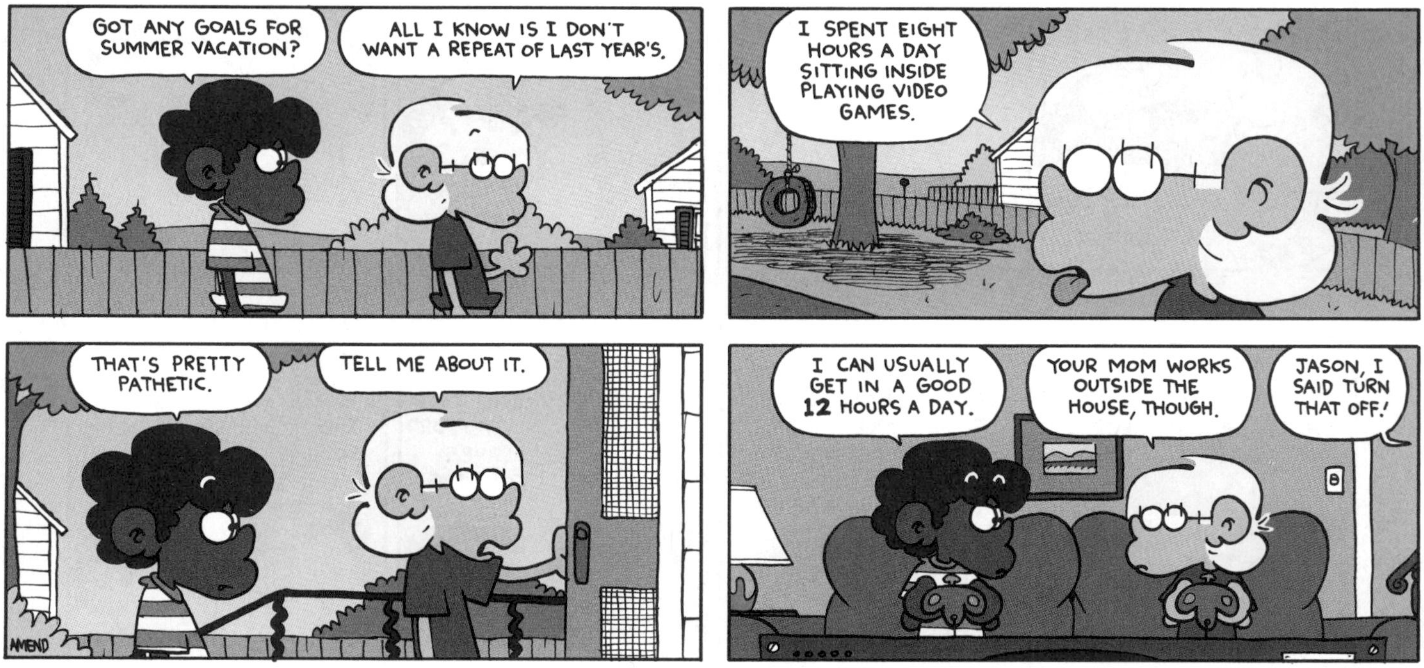
GOT ANY GOALS FOR SUMMER VACATION?
ALL I KNOW IS I DON'T WANT A REPEAT OF LAST YEAR'S.
I SPENT EIGHT HOURS A DAY SITTING INSIDE PLAYING VIDEO GAMES.
THAT'S PRETTY PATHETIC.
TELL ME ABOUT IT.
AMEND
I CAN USUALLY GET IN A GOOD 12 HOURS A DAY.
YOUR MOM WORKS OUTSIDE THE HOUSE, THOUGH.
JASON, I SAID TURN THAT OFF!

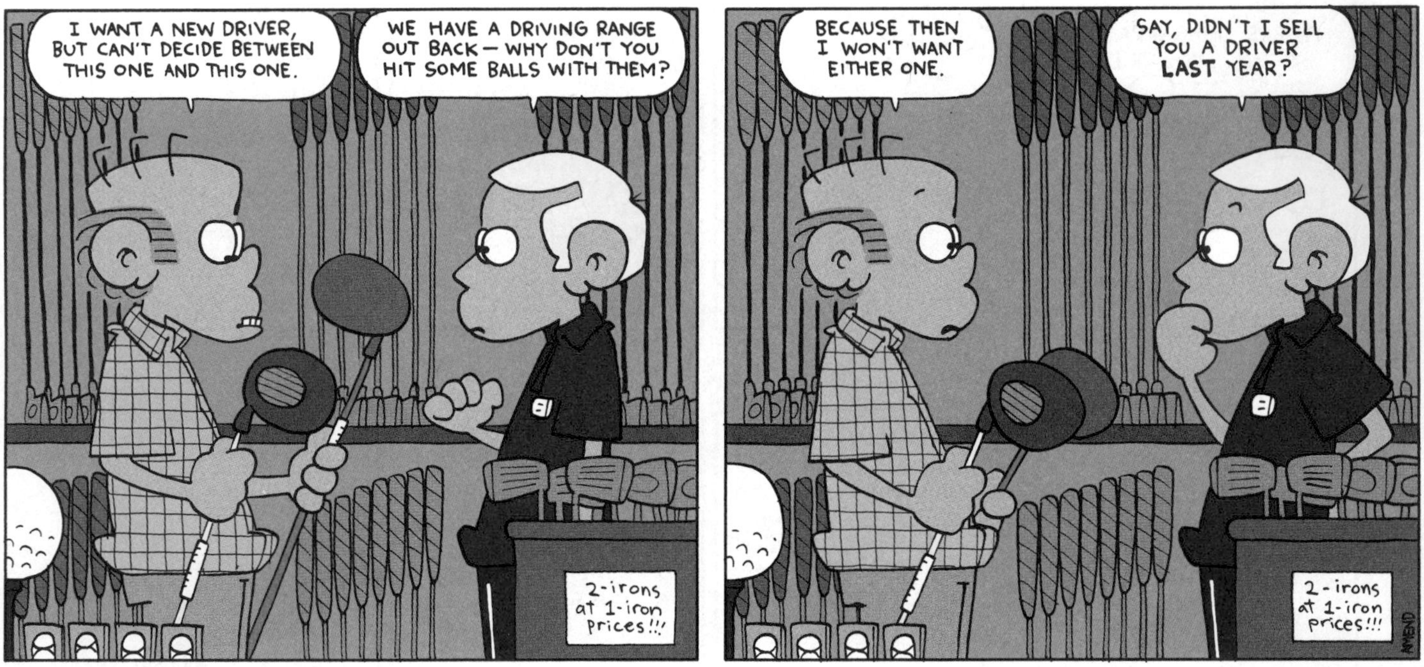
I WANT A NEW DRIVER, BUT CAN'T DECIDE BETWEEN THIS ONE AND THIS ONE.
WE HAVE A DRIVING RANGE OUT BACK — WHY DON'T YOU HIT SOME BALLS WITH THEM?
2-irons at 1-iron prices!!!
BECAUSE THEN I WON'T WANT EITHER ONE.
SAY, DIDN'T I SELL YOU A DRIVER LAST YEAR?
2-irons at 1-iron prices!!!
AMEND

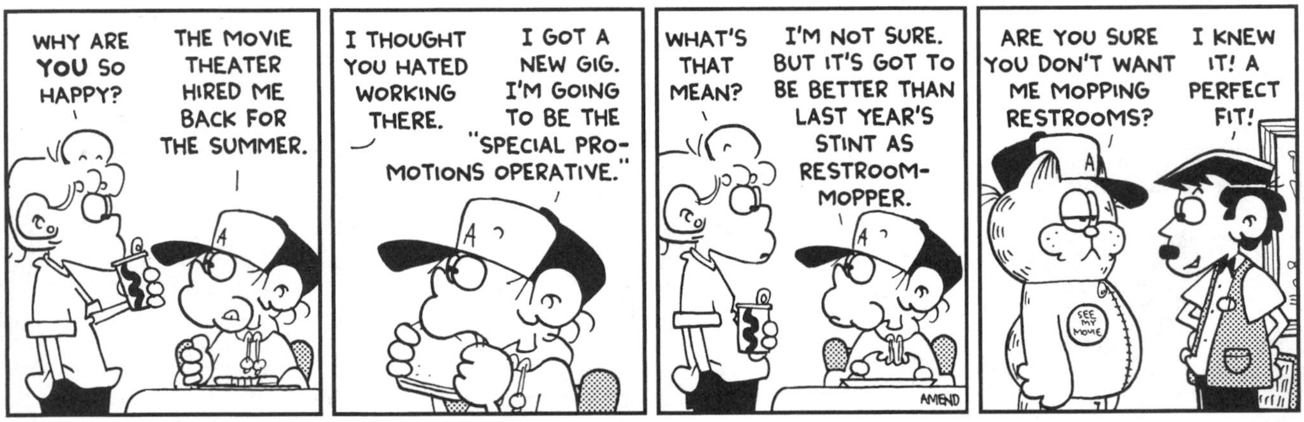
WHY ARE YOU SO HAPPY?
THE MOVIE THEATER HIRED ME BACK FOR THE SUMMER.
I THOUGHT YOU HATED WORKING THERE.
I GOT A NEW GIG. I'M GOING TO BE THE "SPECIAL PROMOTIONS OPERATIVE."
WHAT'S THAT MEAN?
I'M NOT SURE. BUT IT'S GOT TO BE BETTER THAN LAST YEAR'S STINT AS RESTROOM-MOPPER.
AMEND
ARE YOU SURE YOU DON'T WANT ME MOPPING RESTROOMS?
I KNEW IT! A PERFECT FIT!
SEE MY MOVIE

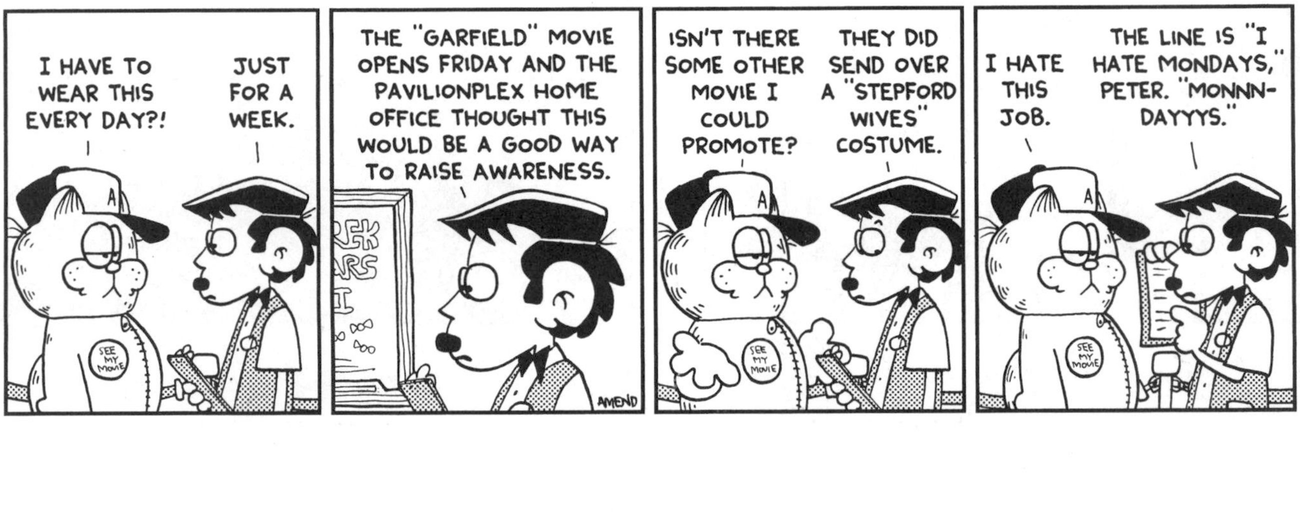
I HAVE TO WEAR THIS EVERY DAY?!
JUST FOR A WEEK.
SEE MY MOVIE
THE "GARFIELD" MOVIE OPENS FRIDAY AND THE PAVILIONPLEX HOME OFFICE THOUGHT THIS WOULD BE A GOOD WAY TO RAISE AWARENESS.
AMEND
ISN'T THERE SOME OTHER MOVIE I COULD PROMOTE?
THEY DID SEND OVER A "STEPFORD WIVES" COSTUME.
SEE MY MOVIE
I HATE THIS JOB.
THE LINE IS "I HATE MONDAYS," PETER. "MONNN-DAYYYS."
SEE MY MOVIE

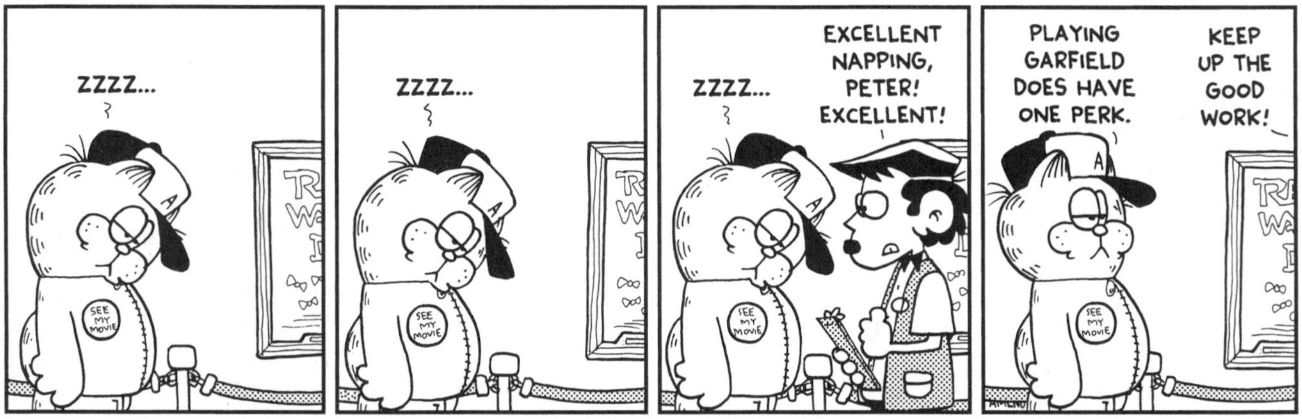
ZZZZ...
ZZZZ...
ZZZZ...
EXCELLENT NAPPING, PETER! EXCELLENT!
PLAYING GARFIELD DOES HAVE ONE PERK.
KEEP UP THE GOOD WORK!
SEE MY MOVIE

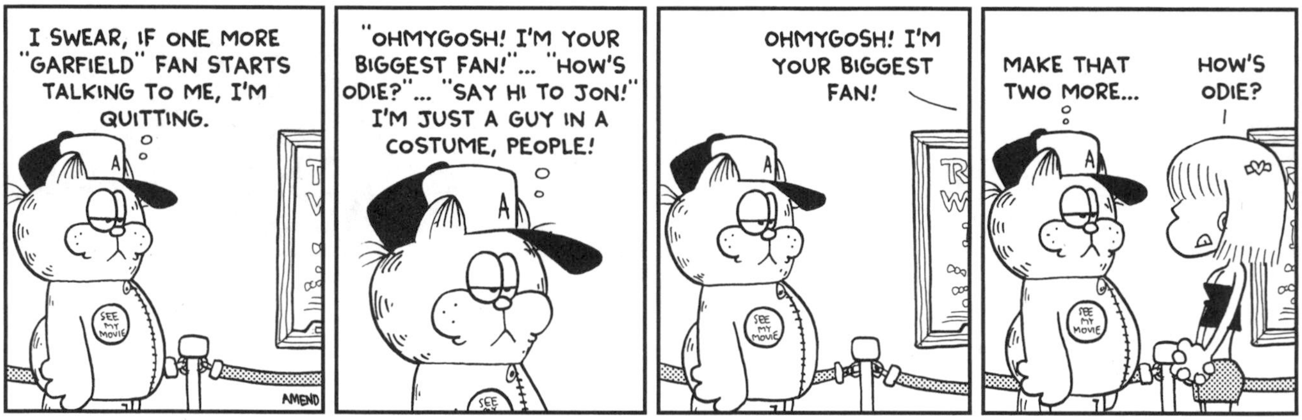
I SWEAR, IF ONE MORE "GARFIELD" FAN STARTS TALKING TO ME, I'M QUITTING.
"OHMYGOSH! I'M YOUR BIGGEST FAN!"... "HOW'S ODIE?"... "SAY HI TO JON!" I'M JUST A GUY IN A COSTUME, PEOPLE!
OHMYGOSH! I'M YOUR BIGGEST FAN!
MAKE THAT TWO MORE...
HOW'S ODIE?
AMEND

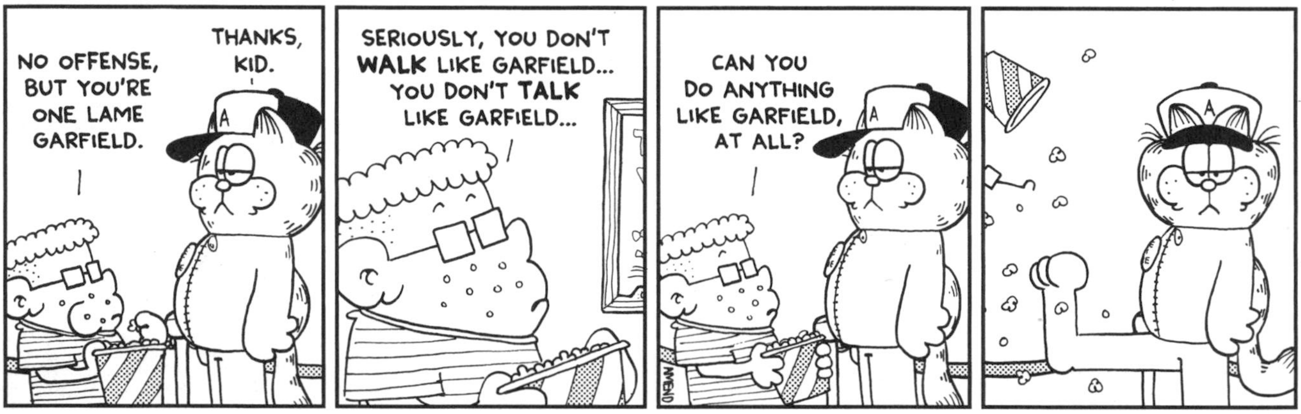
NO OFFENSE, BUT YOU'RE ONE LAME GARFIELD.
THANKS, KID.
SERIOUSLY, YOU DON'T WALK LIKE GARFIELD... YOU DON'T TALK LIKE GARFIELD...
CAN YOU DO ANYTHING LIKE GARFIELD, AT ALL?
AMEND

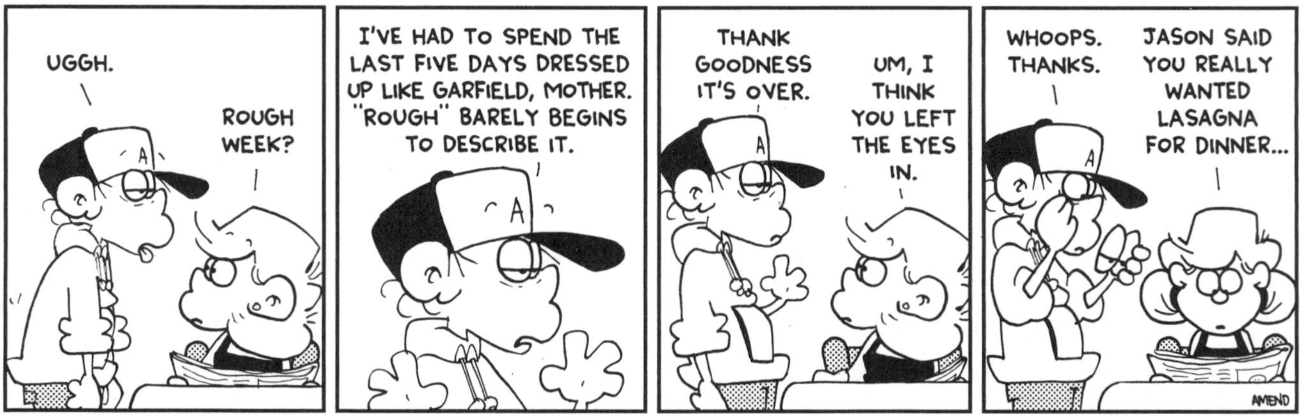
UGGH.
ROUGH WEEK?
I'VE HAD TO SPEND THE LAST FIVE DAYS DRESSED UP LIKE GARFIELD, MOTHER. "ROUGH" BARELY BEGINS TO DESCRIBE IT.
THANK GOODNESS IT'S OVER.
UM, I THINK YOU LEFT THE EYES IN.
WHOOPS. THANKS.
JASON SAID YOU REALLY WANTED LASAGNA FOR DINNER...
AMEND

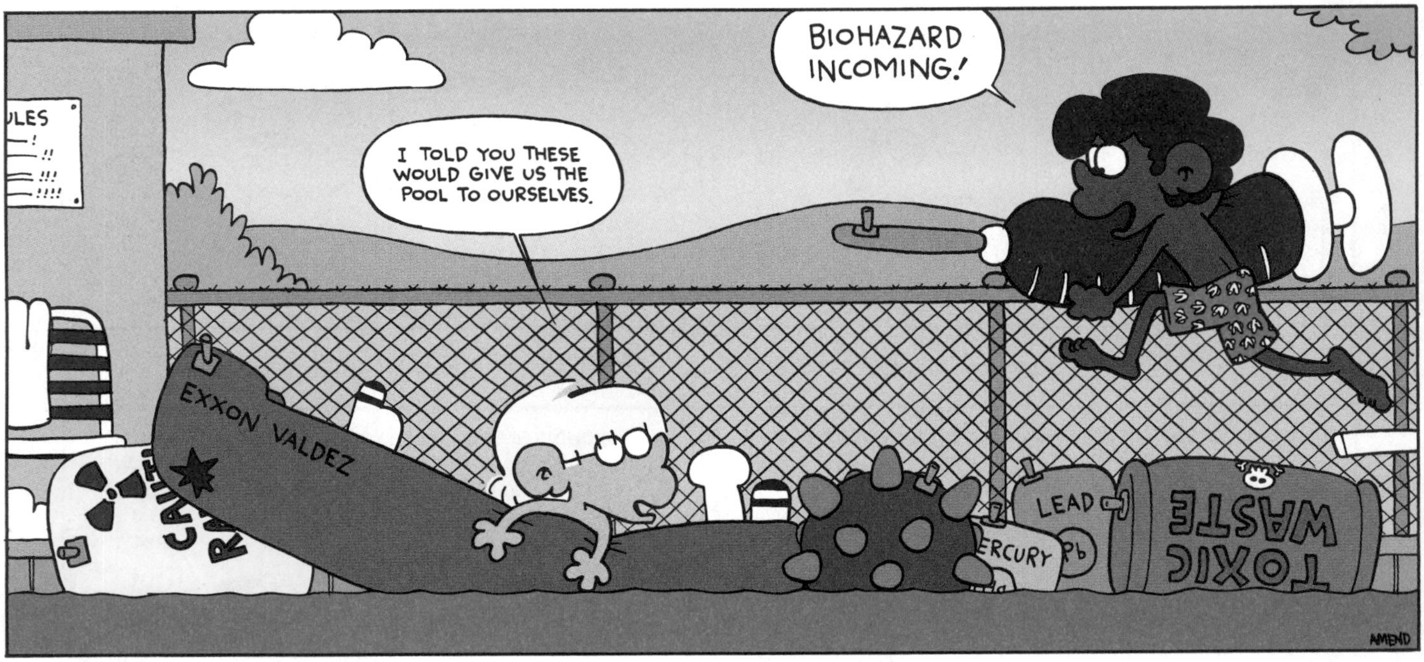
I TOLD YOU THESE WOULD GIVE US THE POOL TO OURSELVES.
BIOHAZARD INCOMING!
EXXON VALDEZ
LEAD
Pb
AMEND

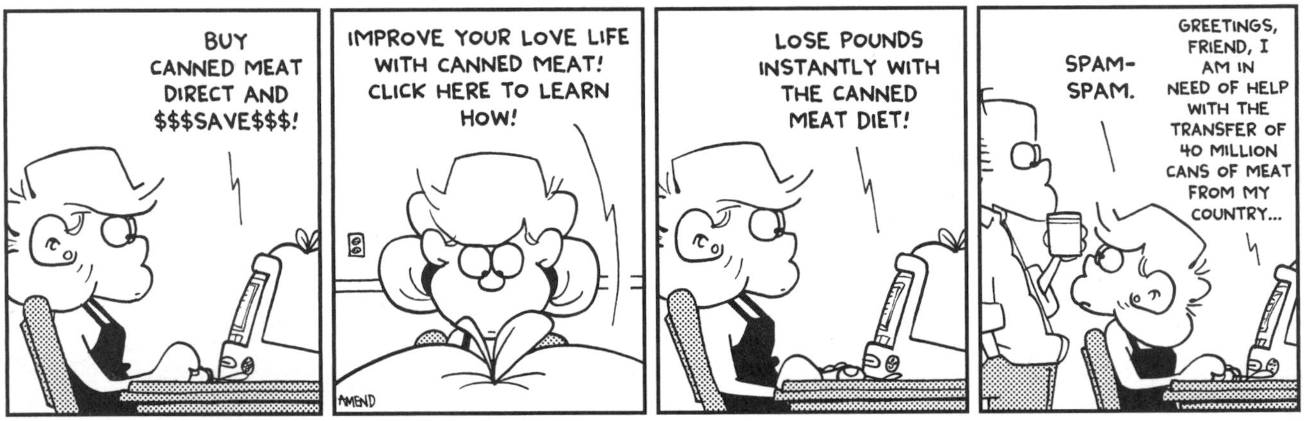
BUY CANNED MEAT DIRECT AND $$$SAVE$$$!
IMPROVE YOUR LOVE LIFE WITH CANNED MEAT! CLICK HERE TO LEARN HOW!
AMEND
LOSE POUNDS INSTANTLY WITH THE CANNED MEAT DIET!
SPAM-SPAM.
GREETINGS, FRIEND, I AM IN NEED OF HELP WITH THE TRANSFER OF 40 MILLION CANS OF MEAT FROM MY COUNTRY...

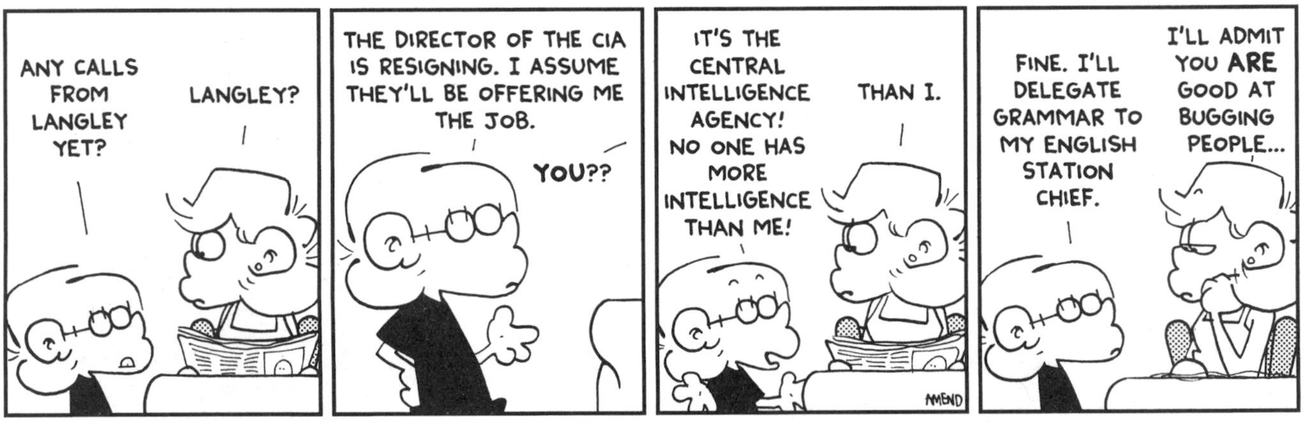
ANY CALLS FROM LANGLEY YET?
LANGLEY?
THE DIRECTOR OF THE CIA IS RESIGNING. I ASSUME THEY'LL BE OFFERING ME THE JOB.
YOU??
IT'S THE CENTRAL INTELLIGENCE AGENCY! NO ONE HAS MORE INTELLIGENCE THAN ME!
THAN I.
AMEND
FINE. I'LL DELEGATE GRAMMAR TO MY ENGLISH STATION CHIEF.
I'LL ADMIT YOU ARE GOOD AT BUGGING PEOPLE...

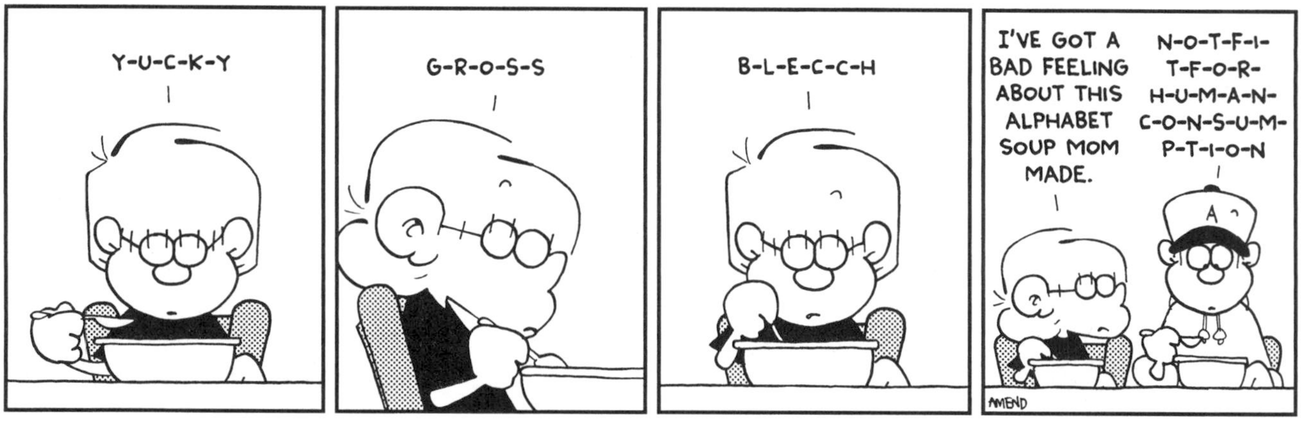
Y-U-C-K-Y
G-R-O-S-S
B-L-E-C-C-H
I'VE GOT A BAD FEELING ABOUT THIS ALPHABET SOUP MOM MADE.
N-O-T-F-I-T-F-O-R-H-U-M-A-N-C-O-N-S-U-M-P-T-I-O-N
AMEND

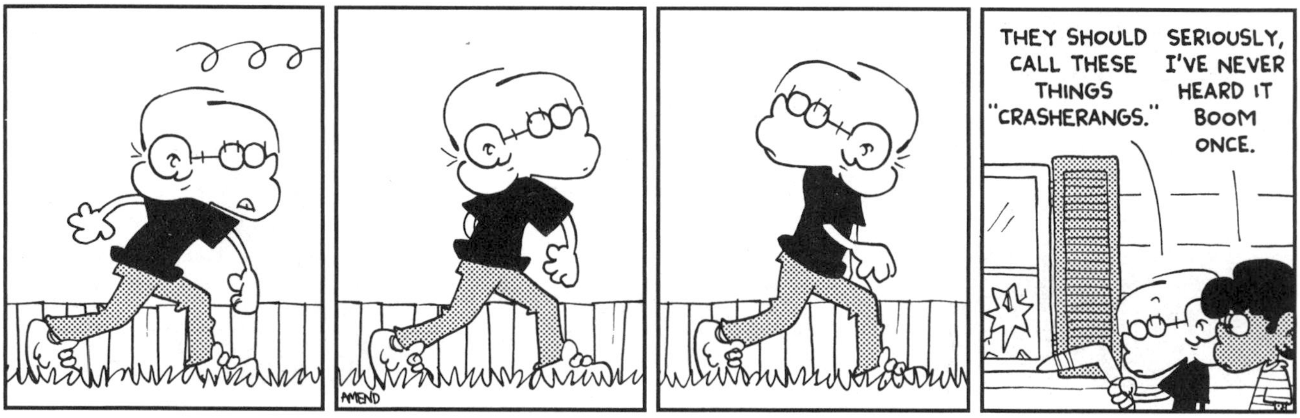
AMEND
THEY SHOULD CALL THESE THINGS "CRASHERANGS."
SERIOUSLY, I'VE NEVER HEARD IT BOOM ONCE.

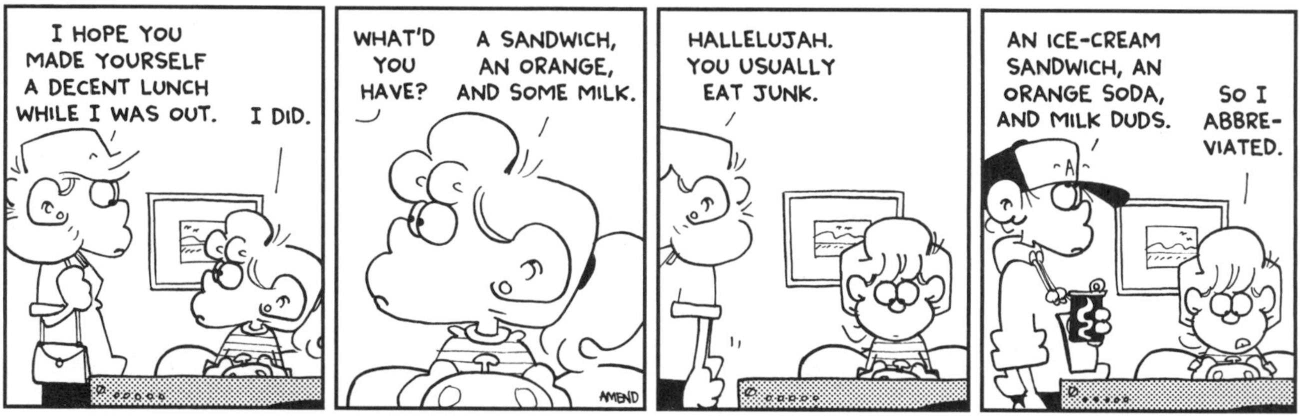
I HOPE YOU MADE YOURSELF A DECENT LUNCH WHILE I WAS OUT.
I DID.
WHAT'D YOU HAVE?
A SANDWICH, AN ORANGE, AND SOME MILK.
AMEND
HALLELUJAH. YOU USUALLY EAT JUNK.
AN ICE-CREAM SANDWICH, AN ORANGE SODA, AND MILK DUDS.
SO I ABBRE-VIATED.

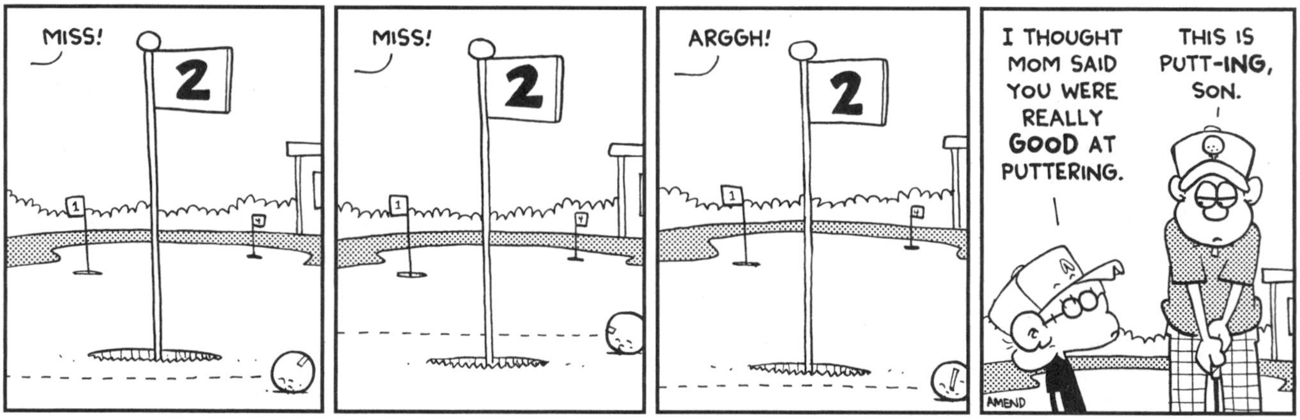
MISS!
2
MISS!
2
ARGGH!
2
I THOUGHT MOM SAID YOU WERE REALLY GOOD AT PUTTERING.
THIS IS PUTT-ING, SON.
AMEND

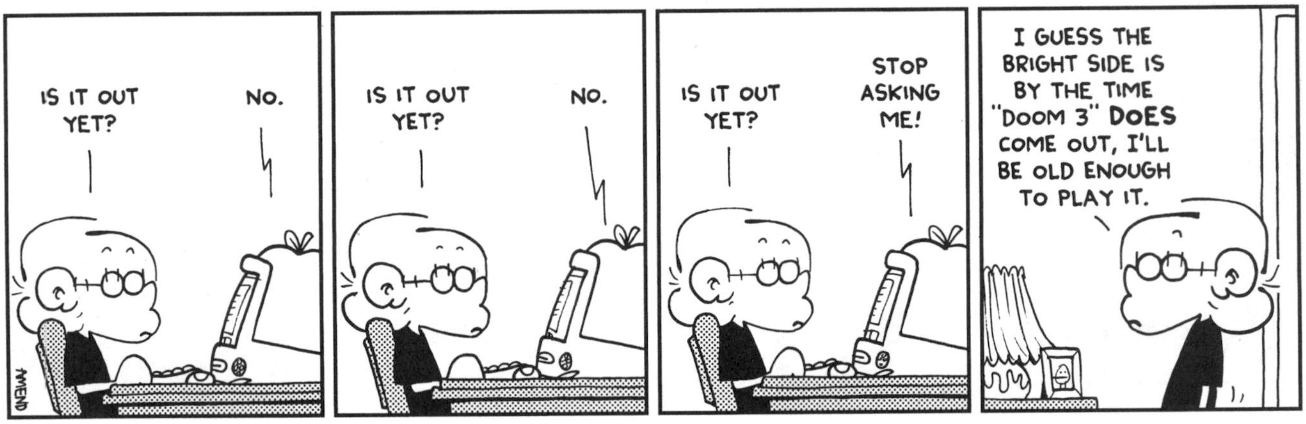
IS IT OUT YET?
NO.
IS IT OUT YET?
NO.
IS IT OUT YET?
STOP ASKING ME!
I GUESS THE BRIGHT SIDE IS BY THE TIME "DOOM 3" **DOES** COME OUT, I'LL BE OLD ENOUGH TO PLAY IT.
AMEND

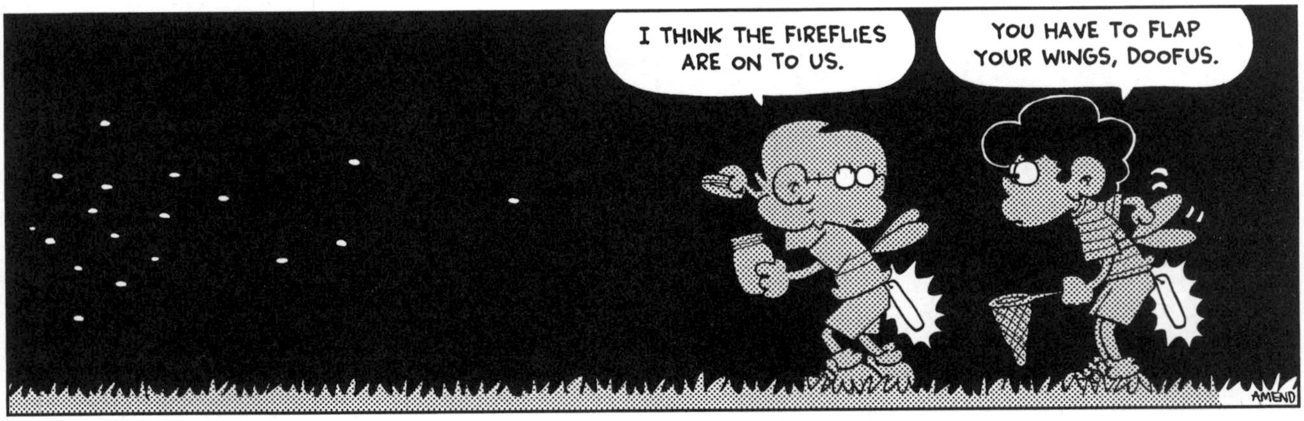
I THINK THE FIREFLIES ARE ON TO US.
YOU HAVE TO FLAP YOUR WINGS, DOOFUS.
AMEND

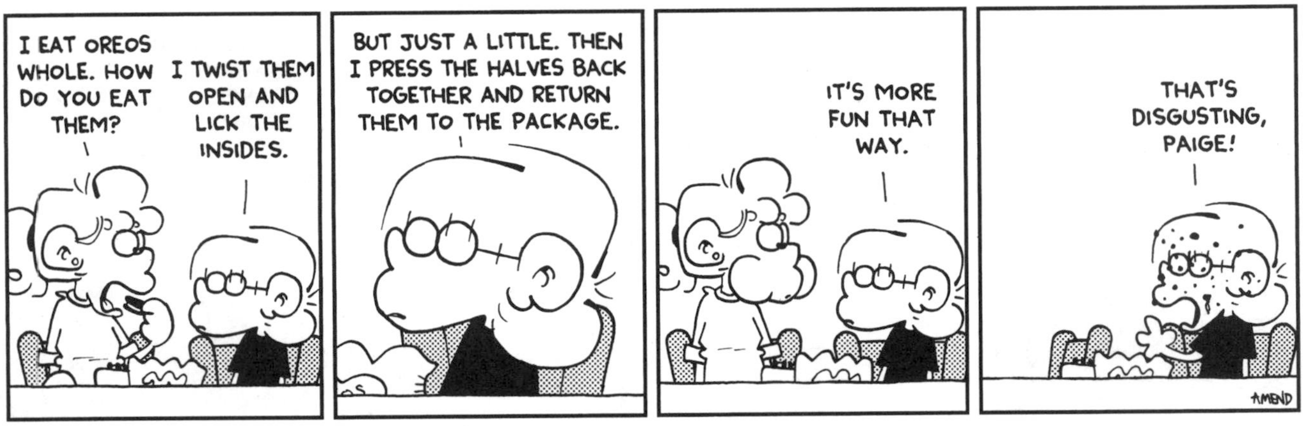
I EAT OREOS WHOLE. HOW DO YOU EAT THEM?
I TWIST THEM OPEN AND LICK THE INSIDES.
BUT JUST A LITTLE. THEN I PRESS THE HALVES BACK TOGETHER AND RETURN THEM TO THE PACKAGE.
IT'S MORE FUN THAT WAY.
THAT'S DISGUSTING, PAIGE!
AMEND

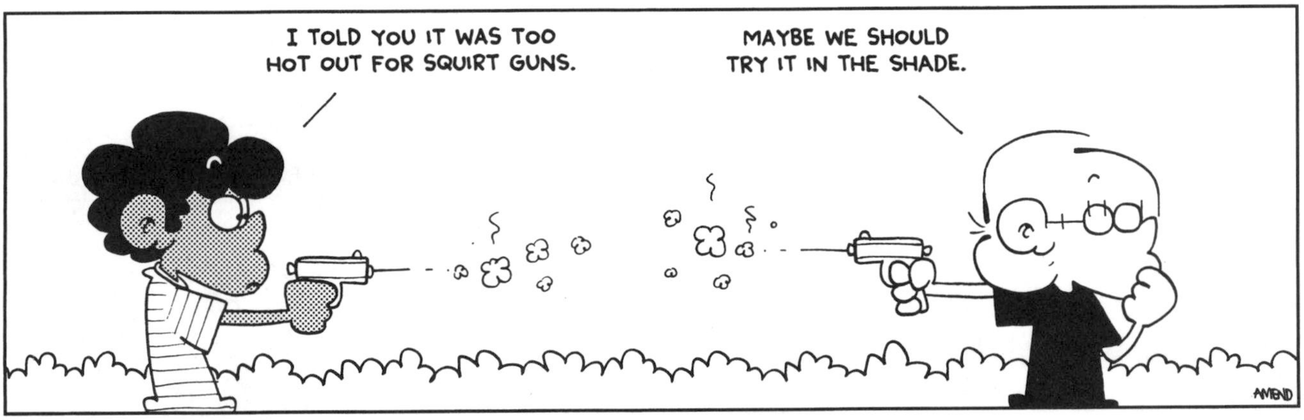
I TOLD YOU IT WAS TOO HOT OUT FOR SQUIRT GUNS.
MAYBE WE SHOULD TRY IT IN THE SHADE.
AMEND

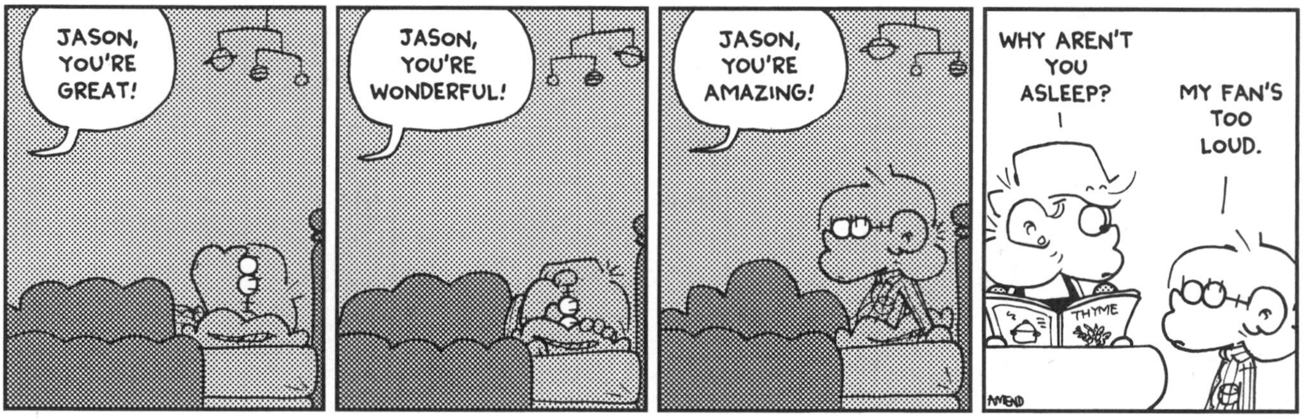
JASON, YOU'RE GREAT!
JASON, YOU'RE WONDERFUL!
JASON, YOU'RE AMAZING!
WHY AREN'T YOU ASLEEP?
MY FAN'S TOO LOUD.
THYME
AMEND

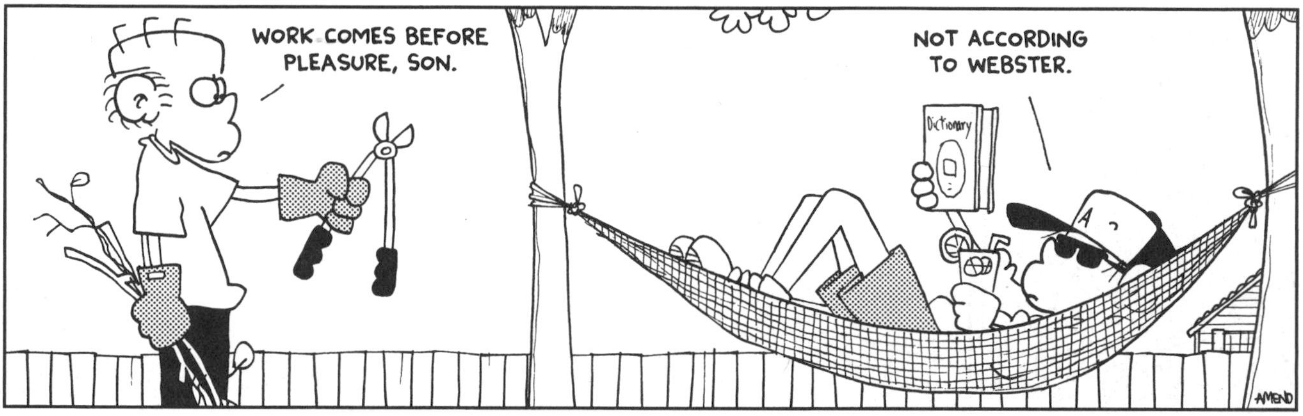
WORK COMES BEFORE PLEASURE, SON.
NOT ACCORDING TO WEBSTER.
Dictionary
A
AMEND

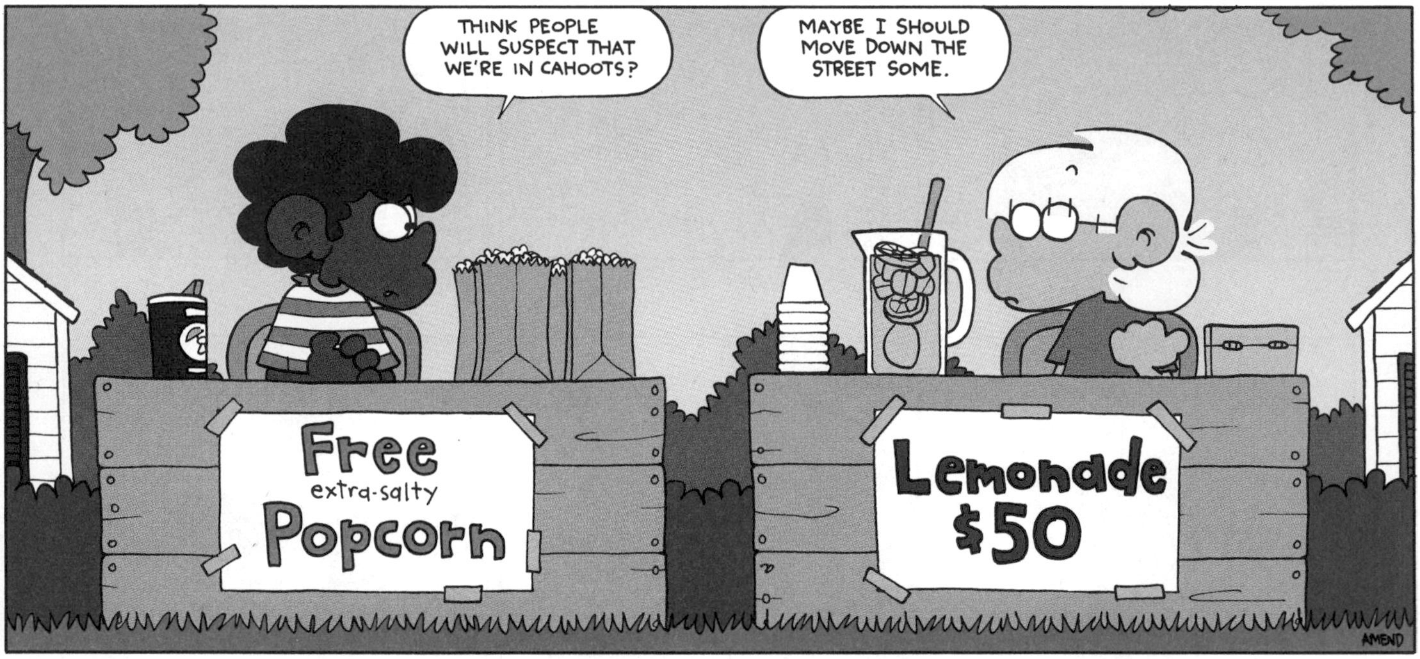
THINK PEOPLE WILL SUSPECT THAT WE'RE IN CAHOOTS?
MAYBE I SHOULD MOVE DOWN THE STREET SOME.
Free
extra-salty
Popcorn
Lemonade
$50
AMEND

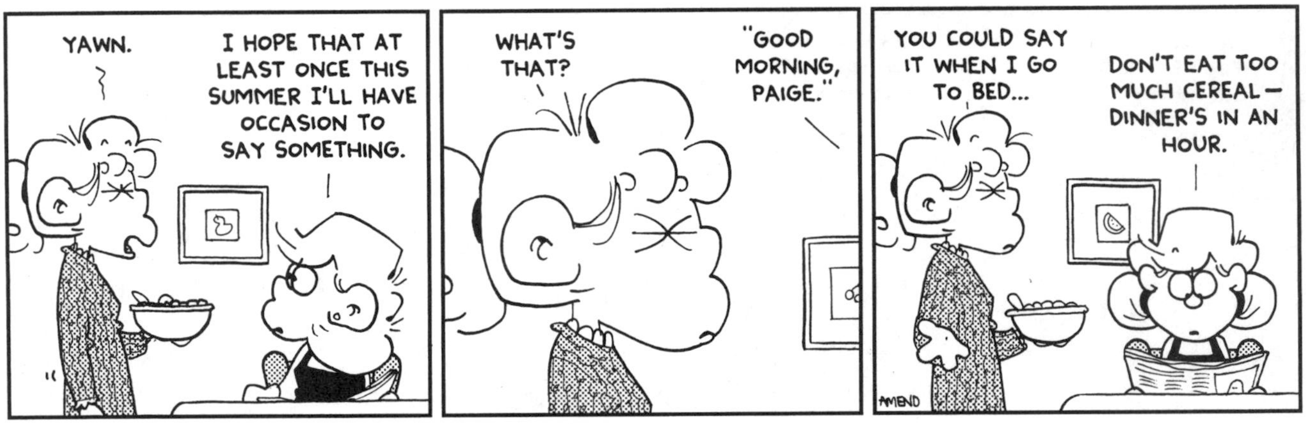
YAWN.
I HOPE THAT AT LEAST ONCE THIS SUMMER I'LL HAVE OCCASION TO SAY SOMETHING.
WHAT'S THAT?
"GOOD MORNING, PAIGE."
YOU COULD SAY IT WHEN I GO TO BED...
DON'T EAT TOO MUCH CEREAL — DINNER'S IN AN HOUR.

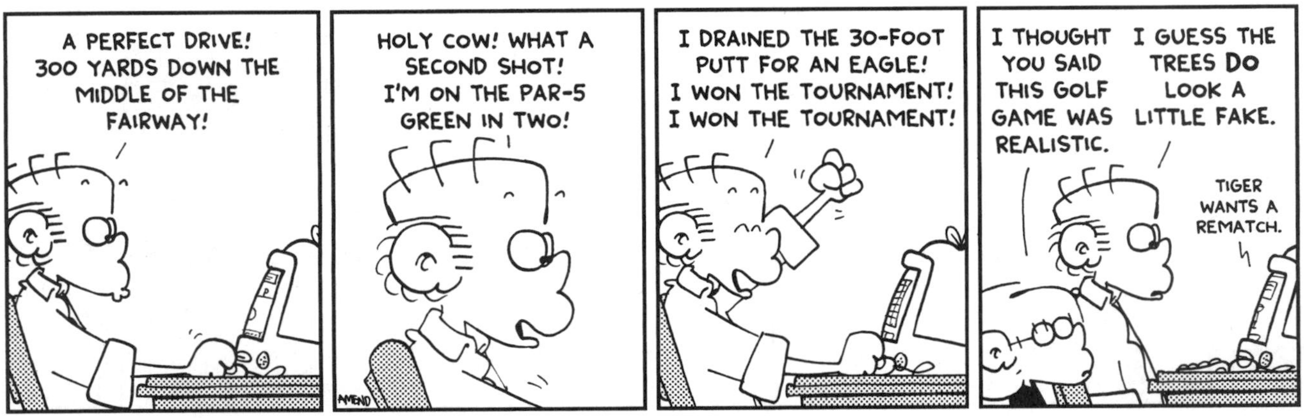
A PERFECT DRIVE! 300 YARDS DOWN THE MIDDLE OF THE FAIRWAY!
HOLY COW! WHAT A SECOND SHOT! I'M ON THE PAR-5 GREEN IN TWO!
I DRAINED THE 30-FOOT PUTT FOR AN EAGLE! I WON THE TOURNAMENT! I WON THE TOURNAMENT!
I THOUGHT YOU SAID THIS GOLF GAME WAS REALISTIC.
I GUESS THE TREES DO LOOK A LITTLE FAKE.
TIGER WANTS A REMATCH.

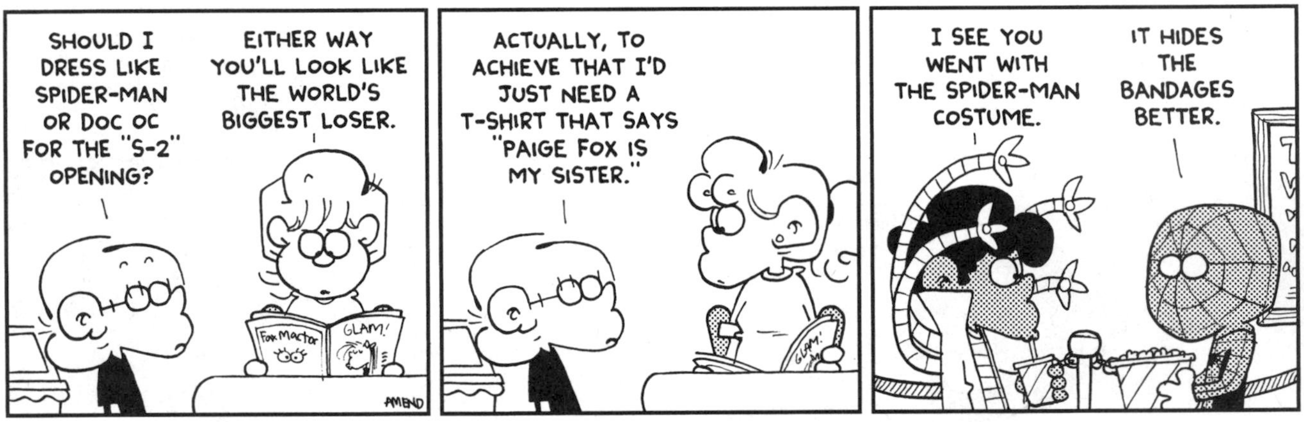
SHOULD I DRESS LIKE SPIDER-MAN OR DOC OC FOR THE "S-2" OPENING?
EITHER WAY YOU'LL LOOK LIKE THE WORLD'S BIGGEST LOSER.
ACTUALLY, TO ACHIEVE THAT I'D JUST NEED A T-SHIRT THAT SAYS "PAIGE FOX IS MY SISTER."
I SEE YOU WENT WITH THE SPIDER-MAN COSTUME.
IT HIDES THE BANDAGES BETTER.

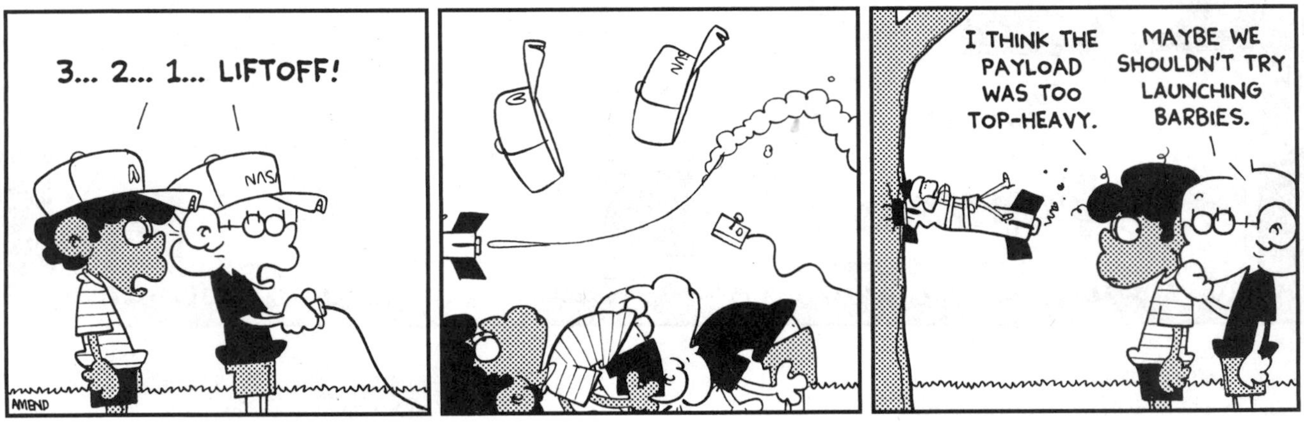
3... 2... 1... LIFTOFF!
I THINK THE PAYLOAD WAS TOO TOP-HEAVY.
MAYBE WE SHOULDN'T TRY LAUNCHING BARBIES.

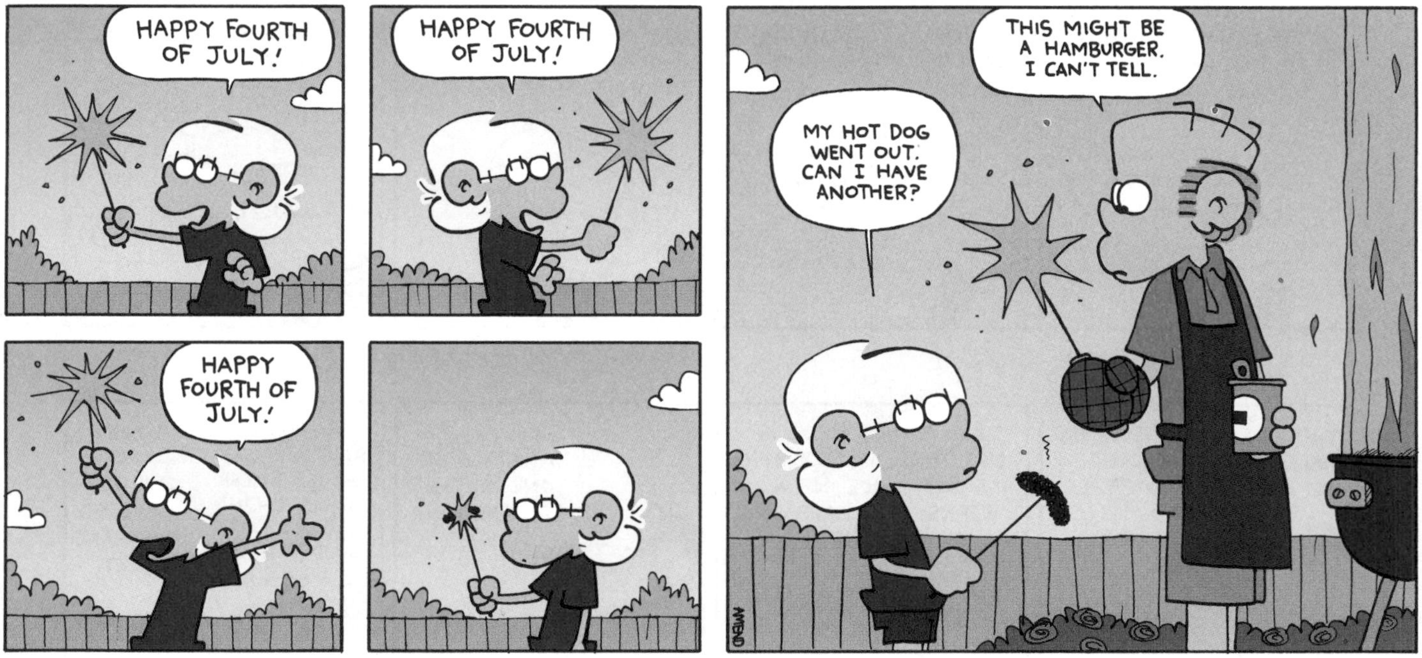
HAPPY FOURTH OF JULY!
HAPPY FOURTH OF JULY!
HAPPY FOURTH OF JULY!
MY HOT DOG WENT OUT. CAN I HAVE ANOTHER?
THIS MIGHT BE A HAMBURGER. I CAN'T TELL.
AMEND

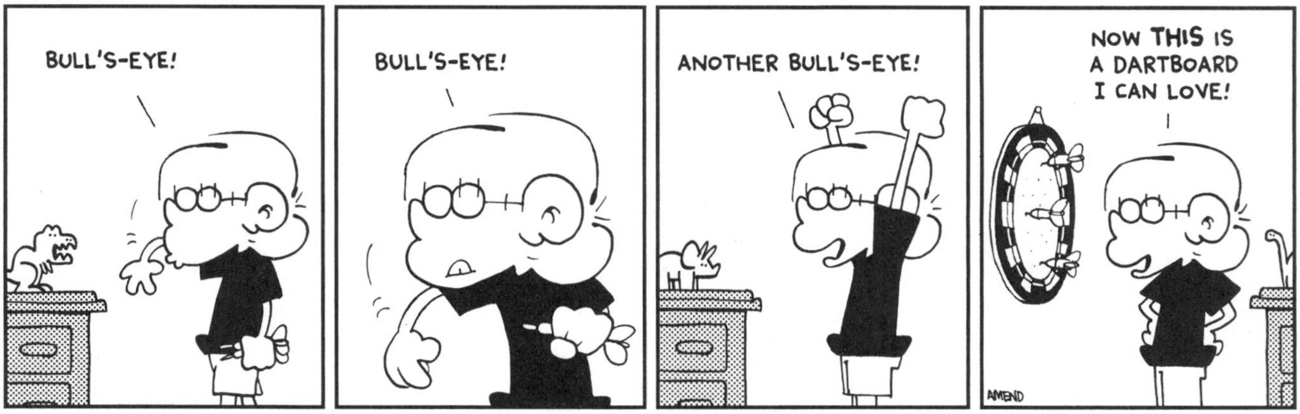
BULL'S-EYE!
BULL'S-EYE!
ANOTHER BULL'S-EYE!
NOW THIS IS A DARTBOARD I CAN LOVE!
AMEND

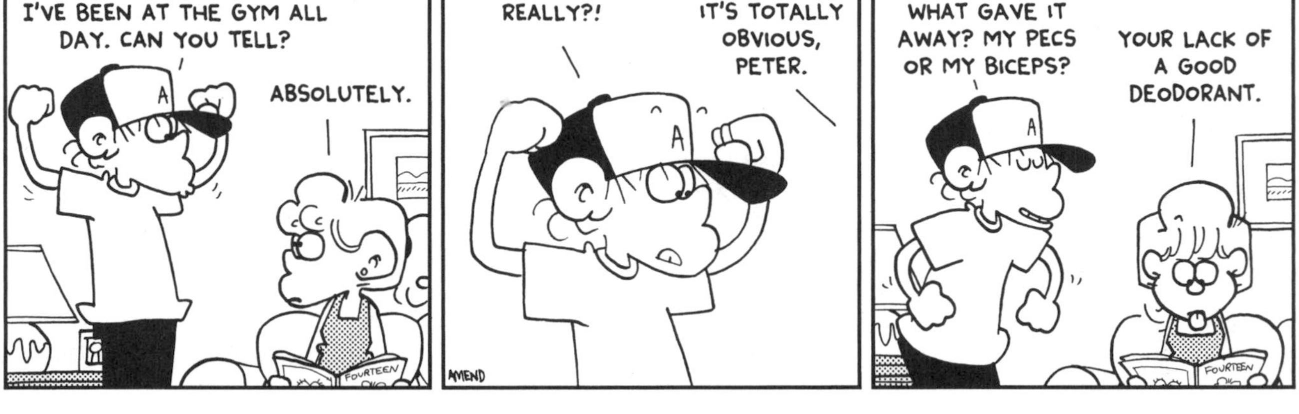
I'VE BEEN AT THE GYM ALL DAY. CAN YOU TELL?
ABSOLUTELY.
FOURTEEN
REALLY?!
IT'S TOTALLY OBVIOUS, PETER.
AMEND
WHAT GAVE IT AWAY? MY PECS OR MY BICEPS?
YOUR LACK OF A GOOD DEODORANT.
FOURTEEN

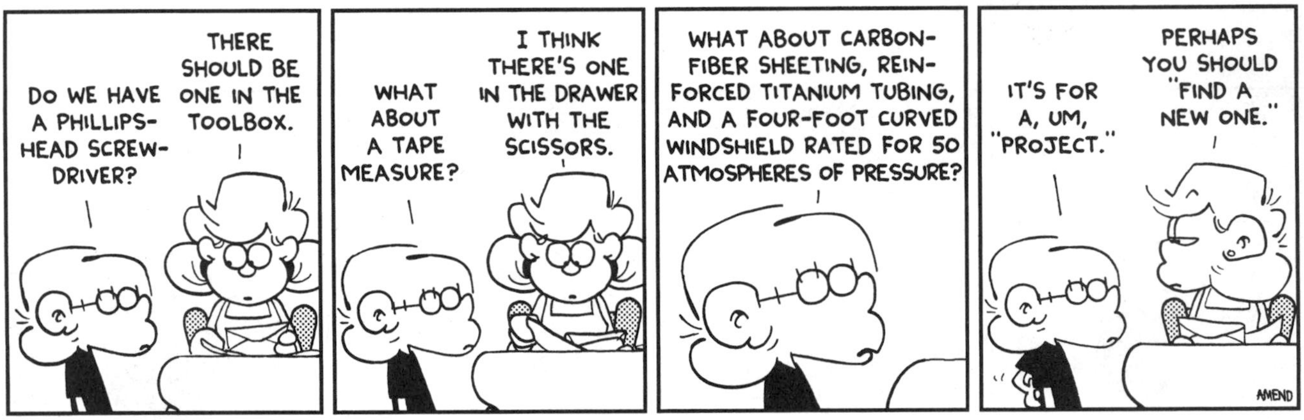
DO WE HAVE A PHILLIPS-HEAD SCREW-DRIVER?
THERE SHOULD BE ONE IN THE TOOLBOX.
WHAT ABOUT A TAPE MEASURE?
I THINK THERE'S ONE IN THE DRAWER WITH THE SCISSORS.
WHAT ABOUT CARBON-FIBER SHEETING, REIN-FORCED TITANIUM TUBING, AND A FOUR-FOOT CURVED WINDSHIELD RATED FOR 50 ATMOSPHERES OF PRESSURE?
IT'S FOR A, UM, "PROJECT."
PERHAPS YOU SHOULD "FIND A NEW ONE."

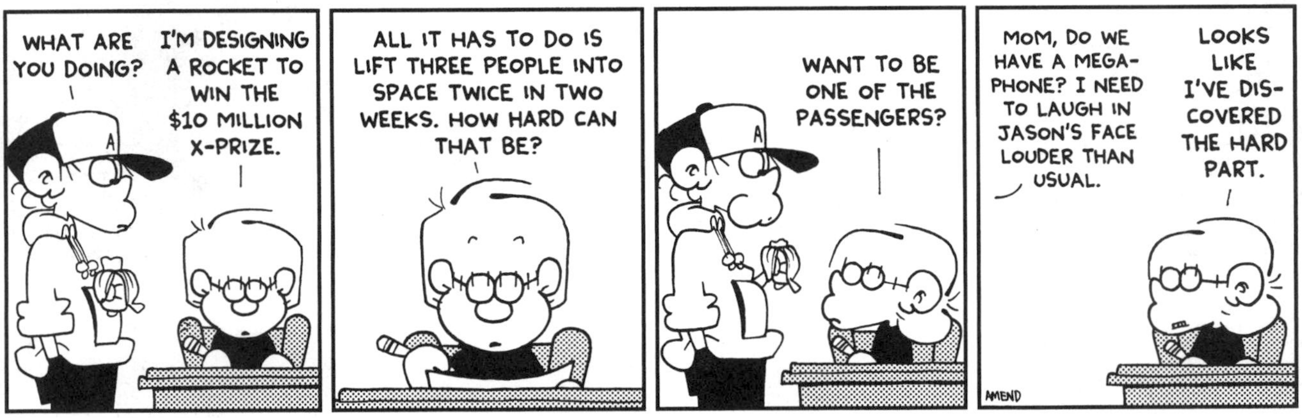
WHAT ARE YOU DOING?
I'M DESIGNING A ROCKET TO WIN THE $10 MILLION X-PRIZE.
ALL IT HAS TO DO IS LIFT THREE PEOPLE INTO SPACE TWICE IN TWO WEEKS. HOW HARD CAN THAT BE?
WANT TO BE ONE OF THE PASSENGERS?
MOM, DO WE HAVE A MEGA-PHONE? I NEED TO LAUGH IN JASON'S FACE LOUDER THAN USUAL.
LOOKS LIKE I'VE DIS-COVERED THE HARD PART.

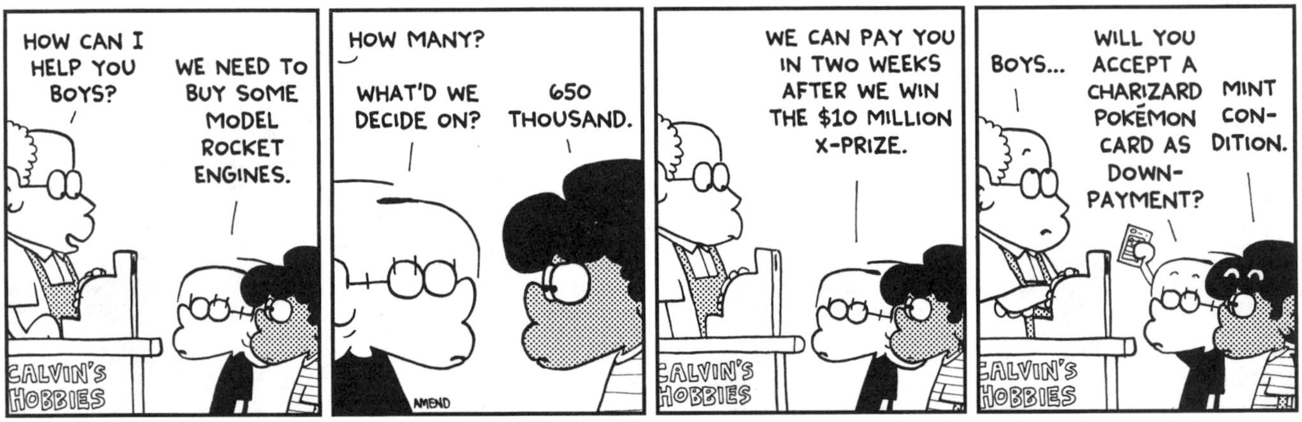
HOW CAN I HELP YOU BOYS?
WE NEED TO BUY SOME MODEL ROCKET ENGINES.
CALVIN'S HOBBIES
HOW MANY?
WHAT'D WE DECIDE ON?
650 THOUSAND.
WE CAN PAY YOU IN TWO WEEKS AFTER WE WIN THE $10 MILLION X-PRIZE.
CALVIN'S HOBBIES
BOYS...
WILL YOU ACCEPT A CHARIZARD POKÉMON CARD AS DOWN-PAYMENT?
MINT CON-DITION.
CALVIN'S HOBBIES

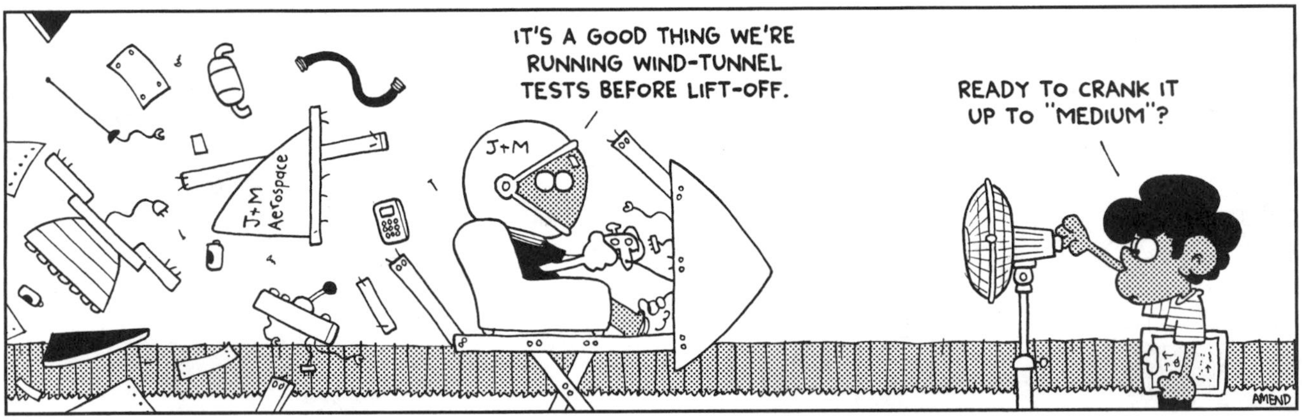
J+M Aerospace
J+M
IT'S A GOOD THING WE'RE RUNNING WIND-TUNNEL TESTS BEFORE LIFT-OFF.
READY TO CRANK IT UP TO "MEDIUM"?

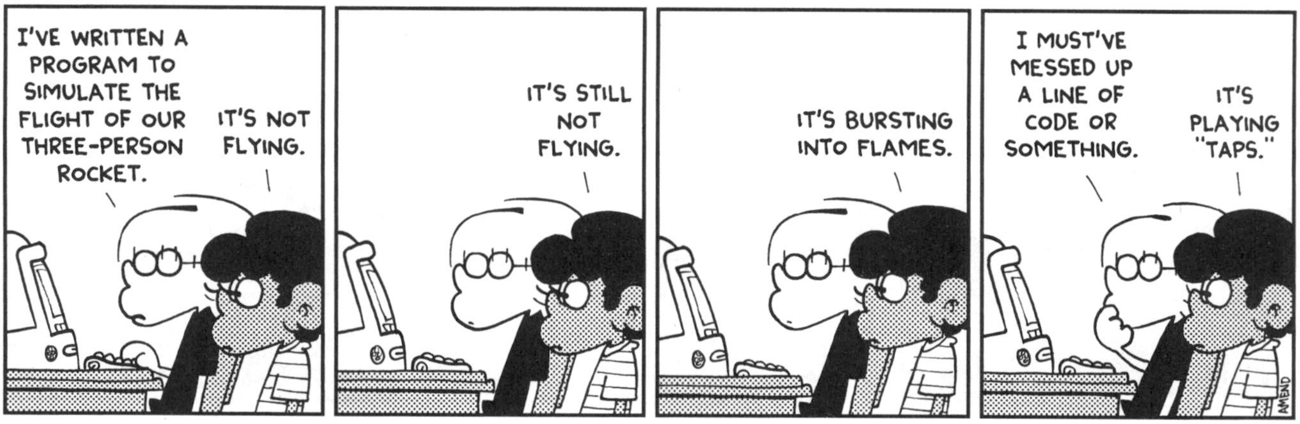
I'VE WRITTEN A PROGRAM TO SIMULATE THE FLIGHT OF OUR THREE-PERSON ROCKET.
IT'S NOT FLYING.
IT'S STILL NOT FLYING.
IT'S BURSTING INTO FLAMES.
I MUST'VE MESSED UP A LINE OF CODE OR SOMETHING.
IT'S PLAYING "TAPS."

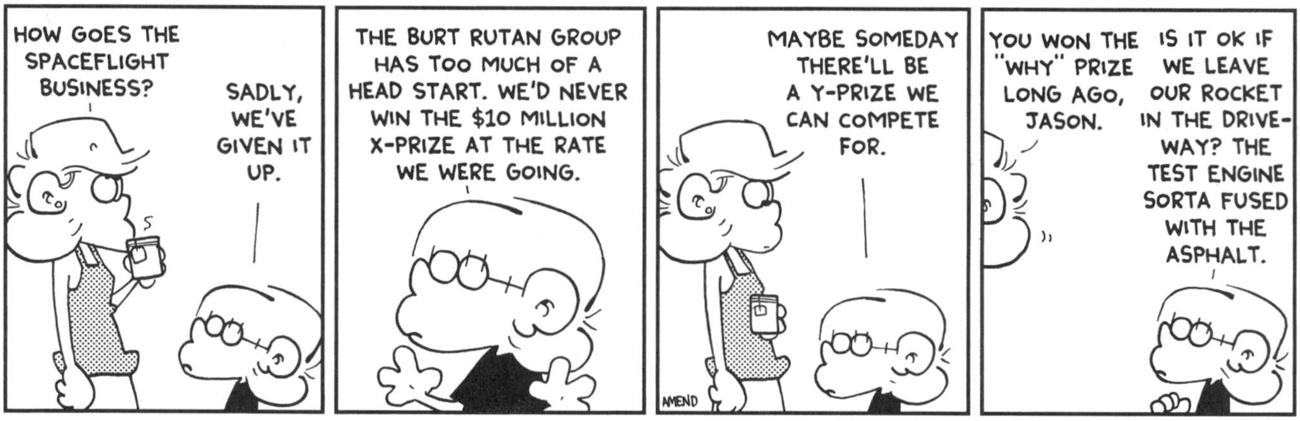
HOW GOES THE SPACEFLIGHT BUSINESS?
SADLY, WE'VE GIVEN IT UP.
THE BURT RUTAN GROUP HAS TOO MUCH OF A HEAD START. WE'D NEVER WIN THE $10 MILLION X-PRIZE AT THE RATE WE WERE GOING.
MAYBE SOMEDAY THERE'LL BE A Y-PRIZE WE CAN COMPETE FOR.
YOU WON THE "WHY" PRIZE LONG AGO, JASON.
IS IT OK IF WE LEAVE OUR ROCKET IN THE DRIVEWAY? THE TEST ENGINE SORTA FUSED WITH THE ASPHALT.

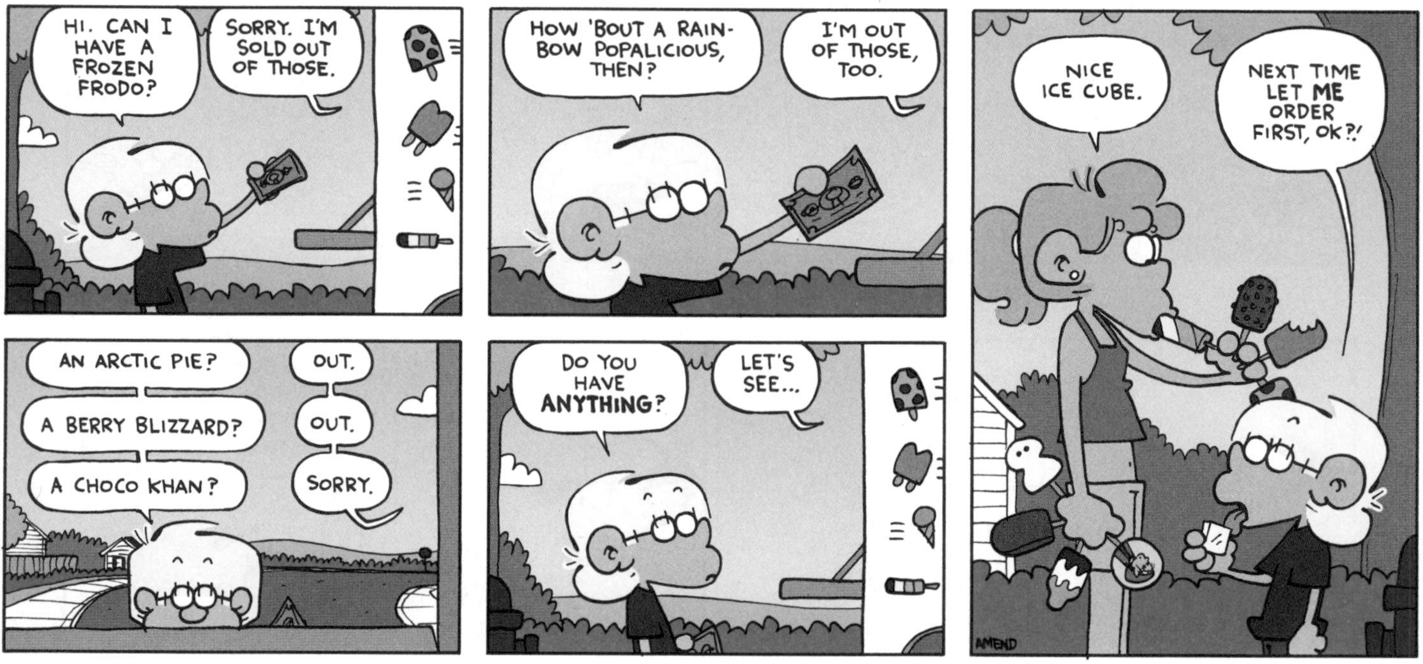
HI. CAN I HAVE A FROZEN FRODO?
SORRY. I'M SOLD OUT OF THOSE.
HOW 'BOUT A RAINBOW POPALICIOUS, THEN?
I'M OUT OF THOSE, TOO.
AN ARCTIC PIE?
OUT.
A BERRY BLIZZARD?
OUT.
A CHOCO KHAN?
SORRY.
DO YOU HAVE **ANYTHING**?
LET'S SEE...
NICE ICE CUBE.
NEXT TIME LET **ME** ORDER FIRST, OK?!

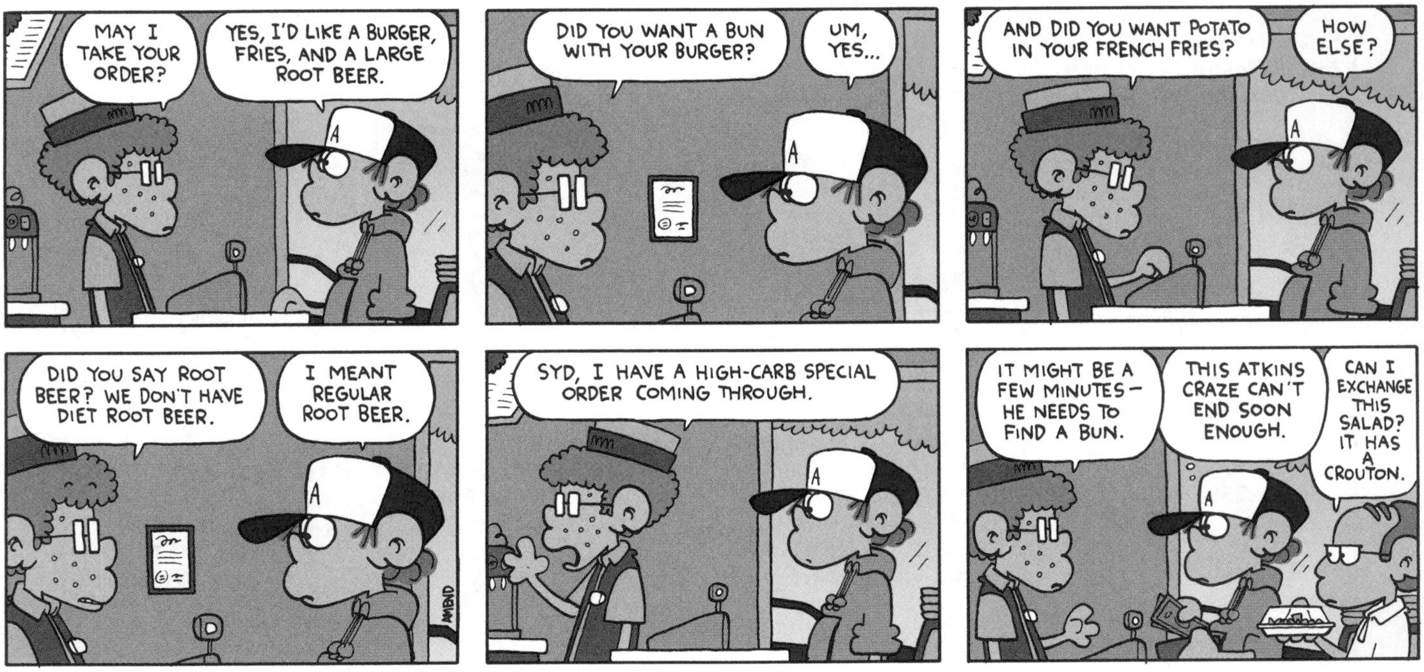
MAY I TAKE YOUR ORDER?
YES, I'D LIKE A BURGER, FRIES, AND A LARGE ROOT BEER.
DID YOU WANT A BUN WITH YOUR BURGER?
UM, YES...
AND DID YOU WANT POTATO IN YOUR FRENCH FRIES?
HOW ELSE?
DID YOU SAY ROOT BEER? WE DON'T HAVE DIET ROOT BEER.
I MEANT REGULAR ROOT BEER.
SYD, I HAVE A HIGH-CARB SPECIAL ORDER COMING THROUGH.
IT MIGHT BE A FEW MINUTES— HE NEEDS TO FIND A BUN.
THIS ATKINS CRAZE CAN'T END SOON ENOUGH.
CAN I EXCHANGE THIS SALAD? IT HAS A CROUTON.
AMEND

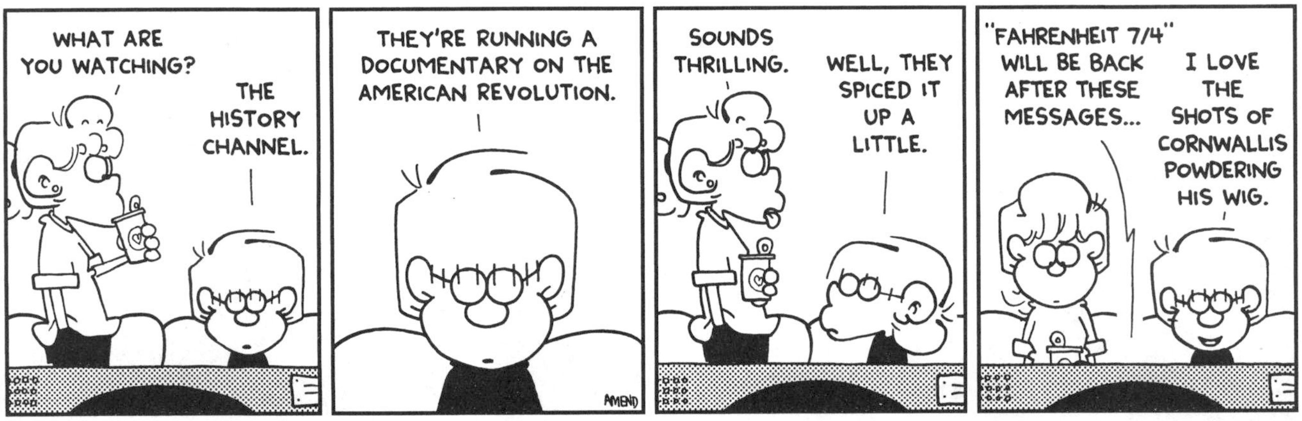
WHAT ARE YOU WATCHING?
THE HISTORY CHANNEL.
THEY'RE RUNNING A DOCUMENTARY ON THE AMERICAN REVOLUTION.
AMEND
SOUNDS THRILLING.
WELL, THEY SPICED IT UP A LITTLE.
"FAHRENHEIT 7/4" WILL BE BACK AFTER THESE MESSAGES...
I LOVE THE SHOTS OF CORNWALLIS POWDERING HIS WIG.

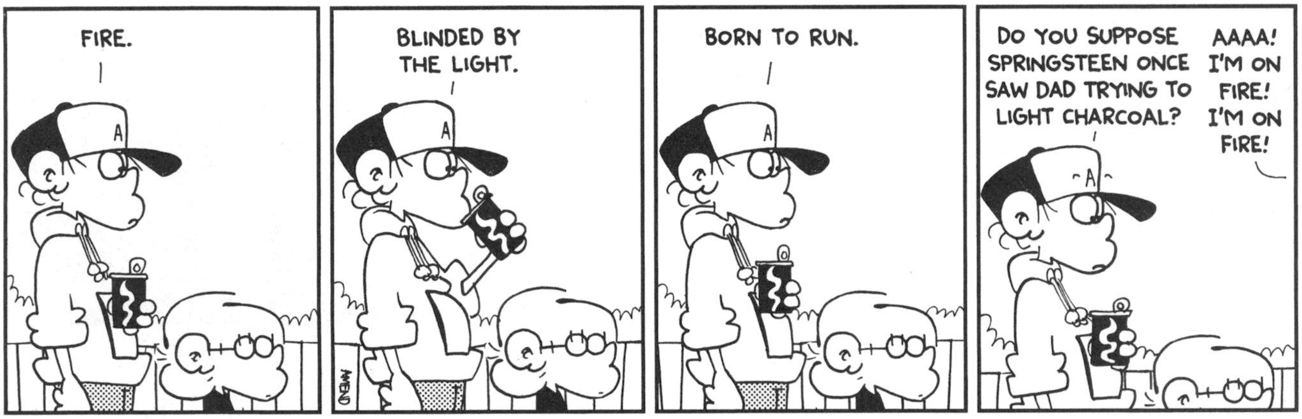
FIRE.
BLINDED BY THE LIGHT.
AMEND
BORN TO RUN.
DO YOU SUPPOSE SPRINGSTEEN ONCE SAW DAD TRYING TO LIGHT CHARCOAL?
AAAA! I'M ON FIRE! I'M ON FIRE!

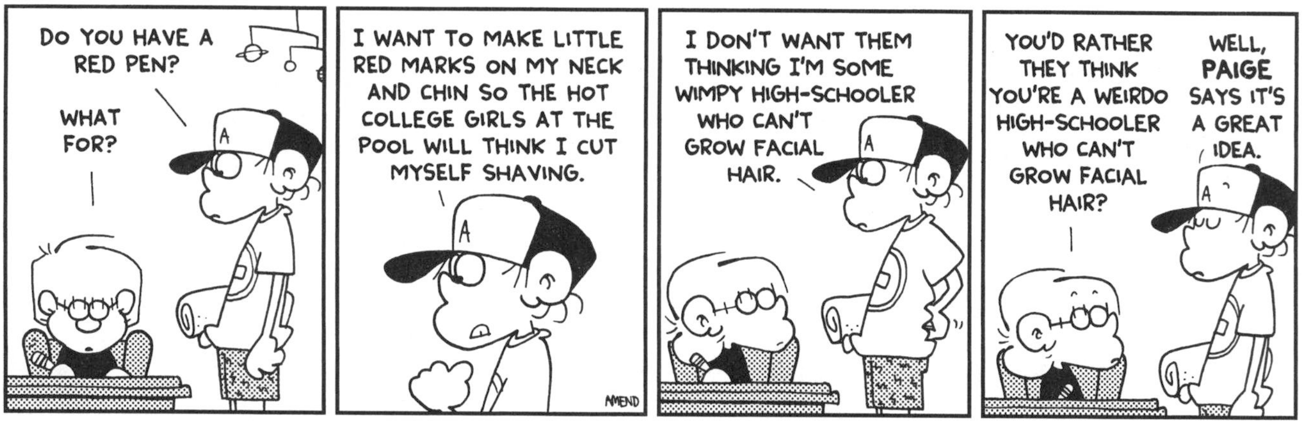
DO YOU HAVE A RED PEN?
WHAT FOR?
I WANT TO MAKE LITTLE RED MARKS ON MY NECK AND CHIN SO THE HOT COLLEGE GIRLS AT THE POOL WILL THINK I CUT MYSELF SHAVING.
AMEND
I DON'T WANT THEM THINKING I'M SOME WIMPY HIGH-SCHOOLER WHO CAN'T GROW FACIAL HAIR.
YOU'D RATHER THEY THINK YOU'RE A WEIRDO HIGH-SCHOOLER WHO CAN'T GROW FACIAL HAIR?
WELL, **PAIGE** SAYS IT'S A GREAT IDEA.

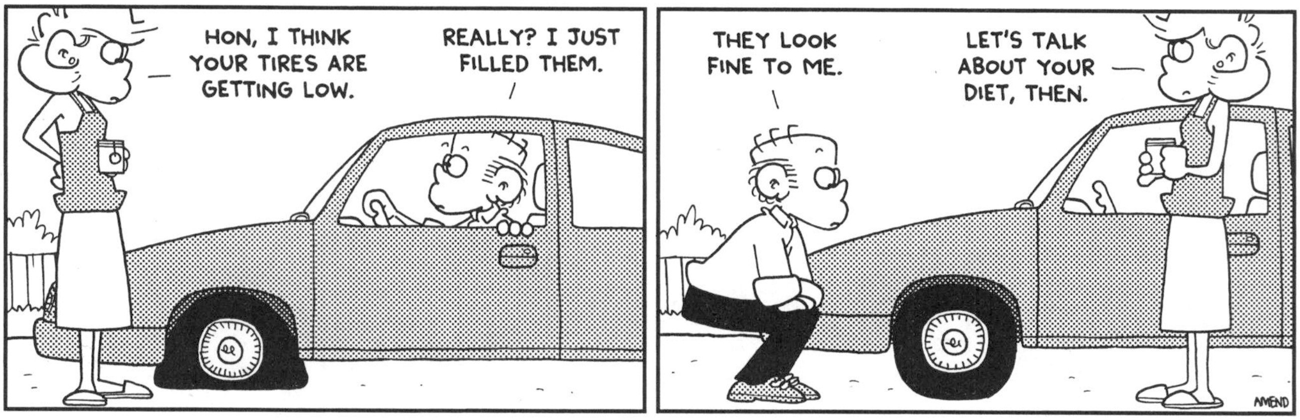
HON, I THINK YOUR TIRES ARE GETTING LOW.
REALLY? I JUST FILLED THEM.
THEY LOOK FINE TO ME.
LET'S TALK ABOUT YOUR DIET, THEN.
AMEND

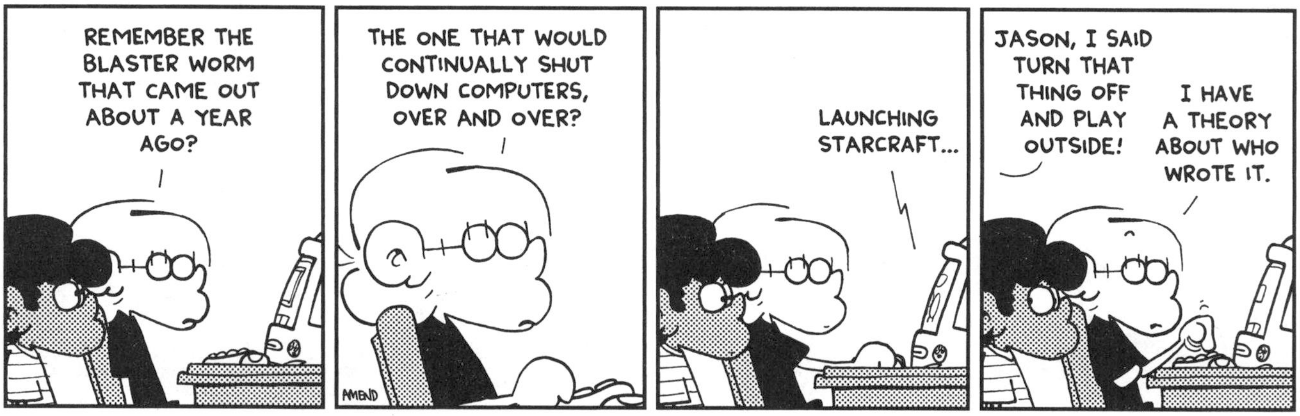
REMEMBER THE BLASTER WORM THAT CAME OUT ABOUT A YEAR AGO?
THE ONE THAT WOULD CONTINUALLY SHUT DOWN COMPUTERS, OVER AND OVER?
AMEND
LAUNCHING STARCRAFT...
JASON, I SAID TURN THAT THING OFF AND PLAY OUTSIDE!
I HAVE A THEORY ABOUT WHO WROTE IT.

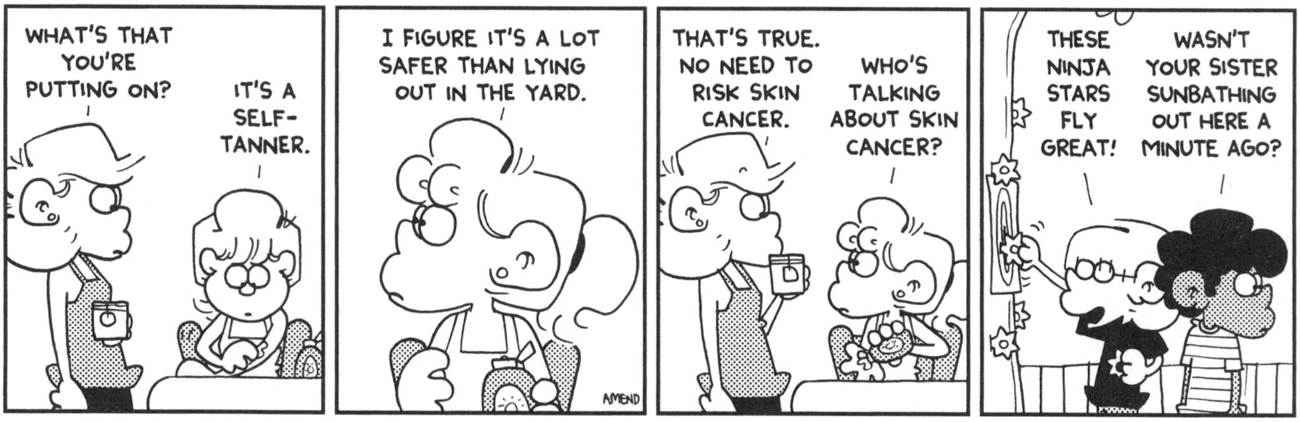
WHAT'S THAT YOU'RE PUTTING ON?
IT'S A SELF-TANNER.
I FIGURE IT'S A LOT SAFER THAN LYING OUT IN THE YARD.
AMEND
THAT'S TRUE. NO NEED TO RISK SKIN CANCER.
WHO'S TALKING ABOUT SKIN CANCER?
THESE NINJA STARS FLY GREAT!
WASN'T YOUR SISTER SUNBATHING OUT HERE A MINUTE AGO?

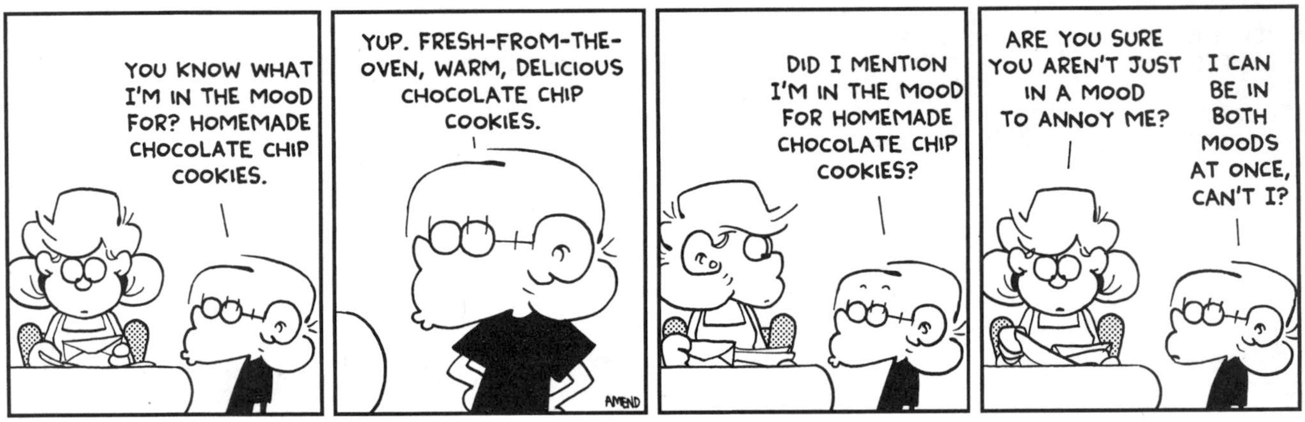
YOU KNOW WHAT I'M IN THE MOOD FOR? HOMEMADE CHOCOLATE CHIP COOKIES.
YUP. FRESH-FROM-THE-OVEN, WARM, DELICIOUS CHOCOLATE CHIP COOKIES.
AMEND
DID I MENTION I'M IN THE MOOD FOR HOMEMADE CHOCOLATE CHIP COOKIES?
ARE YOU SURE YOU AREN'T JUST IN A MOOD TO ANNOY ME?
I CAN BE IN BOTH MOODS AT ONCE, CAN'T I?

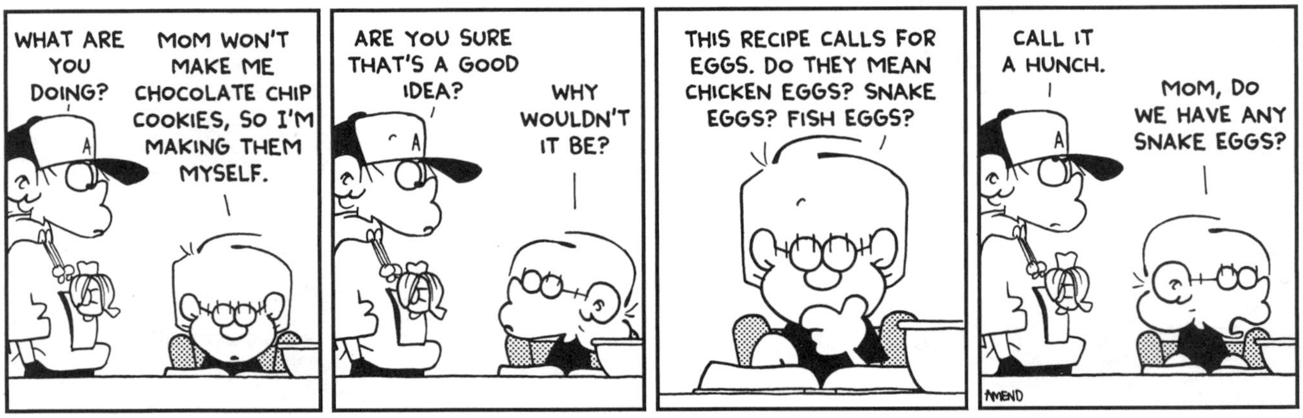
WHAT ARE YOU DOING?
MOM WON'T MAKE ME CHOCOLATE CHIP COOKIES, SO I'M MAKING THEM MYSELF.
ARE YOU SURE THAT'S A GOOD IDEA?
WHY WOULDN'T IT BE?
THIS RECIPE CALLS FOR EGGS. DO THEY MEAN CHICKEN EGGS? SNAKE EGGS? FISH EGGS?
CALL IT A HUNCH.
MOM, DO WE HAVE ANY SNAKE EGGS?
AMEND

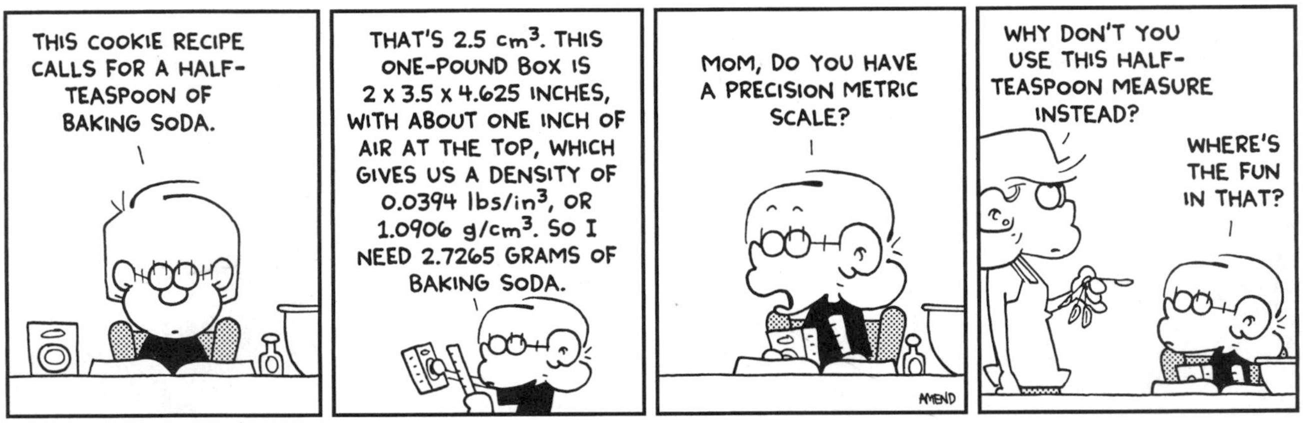
THIS COOKIE RECIPE CALLS FOR A HALF-TEASPOON OF BAKING SODA.
THAT'S 2.5 cm³. THIS ONE-POUND BOX IS 2 x 3.5 x 4.625 INCHES, WITH ABOUT ONE INCH OF AIR AT THE TOP, WHICH GIVES US A DENSITY OF 0.0394 lbs/in³, OR 1.0906 g/cm³. SO I NEED 2.7265 GRAMS OF BAKING SODA.
MOM, DO YOU HAVE A PRECISION METRIC SCALE?
AMEND
WHY DON'T YOU USE THIS HALF-TEASPOON MEASURE INSTEAD?
WHERE'S THE FUN IN THAT?

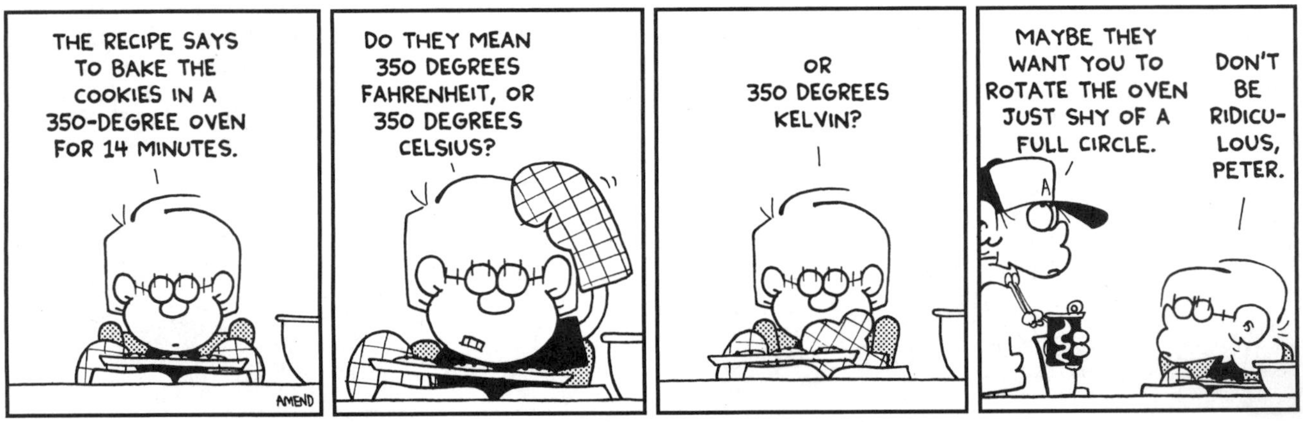
THE RECIPE SAYS TO BAKE THE COOKIES IN A 350-DEGREE OVEN FOR 14 MINUTES.
AMEND
DO THEY MEAN 350 DEGREES FAHRENHEIT, OR 350 DEGREES CELSIUS?
OR 350 DEGREES KELVIN?
MAYBE THEY WANT YOU TO ROTATE THE OVEN JUST SHY OF A FULL CIRCLE.
DON'T BE RIDICULOUS, PETER.

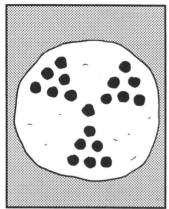

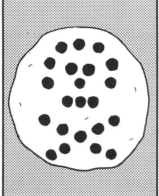

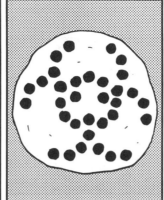

I FIGURE THIS WAY I'LL GET ALL THE COOKIES TO MYSELF.

I DUNNO. THAT BIOHAZARD ONE LOOKS PRETTY TASTY.

HEY, THESE COOKIES YOU MADE TASTE PRETTY GOOD.

THANKS.

SERIOUSLY, WHO KNEW YOU COULD COOK SO WELL?

COOKING'S JUST SCIENCE, PETER.

FOR EXAMPLE, WE WERE OUT OF BROWN SUGAR, SO I SIMPLY WHIPPED UP A SUBSTITUTE USING MY JUNIOR EINSTEIN CHEMISTRY SET.

EXCUSE ME WHILE I FIND A SINK.

THE THINGS YOU CAN DO WITH PLASTICS!

CAN I GET THIS CEREAL?

NOT IF THE FIRST INGREDIENT IS SUGAR.

WHAT ABOUT THIS ONE?

NOT IF THE FIRST INGREDIENT IS SUGAR.

CAN I GET THIS ONE? SUGAR IS THE LAST INGREDIENT.

LET ME SEE THAT.

SUGAR IS THE **ONLY** INGREDIENT, JASON!

IT'S NOT LIKE I WON'T BE ADDING MILK...

FRUCT-Os

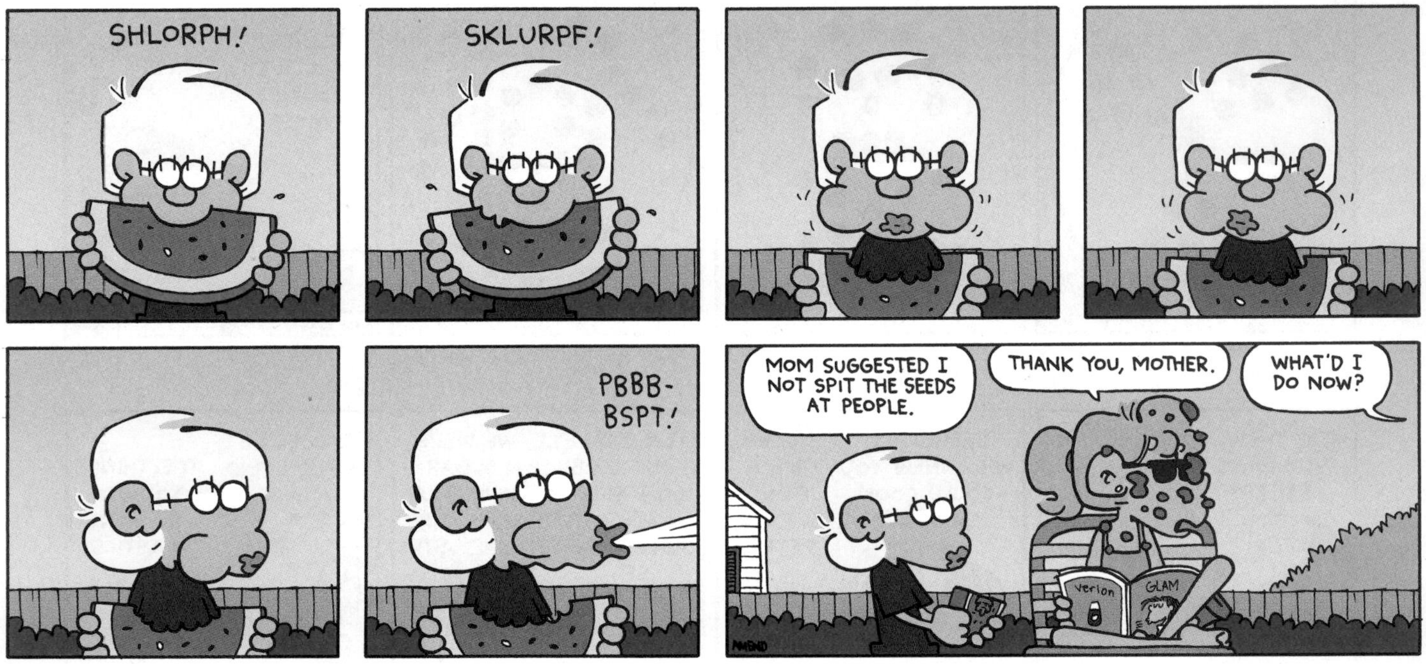
SHLORPH!
SKLURPF!
PBBB-BSPT!
MOM SUGGESTED I NOT SPIT THE SEEDS AT PEOPLE.
THANK YOU, MOTHER.
WHAT'D I DO NOW?
AMEND

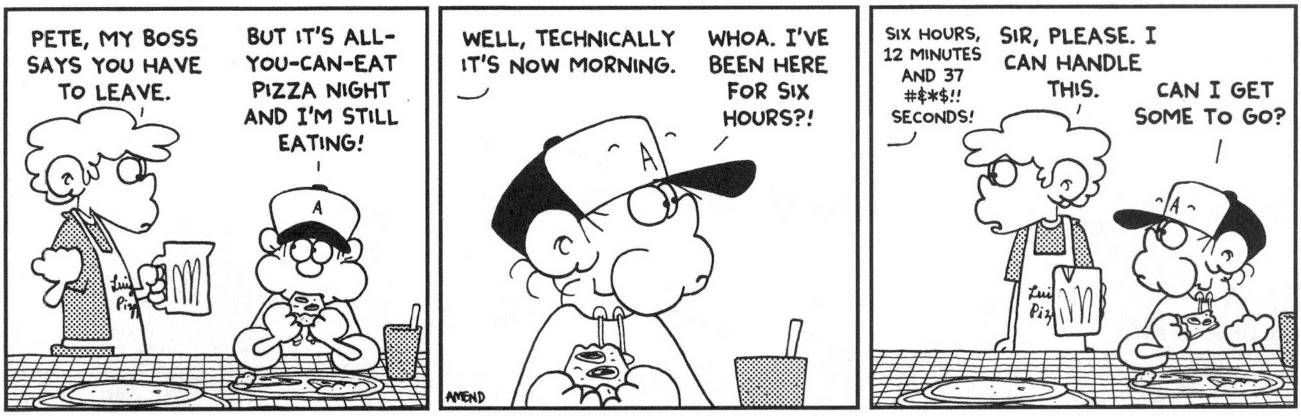
PETE, MY BOSS SAYS YOU HAVE TO LEAVE.
BUT IT'S ALL-YOU-CAN-EAT PIZZA NIGHT AND I'M STILL EATING!
WELL, TECHNICALLY IT'S NOW MORNING.
WHOA. I'VE BEEN HERE FOR SIX HOURS?!
AMEND
SIX HOURS, 12 MINUTES AND 37 #$*$!! SECONDS!
SIR, PLEASE. I CAN HANDLE THIS.
CAN I GET SOME TO GO?

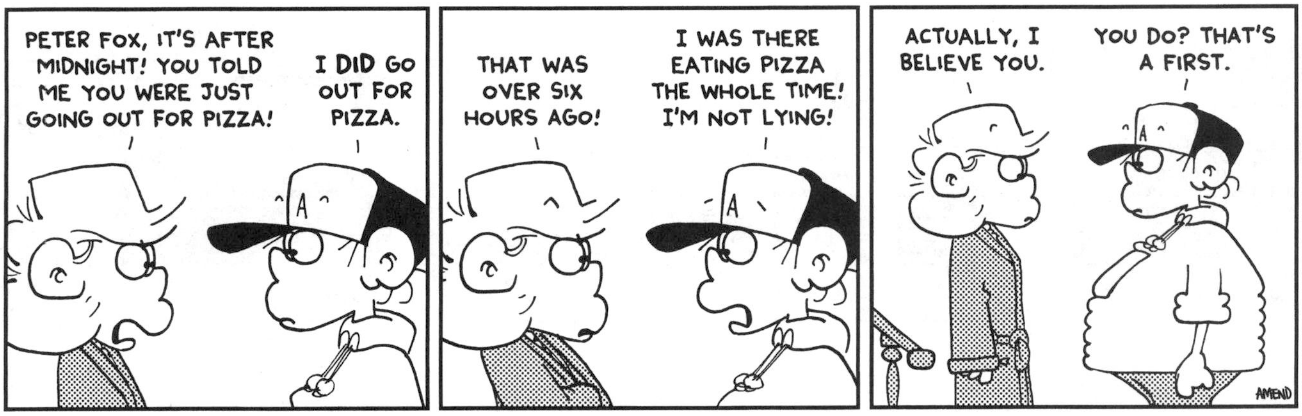
PETER FOX, IT'S AFTER MIDNIGHT! YOU TOLD ME YOU WERE JUST GOING OUT FOR PIZZA!
I **DID** GO OUT FOR PIZZA.
THAT WAS OVER SIX HOURS AGO!
I WAS THERE EATING PIZZA THE WHOLE TIME! I'M NOT LYING!
ACTUALLY, I BELIEVE YOU.
YOU DO? THAT'S A FIRST.
AMEND

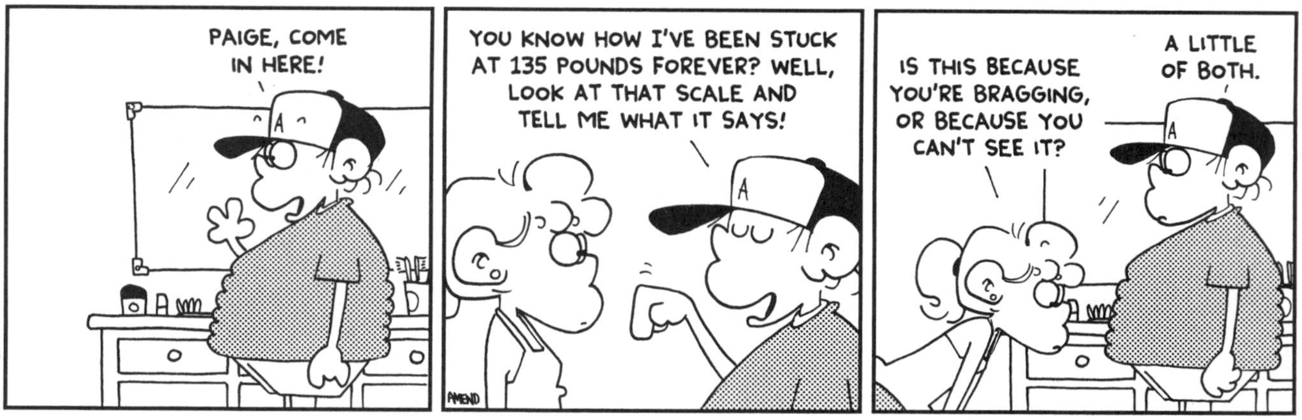
PAIGE, COME IN HERE!
YOU KNOW HOW I'VE BEEN STUCK AT 135 POUNDS FOREVER? WELL, LOOK AT THAT SCALE AND TELL ME WHAT IT SAYS!
IS THIS BECAUSE YOU'RE BRAGGING, OR BECAUSE YOU CAN'T SEE IT?
A LITTLE OF BOTH.
AMEND

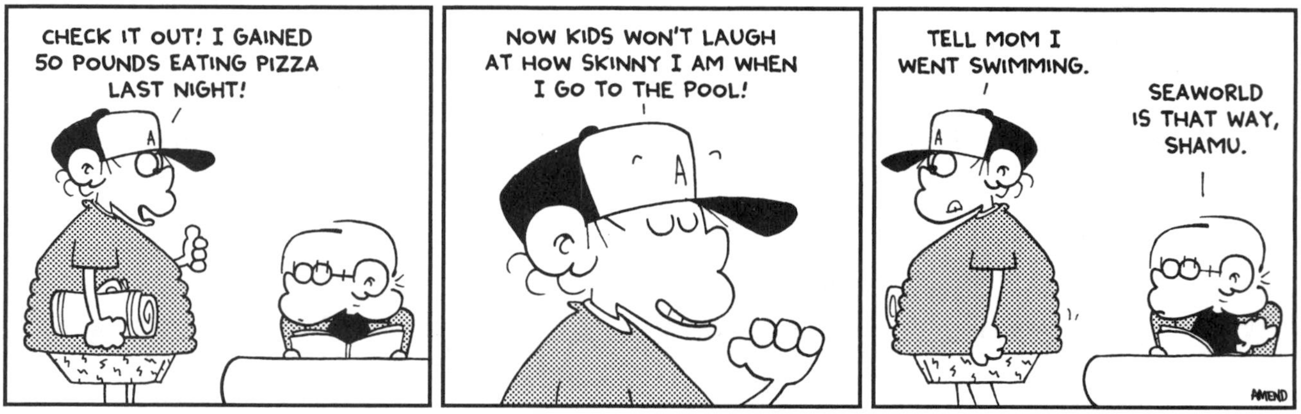
CHECK IT OUT! I GAINED 50 POUNDS EATING PIZZA LAST NIGHT!
NOW KIDS WON'T LAUGH AT HOW SKINNY I AM WHEN I GO TO THE POOL!
TELL MOM I WENT SWIMMING.
SEAWORLD IS THAT WAY, SHAMU.
AMEND

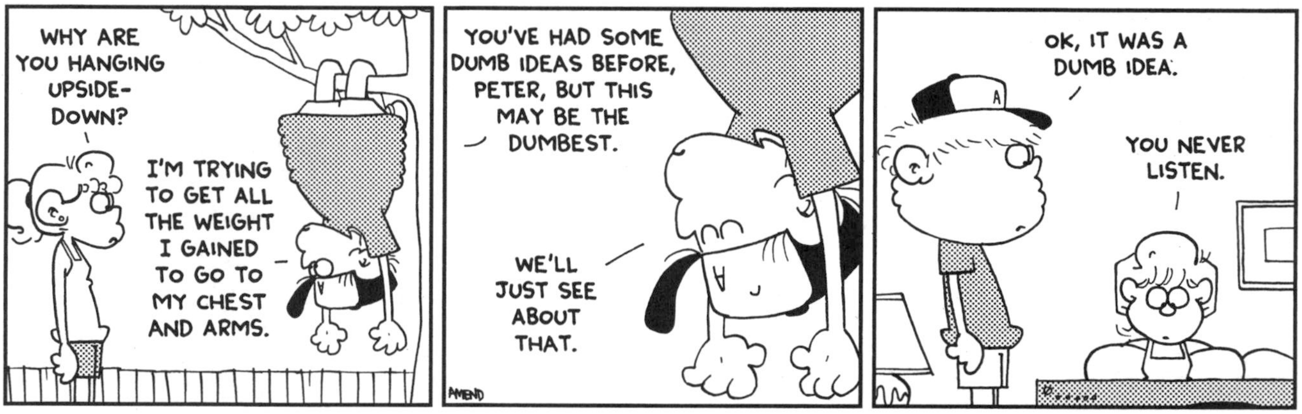
WHY ARE YOU HANGING UPSIDE-DOWN?
I'M TRYING TO GET ALL THE WEIGHT I GAINED TO GO TO MY CHEST AND ARMS.
YOU'VE HAD SOME DUMB IDEAS BEFORE, PETER, BUT THIS MAY BE THE DUMBEST.
WE'LL JUST SEE ABOUT THAT.
AMEND
OK, IT WAS A DUMB IDEA.
YOU NEVER LISTEN.

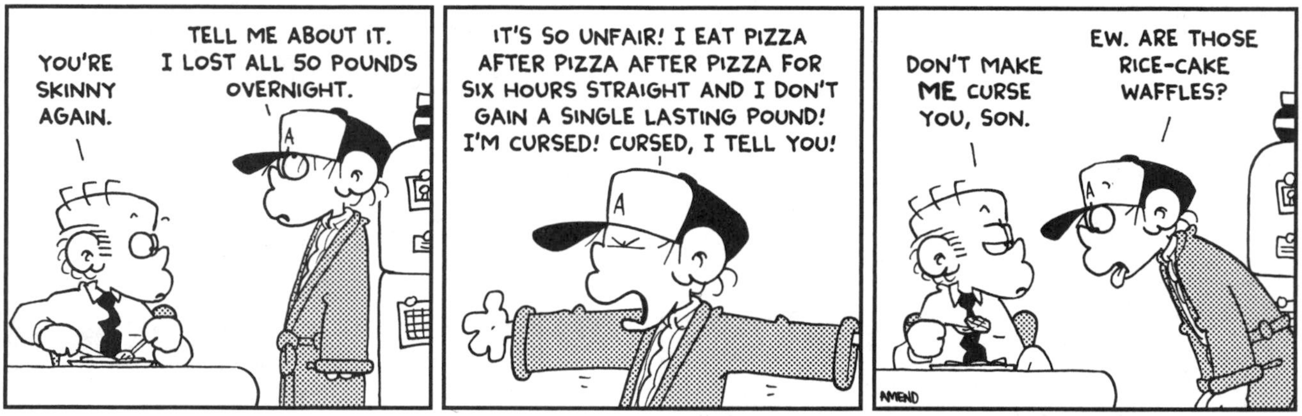
YOU'RE SKINNY AGAIN.
TELL ME ABOUT IT. I LOST ALL 50 POUNDS OVERNIGHT.
IT'S SO UNFAIR! I EAT PIZZA AFTER PIZZA AFTER PIZZA FOR SIX HOURS STRAIGHT AND I DON'T GAIN A SINGLE LASTING POUND! I'M CURSED! CURSED, I TELL YOU!
DON'T MAKE ME CURSE YOU, SON.
EW. ARE THOSE RICE-CAKE WAFFLES?
AMEND

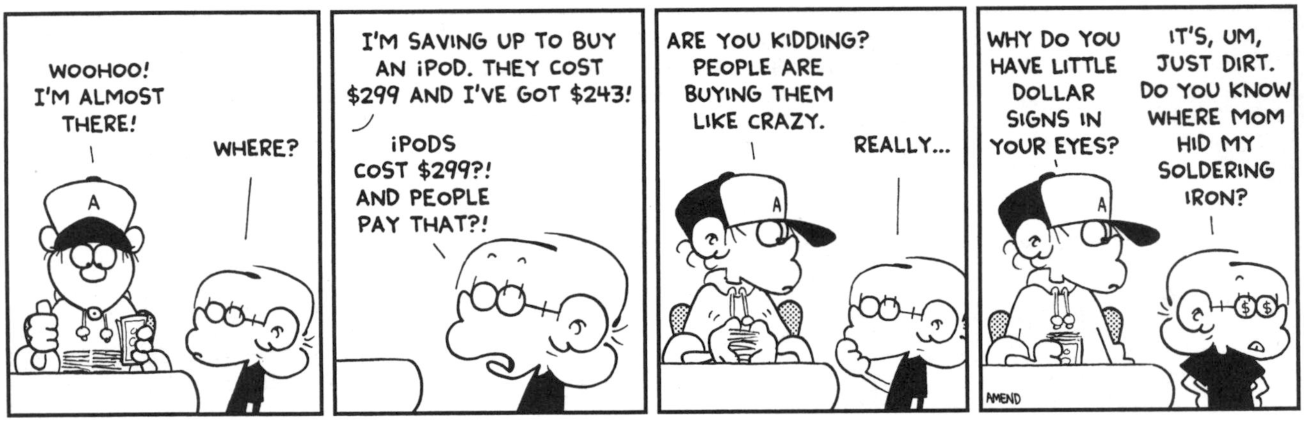
WOOHOO! I'M ALMOST THERE!
WHERE?
I'M SAVING UP TO BUY AN iPOD. THEY COST $299 AND I'VE GOT $243!
iPODS COST $299?! AND PEOPLE PAY THAT?!
ARE YOU KIDDING? PEOPLE ARE BUYING THEM LIKE CRAZY.
REALLY...
WHY DO YOU HAVE LITTLE DOLLAR SIGNS IN YOUR EYES?
IT'S, UM, JUST DIRT. DO YOU KNOW WHERE MOM HID MY SOLDERING IRON?
AMEND

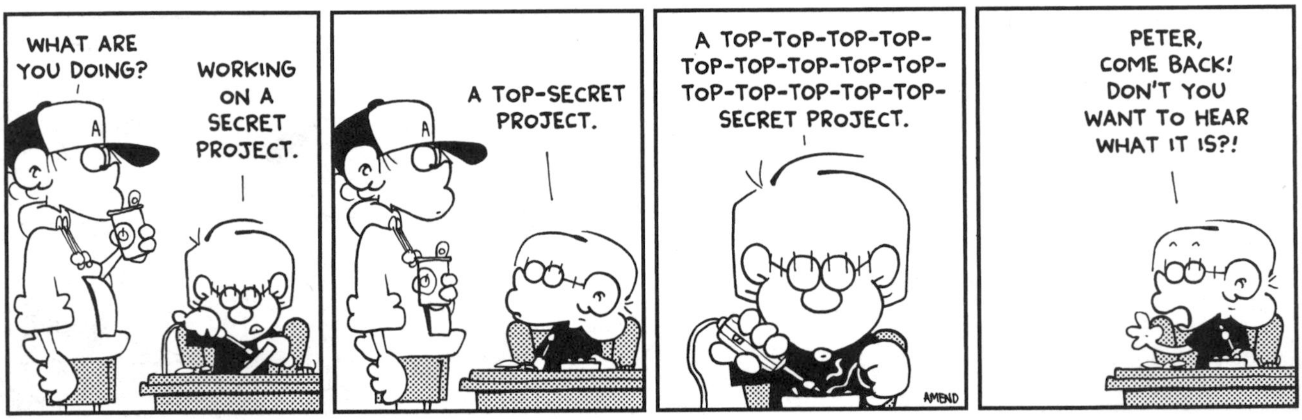
WHAT ARE YOU DOING?
WORKING ON A SECRET PROJECT.
A TOP-SECRET PROJECT.
A TOP-TOP-TOP-TOP-TOP-TOP-TOP-TOP-TOP-TOP-TOP-TOP-TOP-TOP-SECRET PROJECT.
AMEND
PETER, COME BACK! DON'T YOU WANT TO HEAR WHAT IT IS?!

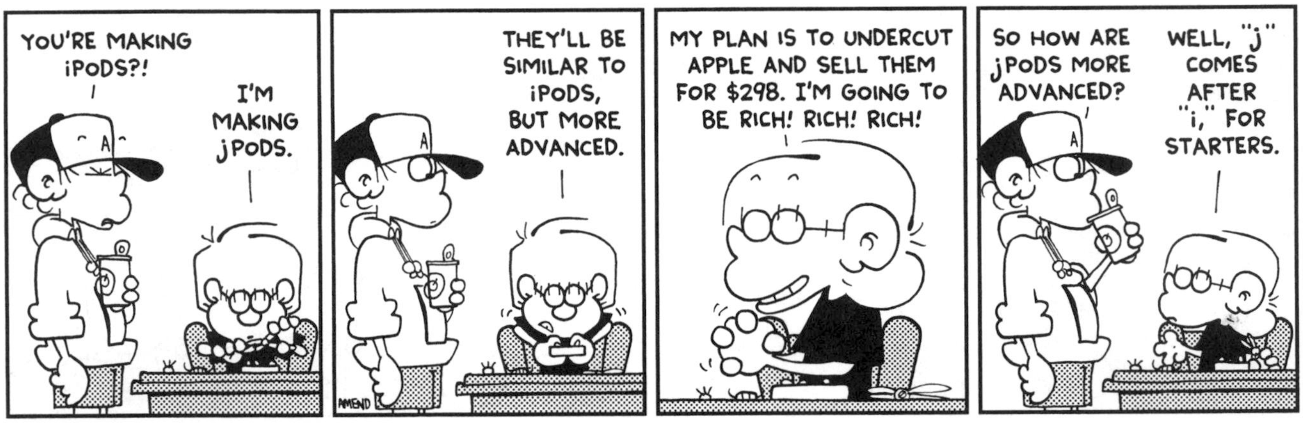
YOU'RE MAKING iPODS?!
I'M MAKING jPODS.
THEY'LL BE SIMILAR TO iPODS, BUT MORE ADVANCED.
AMEND
MY PLAN IS TO UNDERCUT APPLE AND SELL THEM FOR $298. I'M GOING TO BE RICH! RICH! RICH!
SO HOW ARE jPODS MORE ADVANCED?
WELL, "j" COMES AFTER "i," FOR STARTERS.

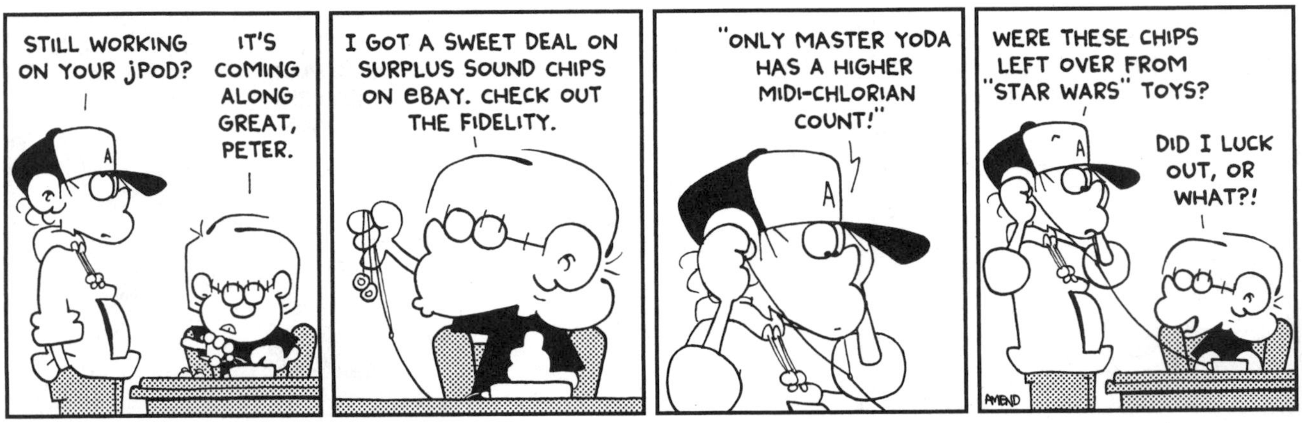
STILL WORKING ON YOUR jPOD?
IT'S COMING ALONG GREAT, PETER.
I GOT A SWEET DEAL ON SURPLUS SOUND CHIPS ON eBAY. CHECK OUT THE FIDELITY.
"ONLY MASTER YODA HAS A HIGHER MIDI-CHLORIAN COUNT!"
WERE THESE CHIPS LEFT OVER FROM "STAR WARS" TOYS?
DID I LUCK OUT, OR WHAT?!
AMEND

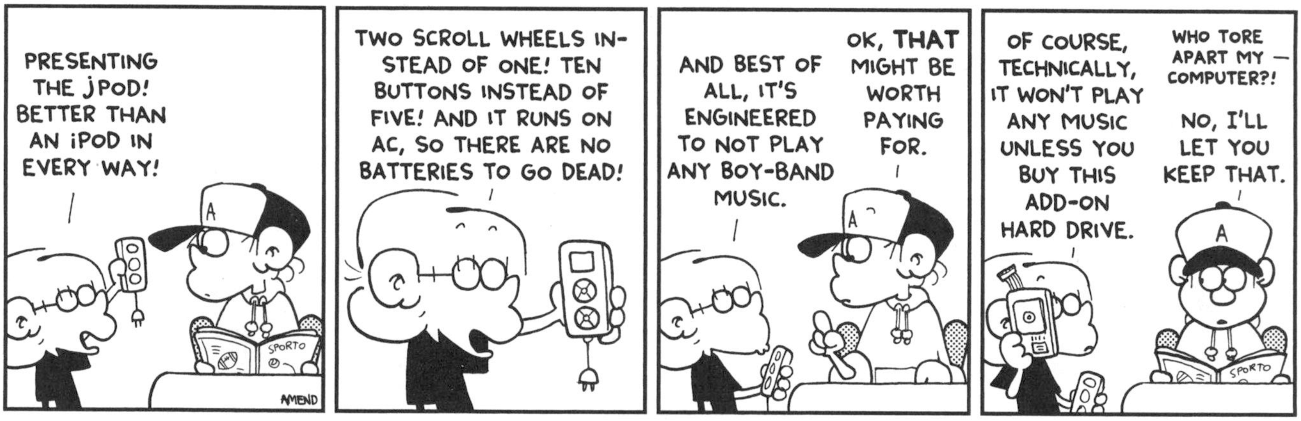
PRESENTING THE jPOD! BETTER THAN AN iPOD IN EVERY WAY!
SPORTO
AMEND
TWO SCROLL WHEELS INSTEAD OF ONE! TEN BUTTONS INSTEAD OF FIVE! AND IT RUNS ON AC, SO THERE ARE NO BATTERIES TO GO DEAD!
AND BEST OF ALL, IT'S ENGINEERED TO NOT PLAY ANY BOY-BAND MUSIC.
OK, THAT MIGHT BE WORTH PAYING FOR.
OF COURSE, TECHNICALLY, IT WON'T PLAY ANY MUSIC UNLESS YOU BUY THIS ADD-ON HARD DRIVE.
WHO TORE APART MY COMPUTER?!
NO, I'LL LET YOU KEEP THAT.
SPORTO

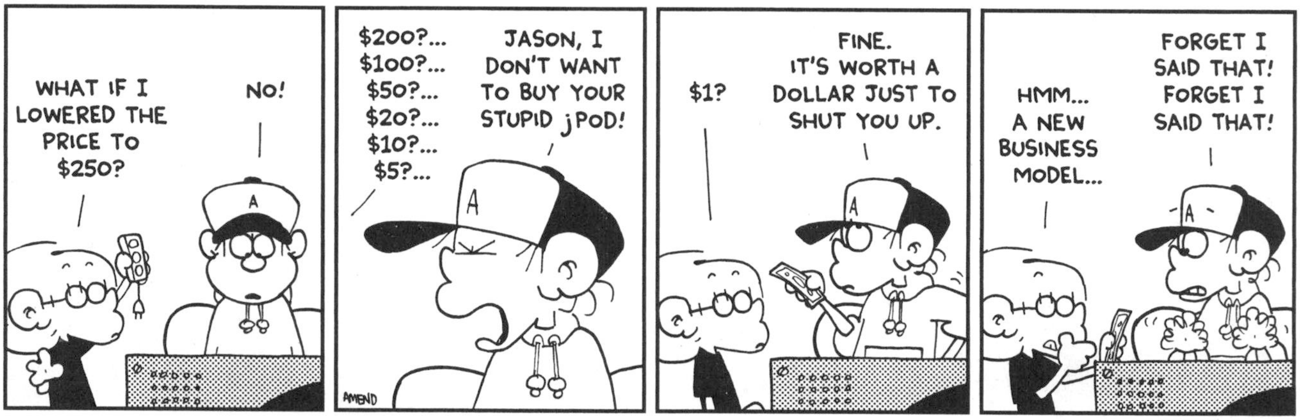
WHAT IF I LOWERED THE PRICE TO $250?
NO!
$200?... $100?... $50?... $20?... $10?... $5?...
JASON, I DON'T WANT TO BUY YOUR STUPID jPOD!
AMEND
$1?
FINE. IT'S WORTH A DOLLAR JUST TO SHUT YOU UP.
HMM... A NEW BUSINESS MODEL...
FORGET I SAID THAT! FORGET I SAID THAT!

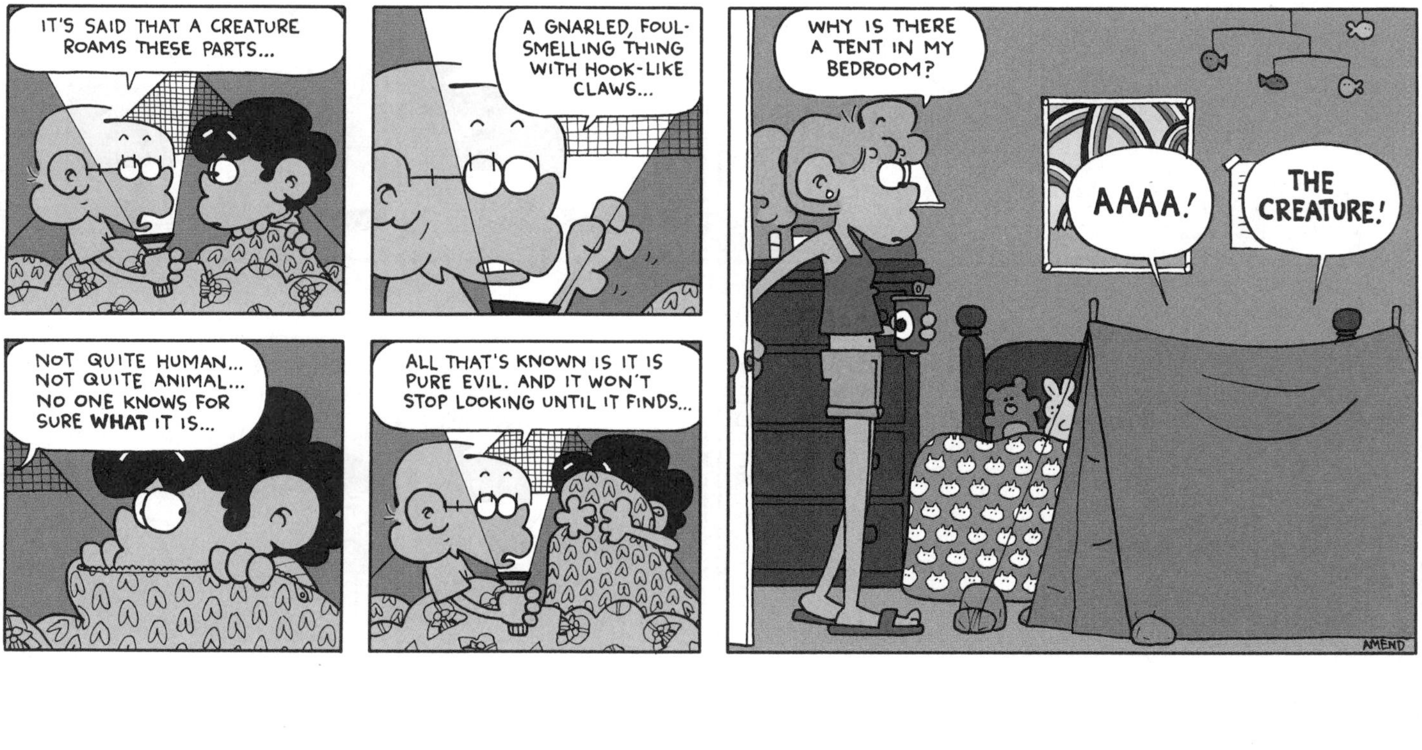
IT'S SAID THAT A CREATURE ROAMS THESE PARTS...
A GNARLED, FOUL-SMELLING THING WITH HOOK-LIKE CLAWS...
NOT QUITE HUMAN... NOT QUITE ANIMAL... NO ONE KNOWS FOR SURE WHAT IT IS...
ALL THAT'S KNOWN IS IT IS PURE EVIL. AND IT WON'T STOP LOOKING UNTIL IT FINDS...
WHY IS THERE A TENT IN MY BEDROOM?
AAAA!
THE CREATURE!
AMEND

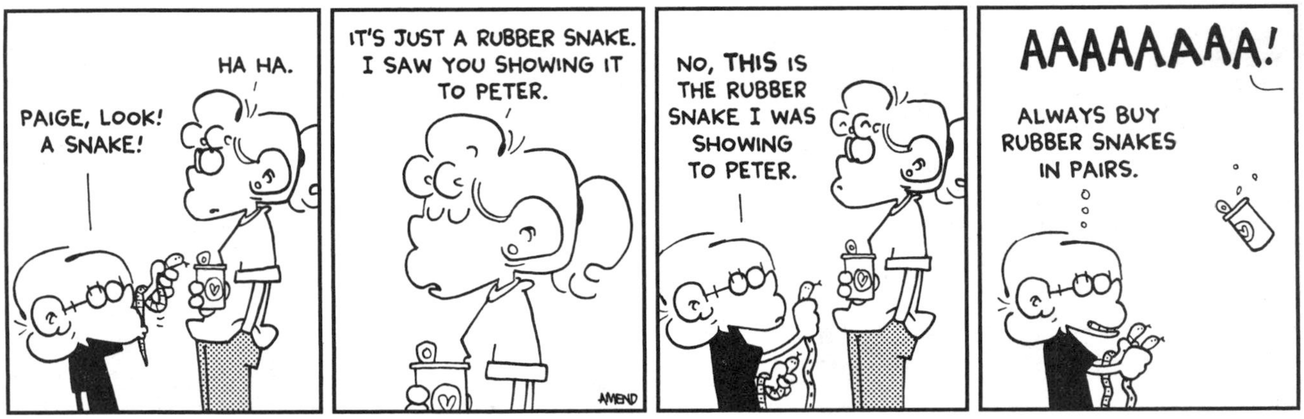
PAIGE, LOOK! A SNAKE!
HA HA.
IT'S JUST A RUBBER SNAKE. I SAW YOU SHOWING IT TO PETER.
NO, THIS IS THE RUBBER SNAKE I WAS SHOWING TO PETER.
AAAAAAAA!
ALWAYS BUY RUBBER SNAKES IN PAIRS.
AMEND

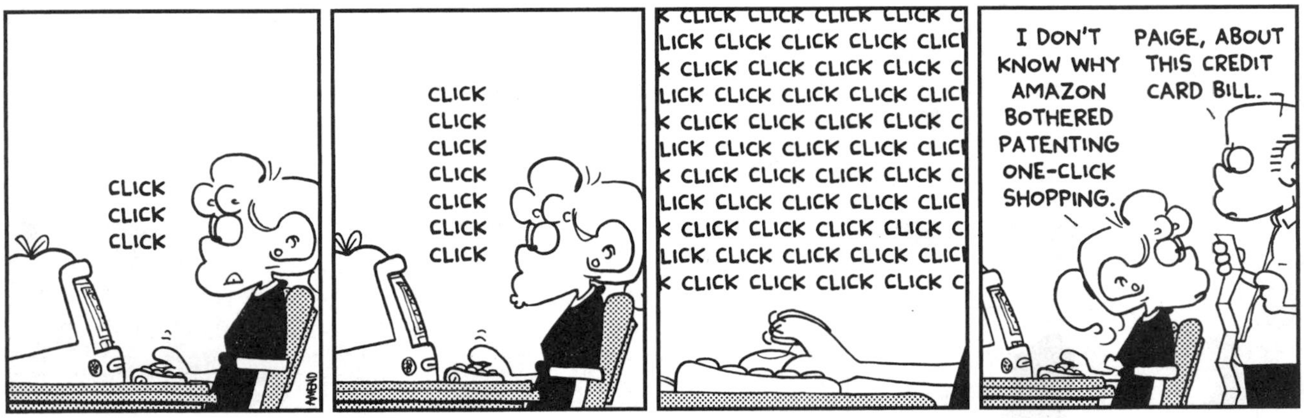
CLICK CLICK CLICK
AMEND
CLICK CLICK CLICK CLICK CLICK CLICK CLICK
K CLICK CLICK CLICK CLICK C
LICK CLICK CLICK CLICK CLICK CLICI
K CLICK CLICK CLICK CLICK C
LICK CLICK CLICK CLICK CLICK CLICI
K CLICK CLICK CLICK CLICK C
LICK CLICK CLICK CLICK CLICK CLICI
K CLICK CLICK CLICK CLICK C
LICK CLICK CLICK CLICK CLICK CLICI
K CLICK CLICK CLICK CLICK C
LICK CLICK CLICK CLICK CLICK CLICI
K CLICK CLICK CLICK CLICK C
I DON'T KNOW WHY AMAZON BOTHERED PATENTING ONE-CLICK SHOPPING.
PAIGE, ABOUT THIS CREDIT CARD BILL.

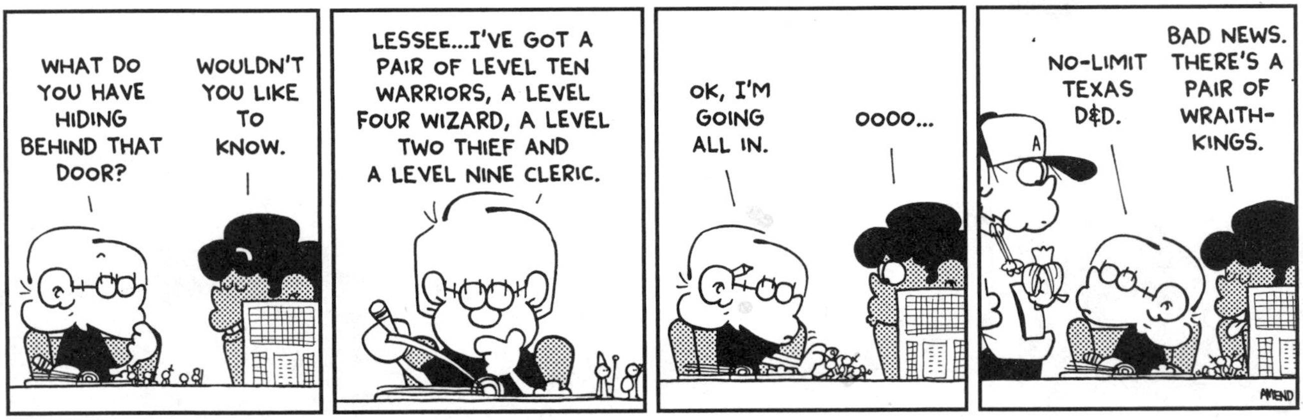
WHAT DO YOU HAVE HIDING BEHIND THAT DOOR?
WOULDN'T YOU LIKE TO KNOW.
LESSEE...I'VE GOT A PAIR OF LEVEL TEN WARRIORS, A LEVEL FOUR WIZARD, A LEVEL TWO THIEF AND A LEVEL NINE CLERIC.
OK, I'M GOING ALL IN.
OOOO...
NO-LIMIT TEXAS D&D.
BAD NEWS. THERE'S A PAIR OF WRAITH-KINGS.
AMEND

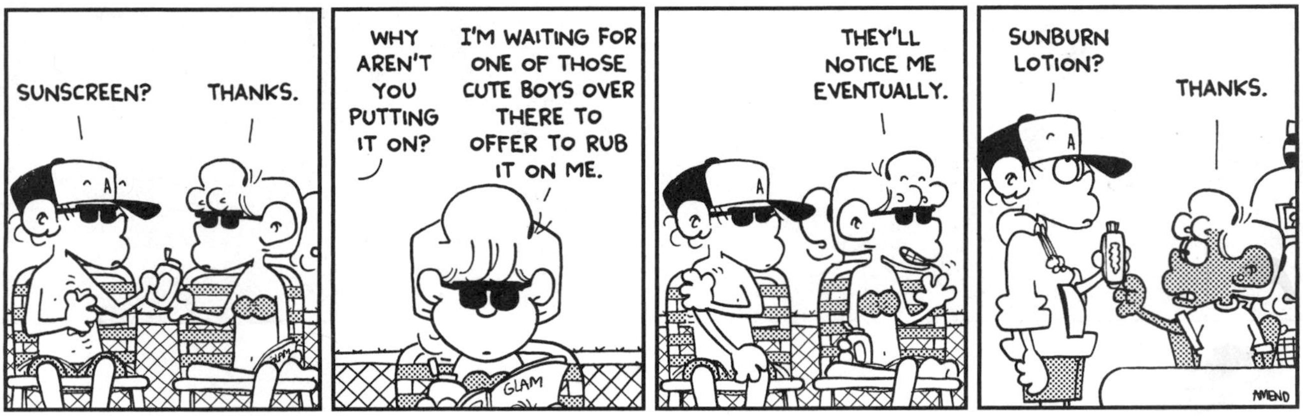
SUNSCREEN?
THANKS.
WHY AREN'T YOU PUTTING IT ON?
I'M WAITING FOR ONE OF THOSE CUTE BOYS OVER THERE TO OFFER TO RUB IT ON ME.
GLAM
THEY'LL NOTICE ME EVENTUALLY.
SUNBURN LOTION?
THANKS.
AMEND

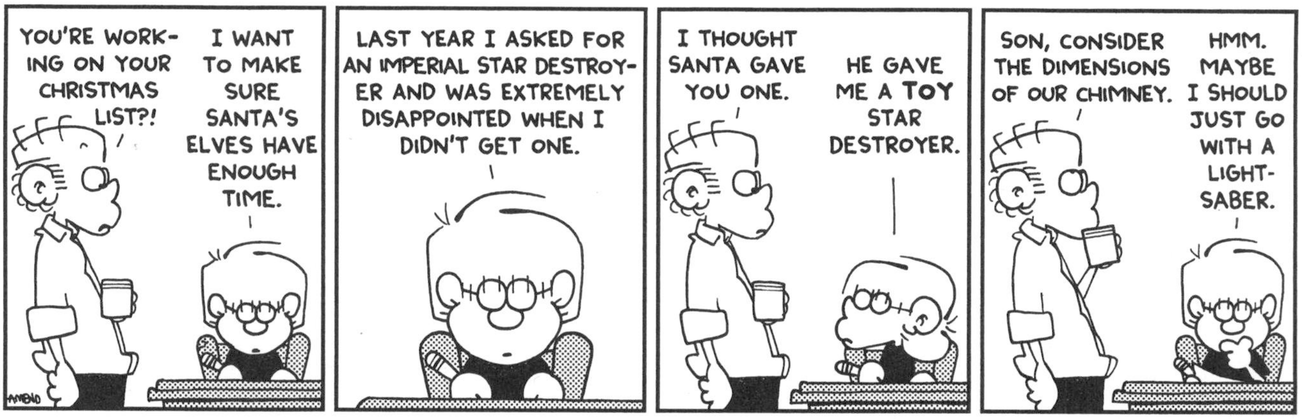
YOU'RE WORKING ON YOUR CHRISTMAS LIST?!
I WANT TO MAKE SURE SANTA'S ELVES HAVE ENOUGH TIME.
LAST YEAR I ASKED FOR AN IMPERIAL STAR DESTROYER AND WAS EXTREMELY DISAPPOINTED WHEN I DIDN'T GET ONE.
I THOUGHT SANTA GAVE YOU ONE.
HE GAVE ME A **TOY** STAR DESTROYER.
SON, CONSIDER THE DIMENSIONS OF OUR CHIMNEY.
HMM. MAYBE I SHOULD JUST GO WITH A LIGHT-SABER.
AMEND

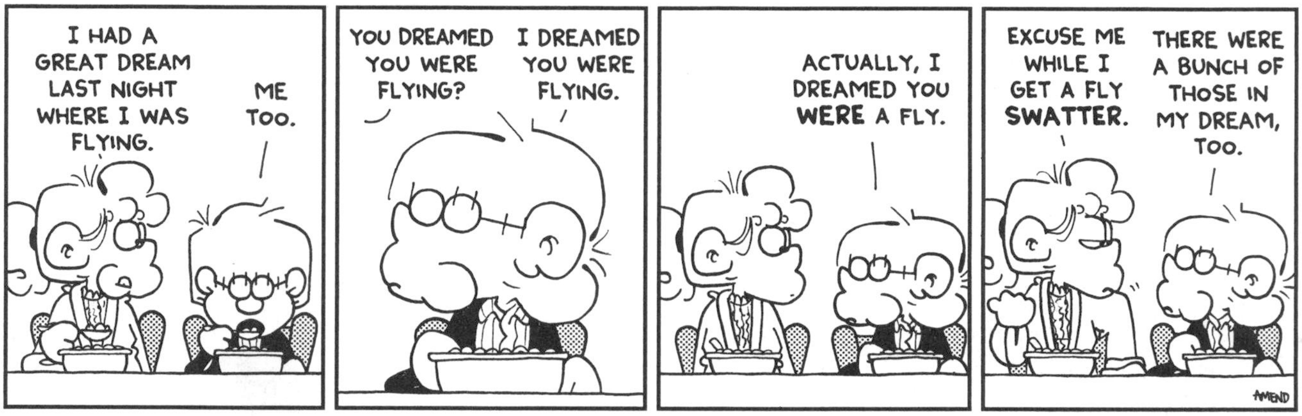
I HAD A GREAT DREAM LAST NIGHT WHERE I WAS FLYING.
ME TOO.
YOU DREAMED YOU WERE FLYING?
I DREAMED YOU WERE FLYING.
ACTUALLY, I DREAMED YOU **WERE** A FLY.
EXCUSE ME WHILE I GET A FLY **SWATTER**.
THERE WERE A BUNCH OF THOSE IN MY DREAM, TOO.
AMEND

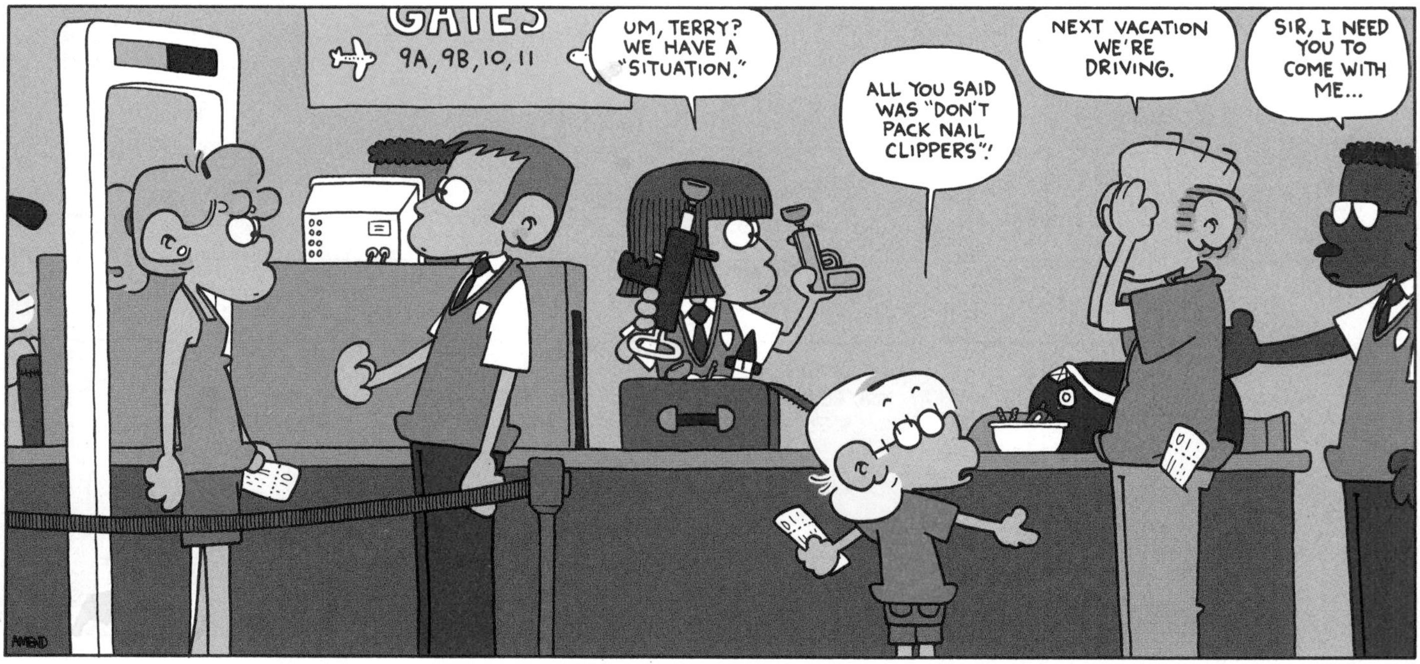
GATES
9A, 9B, 10, 11
UM, TERRY? WE HAVE A "SITUATION."
ALL YOU SAID WAS "DON'T PACK NAIL CLIPPERS"!
NEXT VACATION WE'RE DRIVING.
SIR, I NEED YOU TO COME WITH ME...
AMEND

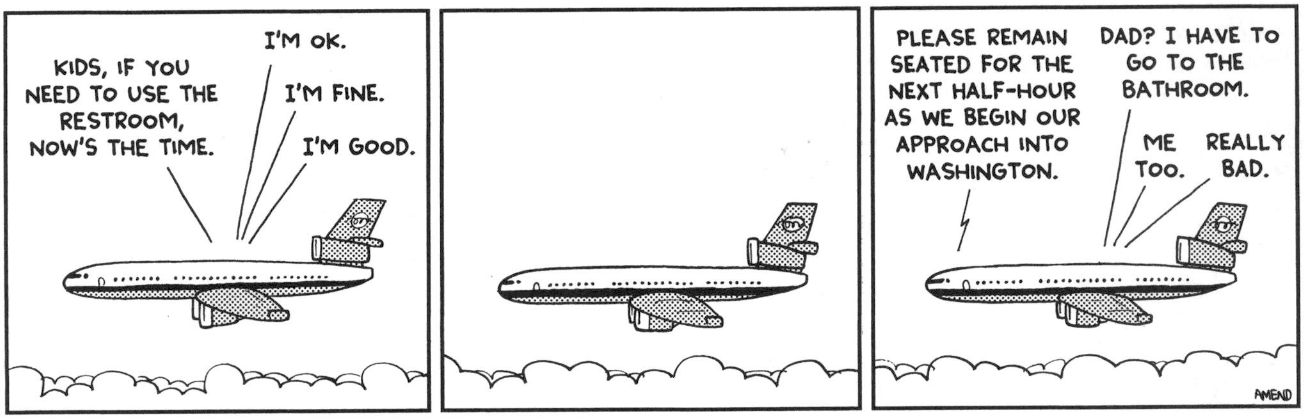

KIDS, IF YOU NEED TO USE THE RESTROOM, NOW'S THE TIME.
I'M OK.
I'M FINE.
I'M GOOD.
PLEASE REMAIN SEATED FOR THE NEXT HALF-HOUR AS WE BEGIN OUR APPROACH INTO WASHINGTON.
DAD? I HAVE TO GO TO THE BATHROOM.
ME TOO.
REALLY BAD.
AMEND

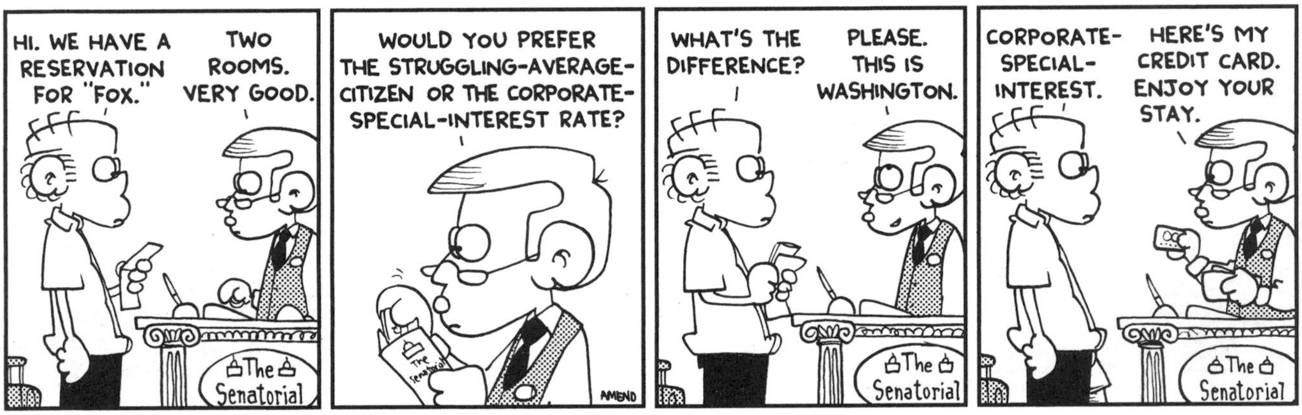

HI. WE HAVE A RESERVATION FOR "FOX."
TWO ROOMS. VERY GOOD.
The Senatorial
WOULD YOU PREFER THE STRUGGLING-AVERAGE-CITIZEN OR THE CORPORATE-SPECIAL-INTEREST RATE?
AMEND
WHAT'S THE DIFFERENCE?
PLEASE. THIS IS WASHINGTON.
The Senatorial
CORPORATE-SPECIAL-INTEREST.
HERE'S MY CREDIT CARD. ENJOY YOUR STAY.
The Senatorial

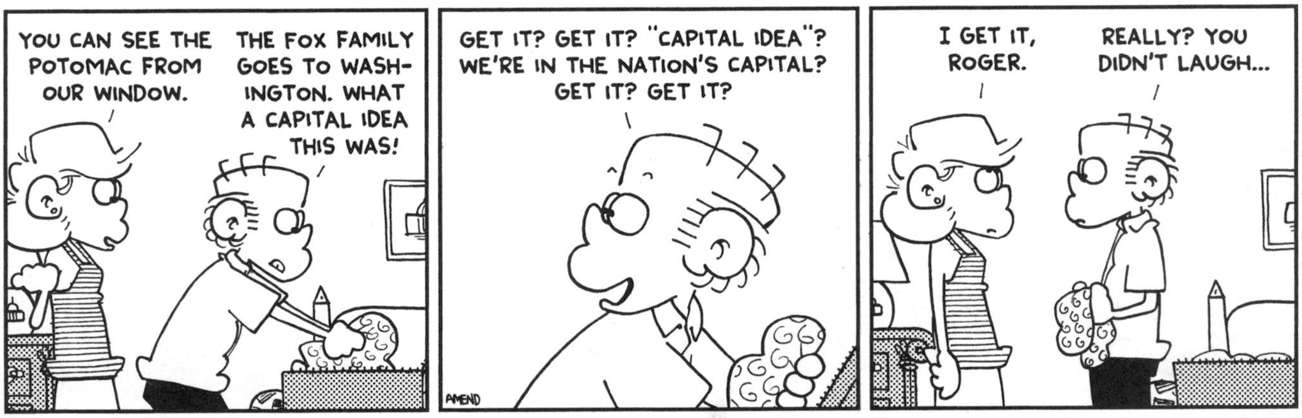

YOU CAN SEE THE POTOMAC FROM OUR WINDOW.
THE FOX FAMILY GOES TO WASHINGTON. WHAT A CAPITAL IDEA THIS WAS!
GET IT? GET IT? "CAPITAL IDEA"? WE'RE IN THE NATION'S CAPITAL? GET IT? GET IT?
AMEND
I GET IT, ROGER.
REALLY? YOU DIDN'T LAUGH...

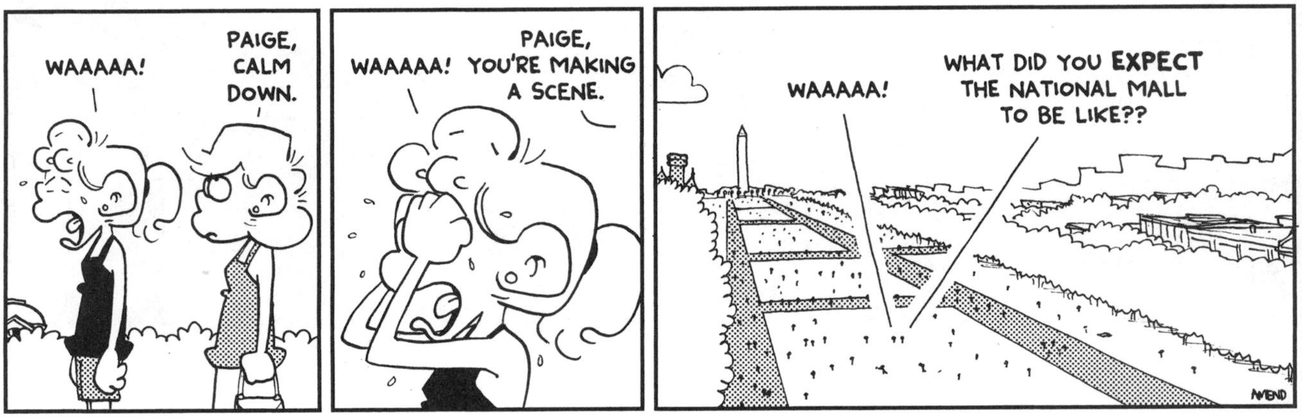

WAAAAA!
PAIGE, CALM DOWN.
WAAAAA!
PAIGE, YOU'RE MAKING A SCENE.
WAAAAA!
WHAT DID YOU **EXPECT** THE NATIONAL MALL TO BE LIKE??
AMEND

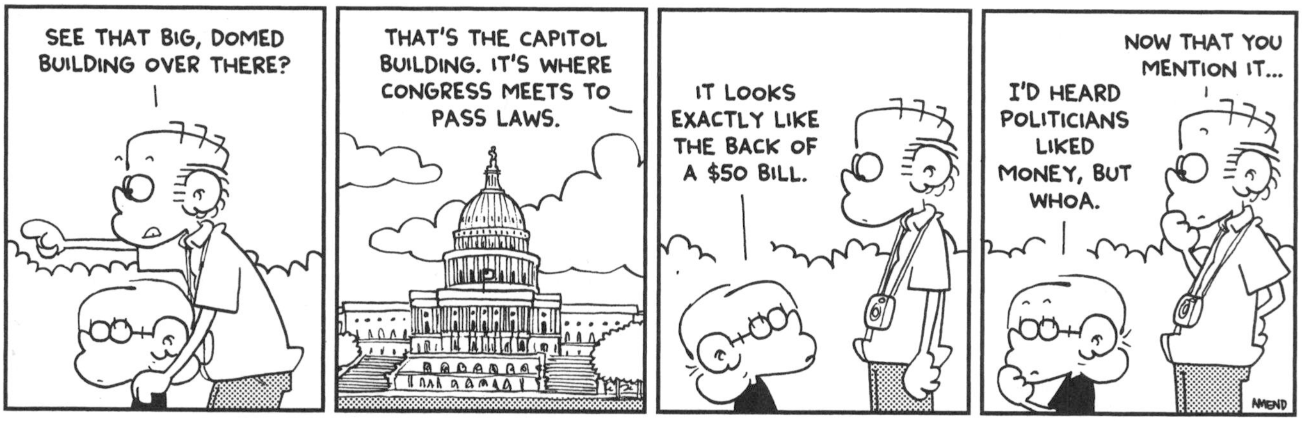
SEE THAT BIG, DOMED BUILDING OVER THERE?
THAT'S THE CAPITOL BUILDING. IT'S WHERE CONGRESS MEETS TO PASS LAWS.
IT LOOKS EXACTLY LIKE THE BACK OF A $50 BILL.
I'D HEARD POLITICIANS LIKED MONEY, BUT WHOA.
NOW THAT YOU MENTION IT...
AMEND

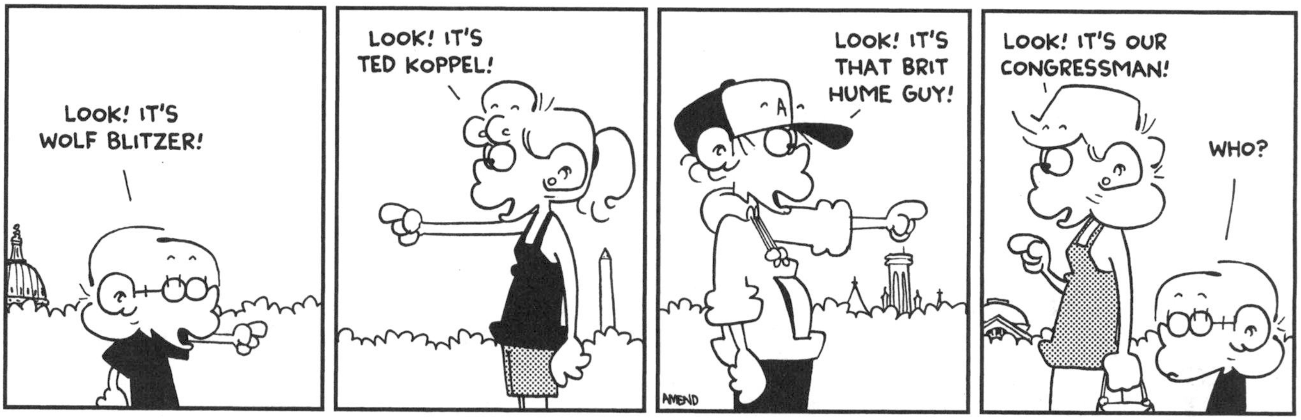
LOOK! IT'S WOLF BLITZER!
LOOK! IT'S TED KOPPEL!
LOOK! IT'S THAT BRIT HUME GUY!
A
AMEND
LOOK! IT'S OUR CONGRESSMAN!
WHO?

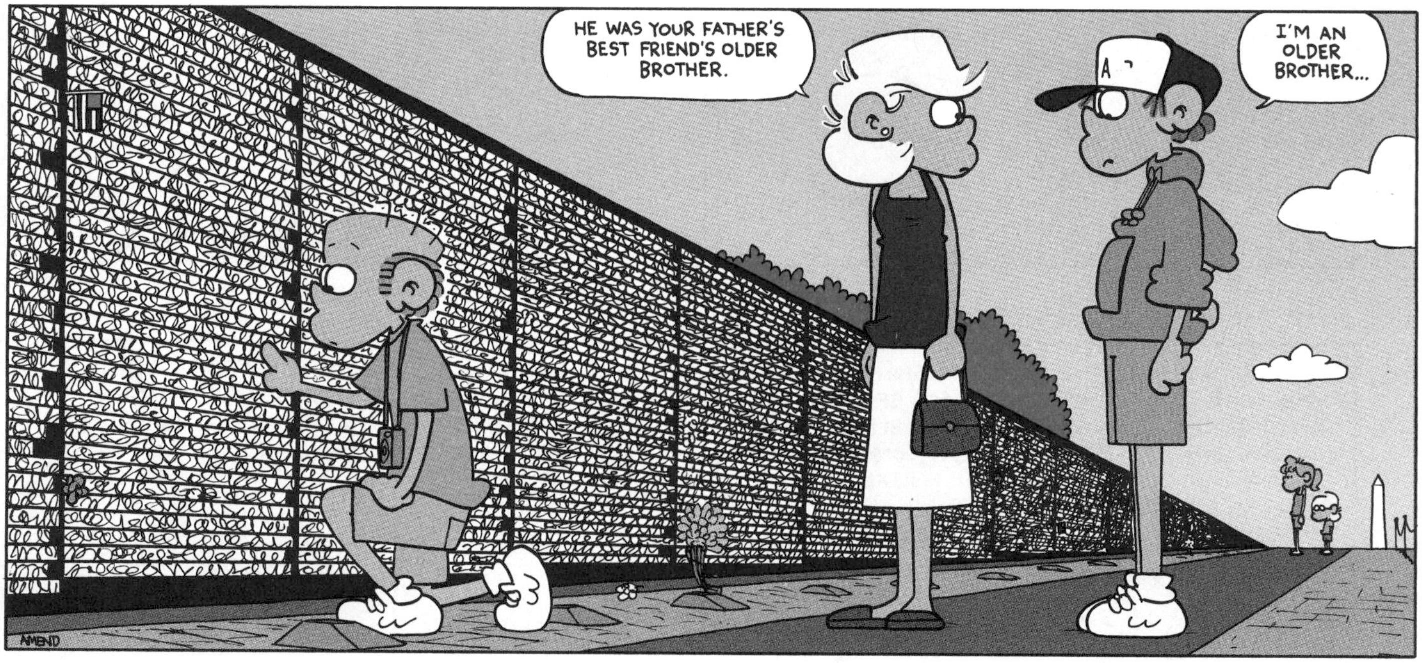
HE WAS YOUR FATHER'S BEST FRIEND'S OLDER BROTHER.
I'M AN OLDER BROTHER...
A
AMEND

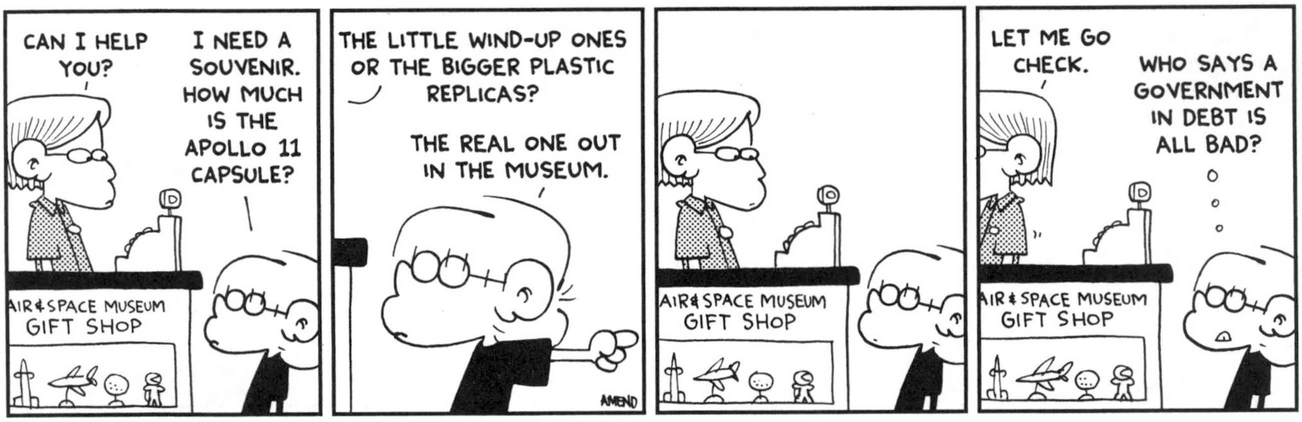
CAN I HELP YOU?
I NEED A SOUVENIR. HOW MUCH IS THE APOLLO 11 CAPSULE?
AIR & SPACE MUSEUM GIFT SHOP
THE LITTLE WIND-UP ONES OR THE BIGGER PLASTIC REPLICAS?
THE REAL ONE OUT IN THE MUSEUM.
AMEND
AIR & SPACE MUSEUM GIFT SHOP
LET ME GO CHECK.
WHO SAYS A GOVERNMENT IN DEBT IS ALL BAD?
AIR & SPACE MUSEUM GIFT SHOP

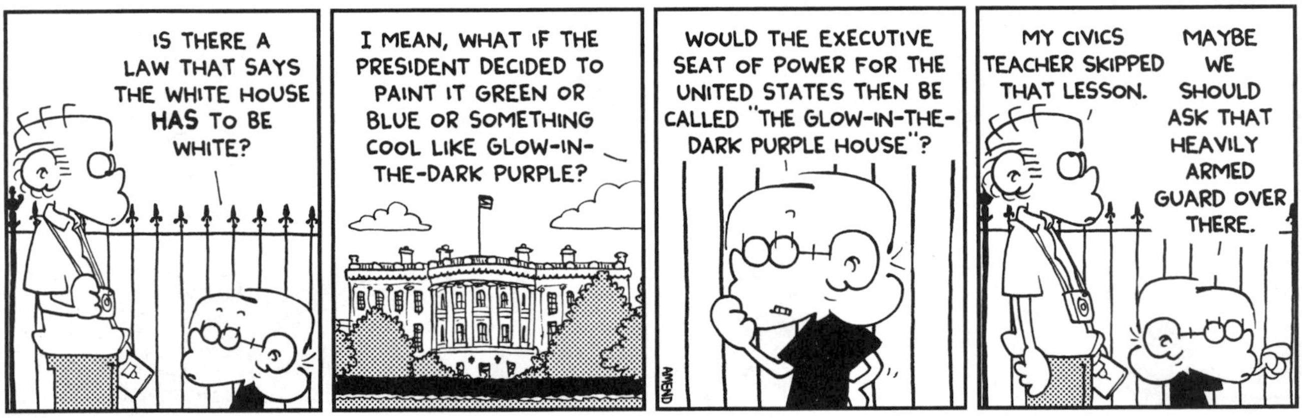
IS THERE A LAW THAT SAYS THE WHITE HOUSE HAS TO BE WHITE?
I MEAN, WHAT IF THE PRESIDENT DECIDED TO PAINT IT GREEN OR BLUE OR SOMETHING COOL LIKE GLOW-IN-THE-DARK PURPLE?
AMEND
WOULD THE EXECUTIVE SEAT OF POWER FOR THE UNITED STATES THEN BE CALLED "THE GLOW-IN-THE-DARK PURPLE HOUSE"?
MY CIVICS TEACHER SKIPPED THAT LESSON.
MAYBE WE SHOULD ASK THAT HEAVILY ARMED GUARD OVER THERE.

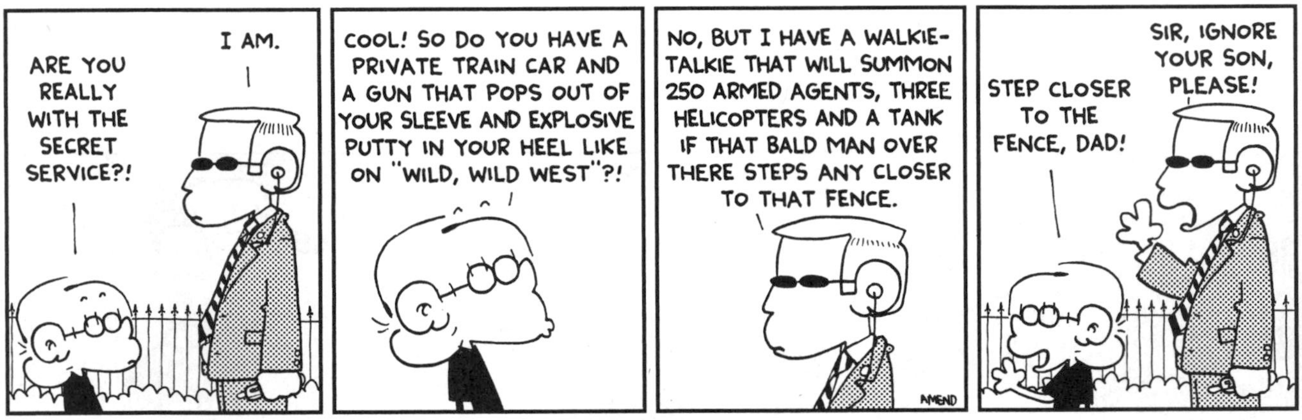
ARE YOU REALLY WITH THE SECRET SERVICE?!
I AM.
COOL! SO DO YOU HAVE A PRIVATE TRAIN CAR AND A GUN THAT POPS OUT OF YOUR SLEEVE AND EXPLOSIVE PUTTY IN YOUR HEEL LIKE ON "WILD, WILD WEST"?!
NO, BUT I HAVE A WALKIE-TALKIE THAT WILL SUMMON 250 ARMED AGENTS, THREE HELICOPTERS AND A TANK IF THAT BALD MAN OVER THERE STEPS ANY CLOSER TO THAT FENCE.
AMEND
STEP CLOSER TO THE FENCE, DAD!
SIR, IGNORE YOUR SON, PLEASE!

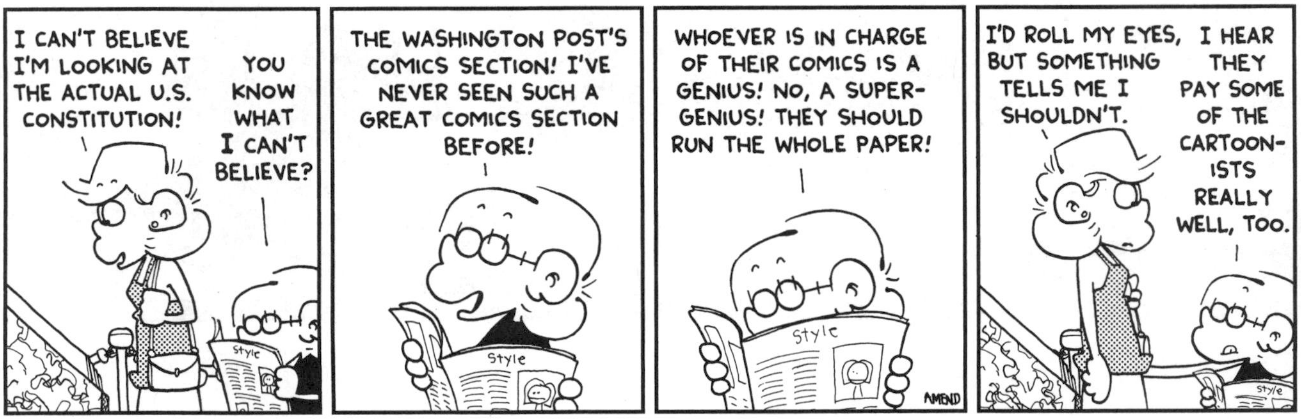
I CAN'T BELIEVE I'M LOOKING AT THE ACTUAL U.S. CONSTITUTION!
YOU KNOW WHAT I CAN'T BELIEVE?
Style
THE WASHINGTON POST'S COMICS SECTION! I'VE NEVER SEEN SUCH A GREAT COMICS SECTION BEFORE!
Style
WHOEVER IS IN CHARGE OF THEIR COMICS IS A GENIUS! NO, A SUPER-GENIUS! THEY SHOULD RUN THE WHOLE PAPER!
Style
AMEND
I'D ROLL MY EYES, BUT SOMETHING TELLS ME I SHOULDN'T.
I HEAR THEY PAY SOME OF THE CARTOONISTS REALLY WELL, TOO.
Style

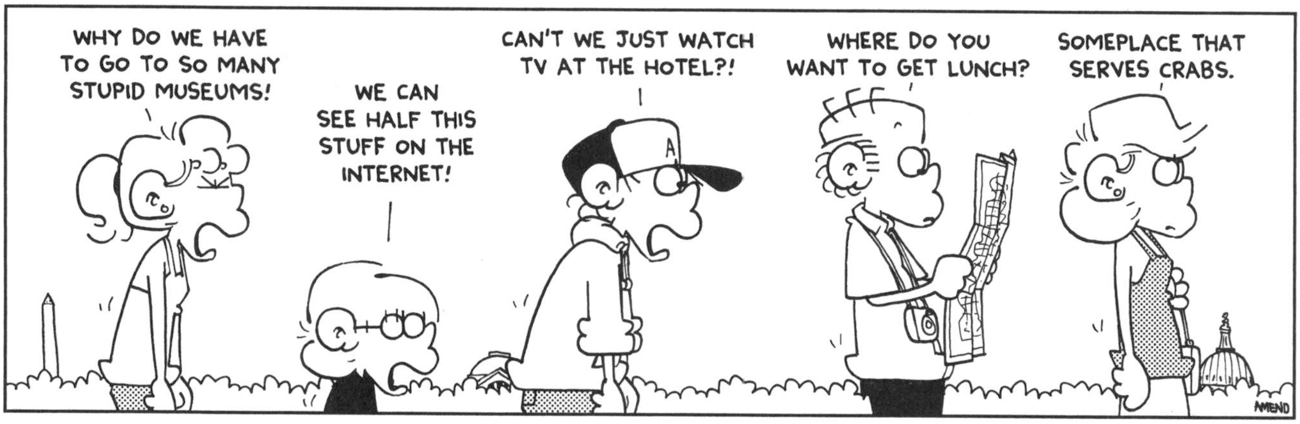
WHY DO WE HAVE TO GO TO SO MANY STUPID MUSEUMS!
WE CAN SEE HALF THIS STUFF ON THE INTERNET!
CAN'T WE JUST WATCH TV AT THE HOTEL?!
WHERE DO YOU WANT TO GET LUNCH?
SOMEPLACE THAT SERVES CRABS.
AMEND

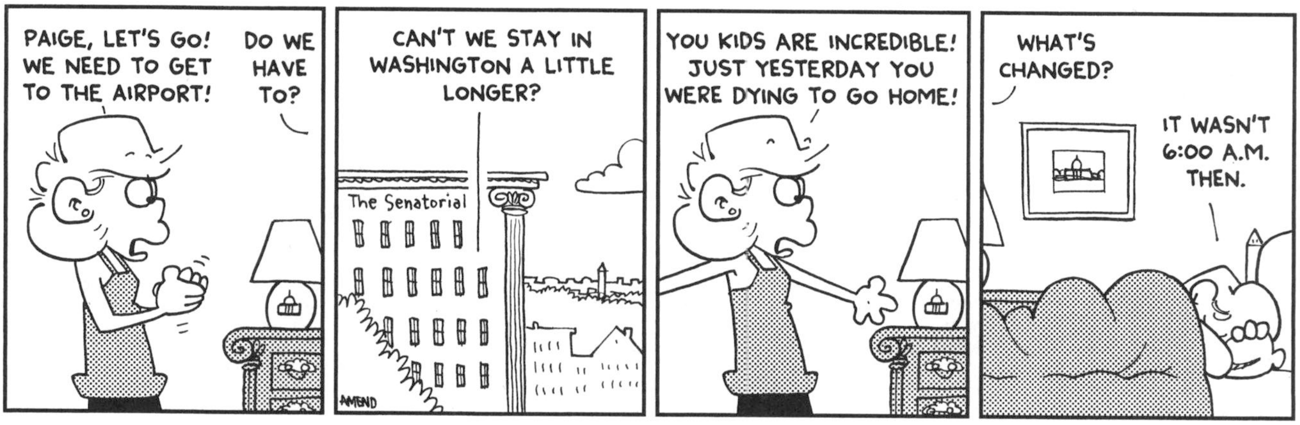
PAIGE, LET'S GO! WE NEED TO GET TO THE AIRPORT!
DO WE HAVE TO?
CAN'T WE STAY IN WASHINGTON A LITTLE LONGER?
The Senatorial
AMEND
YOU KIDS ARE INCREDIBLE! JUST YESTERDAY YOU WERE DYING TO GO HOME!
WHAT'S CHANGED?
IT WASN'T 6:00 A.M. THEN.

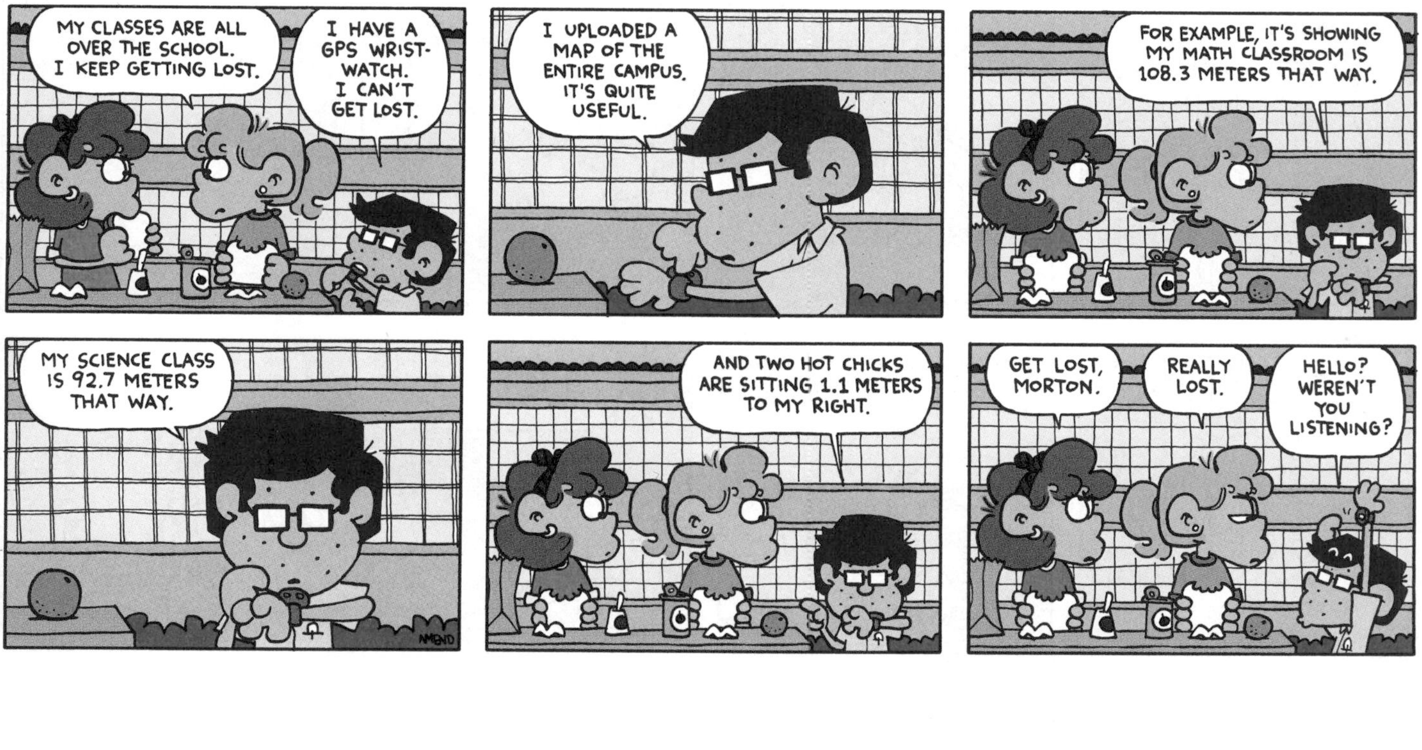
MY CLASSES ARE ALL OVER THE SCHOOL. I KEEP GETTING LOST.
I HAVE A GPS WRIST-WATCH. I CAN'T GET LOST.
I UPLOADED A MAP OF THE ENTIRE CAMPUS. IT'S QUITE USEFUL.
FOR EXAMPLE, IT'S SHOWING MY MATH CLASSROOM IS 108.3 METERS THAT WAY.
MY SCIENCE CLASS IS 92.7 METERS THAT WAY.
AMEND
AND TWO HOT CHICKS ARE SITTING 1.1 METERS TO MY RIGHT.
GET LOST, MORTON.
REALLY LOST.
HELLO? WEREN'T YOU LISTENING?

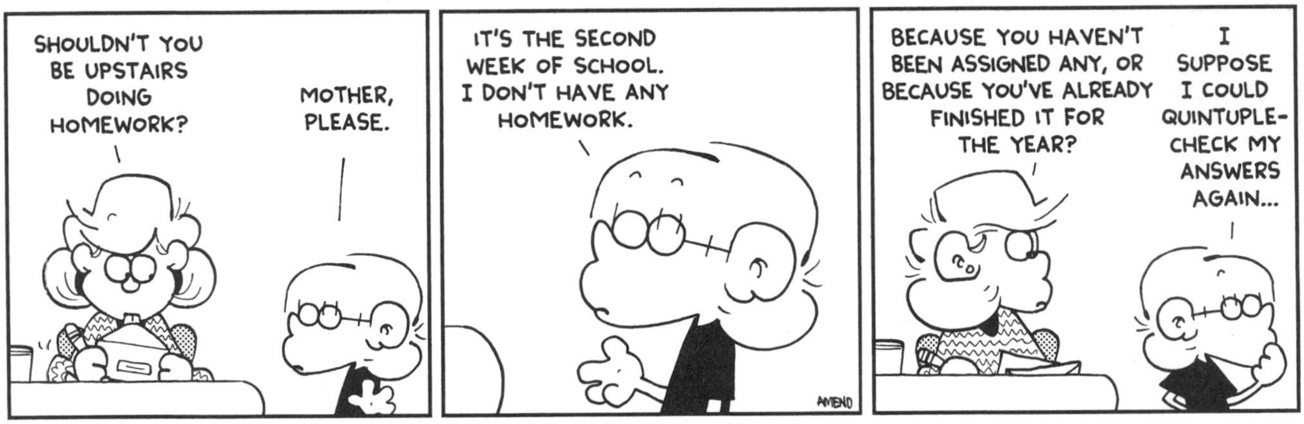
SHOULDN'T YOU BE UPSTAIRS DOING HOMEWORK?
MOTHER, PLEASE.
IT'S THE SECOND WEEK OF SCHOOL. I DON'T HAVE ANY HOMEWORK.
BECAUSE YOU HAVEN'T BEEN ASSIGNED ANY, OR BECAUSE YOU'VE ALREADY FINISHED IT FOR THE YEAR?
I SUPPOSE I COULD QUINTUPLE-CHECK MY ANSWERS AGAIN...
AMEND

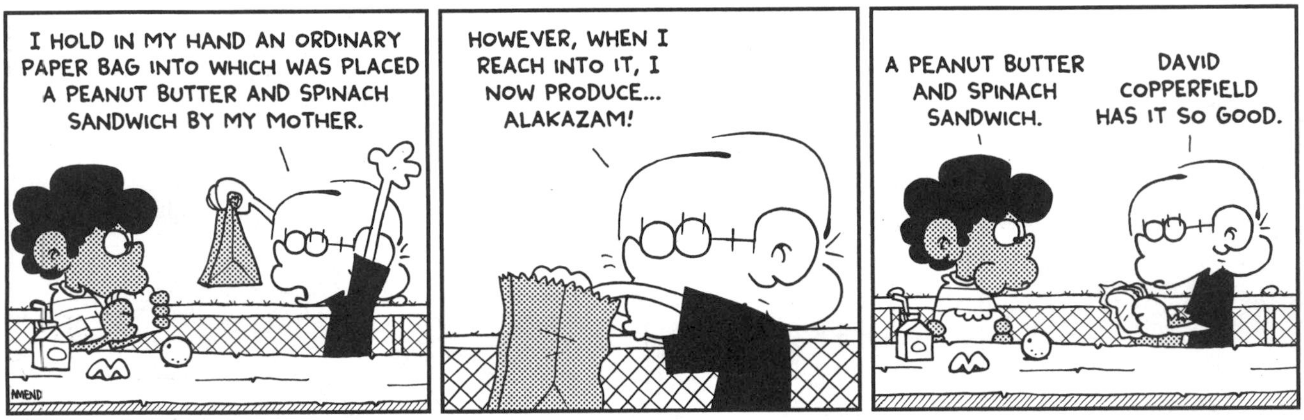
I HOLD IN MY HAND AN ORDINARY PAPER BAG INTO WHICH WAS PLACED A PEANUT BUTTER AND SPINACH SANDWICH BY MY MOTHER.
HOWEVER, WHEN I REACH INTO IT, I NOW PRODUCE... ALAKAZAM!
A PEANUT BUTTER AND SPINACH SANDWICH.
DAVID COPPERFIELD HAS IT SO GOOD.
AMEND

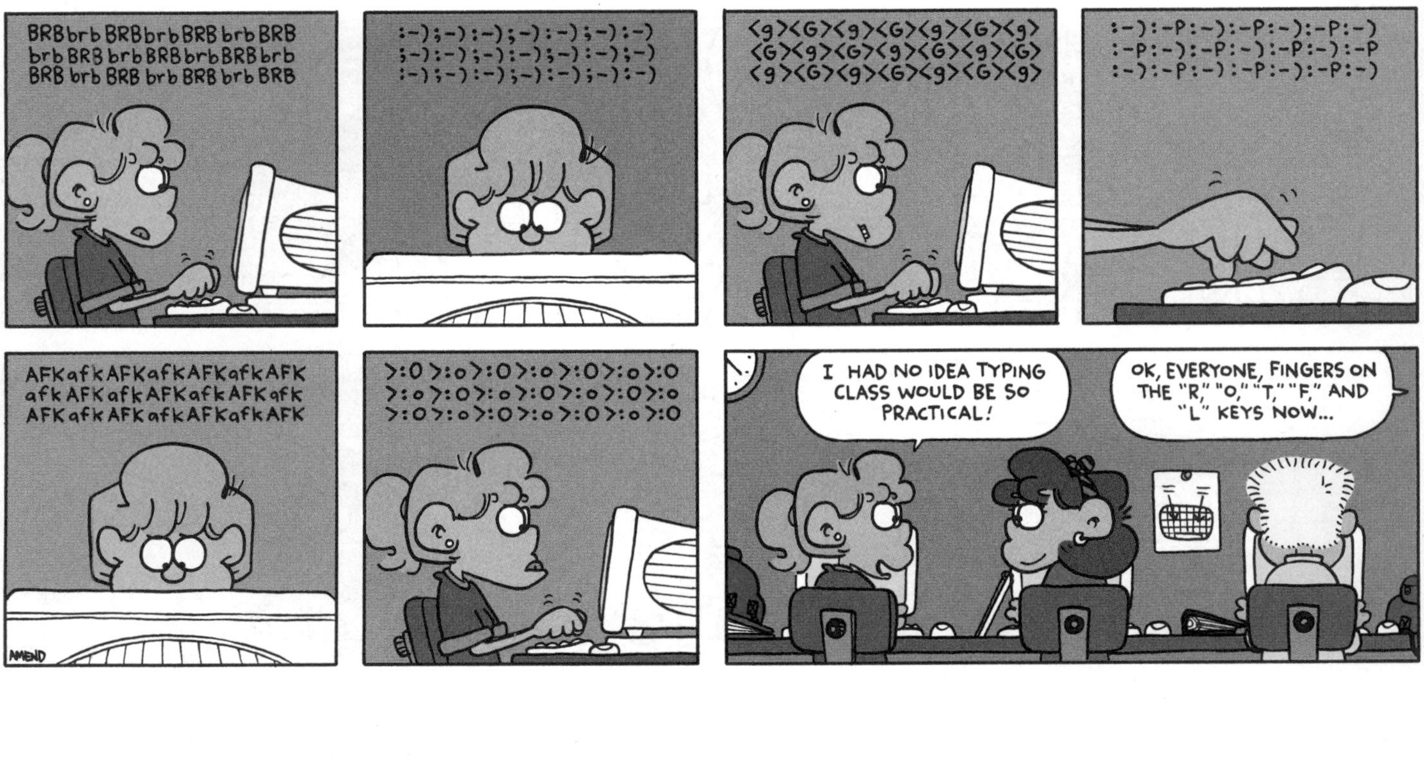
BRBbrbBRBbrbBRBbrbBRB
brbBRBbrbBRBbrbBRBbrb
BRBbrbBRBbrbBRBbrbBRB
:-);-):-);-):-);-):-)
;-):-);-):-);-):-);-)
:-);-):-);-):-);-):-)
<g><G><g><G><g><G><g>
<G><g><G><g><G><g><G>
<g><G><g><G><g><G><g>
:-):-P:-):-P:-):-P:-)
:-P:-):-P:-):-P:-):-P
:-):-P:-):-P:-):-P:-)
AFKafkAFKafkAFKafkAFK
afkAFKafkAFKafkAFKafk
AFKafkAFKafkAFKafkAFK
AMEND
>:O>:o>:O>:o>:O>:o>:O
>:o>:O>:o>:O>:o>:O>:o
>:O>:o>:O>:o>:O>:o>:O
I HAD NO IDEA TYPING CLASS WOULD BE SO PRACTICAL!
OK, EVERYONE, FINGERS ON THE "R," "O," "T," "F," AND "L" KEYS NOW...

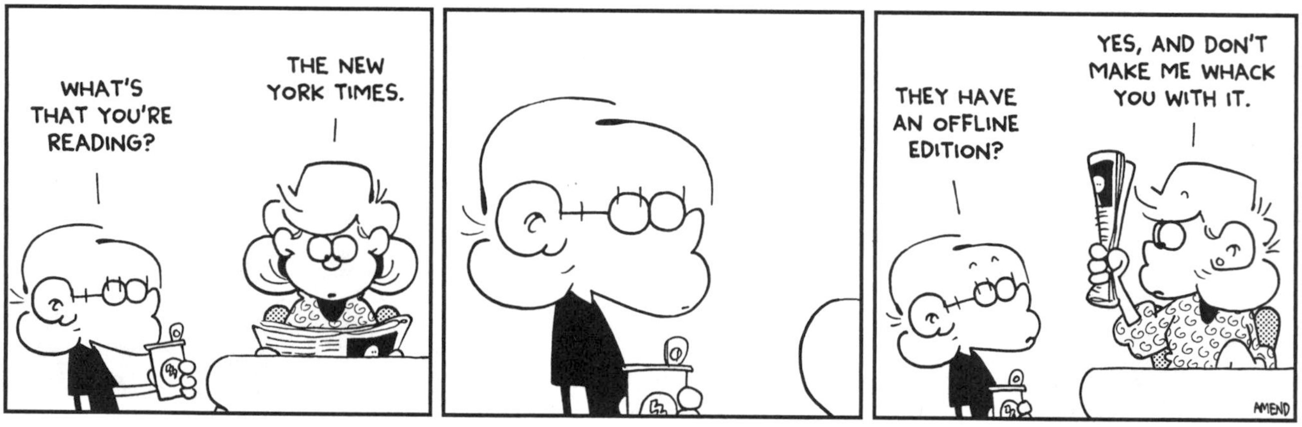
WHAT'S THAT YOU'RE READING?
THE NEW YORK TIMES.
THEY HAVE AN OFFLINE EDITION?
YES, AND DON'T MAKE ME WHACK YOU WITH IT.
AMEND

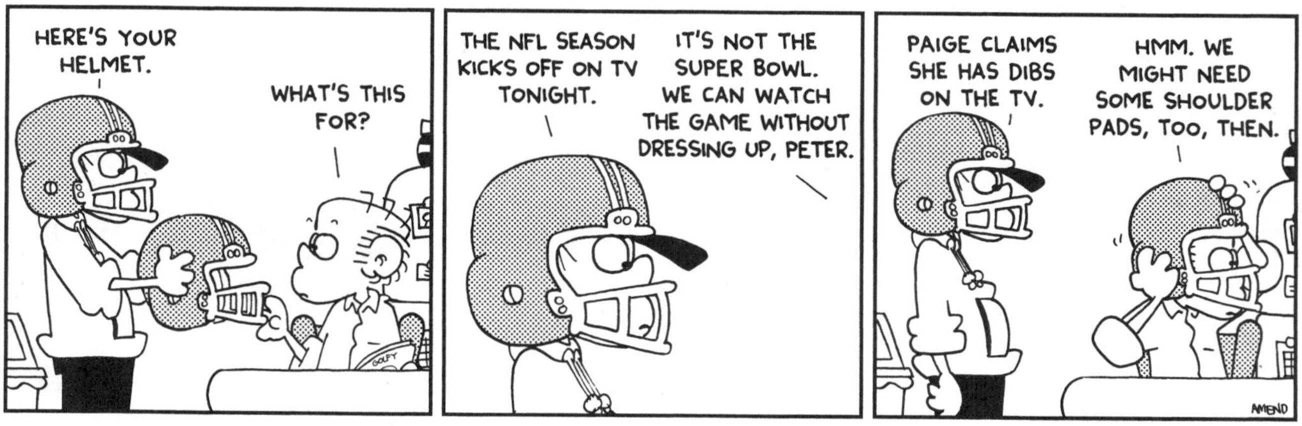
HERE'S YOUR HELMET.
WHAT'S THIS FOR?
THE NFL SEASON KICKS OFF ON TV TONIGHT.
IT'S NOT THE SUPER BOWL. WE CAN WATCH THE GAME WITHOUT DRESSING UP, PETER.
PAIGE CLAIMS SHE HAS DIBS ON THE TV.
HMM. WE MIGHT NEED SOME SHOULDER PADS, TOO, THEN.
AMEND

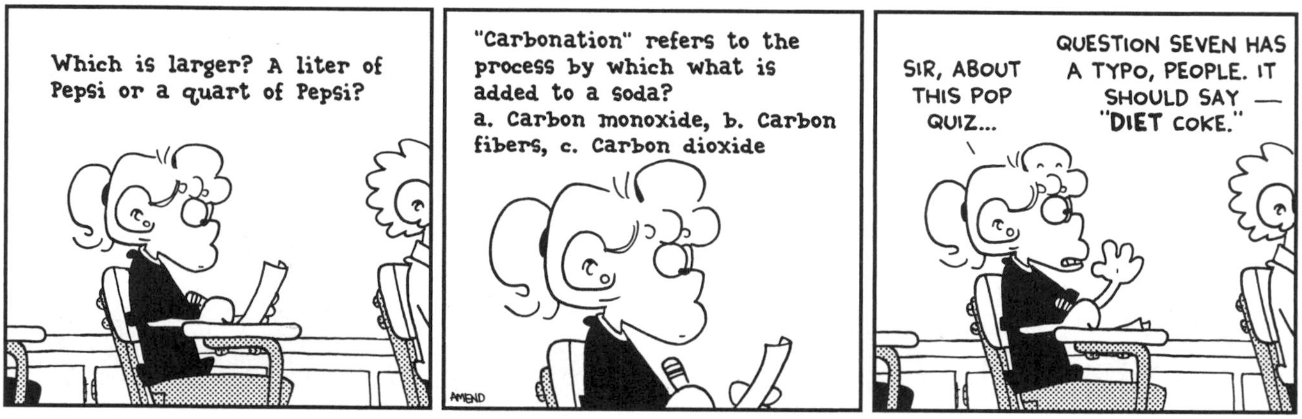
Which is larger? A liter of Pepsi or a quart of Pepsi?
"Carbonation" refers to the process by which what is added to a soda?
a. Carbon monoxide, b. Carbon fibers, c. Carbon dioxide
AMEND
SIR, ABOUT THIS POP QUIZ...
QUESTION SEVEN HAS A TYPO, PEOPLE. IT SHOULD SAY — "DIET COKE."

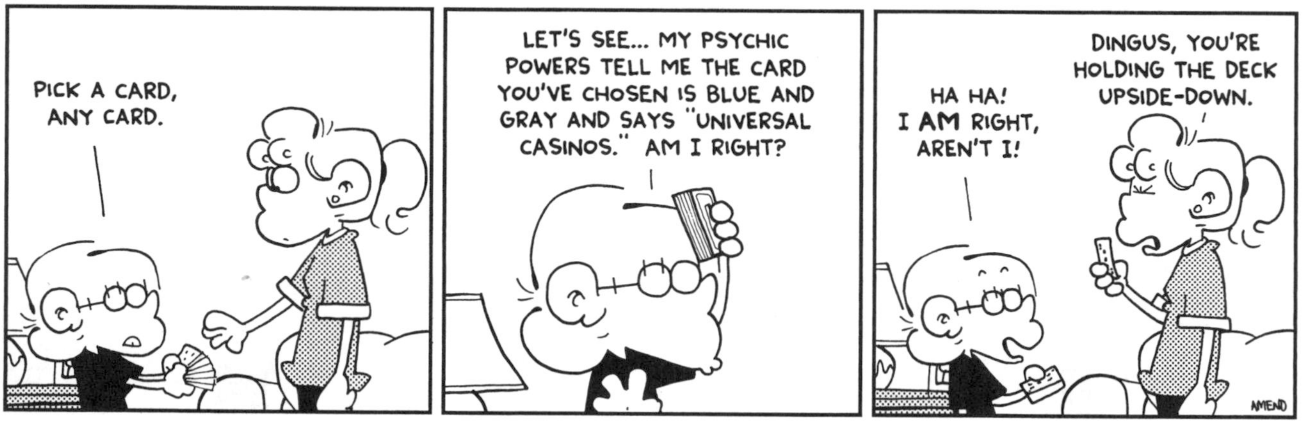
PICK A CARD, ANY CARD.
LET'S SEE... MY PSYCHIC POWERS TELL ME THE CARD YOU'VE CHOSEN IS BLUE AND GRAY AND SAYS "UNIVERSAL CASINOS." AM I RIGHT?
HA HA! I AM RIGHT, AREN'T I!
DINGUS, YOU'RE HOLDING THE DECK UPSIDE-DOWN.
AMEND

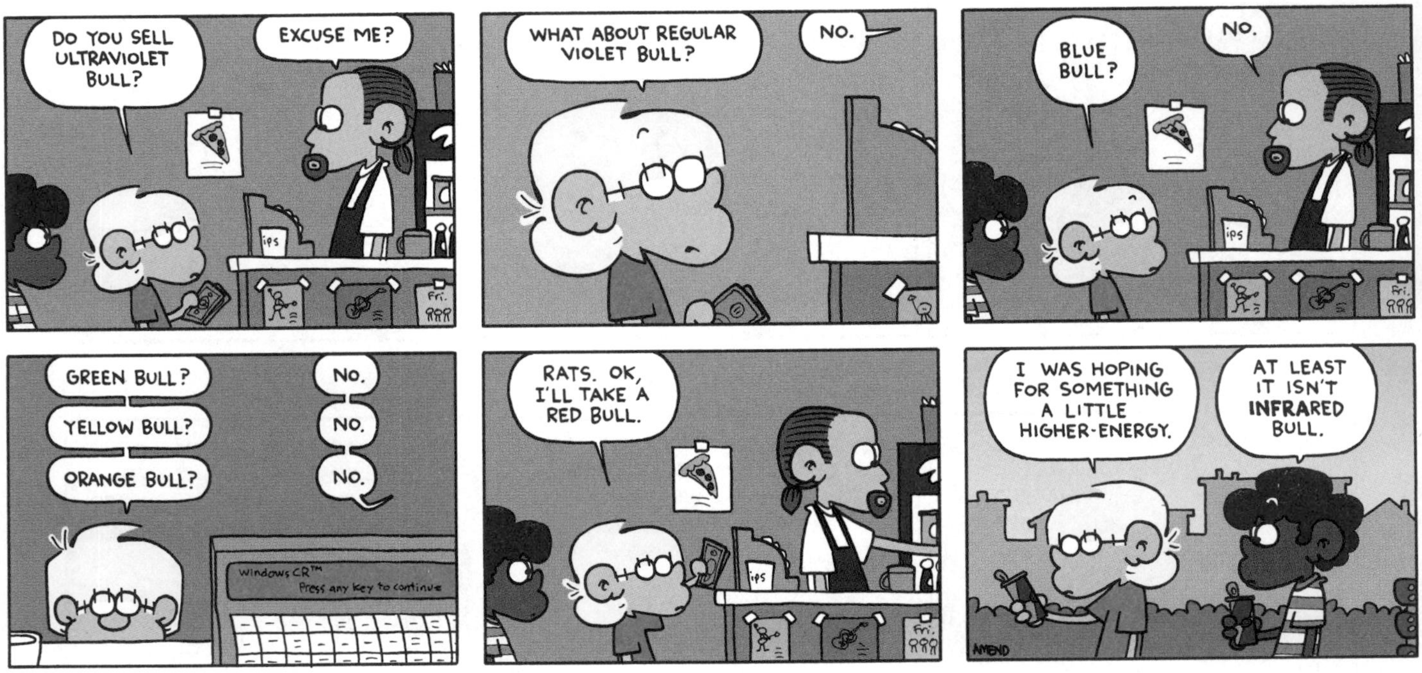
DO YOU SELL ULTRAVIOLET BULL?
EXCUSE ME?
WHAT ABOUT REGULAR VIOLET BULL?
NO.
BLUE BULL?
NO.
GREEN BULL?
NO.
YELLOW BULL?
NO.
ORANGE BULL?
NO.
Windows CR™
Press any key to continue
RATS. OK, I'LL TAKE A RED BULL.
I WAS HOPING FOR SOMETHING A LITTLE HIGHER-ENERGY.
AT LEAST IT ISN'T INFRARED BULL.
AMEND

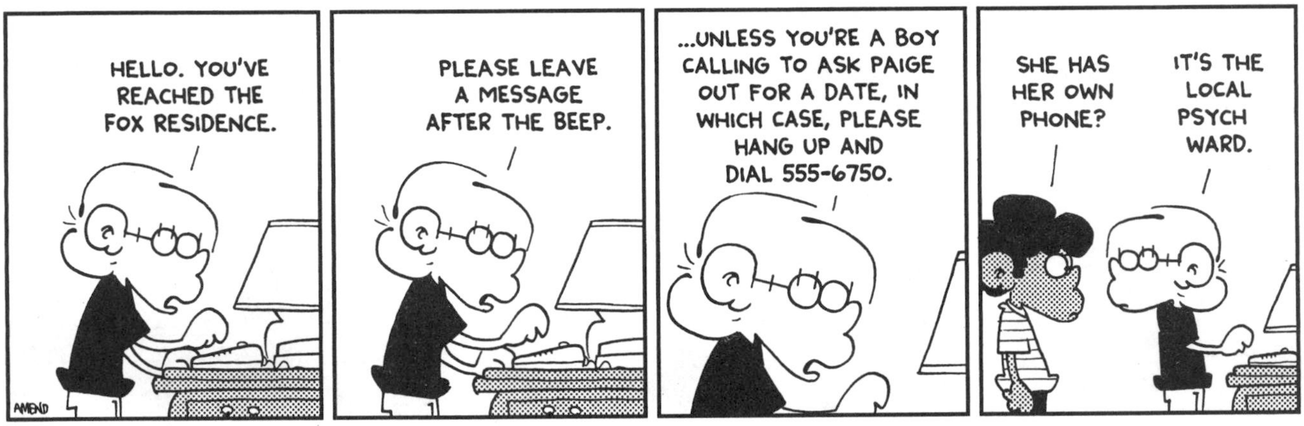
HELLO. YOU'VE REACHED THE FOX RESIDENCE.
AMEND
PLEASE LEAVE A MESSAGE AFTER THE BEEP.
...UNLESS YOU'RE A BOY CALLING TO ASK PAIGE OUT FOR A DATE, IN WHICH CASE, PLEASE HANG UP AND DIAL 555-6750.
SHE HAS HER OWN PHONE?
IT'S THE LOCAL PSYCH WARD.

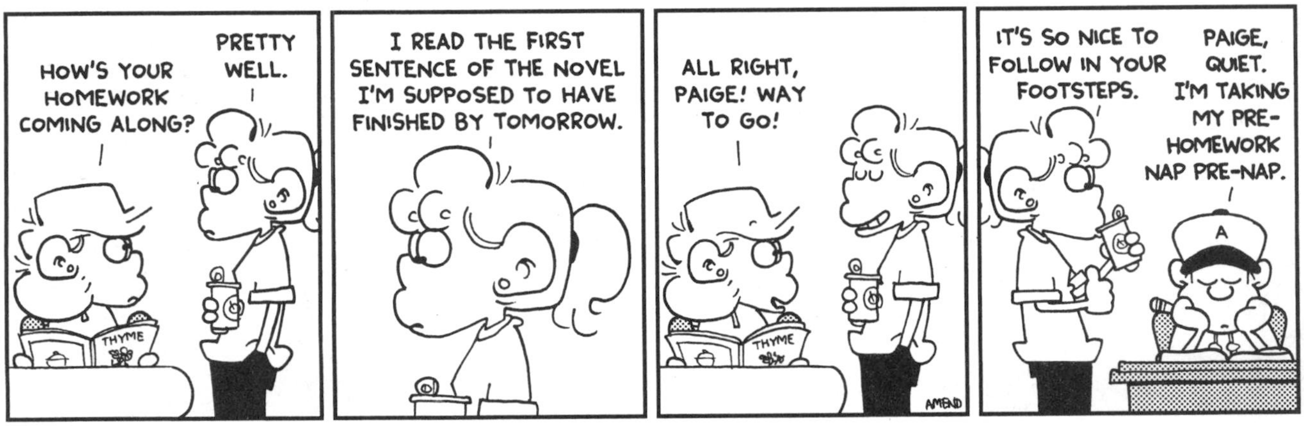
HOW'S YOUR HOMEWORK COMING ALONG?
PRETTY WELL.
THYME
I READ THE FIRST SENTENCE OF THE NOVEL I'M SUPPOSED TO HAVE FINISHED BY TOMORROW.
ALL RIGHT, PAIGE! WAY TO GO!
THYME
AMEND
IT'S SO NICE TO FOLLOW IN YOUR FOOTSTEPS.
PAIGE, QUIET. I'M TAKING MY PRE-HOMEWORK NAP PRE-NAP.

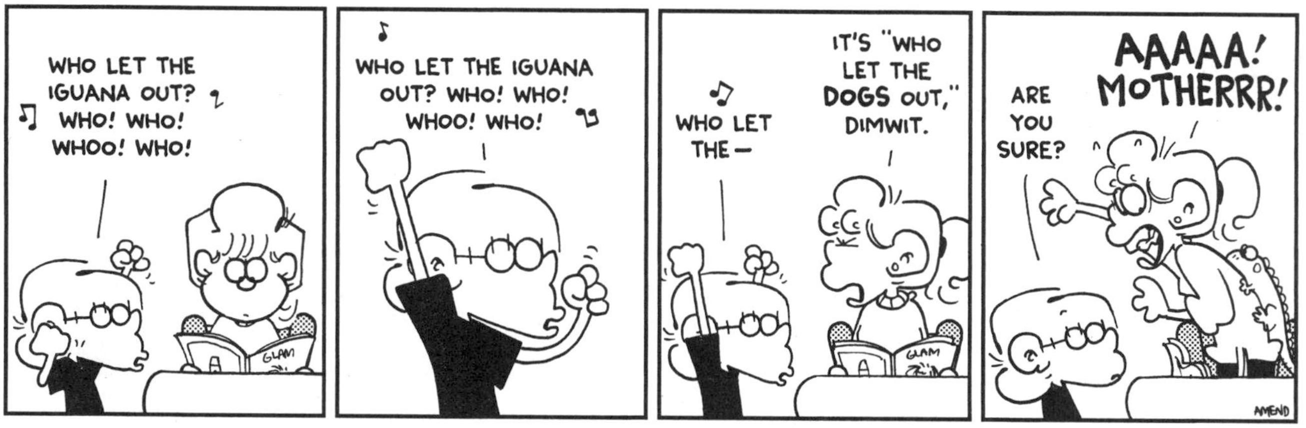
WHO LET THE IGUANA OUT? WHO! WHO! WHOO! WHO!
WHO LET THE IGUANA OUT? WHO! WHO! WHOO! WHO!
WHO LET THE—
IT'S "WHO LET THE DOGS OUT," DIMWIT.
ARE YOU SURE?
AAAAA! MOTHERRR!
AMEND

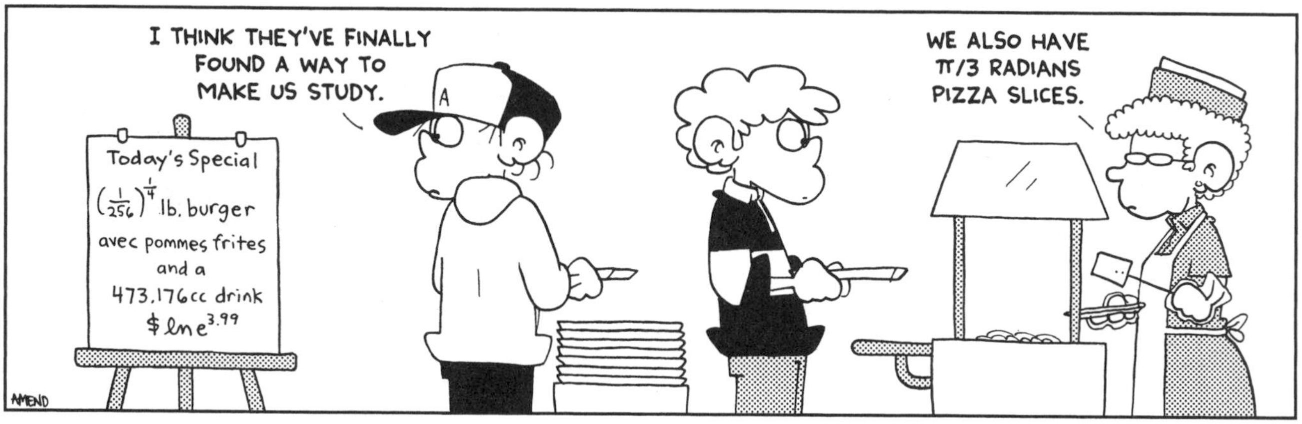
Today's Special
$(\frac{1}{256})^{\frac{1}{4}}$ lb. burger
avec pommes frites
and a
473.176cc drink
$\$ \ln e^{3.99}$
I THINK THEY'VE FINALLY FOUND A WAY TO MAKE US STUDY.
WE ALSO HAVE π/3 RADIANS PIZZA SLICES.
AMEND

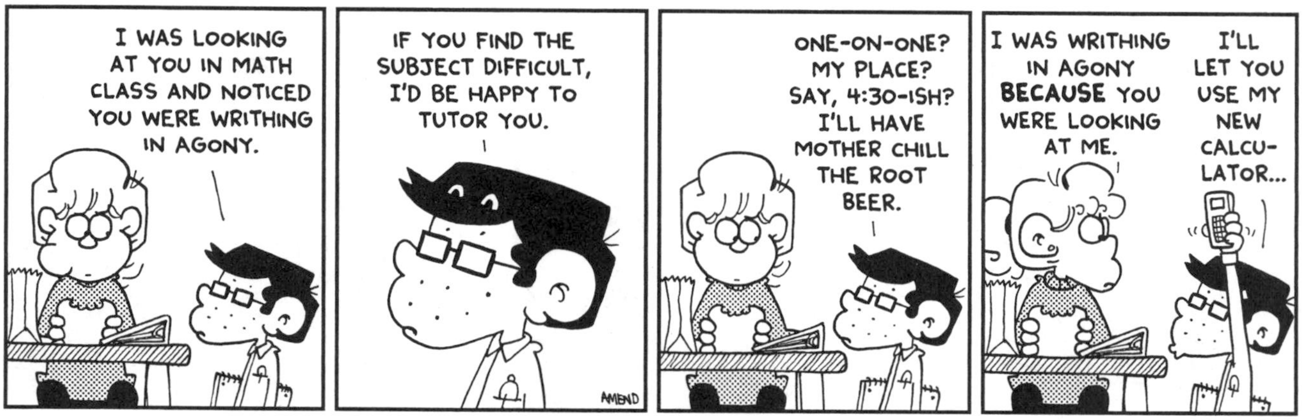
I WAS LOOKING AT YOU IN MATH CLASS AND NOTICED YOU WERE WRITHING IN AGONY.
IF YOU FIND THE SUBJECT DIFFICULT, I'D BE HAPPY TO TUTOR YOU.
ONE-ON-ONE? MY PLACE? SAY, 4:30-ISH? I'LL HAVE MOTHER CHILL THE ROOT BEER.
I WAS WRITHING IN AGONY BECAUSE YOU WERE LOOKING AT ME.
I'LL LET YOU USE MY NEW CALCU-LATOR...
AMEND

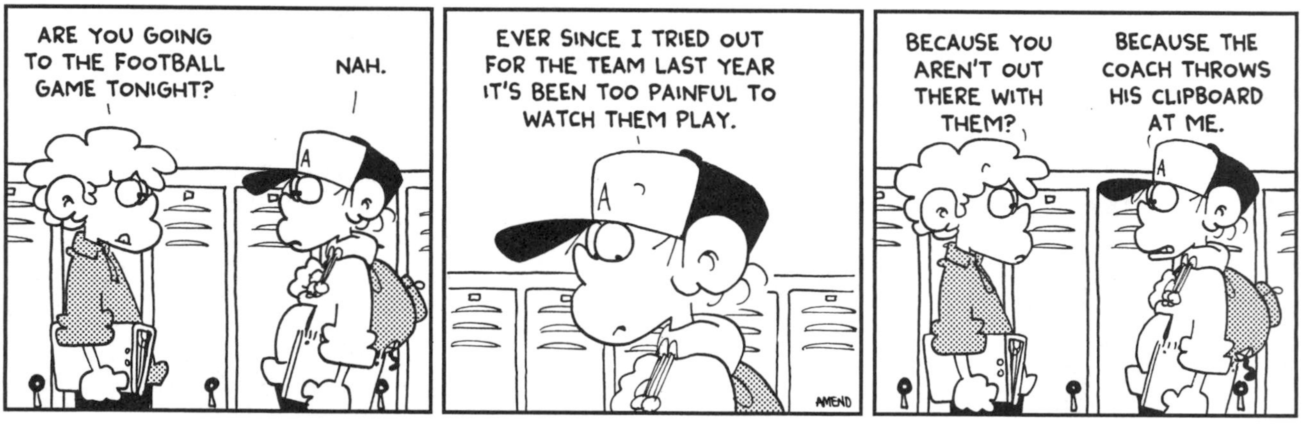
ARE YOU GOING TO THE FOOTBALL GAME TONIGHT?
NAH.
EVER SINCE I TRIED OUT FOR THE TEAM LAST YEAR IT'S BEEN TOO PAINFUL TO WATCH THEM PLAY.
BECAUSE YOU AREN'T OUT THERE WITH THEM?
BECAUSE THE COACH THROWS HIS CLIPBOARD AT ME.
AMEND

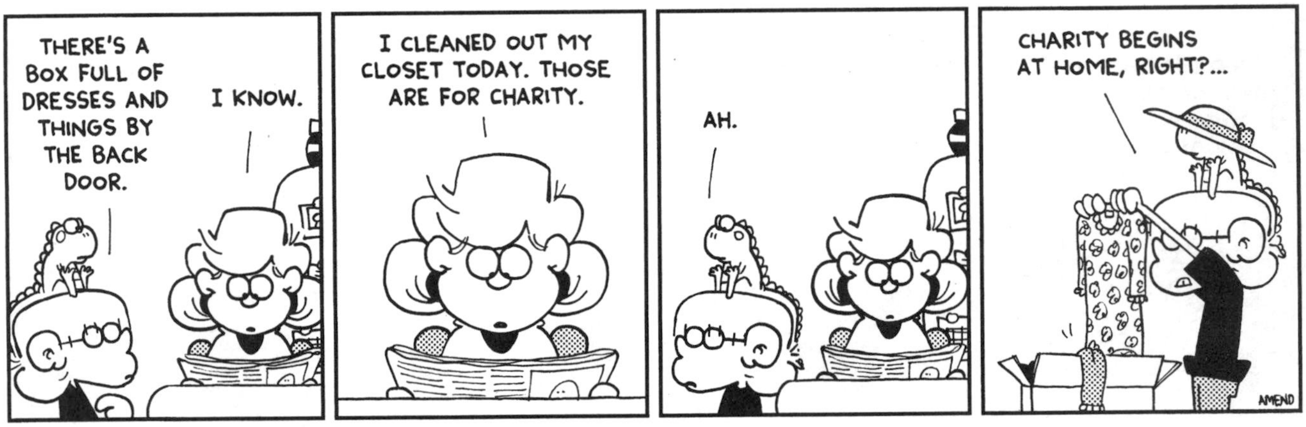
THERE'S A BOX FULL OF DRESSES AND THINGS BY THE BACK DOOR.
I KNOW.
I CLEANED OUT MY CLOSET TODAY. THOSE ARE FOR CHARITY.
AH.
CHARITY BEGINS AT HOME, RIGHT?...
AMEND

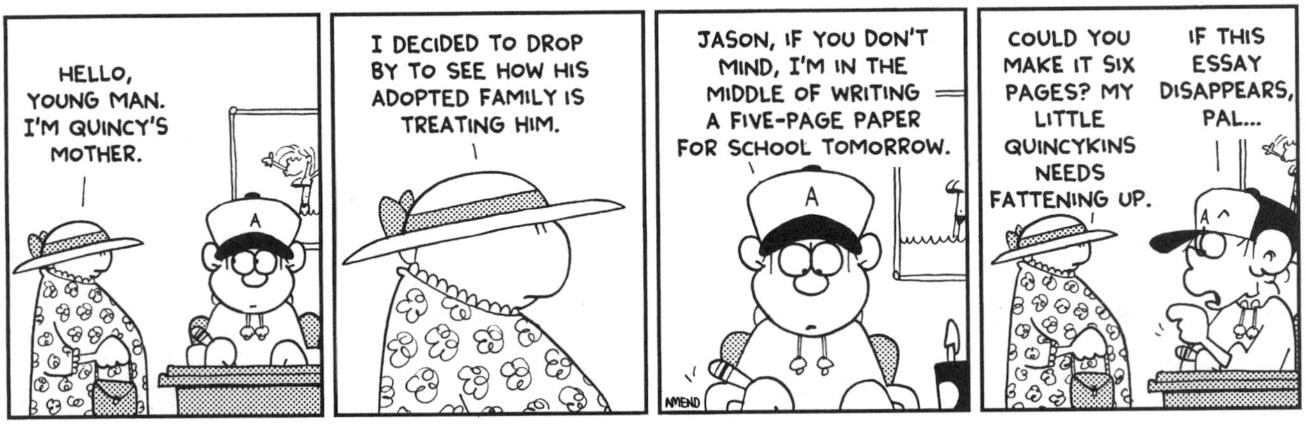
HELLO, YOUNG MAN. I'M QUINCY'S MOTHER.
I DECIDED TO DROP BY TO SEE HOW HIS ADOPTED FAMILY IS TREATING HIM.
JASON, IF YOU DON'T MIND, I'M IN THE MIDDLE OF WRITING A FIVE-PAGE PAPER FOR SCHOOL TOMORROW.
AMEND
COULD YOU MAKE IT SIX PAGES? MY LITTLE QUINCYKINS NEEDS FATTENING UP.
IF THIS ESSAY DISAPPEARS, PAL...

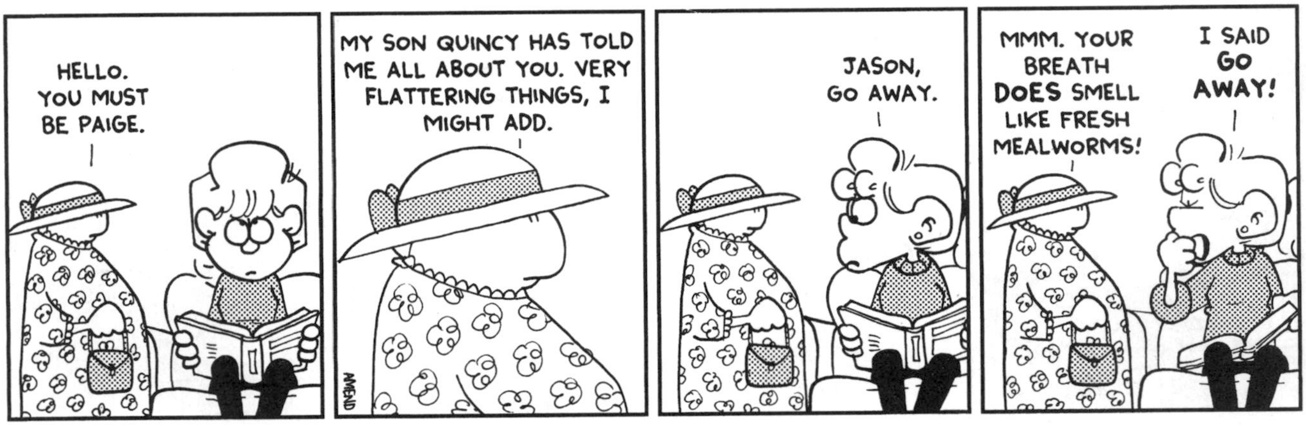
HELLO. YOU MUST BE PAIGE.
MY SON QUINCY HAS TOLD ME ALL ABOUT YOU. VERY FLATTERING THINGS, I MIGHT ADD.
AMEND
JASON, GO AWAY.
MMM. YOUR BREATH DOES SMELL LIKE FRESH MEALWORMS!
I SAID GO AWAY!

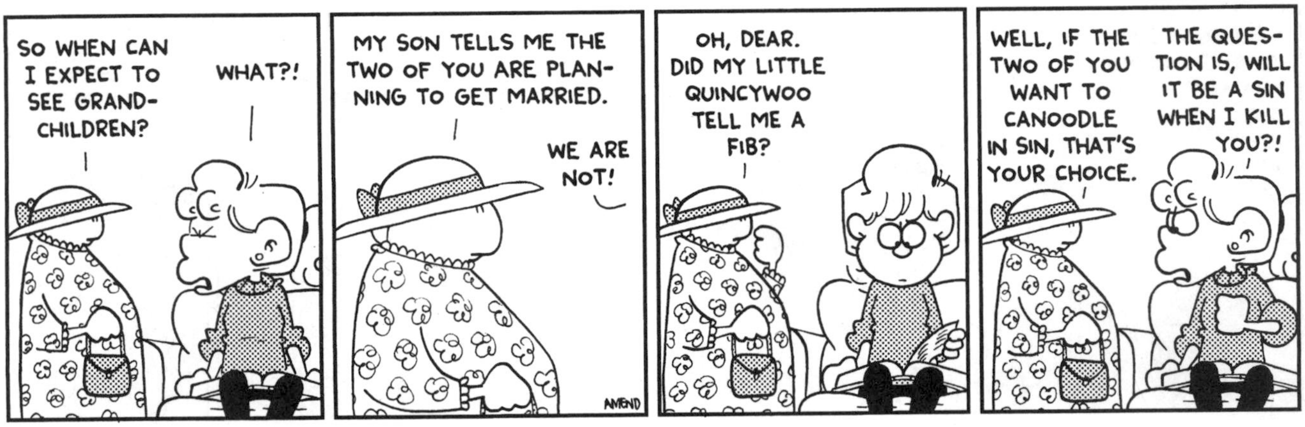
SO WHEN CAN I EXPECT TO SEE GRAND-CHILDREN?
WHAT?!
MY SON TELLS ME THE TWO OF YOU ARE PLAN-NING TO GET MARRIED.
WE ARE NOT!
AMEND
OH, DEAR. DID MY LITTLE QUINCYWOO TELL ME A FIB?
WELL, IF THE TWO OF YOU WANT TO CANOODLE IN SIN, THAT'S YOUR CHOICE.
THE QUES-TION IS, WILL IT BE A SIN WHEN I KILL YOU?!

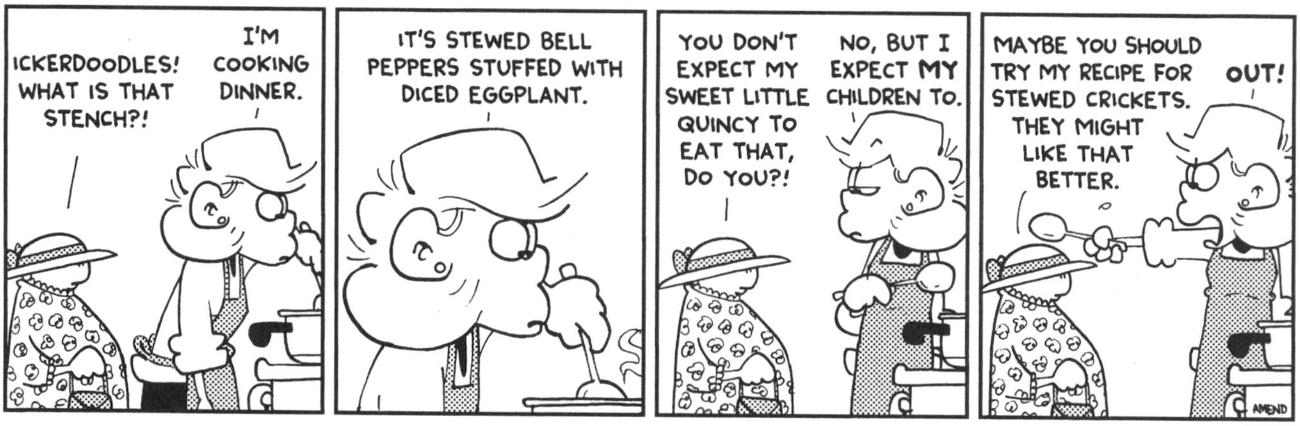
ICKERDOODLES! WHAT IS THAT STENCH?!
I'M COOKING DINNER.
IT'S STEWED BELL PEPPERS STUFFED WITH DICED EGGPLANT.
YOU DON'T EXPECT MY SWEET LITTLE QUINCY TO EAT THAT, DO YOU?!
NO, BUT I EXPECT **MY** CHILDREN TO.
MAYBE YOU SHOULD TRY MY RECIPE FOR STEWED CRICKETS. THEY MIGHT LIKE THAT BETTER.
OUT!
AMEND

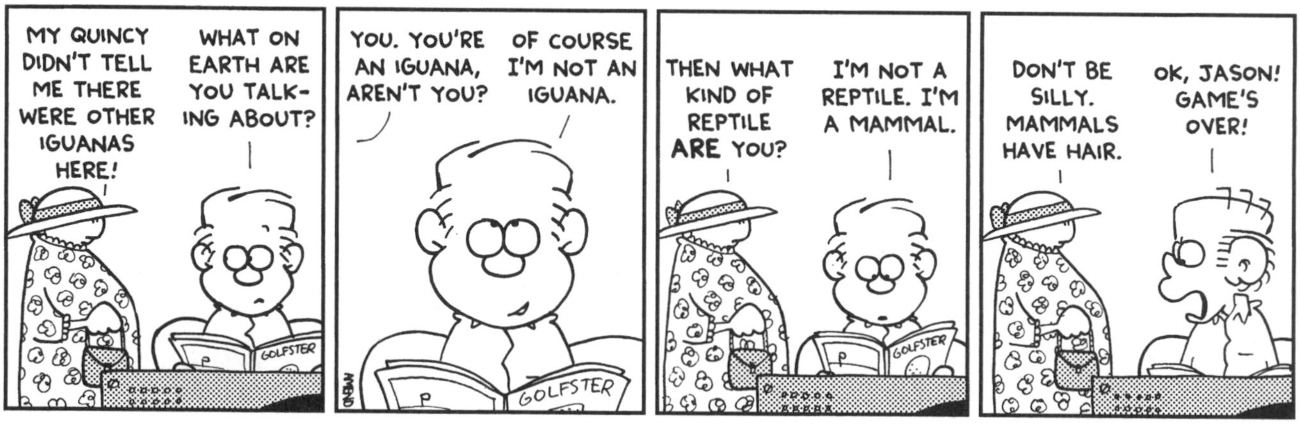
MY QUINCY DIDN'T TELL ME THERE WERE OTHER IGUANAS HERE!
WHAT ON EARTH ARE YOU TALKING ABOUT?
GOLFSTER
YOU. YOU'RE AN IGUANA, AREN'T YOU?
OF COURSE I'M NOT AN IGUANA.
GOLFSTER
THEN WHAT KIND OF REPTILE **ARE** YOU?
I'M NOT A REPTILE. I'M A MAMMAL.
GOLFSTER
DON'T BE SILLY. MAMMALS HAVE HAIR.
OK, JASON! GAME'S OVER!

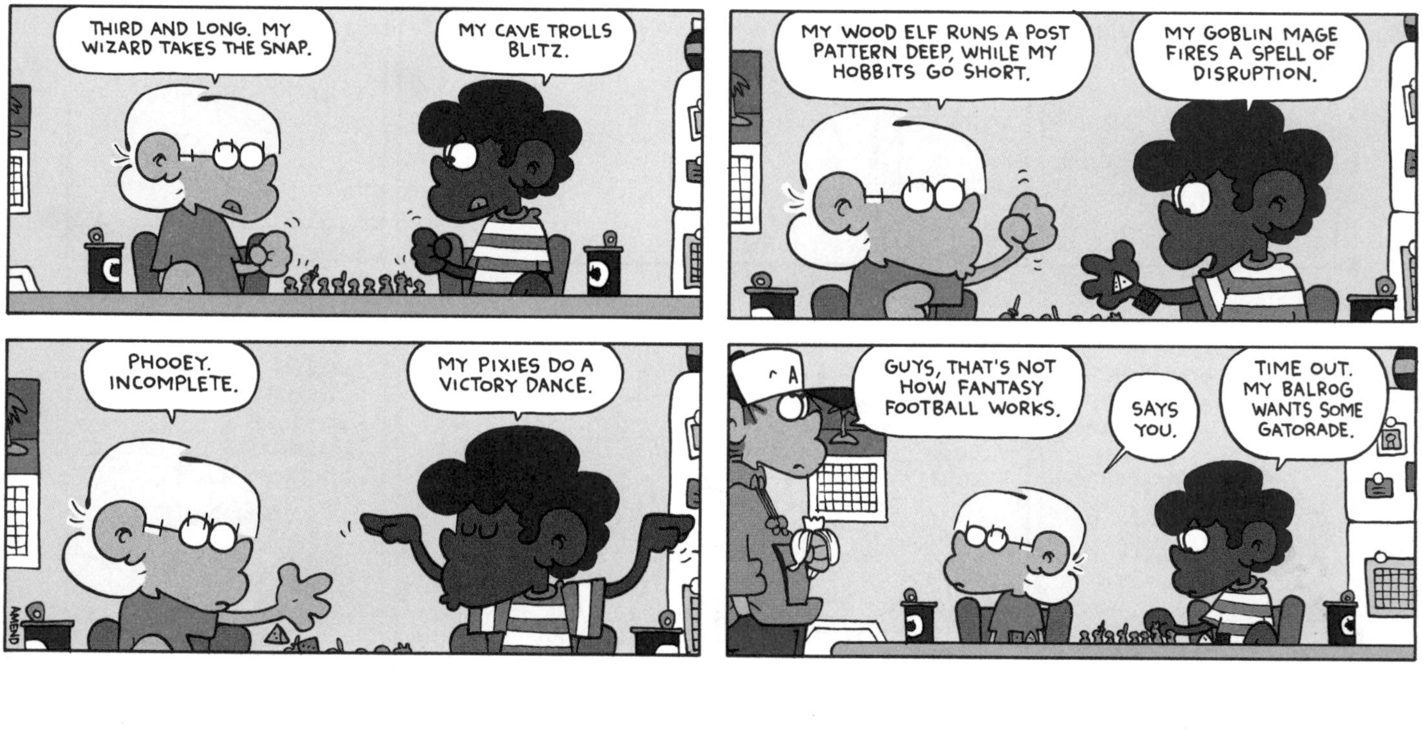
THIRD AND LONG. MY WIZARD TAKES THE SNAP.
MY CAVE TROLLS BLITZ.
MY WOOD ELF RUNS A POST PATTERN DEEP, WHILE MY HOBBITS GO SHORT.
MY GOBLIN MAGE FIRES A SPELL OF DISRUPTION.
PHOOEY. INCOMPLETE.
MY PIXIES DO A VICTORY DANCE.
GUYS, THAT'S NOT HOW FANTASY FOOTBALL WORKS.
SAYS YOU.
TIME OUT. MY BALROG WANTS SOME GATORADE.

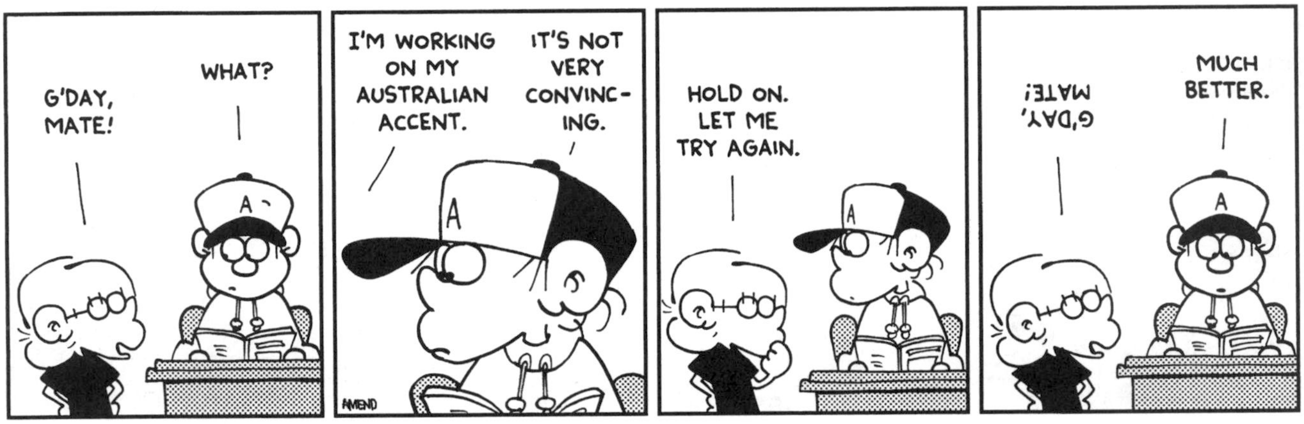
G'DAY, MATE!
WHAT?
I'M WORKING ON MY AUSTRALIAN ACCENT.
IT'S NOT VERY CONVINC- ING.
AMEND
HOLD ON. LET ME TRY AGAIN.
G'DAY, MATE!
MUCH BETTER.

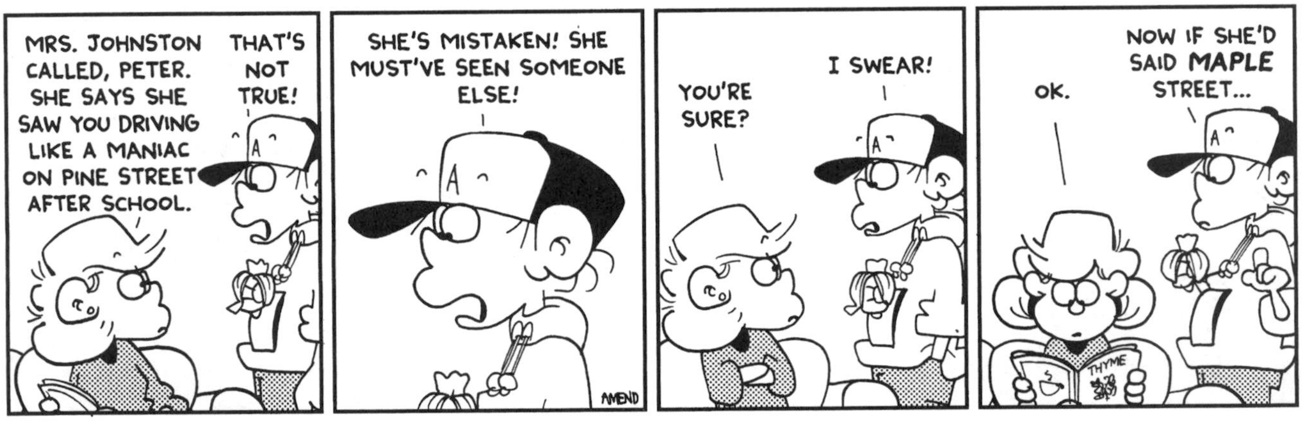
MRS. JOHNSTON CALLED, PETER. SHE SAYS SHE SAW YOU DRIVING LIKE A MANIAC ON PINE STREET AFTER SCHOOL.
THAT'S NOT TRUE!
SHE'S MISTAKEN! SHE MUST'VE SEEN SOMEONE ELSE!
AMEND
YOU'RE SURE?
I SWEAR!
OK.
NOW IF SHE'D SAID **MAPLE** STREET...
THYME

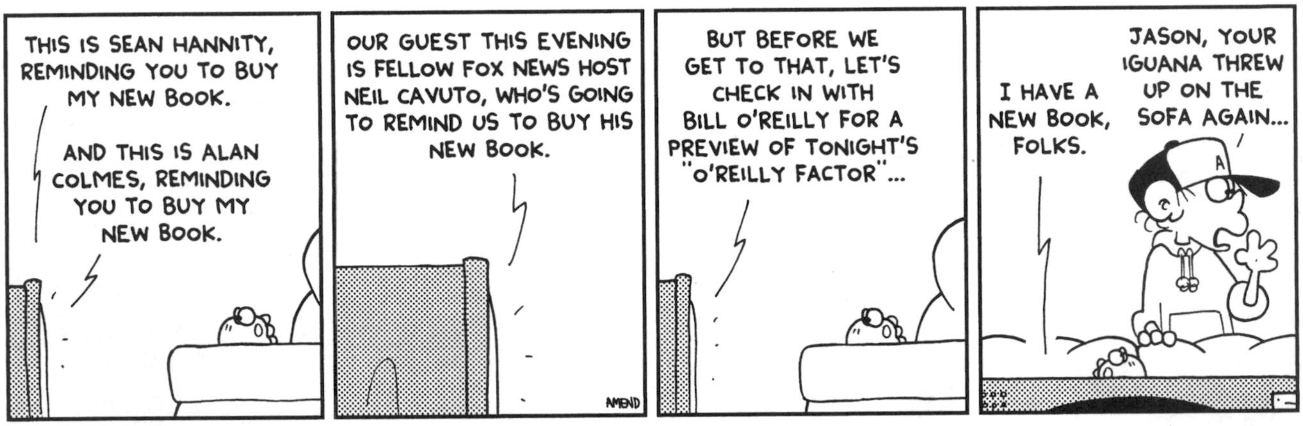
THIS IS SEAN HANNITY, REMINDING YOU TO BUY MY NEW BOOK.
AND THIS IS ALAN COLMES, REMINDING YOU TO BUY MY NEW BOOK.
OUR GUEST THIS EVENING IS FELLOW FOX NEWS HOST NEIL CAVUTO, WHO'S GOING TO REMIND US TO BUY HIS NEW BOOK.
AMEND
BUT BEFORE WE GET TO THAT, LET'S CHECK IN WITH BILL O'REILLY FOR A PREVIEW OF TONIGHT'S "O'REILLY FACTOR"...
I HAVE A NEW BOOK, FOLKS.
JASON, YOUR IGUANA THREW UP ON THE SOFA AGAIN...

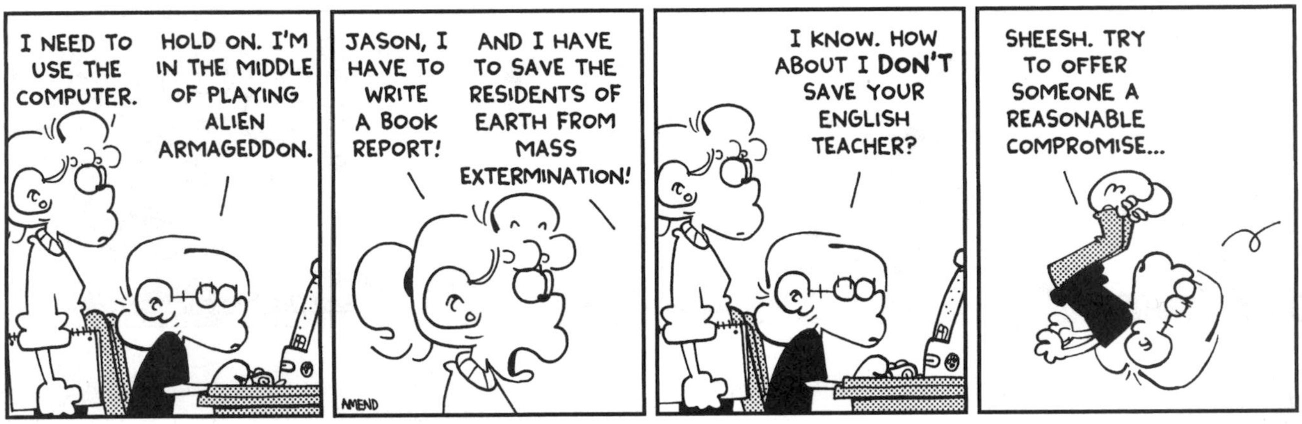
I NEED TO USE THE COMPUTER.
HOLD ON. I'M IN THE MIDDLE OF PLAYING ALIEN ARMAGEDDON.
JASON, I HAVE TO WRITE A BOOK REPORT!
AND I HAVE TO SAVE THE RESIDENTS OF EARTH FROM MASS EXTERMINATION!
AMEND
I KNOW. HOW ABOUT I **DON'T** SAVE YOUR ENGLISH TEACHER?
SHEESH. TRY TO OFFER SOMEONE A REASONABLE COMPROMISE...

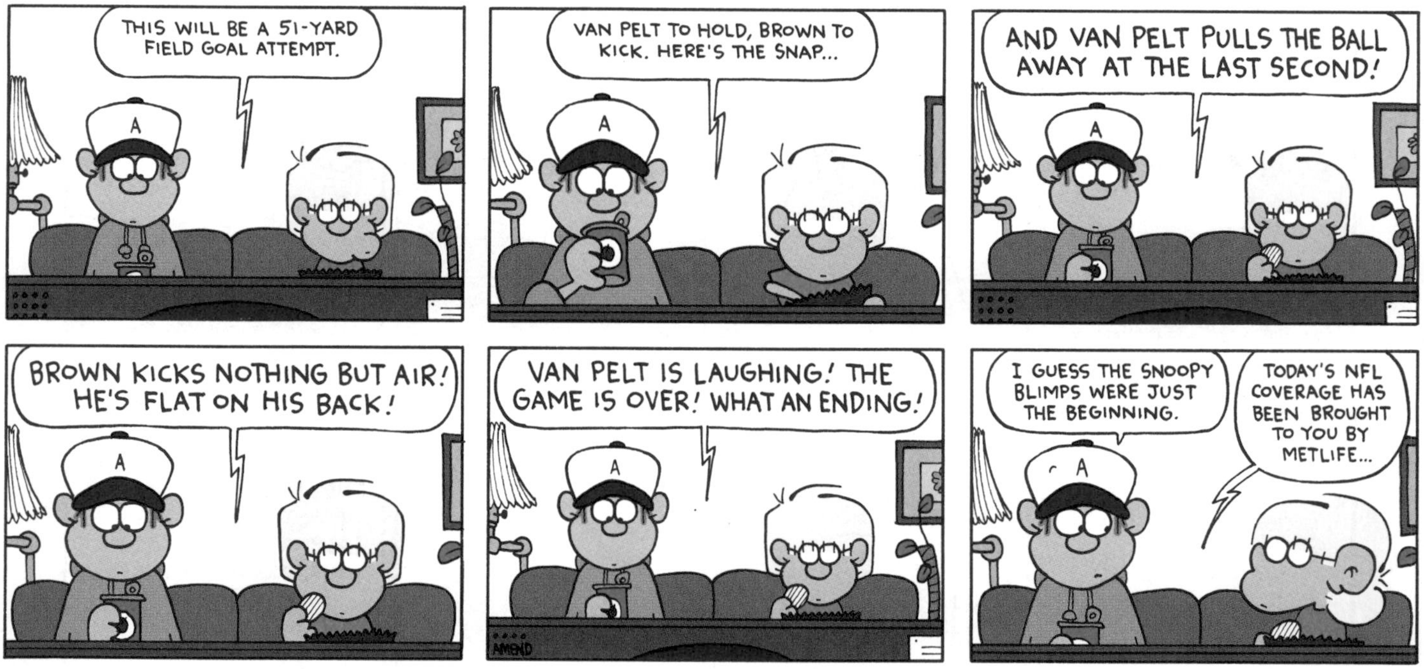
THIS WILL BE A 51-YARD FIELD GOAL ATTEMPT.
VAN PELT TO HOLD, BROWN TO KICK. HERE'S THE SNAP...
AND VAN PELT PULLS THE BALL AWAY AT THE LAST SECOND!
BROWN KICKS NOTHING BUT AIR! HE'S FLAT ON HIS BACK!
VAN PELT IS LAUGHING! THE GAME IS OVER! WHAT AN ENDING!
AMEND
I GUESS THE SNOOPY BLIMPS WERE JUST THE BEGINNING.
TODAY'S NFL COVERAGE HAS BEEN BROUGHT TO YOU BY METLIFE...

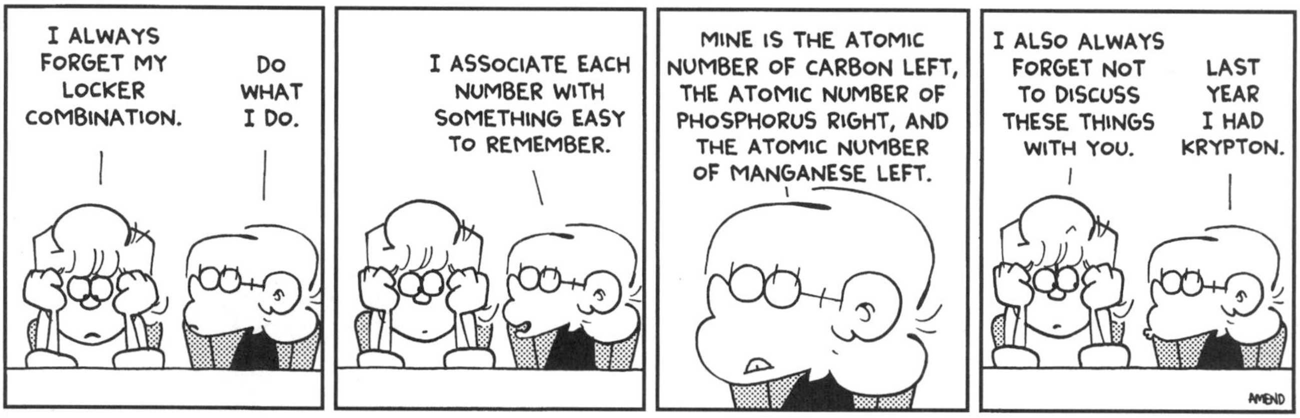
I ALWAYS FORGET MY LOCKER COMBINATION.
DO WHAT I DO.
I ASSOCIATE EACH NUMBER WITH SOMETHING EASY TO REMEMBER.
MINE IS THE ATOMIC NUMBER OF CARBON LEFT, THE ATOMIC NUMBER OF PHOSPHORUS RIGHT, AND THE ATOMIC NUMBER OF MANGANESE LEFT.
I ALSO ALWAYS FORGET NOT TO DISCUSS THESE THINGS WITH YOU.
LAST YEAR I HAD KRYPTON.
AMEND

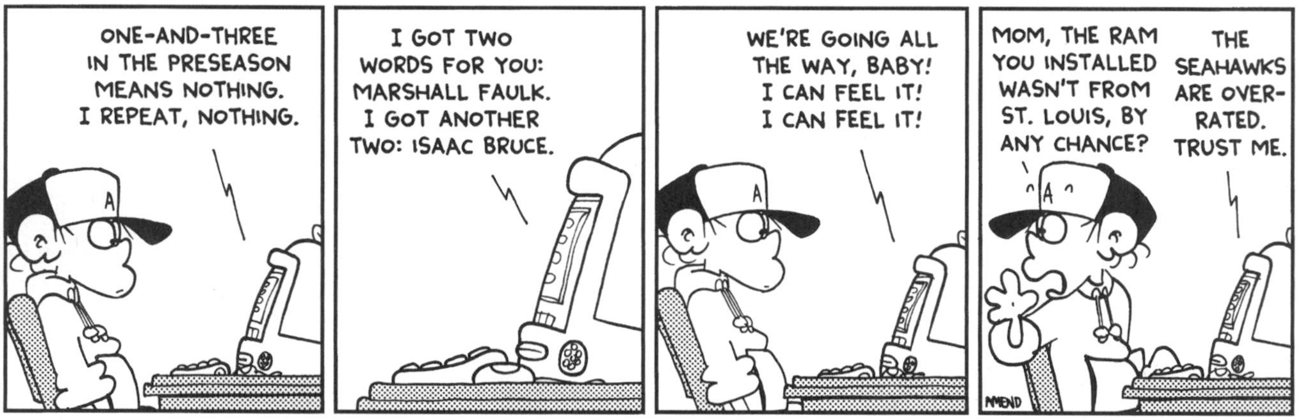
ONE-AND-THREE IN THE PRESEASON MEANS NOTHING. I REPEAT, NOTHING.
I GOT TWO WORDS FOR YOU: MARSHALL FAULK. I GOT ANOTHER TWO: ISAAC BRUCE.
WE'RE GOING ALL THE WAY, BABY! I CAN FEEL IT! I CAN FEEL IT!
MOM, THE RAM YOU INSTALLED WASN'T FROM ST. LOUIS, BY ANY CHANCE?
THE SEAHAWKS ARE OVER-RATED. TRUST ME.
AMEND

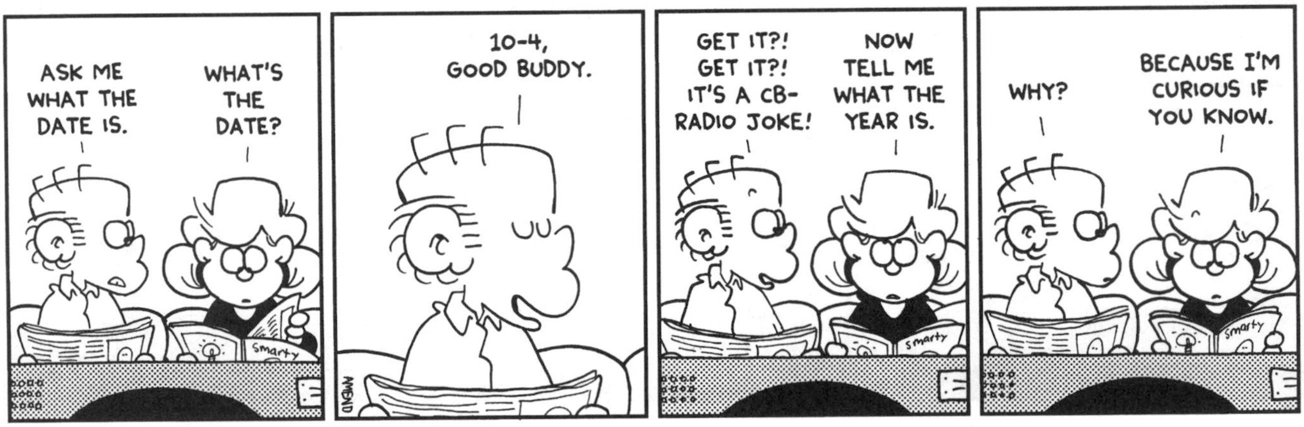
ASK ME WHAT THE DATE IS.
WHAT'S THE DATE?
10-4, GOOD BUDDY.
GET IT?! GET IT?! IT'S A CB-RADIO JOKE!
NOW TELL ME WHAT THE YEAR IS.
WHY?
BECAUSE I'M CURIOUS IF YOU KNOW.
Smarty
AMEND

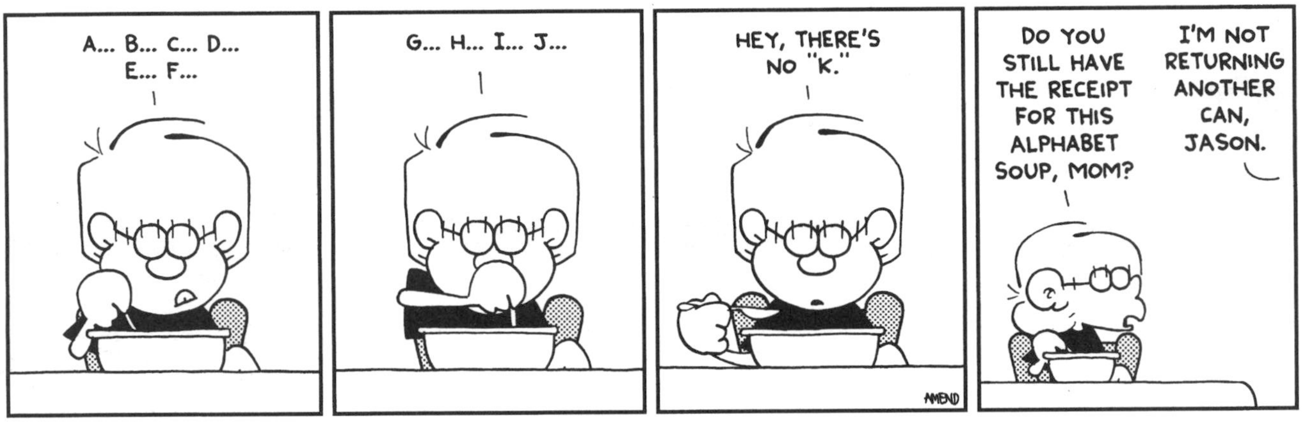
A... B... C... D... E... F...
G... H... I... J...
HEY, THERE'S NO "K."
DO YOU STILL HAVE THE RECEIPT FOR THIS ALPHABET SOUP, MOM?
I'M NOT RETURNING ANOTHER CAN, JASON.
AMEND

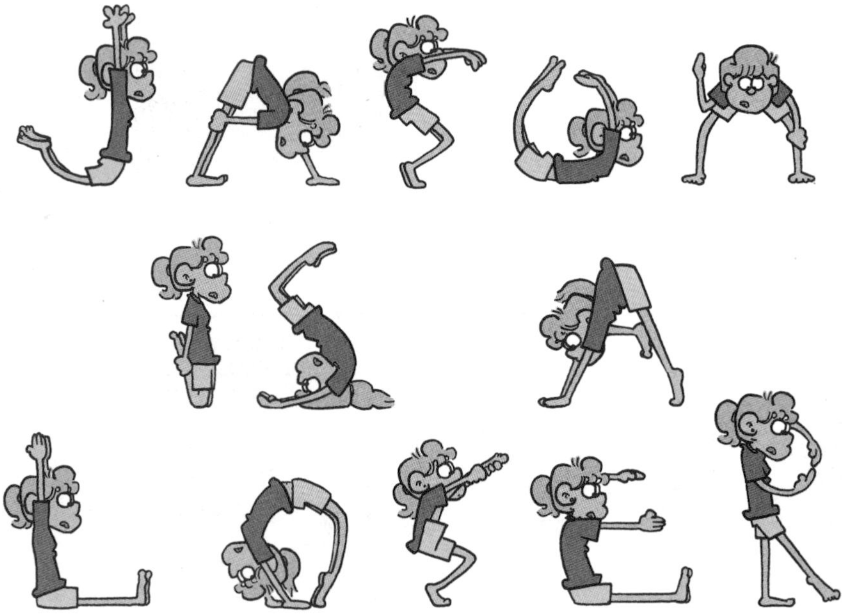

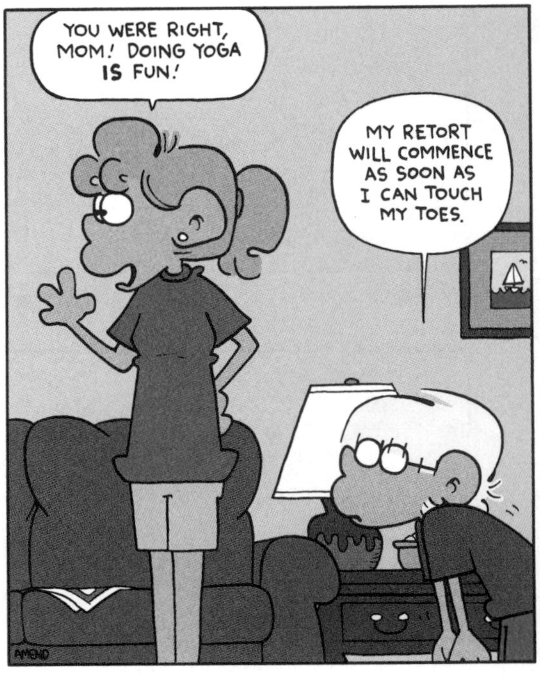
YOU WERE RIGHT, MOM! DOING YOGA **IS** FUN!
MY RETORT WILL COMMENCE AS SOON AS I CAN TOUCH MY TOES.
AMEND

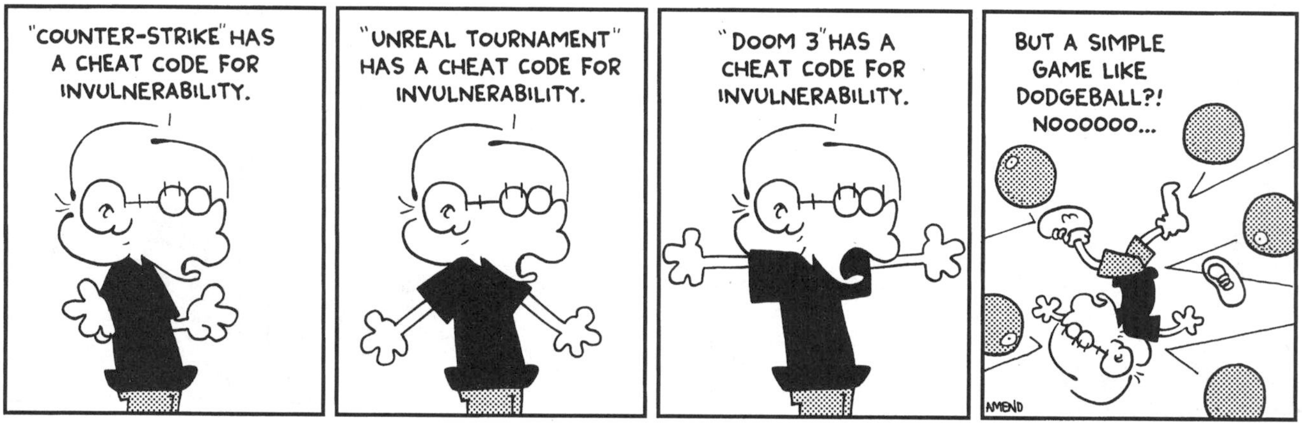
"COUNTER-STRIKE" HAS A CHEAT CODE FOR INVULNERABILITY.
"UNREAL TOURNAMENT" HAS A CHEAT CODE FOR INVULNERABILITY.
"DOOM 3" HAS A CHEAT CODE FOR INVULNERABILITY.
BUT A SIMPLE GAME LIKE DODGEBALL?! NOOOOOO...
AMEND

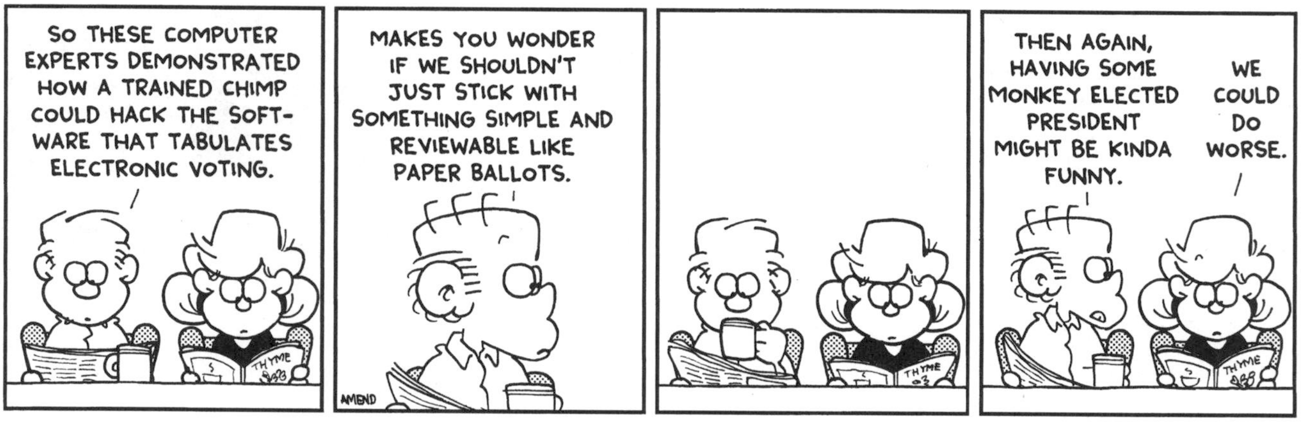
SO THESE COMPUTER EXPERTS DEMONSTRATED HOW A TRAINED CHIMP COULD HACK THE SOFTWARE THAT TABULATES ELECTRONIC VOTING.
THYME
MAKES YOU WONDER IF WE SHOULDN'T JUST STICK WITH SOMETHING SIMPLE AND REVIEWABLE LIKE PAPER BALLOTS.
AMEND
THYME
THEN AGAIN, HAVING SOME MONKEY ELECTED PRESIDENT MIGHT BE KINDA FUNNY.
WE COULD DO WORSE.
THYME

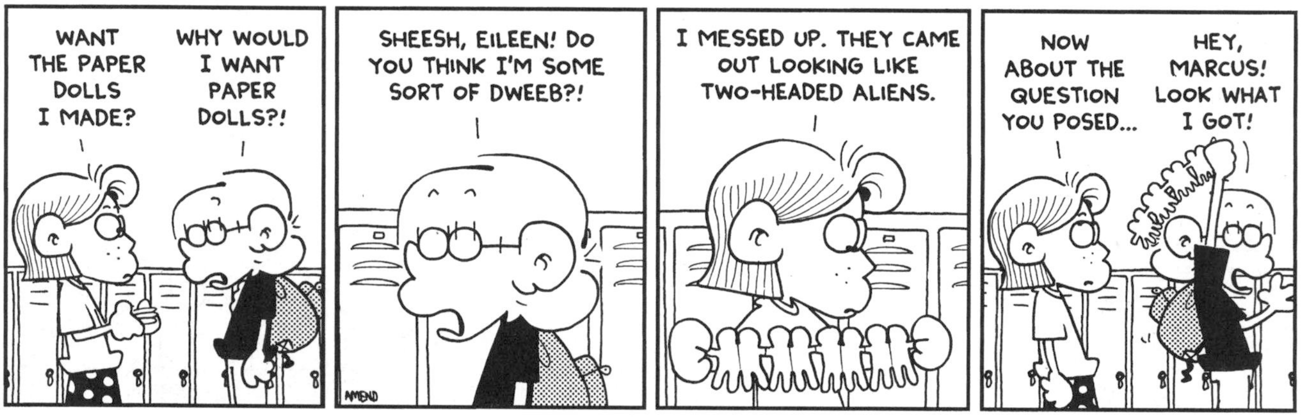
WANT THE PAPER DOLLS I MADE?
WHY WOULD I WANT PAPER DOLLS?!
SHEESH, EILEEN! DO YOU THINK I'M SOME SORT OF DWEEB?!
AMEND
I MESSED UP. THEY CAME OUT LOOKING LIKE TWO-HEADED ALIENS.
NOW ABOUT THE QUESTION YOU POSED...
HEY, MARCUS! LOOK WHAT I GOT!

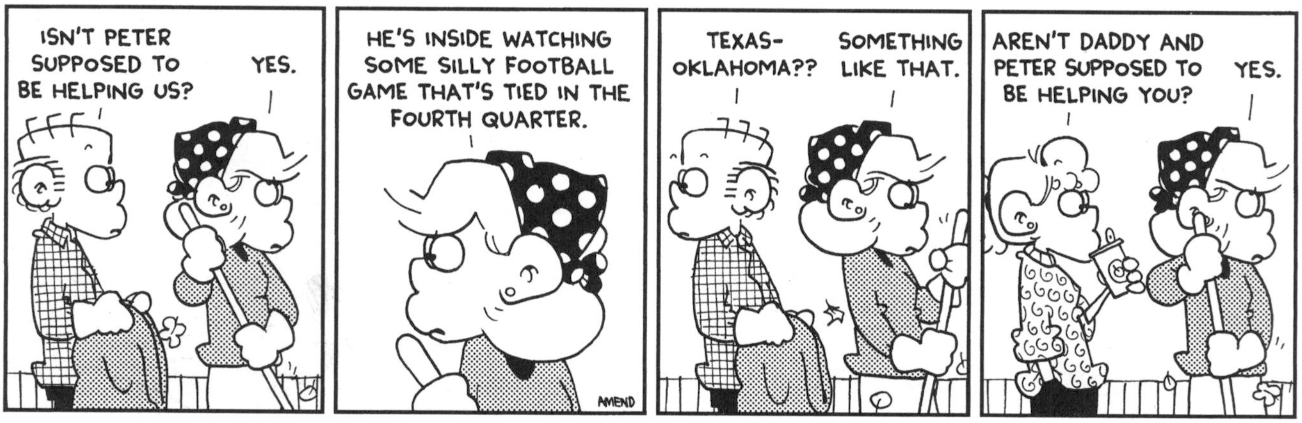
ISN'T PETER SUPPOSED TO BE HELPING US?
YES.
HE'S INSIDE WATCHING SOME SILLY FOOTBALL GAME THAT'S TIED IN THE FOURTH QUARTER.
AMEND
TEXAS-OKLAHOMA??
SOMETHING LIKE THAT.
AREN'T DADDY AND PETER SUPPOSED TO BE HELPING YOU?
YES.

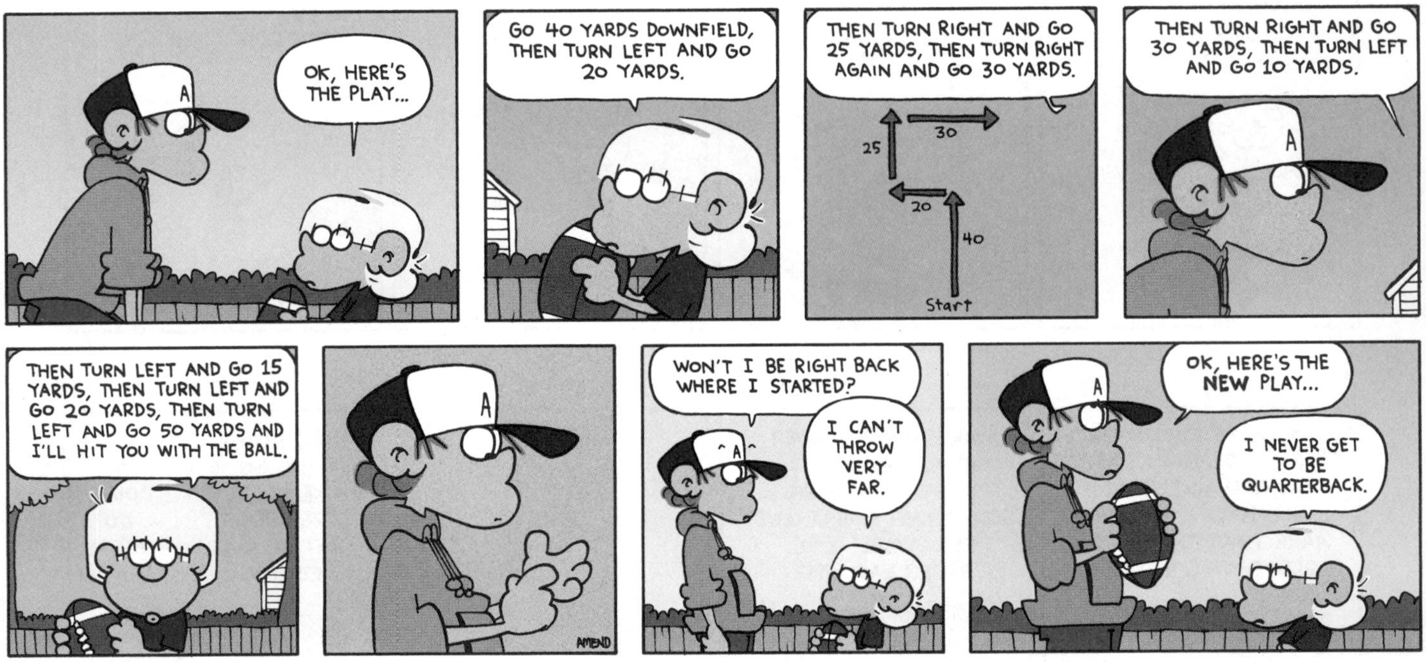
OK, HERE'S THE PLAY...
GO 40 YARDS DOWNFIELD, THEN TURN LEFT AND GO 20 YARDS.
THEN TURN RIGHT AND GO 25 YARDS, THEN TURN RIGHT AGAIN AND GO 30 YARDS.
30
25
20
40
Start
THEN TURN RIGHT AND GO 30 YARDS, THEN TURN LEFT AND GO 10 YARDS.
THEN TURN LEFT AND GO 15 YARDS, THEN TURN LEFT AND GO 20 YARDS, THEN TURN LEFT AND GO 50 YARDS AND I'LL HIT YOU WITH THE BALL.
AMEND
WON'T I BE RIGHT BACK WHERE I STARTED?
I CAN'T THROW VERY FAR.
OK, HERE'S THE NEW PLAY...
I NEVER GET TO BE QUARTERBACK.

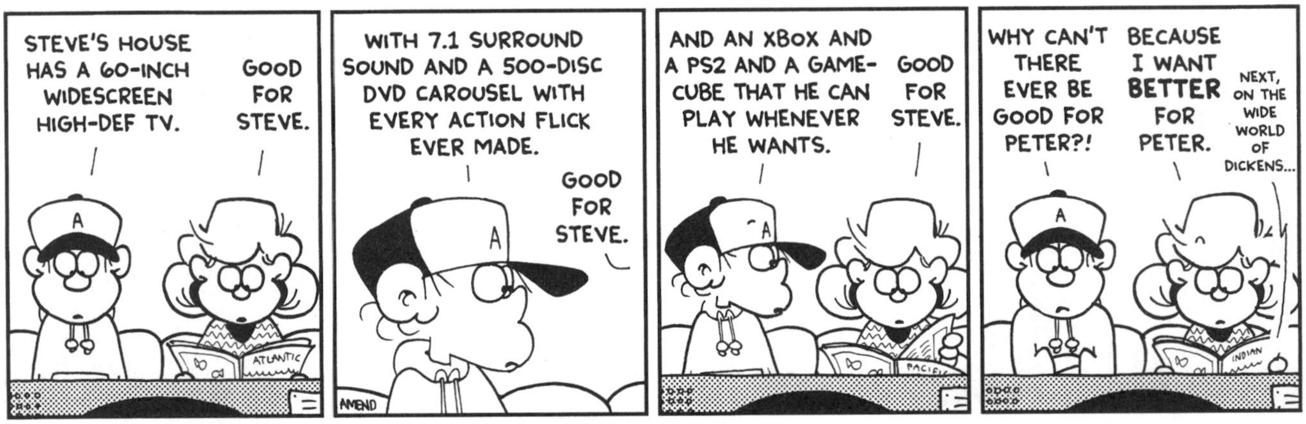
STEVE'S HOUSE HAS A 60-INCH WIDESCREEN HIGH-DEF TV.
GOOD FOR STEVE.
ATLANTIC
WITH 7.1 SURROUND SOUND AND A 500-DISC DVD CAROUSEL WITH EVERY ACTION FLICK EVER MADE.
GOOD FOR STEVE.
AMEND
AND AN XBOX AND A PS2 AND A GAME-CUBE THAT HE CAN PLAY WHENEVER HE WANTS.
GOOD FOR STEVE.
PACIFIC
WHY CAN'T THERE EVER BE GOOD FOR PETER?!
BECAUSE I WANT BETTER FOR PETER.
NEXT, ON THE WIDE WORLD OF DICKENS...
INDIAN

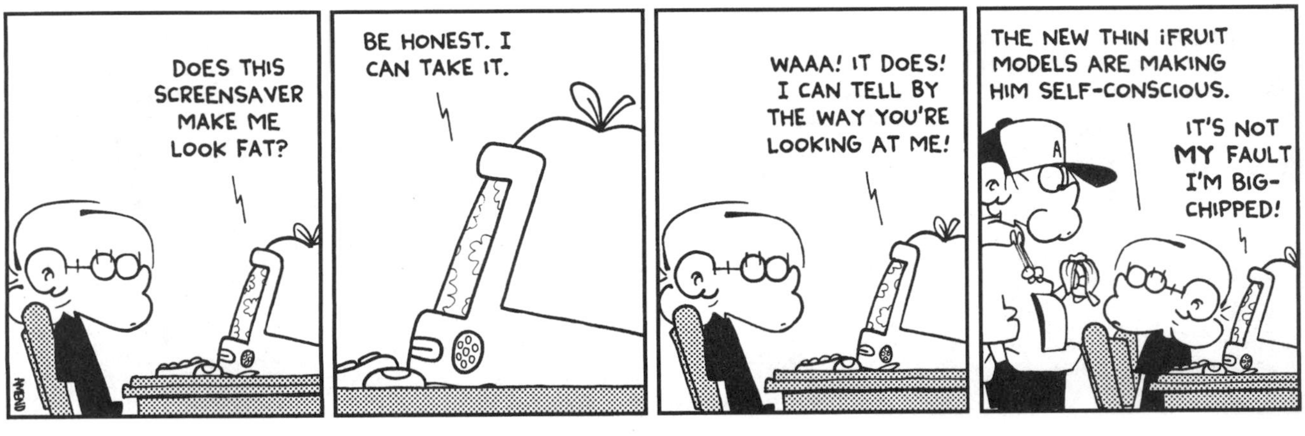
DOES THIS SCREENSAVER MAKE ME LOOK FAT?
AMEND
BE HONEST. I CAN TAKE IT.
WAAA! IT DOES! I CAN TELL BY THE WAY YOU'RE LOOKING AT ME!
THE NEW THIN iFRUIT MODELS ARE MAKING HIM SELF-CONSCIOUS.
IT'S NOT MY FAULT I'M BIG-CHIPPED!

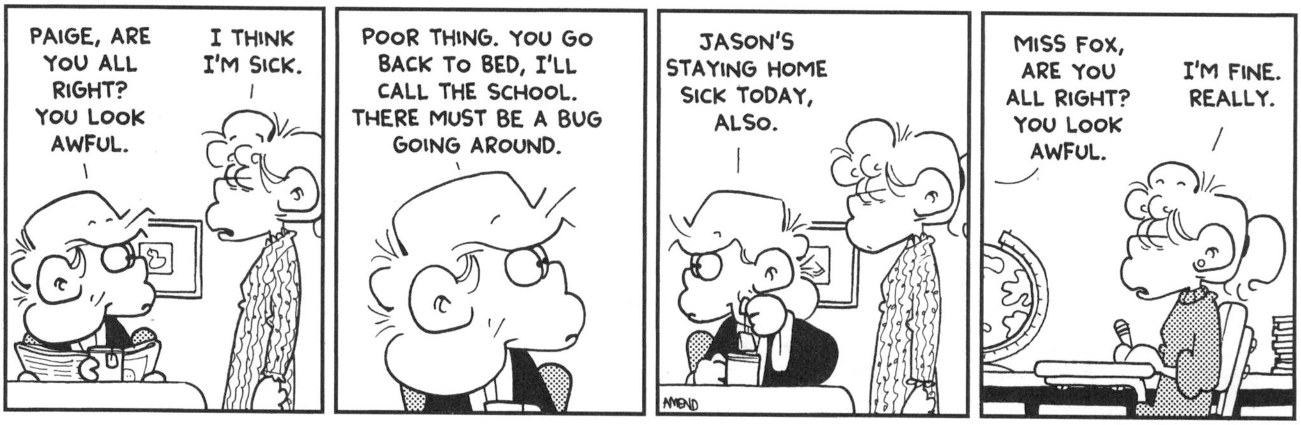
PAIGE, ARE YOU ALL RIGHT? YOU LOOK AWFUL.
I THINK I'M SICK.
POOR THING. YOU GO BACK TO BED, I'LL CALL THE SCHOOL. THERE MUST BE A BUG GOING AROUND.
JASON'S STAYING HOME SICK TODAY, ALSO.
MISS FOX, ARE YOU ALL RIGHT? YOU LOOK AWFUL.
I'M FINE. REALLY.
AMEND

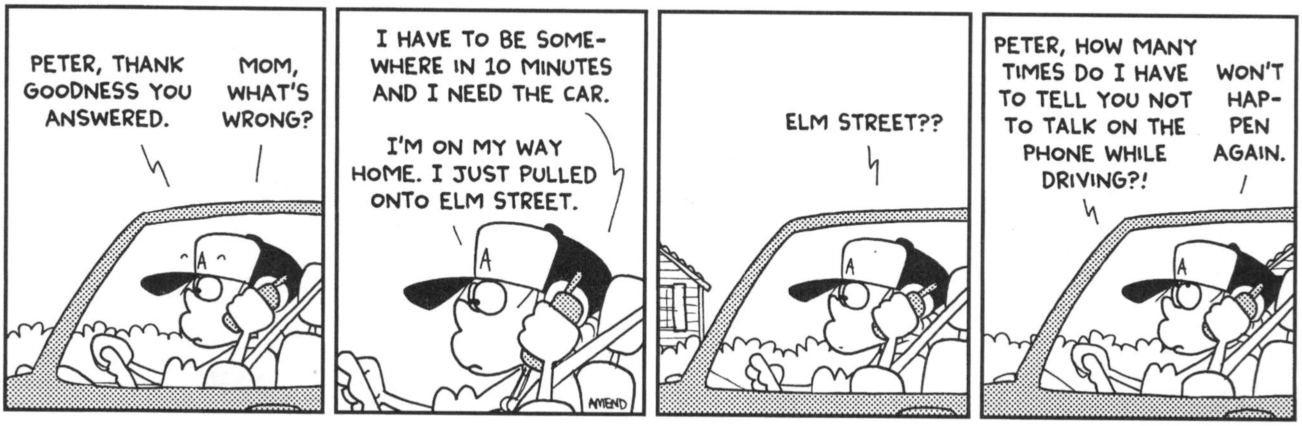
PETER, THANK GOODNESS YOU ANSWERED.
MOM, WHAT'S WRONG?
I HAVE TO BE SOMEWHERE IN 10 MINUTES AND I NEED THE CAR.
I'M ON MY WAY HOME. I JUST PULLED ONTO ELM STREET.
ELM STREET??
PETER, HOW MANY TIMES DO I HAVE TO TELL YOU NOT TO TALK ON THE PHONE WHILE DRIVING?!
WON'T HAPPEN AGAIN.
AMEND

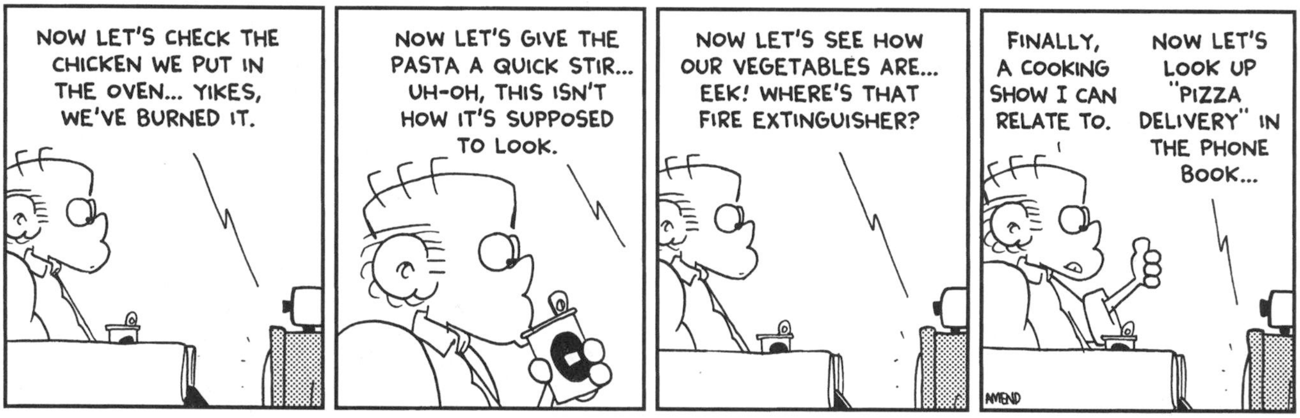
NOW LET'S CHECK THE CHICKEN WE PUT IN THE OVEN... YIKES, WE'VE BURNED IT.
NOW LET'S GIVE THE PASTA A QUICK STIR... UH-OH, THIS ISN'T HOW IT'S SUPPOSED TO LOOK.
NOW LET'S SEE HOW OUR VEGETABLES ARE... EEK! WHERE'S THAT FIRE EXTINGUISHER?
FINALLY, A COOKING SHOW I CAN RELATE TO.
NOW LET'S LOOK UP "PIZZA DELIVERY" IN THE PHONE BOOK...
AMEND

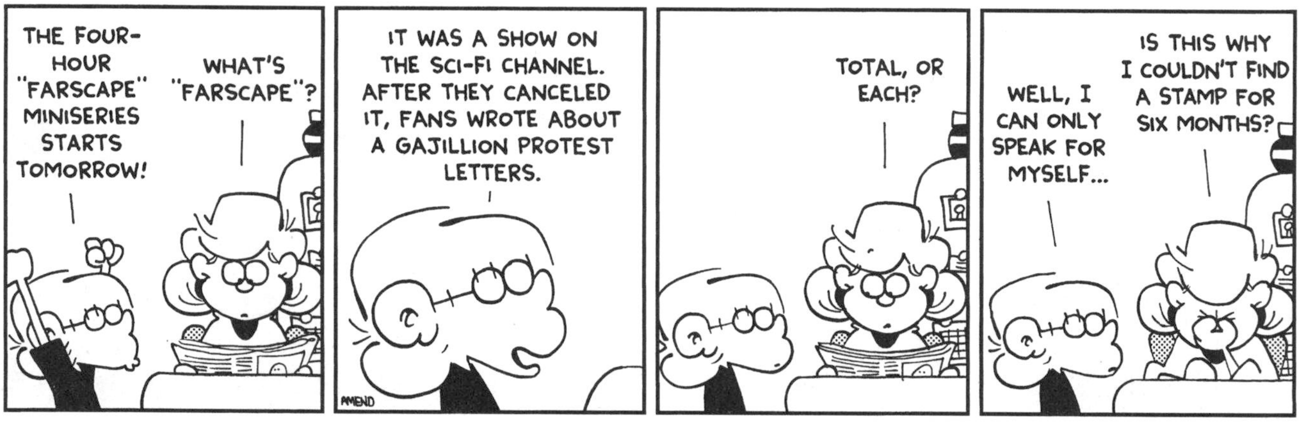
THE FOUR-HOUR "FARSCAPE" MINISERIES STARTS TOMORROW!
WHAT'S "FARSCAPE"?
IT WAS A SHOW ON THE SCI-FI CHANNEL. AFTER THEY CANCELED IT, FANS WROTE ABOUT A GAJILLION PROTEST LETTERS.
TOTAL, OR EACH?
WELL, I CAN ONLY SPEAK FOR MYSELF...
IS THIS WHY I COULDN'T FIND A STAMP FOR SIX MONTHS?
AMEND

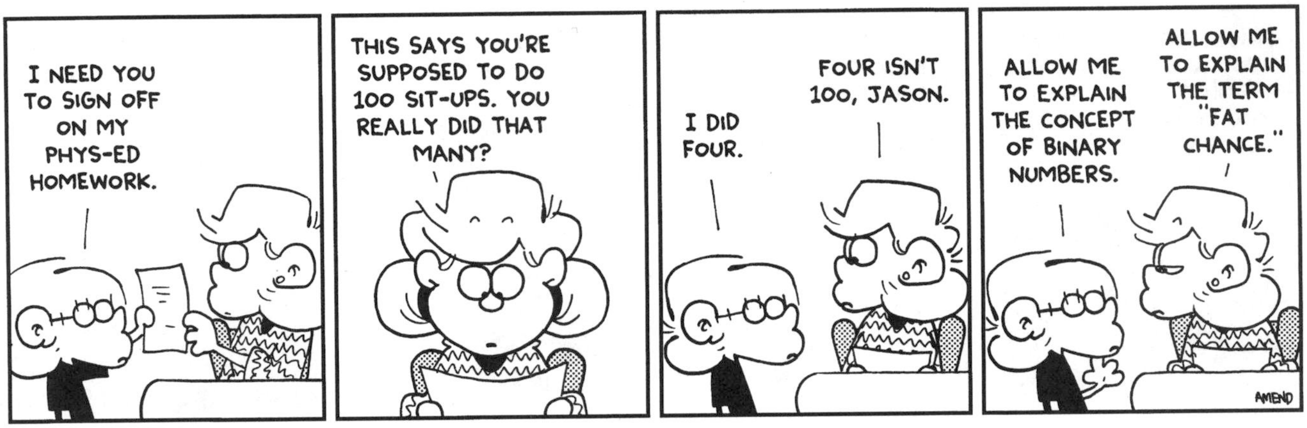
I NEED YOU TO SIGN OFF ON MY PHYS-ED HOMEWORK.
THIS SAYS YOU'RE SUPPOSED TO DO 100 SIT-UPS. YOU REALLY DID THAT MANY?
I DID FOUR.
FOUR ISN'T 100, JASON.
ALLOW ME TO EXPLAIN THE CONCEPT OF BINARY NUMBERS.
ALLOW ME TO EXPLAIN THE TERM "FAT CHANCE."
AMEND

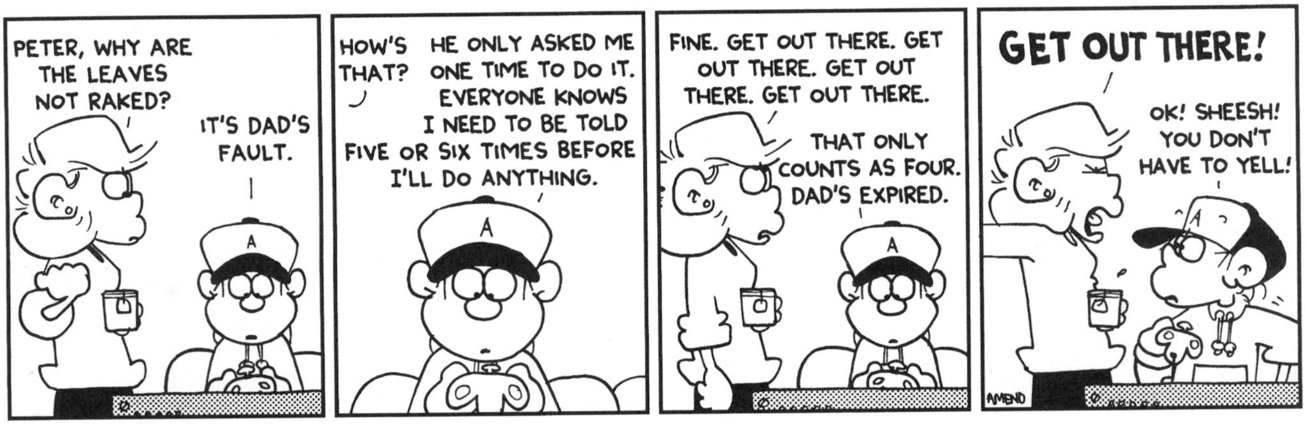
PETER, WHY ARE THE LEAVES NOT RAKED?
IT'S DAD'S FAULT.
HOW'S THAT?
HE ONLY ASKED ME ONE TIME TO DO IT. EVERYONE KNOWS I NEED TO BE TOLD FIVE OR SIX TIMES BEFORE I'LL DO ANYTHING.
FINE. GET OUT THERE. GET OUT THERE. GET OUT THERE. GET OUT THERE.
THAT ONLY COUNTS AS FOUR. DAD'S EXPIRED.
GET OUT THERE!
OK! SHEESH! YOU DON'T HAVE TO YELL!
AMEND

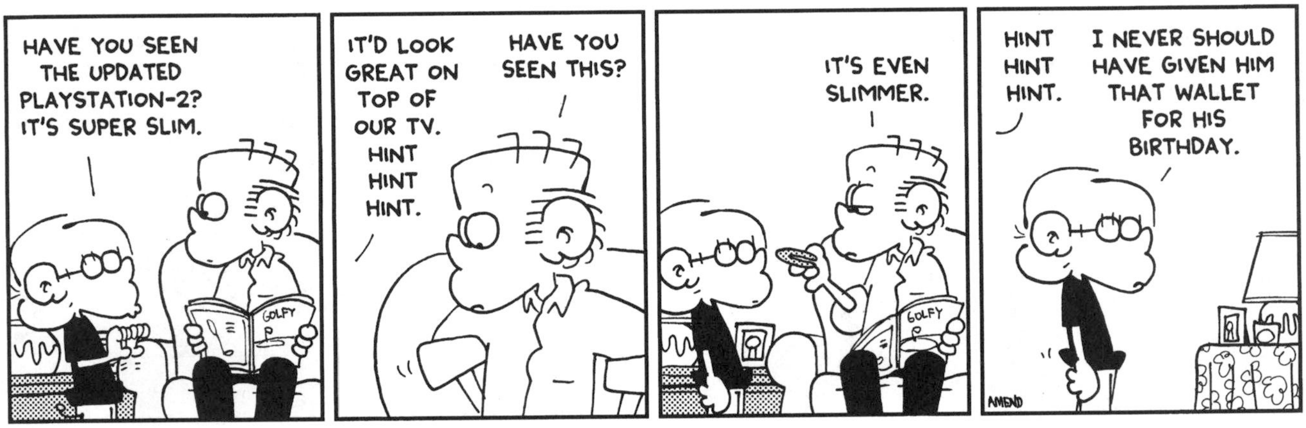
HAVE YOU SEEN THE UPDATED PLAYSTATION-2? IT'S SUPER SLIM.
GOLFY
IT'D LOOK GREAT ON TOP OF OUR TV. HINT HINT HINT.
HAVE YOU SEEN THIS?
IT'S EVEN SLIMMER.
GOLFY
HINT HINT HINT.
I NEVER SHOULD HAVE GIVEN HIM THAT WALLET FOR HIS BIRTHDAY.
AMEND

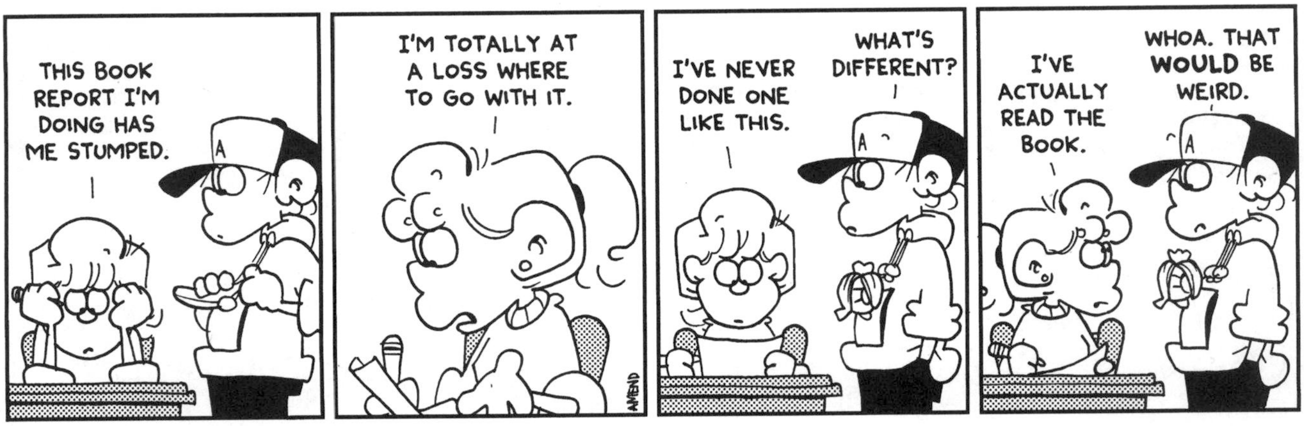
THIS BOOK REPORT I'M DOING HAS ME STUMPED.
I'M TOTALLY AT A LOSS WHERE TO GO WITH IT.
AMEND
I'VE NEVER DONE ONE LIKE THIS.
WHAT'S DIFFERENT?
I'VE ACTUALLY READ THE BOOK.
WHOA. THAT WOULD BE WEIRD.

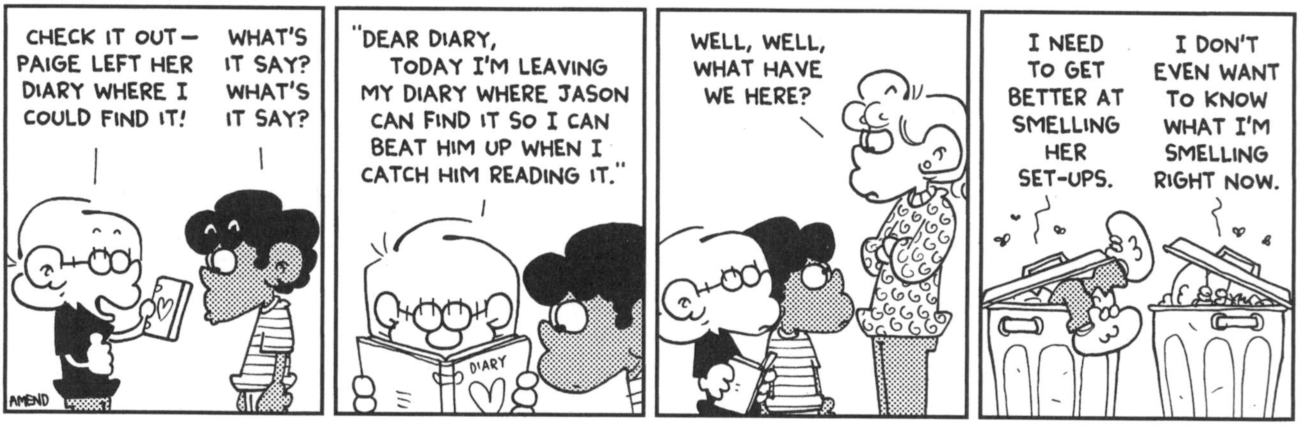
CHECK IT OUT— PAIGE LEFT HER DIARY WHERE I COULD FIND IT!
WHAT'S IT SAY? WHAT'S IT SAY?
"DEAR DIARY, TODAY I'M LEAVING MY DIARY WHERE JASON CAN FIND IT SO I CAN BEAT HIM UP WHEN I CATCH HIM READING IT."
DIARY
WELL, WELL, WHAT HAVE WE HERE?
I NEED TO GET BETTER AT SMELLING HER SET-UPS.
I DON'T EVEN WANT TO KNOW WHAT I'M SMELLING RIGHT NOW.
AMEND

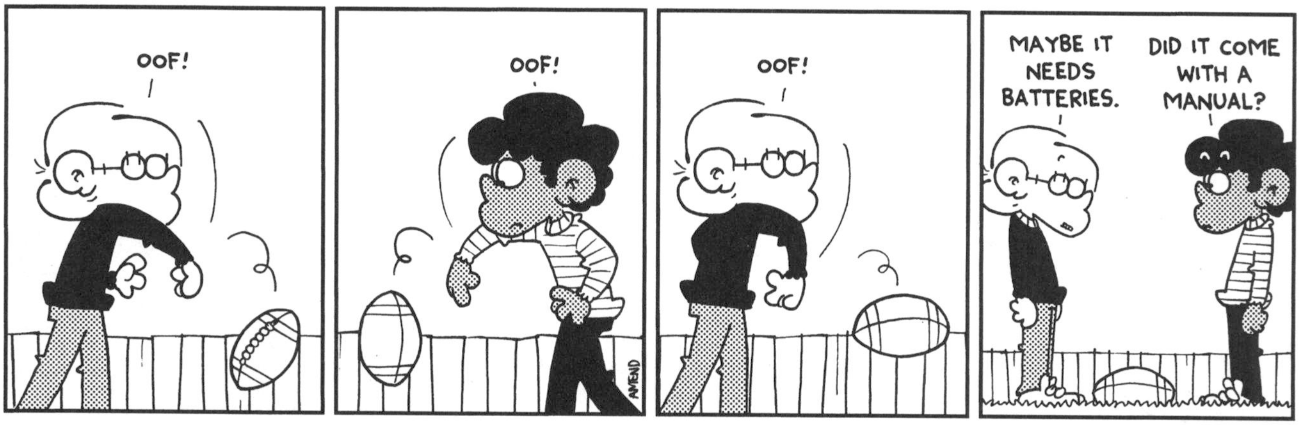
OOF!
OOF!
OOF!
MAYBE IT NEEDS BATTERIES.
DID IT COME WITH A MANUAL?
AMEND

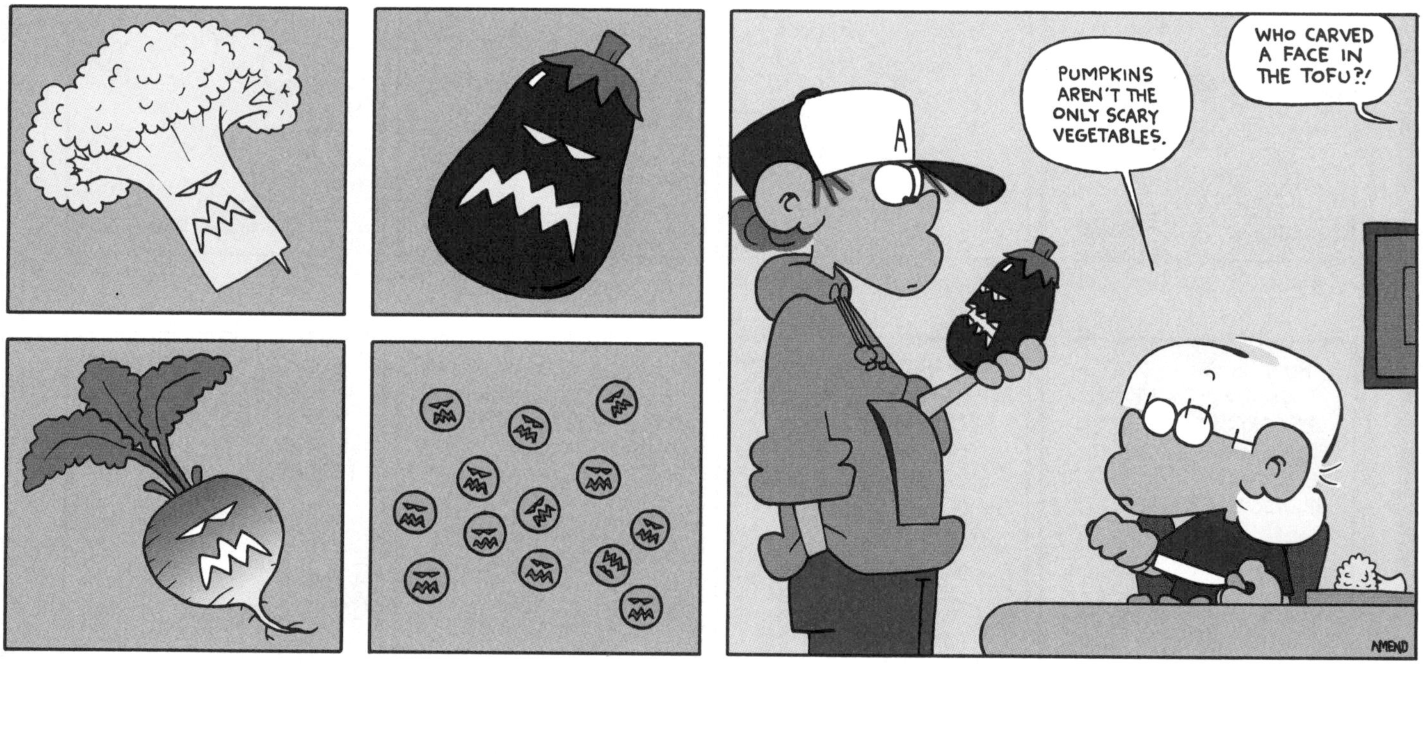
PUMPKINS AREN'T THE ONLY SCARY VEGETABLES.
WHO CARVED A FACE IN THE TOFU?!
A
AMEND

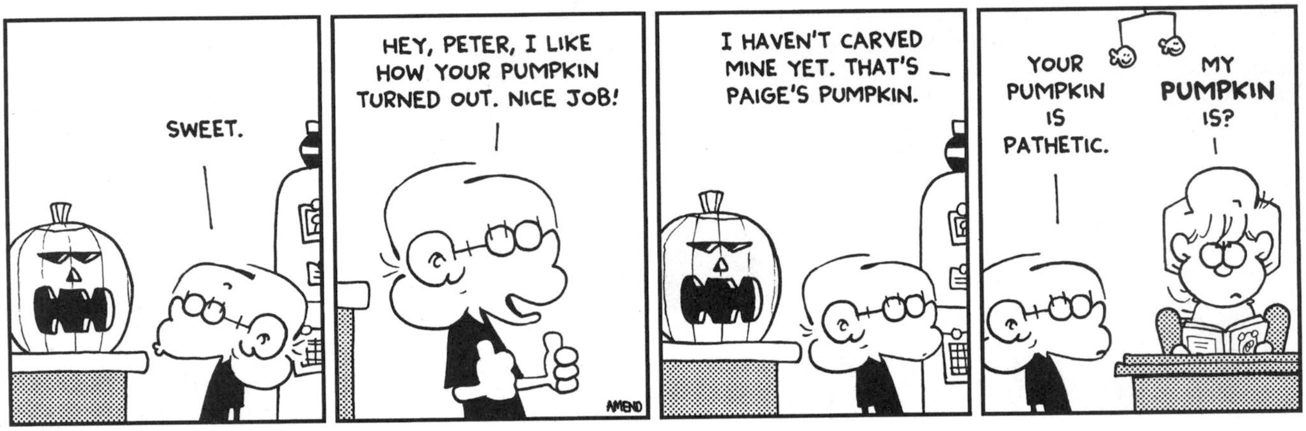
SWEET.
HEY, PETER, I LIKE HOW YOUR PUMPKIN TURNED OUT. NICE JOB!
AMEND
I HAVEN'T CARVED MINE YET. THAT'S PAIGE'S PUMPKIN.
YOUR PUMPKIN IS PATHETIC.
MY **PUMPKIN** IS?

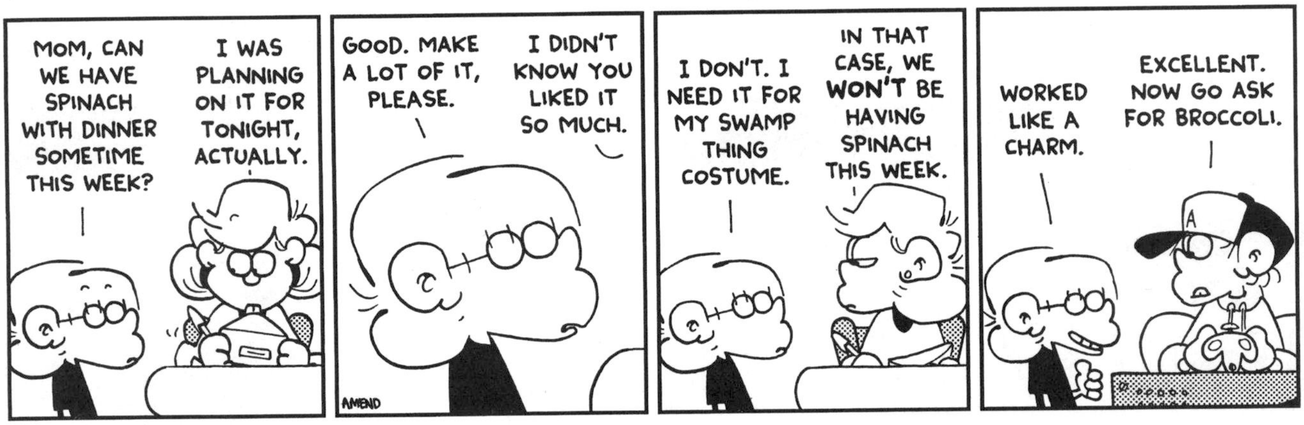
MOM, CAN WE HAVE SPINACH WITH DINNER SOMETIME THIS WEEK?
I WAS PLANNING ON IT FOR TONIGHT, ACTUALLY.
GOOD. MAKE A LOT OF IT, PLEASE.
I DIDN'T KNOW YOU LIKED IT SO MUCH.
AMEND
I DON'T. I NEED IT FOR MY SWAMP THING COSTUME.
IN THAT CASE, WE **WON'T** BE HAVING SPINACH THIS WEEK.
WORKED LIKE A CHARM.
EXCELLENT. NOW GO ASK FOR BROCCOLI.

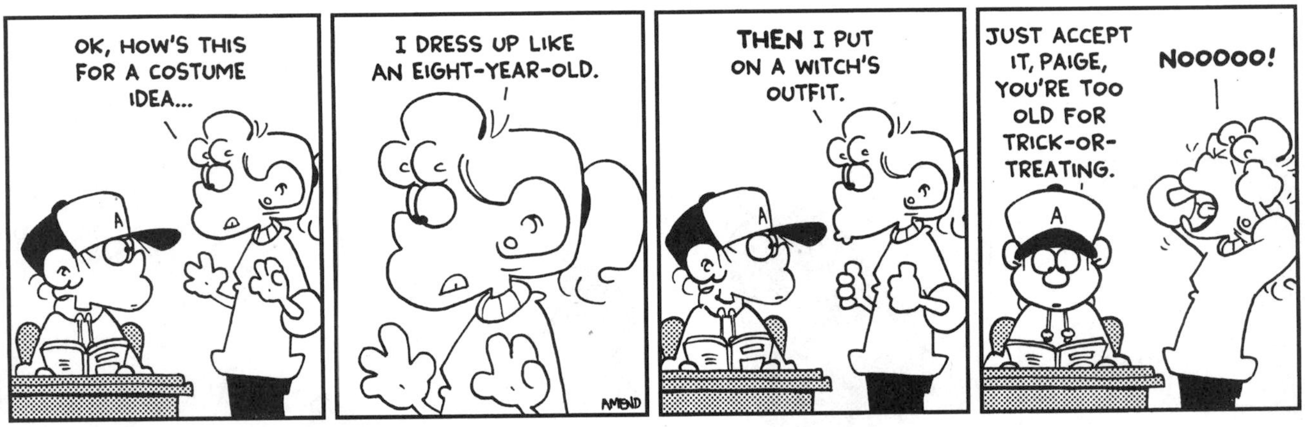
OK, HOW'S THIS FOR A COSTUME IDEA...
I DRESS UP LIKE AN EIGHT-YEAR-OLD.
AMEND
THEN I PUT ON A WITCH'S OUTFIT.
JUST ACCEPT IT, PAIGE, YOU'RE TOO OLD FOR TRICK-OR-TREATING.
NOOOOO!

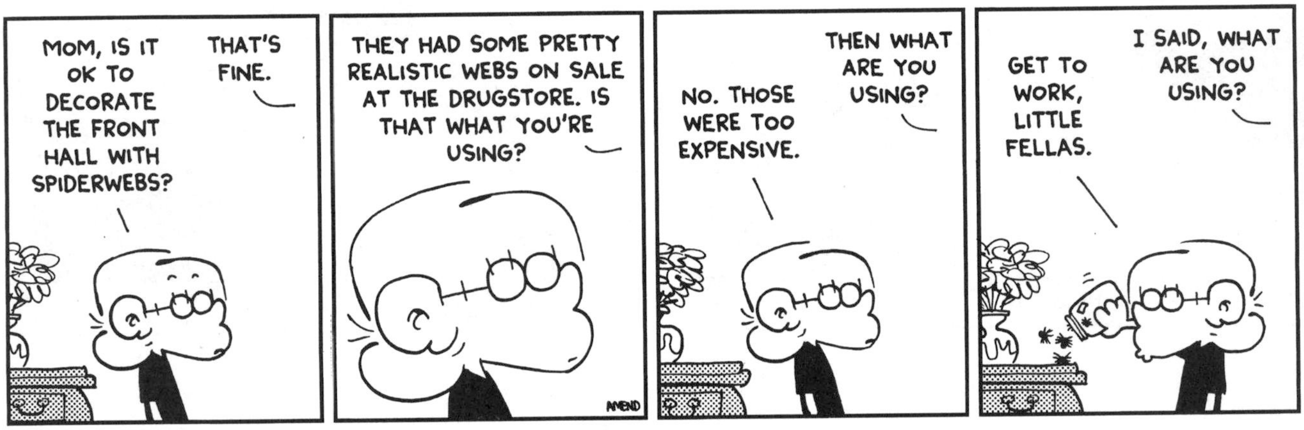
MOM, IS IT OK TO DECORATE THE FRONT HALL WITH SPIDERWEBS?
THAT'S FINE.
THEY HAD SOME PRETTY REALISTIC WEBS ON SALE AT THE DRUGSTORE. IS THAT WHAT YOU'RE USING?
AMEND
NO. THOSE WERE TOO EXPENSIVE.
THEN WHAT ARE YOU USING?
GET TO WORK, LITTLE FELLAS.
I SAID, WHAT ARE YOU USING?

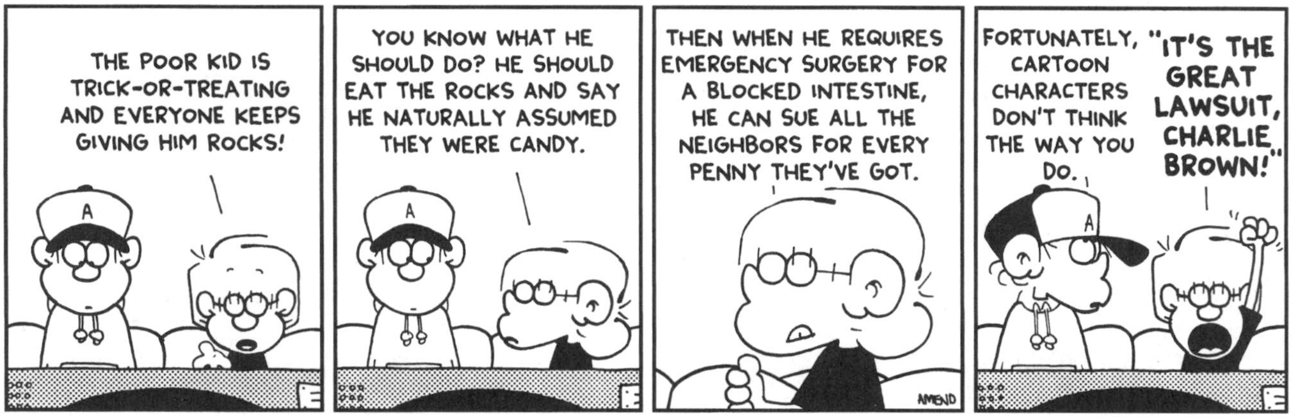
THE POOR KID IS TRICK-OR-TREATING AND EVERYONE KEEPS GIVING HIM ROCKS!
YOU KNOW WHAT HE SHOULD DO? HE SHOULD EAT THE ROCKS AND SAY HE NATURALLY ASSUMED THEY WERE CANDY.
THEN WHEN HE REQUIRES EMERGENCY SURGERY FOR A BLOCKED INTESTINE, HE CAN SUE ALL THE NEIGHBORS FOR EVERY PENNY THEY'VE GOT.
FORTUNATELY, CARTOON CHARACTERS DON'T THINK THE WAY YOU DO.
"IT'S THE GREAT LAWSUIT, CHARLIE BROWN!"

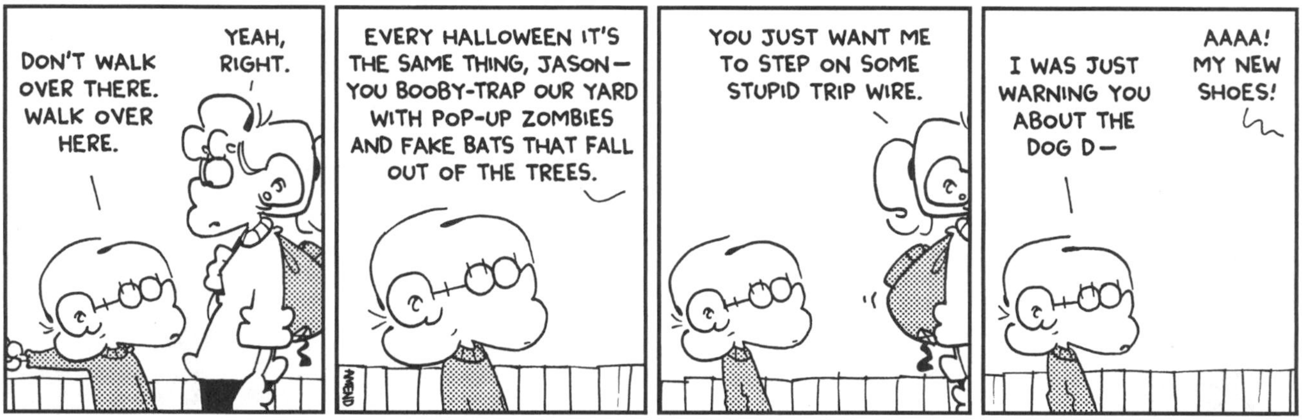
DON'T WALK OVER THERE. WALK OVER HERE.
YEAH, RIGHT.
EVERY HALLOWEEN IT'S THE SAME THING, JASON— YOU BOOBY-TRAP OUR YARD WITH POP-UP ZOMBIES AND FAKE BATS THAT FALL OUT OF THE TREES.
YOU JUST WANT ME TO STEP ON SOME STUPID TRIP WIRE.
I WAS JUST WARNING YOU ABOUT THE DOG D—
AAAA! MY NEW SHOES!

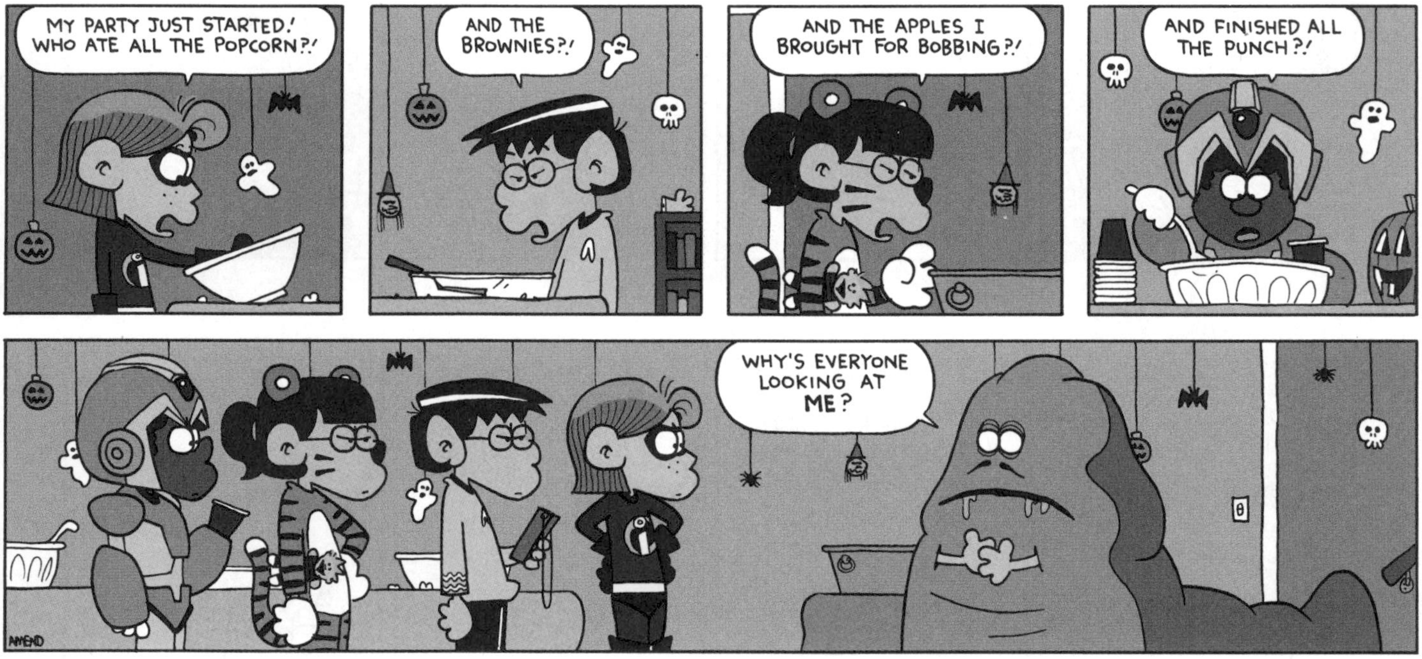
MY PARTY JUST STARTED?! WHO ATE ALL THE POPCORN?!
AND THE BROWNIES?!
AND THE APPLES I BROUGHT FOR BOBBING?!
AND FINISHED ALL THE PUNCH?!
WHY'S EVERYONE LOOKING AT ME?

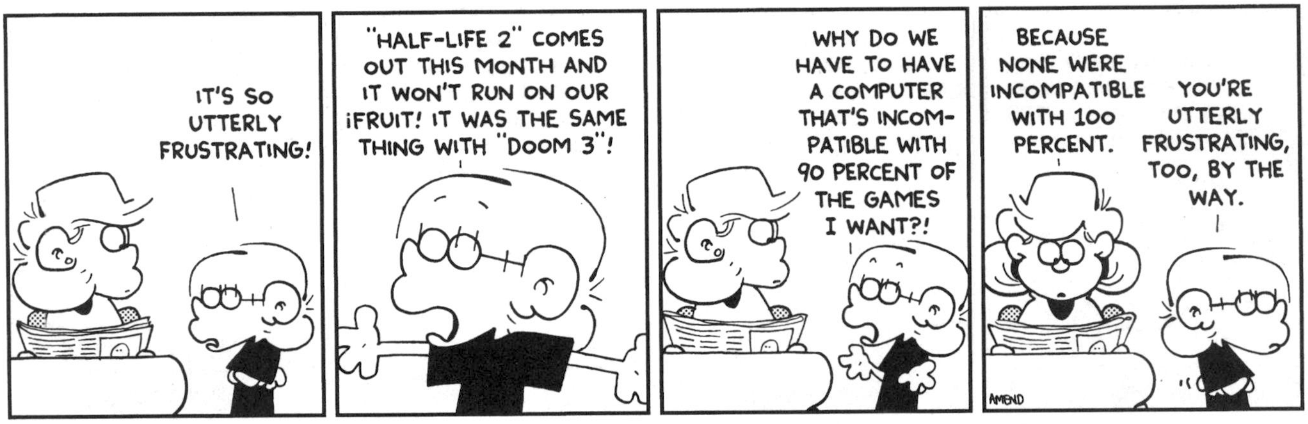
IT'S SO UTTERLY FRUSTRATING!
"HALF-LIFE 2" COMES OUT THIS MONTH AND IT WON'T RUN ON OUR iFRUIT! IT WAS THE SAME THING WITH "DOOM 3"!
WHY DO WE HAVE TO HAVE A COMPUTER THAT'S INCOMPATIBLE WITH 90 PERCENT OF THE GAMES I WANT?!
BECAUSE NONE WERE INCOMPATIBLE WITH 100 PERCENT.
YOU'RE UTTERLY FRUSTRATING, TOO, BY THE WAY.
AMEND

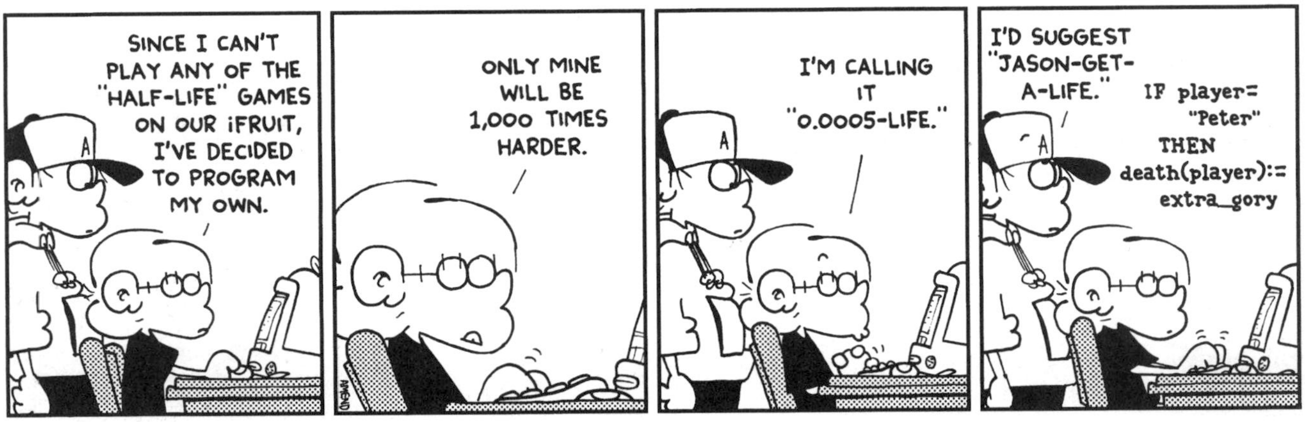
SINCE I CAN'T PLAY ANY OF THE "HALF-LIFE" GAMES ON OUR iFRUIT, I'VE DECIDED TO PROGRAM MY OWN.
ONLY MINE WILL BE 1,000 TIMES HARDER.
AMEND
I'M CALLING IT "0.0005-LIFE."
I'D SUGGEST "JASON-GET-A-LIFE."
IF player= "Peter" THEN death(player):= extra_gory

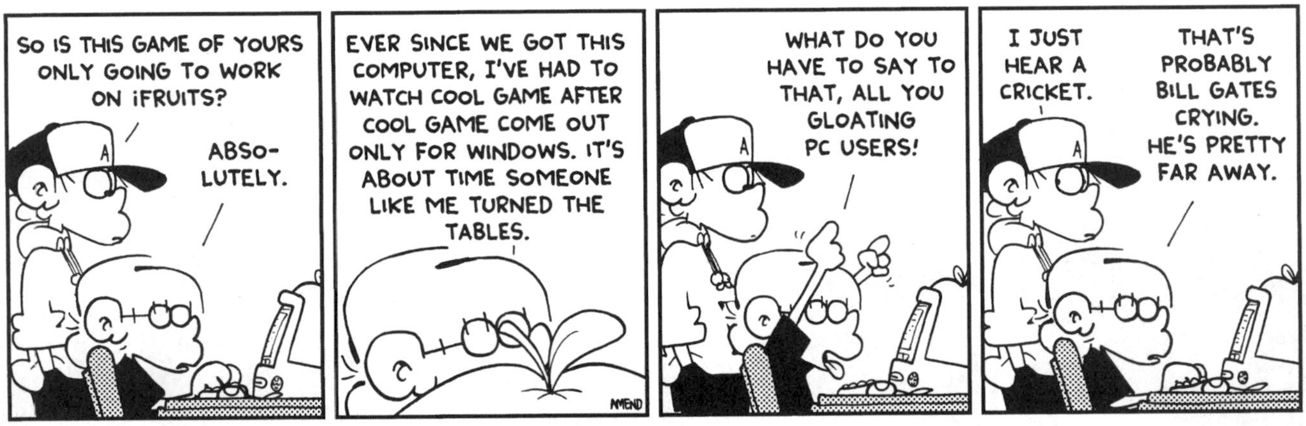
SO IS THIS GAME OF YOURS ONLY GOING TO WORK ON iFRUITS?
ABSO-LUTELY.
EVER SINCE WE GOT THIS COMPUTER, I'VE HAD TO WATCH COOL GAME AFTER COOL GAME COME OUT ONLY FOR WINDOWS. IT'S ABOUT TIME SOMEONE LIKE ME TURNED THE TABLES.
AMEND
WHAT DO YOU HAVE TO SAY TO THAT, ALL YOU GLOATING PC USERS!
I JUST HEAR A CRICKET.
THAT'S PROBABLY BILL GATES CRYING. HE'S PRETTY FAR AWAY.

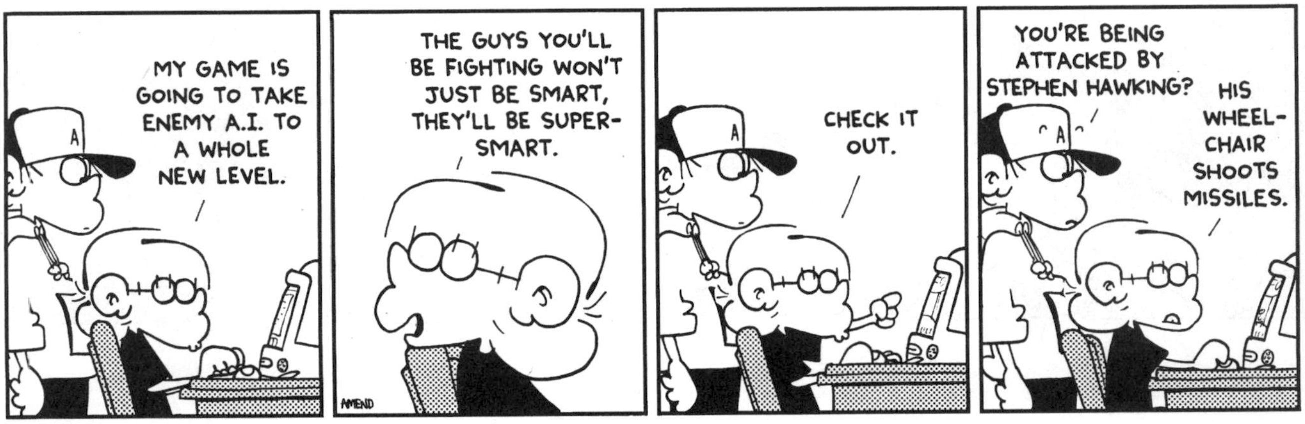
MY GAME IS GOING TO TAKE ENEMY A.I. TO A WHOLE NEW LEVEL.
THE GUYS YOU'LL BE FIGHTING WON'T JUST BE SMART, THEY'LL BE SUPER-SMART.
AMEND
CHECK IT OUT.
YOU'RE BEING ATTACKED BY STEPHEN HAWKING?
HIS WHEEL-CHAIR SHOOTS MISSILES.

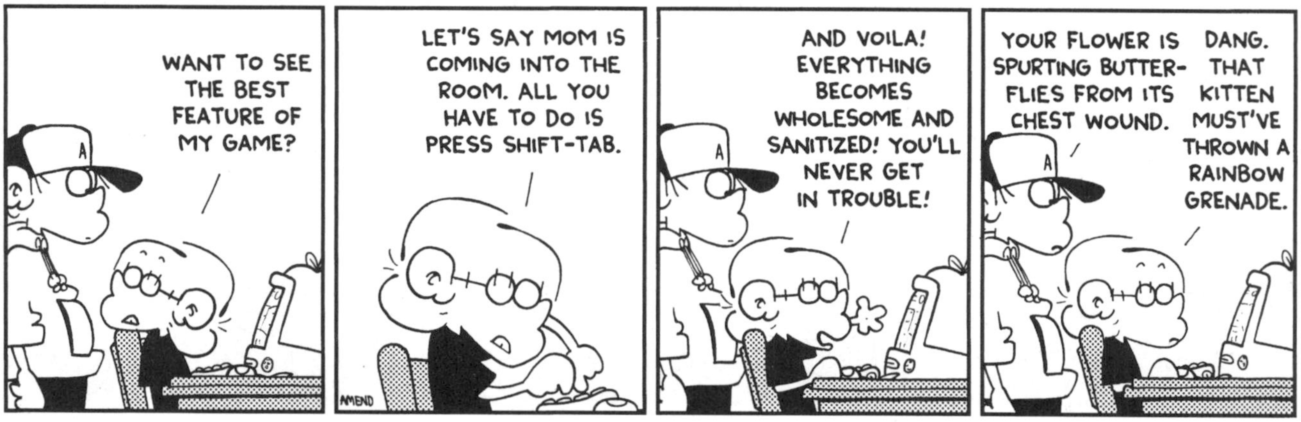
WANT TO SEE THE BEST FEATURE OF MY GAME?
LET'S SAY MOM IS COMING INTO THE ROOM. ALL YOU HAVE TO DO IS PRESS SHIFT-TAB.
AMEND
AND VOILA! EVERYTHING BECOMES WHOLESOME AND SANITIZED! YOU'LL NEVER GET IN TROUBLE!
YOUR FLOWER IS SPURTING BUTTER-FLIES FROM ITS CHEST WOUND.
DANG. THAT KITTEN MUST'VE THROWN A RAINBOW GRENADE.

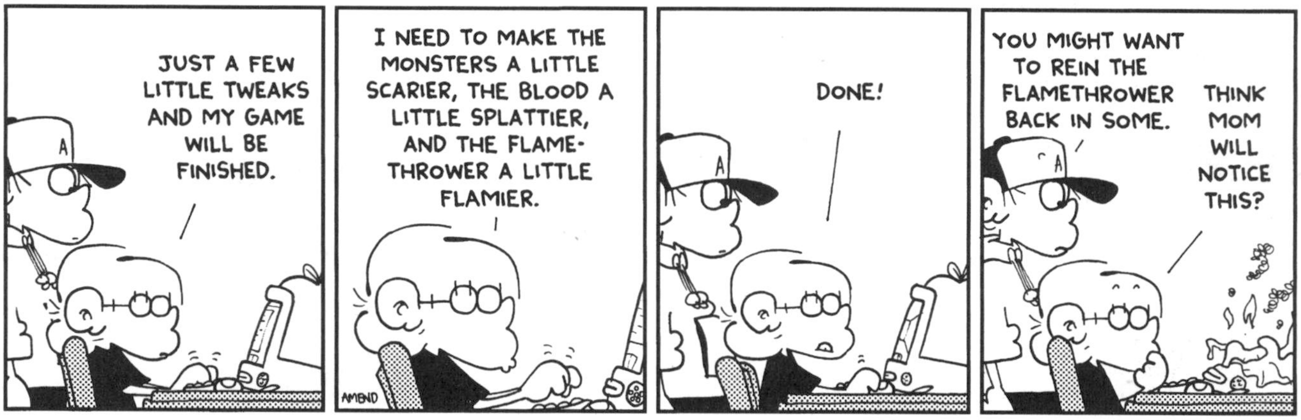
JUST A FEW LITTLE TWEAKS AND MY GAME WILL BE FINISHED.
I NEED TO MAKE THE MONSTERS A LITTLE SCARIER, THE BLOOD A LITTLE SPLATTIER, AND THE FLAME-THROWER A LITTLE FLAMIER.
AMEND
DONE!
YOU MIGHT WANT TO REIN THE FLAMETHROWER BACK IN SOME.
THINK MOM WILL NOTICE THIS?

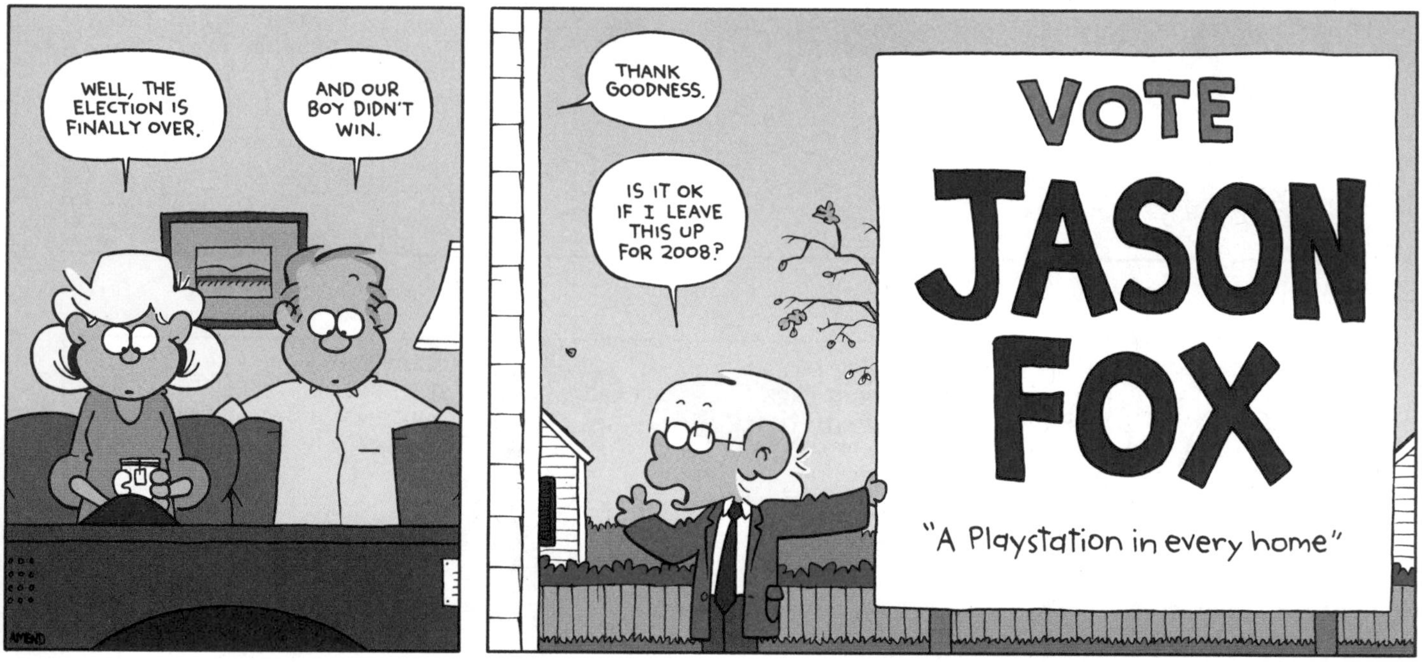
WELL, THE ELECTION IS FINALLY OVER.
AND OUR BOY DIDN'T WIN.
AMEND
THANK GOODNESS.
IS IT OK IF I LEAVE THIS UP FOR 2008?
VOTE
JASON FOX
"A Playstation in every home"

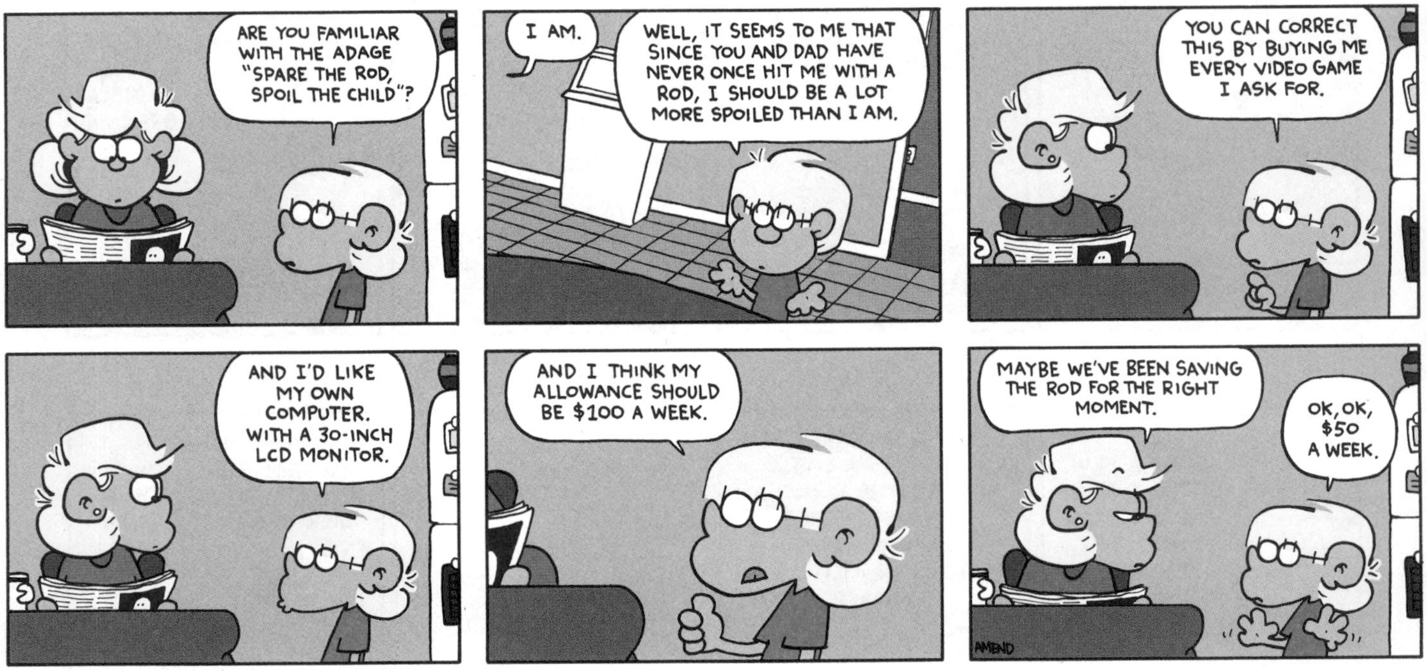
ARE YOU FAMILIAR WITH THE ADAGE "SPARE THE ROD, SPOIL THE CHILD"?
I AM.
WELL, IT SEEMS TO ME THAT SINCE YOU AND DAD HAVE NEVER ONCE HIT ME WITH A ROD, I SHOULD BE A LOT MORE SPOILED THAN I AM.
YOU CAN CORRECT THIS BY BUYING ME EVERY VIDEO GAME I ASK FOR.
AND I'D LIKE MY OWN COMPUTER. WITH A 30-INCH LCD MONITOR.
AND I THINK MY ALLOWANCE SHOULD BE $100 A WEEK.
MAYBE WE'VE BEEN SAVING THE ROD FOR THE RIGHT MOMENT.
OK, OK, $50 A WEEK.
AMEND

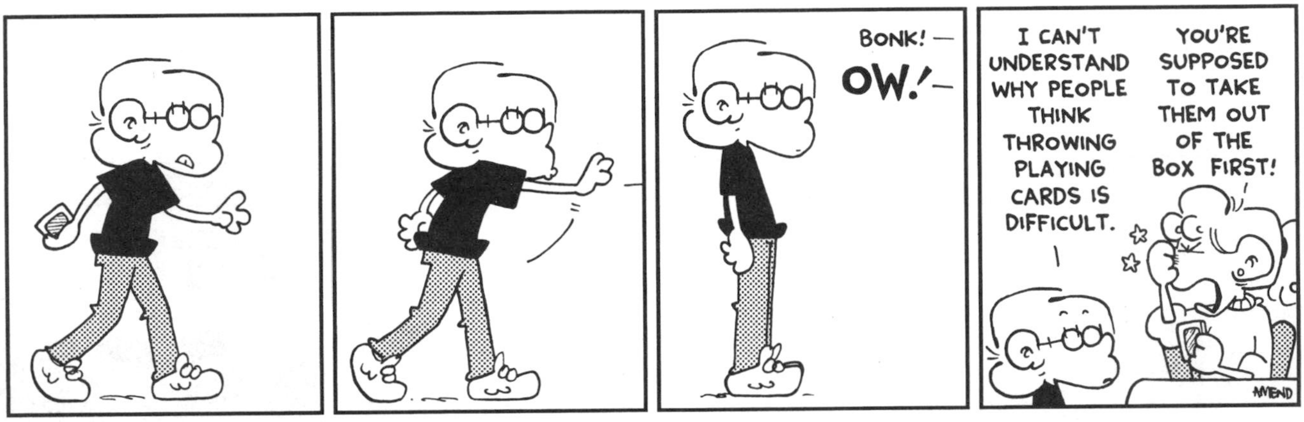
BONK!
OW!
I CAN'T UNDERSTAND WHY PEOPLE THINK THROWING PLAYING CARDS IS DIFFICULT.
YOU'RE SUPPOSED TO TAKE THEM OUT OF THE BOX FIRST!
AMEND

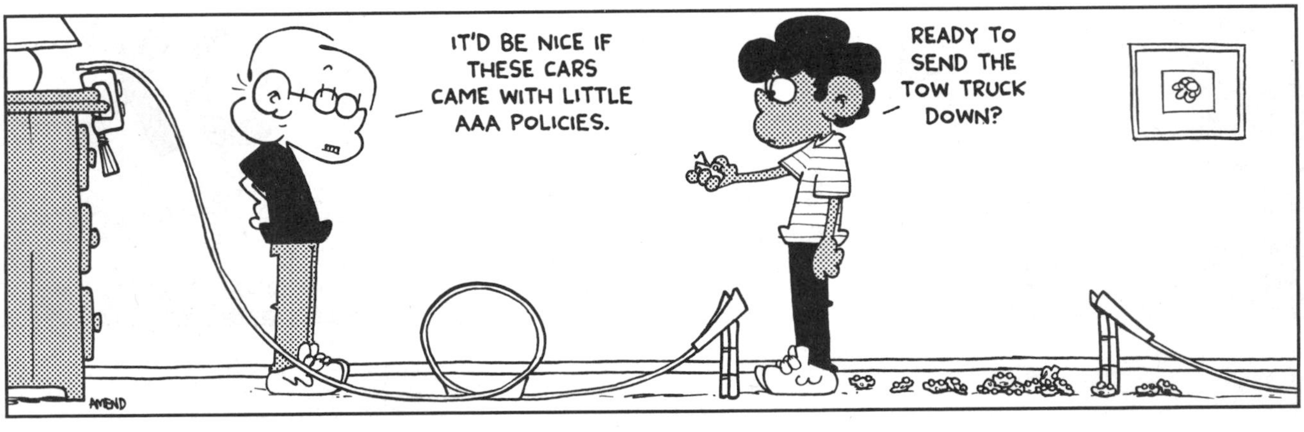
IT'D BE NICE IF THESE CARS CAME WITH LITTLE AAA POLICIES.
READY TO SEND THE TOW TRUCK DOWN?
AMEND

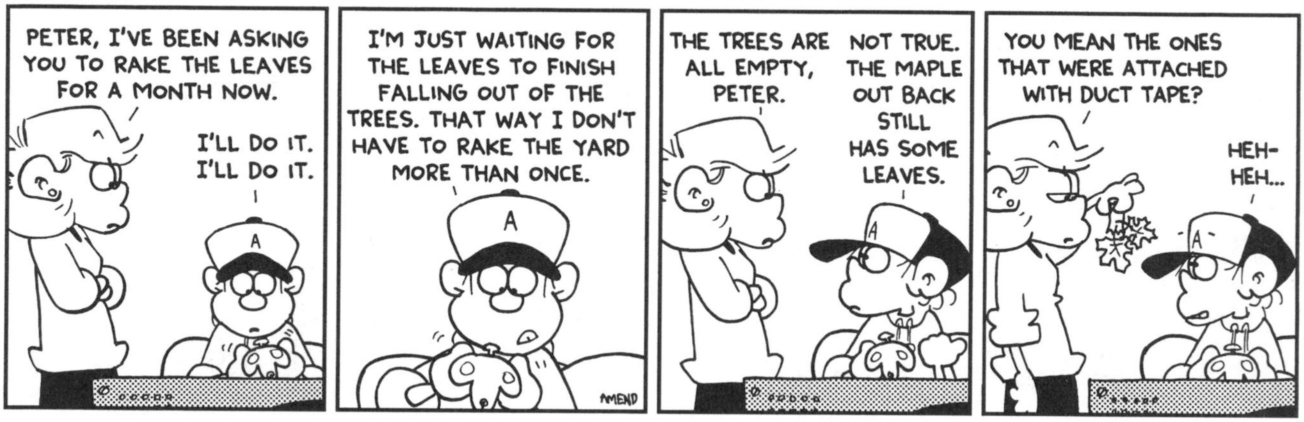
PETER, I'VE BEEN ASKING YOU TO RAKE THE LEAVES FOR A MONTH NOW.
I'LL DO IT. I'LL DO IT.
I'M JUST WAITING FOR THE LEAVES TO FINISH FALLING OUT OF THE TREES. THAT WAY I DON'T HAVE TO RAKE THE YARD MORE THAN ONCE.
THE TREES ARE ALL EMPTY, PETER.
NOT TRUE. THE MAPLE OUT BACK STILL HAS SOME LEAVES.
YOU MEAN THE ONES THAT WERE ATTACHED WITH DUCT TAPE?
HEH-HEH...

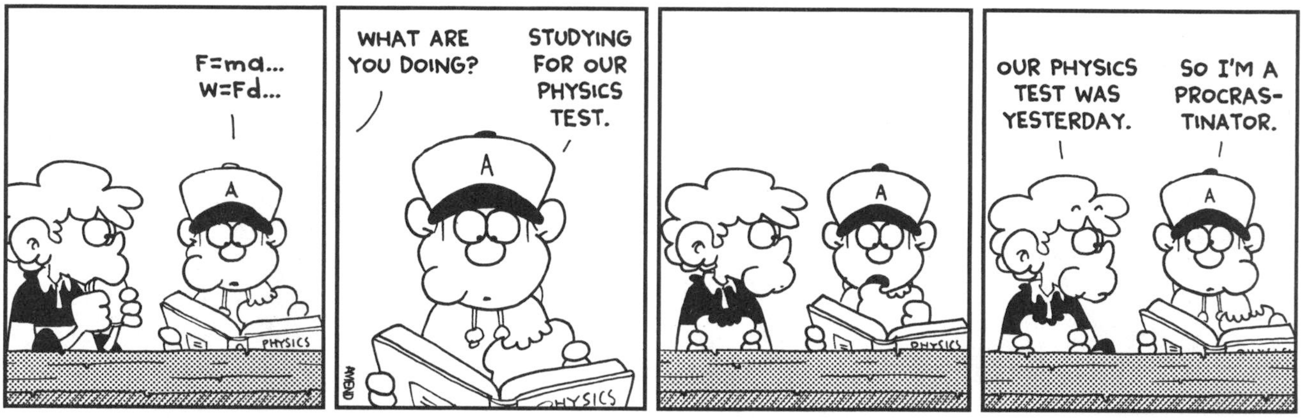
F=ma... W=Fd...
PHYSICS
WHAT ARE YOU DOING?
STUDYING FOR OUR PHYSICS TEST.
PHYSICS
PHYSICS
OUR PHYSICS TEST WAS YESTERDAY.
SO I'M A PROCRASTINATOR.

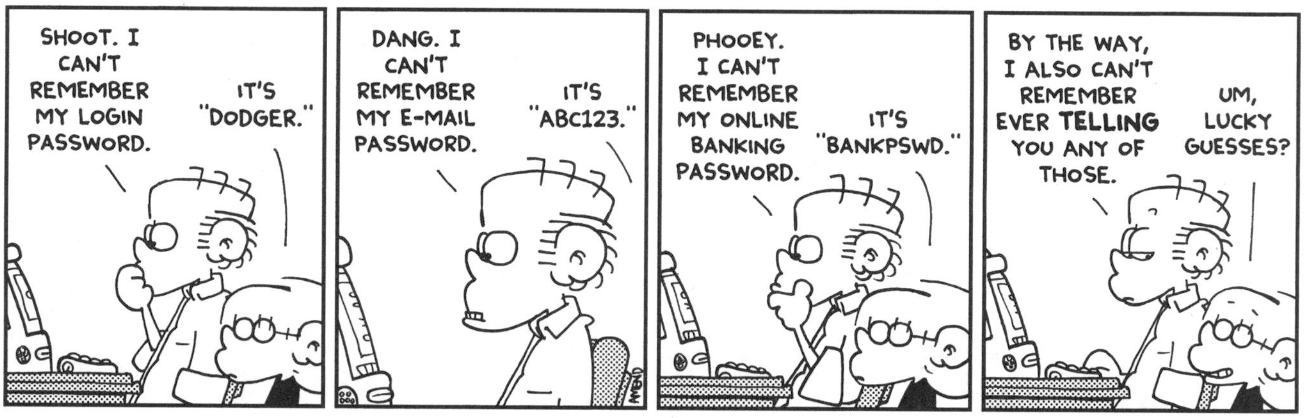
SHOOT. I CAN'T REMEMBER MY LOGIN PASSWORD.
IT'S "DODGER."
DANG. I CAN'T REMEMBER MY E-MAIL PASSWORD.
IT'S "ABC123."
PHOOEY. I CAN'T REMEMBER MY ONLINE BANKING PASSWORD.
IT'S "BANKPSWD."
BY THE WAY, I ALSO CAN'T REMEMBER EVER **TELLING** YOU ANY OF THOSE.
UM, LUCKY GUESSES?

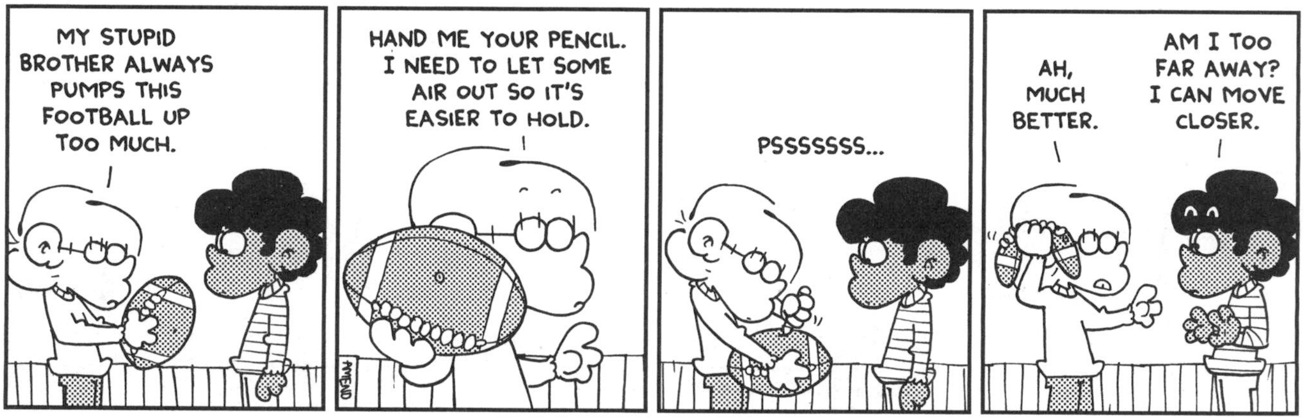
MY STUPID BROTHER ALWAYS PUMPS THIS FOOTBALL UP TOO MUCH.
HAND ME YOUR PENCIL. I NEED TO LET SOME AIR OUT SO IT'S EASIER TO HOLD.
PSSSSSSS...
AH, MUCH BETTER.
AM I TOO FAR AWAY? I CAN MOVE CLOSER.

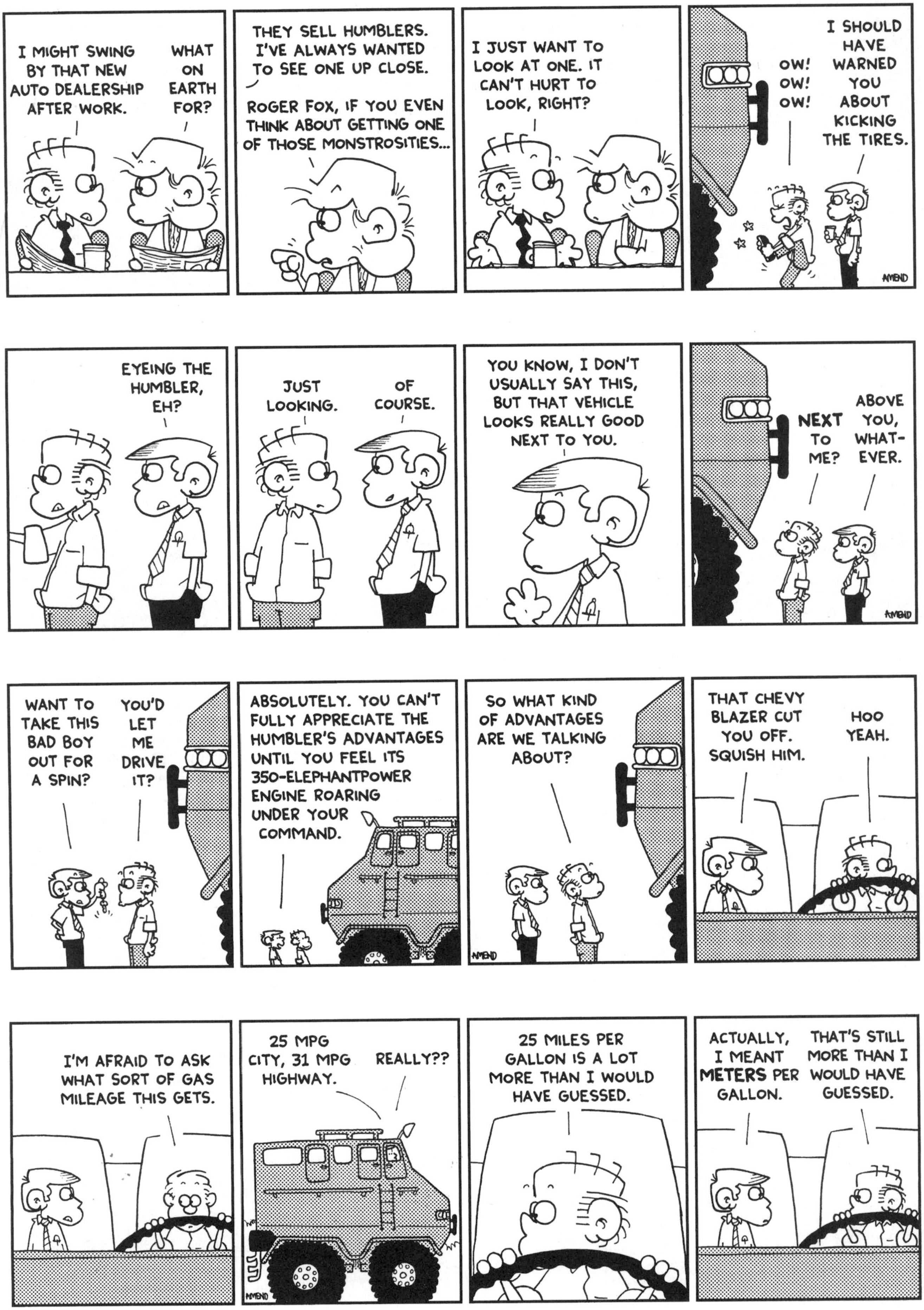
I MIGHT SWING BY THAT NEW AUTO DEALERSHIP AFTER WORK.
WHAT ON EARTH FOR?
THEY SELL HUMBLERS. I'VE ALWAYS WANTED TO SEE ONE UP CLOSE.
ROGER FOX, IF YOU EVEN THINK ABOUT GETTING ONE OF THOSE MONSTROSITIES...
I JUST WANT TO LOOK AT ONE. IT CAN'T HURT TO LOOK, RIGHT?
OW! OW! OW!
I SHOULD HAVE WARNED YOU ABOUT KICKING THE TIRES.
AMEND
EYEING THE HUMBLER, EH?
JUST LOOKING.
OF COURSE.
YOU KNOW, I DON'T USUALLY SAY THIS, BUT THAT VEHICLE LOOKS REALLY GOOD NEXT TO YOU.
NEXT TO ME?
ABOVE YOU, WHAT-EVER.
AMEND
WANT TO TAKE THIS BAD BOY OUT FOR A SPIN?
YOU'D LET ME DRIVE IT?
ABSOLUTELY. YOU CAN'T FULLY APPRECIATE THE HUMBLER'S ADVANTAGES UNTIL YOU FEEL ITS 350-ELEPHANTPOWER ENGINE ROARING UNDER YOUR COMMAND.
SO WHAT KIND OF ADVANTAGES ARE WE TALKING ABOUT?
AMEND
THAT CHEVY BLAZER CUT YOU OFF. SQUISH HIM.
HOO YEAH.
I'M AFRAID TO ASK WHAT SORT OF GAS MILEAGE THIS GETS.
25 MPG CITY, 31 MPG HIGHWAY.
REALLY??
AMEND
25 MILES PER GALLON IS A LOT MORE THAN I WOULD HAVE GUESSED.
ACTUALLY, I MEANT **METERS** PER GALLON.
THAT'S STILL MORE THAN I WOULD HAVE GUESSED.

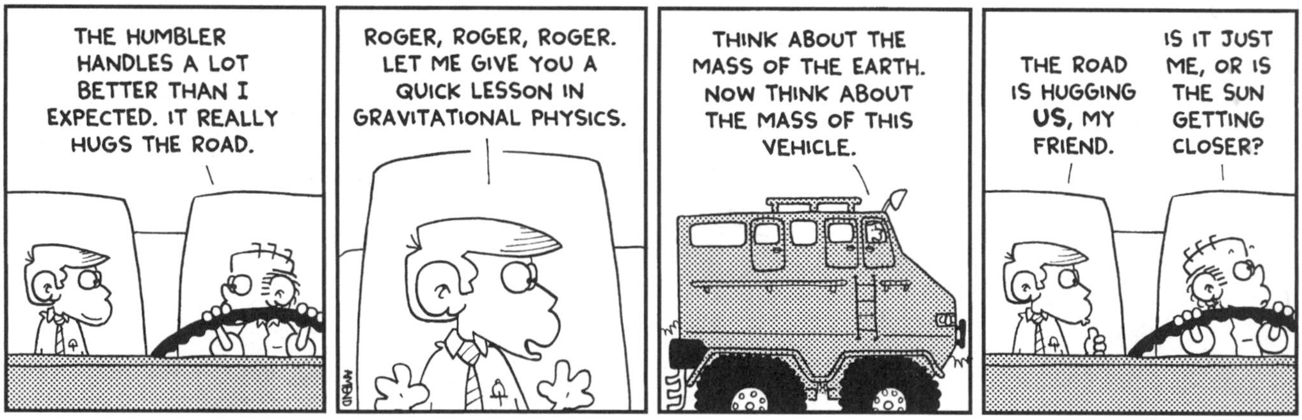
THE HUMBLER HANDLES A LOT BETTER THAN I EXPECTED. IT REALLY HUGS THE ROAD.
ROGER, ROGER, ROGER. LET ME GIVE YOU A QUICK LESSON IN GRAVITATIONAL PHYSICS.
THINK ABOUT THE MASS OF THE EARTH. NOW THINK ABOUT THE MASS OF THIS VEHICLE.
THE ROAD IS HUGGING **US**, MY FRIEND.
IS IT JUST ME, OR IS THE SUN GETTING CLOSER?
AMEND

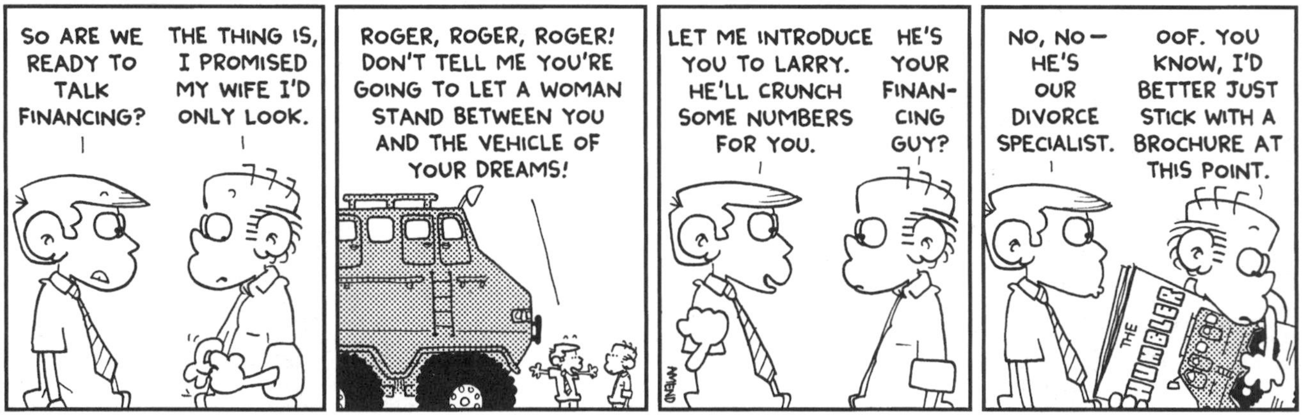
SO ARE WE READY TO TALK FINANCING?
THE THING IS, I PROMISED MY WIFE I'D ONLY LOOK.
ROGER, ROGER, ROGER! DON'T TELL ME YOU'RE GOING TO LET A WOMAN STAND BETWEEN YOU AND THE VEHICLE OF YOUR DREAMS!
LET ME INTRODUCE YOU TO LARRY. HE'LL CRUNCH SOME NUMBERS FOR YOU.
HE'S YOUR FINAN-CING GUY?
NO, NO — HE'S OUR DIVORCE SPECIALIST.
OOF. YOU KNOW, I'D BETTER JUST STICK WITH A BROCHURE AT THIS POINT.
THE HUMBLER
AMEND

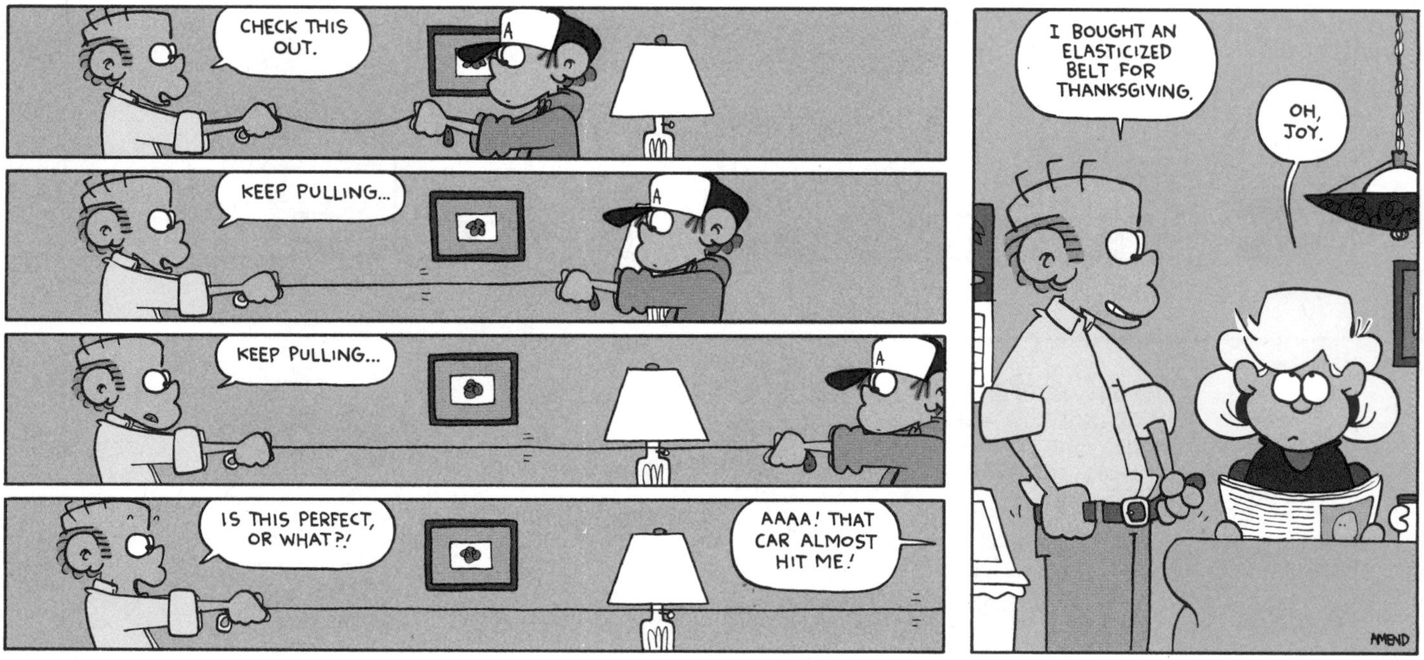
CHECK THIS OUT.
KEEP PULLING...
KEEP PULLING...
IS THIS PERFECT, OR WHAT?!
AAAA! THAT CAR ALMOST HIT ME!
I BOUGHT AN ELASTICIZED BELT FOR THANKSGIVING.
OH, JOY.
AMEND

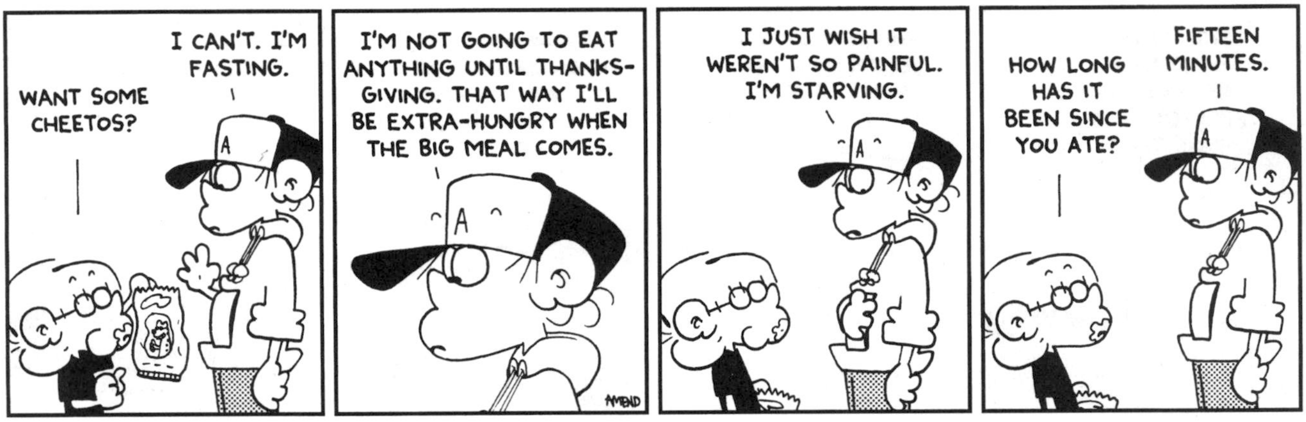

WANT SOME CHEETOS?
I CAN'T. I'M FASTING.
I'M NOT GOING TO EAT ANYTHING UNTIL THANKSGIVING. THAT WAY I'LL BE EXTRA-HUNGRY WHEN THE BIG MEAL COMES.
I JUST WISH IT WEREN'T SO PAINFUL. I'M STARVING.
HOW LONG HAS IT BEEN SINCE YOU ATE?
FIFTEEN MINUTES.
AMEND

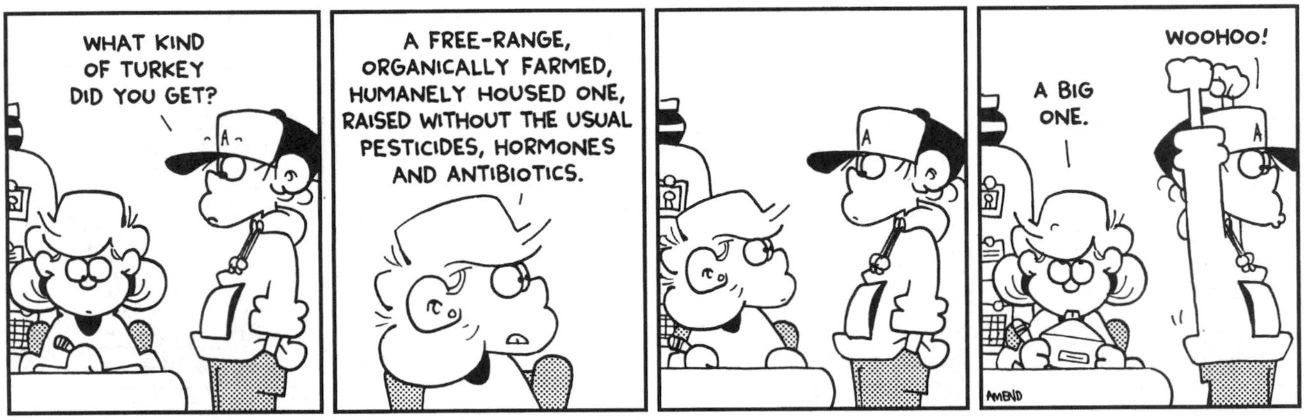

WHAT KIND OF TURKEY DID YOU GET?
A FREE-RANGE, ORGANICALLY FARMED, HUMANELY HOUSED ONE, RAISED WITHOUT THE USUAL PESTICIDES, HORMONES AND ANTIBIOTICS.
A BIG ONE.
WOOHOO!
AMEND

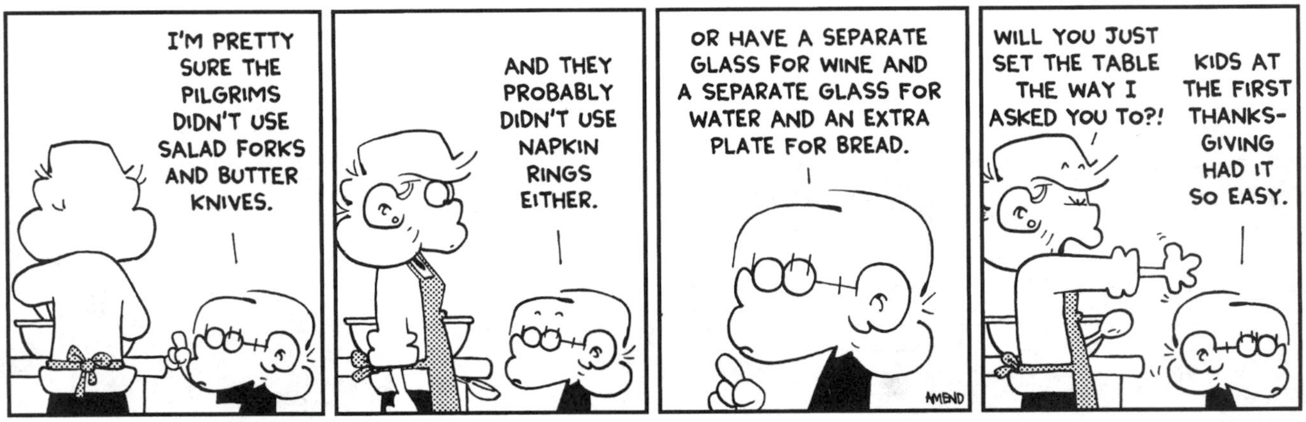

I'M PRETTY SURE THE PILGRIMS DIDN'T USE SALAD FORKS AND BUTTER KNIVES.
AND THEY PROBABLY DIDN'T USE NAPKIN RINGS EITHER.
OR HAVE A SEPARATE GLASS FOR WINE AND A SEPARATE GLASS FOR WATER AND AN EXTRA PLATE FOR BREAD.
AMEND
WILL YOU JUST SET THE TABLE THE WAY I ASKED YOU TO?!
KIDS AT THE FIRST THANKSGIVING HAD IT SO EASY.

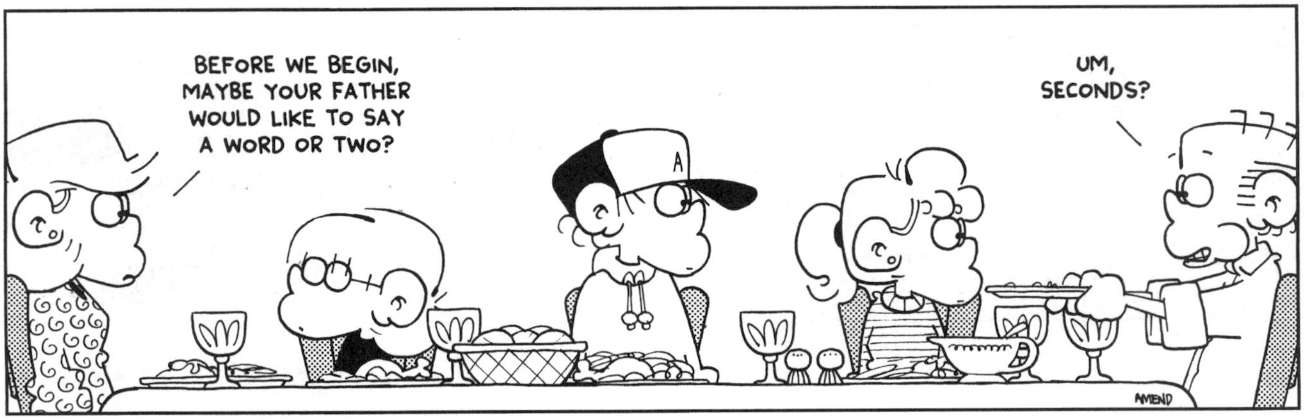

BEFORE WE BEGIN, MAYBE YOUR FATHER WOULD LIKE TO SAY A WORD OR TWO?
UM, SECONDS?
AMEND

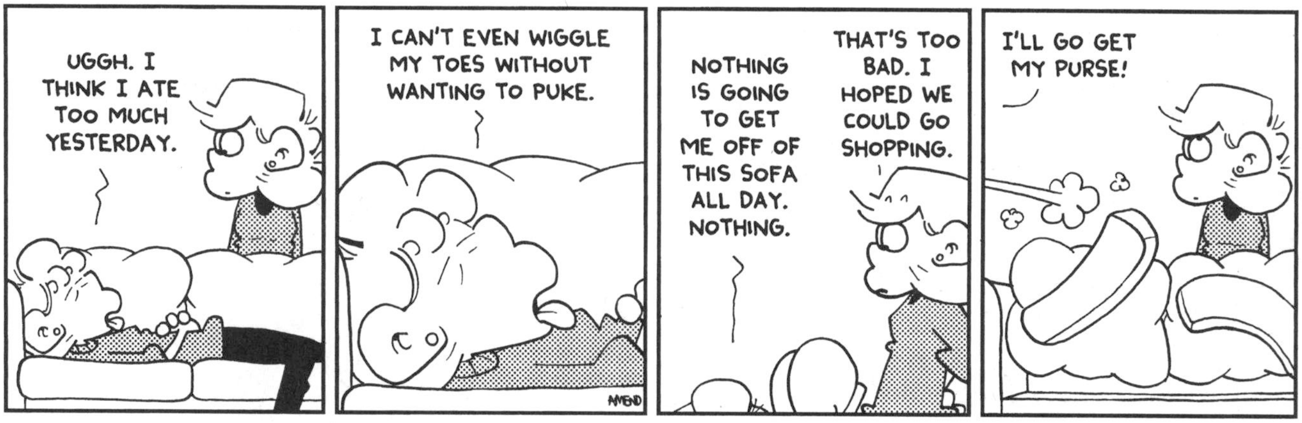
UGGH. I THINK I ATE TOO MUCH YESTERDAY.
I CAN'T EVEN WIGGLE MY TOES WITHOUT WANTING TO PUKE.
NOTHING IS GOING TO GET ME OFF OF THIS SOFA ALL DAY. NOTHING.
THAT'S TOO BAD. I HOPED WE COULD GO SHOPPING.
I'LL GO GET MY PURSE!
AMEND

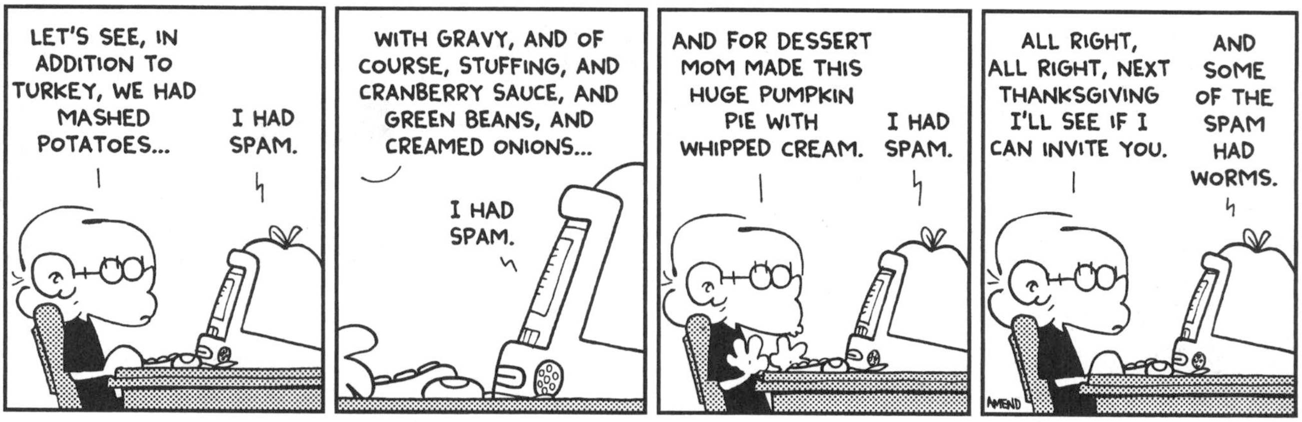
LET'S SEE, IN ADDITION TO TURKEY, WE HAD MASHED POTATOES...
I HAD SPAM.
WITH GRAVY, AND OF COURSE, STUFFING, AND CRANBERRY SAUCE, AND GREEN BEANS, AND CREAMED ONIONS...
I HAD SPAM.
AND FOR DESSERT MOM MADE THIS HUGE PUMPKIN PIE WITH WHIPPED CREAM.
I HAD SPAM.
ALL RIGHT, ALL RIGHT, NEXT THANKSGIVING I'LL SEE IF I CAN INVITE YOU.
AND SOME OF THE SPAM HAD WORMS.
AMEND

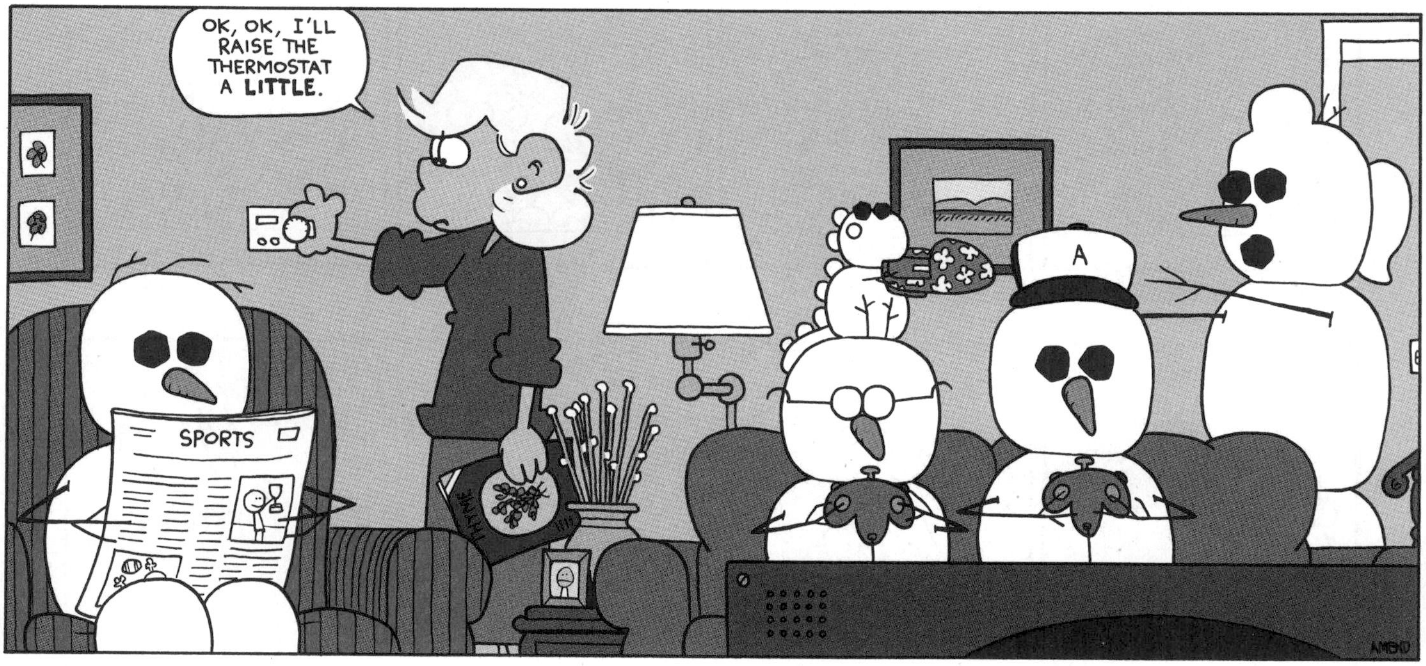
OK, OK, I'LL RAISE THE THERMOSTAT A **LITTLE**.
SPORTS
THYME
A
AMEND

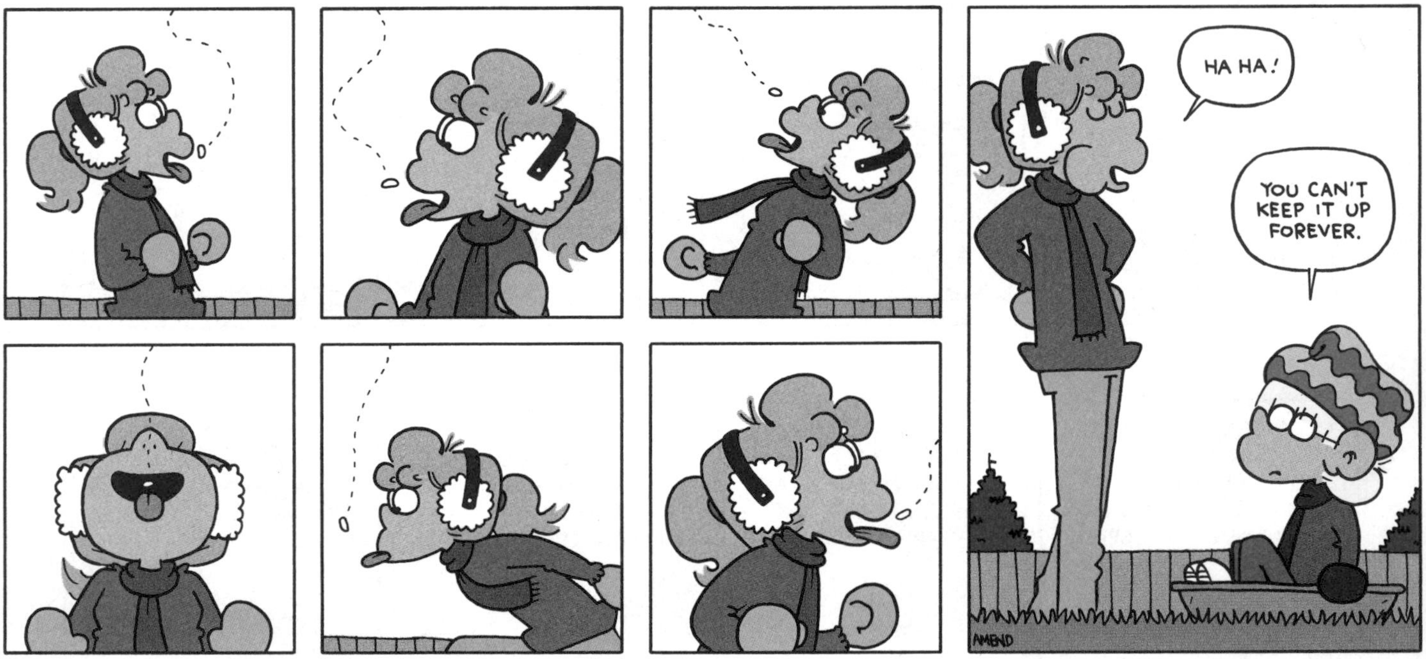
HA HA!
YOU CAN'T KEEP IT UP FOREVER.
AMEND

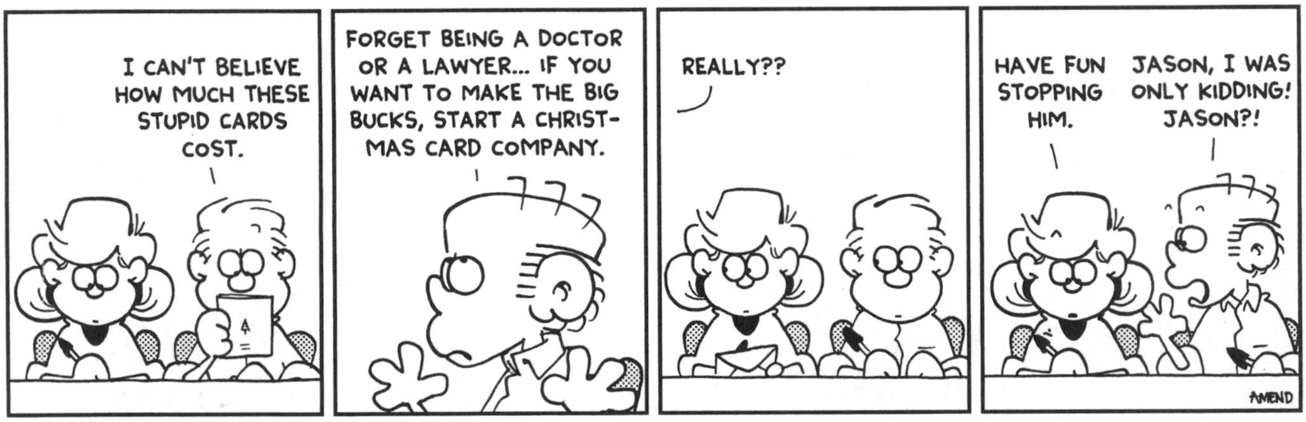
I CAN'T BELIEVE HOW MUCH THESE STUPID CARDS COST.
FORGET BEING A DOCTOR OR A LAWYER... IF YOU WANT TO MAKE THE BIG BUCKS, START A CHRISTMAS CARD COMPANY.
REALLY??
HAVE FUN STOPPING HIM.
JASON, I WAS ONLY KIDDING! JASON?!
AMEND

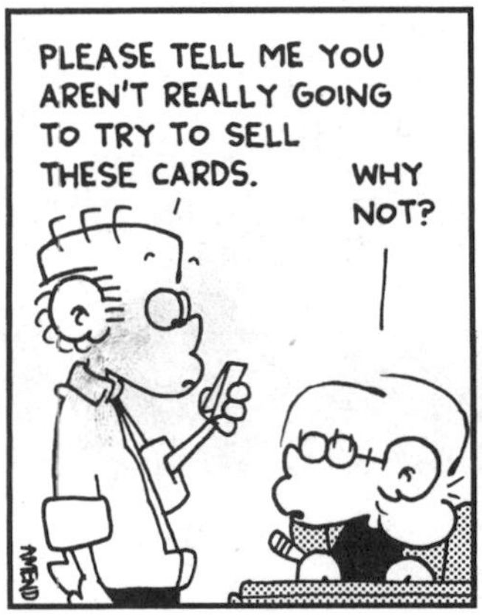
PLEASE TELL ME YOU AREN'T REALLY GOING TO TRY TO SELL THESE CARDS.
WHY NOT?
AMEND

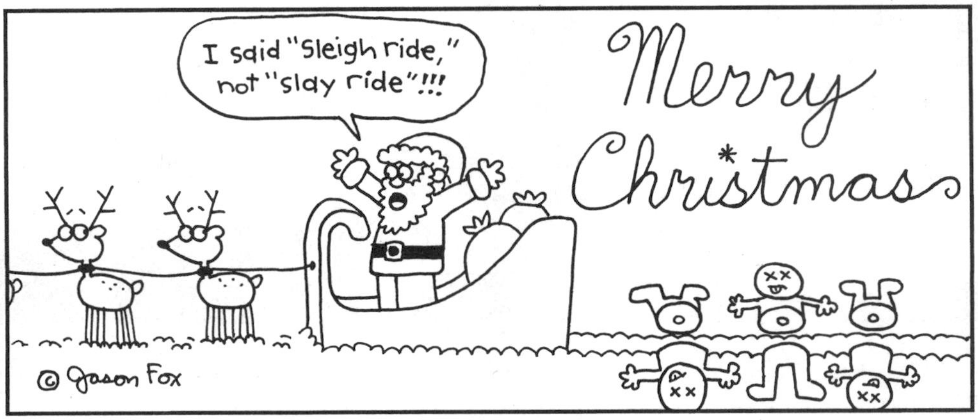
I said "Sleigh ride," not "slay ride"!!!
Merry Christmas
© Jason Fox

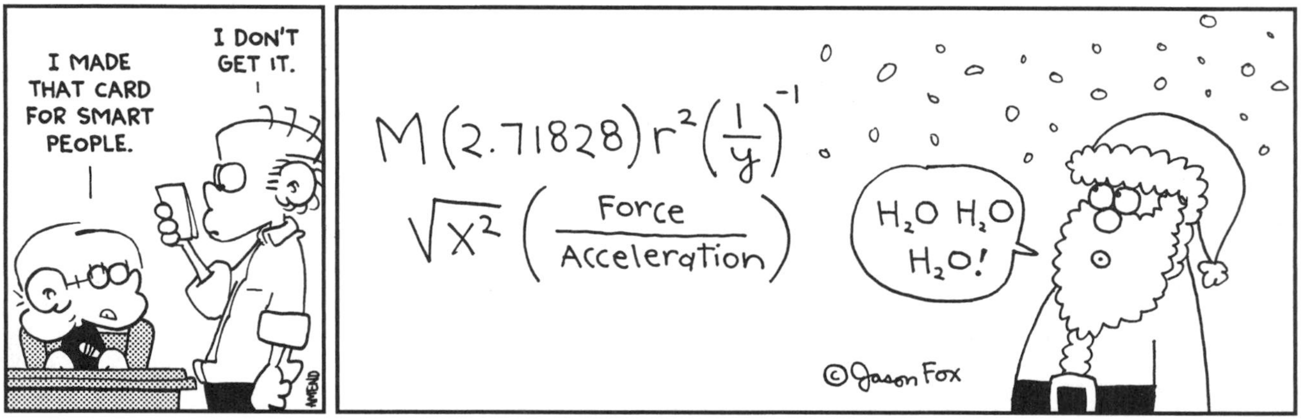
I MADE THAT CARD FOR SMART PEOPLE.
I DON'T GET IT.
$M(2.71828)r^2\left(\frac{1}{y}\right)^{-1}\sqrt{x^2}\left(\frac{\text{Force}}{\text{Acceleration}}\right)$
H_2O H_2O H_2O!
©Jason Fox
AMEND

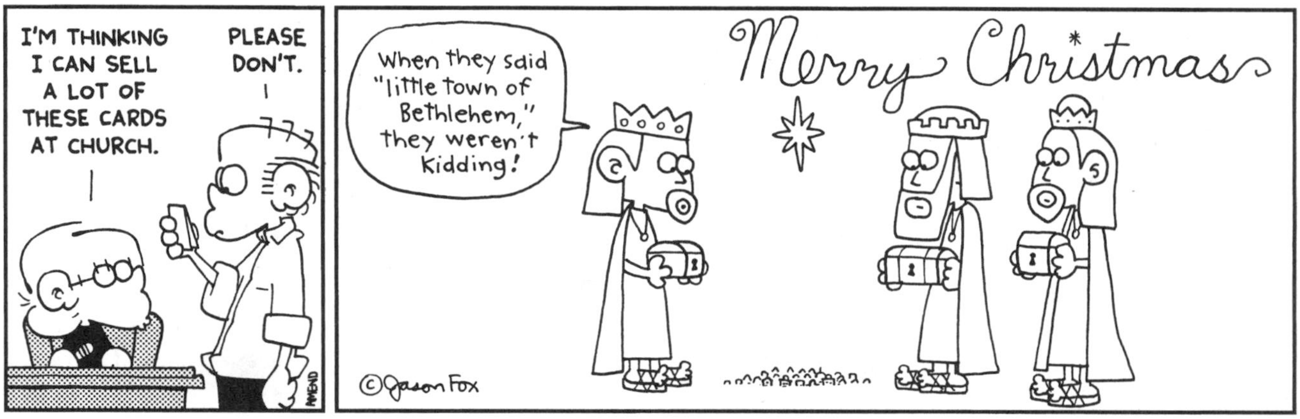
I'M THINKING I CAN SELL A LOT OF THESE CARDS AT CHURCH.
PLEASE DON'T.
When they said "little town of Bethlehem," they weren't kidding!
Merry Christmas
©Jason Fox
AMEND

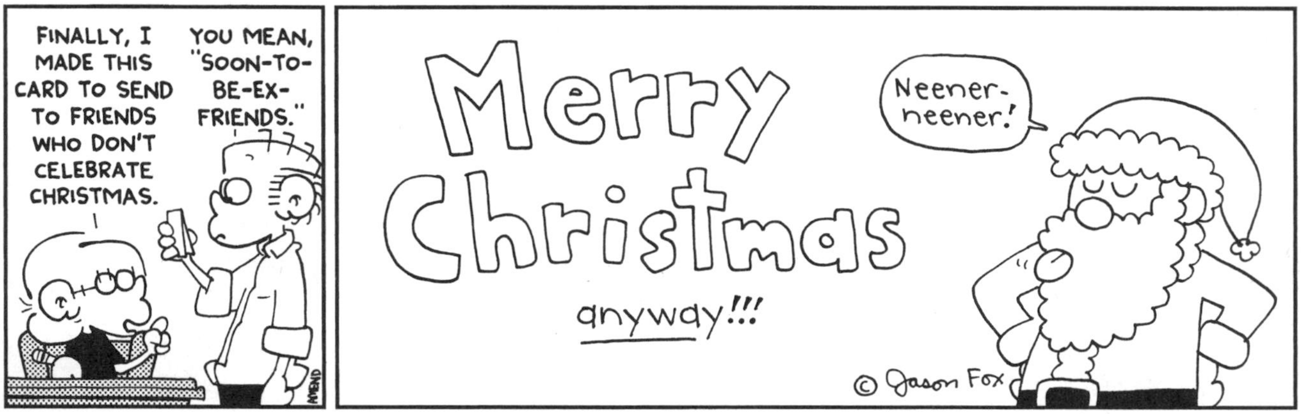
FINALLY, I MADE THIS CARD TO SEND TO FRIENDS WHO DON'T CELEBRATE CHRISTMAS.
YOU MEAN, "SOON-TO-BE-EX-FRIENDS."
Merry Christmas
anyway!!!
Neener-neener!
© Jason Fox
AMEND

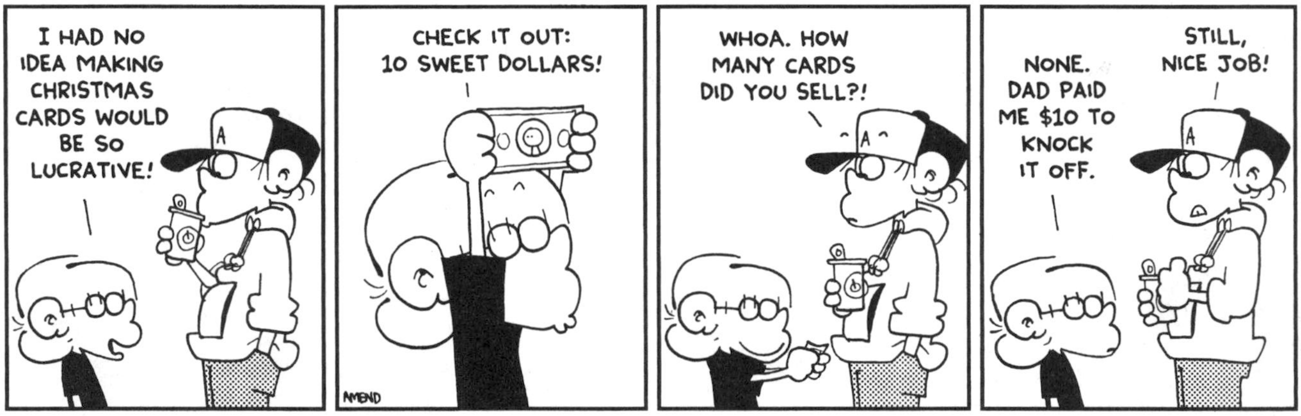
I HAD NO IDEA MAKING CHRISTMAS CARDS WOULD BE SO LUCRATIVE!
CHECK IT OUT: 10 SWEET DOLLARS!
WHOA. HOW MANY CARDS DID YOU SELL?!
NONE. DAD PAID ME $10 TO KNOCK IT OFF.
STILL, NICE JOB!
AMEND

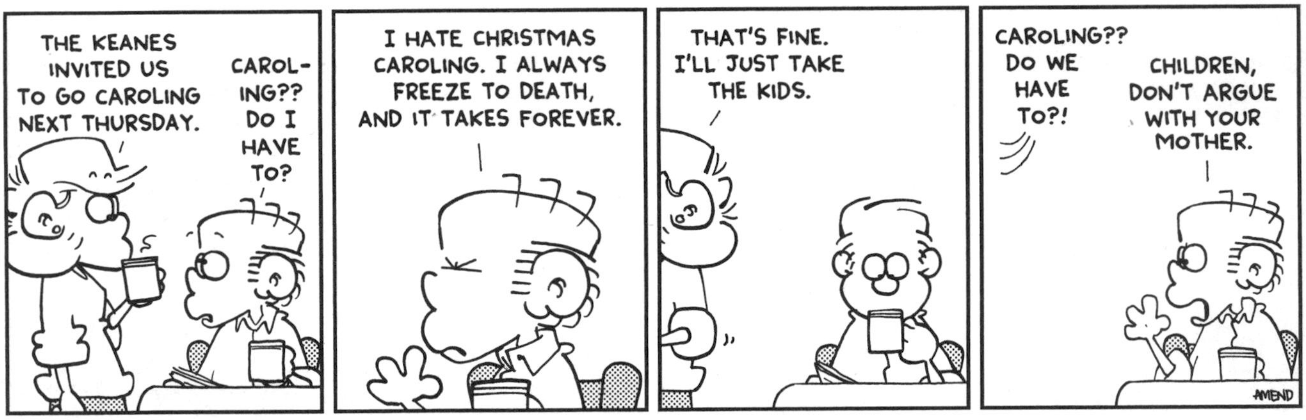
THE KEANES INVITED US TO GO CAROLING NEXT THURSDAY.
CAROL-ING?? DO I HAVE TO?
I HATE CHRISTMAS CAROLING. I ALWAYS FREEZE TO DEATH, AND IT TAKES FOREVER.
THAT'S FINE. I'LL JUST TAKE THE KIDS.
CAROLING?? DO WE HAVE TO?!
CHILDREN, DON'T ARGUE WITH YOUR MOTHER.
AMEND

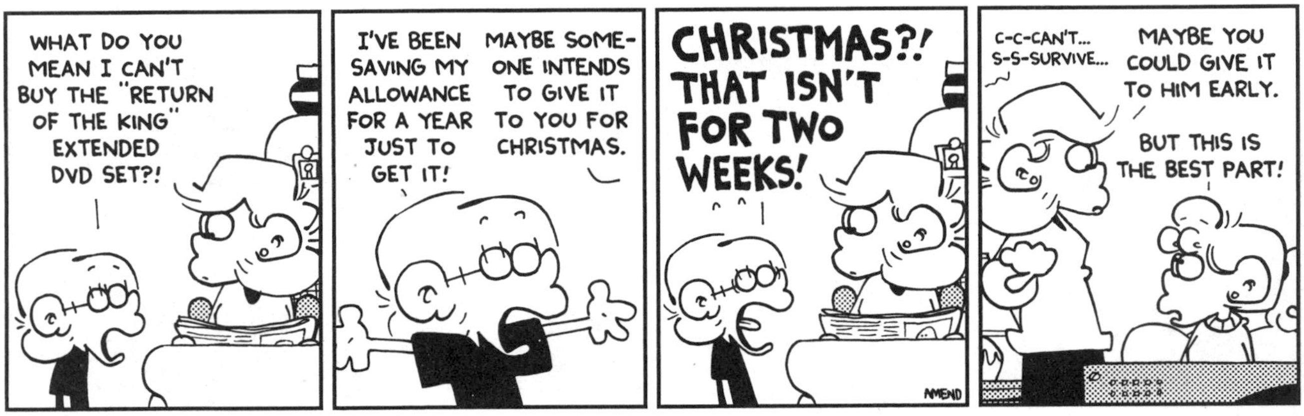
WHAT DO YOU MEAN I CAN'T BUY THE "RETURN OF THE KING" EXTENDED DVD SET?!
I'VE BEEN SAVING MY ALLOWANCE FOR A YEAR JUST TO GET IT!
MAYBE SOME-ONE INTENDS TO GIVE IT TO YOU FOR CHRISTMAS.
CHRISTMAS?! THAT ISN'T FOR TWO WEEKS!
C-C-CAN'T... S-S-SURVIVE...
MAYBE YOU COULD GIVE IT TO HIM EARLY.
BUT THIS IS THE BEST PART!
AMEND

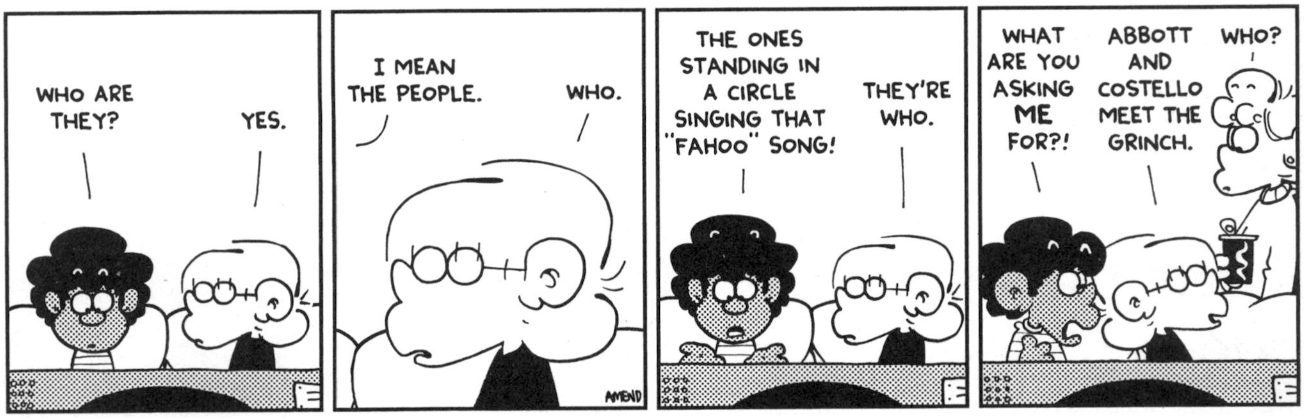
WHO ARE THEY?
YES.
I MEAN THE PEOPLE.
WHO.
THE ONES STANDING IN A CIRCLE SINGING THAT "FAHOO" SONG!
THEY'RE WHO.
WHAT ARE YOU ASKING ME FOR?!
ABBOTT AND COSTELLO MEET THE GRINCH.
WHO?
AMEND

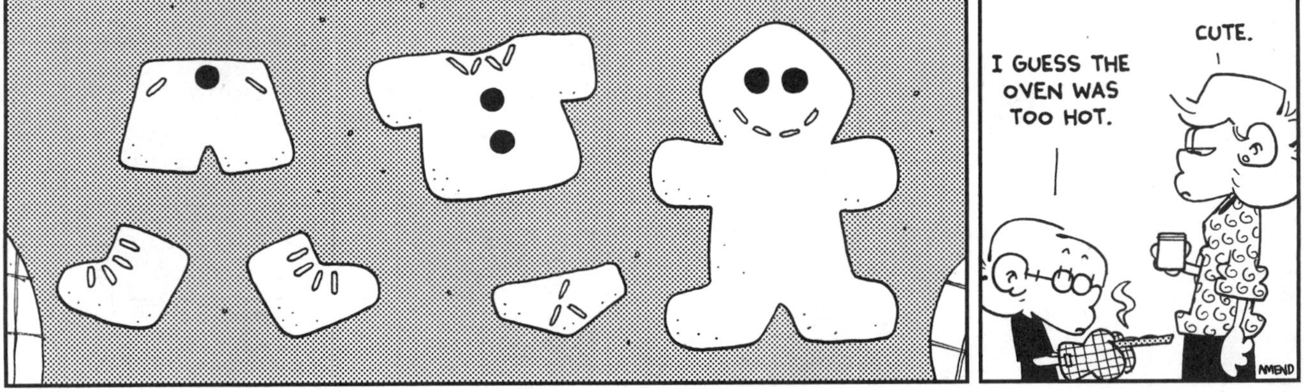
I GUESS THE OVEN WAS TOO HOT.
CUTE.
AMEND

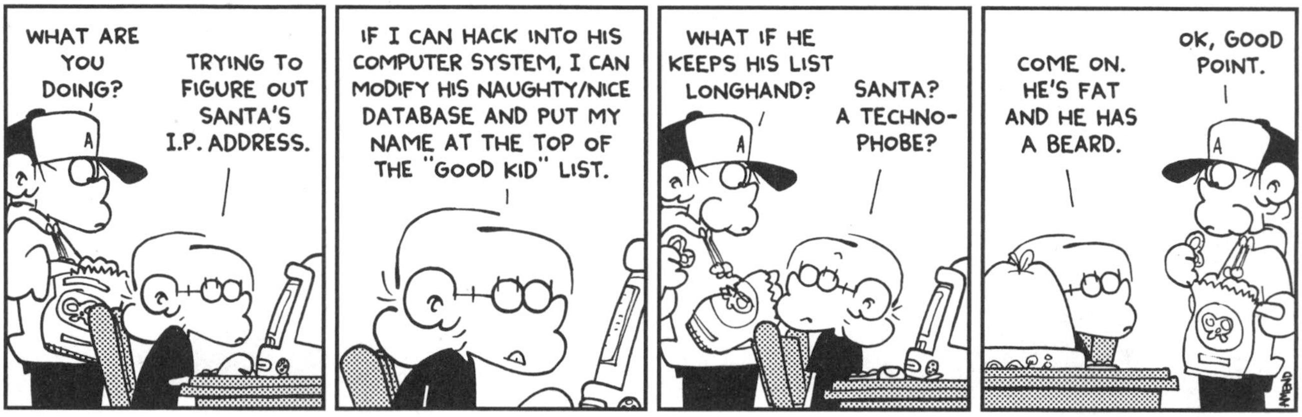
WHAT ARE YOU DOING?
TRYING TO FIGURE OUT SANTA'S I.P. ADDRESS.
IF I CAN HACK INTO HIS COMPUTER SYSTEM, I CAN MODIFY HIS NAUGHTY/NICE DATABASE AND PUT MY NAME AT THE TOP OF THE "GOOD KID" LIST.
WHAT IF HE KEEPS HIS LIST LONGHAND?
SANTA? A TECHNO-PHOBE?
COME ON. HE'S FAT AND HE HAS A BEARD.
OK, GOOD POINT.
AMEND

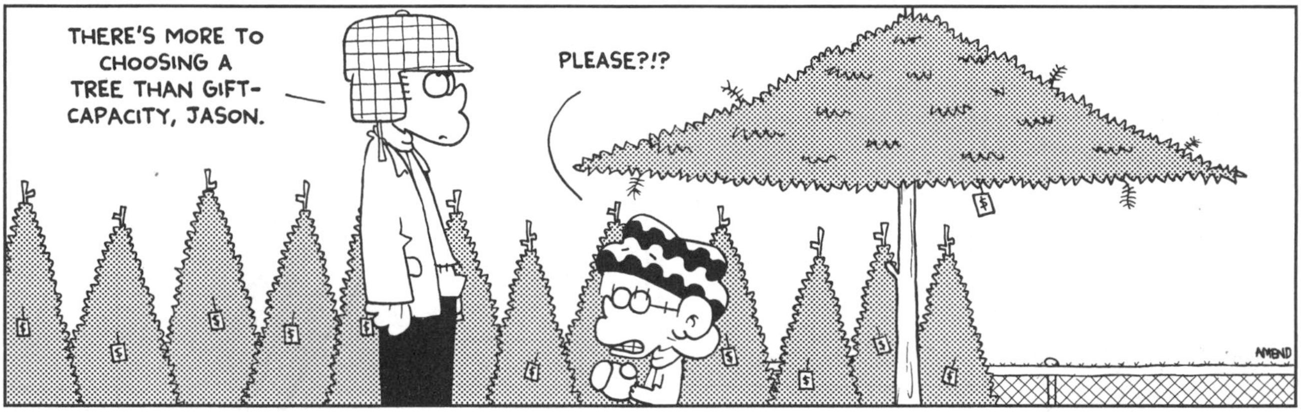
THERE'S MORE TO CHOOSING A TREE THAN GIFT-CAPACITY, JASON.
PLEASE?!?
AMEND

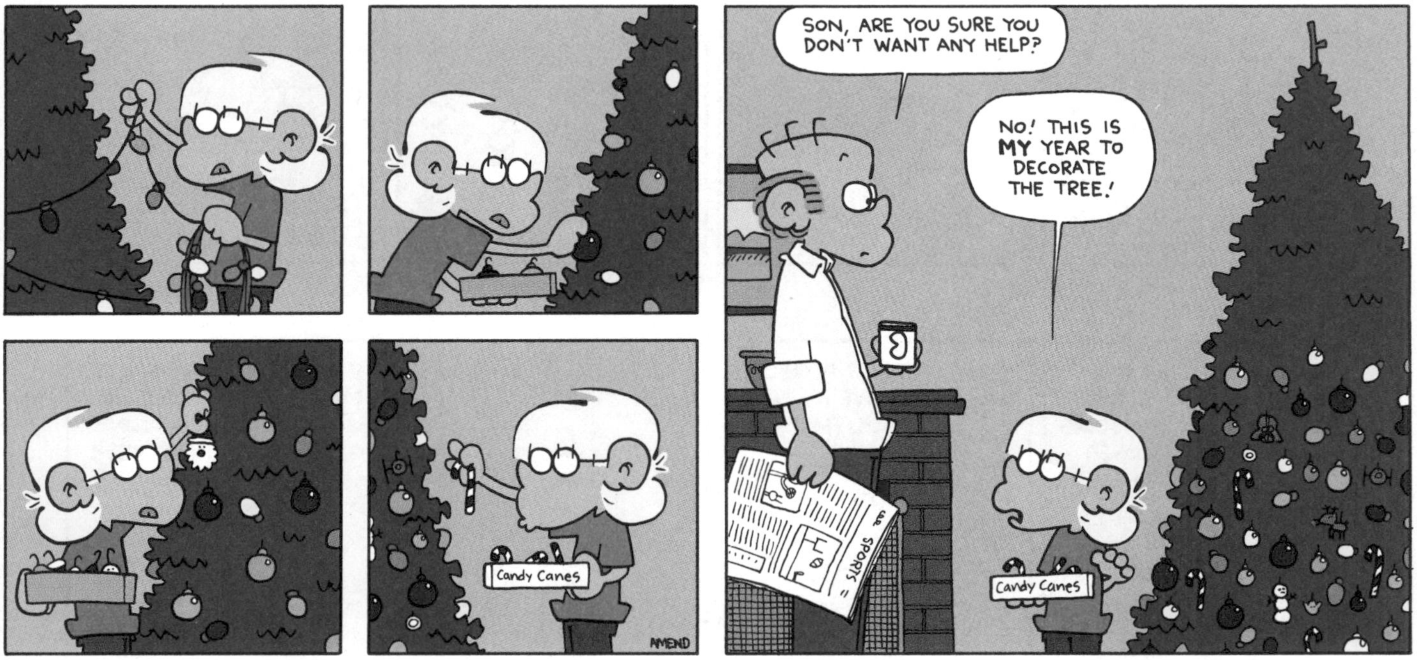
Candy Canes
AMEND
SON, ARE YOU SURE YOU DON'T WANT ANY HELP?
NO! THIS IS MY YEAR TO DECORATE THE TREE!
SPORTS
Candy Canes

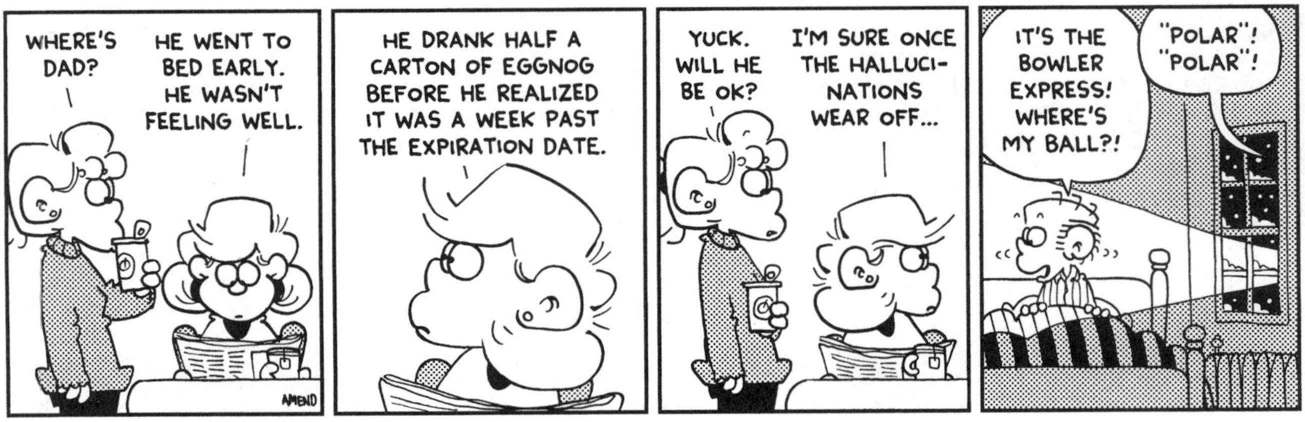
WHERE'S DAD?
HE WENT TO BED EARLY. HE WASN'T FEELING WELL.
HE DRANK HALF A CARTON OF EGGNOG BEFORE HE REALIZED IT WAS A WEEK PAST THE EXPIRATION DATE.
YUCK. WILL HE BE OK?
I'M SURE ONCE THE HALLUCI-NATIONS WEAR OFF...
IT'S THE BOWLER EXPRESS! WHERE'S MY BALL?!
"POLAR"! "POLAR"!
AMEND

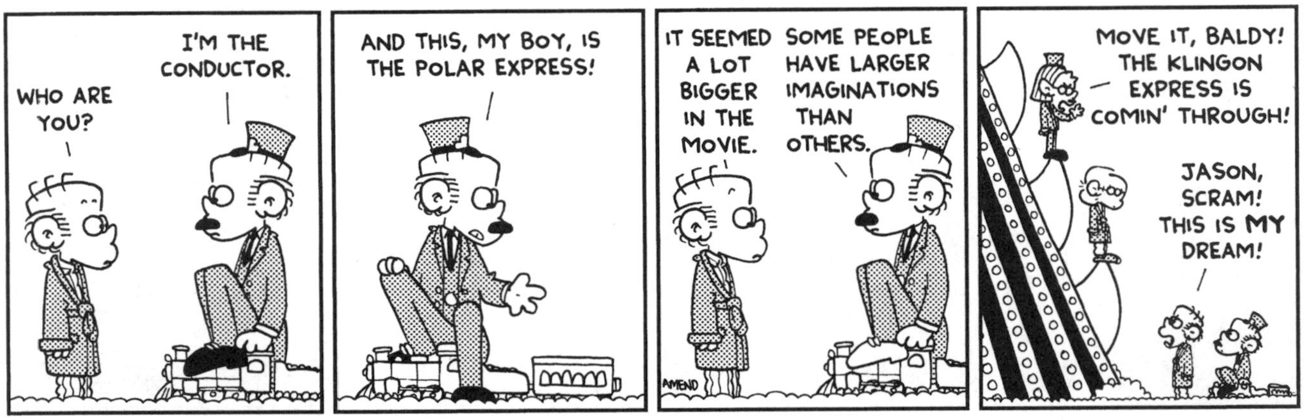
WHO ARE YOU?
I'M THE CONDUCTOR.
AND THIS, MY BOY, IS THE POLAR EXPRESS!
IT SEEMED A LOT BIGGER IN THE MOVIE.
SOME PEOPLE HAVE LARGER IMAGINATIONS THAN OTHERS.
MOVE IT, BALDY! THE KLINGON EXPRESS IS COMIN' THROUGH!
JASON, SCRAM! THIS IS MY DREAM!
AMEND

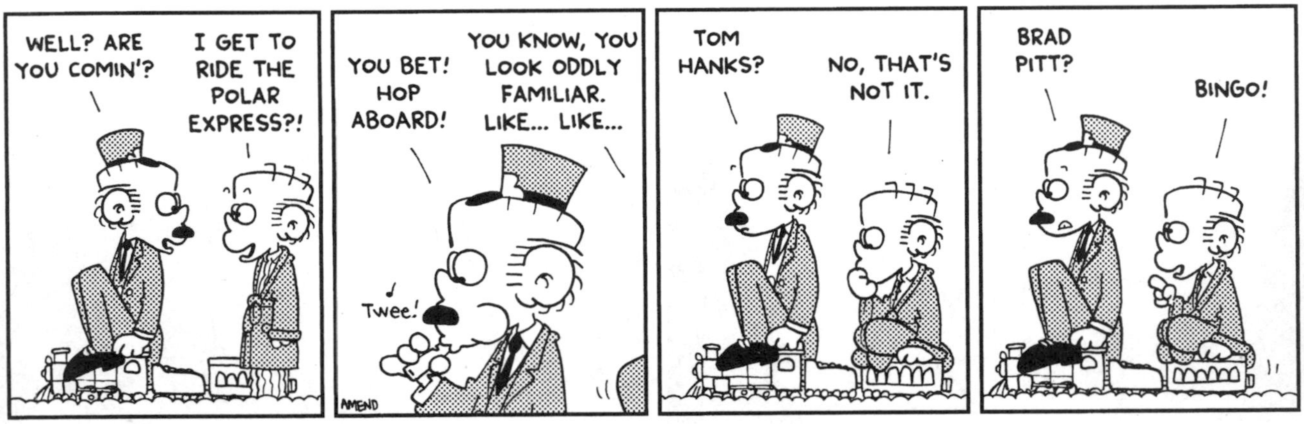
WELL? ARE YOU COMIN'?
I GET TO RIDE THE POLAR EXPRESS?!
YOU BET! HOP ABOARD!
YOU KNOW, YOU LOOK ODDLY FAMILIAR. LIKE... LIKE...
Twee!
TOM HANKS?
NO, THAT'S NOT IT.
BRAD PITT?
BINGO!
AMEND

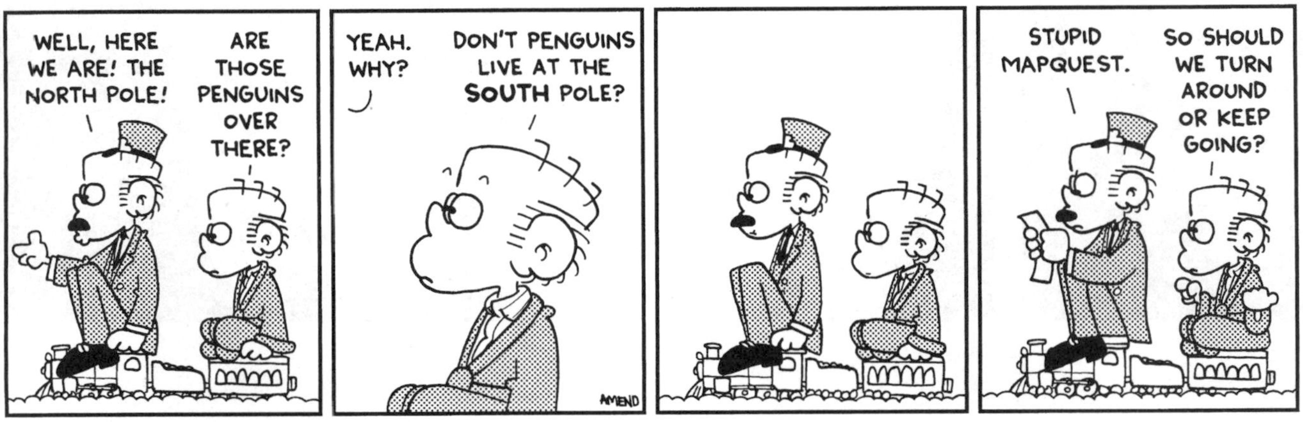
WELL, HERE WE ARE! THE NORTH POLE!
ARE THOSE PENGUINS OVER THERE?
YEAH. WHY?
DON'T PENGUINS LIVE AT THE SOUTH POLE?
STUPID MAPQUEST.
SO SHOULD WE TURN AROUND OR KEEP GOING?
AMEND

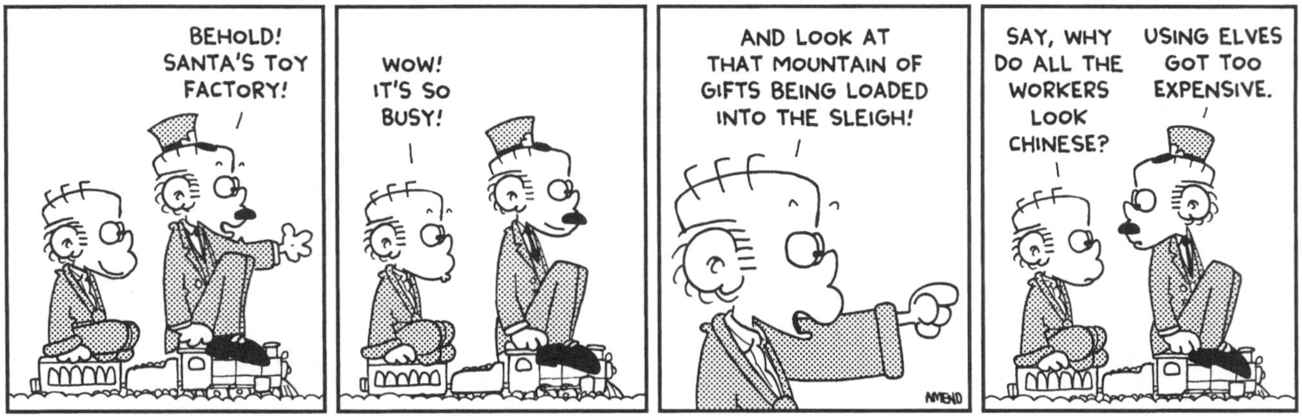
BEHOLD! SANTA'S TOY FACTORY!
WOW! IT'S SO BUSY!
AND LOOK AT THAT MOUNTAIN OF GIFTS BEING LOADED INTO THE SLEIGH!
SAY, WHY DO ALL THE WORKERS LOOK CHINESE?
USING ELVES GOT TOO EXPENSIVE.
AMEND

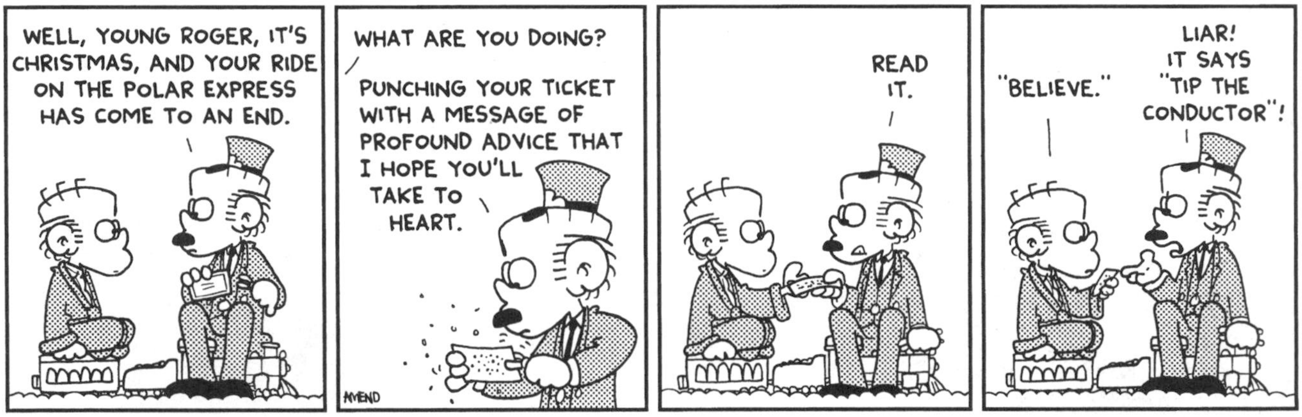
WELL, YOUNG ROGER, IT'S CHRISTMAS, AND YOUR RIDE ON THE POLAR EXPRESS HAS COME TO AN END.
WHAT ARE YOU DOING?
PUNCHING YOUR TICKET WITH A MESSAGE OF PROFOUND ADVICE THAT I HOPE YOU'LL TAKE TO HEART.
AMEND
READ IT.
"BELIEVE."
LIAR! IT SAYS "TIP THE CONDUCTOR"!

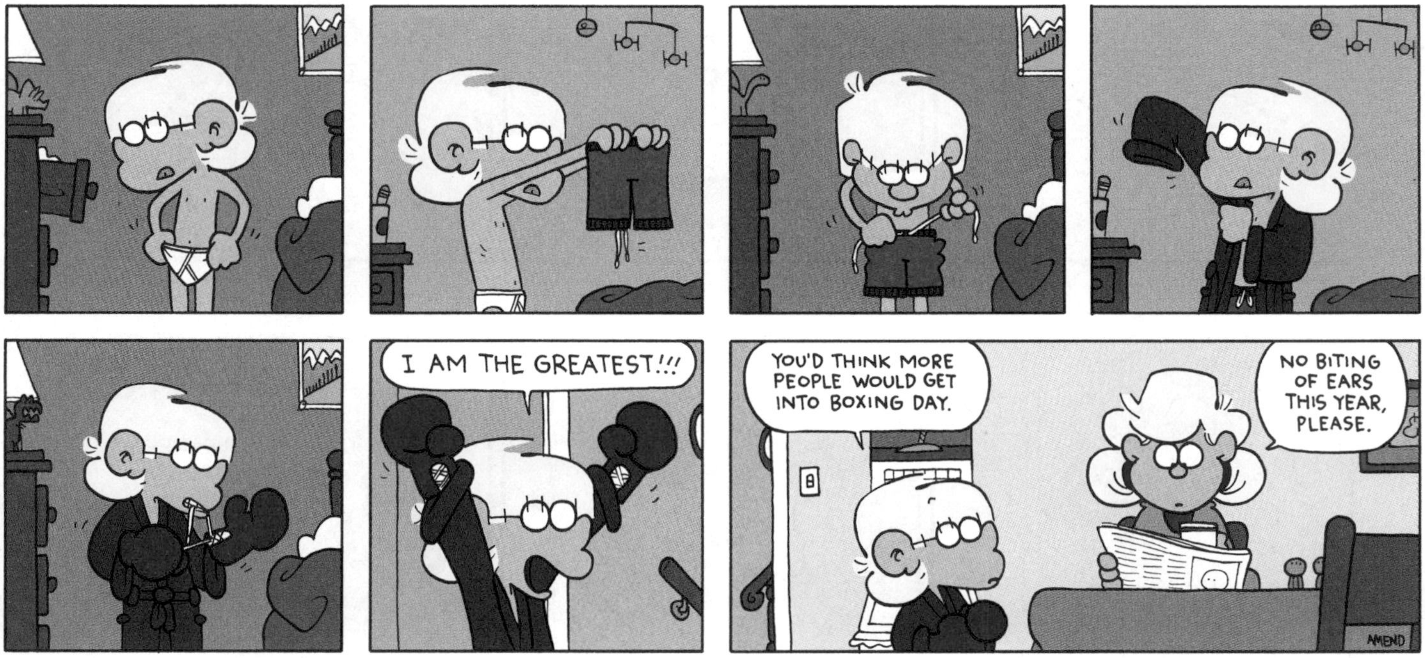
I AM THE GREATEST!!!
YOU'D THINK MORE PEOPLE WOULD GET INTO BOXING DAY.
NO BITING OF EARS THIS YEAR, PLEASE.
AMEND

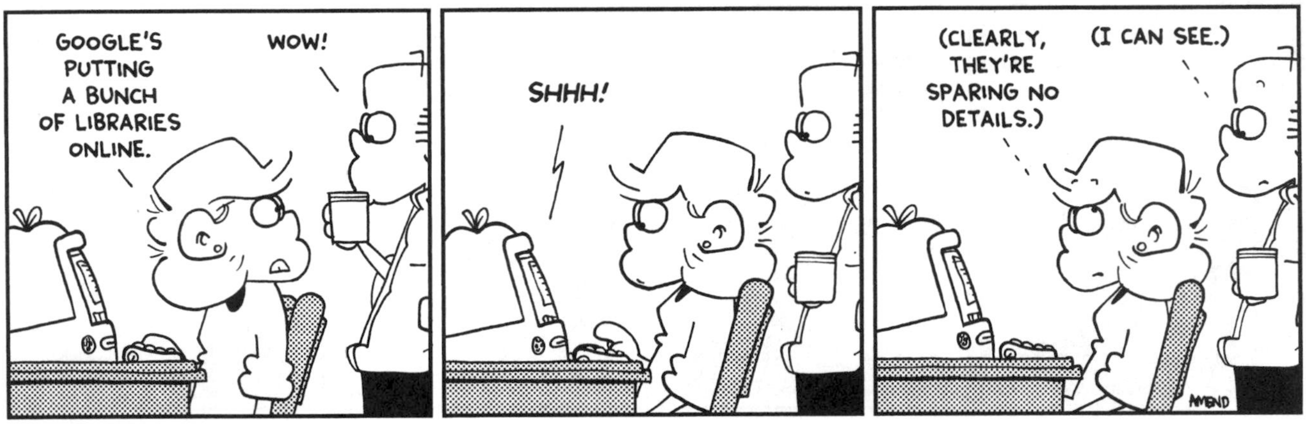
GOOGLE'S PUTTING A BUNCH OF LIBRARIES ONLINE.
WOW!
SHHH!
(CLEARLY, THEY'RE SPARING NO DETAILS.)
(I CAN SEE.)
AMEND

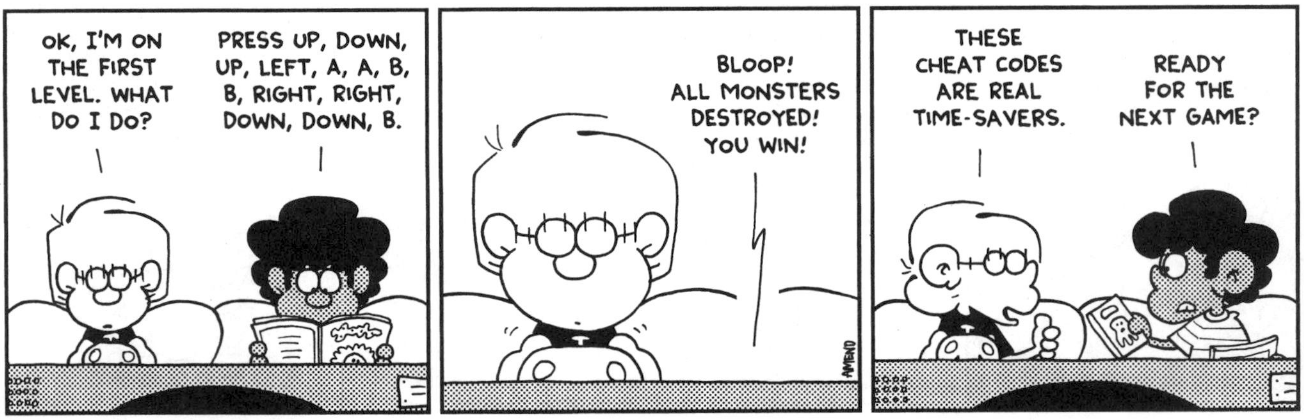
OK, I'M ON THE FIRST LEVEL. WHAT DO I DO?
PRESS UP, DOWN, UP, LEFT, A, A, B, B, RIGHT, RIGHT, DOWN, DOWN, B.
BLOOP! ALL MONSTERS DESTROYED! YOU WIN!
AMEND
THESE CHEAT CODES ARE REAL TIME-SAVERS.
READY FOR THE NEXT GAME?

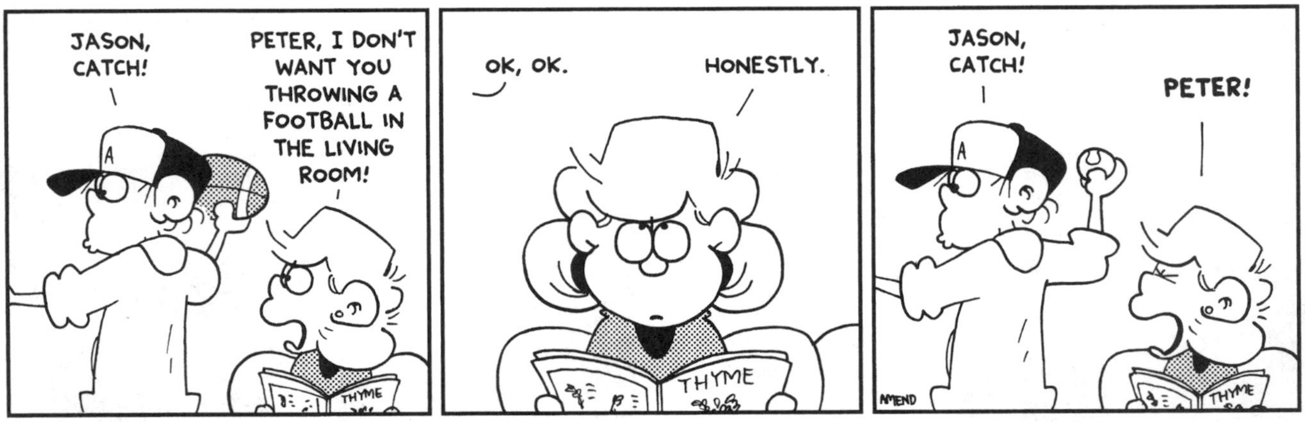
JASON, CATCH!
PETER, I DON'T WANT YOU THROWING A FOOTBALL IN THE LIVING ROOM!
THYME
OK, OK.
HONESTLY.
THYME
JASON, CATCH!
PETER!
THYME
AMEND

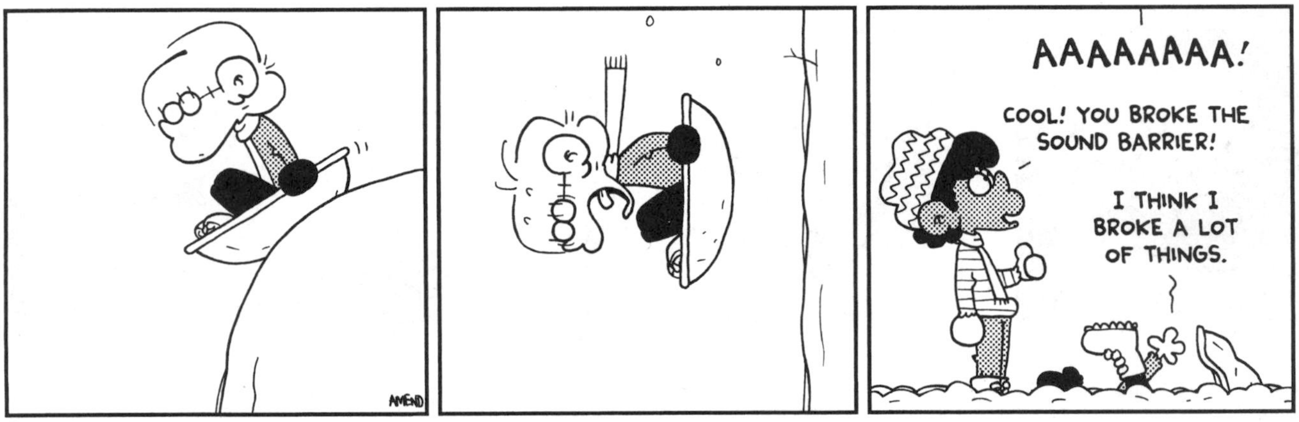
AMEND
AAAAAAAA!
COOL! YOU BROKE THE SOUND BARRIER!
I THINK I BROKE A LOT OF THINGS.

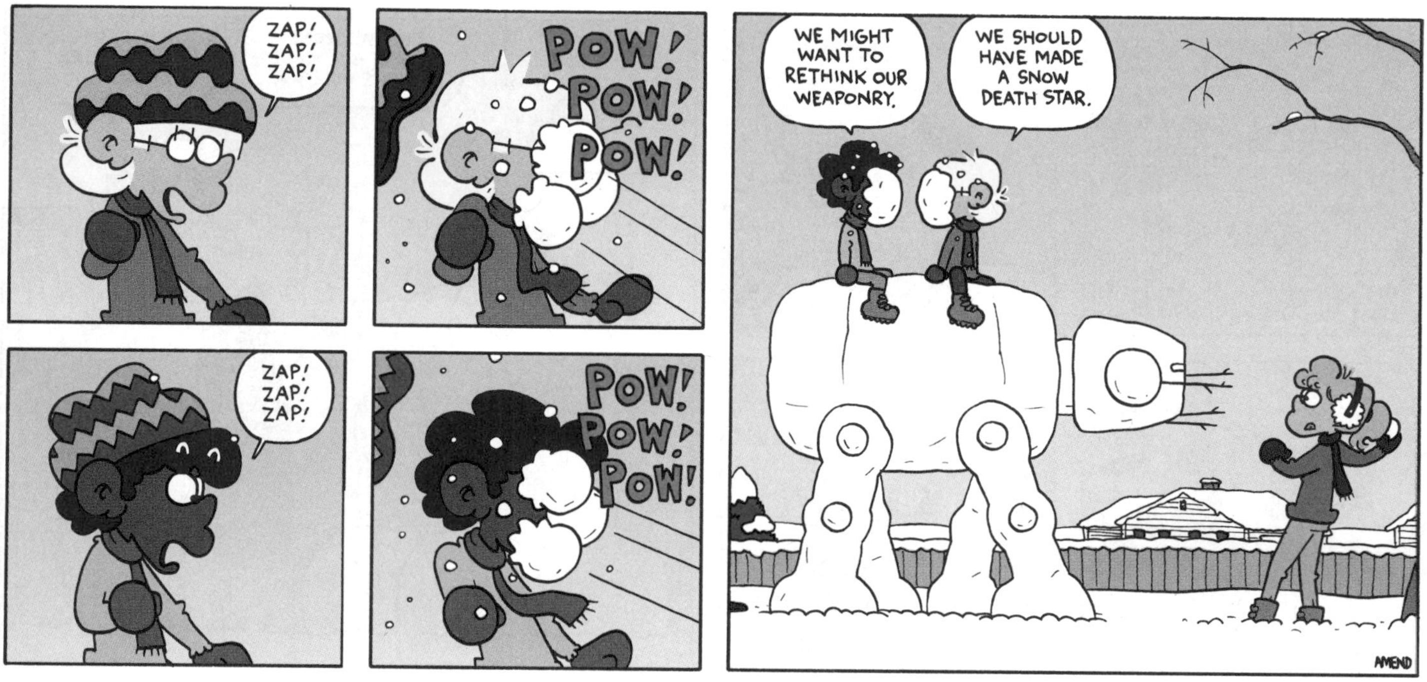
ZAP! ZAP! ZAP!
POW! POW! POW!
ZAP! ZAP! ZAP!
POW! POW! POW!
WE MIGHT WANT TO RETHINK OUR WEAPONRY.
WE SHOULD HAVE MADE A SNOW DEATH STAR.
AMEND

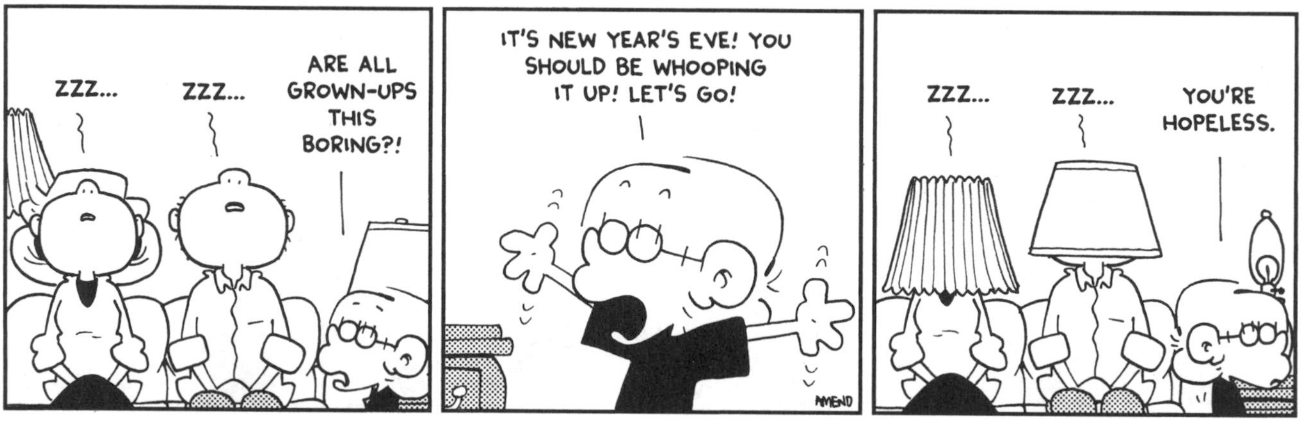
ZZZ...
ZZZ...
ARE ALL GROWN-UPS THIS BORING?!
IT'S NEW YEAR'S EVE! YOU SHOULD BE WHOOPING IT UP! LET'S GO!
AMEND
ZZZ...
ZZZ...
YOU'RE HOPELESS.

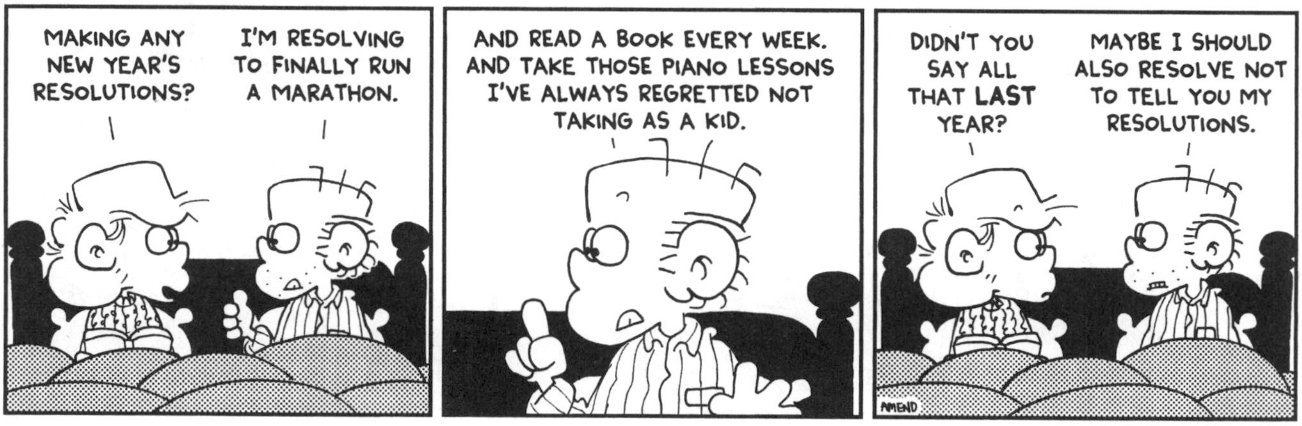
MAKING ANY NEW YEAR'S RESOLUTIONS?
I'M RESOLVING TO FINALLY RUN A MARATHON.
AND READ A BOOK EVERY WEEK. AND TAKE THOSE PIANO LESSONS I'VE ALWAYS REGRETTED NOT TAKING AS A KID.
DIDN'T YOU SAY ALL THAT LAST YEAR?
MAYBE I SHOULD ALSO RESOLVE NOT TO TELL YOU MY RESOLUTIONS.
AMEND

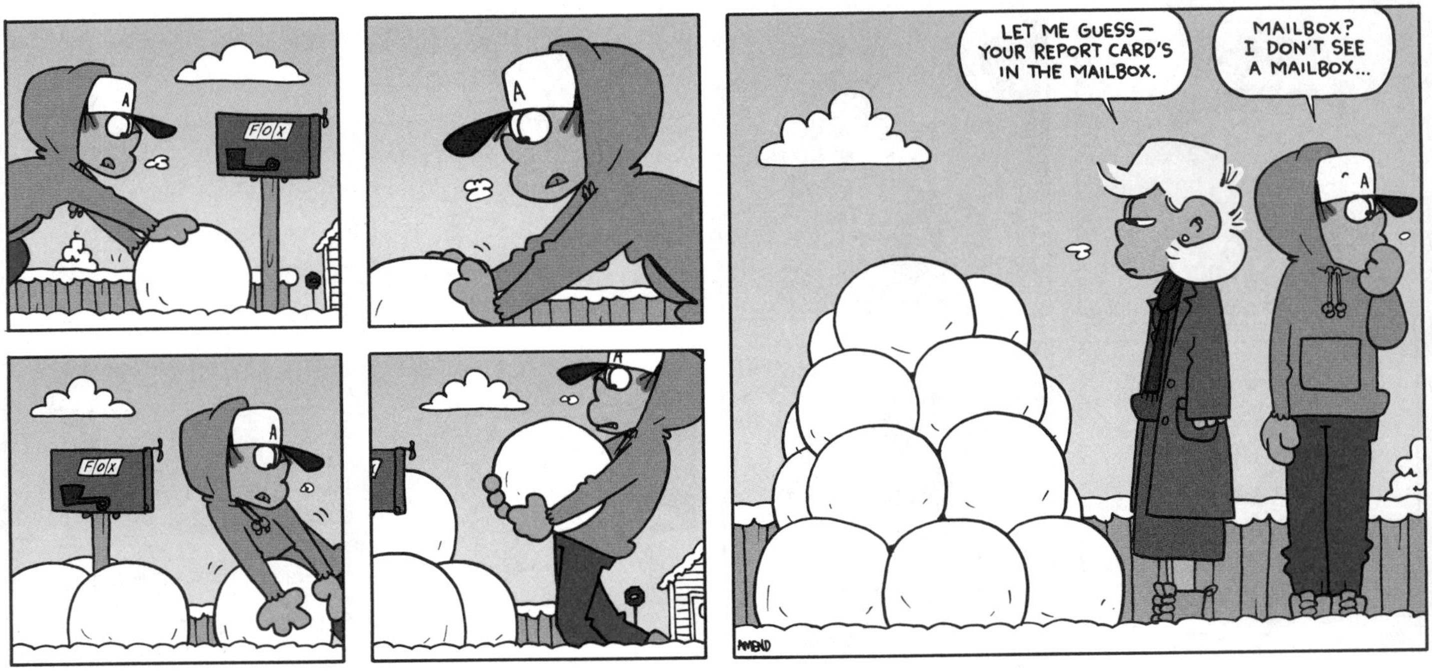
FOX
FOX
LET ME GUESS— YOUR REPORT CARD'S IN THE MAILBOX.
MAILBOX? I DON'T SEE A MAILBOX...
AMEND

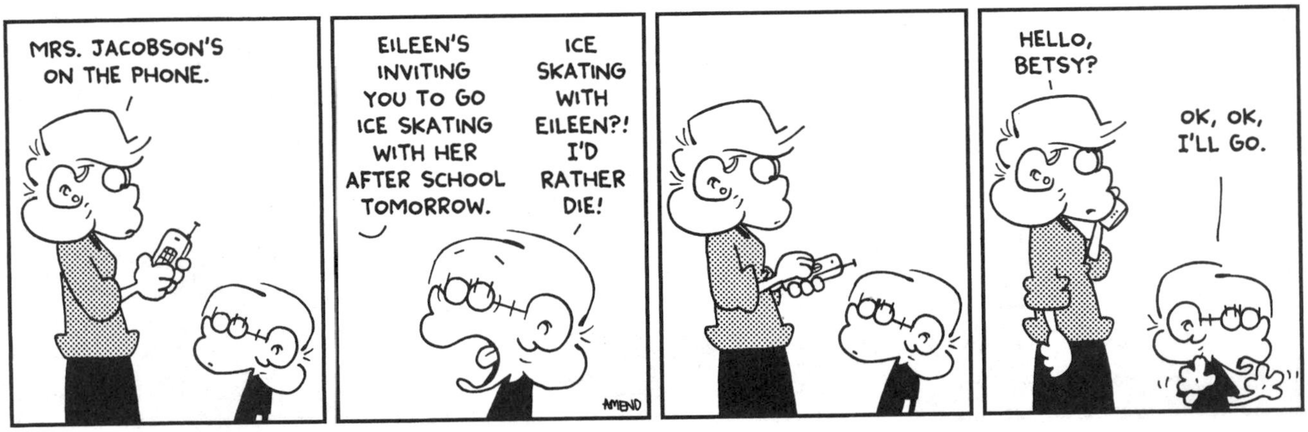
MRS. JACOBSON'S ON THE PHONE.
EILEEN'S INVITING YOU TO GO ICE SKATING WITH HER AFTER SCHOOL TOMORROW.
ICE SKATING WITH EILEEN?! I'D RATHER DIE!
AMEND
HELLO, BETSY?
OK, OK, I'LL GO.

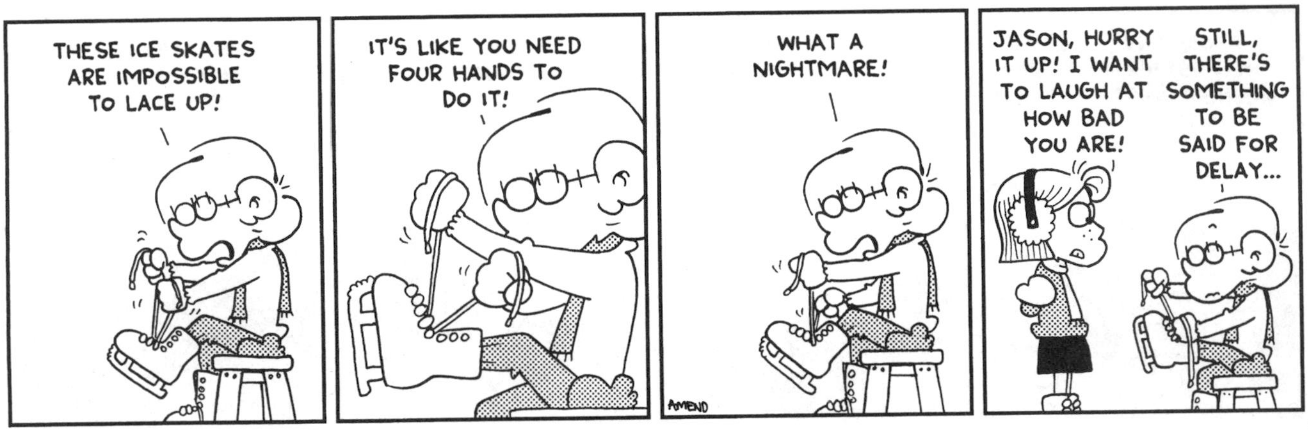
THESE ICE SKATES ARE IMPOSSIBLE TO LACE UP!
IT'S LIKE YOU NEED FOUR HANDS TO DO IT!
WHAT A NIGHTMARE!
AMEND
JASON, HURRY IT UP! I WANT TO LAUGH AT HOW BAD YOU ARE!
STILL, THERE'S SOMETHING TO BE SAID FOR DELAY...

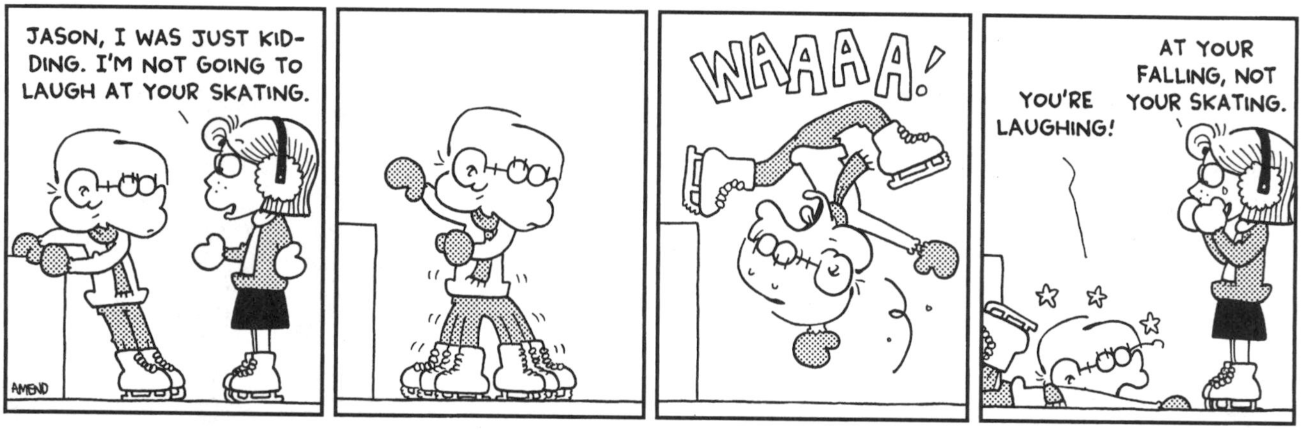
JASON, I WAS JUST KIDDING. I'M NOT GOING TO LAUGH AT YOUR SKATING.
WAAAA!
YOU'RE LAUGHING!
AT YOUR FALLING, NOT YOUR SKATING.
AMEND

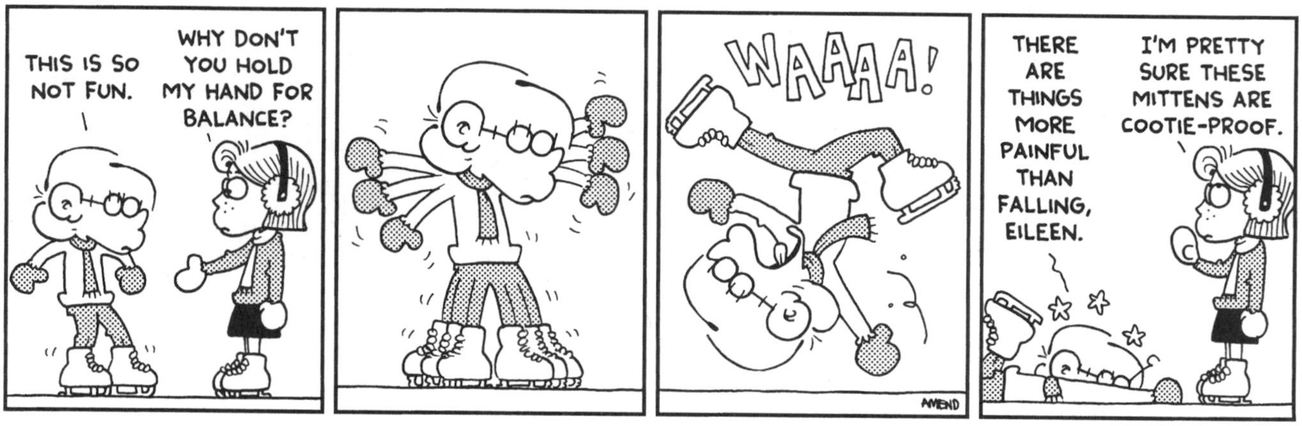
THIS IS SO NOT FUN.
WHY DON'T YOU HOLD MY HAND FOR BALANCE?
WAAAA!
THERE ARE THINGS MORE PAINFUL THAN FALLING, EILEEN.
I'M PRETTY SURE THESE MITTENS ARE COOTIE-PROOF.
AMEND

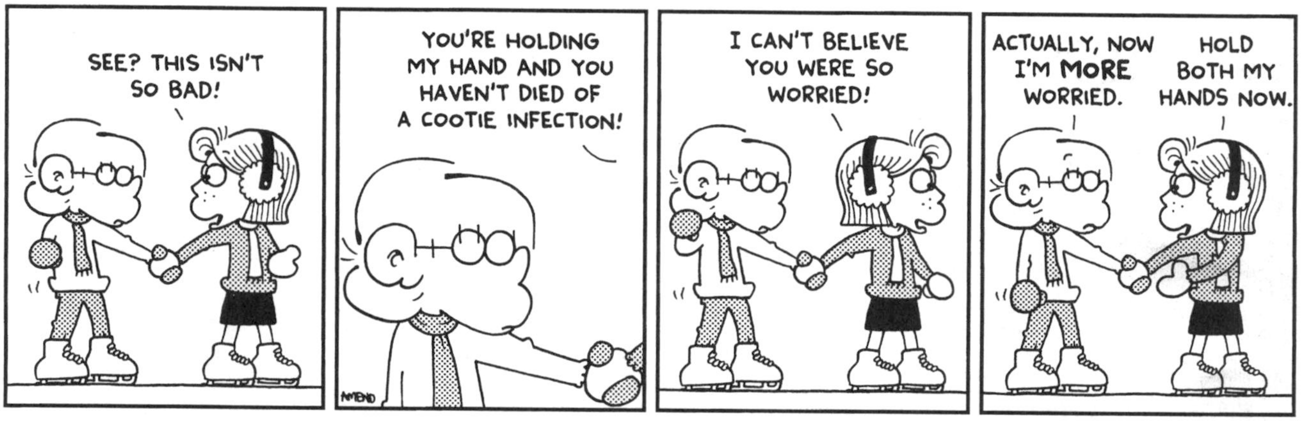
SEE? THIS ISN'T SO BAD!
YOU'RE HOLDING MY HAND AND YOU HAVEN'T DIED OF A COOTIE INFECTION!
I CAN'T BELIEVE YOU WERE SO WORRIED!
ACTUALLY, NOW I'M MORE WORRIED.
HOLD BOTH MY HANDS NOW.
AMEND

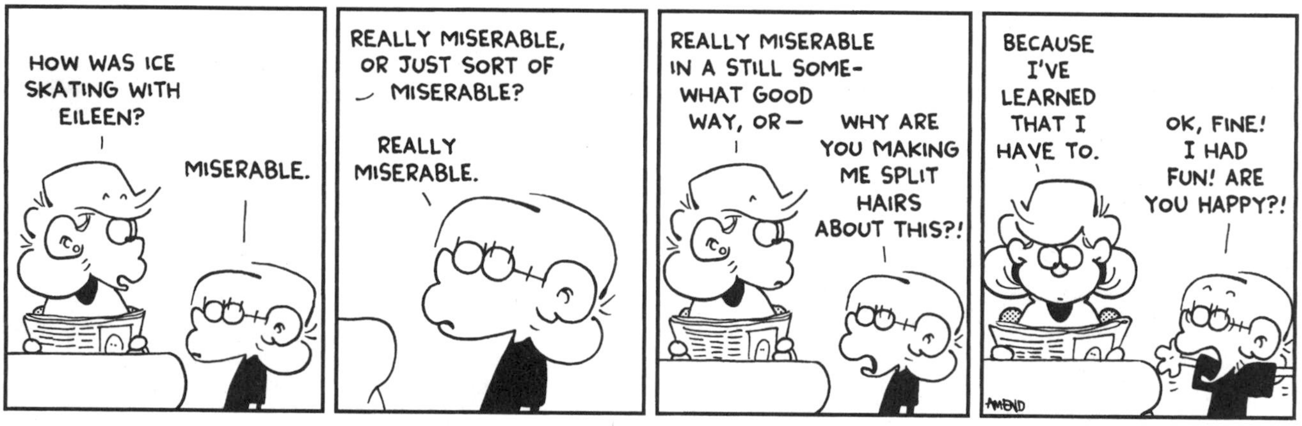
HOW WAS ICE SKATING WITH EILEEN?
MISERABLE.
REALLY MISERABLE, OR JUST SORT OF MISERABLE?
REALLY MISERABLE.
REALLY MISERABLE IN A STILL SOMEWHAT GOOD WAY, OR—
WHY ARE YOU MAKING ME SPLIT HAIRS ABOUT THIS?!
BECAUSE I'VE LEARNED THAT I HAVE TO.
OK, FINE! I HAD FUN! ARE YOU HAPPY?!
AMEND

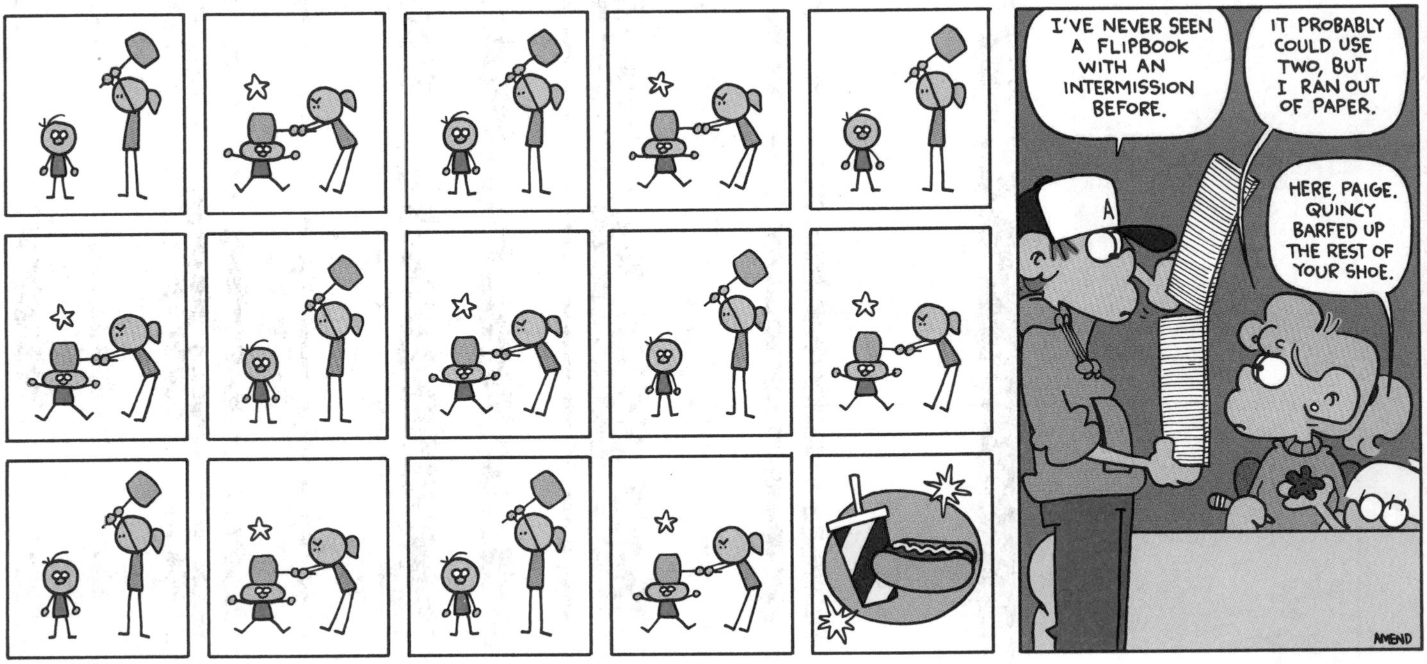
I'VE NEVER SEEN A FLIPBOOK WITH AN INTERMISSION BEFORE.
IT PROBABLY COULD USE TWO, BUT I RAN OUT OF PAPER.
HERE, PAIGE. QUINCY BARFED UP THE REST OF YOUR SHOE.
AMEND

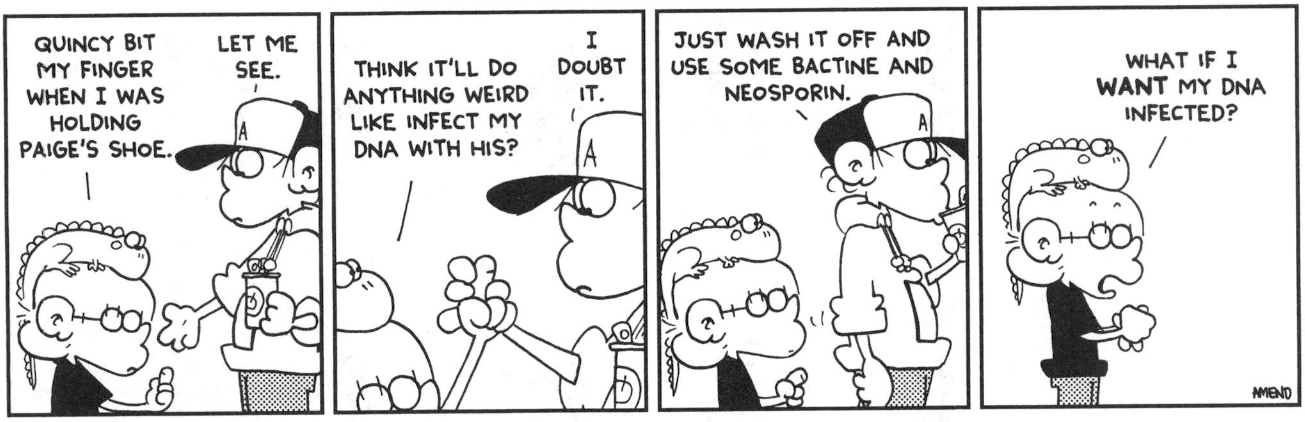
QUINCY BIT MY FINGER WHEN I WAS HOLDING PAIGE'S SHOE.
LET ME SEE.
THINK IT'LL DO ANYTHING WEIRD LIKE INFECT MY DNA WITH HIS?
I DOUBT IT.
JUST WASH IT OFF AND USE SOME BACTINE AND NEOSPORIN.
WHAT IF I **WANT** MY DNA INFECTED?
AMEND

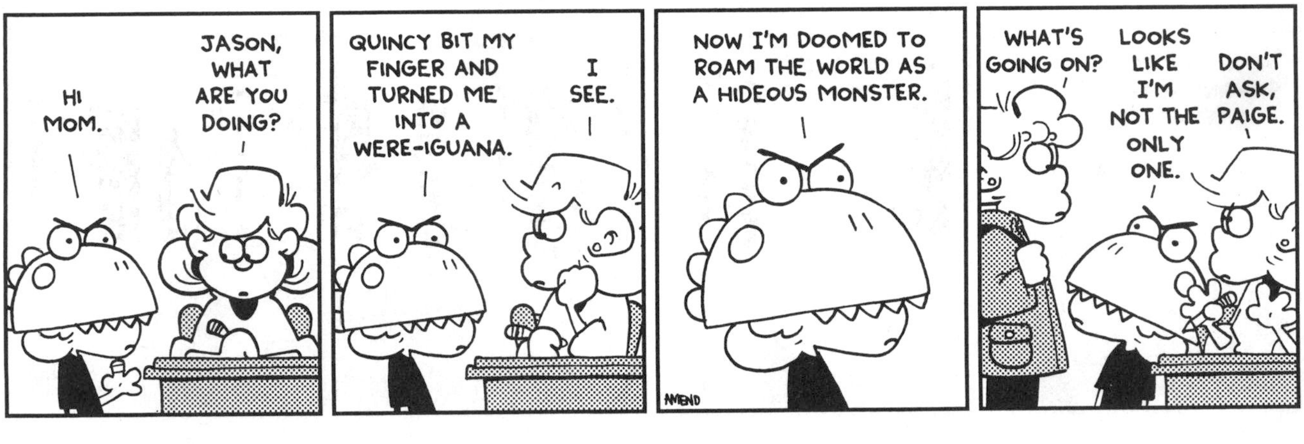
HI MOM.
JASON, WHAT ARE YOU DOING?
QUINCY BIT MY FINGER AND TURNED ME INTO A WERE-IGUANA.
I SEE.
NOW I'M DOOMED TO ROAM THE WORLD AS A HIDEOUS MONSTER.
AMEND
WHAT'S GOING ON?
LOOKS LIKE I'M NOT THE ONLY ONE.
DON'T ASK, PAIGE.

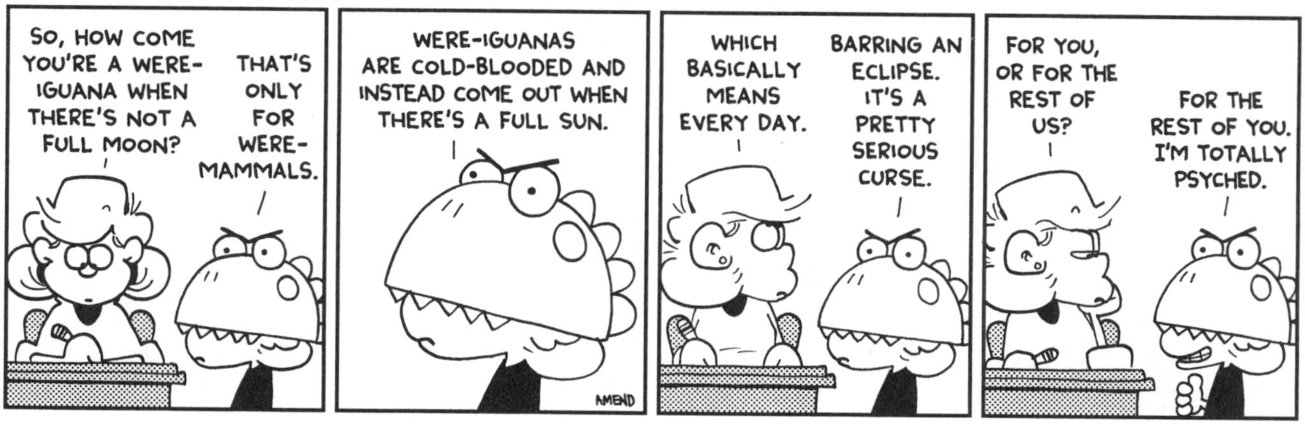
SO, HOW COME YOU'RE A WERE-IGUANA WHEN THERE'S NOT A FULL MOON?
THAT'S ONLY FOR WERE-MAMMALS.
WERE-IGUANAS ARE COLD-BLOODED AND INSTEAD COME OUT WHEN THERE'S A FULL SUN.
AMEND
WHICH BASICALLY MEANS EVERY DAY.
BARRING AN ECLIPSE. IT'S A PRETTY SERIOUS CURSE.
FOR YOU, OR FOR THE REST OF US?
FOR THE REST OF YOU. I'M TOTALLY PSYCHED.

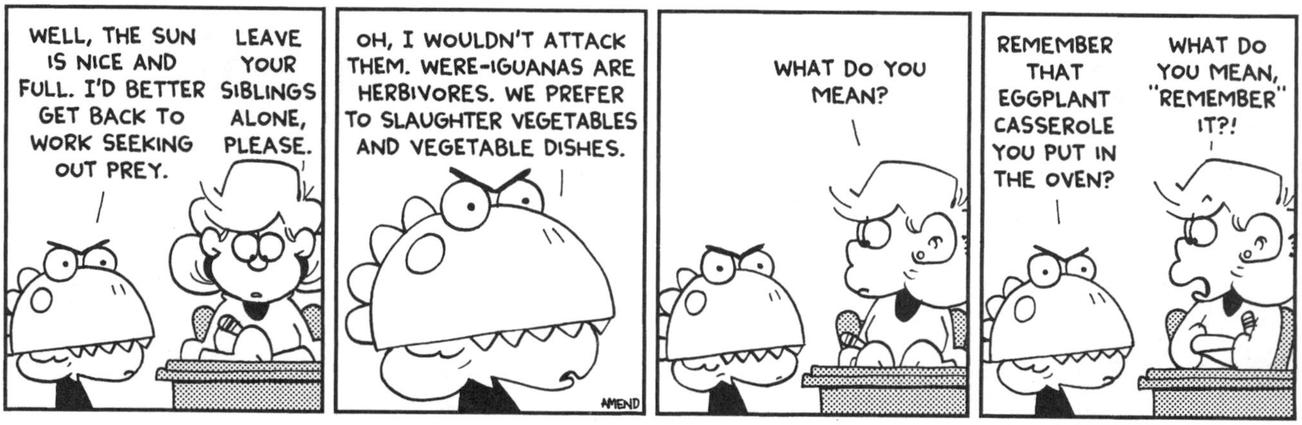
WELL, THE SUN IS NICE AND FULL. I'D BETTER GET BACK TO WORK SEEKING OUT PREY.
LEAVE YOUR SIBLINGS ALONE, PLEASE.
OH, I WOULDN'T ATTACK THEM. WERE-IGUANAS ARE HERBIVORES. WE PREFER TO SLAUGHTER VEGETABLES AND VEGETABLE DISHES.
AMEND
WHAT DO YOU MEAN?
REMEMBER THAT EGGPLANT CASSEROLE YOU PUT IN THE OVEN?
WHAT DO YOU MEAN, "REMEMBER" IT?!

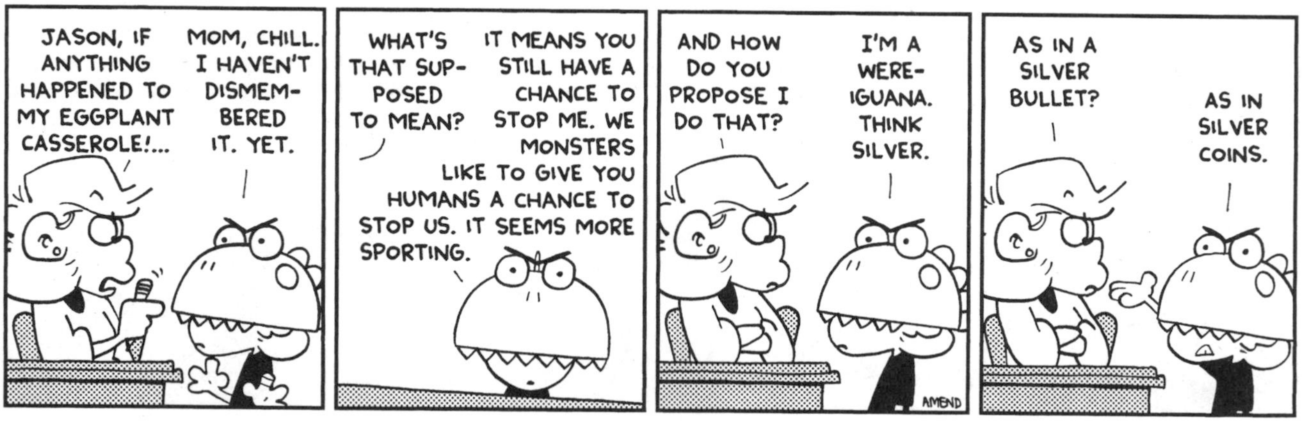
JASON, IF ANYTHING HAPPENED TO MY EGGPLANT CASSEROLE!...
MOM, CHILL. I HAVEN'T DISMEMBERED IT. YET.
WHAT'S THAT SUPPOSED TO MEAN?
IT MEANS YOU STILL HAVE A CHANCE TO STOP ME. WE MONSTERS LIKE TO GIVE YOU HUMANS A CHANCE TO STOP US. IT SEEMS MORE SPORTING.
AND HOW DO YOU PROPOSE I DO THAT?
I'M A WERE-IGUANA. THINK SILVER.
AMEND
AS IN A SILVER BULLET?
AS IN SILVER COINS.

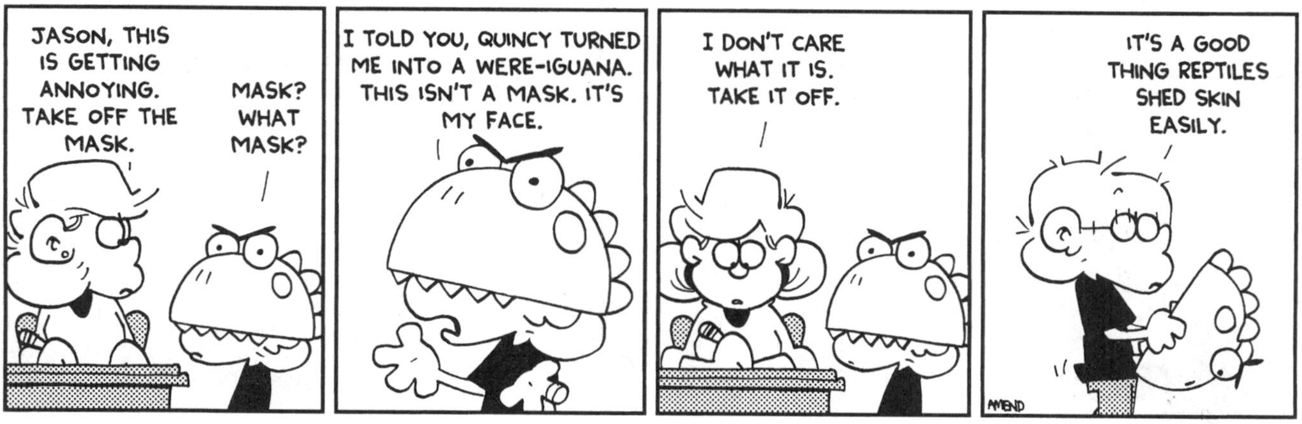
JASON, THIS IS GETTING ANNOYING. TAKE OFF THE MASK.
MASK? WHAT MASK?
I TOLD YOU, QUINCY TURNED ME INTO A WERE-IGUANA. THIS ISN'T A MASK. IT'S MY FACE.
I DON'T CARE WHAT IT IS. TAKE IT OFF.
IT'S A GOOD THING REPTILES SHED SKIN EASILY.
AMEND

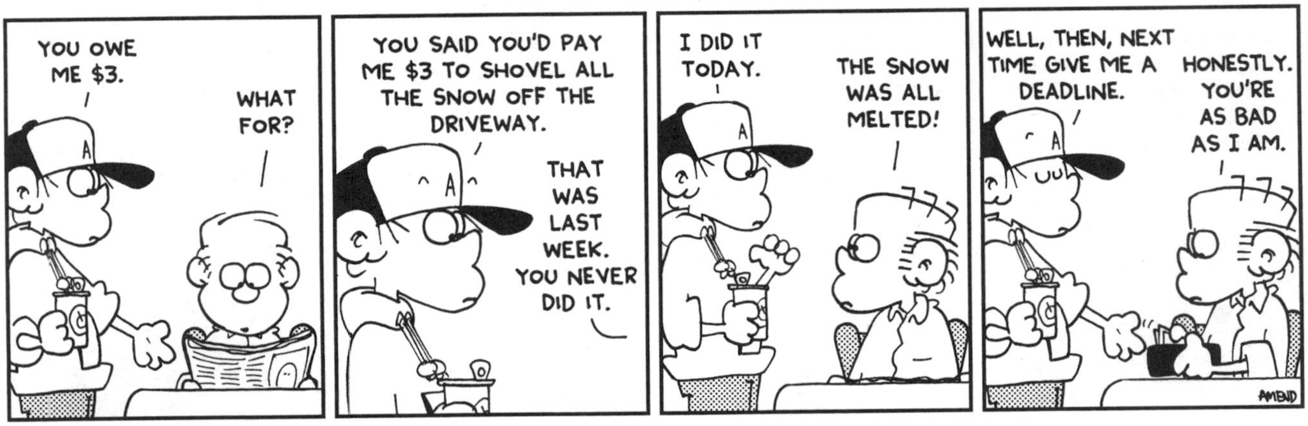
YOU OWE ME $3.
WHAT FOR?
YOU SAID YOU'D PAY ME $3 TO SHOVEL ALL THE SNOW OFF THE DRIVEWAY.
THAT WAS LAST WEEK. YOU NEVER DID IT.
I DID IT TODAY.
THE SNOW WAS ALL MELTED!
WELL, THEN, NEXT TIME GIVE ME A DEADLINE.
HONESTLY. YOU'RE AS BAD AS I AM.
AMEND

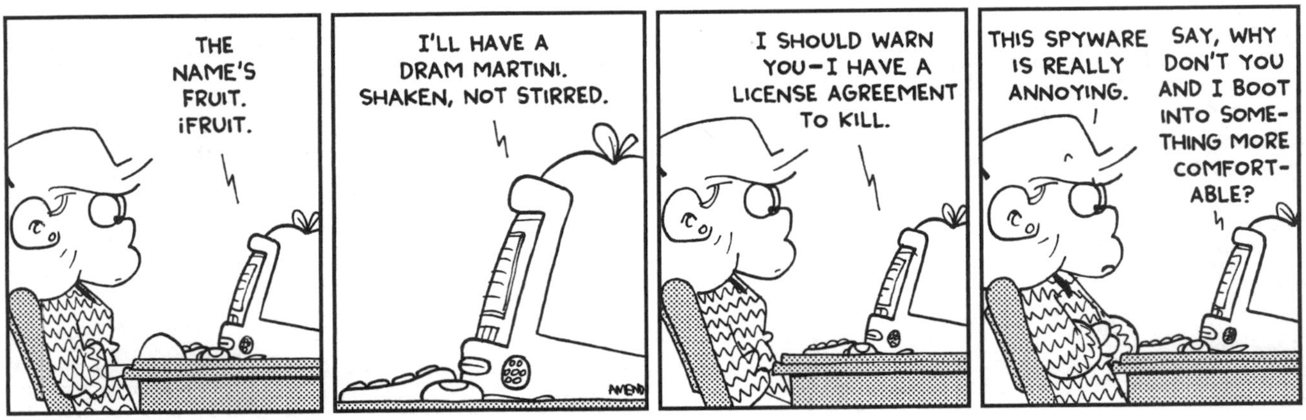
THE NAME'S FRUIT. iFRUIT.
I'LL HAVE A DRAM MARTINI. SHAKEN, NOT STIRRED.
AMEND
I SHOULD WARN YOU—I HAVE A LICENSE AGREEMENT TO KILL.
THIS SPYWARE IS REALLY ANNOYING.
SAY, WHY DON'T YOU AND I BOOT INTO SOME-THING MORE COMFORT-ABLE?

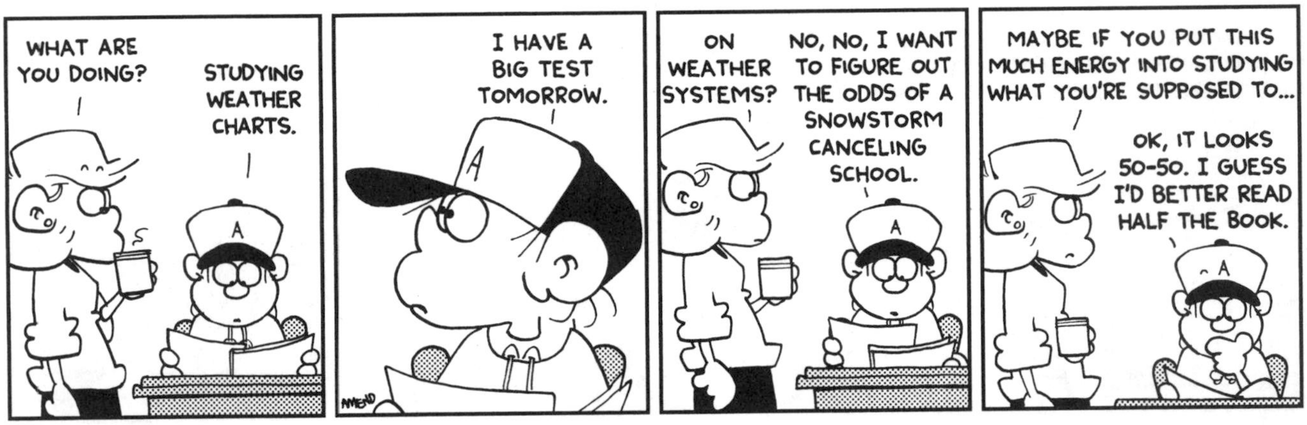
WHAT ARE YOU DOING?
STUDYING WEATHER CHARTS.
I HAVE A BIG TEST TOMORROW.
AMEND
ON WEATHER SYSTEMS?
NO, NO, I WANT TO FIGURE OUT THE ODDS OF A SNOWSTORM CANCELING SCHOOL.
MAYBE IF YOU PUT THIS MUCH ENERGY INTO STUDYING WHAT YOU'RE SUPPOSED TO...
OK, IT LOOKS 50-50. I GUESS I'D BETTER READ HALF THE BOOK.

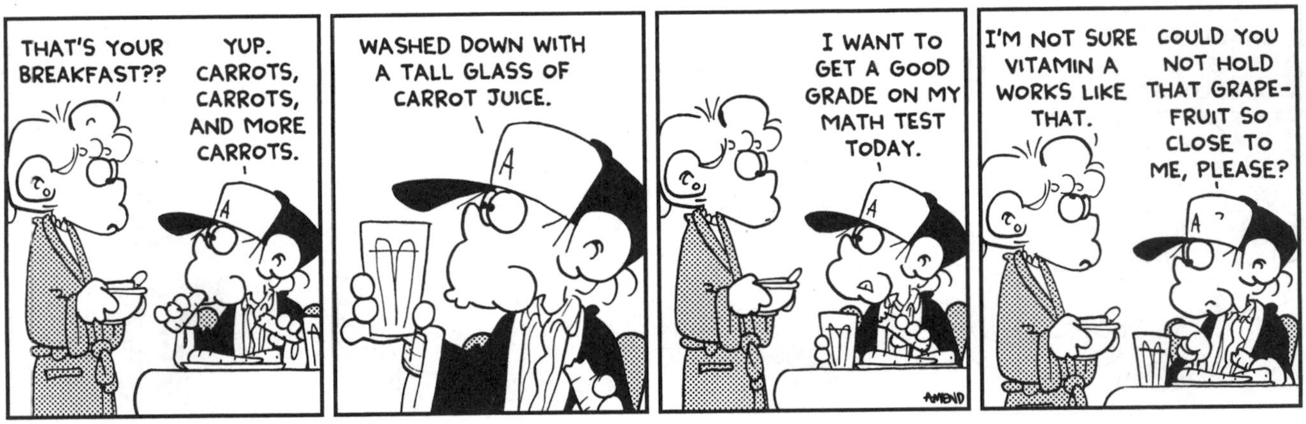
THAT'S YOUR BREAKFAST??
YUP. CARROTS, CARROTS, AND MORE CARROTS.
WASHED DOWN WITH A TALL GLASS OF CARROT JUICE.
I WANT TO GET A GOOD GRADE ON MY MATH TEST TODAY.
AMEND
I'M NOT SURE VITAMIN A WORKS LIKE THAT.
COULD YOU NOT HOLD THAT GRAPE-FRUIT SO CLOSE TO ME, PLEASE?

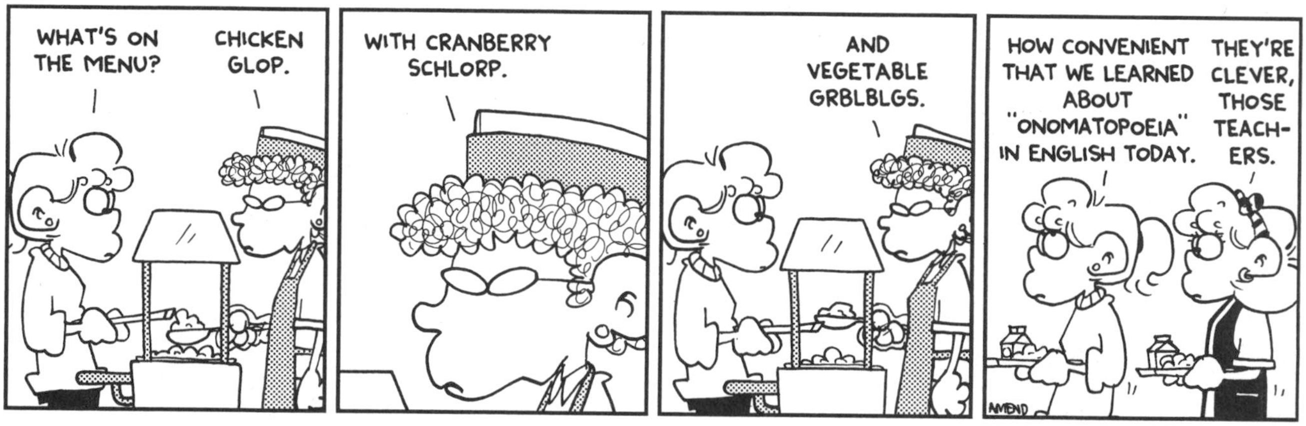
WHAT'S ON THE MENU?
CHICKEN GLOP.
WITH CRANBERRY SCHLORP.
AND VEGETABLE GRBLBLGS.
HOW CONVENIENT THAT WE LEARNED ABOUT "ONOMATOPOEIA" IN ENGLISH TODAY.
THEY'RE CLEVER, THOSE TEACHERS.
AMEND

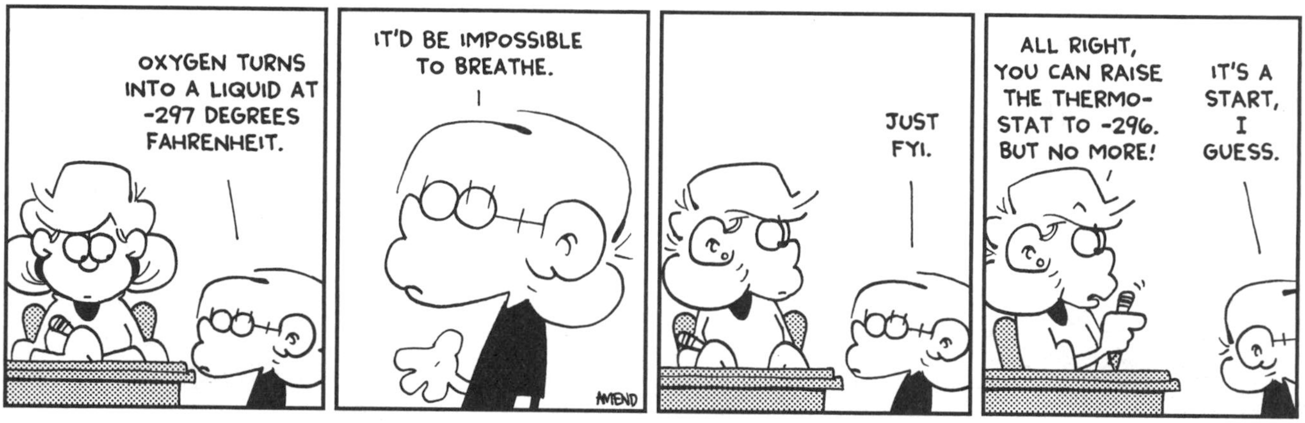
OXYGEN TURNS INTO A LIQUID AT -297 DEGREES FAHRENHEIT.
IT'D BE IMPOSSIBLE TO BREATHE.
AMEND
JUST FYI.
ALL RIGHT, YOU CAN RAISE THE THERMOSTAT TO -296. BUT NO MORE!
IT'S A START, I GUESS.

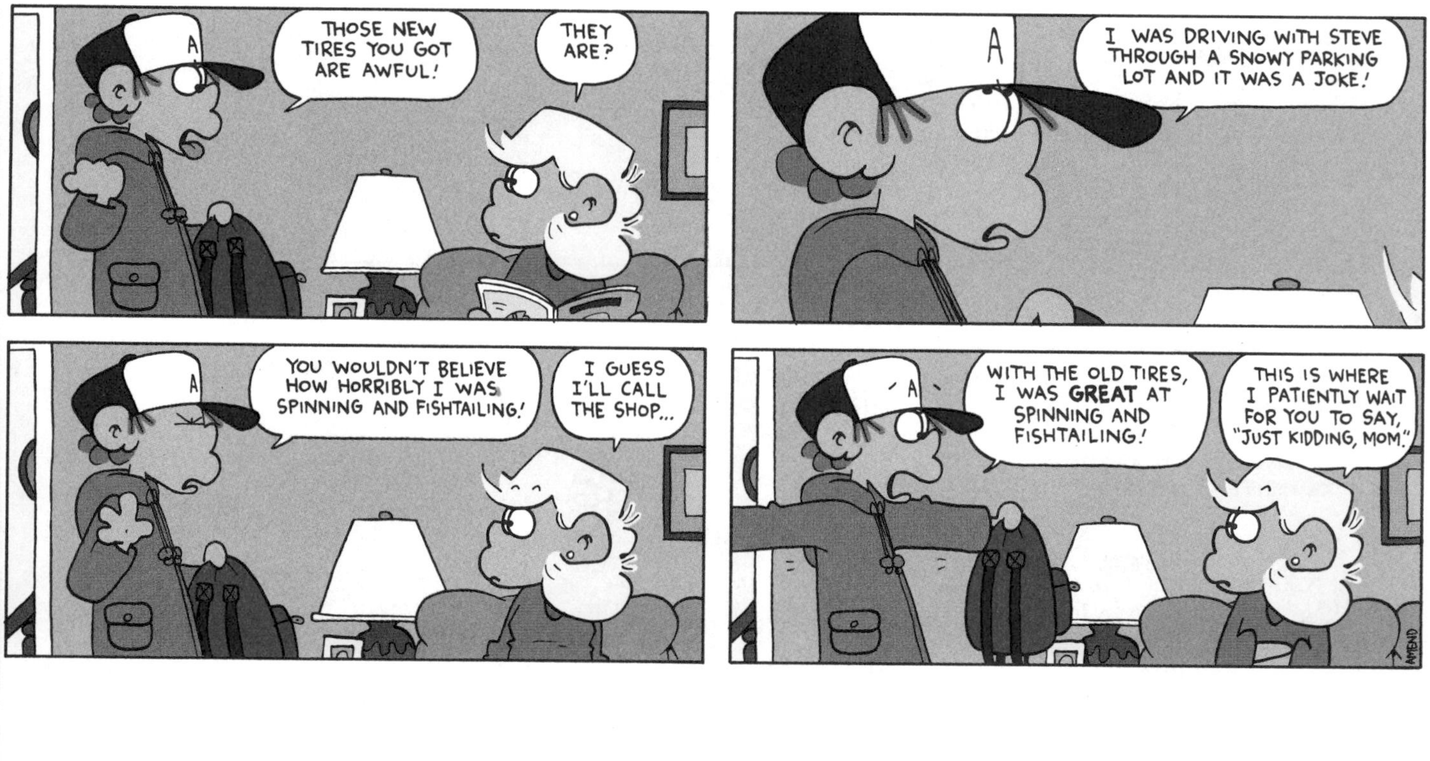
A
THOSE NEW TIRES YOU GOT ARE AWFUL!
THEY ARE?
I WAS DRIVING WITH STEVE THROUGH A SNOWY PARKING LOT AND IT WAS A JOKE!
YOU WOULDN'T BELIEVE HOW HORRIBLY I WAS SPINNING AND FISHTAILING!
I GUESS I'LL CALL THE SHOP...
WITH THE OLD TIRES, I WAS **GREAT** AT SPINNING AND FISHTAILING!
THIS IS WHERE I PATIENTLY WAIT FOR YOU TO SAY, "JUST KIDDING, MOM."
AMEND

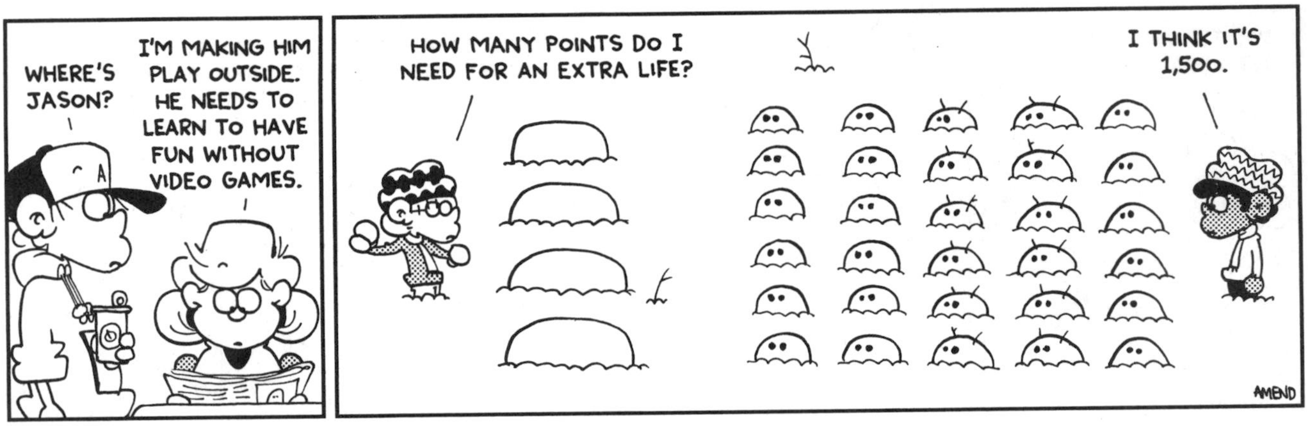
WHERE'S JASON?
I'M MAKING HIM PLAY OUTSIDE. HE NEEDS TO LEARN TO HAVE FUN WITHOUT VIDEO GAMES.
HOW MANY POINTS DO I NEED FOR AN EXTRA LIFE?
I THINK IT'S 1,500.
AMEND

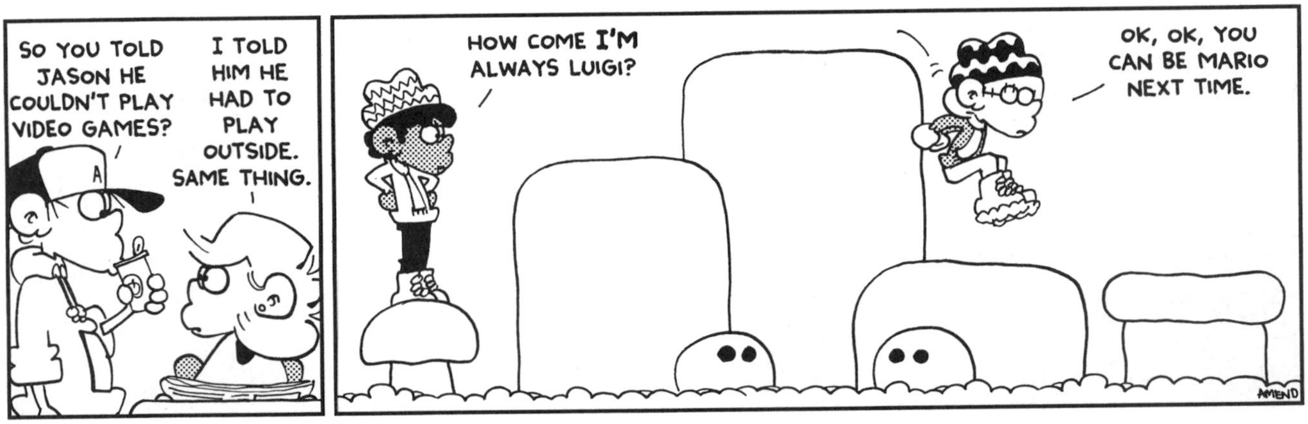
SO YOU TOLD JASON HE COULDN'T PLAY VIDEO GAMES?
I TOLD HIM HE HAD TO PLAY OUTSIDE. SAME THING.
HOW COME I'M ALWAYS LUIGI?
OK, OK, YOU CAN BE MARIO NEXT TIME.
AMEND

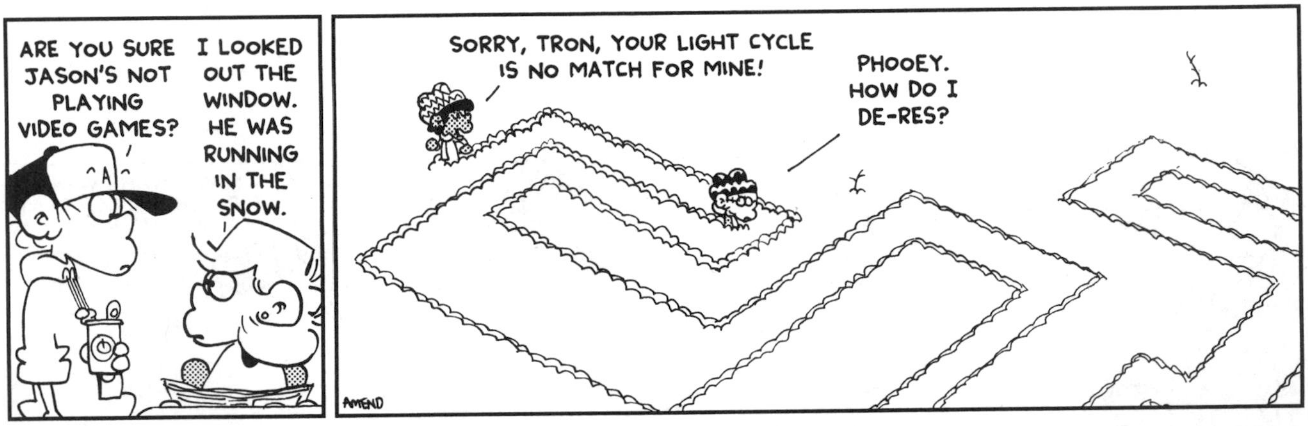
ARE YOU SURE JASON'S NOT PLAYING VIDEO GAMES?
I LOOKED OUT THE WINDOW. HE WAS RUNNING IN THE SNOW.
SORRY, TRON, YOUR LIGHT CYCLE IS NO MATCH FOR MINE!
PHOOEY. HOW DO I DE-RES?
AMEND

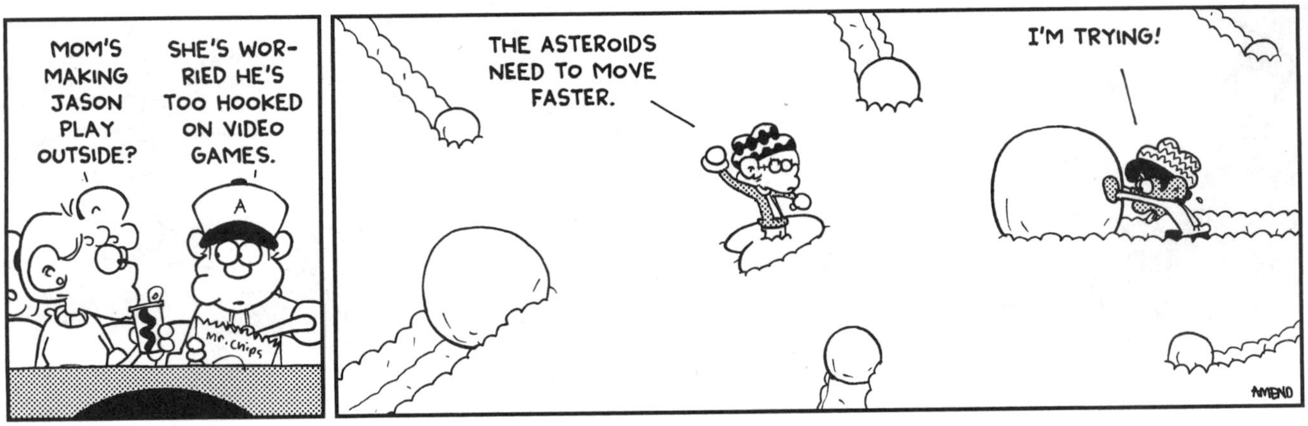
MOM'S MAKING JASON PLAY OUTSIDE?
SHE'S WORRIED HE'S TOO HOOKED ON VIDEO GAMES.
Mr. Chips
THE ASTEROIDS NEED TO MOVE FASTER.
I'M TRYING!
AMEND

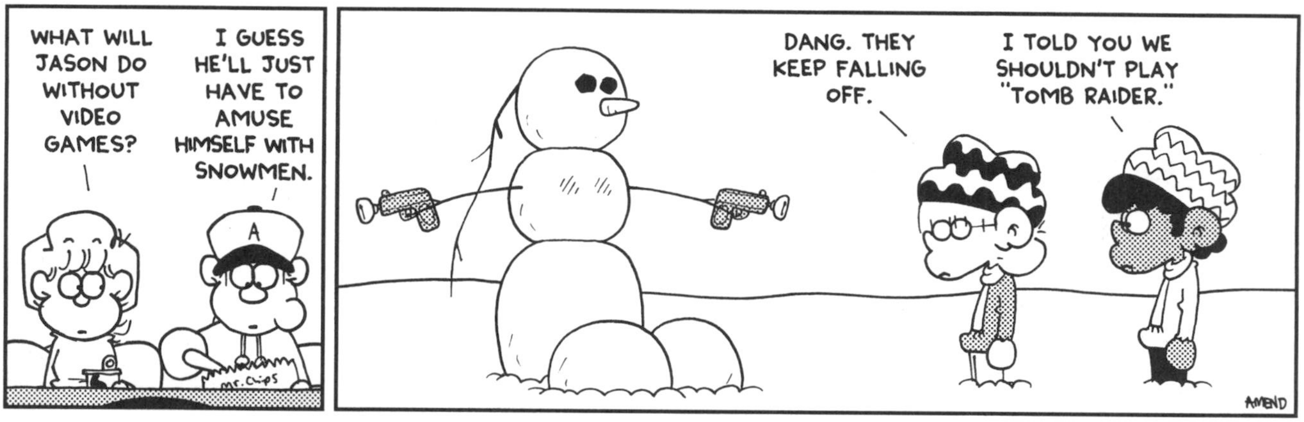
WHAT WILL JASON DO WITHOUT VIDEO GAMES?
I GUESS HE'LL JUST HAVE TO AMUSE HIMSELF WITH SNOWMEN.
DANG. THEY KEEP FALLING OFF.
I TOLD YOU WE SHOULDN'T PLAY "TOMB RAIDER."
AMEND

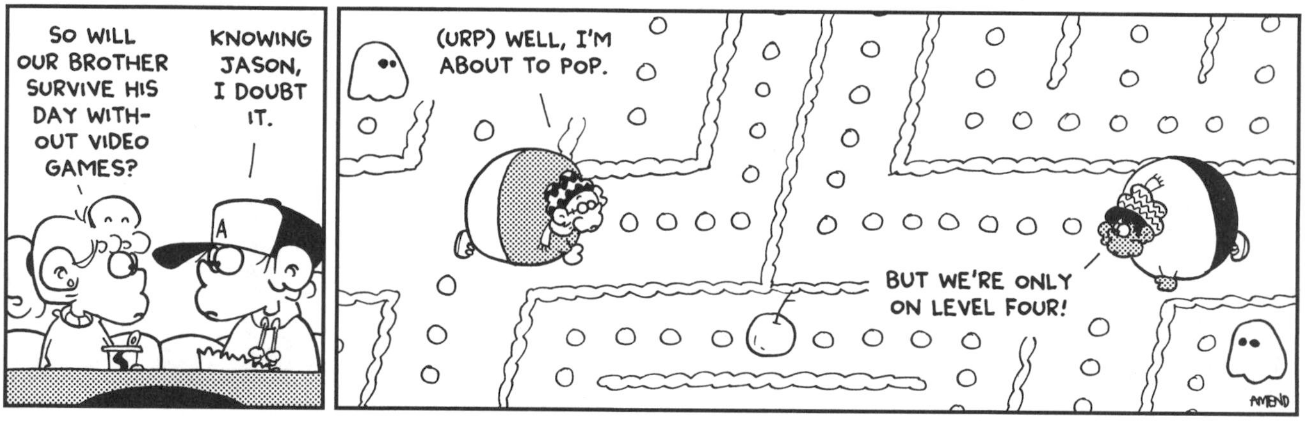
SO WILL OUR BROTHER SURVIVE HIS DAY WITH-OUT VIDEO GAMES?
KNOWING JASON, I DOUBT IT.
(URP) WELL, I'M ABOUT TO POP.
BUT WE'RE ONLY ON LEVEL FOUR!
AMEND

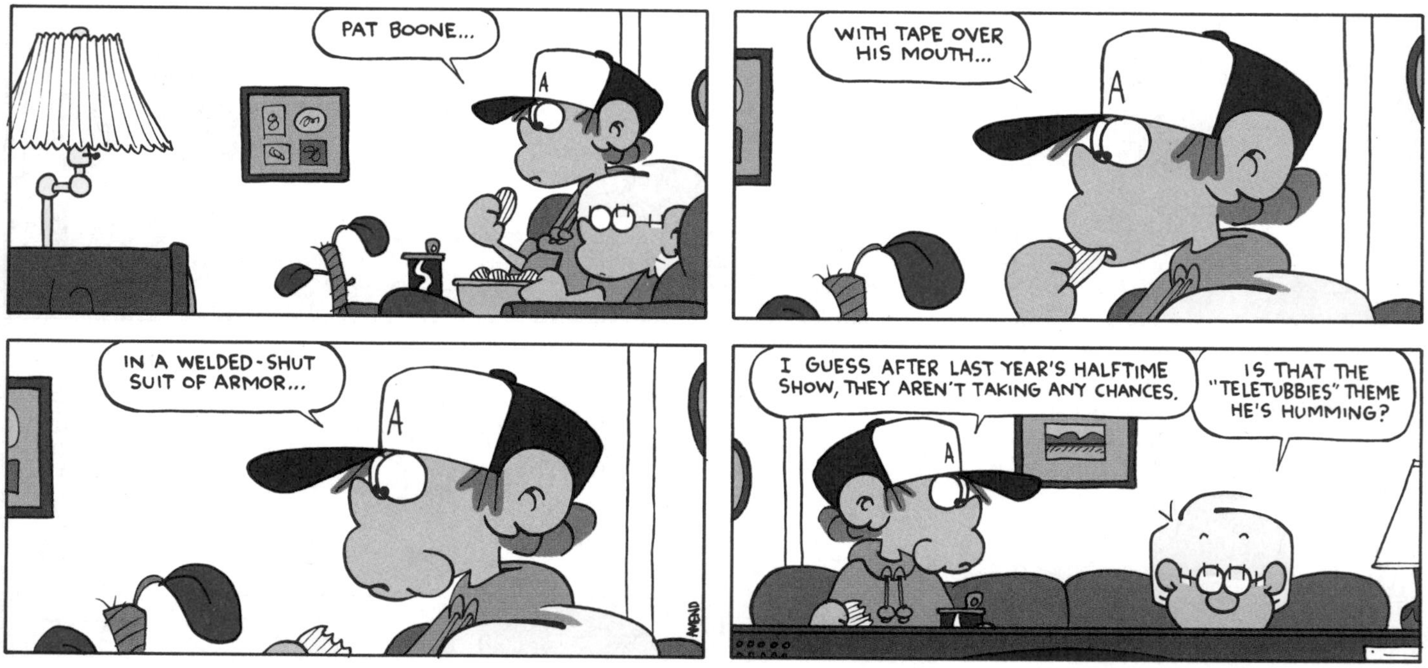
PAT BOONE...
WITH TAPE OVER HIS MOUTH...
IN A WELDED-SHUT SUIT OF ARMOR...
AMEND
I GUESS AFTER LAST YEAR'S HALFTIME SHOW, THEY AREN'T TAKING ANY CHANCES.
IS THAT THE "TELETUBBIES" THEME HE'S HUMMING?

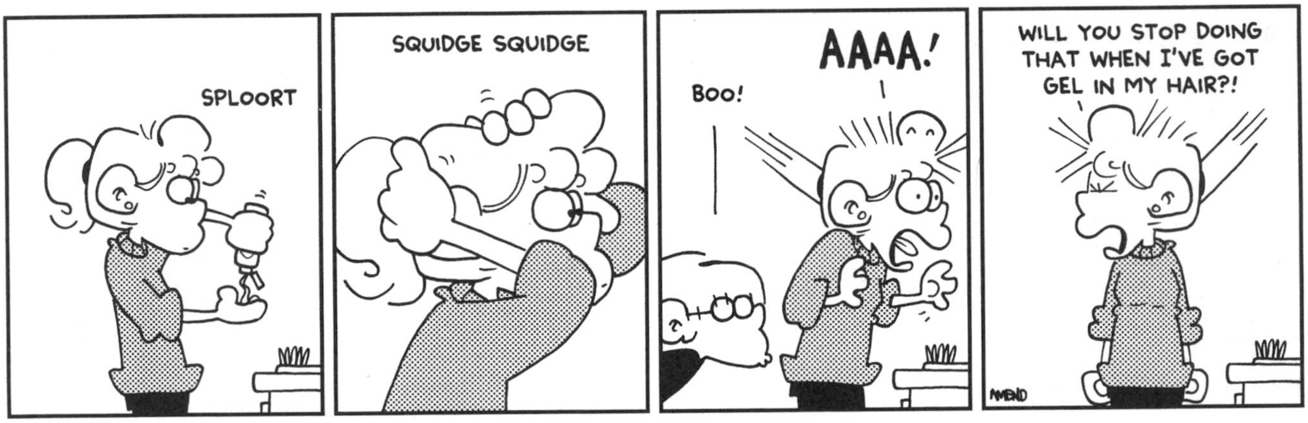
SPLOORT
SQUIDGE SQUIDGE
BOO!
AAAA!
WILL YOU STOP DOING THAT WHEN I'VE GOT GEL IN MY HAIR?!
AMEND

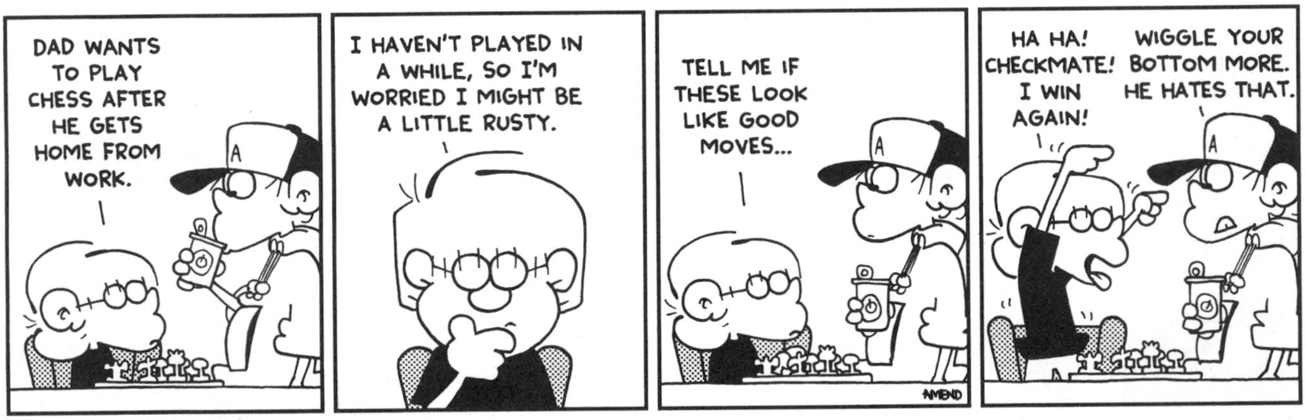
DAD WANTS TO PLAY CHESS AFTER HE GETS HOME FROM WORK.
I HAVEN'T PLAYED IN A WHILE, SO I'M WORRIED I MIGHT BE A LITTLE RUSTY.
TELL ME IF THESE LOOK LIKE GOOD MOVES...
HA HA! CHECKMATE! I WIN AGAIN!
WIGGLE YOUR BOTTOM MORE. HE HATES THAT.
AMEND

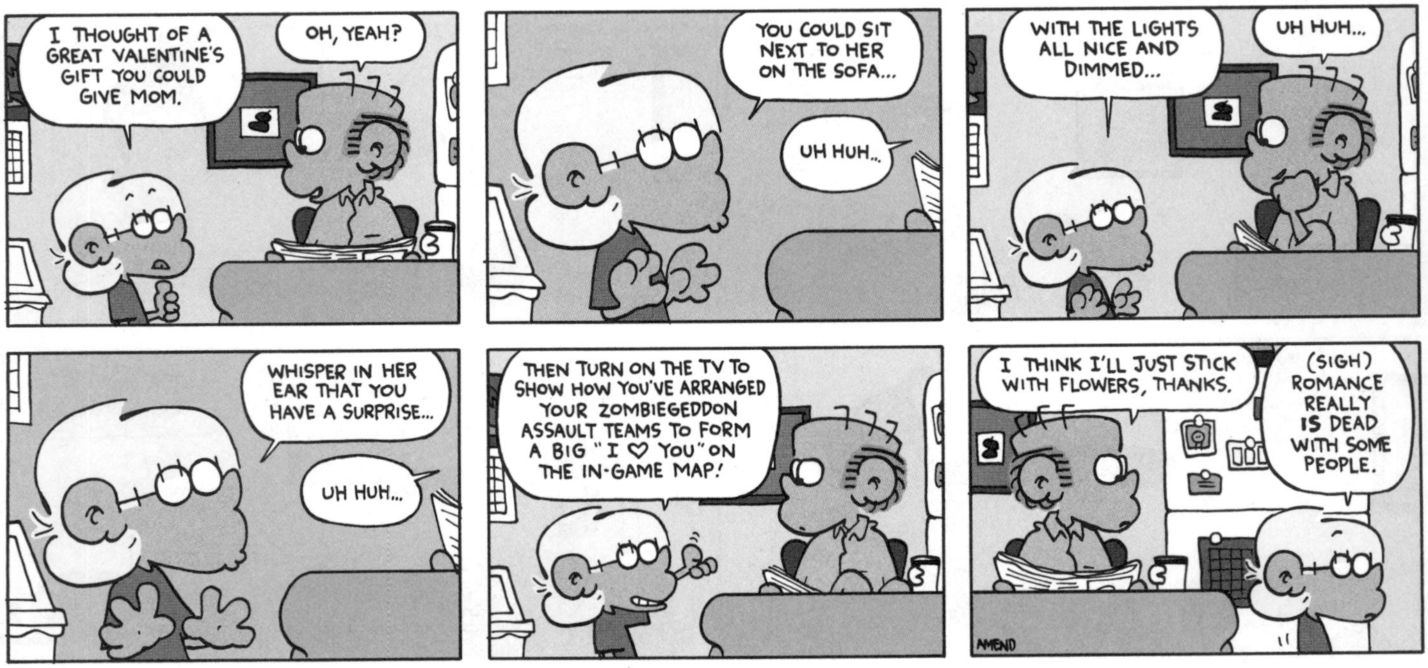
I THOUGHT OF A GREAT VALENTINE'S GIFT YOU COULD GIVE MOM.
OH, YEAH?
YOU COULD SIT NEXT TO HER ON THE SOFA...
UH HUH...
WITH THE LIGHTS ALL NICE AND DIMMED...
UH HUH...
WHISPER IN HER EAR THAT YOU HAVE A SURPRISE...
UH HUH...
THEN TURN ON THE TV TO SHOW HOW YOU'VE ARRANGED YOUR ZOMBIEGEDDON ASSAULT TEAMS TO FORM A BIG "I ♡ YOU" ON THE IN-GAME MAP!
I THINK I'LL JUST STICK WITH FLOWERS, THANKS.
(SIGH) ROMANCE REALLY IS DEAD WITH SOME PEOPLE.
AMEND

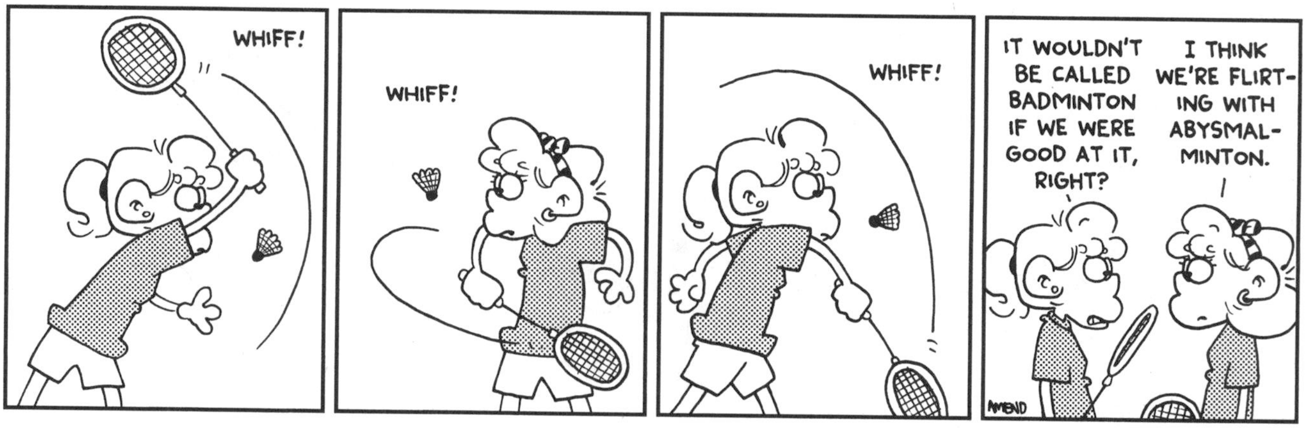
WHIFF!
WHIFF!
WHIFF!
IT WOULDN'T BE CALLED BADMINTON IF WE WERE GOOD AT IT, RIGHT?
I THINK WE'RE FLIRTING WITH ABYSMAL-MINTON.
AMEND

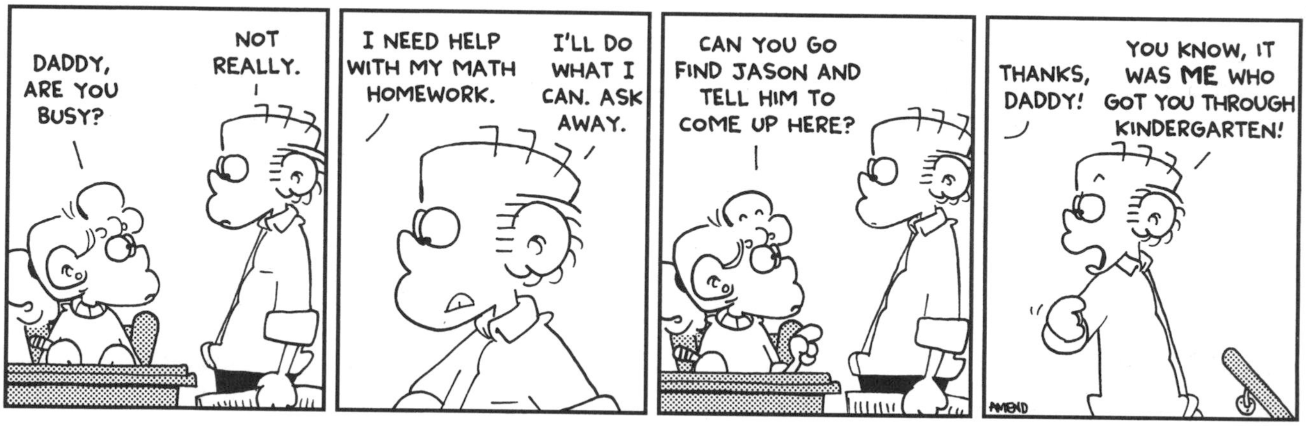
DADDY, ARE YOU BUSY?
NOT REALLY.
I NEED HELP WITH MY MATH HOMEWORK.
I'LL DO WHAT I CAN. ASK AWAY.
CAN YOU GO FIND JASON AND TELL HIM TO COME UP HERE?
THANKS, DADDY!
YOU KNOW, IT WAS ME WHO GOT YOU THROUGH KINDERGARTEN!
AMEND

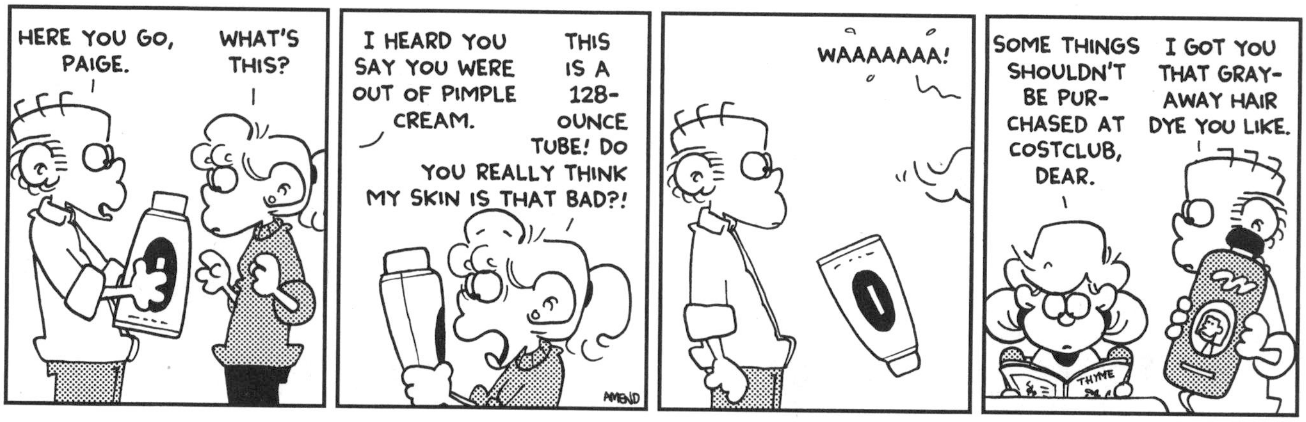
HERE YOU GO, PAIGE.
WHAT'S THIS?
I HEARD YOU SAY YOU WERE OUT OF PIMPLE CREAM.
THIS IS A 128-OUNCE TUBE! DO YOU REALLY THINK MY SKIN IS THAT BAD?!
AMEND
WAAAAAAA!
SOME THINGS SHOULDN'T BE PURCHASED AT COSTCLUB, DEAR.
I GOT YOU THAT GRAY-AWAY HAIR DYE YOU LIKE.
THYME

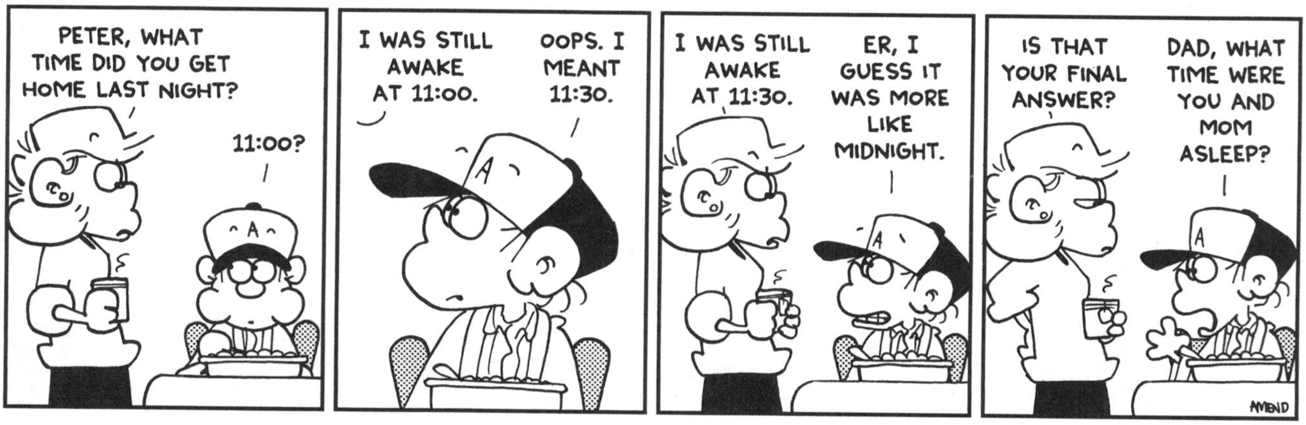
PETER, WHAT TIME DID YOU GET HOME LAST NIGHT?
11:00?
I WAS STILL AWAKE AT 11:00.
OOPS. I MEANT 11:30.
I WAS STILL AWAKE AT 11:30.
ER, I GUESS IT WAS MORE LIKE MIDNIGHT.
IS THAT YOUR FINAL ANSWER?
DAD, WHAT TIME WERE YOU AND MOM ASLEEP?
AMEND

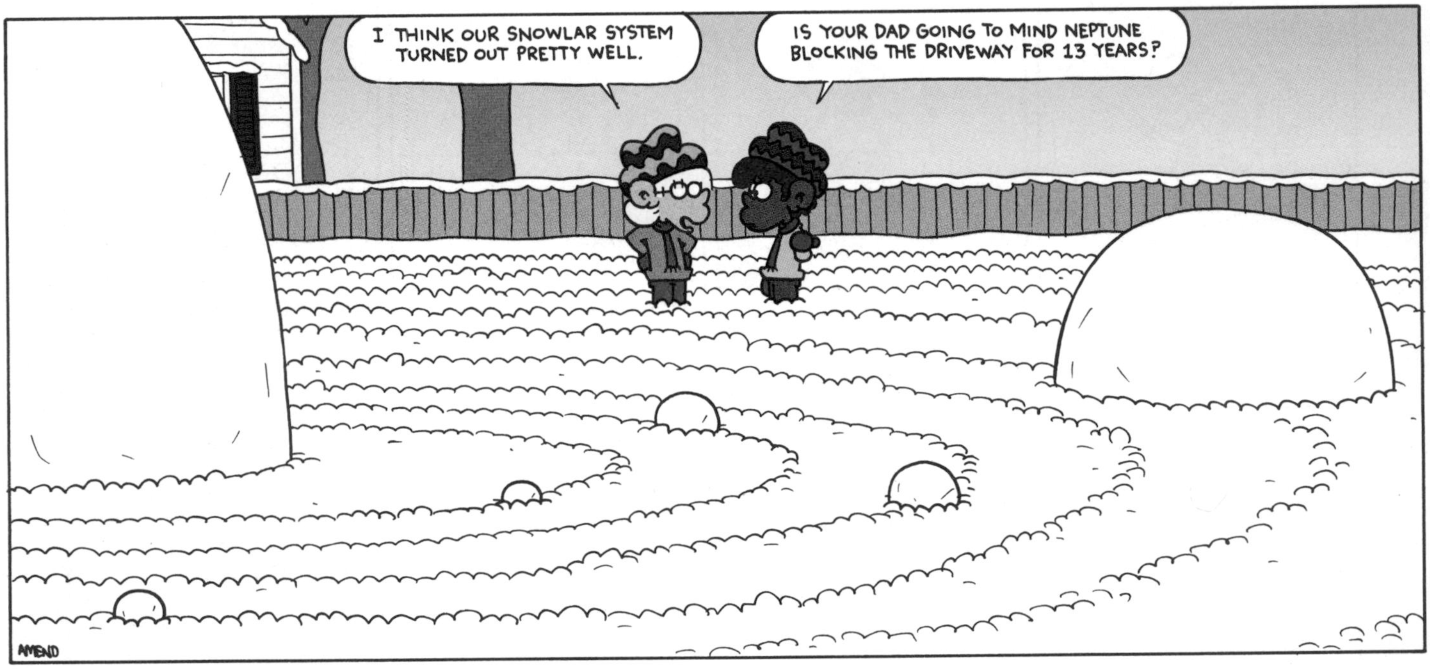
I THINK OUR SNOWLAR SYSTEM TURNED OUT PRETTY WELL.
IS YOUR DAD GOING TO MIND NEPTUNE BLOCKING THE DRIVEWAY FOR 13 YEARS?
AMEND

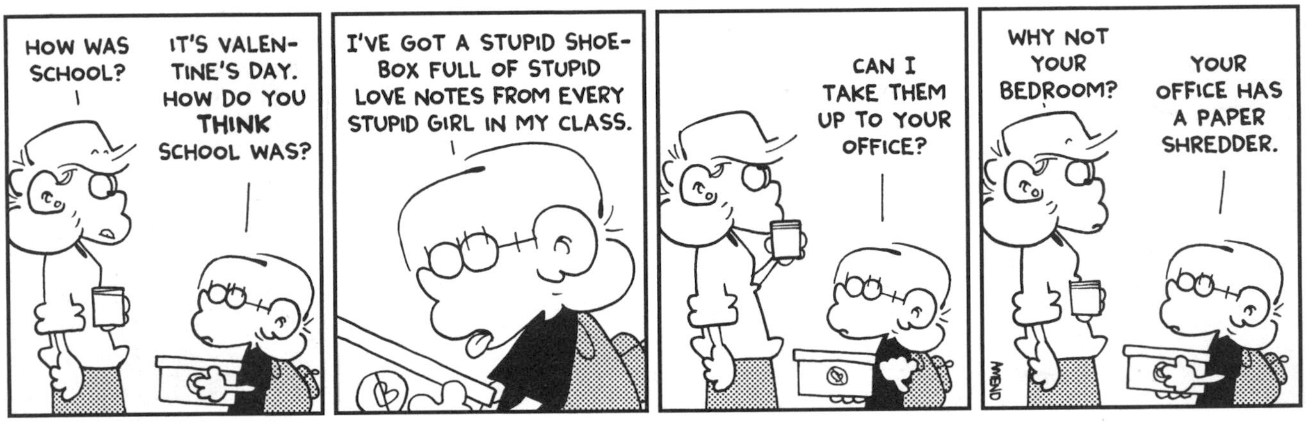
HOW WAS SCHOOL?
IT'S VALEN-TINE'S DAY. HOW DO YOU THINK SCHOOL WAS?
I'VE GOT A STUPID SHOE-BOX FULL OF STUPID LOVE NOTES FROM EVERY STUPID GIRL IN MY CLASS.
CAN I TAKE THEM UP TO YOUR OFFICE?
WHY NOT YOUR BEDROOM?
YOUR OFFICE HAS A PAPER SHREDDER.
AMEND

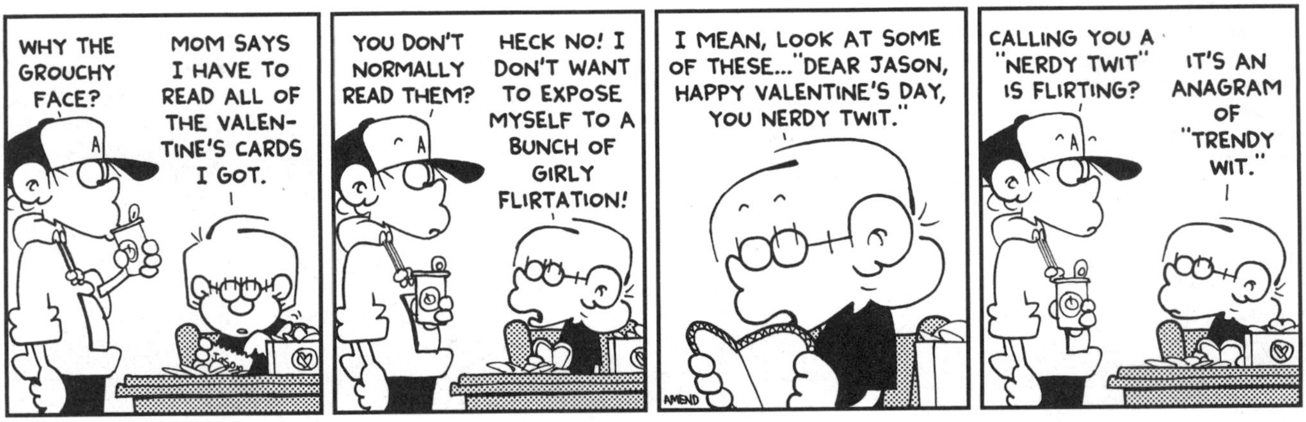
WHY THE GROUCHY FACE?
MOM SAYS I HAVE TO READ ALL OF THE VALEN-TINE'S CARDS I GOT.
YOU DON'T NORMALLY READ THEM?
HECK NO! I DON'T WANT TO EXPOSE MYSELF TO A BUNCH OF GIRLY FLIRTATION!
I MEAN, LOOK AT SOME OF THESE..."DEAR JASON, HAPPY VALENTINE'S DAY, YOU NERDY TWIT."
CALLING YOU A "NERDY TWIT" IS FLIRTING?
IT'S AN ANAGRAM OF "TRENDY WIT."
AMEND

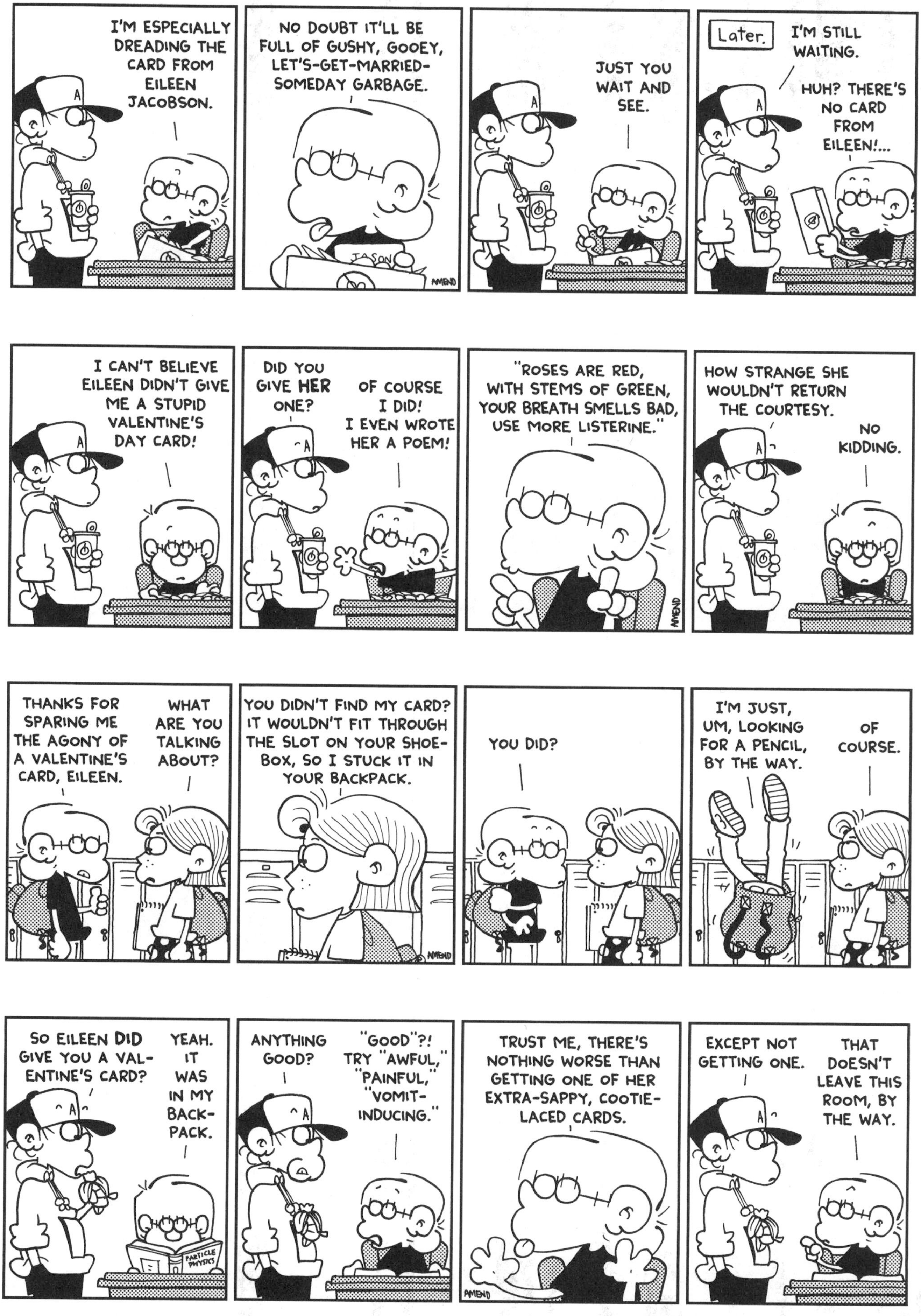
I'M ESPECIALLY DREADING THE CARD FROM EILEEN JACOBSON.
NO DOUBT IT'LL BE FULL OF GUSHY, GOOEY, LET'S-GET-MARRIED-SOMEDAY GARBAGE.
JASON
JUST YOU WAIT AND SEE.
Later.
I'M STILL WAITING.
HUH? THERE'S NO CARD FROM EILEEN!...
I CAN'T BELIEVE EILEEN DIDN'T GIVE ME A STUPID VALENTINE'S DAY CARD!
DID YOU GIVE HER ONE?
OF COURSE I DID! I EVEN WROTE HER A POEM!
"ROSES ARE RED, WITH STEMS OF GREEN, YOUR BREATH SMELLS BAD, USE MORE LISTERINE."
HOW STRANGE SHE WOULDN'T RETURN THE COURTESY.
NO KIDDING.
THANKS FOR SPARING ME THE AGONY OF A VALENTINE'S CARD, EILEEN.
WHAT ARE YOU TALKING ABOUT?
YOU DIDN'T FIND MY CARD? IT WOULDN'T FIT THROUGH THE SLOT ON YOUR SHOE-BOX, SO I STUCK IT IN YOUR BACKPACK.
YOU DID?
I'M JUST, UM, LOOKING FOR A PENCIL, BY THE WAY.
OF COURSE.
SO EILEEN DID GIVE YOU A VAL-ENTINE'S CARD?
YEAH. IT WAS IN MY BACK-PACK.
PARTICLE PHYSICS
ANYTHING GOOD?
"GOOD"?! TRY "AWFUL," "PAINFUL," "VOMIT-INDUCING."
TRUST ME, THERE'S NOTHING WORSE THAN GETTING ONE OF HER EXTRA-SAPPY, COOTIE-LACED CARDS.
EXCEPT NOT GETTING ONE.
THAT DOESN'T LEAVE THIS ROOM, BY THE WAY.

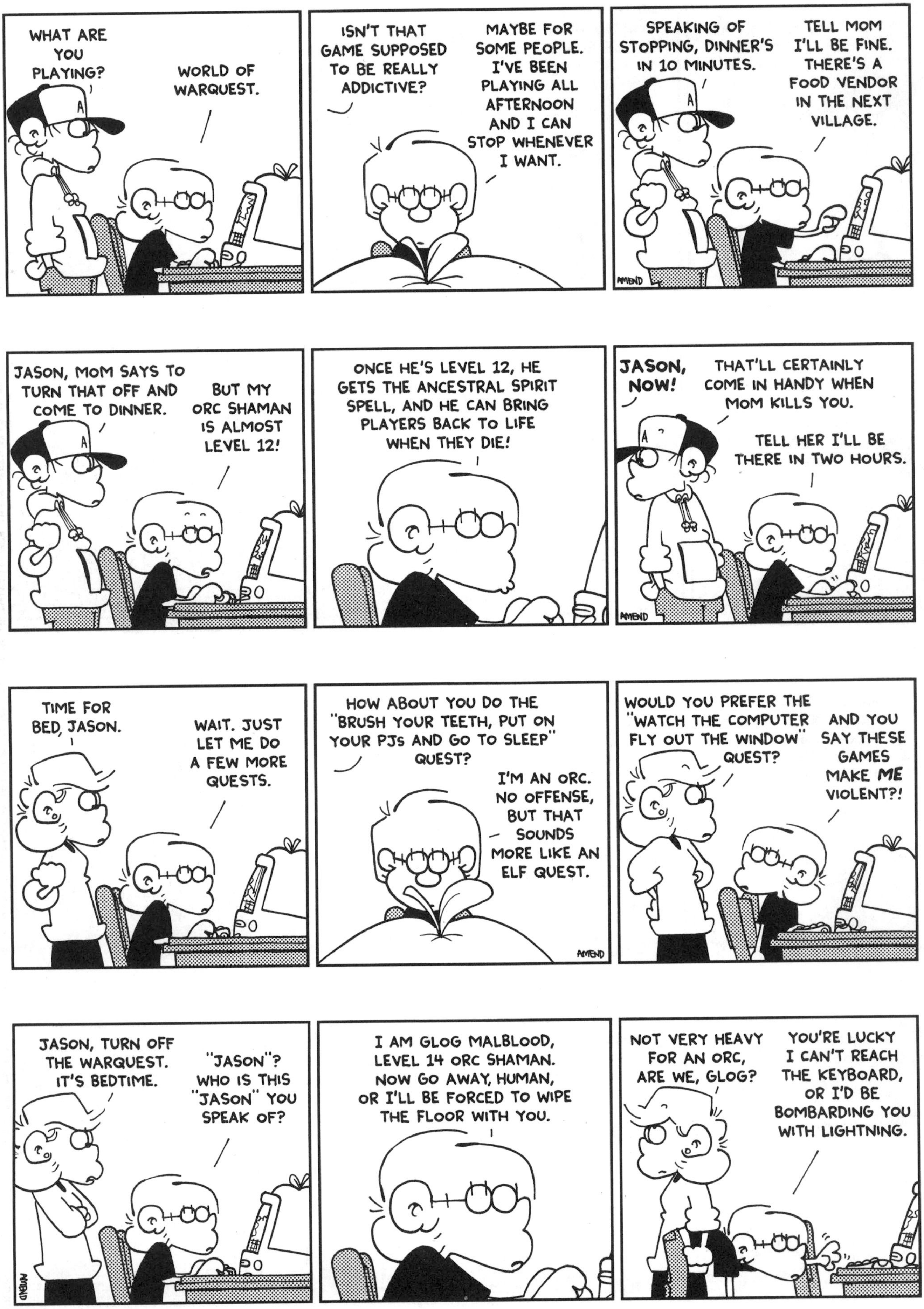
WHAT ARE YOU PLAYING?
WORLD OF WARQUEST.
ISN'T THAT GAME SUPPOSED TO BE REALLY ADDICTIVE?
MAYBE FOR SOME PEOPLE. I'VE BEEN PLAYING ALL AFTERNOON AND I CAN STOP WHENEVER I WANT.
SPEAKING OF STOPPING, DINNER'S IN 10 MINUTES.
TELL MOM I'LL BE FINE. THERE'S A FOOD VENDOR IN THE NEXT VILLAGE.
AMEND
JASON, MOM SAYS TO TURN THAT OFF AND COME TO DINNER.
BUT MY ORC SHAMAN IS ALMOST LEVEL 12!
ONCE HE'S LEVEL 12, HE GETS THE ANCESTRAL SPIRIT SPELL, AND HE CAN BRING PLAYERS BACK TO LIFE WHEN THEY DIE!
JASON, NOW!
THAT'LL CERTAINLY COME IN HANDY WHEN MOM KILLS YOU.
TELL HER I'LL BE THERE IN TWO HOURS.
AMEND
TIME FOR BED, JASON.
WAIT. JUST LET ME DO A FEW MORE QUESTS.
HOW ABOUT YOU DO THE "BRUSH YOUR TEETH, PUT ON YOUR PJs AND GO TO SLEEP" QUEST?
I'M AN ORC. NO OFFENSE, BUT THAT SOUNDS MORE LIKE AN ELF QUEST.
AMEND
WOULD YOU PREFER THE "WATCH THE COMPUTER FLY OUT THE WINDOW" QUEST?
AND YOU SAY THESE GAMES MAKE **ME** VIOLENT?!
JASON, TURN OFF THE WARQUEST. IT'S BEDTIME.
"JASON"? WHO IS THIS "JASON" YOU SPEAK OF?
AMEND
I AM GLOG MALBLOOD, LEVEL 14 ORC SHAMAN. NOW GO AWAY, HUMAN, OR I'LL BE FORCED TO WIPE THE FLOOR WITH YOU.
NOT VERY HEAVY FOR AN ORC, ARE WE, GLOG?
YOU'RE LUCKY I CAN'T REACH THE KEYBOARD, OR I'D BE BOMBARDING YOU WITH LIGHTNING.

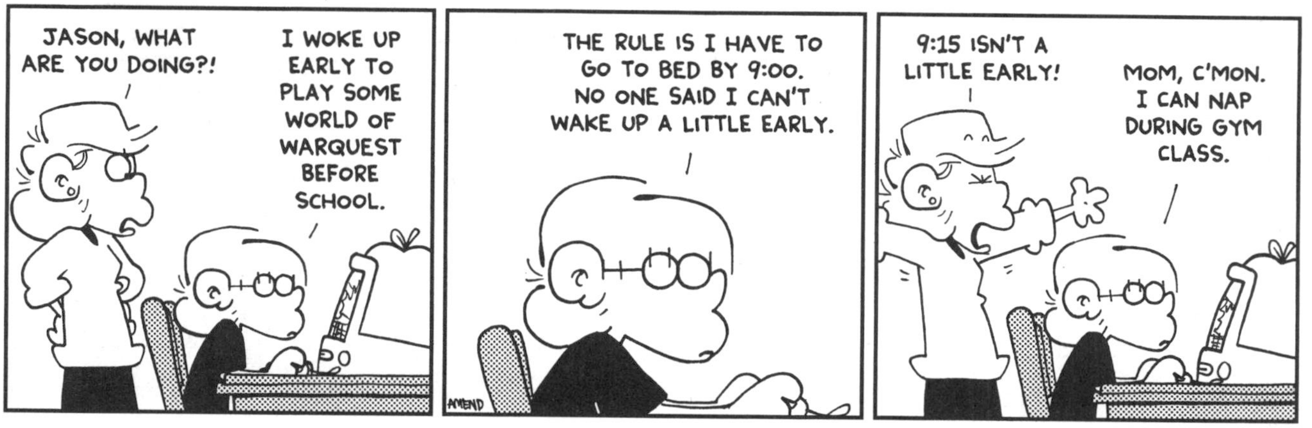
JASON, WHAT ARE YOU DOING?!
I WOKE UP EARLY TO PLAY SOME WORLD OF WARQUEST BEFORE SCHOOL.
THE RULE IS I HAVE TO GO TO BED BY 9:00. NO ONE SAID I CAN'T WAKE UP A LITTLE EARLY.
9:15 ISN'T A LITTLE EARLY!
MOM, C'MON. I CAN NAP DURING GYM CLASS.
AMEND

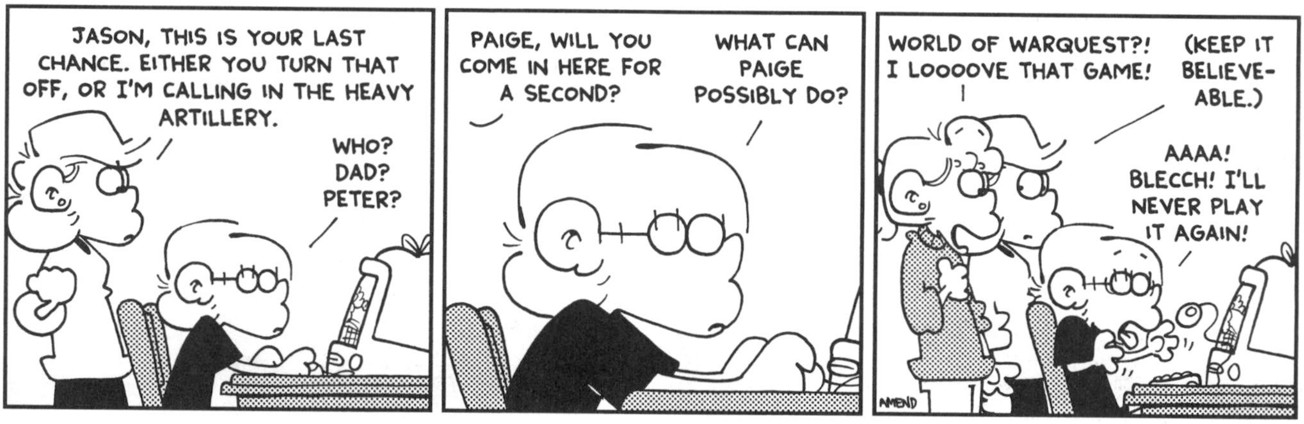
JASON, THIS IS YOUR LAST CHANCE. EITHER YOU TURN THAT OFF, OR I'M CALLING IN THE HEAVY ARTILLERY.
WHO? DAD? PETER?
PAIGE, WILL YOU COME IN HERE FOR A SECOND?
WHAT CAN PAIGE POSSIBLY DO?
WORLD OF WARQUEST?! I LOOOOVE THAT GAME!
(KEEP IT BELIEVE-ABLE.)
AAAA! BLECCH! I'LL NEVER PLAY IT AGAIN!
AMEND

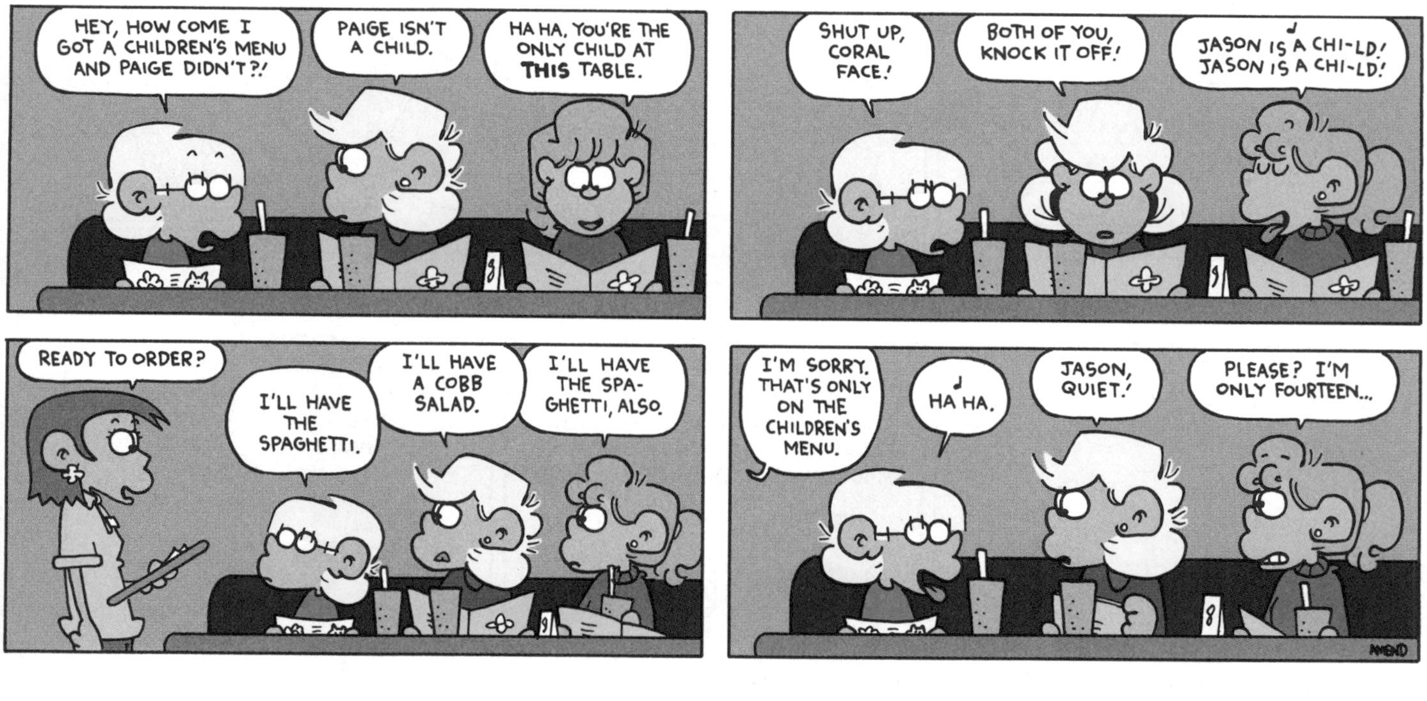
HEY, HOW COME I GOT A CHILDREN'S MENU AND PAIGE DIDN'T?!
PAIGE ISN'T A CHILD.
HA HA, YOU'RE THE ONLY CHILD AT THIS TABLE.
SHUT UP, CORAL FACE!
BOTH OF YOU, KNOCK IT OFF!
JASON IS A CHI-LD! JASON IS A CHI-LD!
READY TO ORDER?
I'LL HAVE THE SPAGHETTI.
I'LL HAVE A COBB SALAD.
I'LL HAVE THE SPA-GHETTI, ALSO.
I'M SORRY. THAT'S ONLY ON THE CHILDREN'S MENU.
HA HA.
JASON, QUIET!
PLEASE? I'M ONLY FOURTEEN...
AMEND

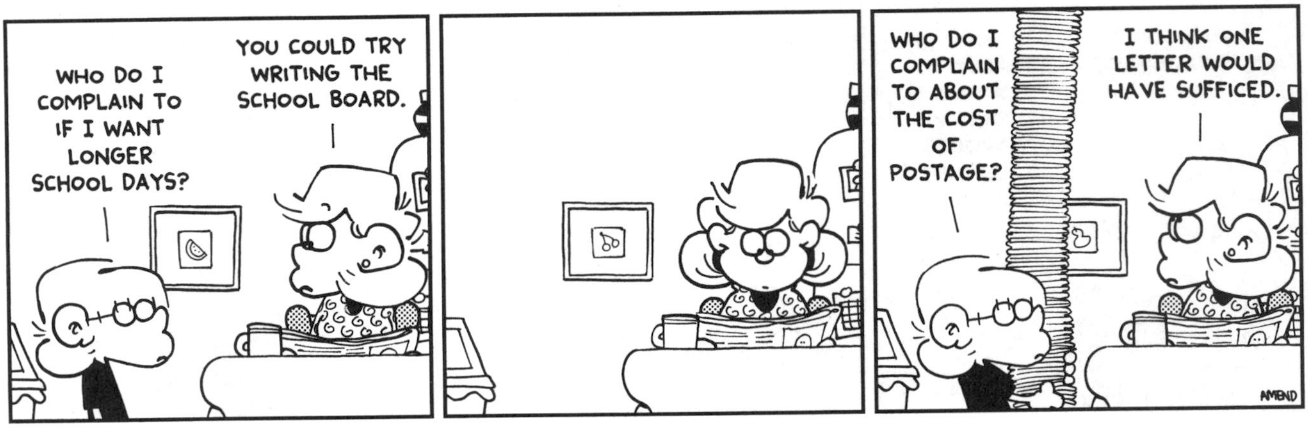
WHO DO I COMPLAIN TO IF I WANT LONGER SCHOOL DAYS?
YOU COULD TRY WRITING THE SCHOOL BOARD.
WHO DO I COMPLAIN TO ABOUT THE COST OF POSTAGE?
I THINK ONE LETTER WOULD HAVE SUFFICED.
AMEND

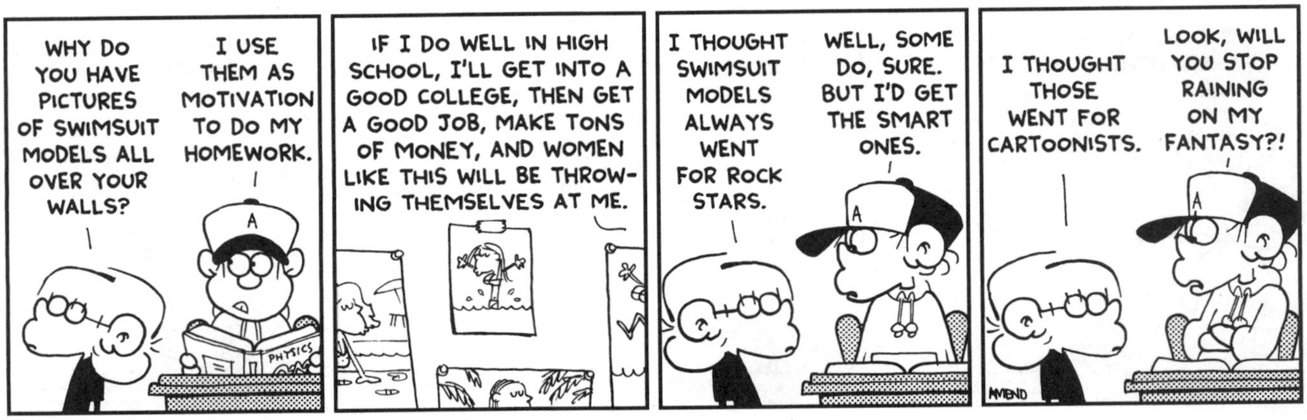
WHY DO YOU HAVE PICTURES OF SWIMSUIT MODELS ALL OVER YOUR WALLS?
I USE THEM AS MOTIVATION TO DO MY HOMEWORK.
PHYSICS
IF I DO WELL IN HIGH SCHOOL, I'LL GET INTO A GOOD COLLEGE, THEN GET A GOOD JOB, MAKE TONS OF MONEY, AND WOMEN LIKE THIS WILL BE THROWING THEMSELVES AT ME.
I THOUGHT SWIMSUIT MODELS ALWAYS WENT FOR ROCK STARS.
WELL, SOME DO, SURE. BUT I'D GET THE SMART ONES.
I THOUGHT THOSE WENT FOR CARTOONISTS.
LOOK, WILL YOU STOP RAINING ON MY FANTASY?!
AMEND

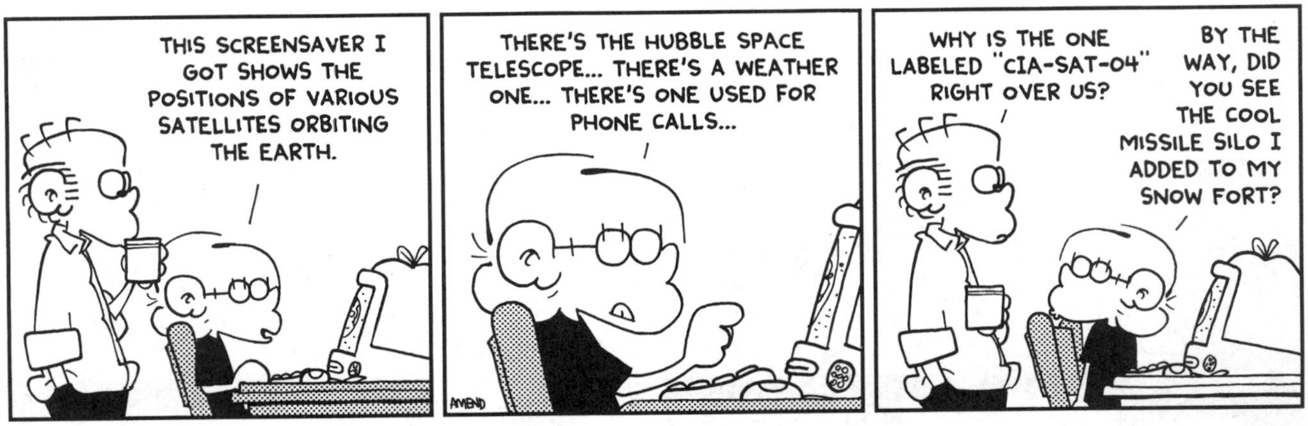
THIS SCREENSAVER I GOT SHOWS THE POSITIONS OF VARIOUS SATELLITES ORBITING THE EARTH.
AMEND
THERE'S THE HUBBLE SPACE TELESCOPE... THERE'S A WEATHER ONE... THERE'S ONE USED FOR PHONE CALLS...
WHY IS THE ONE LABELED "CIA-SAT-04" RIGHT OVER US?
BY THE WAY, DID YOU SEE THE COOL MISSILE SILO I ADDED TO MY SNOW FORT?

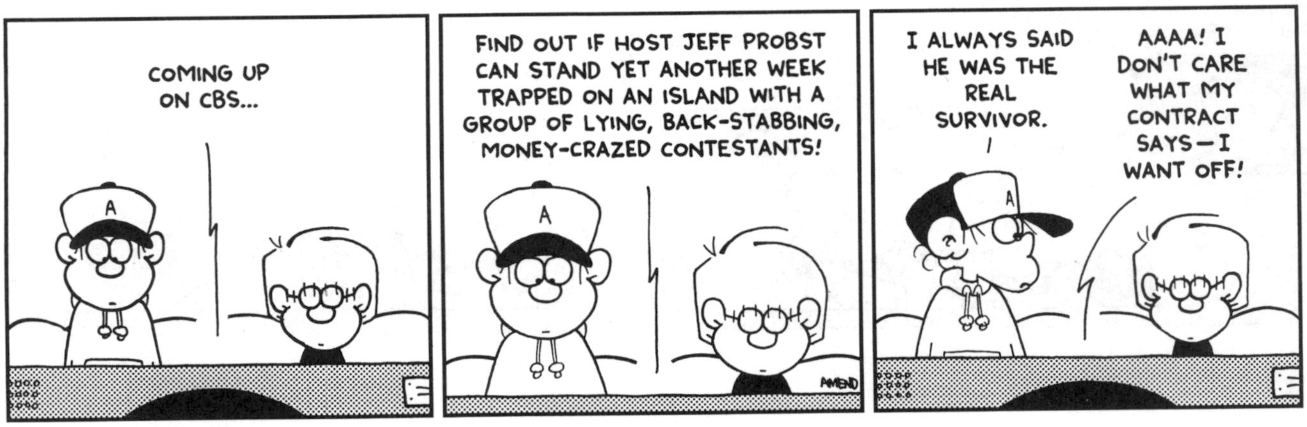
COMING UP ON CBS...
FIND OUT IF HOST JEFF PROBST CAN STAND YET ANOTHER WEEK TRAPPED ON AN ISLAND WITH A GROUP OF LYING, BACK-STABBING, MONEY-CRAZED CONTESTANTS!
AMEND
I ALWAYS SAID HE WAS THE REAL SURVIVOR.
AAAA! I DON'T CARE WHAT MY CONTRACT SAYS—I WANT OFF!

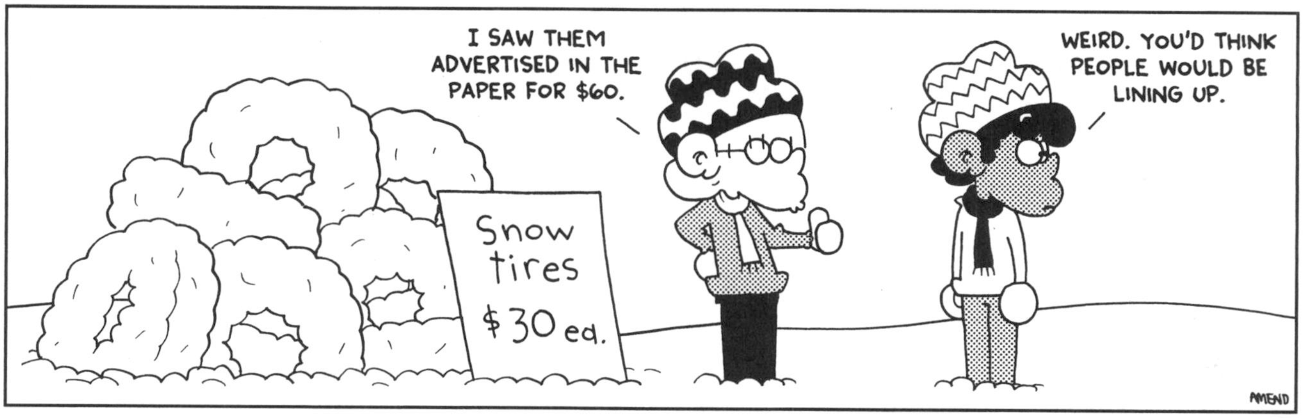
I SAW THEM ADVERTISED IN THE PAPER FOR $60.
WEIRD. YOU'D THINK PEOPLE WOULD BE LINING UP.
Snow tires $30 ea.
AMEND

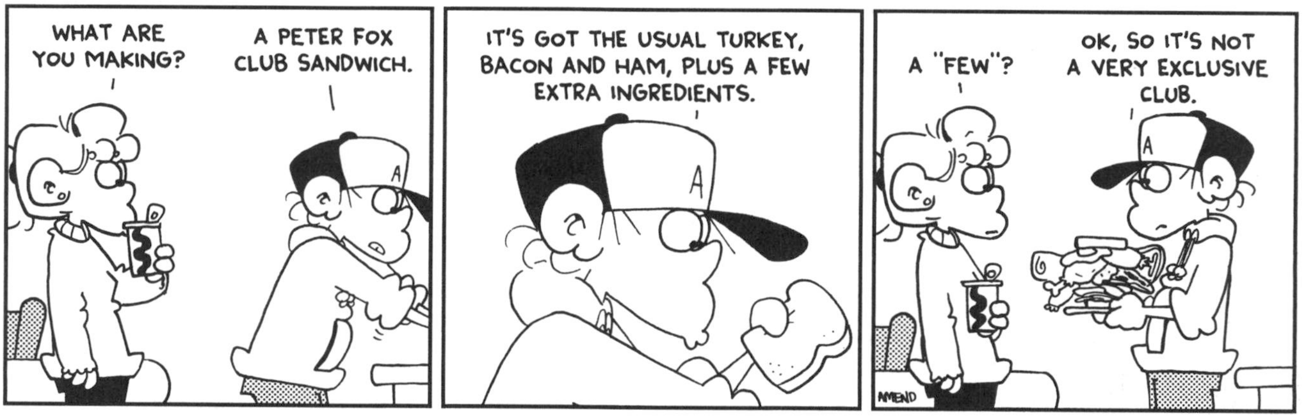
WHAT ARE YOU MAKING?
A PETER FOX CLUB SANDWICH.
IT'S GOT THE USUAL TURKEY, BACON AND HAM, PLUS A FEW EXTRA INGREDIENTS.
A "FEW"?
OK, SO IT'S NOT A VERY EXCLUSIVE CLUB.
AMEND

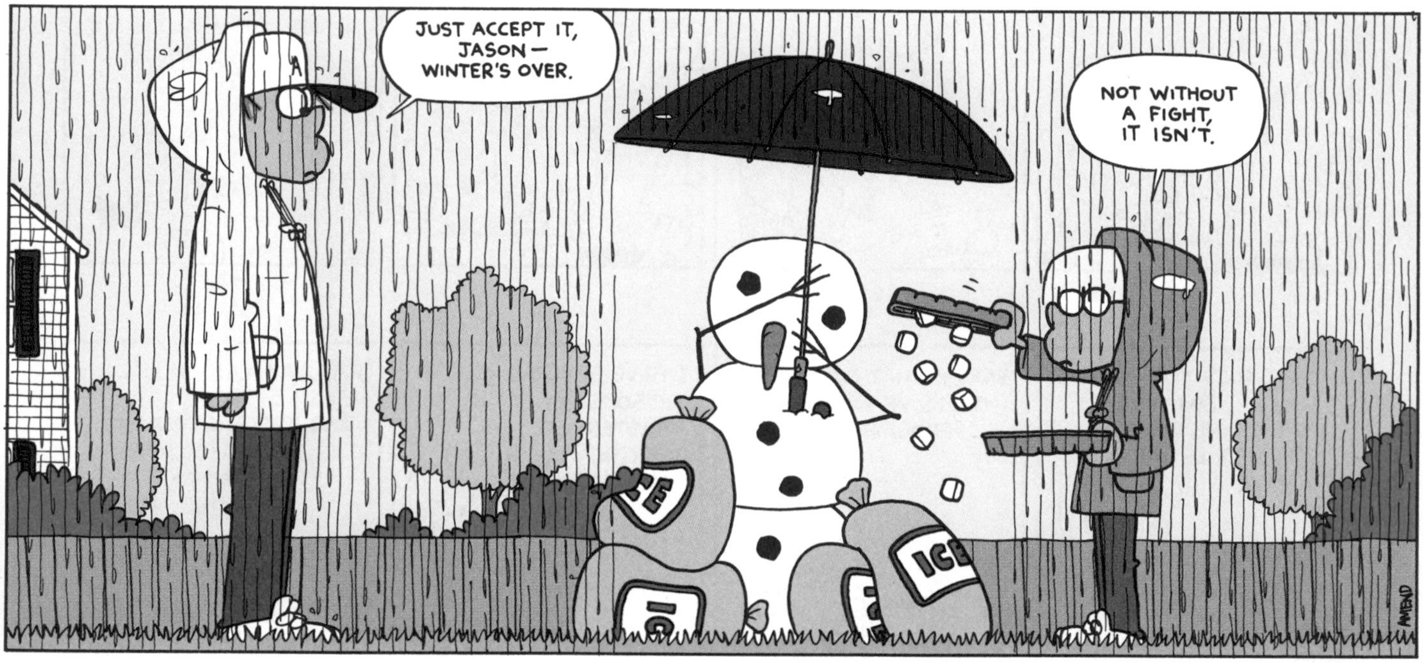
JUST ACCEPT IT, JASON— WINTER'S OVER.
NOT WITHOUT A FIGHT, IT ISN'T.
ICE
ICE
AMEND

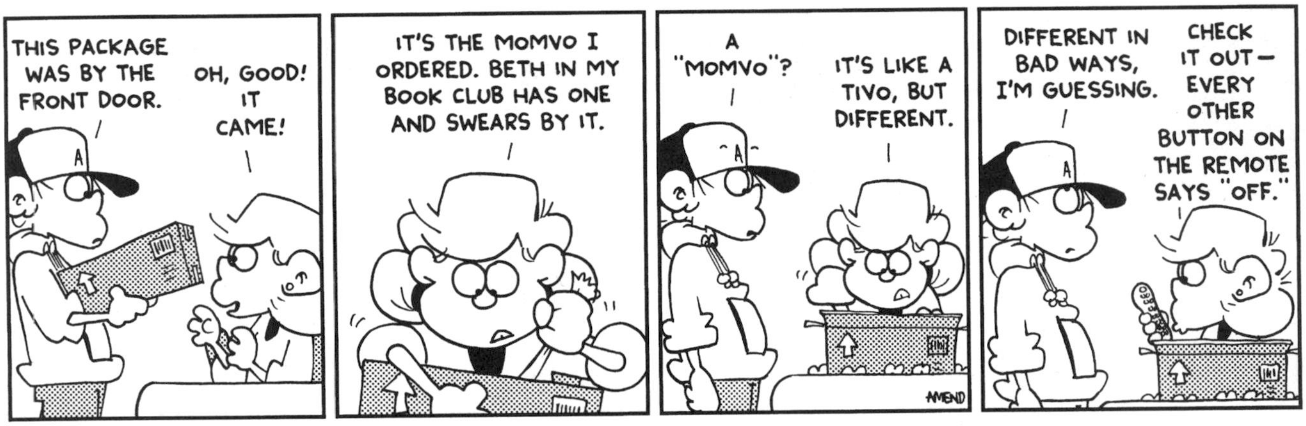
THIS PACKAGE WAS BY THE FRONT DOOR.
OH, GOOD! IT CAME!
IT'S THE MOMVO I ORDERED. BETH IN MY BOOK CLUB HAS ONE AND SWEARS BY IT.
A "MOMVO"?
IT'S LIKE A TIVO, BUT DIFFERENT.
DIFFERENT IN BAD WAYS, I'M GUESSING.
CHECK IT OUT— EVERY OTHER BUTTON ON THE REMOTE SAYS "OFF."

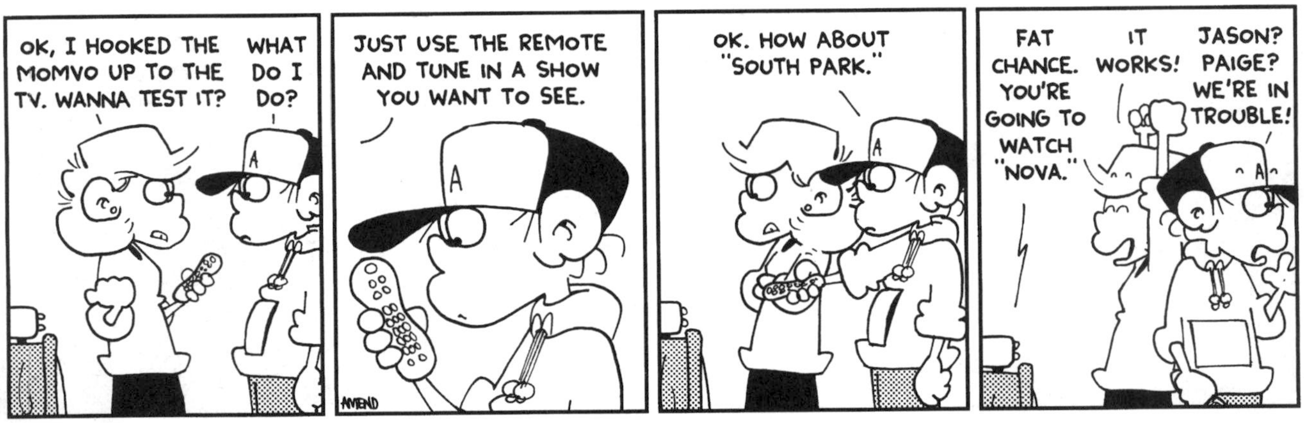
OK, I HOOKED THE MOMVO UP TO THE TV. WANNA TEST IT?
WHAT DO I DO?
JUST USE THE REMOTE AND TUNE IN A SHOW YOU WANT TO SEE.
OK. HOW ABOUT "SOUTH PARK."
FAT CHANCE. YOU'RE GOING TO WATCH "NOVA."
IT WORKS!
JASON? PAIGE? WE'RE IN TROUBLE!

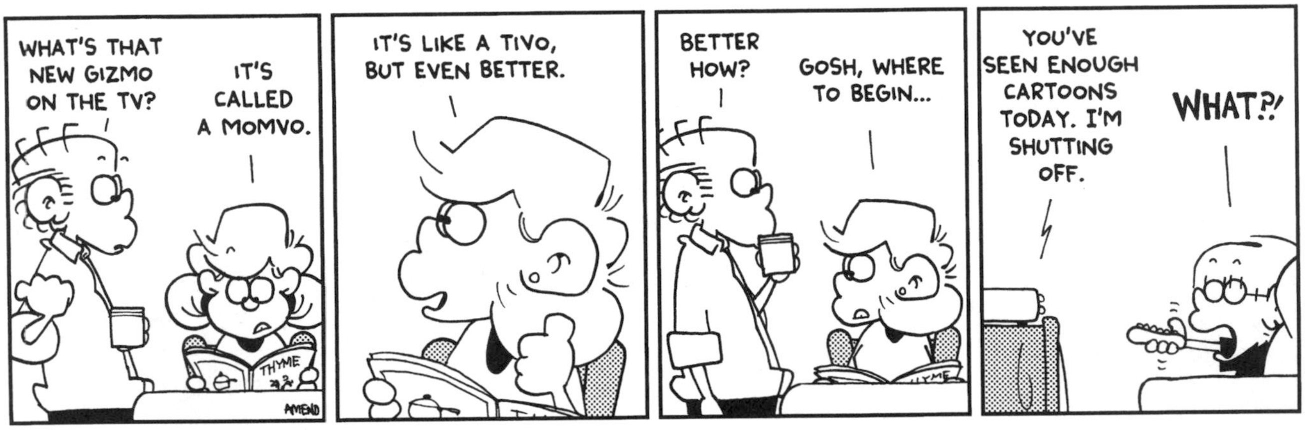
WHAT'S THAT NEW GIZMO ON THE TV?
IT'S CALLED A MOMVO.
IT'S LIKE A TIVO, BUT EVEN BETTER.
BETTER HOW?
GOSH, WHERE TO BEGIN...
YOU'VE SEEN ENOUGH CARTOONS TODAY. I'M SHUTTING OFF.
WHAT?!

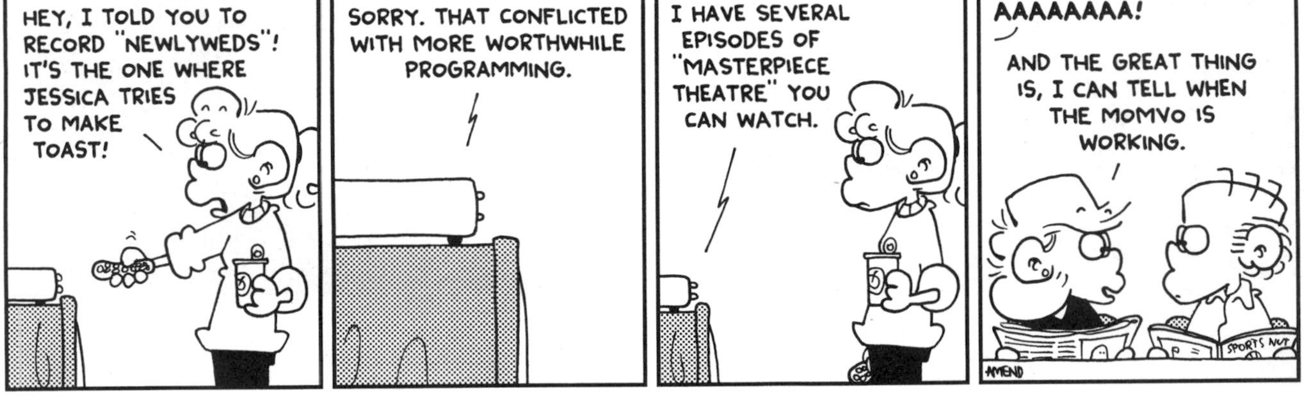
HEY, I TOLD YOU TO RECORD "NEWLYWEDS"! IT'S THE ONE WHERE JESSICA TRIES TO MAKE TOAST!
SORRY. THAT CONFLICTED WITH MORE WORTHWHILE PROGRAMMING.
I HAVE SEVERAL EPISODES OF "MASTERPIECE THEATRE" YOU CAN WATCH.
AAAAAAAA!
AND THE GREAT THING IS, I CAN TELL WHEN THE MOMVO IS WORKING.

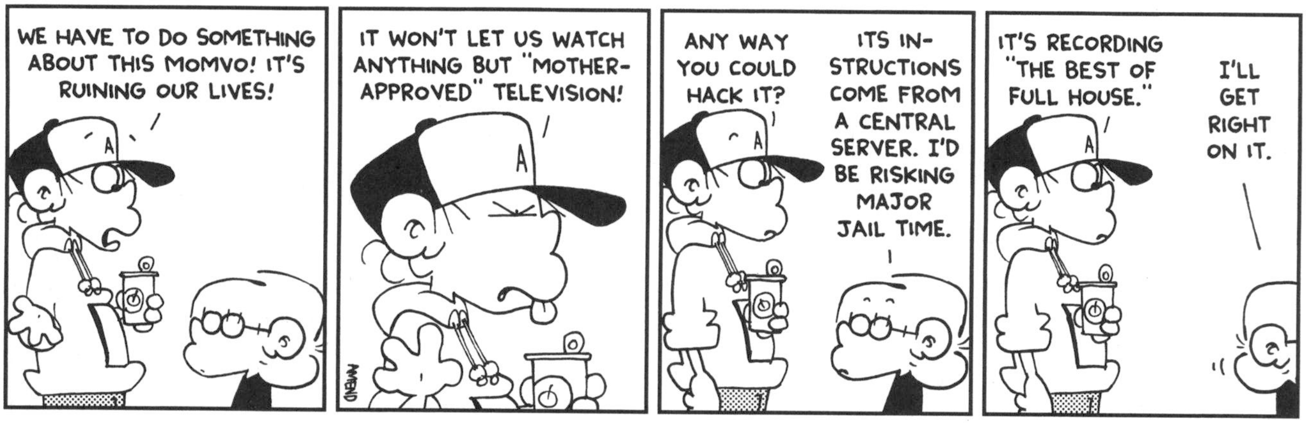
WE HAVE TO DO SOMETHING ABOUT THIS MOMVO! IT'S RUINING OUR LIVES!
IT WON'T LET US WATCH ANYTHING BUT "MOTHER-APPROVED" TELEVISION!
ANY WAY YOU COULD HACK IT?
ITS INSTRUCTIONS COME FROM A CENTRAL SERVER. I'D BE RISKING MAJOR JAIL TIME.
IT'S RECORDING "THE BEST OF FULL HOUSE."
I'LL GET RIGHT ON IT.

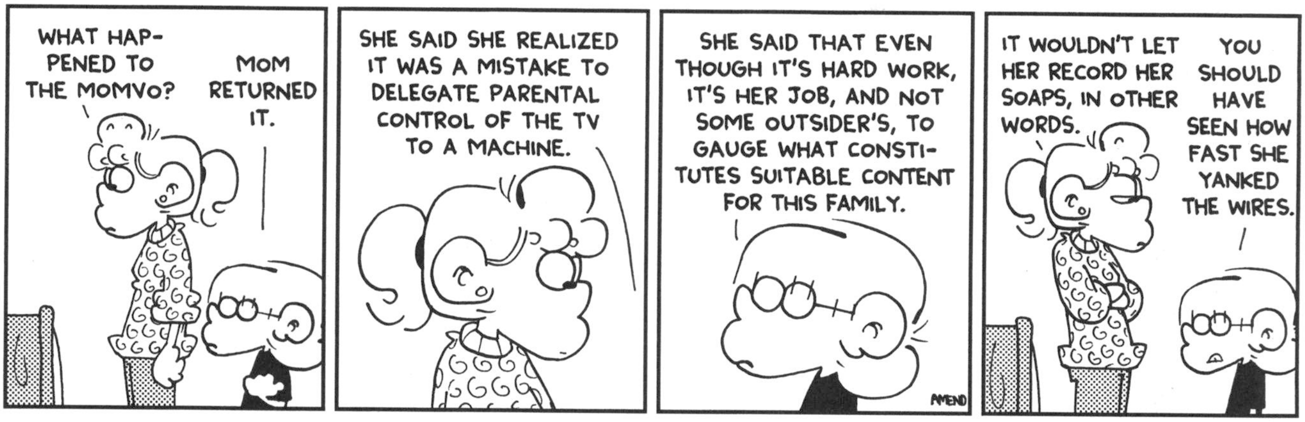
WHAT HAPPENED TO THE MOMVO?
MOM RETURNED IT.
SHE SAID SHE REALIZED IT WAS A MISTAKE TO DELEGATE PARENTAL CONTROL OF THE TV TO A MACHINE.
SHE SAID THAT EVEN THOUGH IT'S HARD WORK, IT'S HER JOB, AND NOT SOME OUTSIDER'S, TO GAUGE WHAT CONSTITUTES SUITABLE CONTENT FOR THIS FAMILY.
IT WOULDN'T LET HER RECORD HER SOAPS, IN OTHER WORDS.
YOU SHOULD HAVE SEEN HOW FAST SHE YANKED THE WIRES.

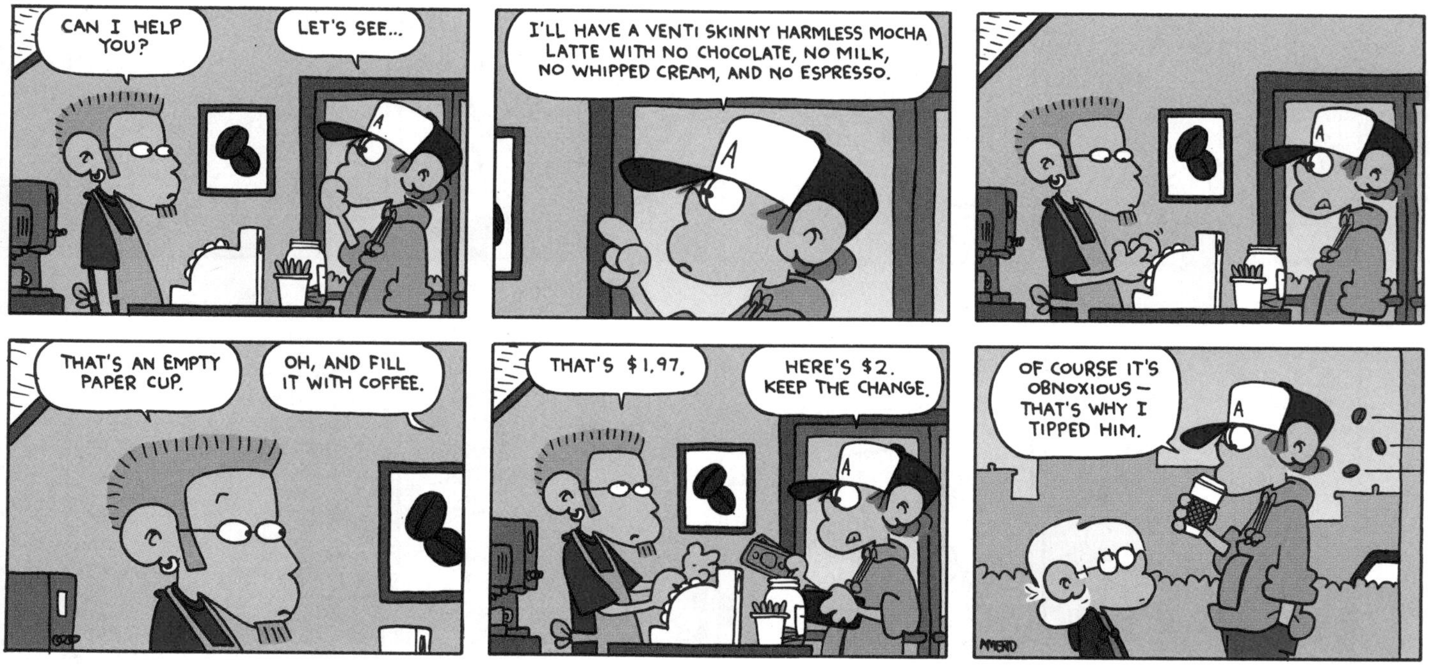
CAN I HELP YOU?
LET'S SEE...
I'LL HAVE A VENTI SKINNY HARMLESS MOCHA LATTE WITH NO CHOCOLATE, NO MILK, NO WHIPPED CREAM, AND NO ESPRESSO.
THAT'S AN EMPTY PAPER CUP.
OH, AND FILL IT WITH COFFEE.
THAT'S $1.97.
HERE'S $2. KEEP THE CHANGE.
OF COURSE IT'S OBNOXIOUS — THAT'S WHY I TIPPED HIM.

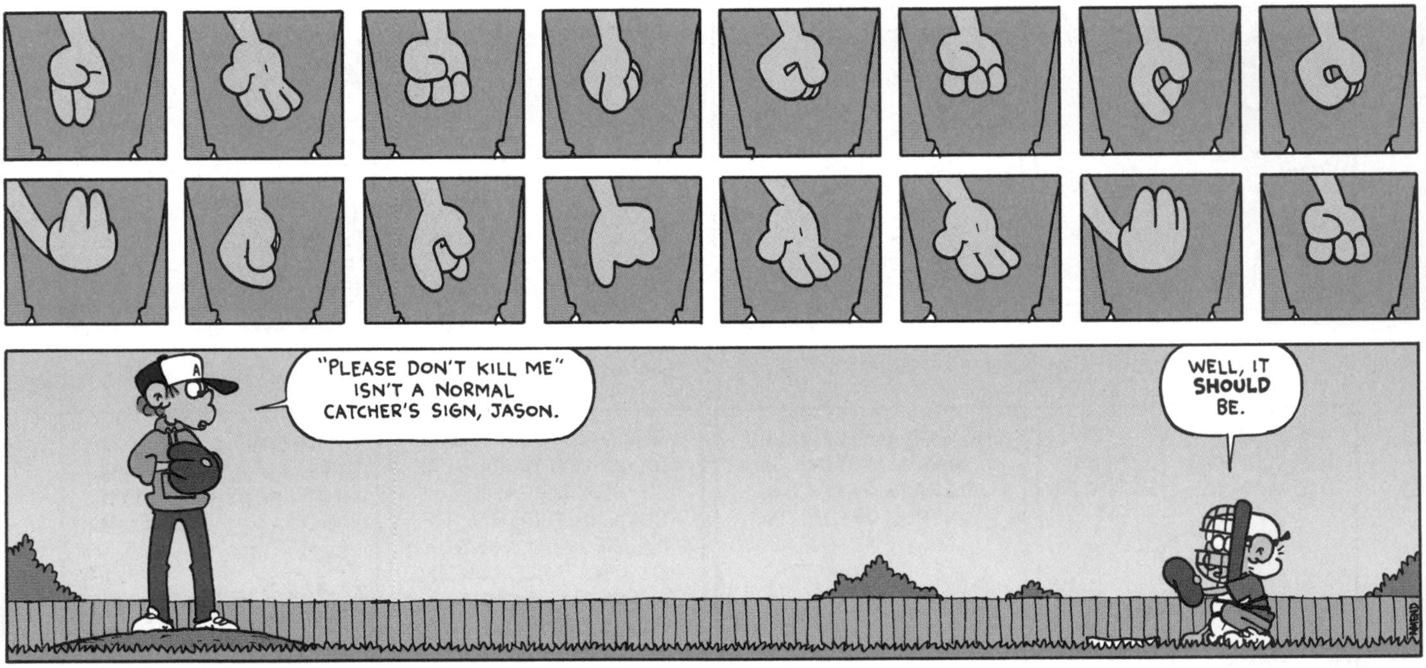
"PLEASE DON'T KILL ME" ISN'T A NORMAL CATCHER'S SIGN, JASON.
WELL, IT SHOULD BE.
AMEND

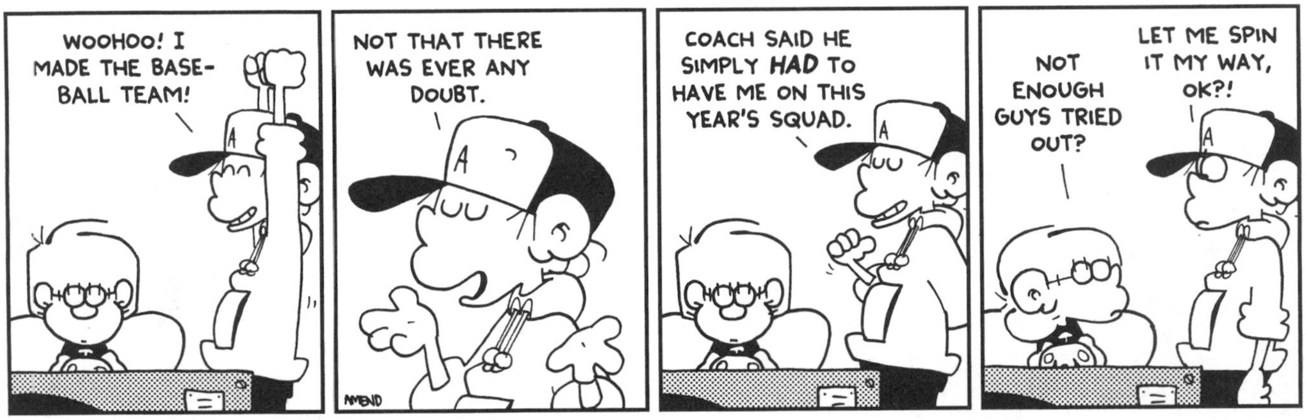
WOOHOO! I MADE THE BASE-BALL TEAM!
NOT THAT THERE WAS EVER ANY DOUBT.
AMEND
COACH SAID HE SIMPLY HAD TO HAVE ME ON THIS YEAR'S SQUAD.
NOT ENOUGH GUYS TRIED OUT?
LET ME SPIN IT MY WAY, OK?!

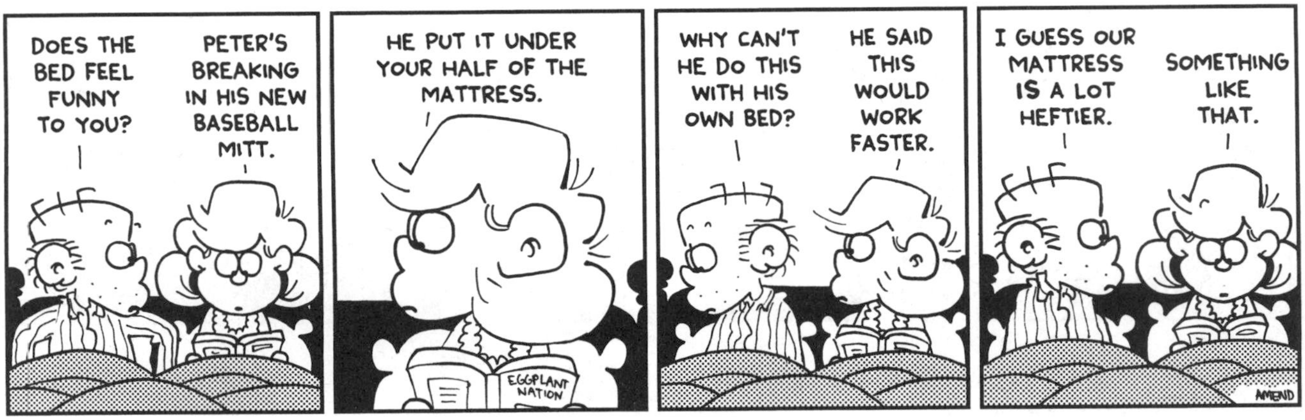
DOES THE BED FEEL FUNNY TO YOU?
PETER'S BREAKING IN HIS NEW BASEBALL MITT.
HE PUT IT UNDER YOUR HALF OF THE MATTRESS.
EGGPLANT NATION
WHY CAN'T HE DO THIS WITH HIS OWN BED?
HE SAID THIS WOULD WORK FASTER.
I GUESS OUR MATTRESS IS A LOT HEFTIER.
SOMETHING LIKE THAT.
AMEND

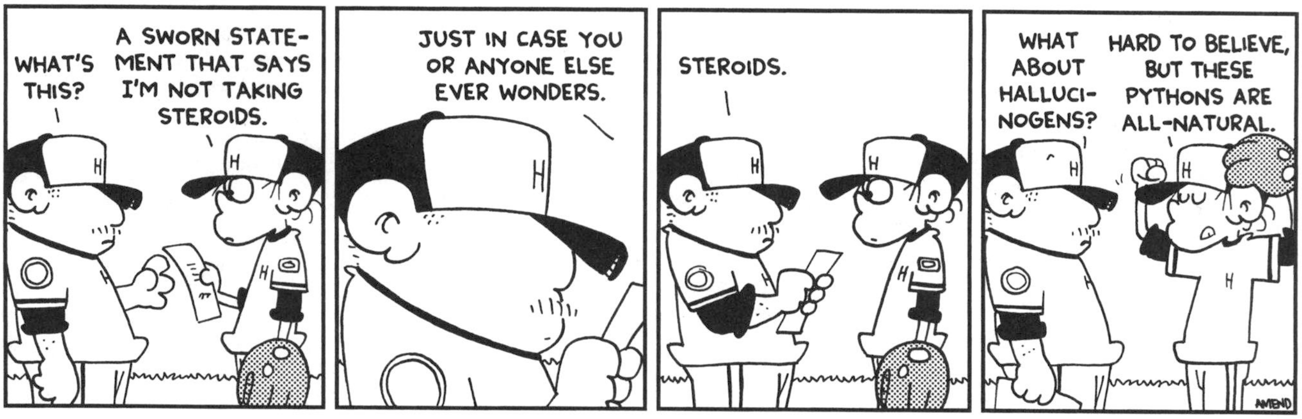
WHAT'S THIS?
A SWORN STATEMENT THAT SAYS I'M NOT TAKING STEROIDS.
JUST IN CASE YOU OR ANYONE ELSE EVER WONDERS.
STEROIDS.
WHAT ABOUT HALLUCINOGENS?
HARD TO BELIEVE, BUT THESE PYTHONS ARE ALL-NATURAL.
AMEND

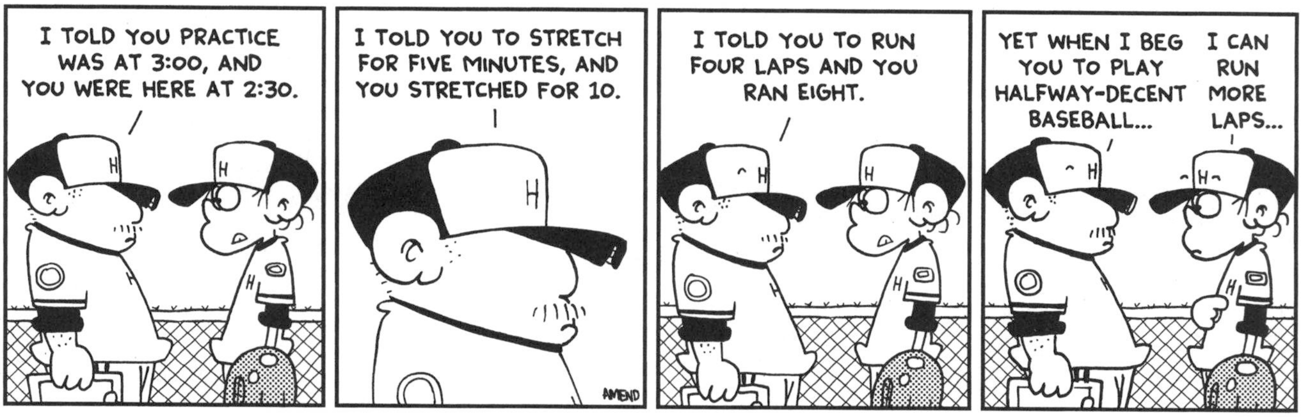
I TOLD YOU PRACTICE WAS AT 3:00, AND YOU WERE HERE AT 2:30.
I TOLD YOU TO STRETCH FOR FIVE MINUTES, AND YOU STRETCHED FOR 10.
AMEND
I TOLD YOU TO RUN FOUR LAPS AND YOU RAN EIGHT.
YET WHEN I BEG YOU TO PLAY HALFWAY-DECENT BASEBALL...
I CAN RUN MORE LAPS...

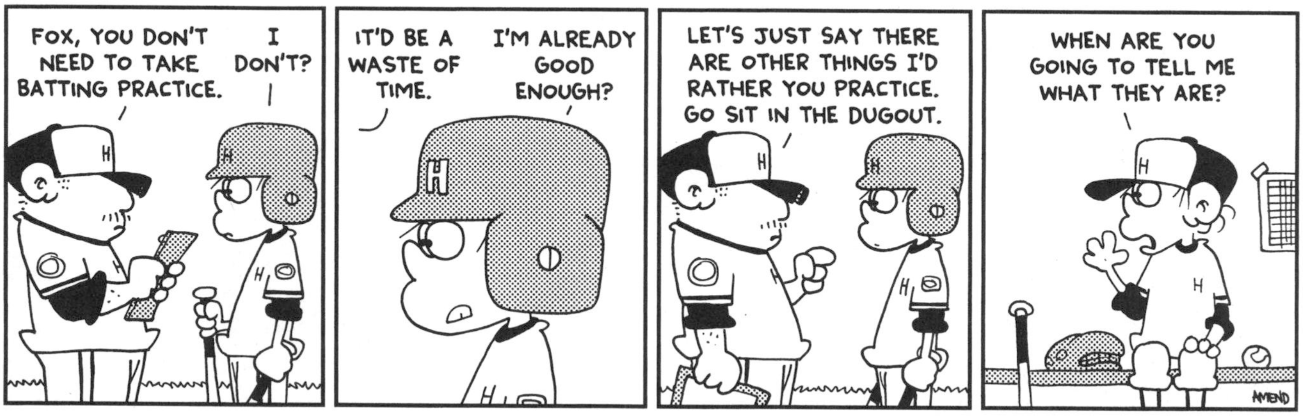
FOX, YOU DON'T NEED TO TAKE BATTING PRACTICE.
I DON'T?
IT'D BE A WASTE OF TIME.
I'M ALREADY GOOD ENOUGH?
LET'S JUST SAY THERE ARE OTHER THINGS I'D RATHER YOU PRACTICE. GO SIT IN THE DUGOUT.
WHEN ARE YOU GOING TO TELL ME WHAT THEY ARE?
AMEND

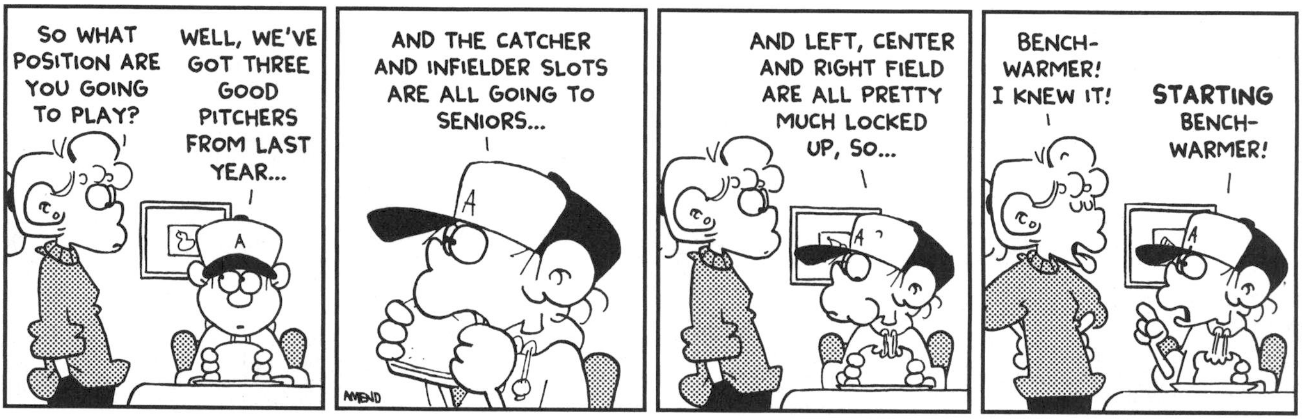
SO WHAT POSITION ARE YOU GOING TO PLAY?
WELL, WE'VE GOT THREE GOOD PITCHERS FROM LAST YEAR...
AND THE CATCHER AND INFIELDER SLOTS ARE ALL GOING TO SENIORS...
AMEND
AND LEFT, CENTER AND RIGHT FIELD ARE ALL PRETTY MUCH LOCKED UP, SO...
BENCH-WARMER! I KNEW IT!
STARTING BENCH-WARMER!

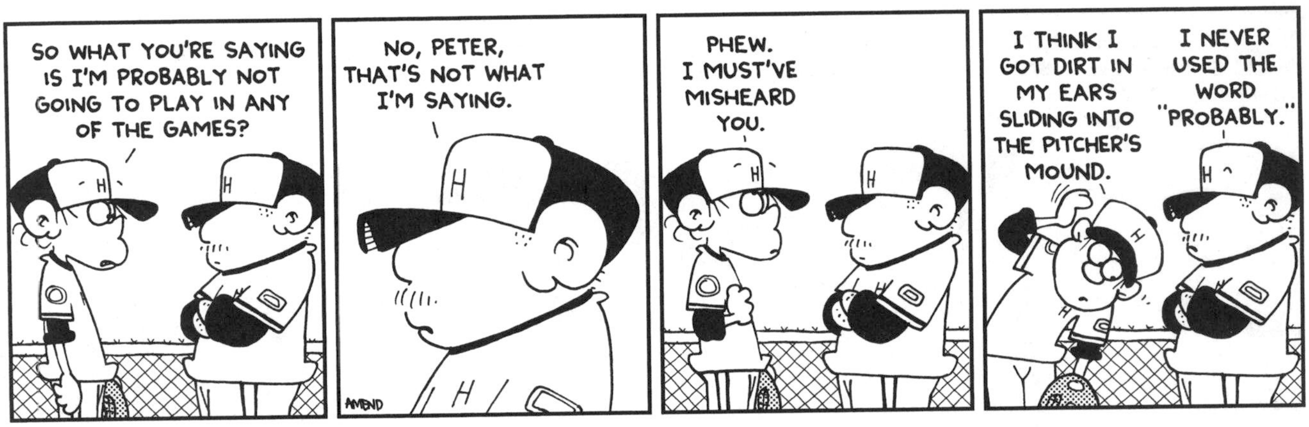
SO WHAT YOU'RE SAYING IS I'M PROBABLY NOT GOING TO PLAY IN ANY OF THE GAMES?
NO, PETER, THAT'S NOT WHAT I'M SAYING.
AMEND
PHEW. I MUST'VE MISHEARD YOU.
I THINK I GOT DIRT IN MY EARS SLIDING INTO THE PITCHER'S MOUND.
I NEVER USED THE WORD "PROBABLY."

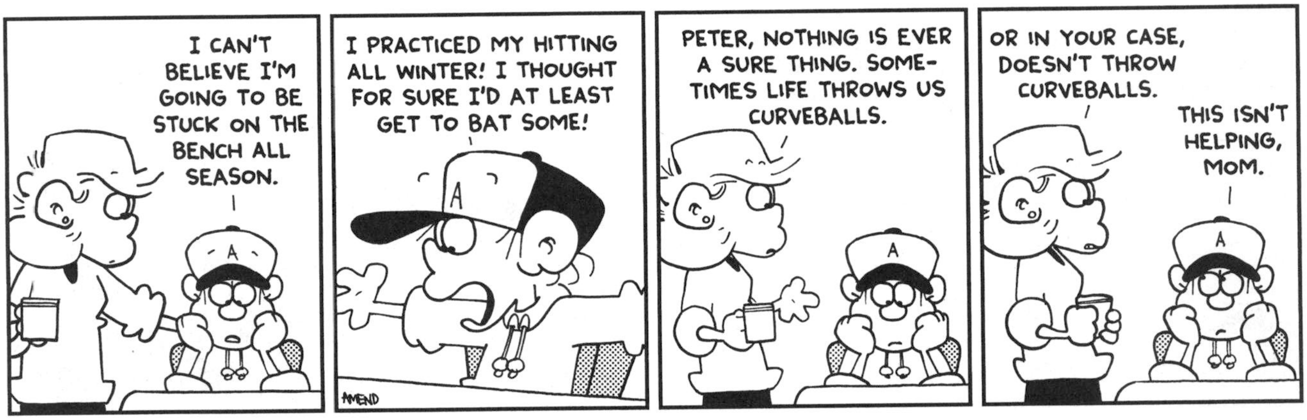
I CAN'T BELIEVE I'M GOING TO BE STUCK ON THE BENCH ALL SEASON.
I PRACTICED MY HITTING ALL WINTER! I THOUGHT FOR SURE I'D AT LEAST GET TO BAT SOME!
AMEND
PETER, NOTHING IS EVER A SURE THING. SOMETIMES LIFE THROWS US CURVEBALLS.
OR IN YOUR CASE, DOESN'T THROW CURVEBALLS.
THIS ISN'T HELPING, MOM.

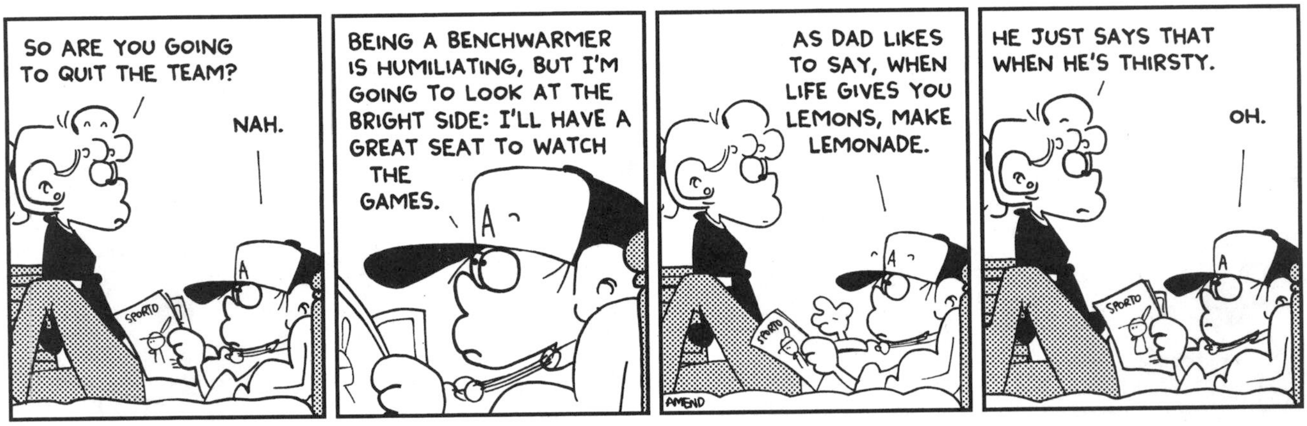
SO ARE YOU GOING TO QUIT THE TEAM?
NAH.
SPORTO
BEING A BENCHWARMER IS HUMILIATING, BUT I'M GOING TO LOOK AT THE BRIGHT SIDE: I'LL HAVE A GREAT SEAT TO WATCH THE GAMES.
AS DAD LIKES TO SAY, WHEN LIFE GIVES YOU LEMONS, MAKE LEMONADE.
AMEND
HE JUST SAYS THAT WHEN HE'S THIRSTY.
OH.

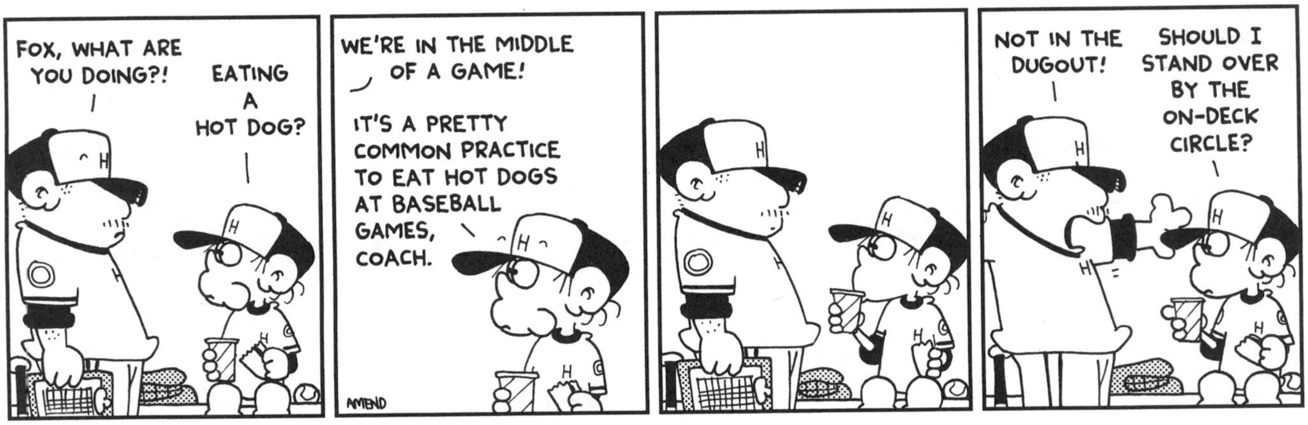
FOX, WHAT ARE YOU DOING?!
EATING A HOT DOG?
WE'RE IN THE MIDDLE OF A GAME!
IT'S A PRETTY COMMON PRACTICE TO EAT HOT DOGS AT BASEBALL GAMES, COACH.
AMEND
NOT IN THE DUGOUT!
SHOULD I STAND OVER BY THE ON-DECK CIRCLE?

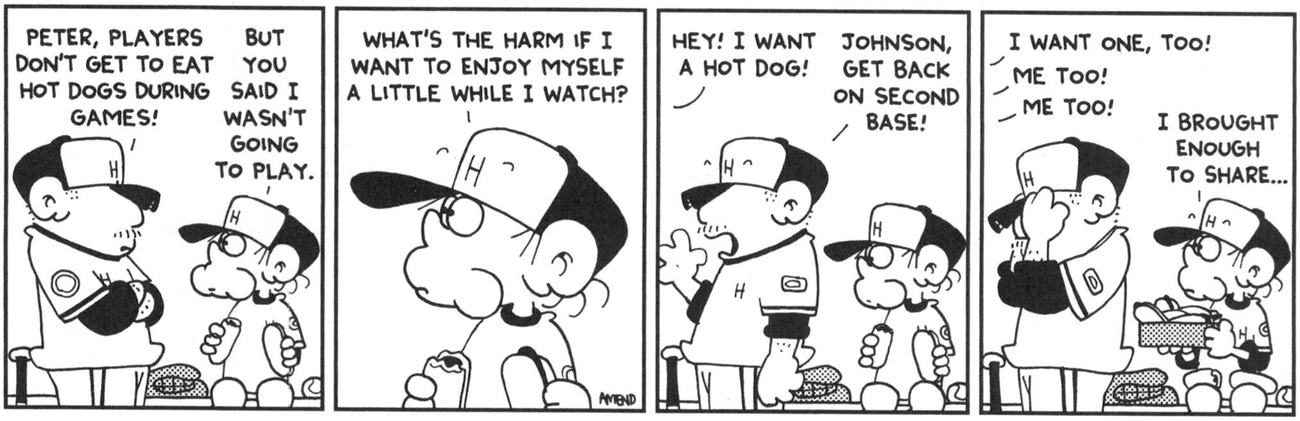
PETER, PLAYERS DON'T GET TO EAT HOT DOGS DURING GAMES!
BUT YOU SAID I WASN'T GOING TO PLAY.
WHAT'S THE HARM IF I WANT TO ENJOY MYSELF A LITTLE WHILE I WATCH?
HEY! I WANT A HOT DOG!
JOHNSON, GET BACK ON SECOND BASE!
I WANT ONE, TOO!
ME TOO!
ME TOO!
I BROUGHT ENOUGH TO SHARE...
AMEND

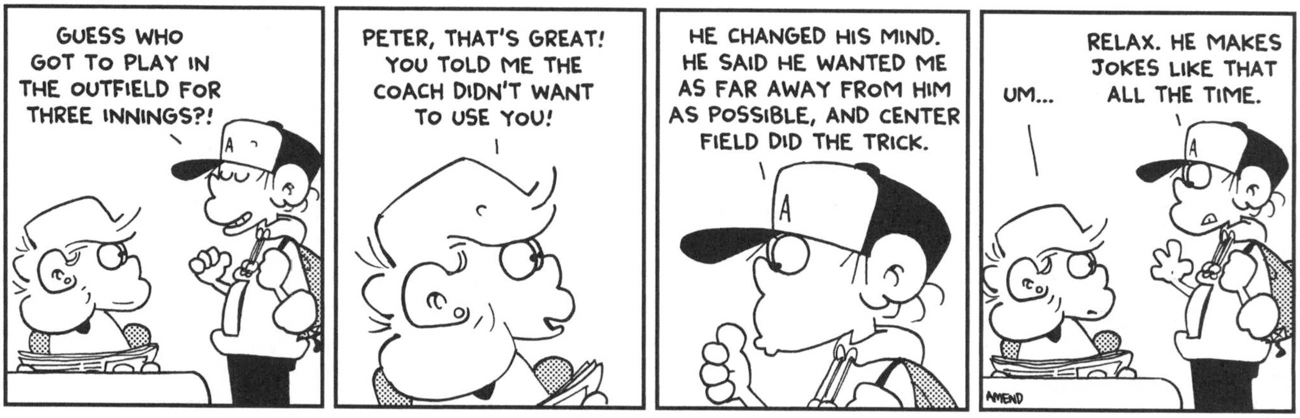
GUESS WHO GOT TO PLAY IN THE OUTFIELD FOR THREE INNINGS?!
PETER, THAT'S GREAT! YOU TOLD ME THE COACH DIDN'T WANT TO USE YOU!
HE CHANGED HIS MIND. HE SAID HE WANTED ME AS FAR AWAY FROM HIM AS POSSIBLE, AND CENTER FIELD DID THE TRICK.
UM...
RELAX. HE MAKES JOKES LIKE THAT ALL THE TIME.
AMEND

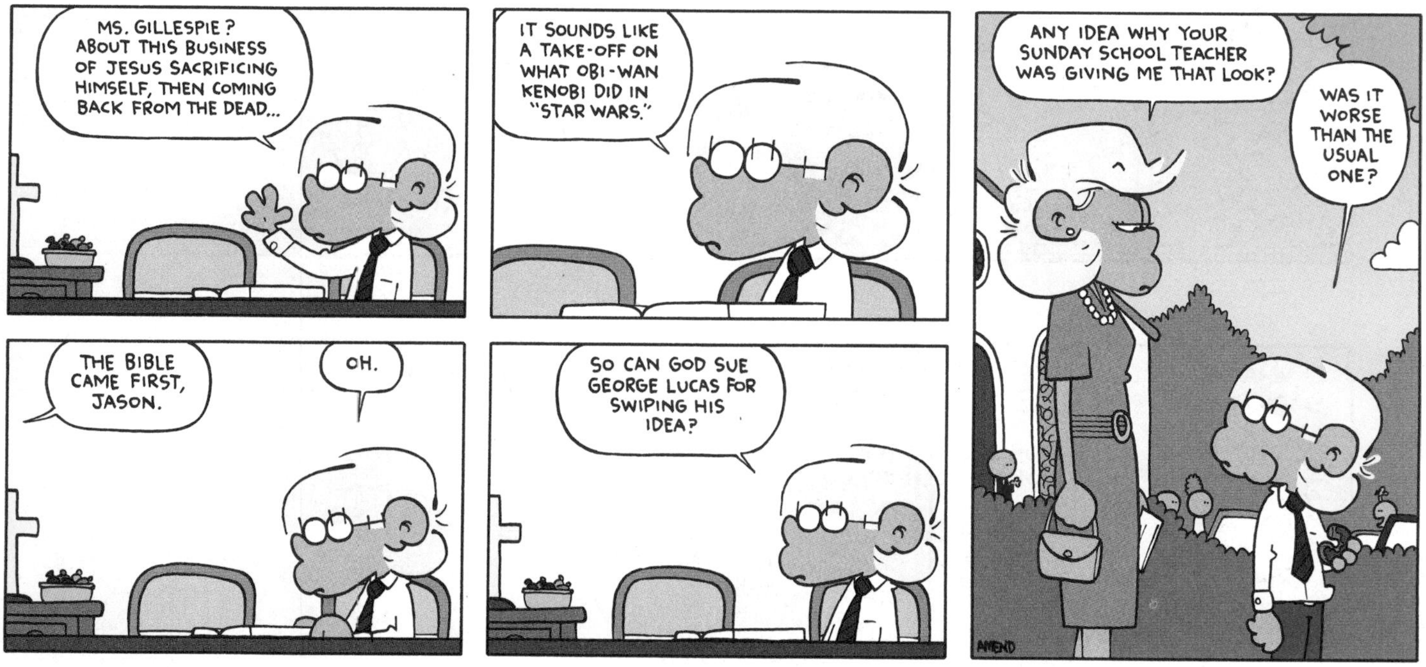
MS. GILLESPIE? ABOUT THIS BUSINESS OF JESUS SACRIFICING HIMSELF, THEN COMING BACK FROM THE DEAD...
IT SOUNDS LIKE A TAKE-OFF ON WHAT OBI-WAN KENOBI DID IN "STAR WARS."
THE BIBLE CAME FIRST, JASON.
OH.
SO CAN GOD SUE GEORGE LUCAS FOR SWIPING HIS IDEA?
ANY IDEA WHY YOUR SUNDAY SCHOOL TEACHER WAS GIVING ME THAT LOOK?
WAS IT WORSE THAN THE USUAL ONE?
AMEND

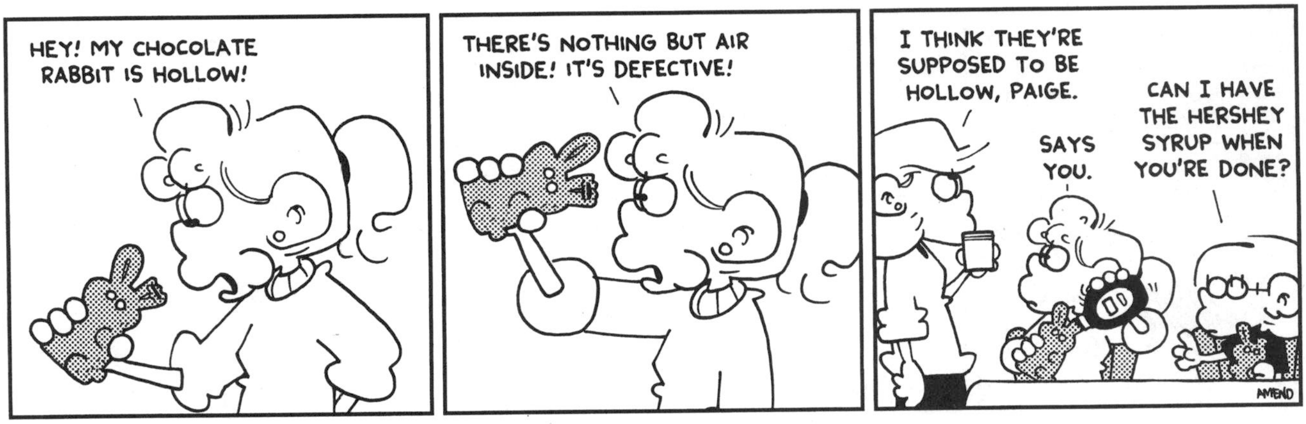
HEY! MY CHOCOLATE RABBIT IS HOLLOW!
THERE'S NOTHING BUT AIR INSIDE! IT'S DEFECTIVE!
I THINK THEY'RE SUPPOSED TO BE HOLLOW, PAIGE.
SAYS YOU.
CAN I HAVE THE HERSHEY SYRUP WHEN YOU'RE DONE?
AMEND

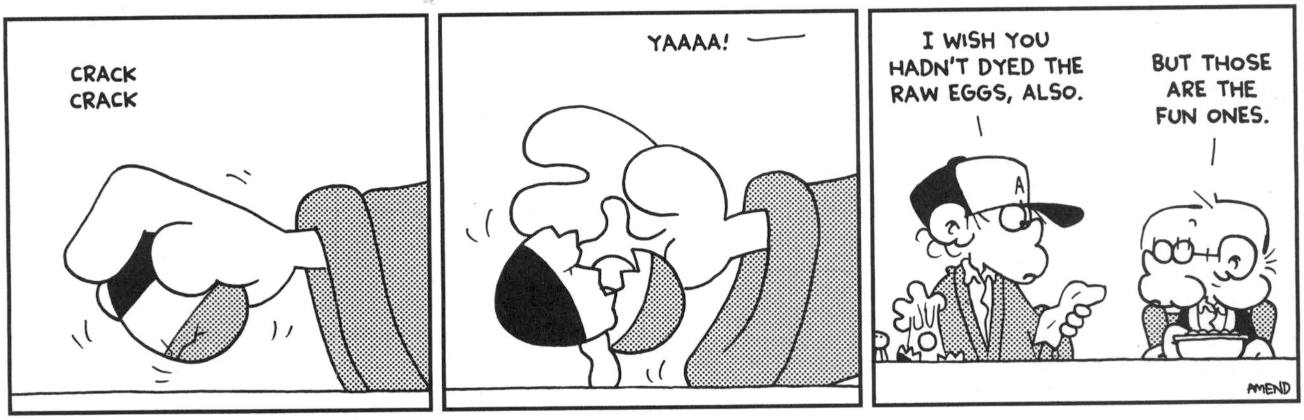
CRACK
CRACK
YAAAA!
I WISH YOU HADN'T DYED THE RAW EGGS, ALSO.
BUT THOSE ARE THE FUN ONES.
AMEND

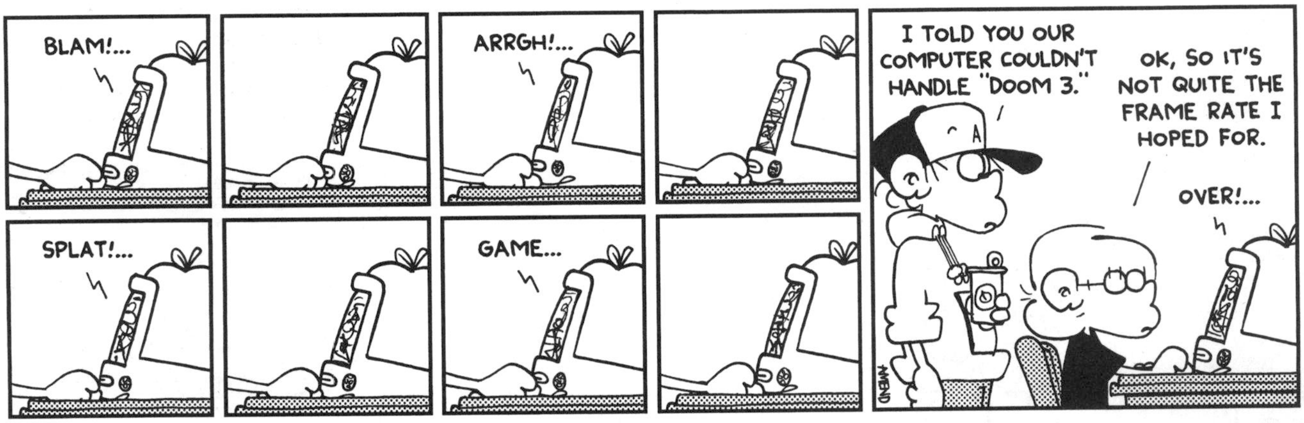
BLAM!...
ARRGH!...
SPLAT!...
GAME...
I TOLD YOU OUR COMPUTER COULDN'T HANDLE "DOOM 3."
OK, SO IT'S NOT QUITE THE FRAME RATE I HOPED FOR.
OVER!...
AMEND

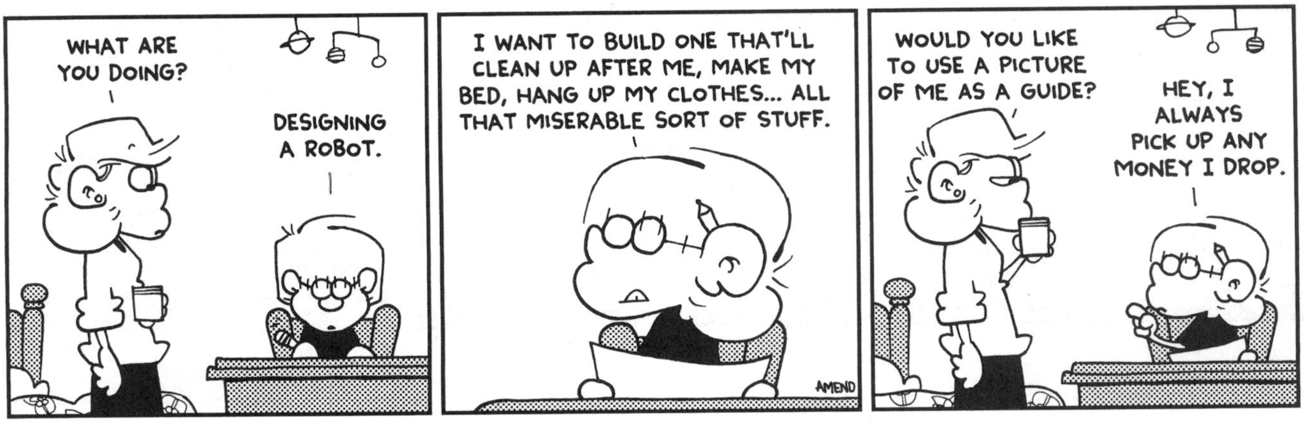
WHAT ARE YOU DOING?
DESIGNING A ROBOT.
I WANT TO BUILD ONE THAT'LL CLEAN UP AFTER ME, MAKE MY BED, HANG UP MY CLOTHES... ALL THAT MISERABLE SORT OF STUFF.
AMEND
WOULD YOU LIKE TO USE A PICTURE OF ME AS A GUIDE?
HEY, I ALWAYS PICK UP ANY MONEY I DROP.

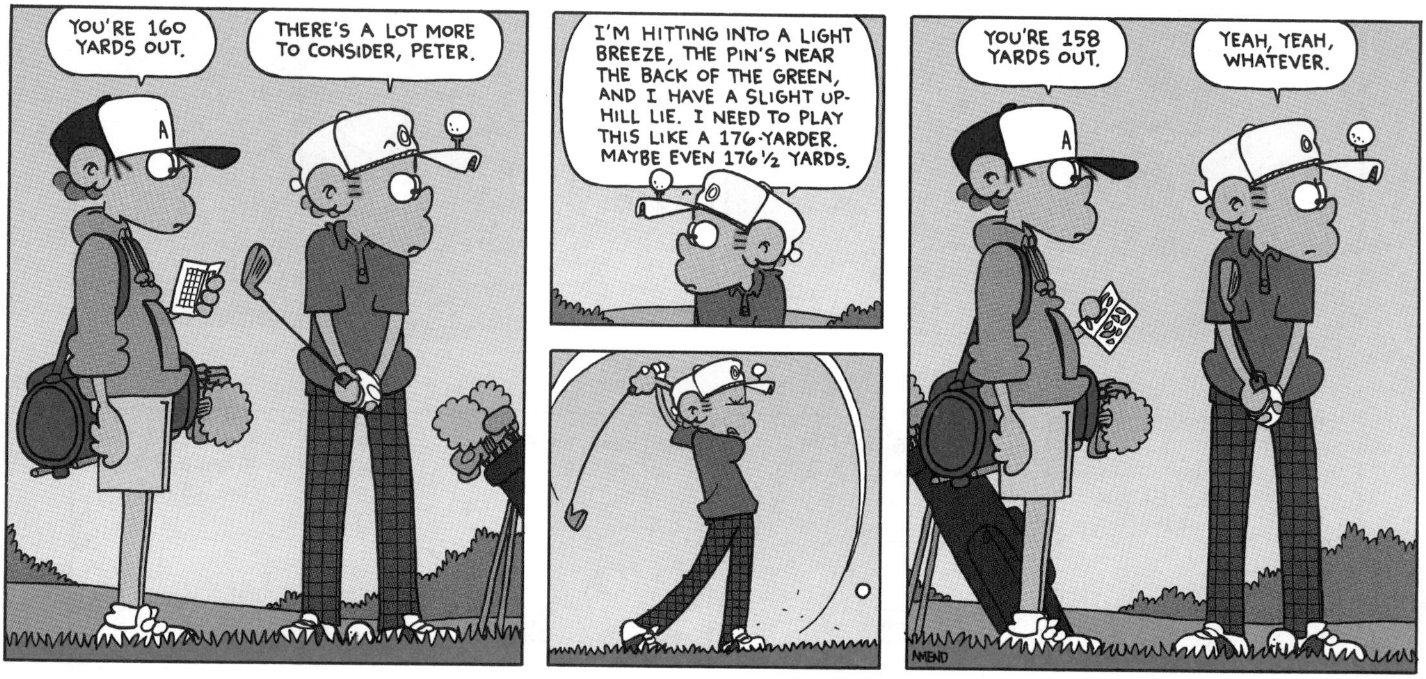
YOU'RE 160 YARDS OUT.
THERE'S A LOT MORE TO CONSIDER, PETER.
I'M HITTING INTO A LIGHT BREEZE, THE PIN'S NEAR THE BACK OF THE GREEN, AND I HAVE A SLIGHT UP-HILL LIE. I NEED TO PLAY THIS LIKE A 176-YARDER. MAYBE EVEN 176 1/2 YARDS.
YOU'RE 158 YARDS OUT.
YEAH, YEAH, WHATEVER.
AMEND

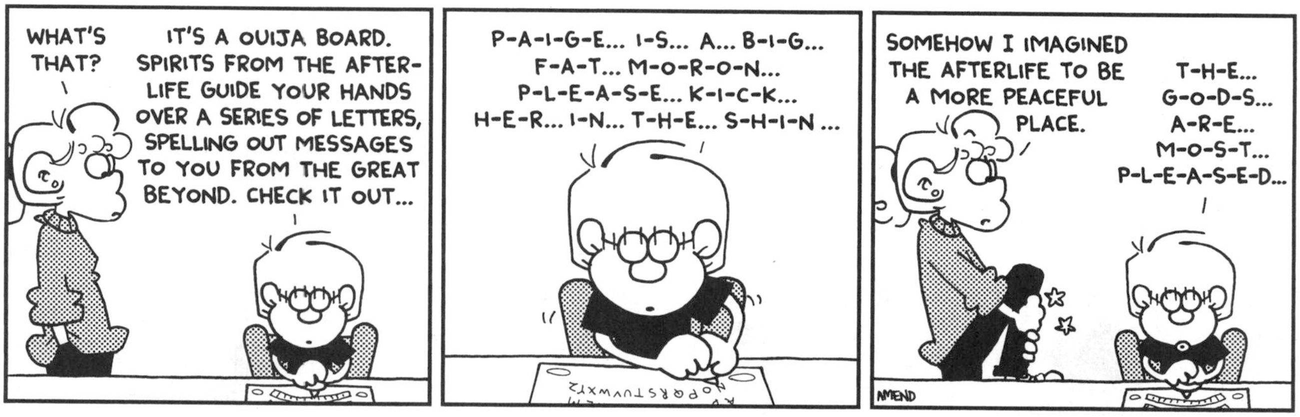
WHAT'S THAT?
IT'S A OUIJA BOARD. SPIRITS FROM THE AFTER-LIFE GUIDE YOUR HANDS OVER A SERIES OF LETTERS, SPELLING OUT MESSAGES TO YOU FROM THE GREAT BEYOND. CHECK IT OUT...
P-A-I-G-E... I-S... A... B-I-G... F-A-T... M-O-R-O-N... P-L-E-A-S-E... K-I-C-K... H-E-R... I-N... T-H-E... S-H-I-N ...
SOMEHOW I IMAGINED THE AFTERLIFE TO BE A MORE PEACEFUL PLACE.
T-H-E... G-O-D-S... A-R-E... M-O-S-T... P-L-E-A-S-E-D...
AMEND

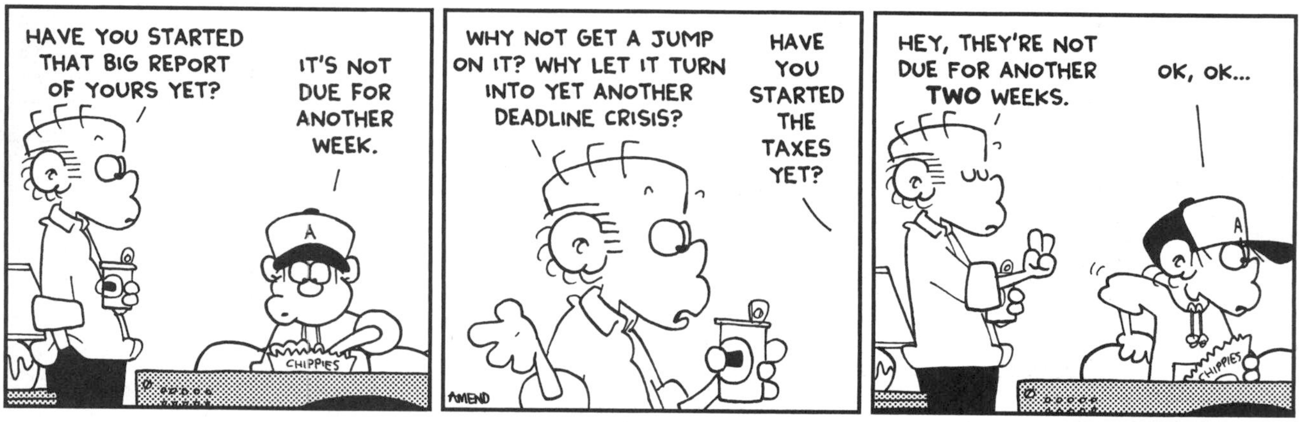
HAVE YOU STARTED THAT BIG REPORT OF YOURS YET?
IT'S NOT DUE FOR ANOTHER WEEK.
CHIPPIES
WHY NOT GET A JUMP ON IT? WHY LET IT TURN INTO YET ANOTHER DEADLINE CRISIS?
HAVE YOU STARTED THE TAXES YET?
AMEND
HEY, THEY'RE NOT DUE FOR ANOTHER **TWO** WEEKS.
OK, OK...
CHIPPIES

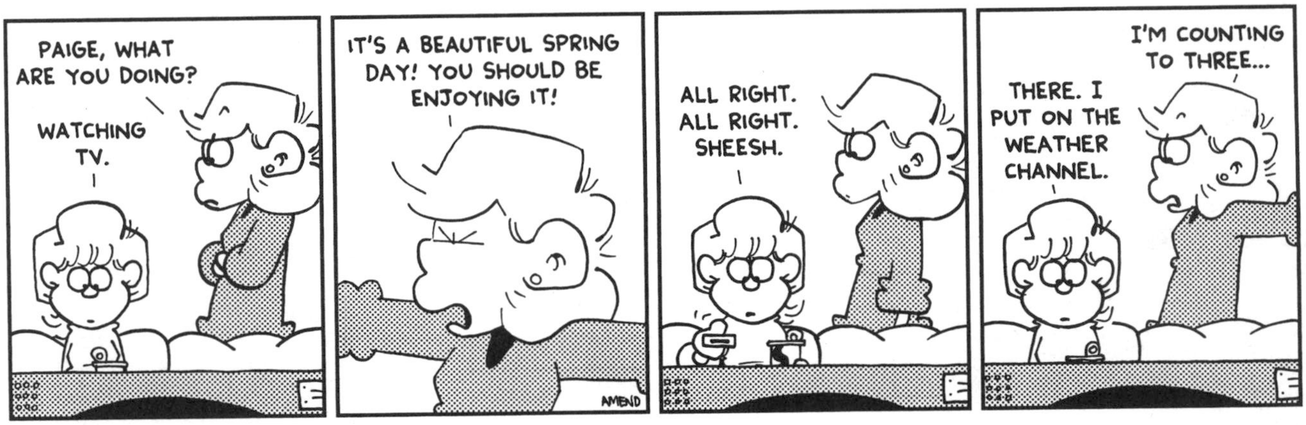
PAIGE, WHAT ARE YOU DOING?
WATCHING TV.
IT'S A BEAUTIFUL SPRING DAY! YOU SHOULD BE ENJOYING IT!
ALL RIGHT. ALL RIGHT. SHEESH.
THERE. I PUT ON THE WEATHER CHANNEL.
I'M COUNTING TO THREE...
AMEND

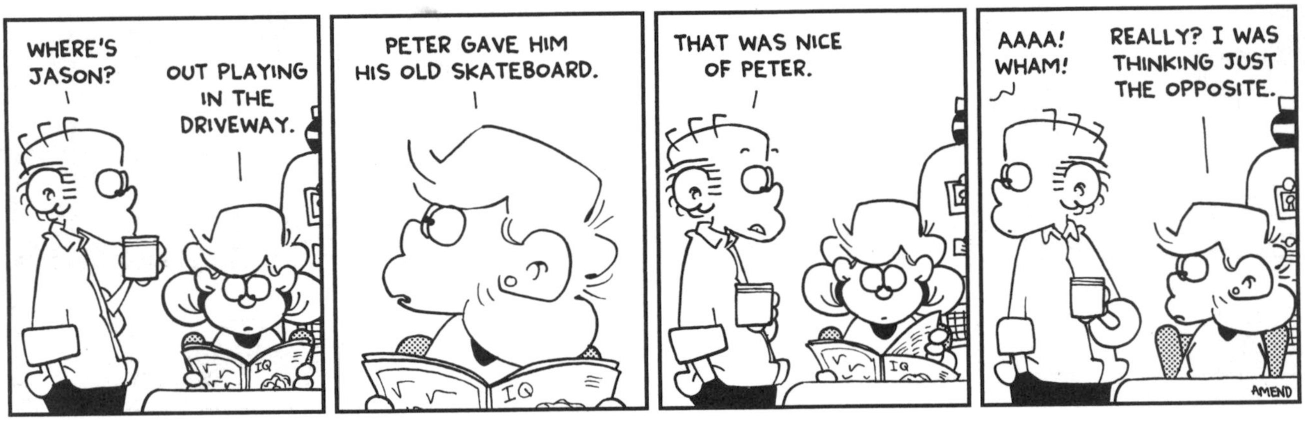
WHERE'S JASON?
OUT PLAYING IN THE DRIVEWAY.
PETER GAVE HIM HIS OLD SKATEBOARD.
THAT WAS NICE OF PETER.
AAAA! WHAM!
REALLY? I WAS THINKING JUST THE OPPOSITE.
AMEND

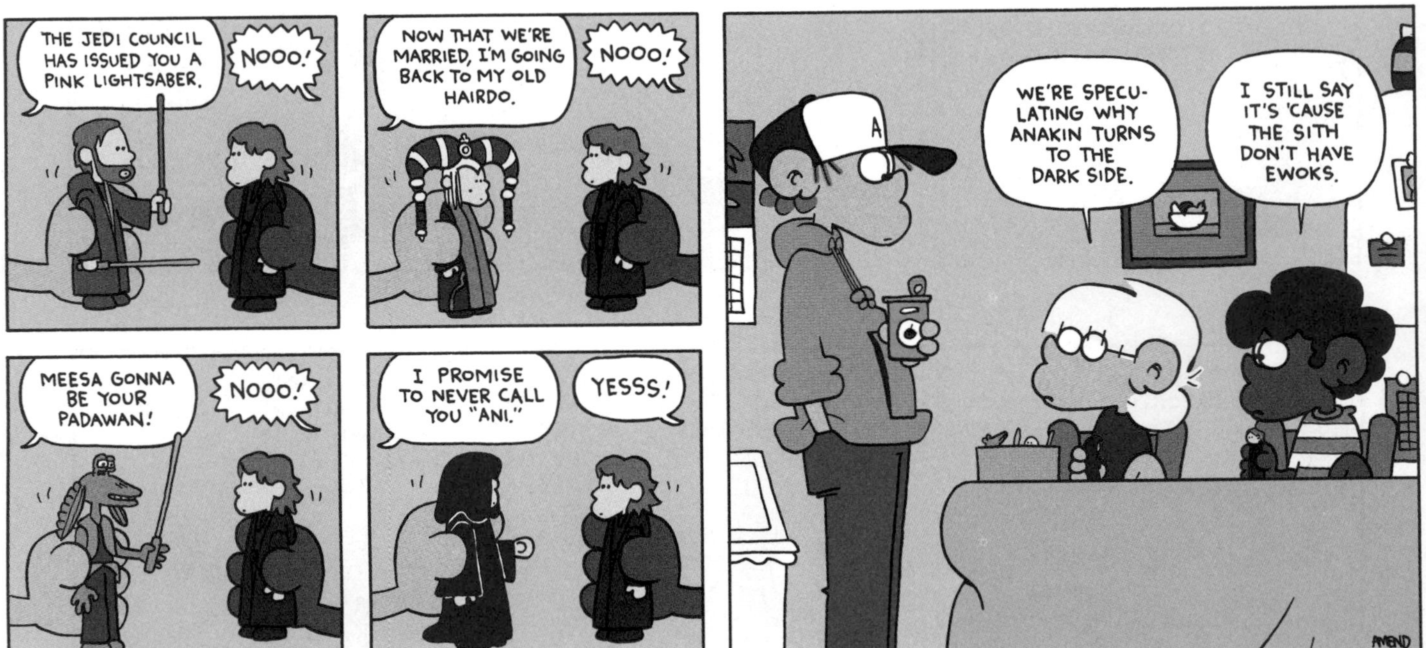
THE JEDI COUNCIL HAS ISSUED YOU A PINK LIGHTSABER.
NOOO!
NOW THAT WE'RE MARRIED, I'M GOING BACK TO MY OLD HAIRDO.
NOOO!
MEESA GONNA BE YOUR PADAWAN!
NOOO!
I PROMISE TO NEVER CALL YOU "ANI."
YESSS!
WE'RE SPECU-LATING WHY ANAKIN TURNS TO THE DARK SIDE.
I STILL SAY IT'S 'CAUSE THE SITH DON'T HAVE EWOKS.
AMEND

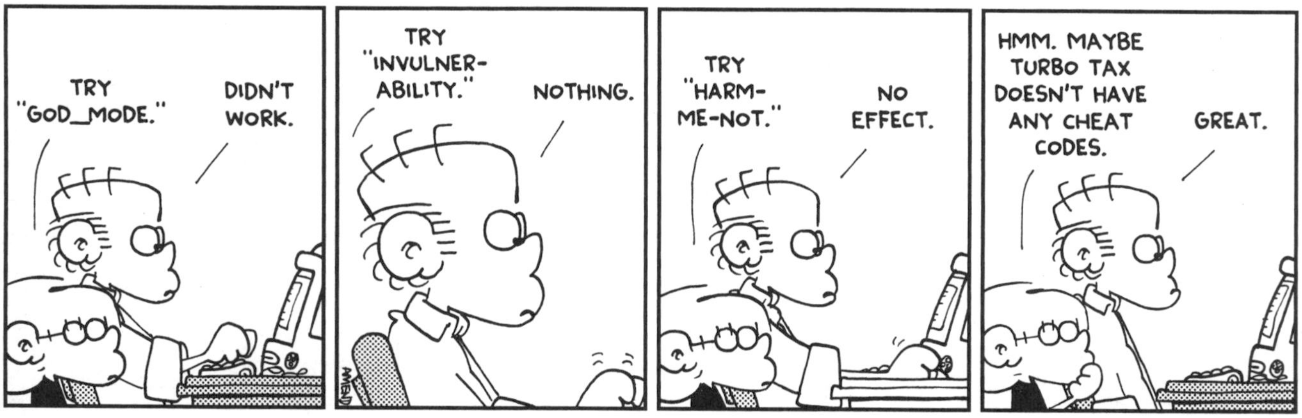
TRY "GOD_MODE."
DIDN'T WORK.
TRY "INVULNER-ABILITY."
NOTHING.
TRY "HARM-ME-NOT."
NO EFFECT.
HMM. MAYBE TURBO TAX DOESN'T HAVE ANY CHEAT CODES.
GREAT.
AMEND

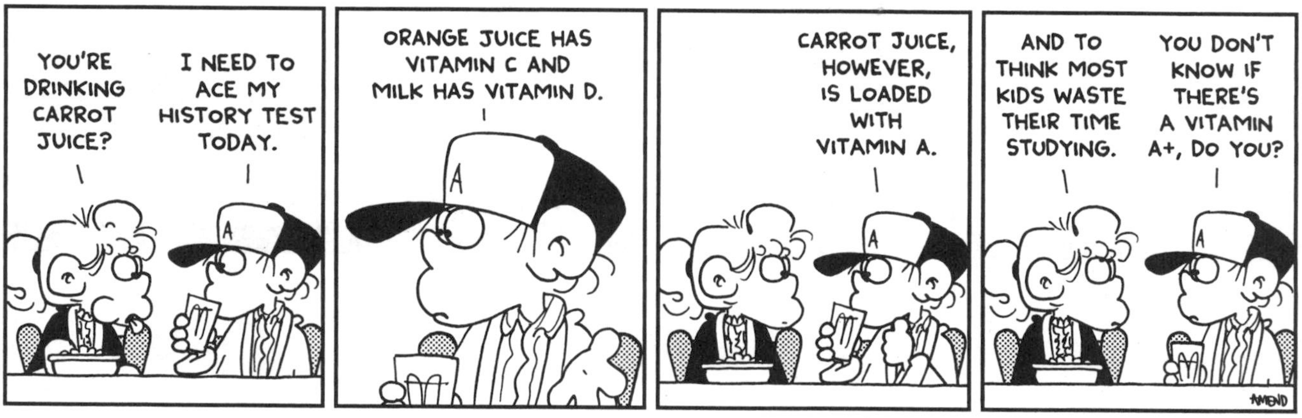
YOU'RE DRINKING CARROT JUICE?
I NEED TO ACE MY HISTORY TEST TODAY.
ORANGE JUICE HAS VITAMIN C AND MILK HAS VITAMIN D.
CARROT JUICE, HOWEVER, IS LOADED WITH VITAMIN A.
AND TO THINK MOST KIDS WASTE THEIR TIME STUDYING.
YOU DON'T KNOW IF THERE'S A VITAMIN A+, DO YOU?
AMEND

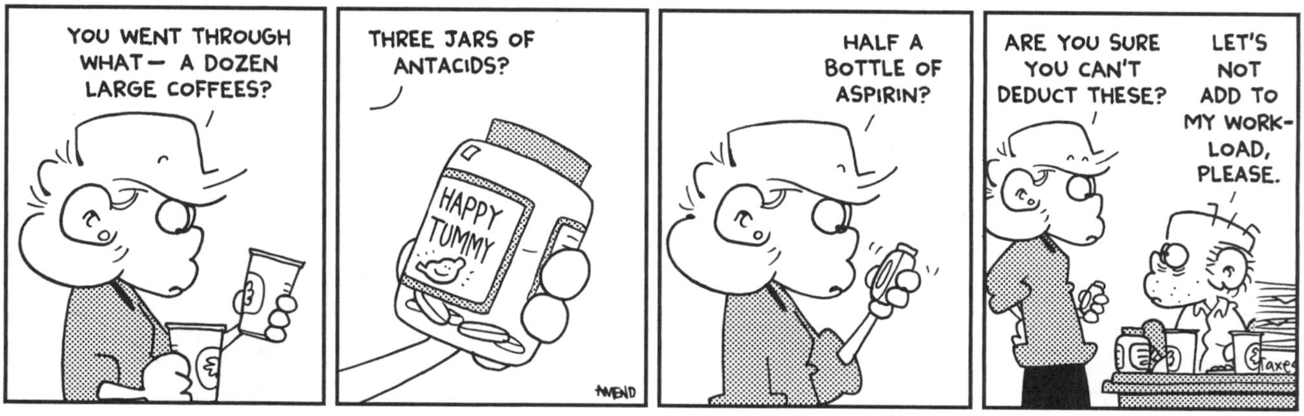
YOU WENT THROUGH WHAT— A DOZEN LARGE COFFEES?
THREE JARS OF ANTACIDS?
HAPPY TUMMY
AMEND
HALF A BOTTLE OF ASPIRIN?
ARE YOU SURE YOU CAN'T DEDUCT THESE?
LET'S NOT ADD TO MY WORK-LOAD, PLEASE.
Taxes

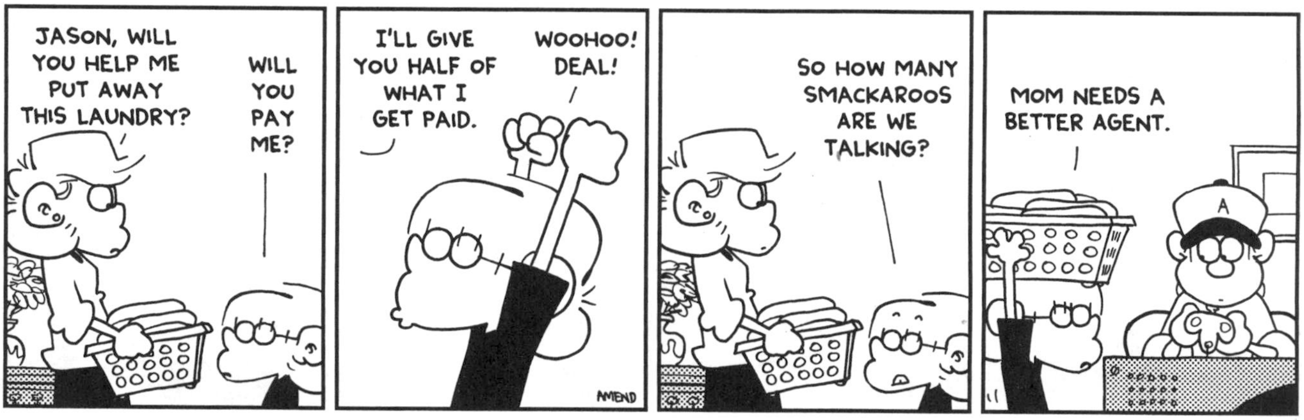
JASON, WILL YOU HELP ME PUT AWAY THIS LAUNDRY?
WILL YOU PAY ME?
I'LL GIVE YOU HALF OF WHAT I GET PAID.
WOOHOO! DEAL!
AMEND
SO HOW MANY SMACKAROOS ARE WE TALKING?
MOM NEEDS A BETTER AGENT.

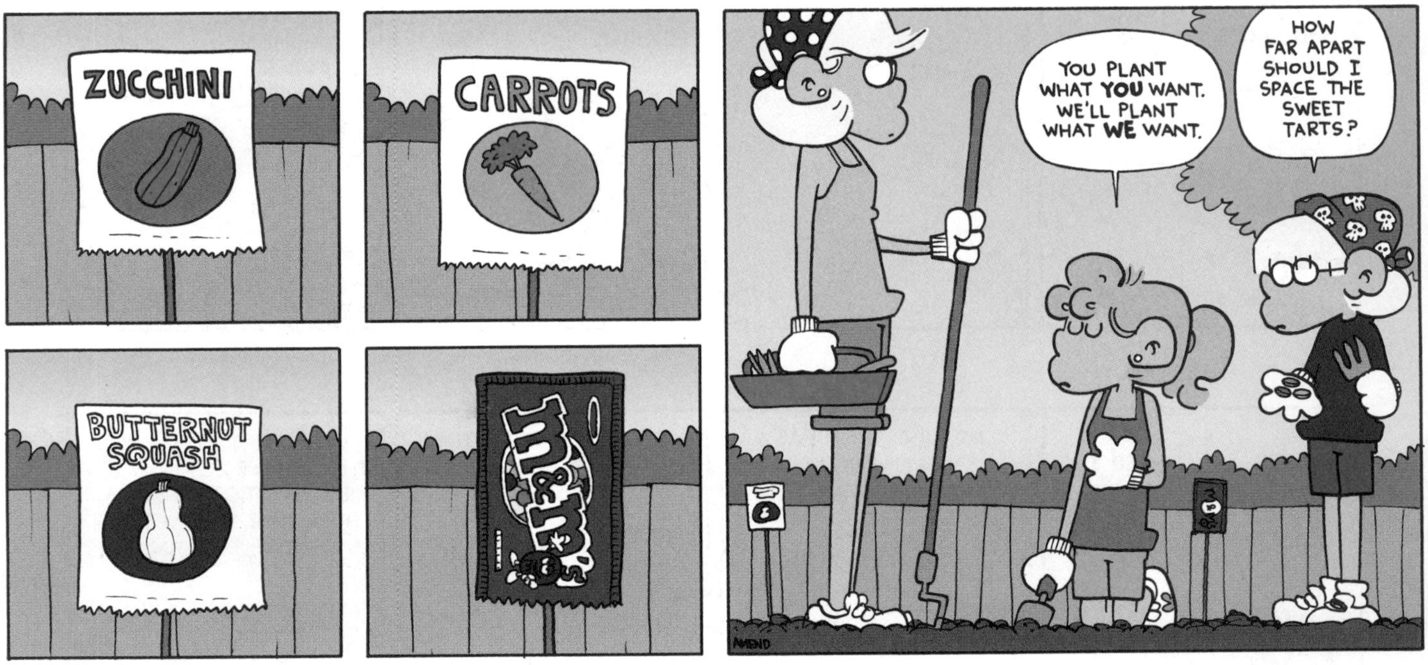
ZUCCHINI
CARROTS
BUTTERNUT SQUASH
m&m's
YOU PLANT WHAT YOU WANT. WE'LL PLANT WHAT WE WANT.
HOW FAR APART SHOULD I SPACE THE SWEET TARTS?
AMEND

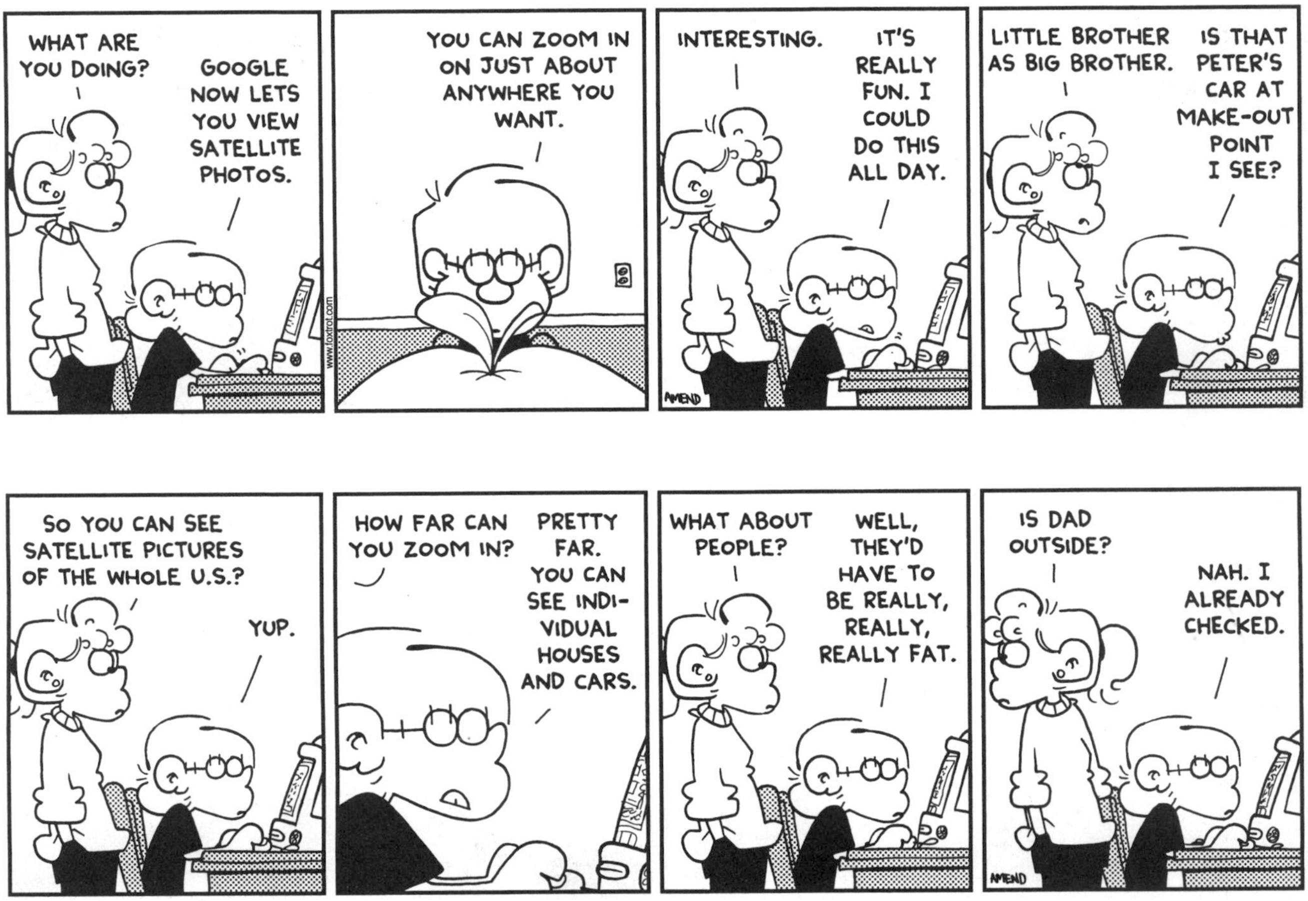
WHAT ARE YOU DOING?
GOOGLE NOW LETS YOU VIEW SATELLITE PHOTOS.
YOU CAN ZOOM IN ON JUST ABOUT ANYWHERE YOU WANT.
INTERESTING.
IT'S REALLY FUN. I COULD DO THIS ALL DAY.
LITTLE BROTHER AS BIG BROTHER.
IS THAT PETER'S CAR AT MAKE-OUT POINT I SEE?
SO YOU CAN SEE SATELLITE PICTURES OF THE WHOLE U.S.?
YUP.
HOW FAR CAN YOU ZOOM IN?
PRETTY FAR. YOU CAN SEE INDI-VIDUAL HOUSES AND CARS.
WHAT ABOUT PEOPLE?
WELL, THEY'D HAVE TO BE REALLY, REALLY, REALLY FAT.
IS DAD OUTSIDE?
NAH. I ALREADY CHECKED.
AMEND

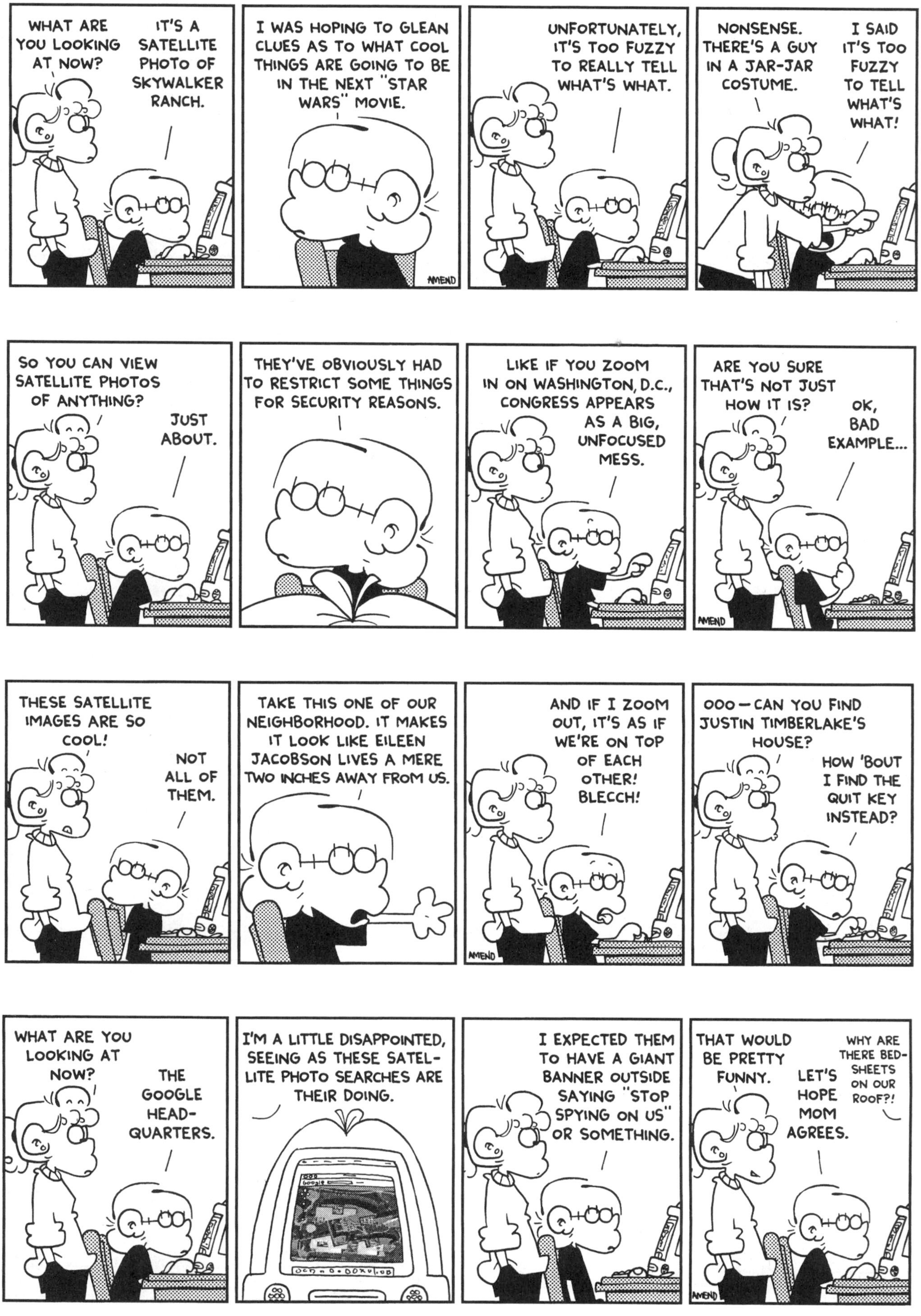
WHAT ARE YOU LOOKING AT NOW?
IT'S A SATELLITE PHOTO OF SKYWALKER RANCH.
I WAS HOPING TO GLEAN CLUES AS TO WHAT COOL THINGS ARE GOING TO BE IN THE NEXT "STAR WARS" MOVIE.
UNFORTUNATELY, IT'S TOO FUZZY TO REALLY TELL WHAT'S WHAT.
NONSENSE. THERE'S A GUY IN A JAR-JAR COSTUME.
I SAID IT'S TOO FUZZY TO TELL WHAT'S WHAT!
AMEND
SO YOU CAN VIEW SATELLITE PHOTOS OF ANYTHING?
JUST ABOUT.
THEY'VE OBVIOUSLY HAD TO RESTRICT SOME THINGS FOR SECURITY REASONS.
LIKE IF YOU ZOOM IN ON WASHINGTON, D.C., CONGRESS APPEARS AS A BIG, UNFOCUSED MESS.
ARE YOU SURE THAT'S NOT JUST HOW IT IS?
OK, BAD EXAMPLE...
AMEND
THESE SATELLITE IMAGES ARE SO COOL!
NOT ALL OF THEM.
TAKE THIS ONE OF OUR NEIGHBORHOOD. IT MAKES IT LOOK LIKE EILEEN JACOBSON LIVES A MERE TWO INCHES AWAY FROM US.
AND IF I ZOOM OUT, IT'S AS IF WE'RE ON TOP OF EACH OTHER! BLECCH!
AMEND
OOO—CAN YOU FIND JUSTIN TIMBERLAKE'S HOUSE?
HOW 'BOUT I FIND THE QUIT KEY INSTEAD?
WHAT ARE YOU LOOKING AT NOW?
THE GOOGLE HEAD-QUARTERS.
I'M A LITTLE DISAPPOINTED, SEEING AS THESE SATEL-LITE PHOTO SEARCHES ARE THEIR DOING.
I EXPECTED THEM TO HAVE A GIANT BANNER OUTSIDE SAYING "STOP SPYING ON US" OR SOMETHING.
THAT WOULD BE PRETTY FUNNY.
LET'S HOPE MOM AGREES.
WHY ARE THERE BED-SHEETS ON OUR ROOF?!
AMEND

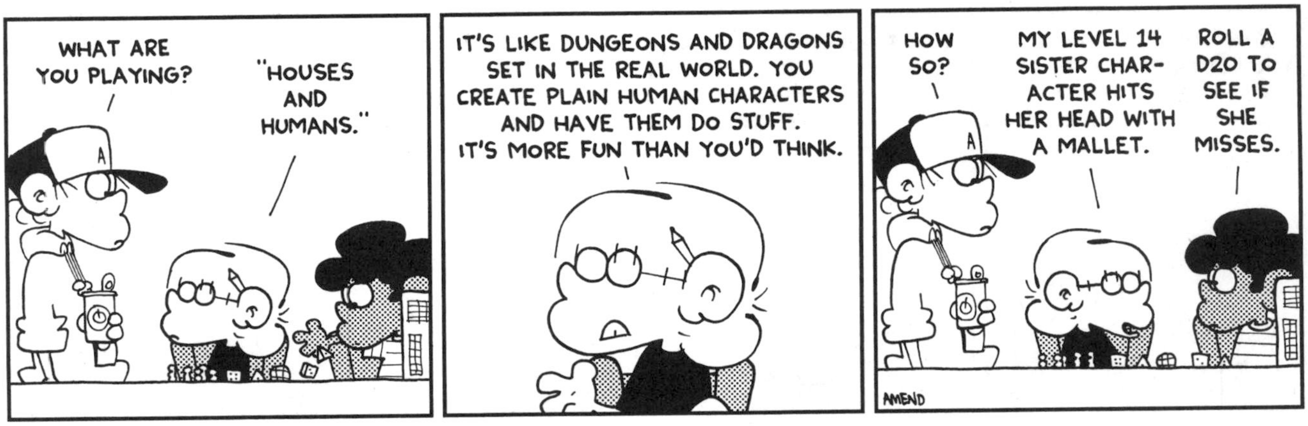
WHAT ARE YOU PLAYING?
"HOUSES AND HUMANS."
IT'S LIKE DUNGEONS AND DRAGONS SET IN THE REAL WORLD. YOU CREATE PLAIN HUMAN CHARACTERS AND HAVE THEM DO STUFF. IT'S MORE FUN THAN YOU'D THINK.
HOW SO?
MY LEVEL 14 SISTER CHARACTER HITS HER HEAD WITH A MALLET.
ROLL A D20 TO SEE IF SHE MISSES.
AMEND

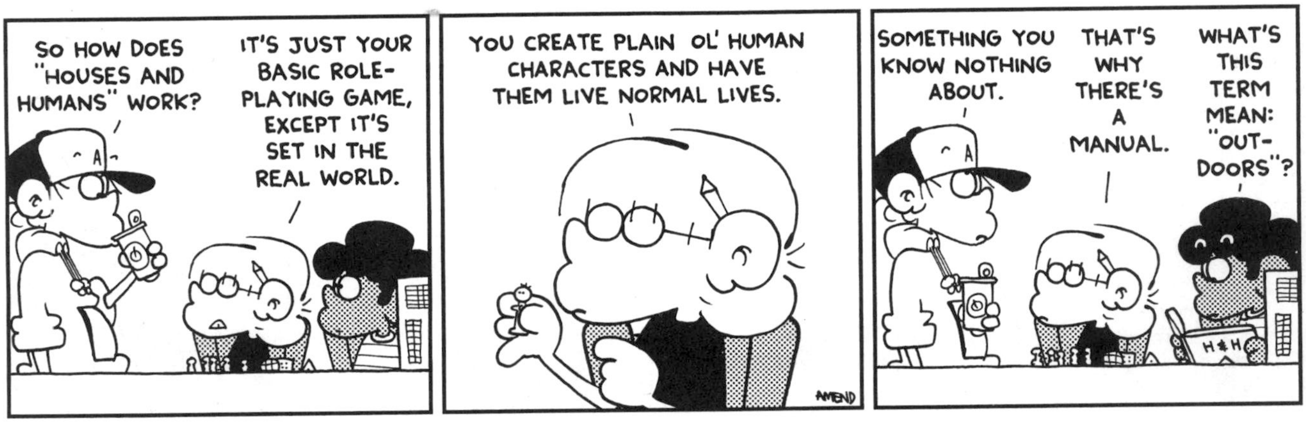
SO HOW DOES "HOUSES AND HUMANS" WORK?
IT'S JUST YOUR BASIC ROLE-PLAYING GAME, EXCEPT IT'S SET IN THE REAL WORLD.
YOU CREATE PLAIN OL' HUMAN CHARACTERS AND HAVE THEM LIVE NORMAL LIVES.
AMEND
SOMETHING YOU KNOW NOTHING ABOUT.
THAT'S WHY THERE'S A MANUAL.
WHAT'S THIS TERM MEAN: "OUT-DOORS"?
H & H

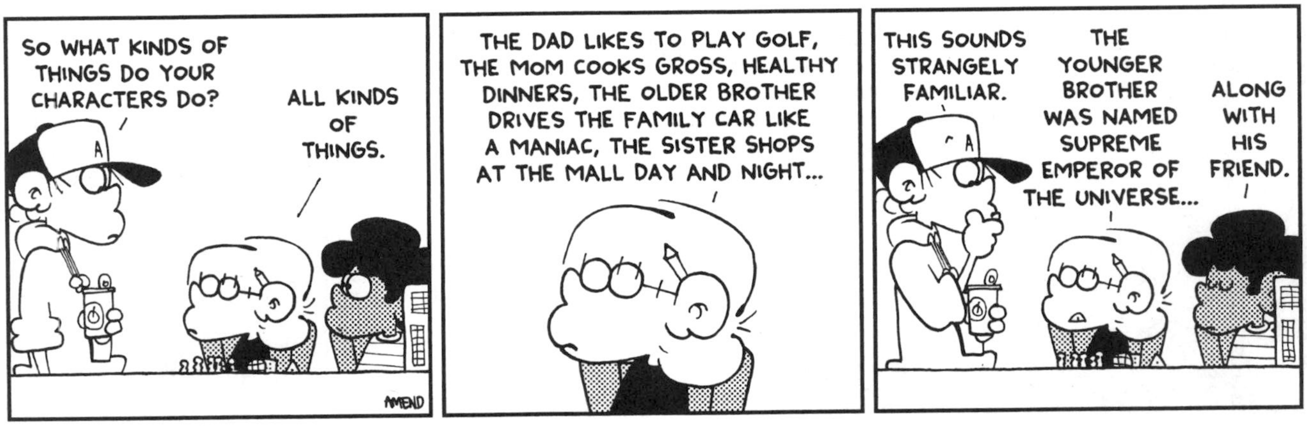
SO WHAT KINDS OF THINGS DO YOUR CHARACTERS DO?
ALL KINDS OF THINGS.
AMEND
THE DAD LIKES TO PLAY GOLF, THE MOM COOKS GROSS, HEALTHY DINNERS, THE OLDER BROTHER DRIVES THE FAMILY CAR LIKE A MANIAC, THE SISTER SHOPS AT THE MALL DAY AND NIGHT...
THIS SOUNDS STRANGELY FAMILIAR.
THE YOUNGER BROTHER WAS NAMED SUPREME EMPEROR OF THE UNIVERSE...
ALONG WITH HIS FRIEND.

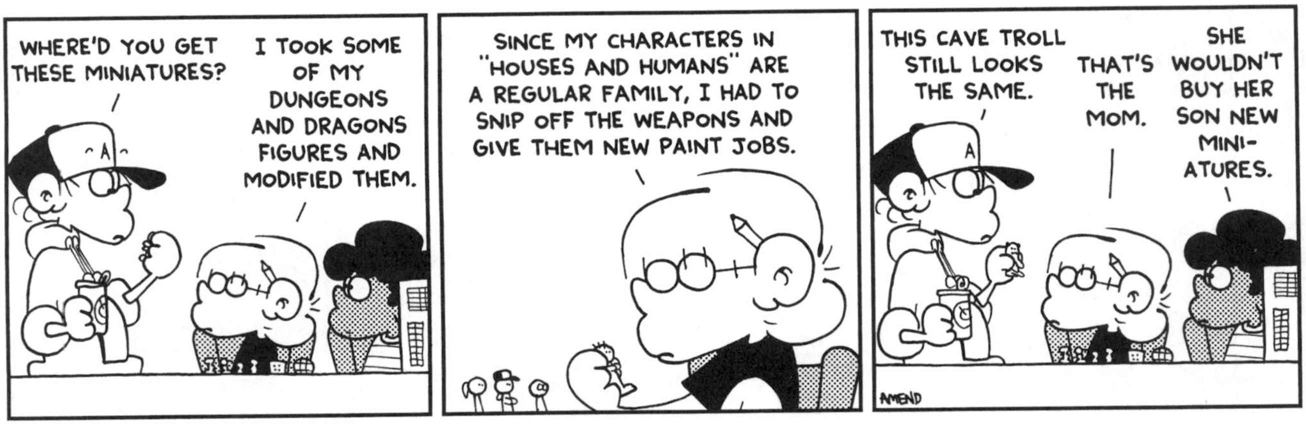
WHERE'D YOU GET THESE MINIATURES?
I TOOK SOME OF MY DUNGEONS AND DRAGONS FIGURES AND MODIFIED THEM.
SINCE MY CHARACTERS IN "HOUSES AND HUMANS" ARE A REGULAR FAMILY, I HAD TO SNIP OFF THE WEAPONS AND GIVE THEM NEW PAINT JOBS.
THIS CAVE TROLL STILL LOOKS THE SAME.
THAT'S THE MOM.
SHE WOULDN'T BUY HER SON NEW MINI-ATURES.
AMEND

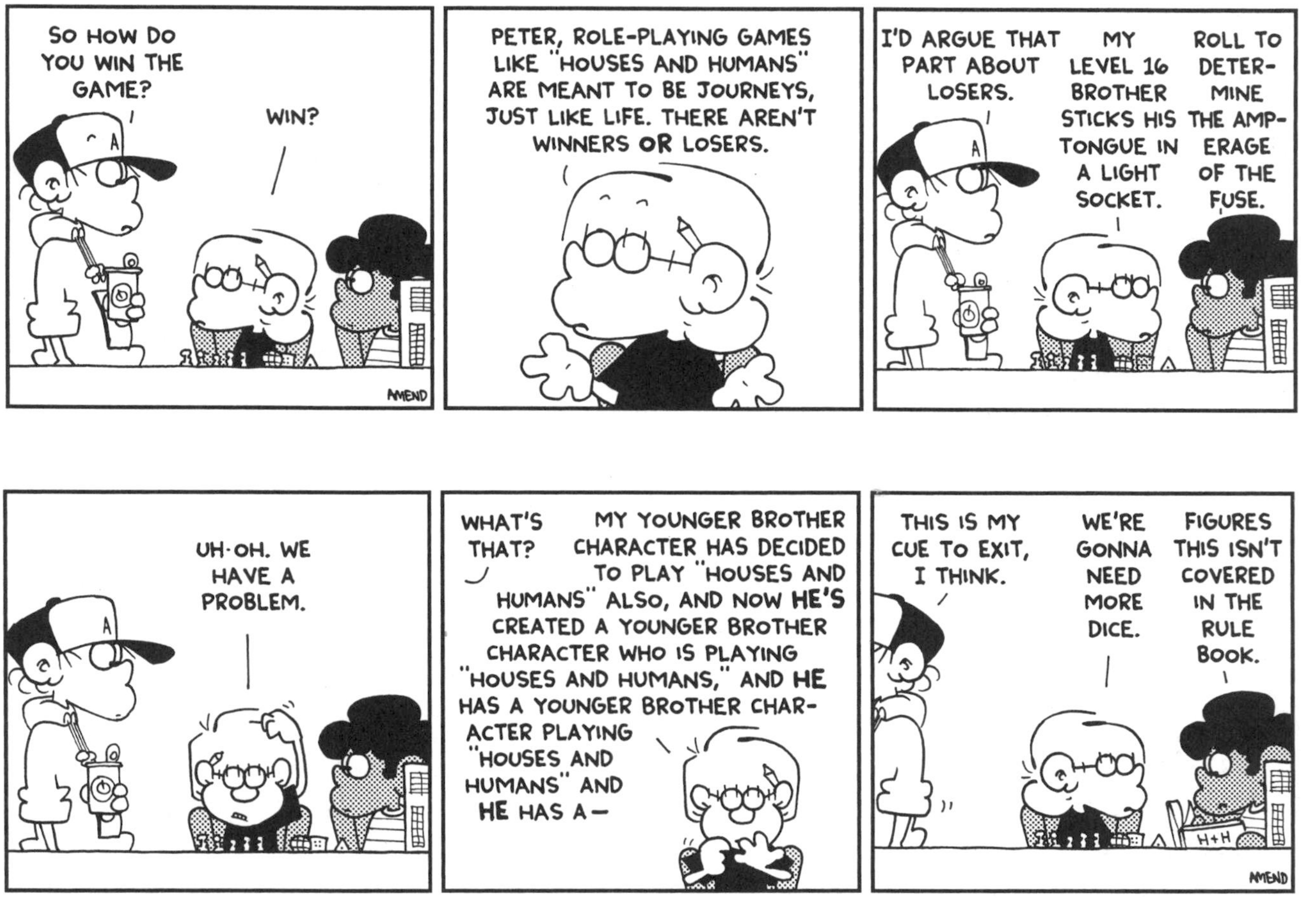
SO HOW DO YOU WIN THE GAME?
WIN?
PETER, ROLE-PLAYING GAMES LIKE "HOUSES AND HUMANS" ARE MEANT TO BE JOURNEYS, JUST LIKE LIFE. THERE AREN'T WINNERS **OR** LOSERS.
I'D ARGUE THAT PART ABOUT LOSERS.
MY LEVEL 16 BROTHER STICKS HIS TONGUE IN A LIGHT SOCKET.
ROLL TO DETERMINE THE AMPERAGE OF THE FUSE.
UH-OH. WE HAVE A PROBLEM.
WHAT'S THAT?
MY YOUNGER BROTHER CHARACTER HAS DECIDED TO PLAY "HOUSES AND HUMANS" ALSO, AND NOW **HE'S** CREATED A YOUNGER BROTHER CHARACTER WHO IS PLAYING "HOUSES AND HUMANS," AND **HE** HAS A YOUNGER BROTHER CHARACTER PLAYING "HOUSES AND HUMANS" AND **HE** HAS A—
THIS IS MY CUE TO EXIT, I THINK.
WE'RE GONNA NEED MORE DICE.
FIGURES THIS ISN'T COVERED IN THE RULE BOOK.
H+H
AMEND

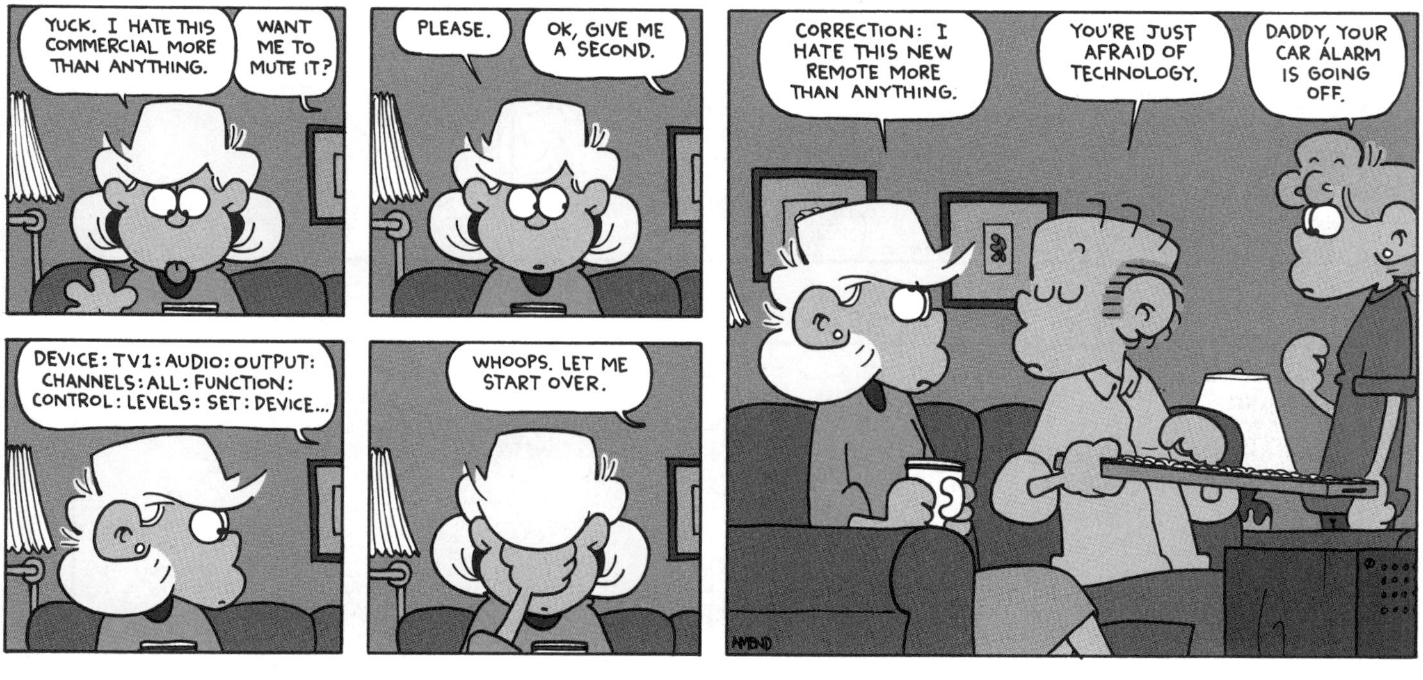
YUCK. I HATE THIS COMMERCIAL MORE THAN ANYTHING.
WANT ME TO MUTE IT?
PLEASE.
OK, GIVE ME A SECOND.
DEVICE: TV1: AUDIO: OUTPUT: CHANNELS: ALL: FUNCTION: CONTROL: LEVELS: SET: DEVICE...
WHOOPS. LET ME START OVER.
CORRECTION: I HATE THIS NEW REMOTE MORE THAN ANYTHING.
YOU'RE JUST AFRAID OF TECHNOLOGY.
DADDY, YOUR CAR ALARM IS GOING OFF.
AMEND

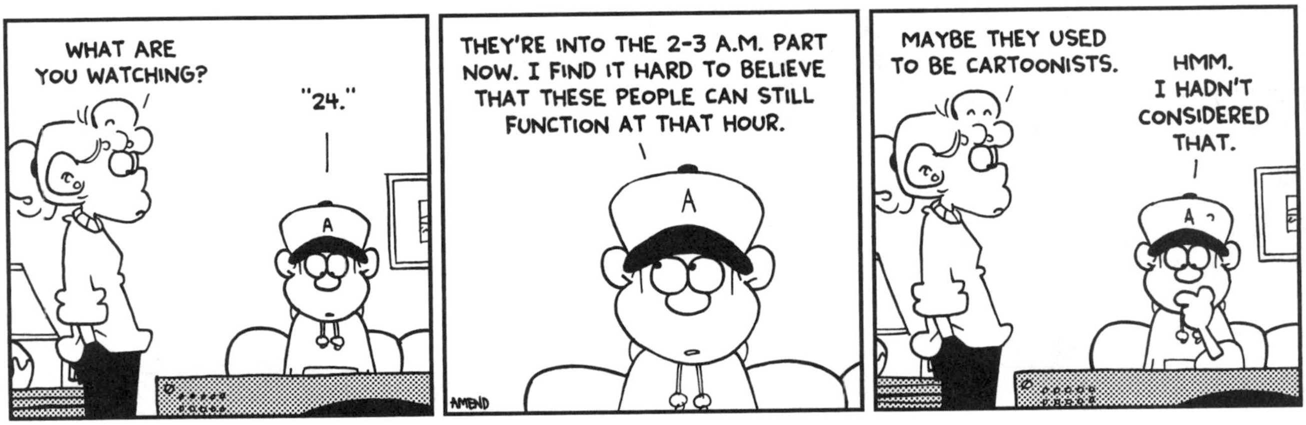
WHAT ARE YOU WATCHING?
"24."
THEY'RE INTO THE 2-3 A.M. PART NOW. I FIND IT HARD TO BELIEVE THAT THESE PEOPLE CAN STILL FUNCTION AT THAT HOUR.
MAYBE THEY USED TO BE CARTOONISTS.
HMM. I HADN'T CONSIDERED THAT.

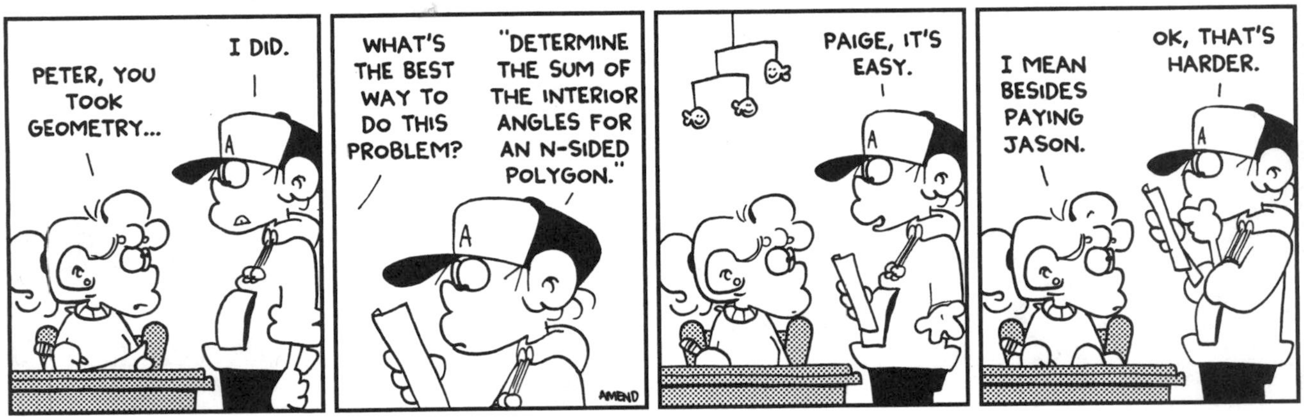
PETER, YOU TOOK GEOMETRY...
I DID.
WHAT'S THE BEST WAY TO DO THIS PROBLEM?
"DETERMINE THE SUM OF THE INTERIOR ANGLES FOR AN N-SIDED POLYGON."
PAIGE, IT'S EASY.
I MEAN BESIDES PAYING JASON.
OK, THAT'S HARDER.

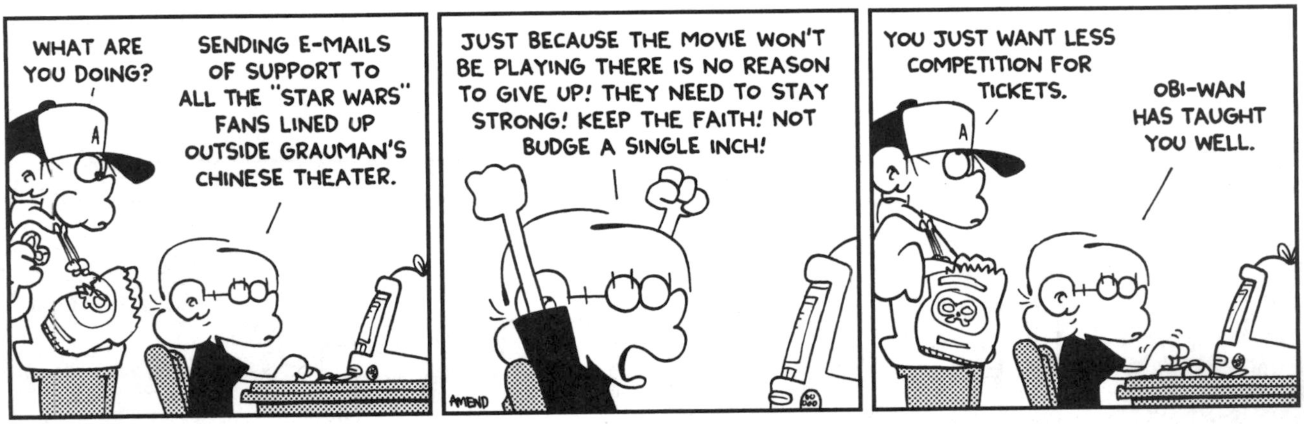
WHAT ARE YOU DOING?
SENDING E-MAILS OF SUPPORT TO ALL THE "STAR WARS" FANS LINED UP OUTSIDE GRAUMAN'S CHINESE THEATER.
JUST BECAUSE THE MOVIE WON'T BE PLAYING THERE IS NO REASON TO GIVE UP! THEY NEED TO STAY STRONG! KEEP THE FAITH! NOT BUDGE A SINGLE INCH!
YOU JUST WANT LESS COMPETITION FOR TICKETS.
OBI-WAN HAS TAUGHT YOU WELL.

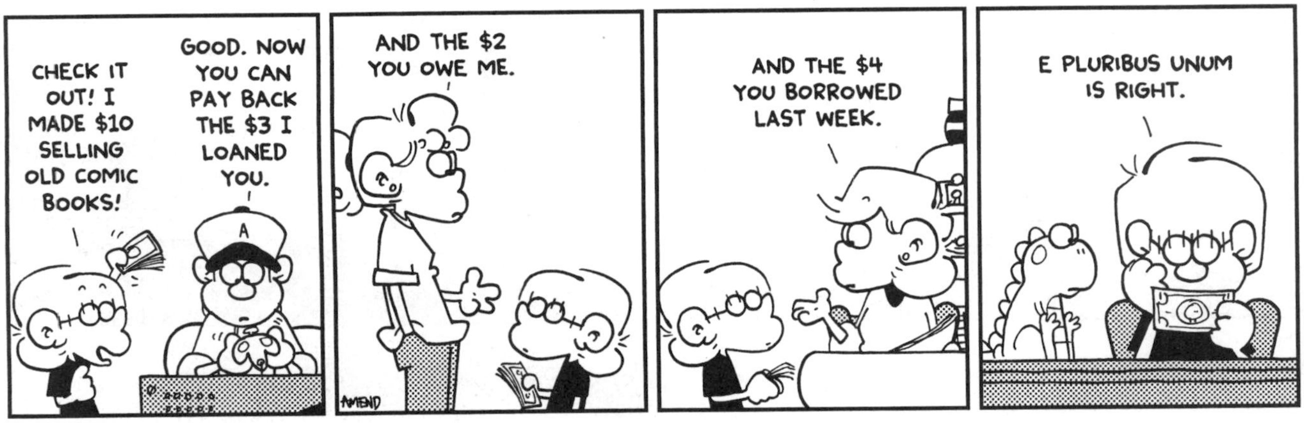
CHECK IT OUT! I MADE $10 SELLING OLD COMIC BOOKS!
GOOD. NOW YOU CAN PAY BACK THE $3 I LOANED YOU.
AND THE $2 YOU OWE ME.
AND THE $4 YOU BORROWED LAST WEEK.
E PLURIBUS UNUM IS RIGHT.

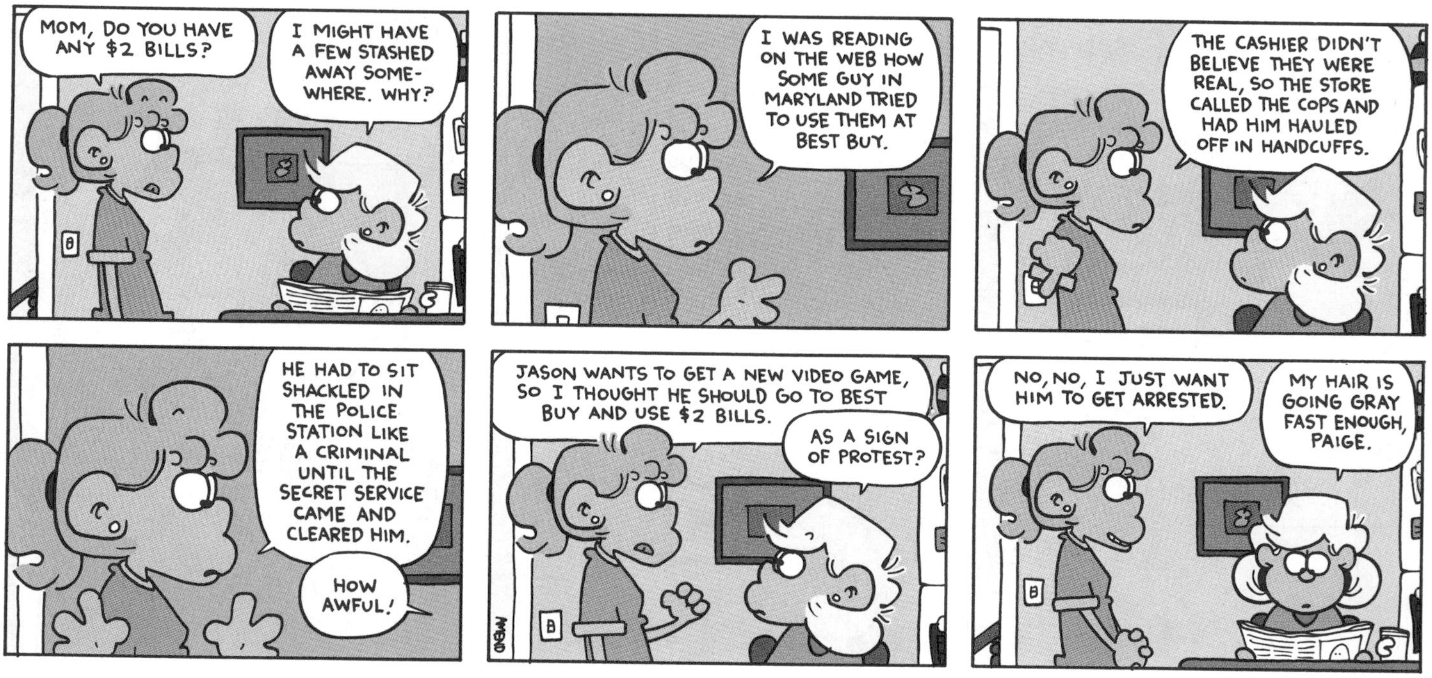
MOM, DO YOU HAVE ANY $2 BILLS?
I MIGHT HAVE A FEW STASHED AWAY SOME-WHERE. WHY?
I WAS READING ON THE WEB HOW SOME GUY IN MARYLAND TRIED TO USE THEM AT BEST BUY.
THE CASHIER DIDN'T BELIEVE THEY WERE REAL, SO THE STORE CALLED THE COPS AND HAD HIM HAULED OFF IN HANDCUFFS.
HE HAD TO SIT SHACKLED IN THE POLICE STATION LIKE A CRIMINAL UNTIL THE SECRET SERVICE CAME AND CLEARED HIM.
HOW AWFUL!
JASON WANTS TO GET A NEW VIDEO GAME, SO I THOUGHT HE SHOULD GO TO BEST BUY AND USE $2 BILLS.
AS A SIGN OF PROTEST?
NO, NO, I JUST WANT HIM TO GET ARRESTED.
MY HAIR IS GOING GRAY FAST ENOUGH, PAIGE.
AMEND

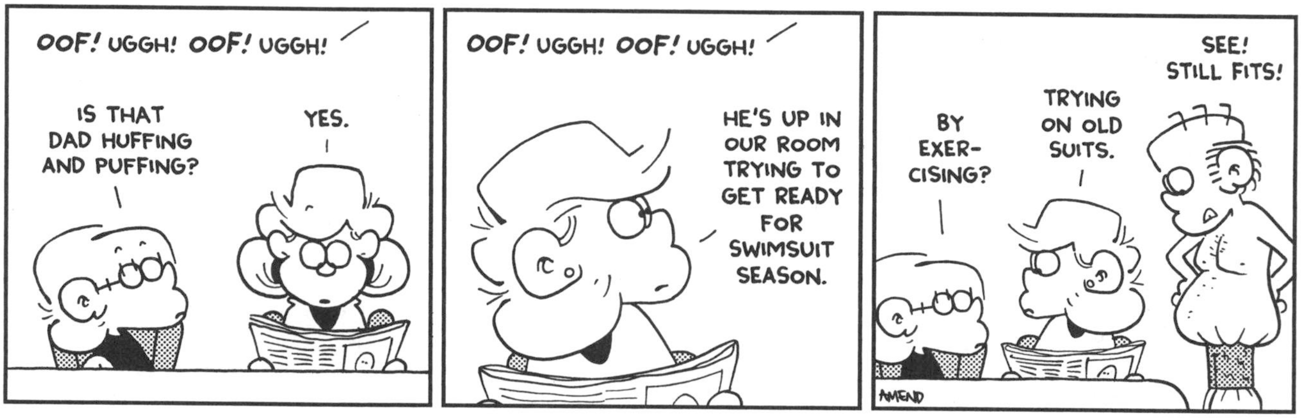
OOF! UGGH! OOF! UGGH!
IS THAT DAD HUFFING AND PUFFING?
YES.
OOF! UGGH! OOF! UGGH!
HE'S UP IN OUR ROOM TRYING TO GET READY FOR SWIMSUIT SEASON.
BY EXER-CISING?
TRYING ON OLD SUITS.
SEE! STILL FITS!
AMEND

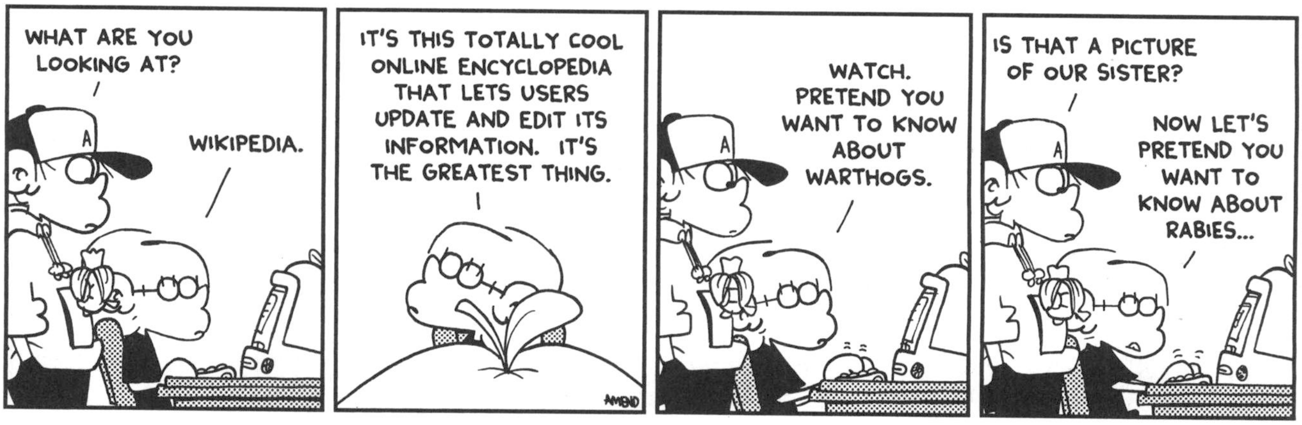
WHAT ARE YOU LOOKING AT?
WIKIPEDIA.
IT'S THIS TOTALLY COOL ONLINE ENCYCLOPEDIA THAT LETS USERS UPDATE AND EDIT ITS INFORMATION. IT'S THE GREATEST THING.
AMEND
WATCH. PRETEND YOU WANT TO KNOW ABOUT WARTHOGS.
IS THAT A PICTURE OF OUR SISTER?
NOW LET'S PRETEND YOU WANT TO KNOW ABOUT RABIES...

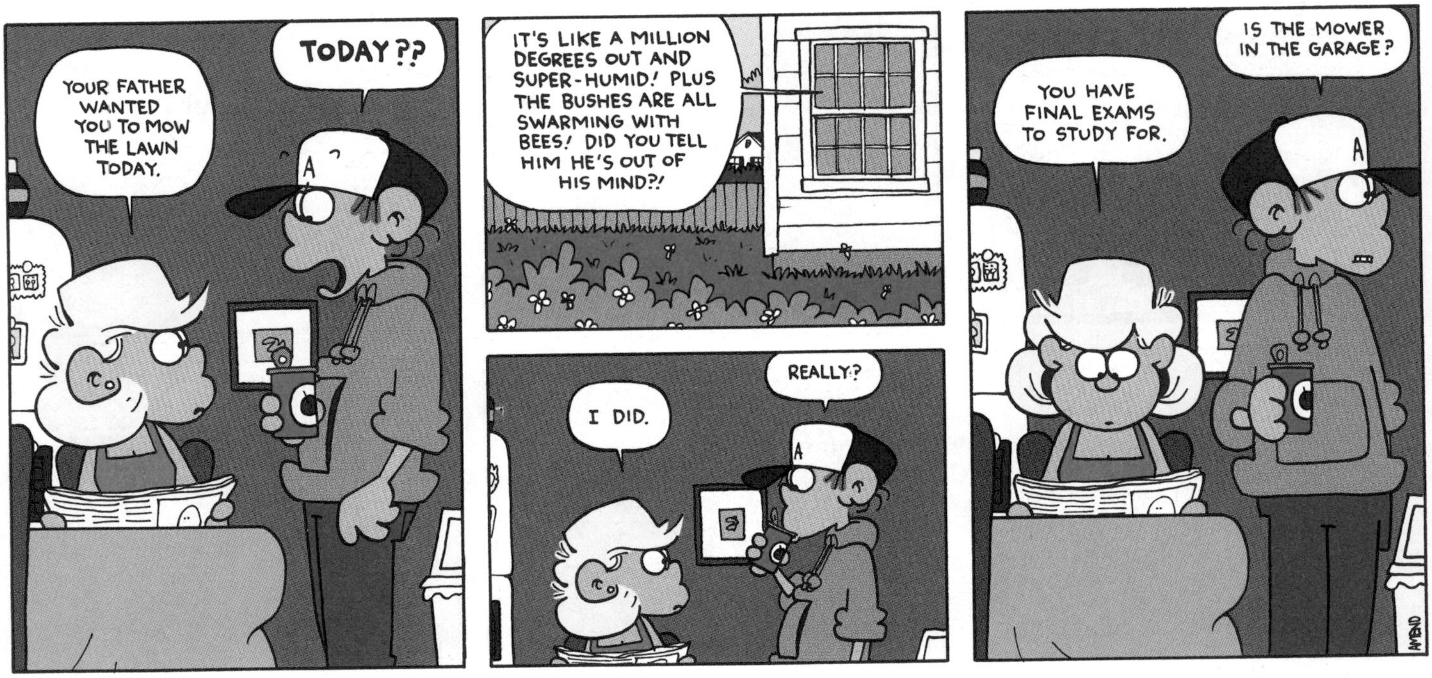
YOUR FATHER WANTED YOU TO MOW THE LAWN TODAY.
TODAY??
IT'S LIKE A MILLION DEGREES OUT AND SUPER-HUMID! PLUS THE BUSHES ARE ALL SWARMING WITH BEES! DID YOU TELL HIM HE'S OUT OF HIS MIND?!
I DID.
REALLY?
YOU HAVE FINAL EXAMS TO STUDY FOR.
IS THE MOWER IN THE GARAGE?
AMEND

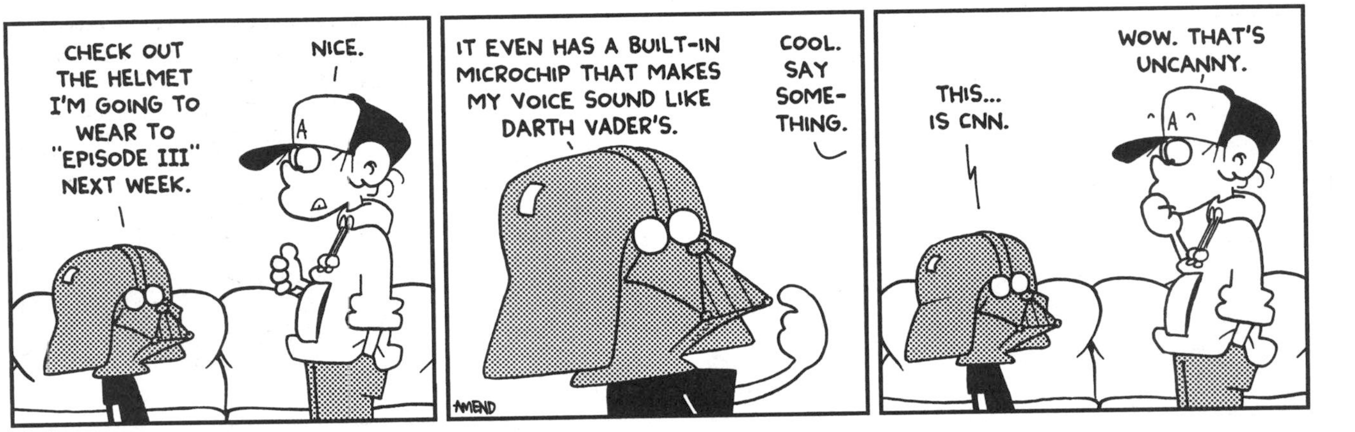
CHECK OUT THE HELMET I'M GOING TO WEAR TO "EPISODE III" NEXT WEEK.
NICE.
IT EVEN HAS A BUILT-IN MICROCHIP THAT MAKES MY VOICE SOUND LIKE DARTH VADER'S.
COOL. SAY SOME-THING.
AMEND
THIS... IS CNN.
WOW. THAT'S UNCANNY.

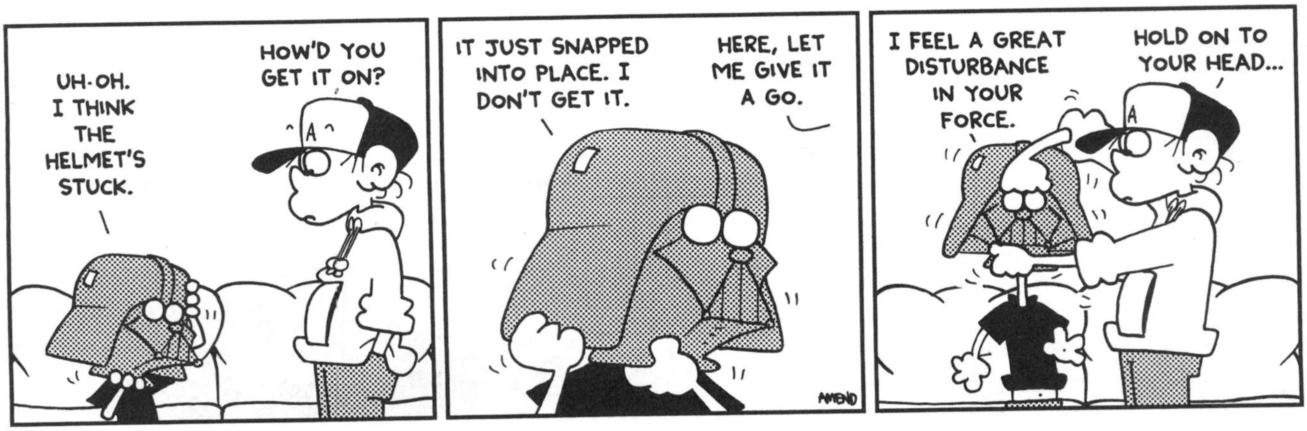
UH-OH. I THINK THE HELMET'S STUCK.
HOW'D YOU GET IT ON?
IT JUST SNAPPED INTO PLACE. I DON'T GET IT.
HERE, LET ME GIVE IT A GO.
AMEND
I FEEL A GREAT DISTURBANCE IN YOUR FORCE.
HOLD ON TO YOUR HEAD...

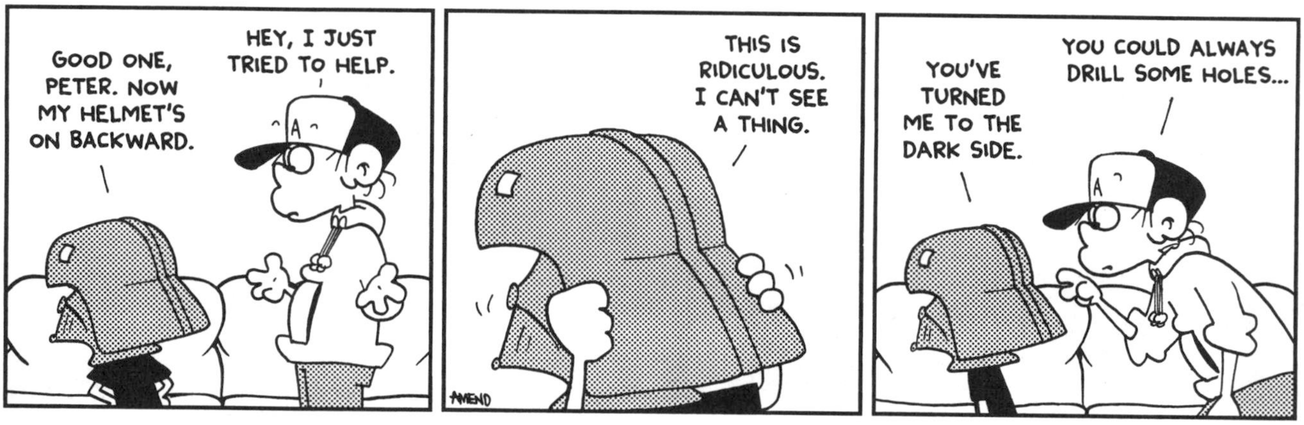
GOOD ONE, PETER. NOW MY HELMET'S ON BACKWARD.
HEY, I JUST TRIED TO HELP.
THIS IS RIDICULOUS. I CAN'T SEE A THING.
YOU'VE TURNED ME TO THE DARK SIDE.
YOU COULD ALWAYS DRILL SOME HOLES...
AMEND

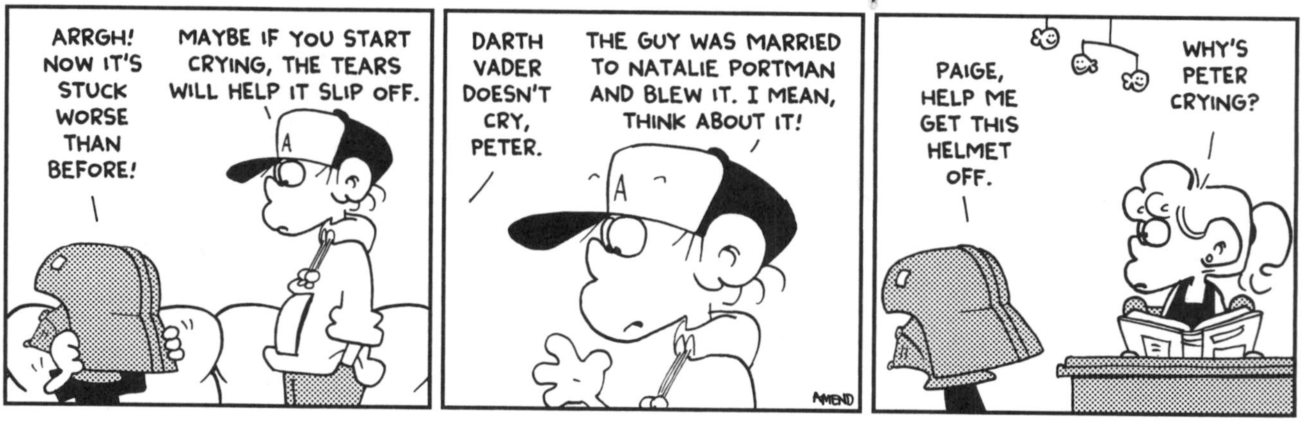
ARRGH! NOW IT'S STUCK WORSE THAN BEFORE!
MAYBE IF YOU START CRYING, THE TEARS WILL HELP IT SLIP OFF.
DARTH VADER DOESN'T CRY, PETER.
THE GUY WAS MARRIED TO NATALIE PORTMAN AND BLEW IT. I MEAN, THINK ABOUT IT!
AMEND
PAIGE, HELP ME GET THIS HELMET OFF.
WHY'S PETER CRYING?

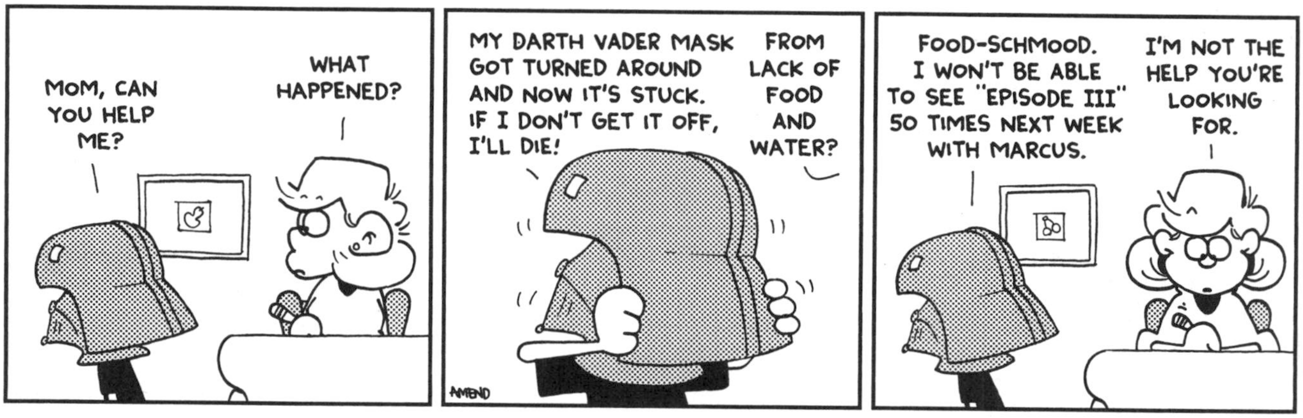
MOM, CAN YOU HELP ME?
WHAT HAPPENED?
MY DARTH VADER MASK GOT TURNED AROUND AND NOW IT'S STUCK. IF I DON'T GET IT OFF, I'LL DIE!
FROM LACK OF FOOD AND WATER?
AMEND
FOOD-SCHMOOD. I WON'T BE ABLE TO SEE "EPISODE III" 50 TIMES NEXT WEEK WITH MARCUS.
I'M NOT THE HELP YOU'RE LOOKING FOR.

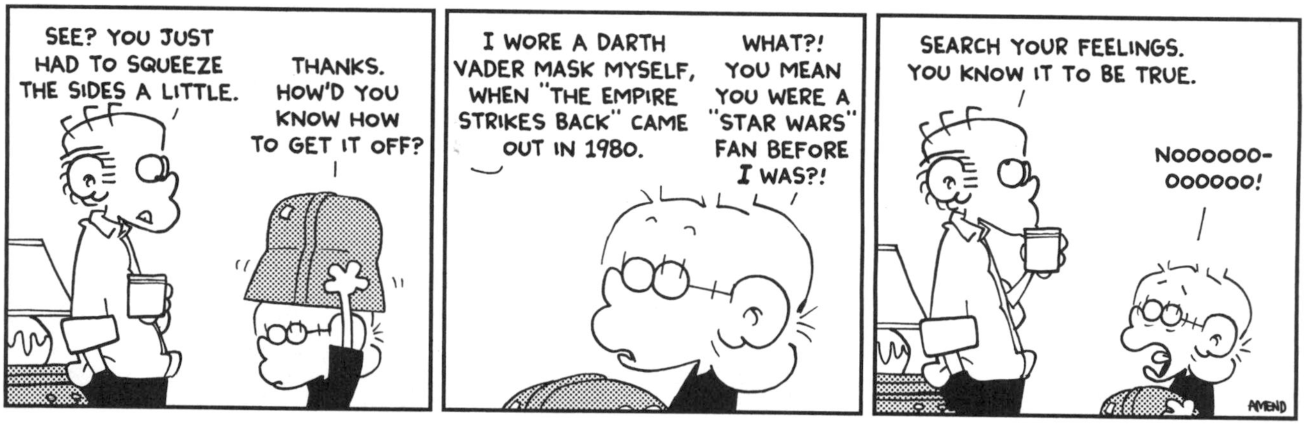
SEE? YOU JUST HAD TO SQUEEZE THE SIDES A LITTLE.
THANKS. HOW'D YOU KNOW HOW TO GET IT OFF?
I WORE A DARTH VADER MASK MYSELF, WHEN "THE EMPIRE STRIKES BACK" CAME OUT IN 1980.
WHAT?! YOU MEAN YOU WERE A "STAR WARS" FAN BEFORE I WAS?!
SEARCH YOUR FEELINGS. YOU KNOW IT TO BE TRUE.
NOOOOOO-OOOOOO!
AMEND

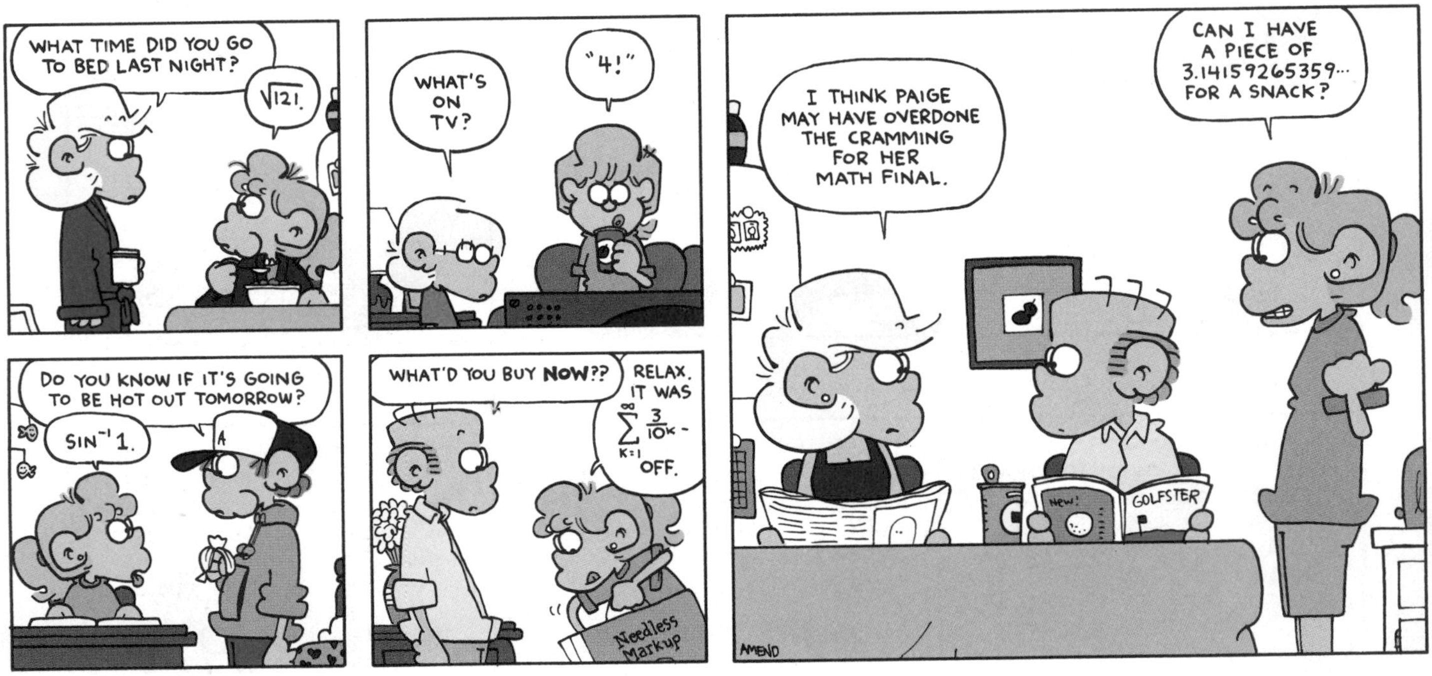
WHAT TIME DID YOU GO TO BED LAST NIGHT?
$\sqrt{121}$.
WHAT'S ON TV?
"4!"
DO YOU KNOW IF IT'S GOING TO BE HOT OUT TOMORROW?
$\sin^{-1} 1$.
WHAT'D YOU BUY **NOW**??
RELAX. IT WAS $\sum_{k=1}^{\infty} \frac{3}{10^k}$-OFF.
Needless Markup
I THINK PAIGE MAY HAVE OVERDONE THE CRAMMING FOR HER MATH FINAL.
CAN I HAVE A PIECE OF 3.14159265359... FOR A SNACK?
New!
GOLFSTER
AMEND

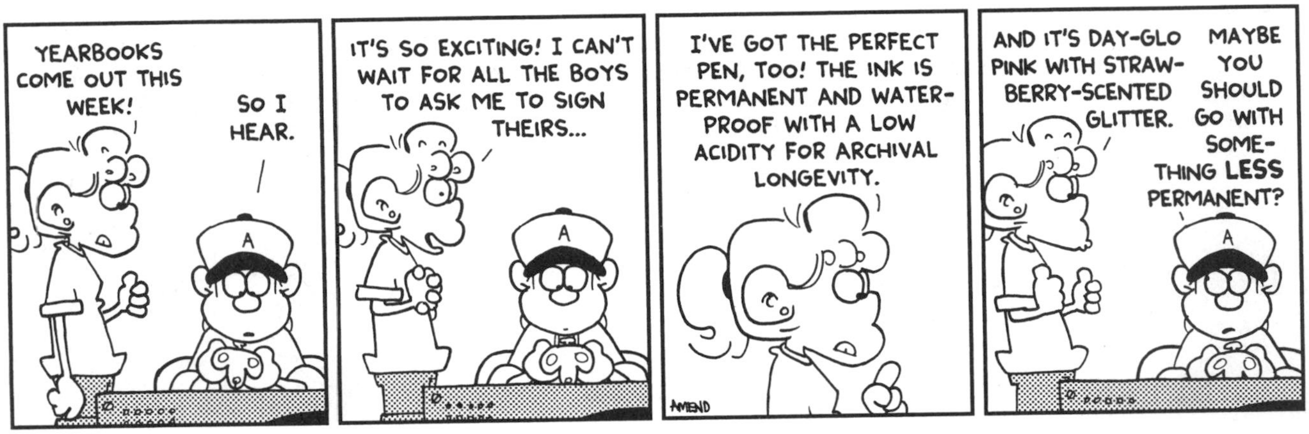
YEARBOOKS COME OUT THIS WEEK!
SO I HEAR.
IT'S SO EXCITING! I CAN'T WAIT FOR ALL THE BOYS TO ASK ME TO SIGN THEIRS...
I'VE GOT THE PERFECT PEN, TOO! THE INK IS PERMANENT AND WATER-PROOF WITH A LOW ACIDITY FOR ARCHIVAL LONGEVITY.
AMEND
AND IT'S DAY-GLO PINK WITH STRAW-BERRY-SCENTED GLITTER.
MAYBE YOU SHOULD GO WITH SOME-THING **LESS** PERMANENT?

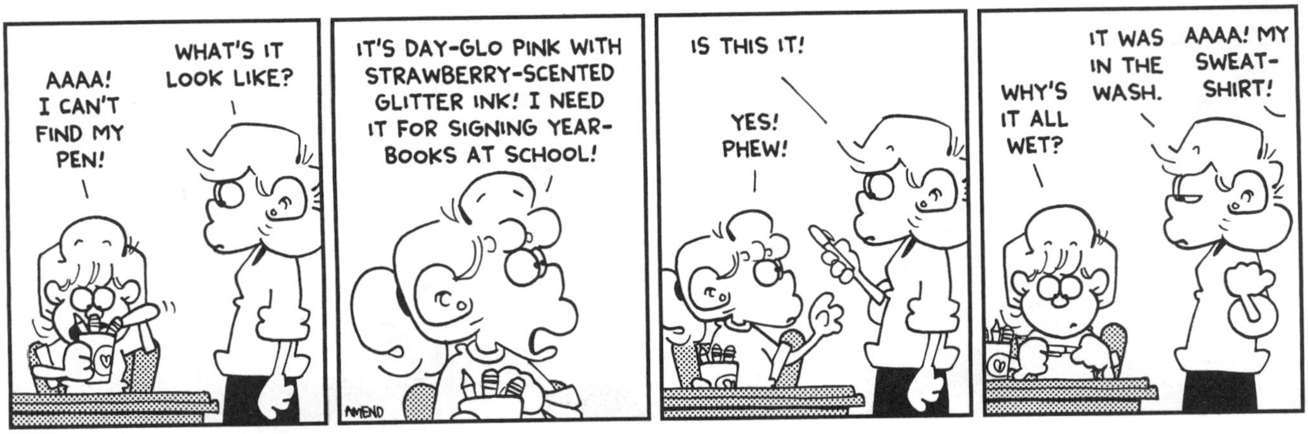
AAAA! I CAN'T FIND MY PEN!
WHAT'S IT LOOK LIKE?
IT'S DAY-GLO PINK WITH STRAWBERRY-SCENTED GLITTER INK! I NEED IT FOR SIGNING YEAR-BOOKS AT SCHOOL!
AMEND
IS THIS IT!
YES! PHEW!
WHY'S IT ALL WET?
IT WAS IN THE WASH.
AAAA! MY SWEAT-SHIRT!

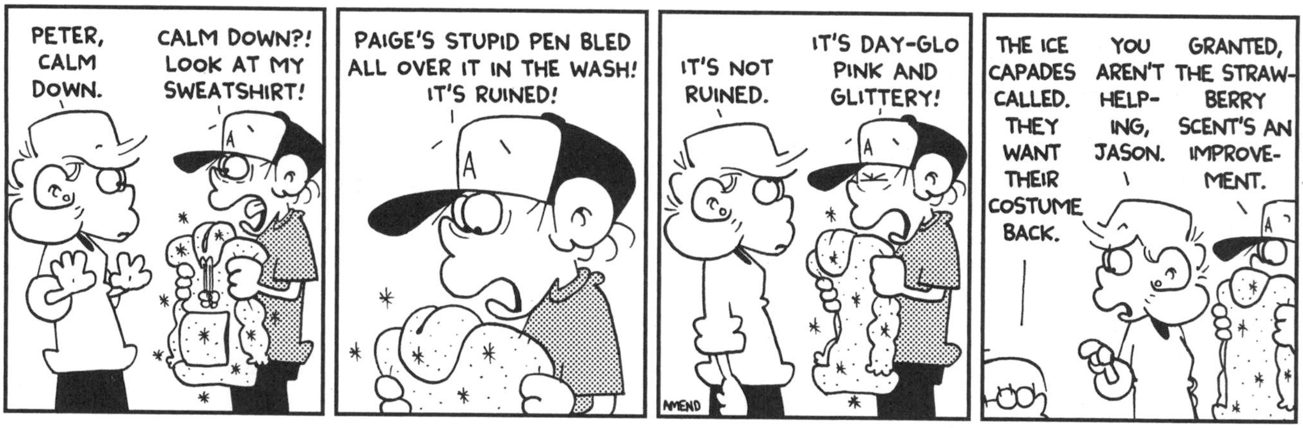
PETER, CALM DOWN.
CALM DOWN?! LOOK AT MY SWEATSHIRT!
PAIGE'S STUPID PEN BLED ALL OVER IT IN THE WASH! IT'S RUINED!
IT'S NOT RUINED.
IT'S DAY-GLO PINK AND GLITTERY!
AMEND
THE ICE CAPADES CALLED. THEY WANT THEIR COSTUME BACK.
YOU AREN'T HELPING, JASON.
GRANTED, THE STRAWBERRY SCENT'S AN IMPROVEMENT.

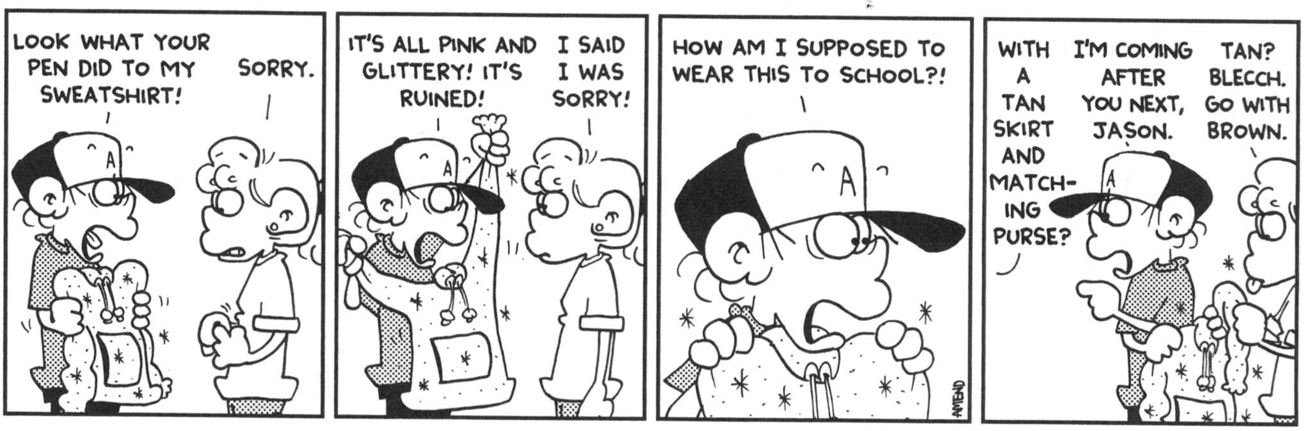
LOOK WHAT YOUR PEN DID TO MY SWEATSHIRT!
SORRY.
IT'S ALL PINK AND GLITTERY! IT'S RUINED!
I SAID I WAS SORRY!
HOW AM I SUPPOSED TO WEAR THIS TO SCHOOL?!
AMEND
WITH A TAN SKIRT AND MATCHING PURSE?
I'M COMING AFTER YOU NEXT, JASON.
TAN? BLECCH. GO WITH BROWN.

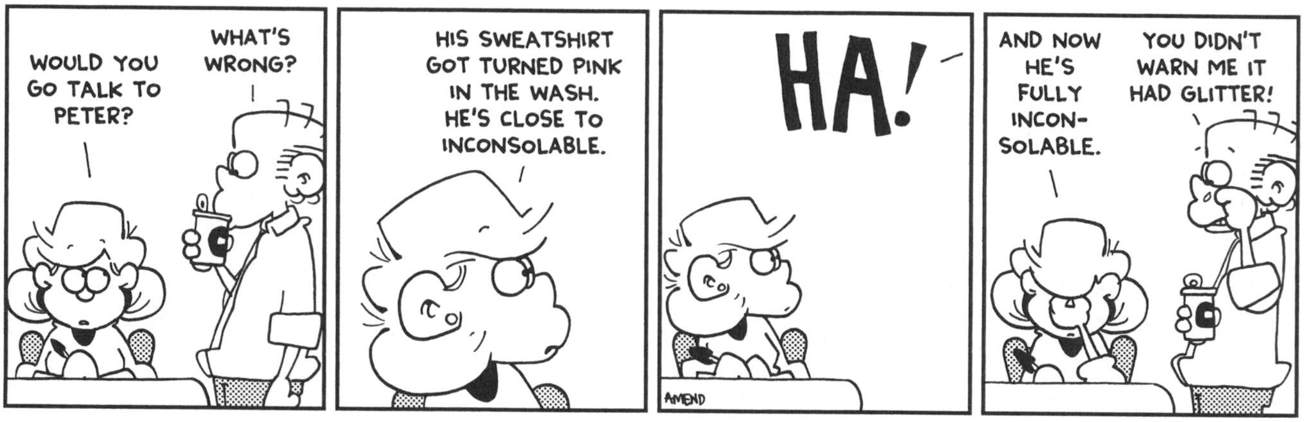
WOULD YOU GO TALK TO PETER?
WHAT'S WRONG?
HIS SWEATSHIRT GOT TURNED PINK IN THE WASH. HE'S CLOSE TO INCONSOLABLE.
HA!
AMEND
AND NOW HE'S FULLY INCONSOLABLE.
YOU DIDN'T WARN ME IT HAD GLITTER!

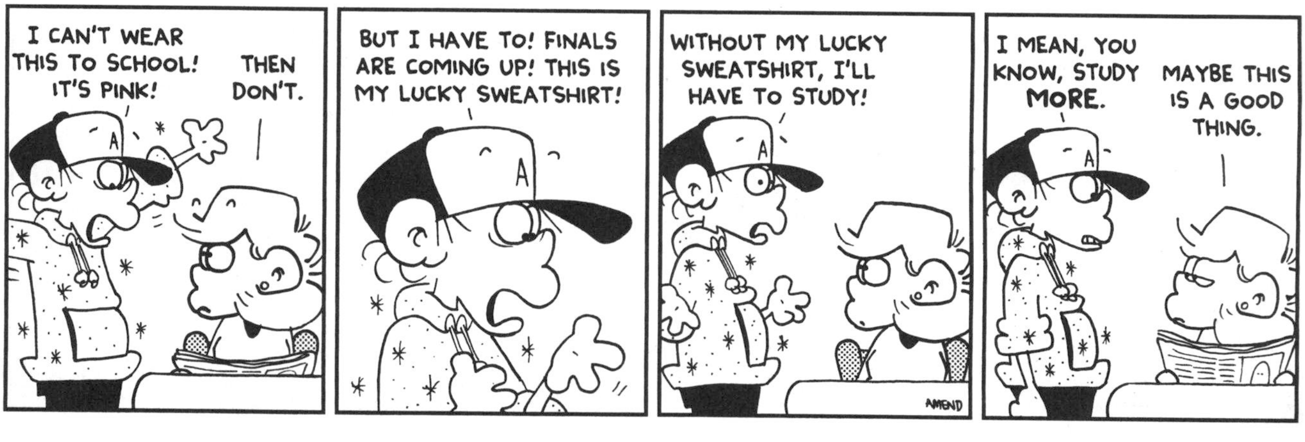
I CAN'T WEAR THIS TO SCHOOL! IT'S PINK!
THEN DON'T.
BUT I HAVE TO! FINALS ARE COMING UP! THIS IS MY LUCKY SWEATSHIRT!
WITHOUT MY LUCKY SWEATSHIRT, I'LL HAVE TO STUDY!
AMEND
I MEAN, YOU KNOW, STUDY MORE.
MAYBE THIS IS A GOOD THING.

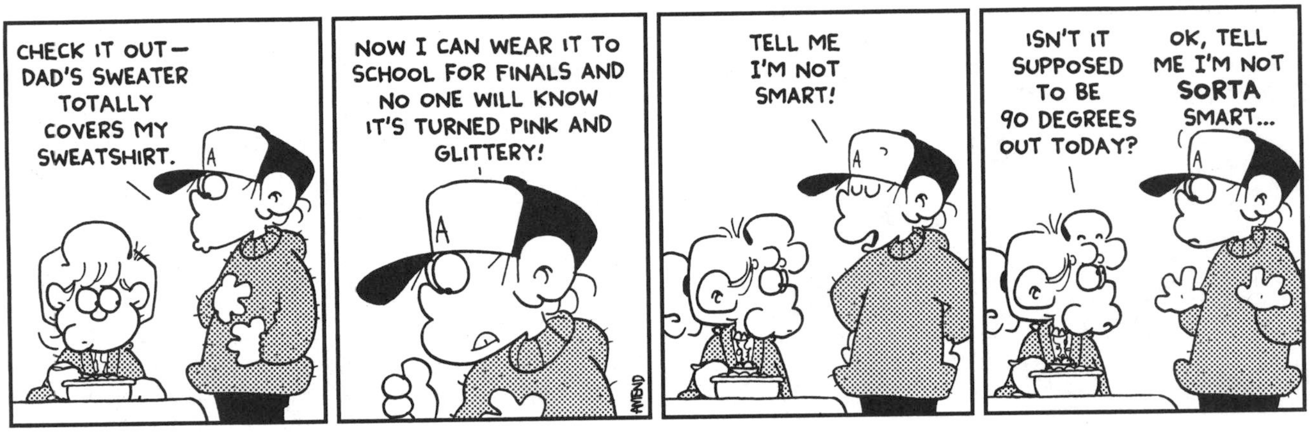
CHECK IT OUT— DAD'S SWEATER TOTALLY COVERS MY SWEATSHIRT.
NOW I CAN WEAR IT TO SCHOOL FOR FINALS AND NO ONE WILL KNOW IT'S TURNED PINK AND GLITTERY!
TELL ME I'M NOT SMART!
ISN'T IT SUPPOSED TO BE 90 DEGREES OUT TODAY?
OK, TELL ME I'M NOT SORTA SMART...

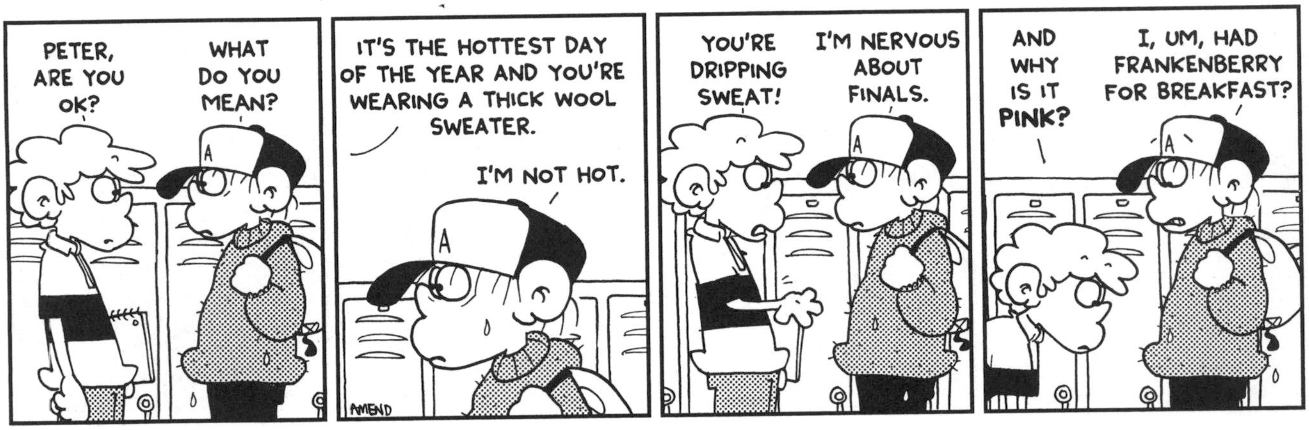
PETER, ARE YOU OK?
WHAT DO YOU MEAN?
IT'S THE HOTTEST DAY OF THE YEAR AND YOU'RE WEARING A THICK WOOL SWEATER.
I'M NOT HOT.
YOU'RE DRIPPING SWEAT!
I'M NERVOUS ABOUT FINALS.
AND WHY IS IT PINK?
I, UM, HAD FRANKENBERRY FOR BREAKFAST?

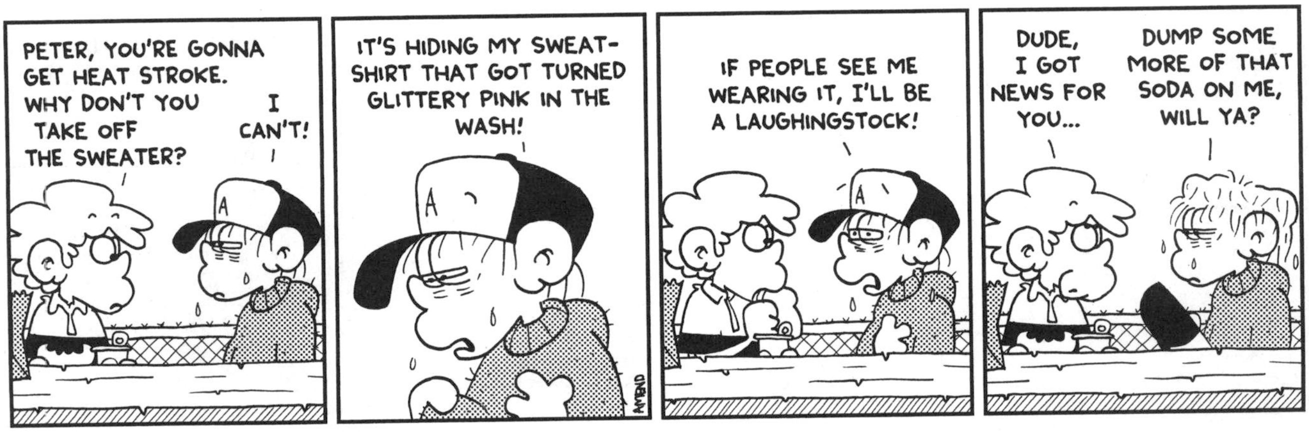
PETER, YOU'RE GONNA GET HEAT STROKE. WHY DON'T YOU TAKE OFF THE SWEATER?
I CAN'T!
IT'S HIDING MY SWEAT-SHIRT THAT GOT TURNED GLITTERY PINK IN THE WASH!
IF PEOPLE SEE ME WEARING IT, I'LL BE A LAUGHINGSTOCK!
DUDE, I GOT NEWS FOR YOU...
DUMP SOME MORE OF THAT SODA ON ME, WILL YA?

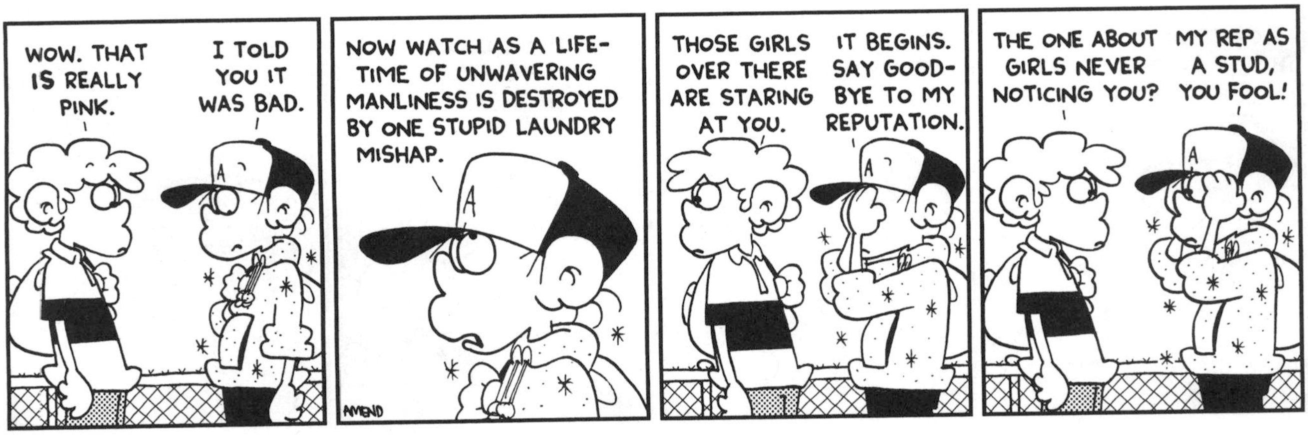
WOW. THAT IS REALLY PINK.
I TOLD YOU IT WAS BAD.
NOW WATCH AS A LIFE-TIME OF UNWAVERING MANLINESS IS DESTROYED BY ONE STUPID LAUNDRY MISHAP.
THOSE GIRLS OVER THERE ARE STARING AT YOU.
IT BEGINS. SAY GOOD-BYE TO MY REPUTATION.
THE ONE ABOUT GIRLS NEVER NOTICING YOU?
MY REP AS A STUD, YOU FOOL!

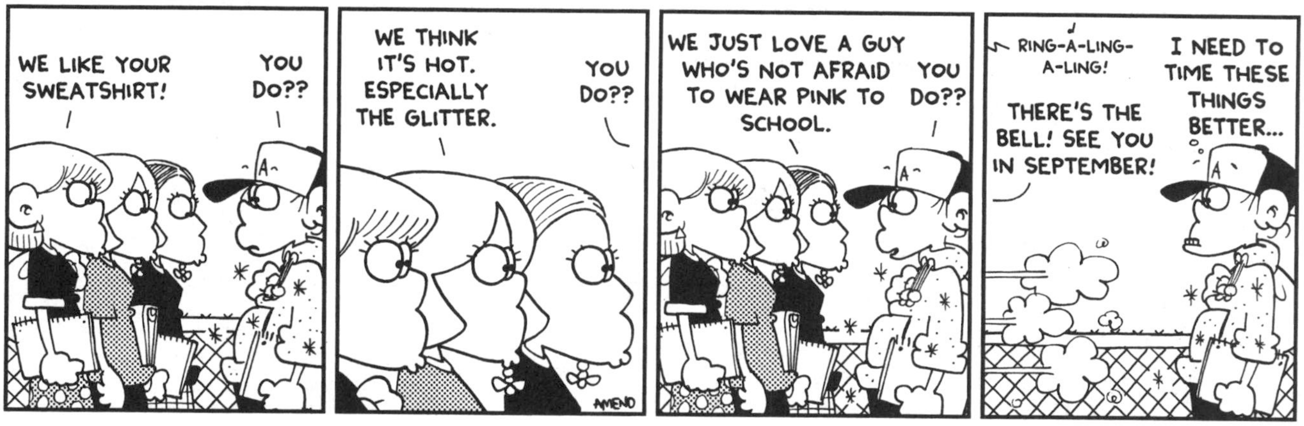
WE LIKE YOUR SWEATSHIRT!
YOU DO??
WE THINK IT'S HOT. ESPECIALLY THE GLITTER.
YOU DO??
WE JUST LOVE A GUY WHO'S NOT AFRAID TO WEAR PINK TO SCHOOL.
YOU DO??
RING-A-LING-A-LING!
THERE'S THE BELL! SEE YOU IN SEPTEMBER!
I NEED TO TIME THESE THINGS BETTER...
AMEND

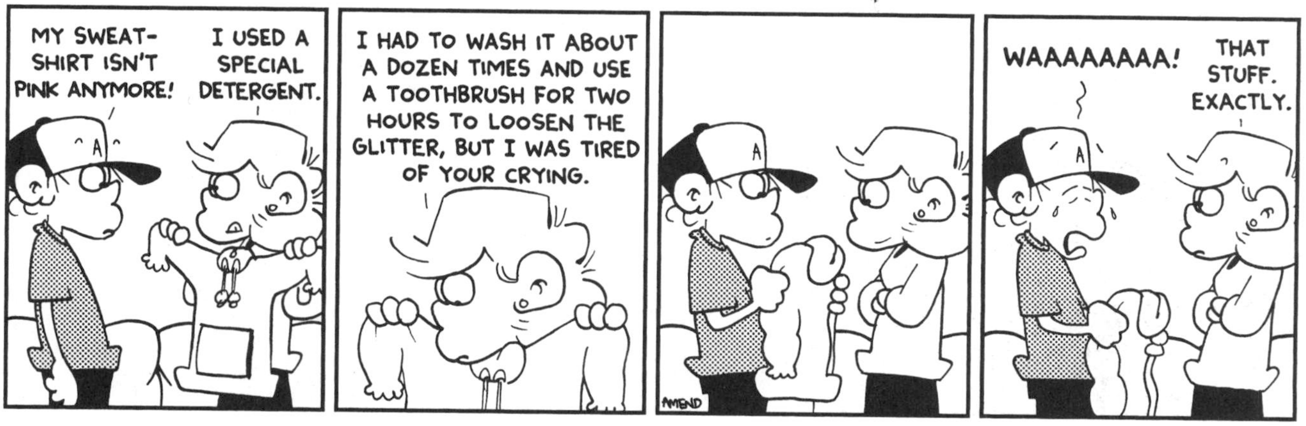
MY SWEAT-SHIRT ISN'T PINK ANYMORE!
I USED A SPECIAL DETERGENT.
I HAD TO WASH IT ABOUT A DOZEN TIMES AND USE A TOOTHBRUSH FOR TWO HOURS TO LOOSEN THE GLITTER, BUT I WAS TIRED OF YOUR CRYING.
WAAAAAAAA!
THAT STUFF. EXACTLY.
AMEND

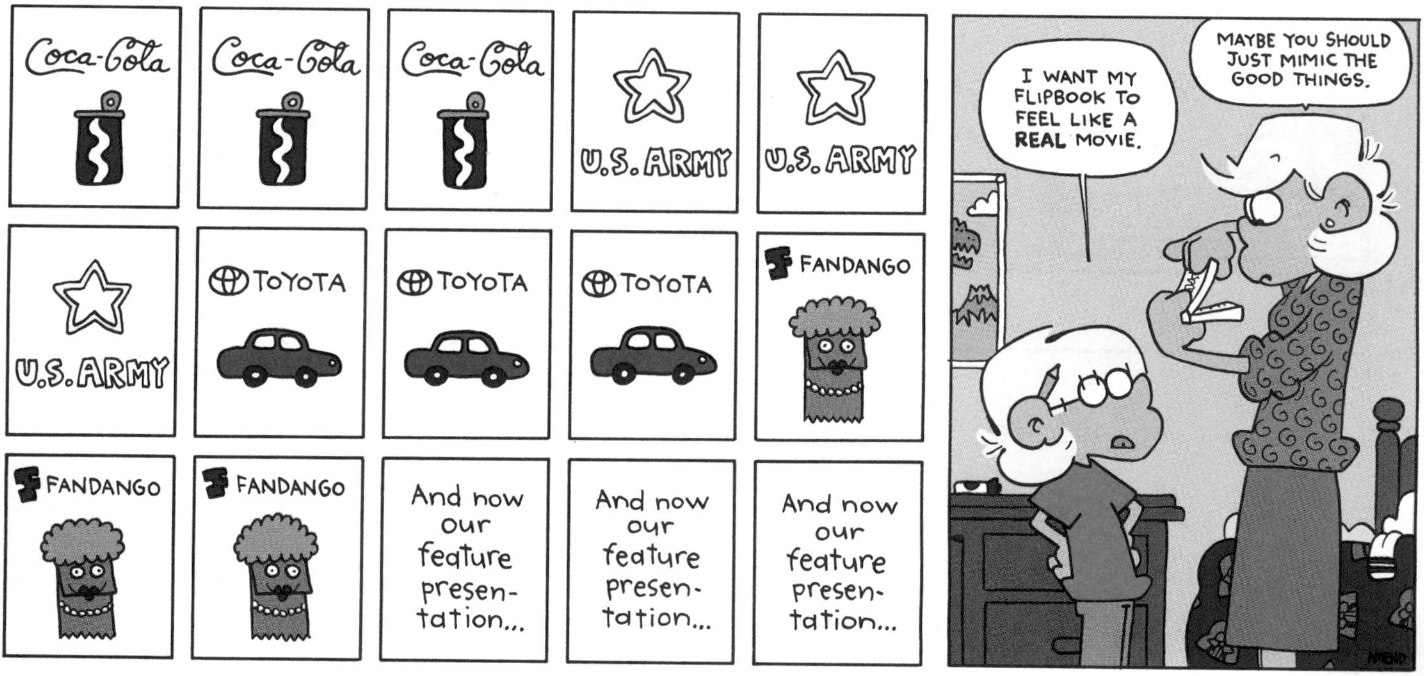
Coca-Cola
Coca-Cola
Coca-Cola
U.S. ARMY
U.S. ARMY
U.S. ARMY
TOYOTA
TOYOTA
TOYOTA
FANDANGO
FANDANGO
FANDANGO
And now our feature presen-tation...
And now our feature presen-tation...
And now our feature presen-tation...
I WANT MY FLIPBOOK TO FEEL LIKE A REAL MOVIE.
MAYBE YOU SHOULD JUST MIMIC THE GOOD THINGS.
AMEND

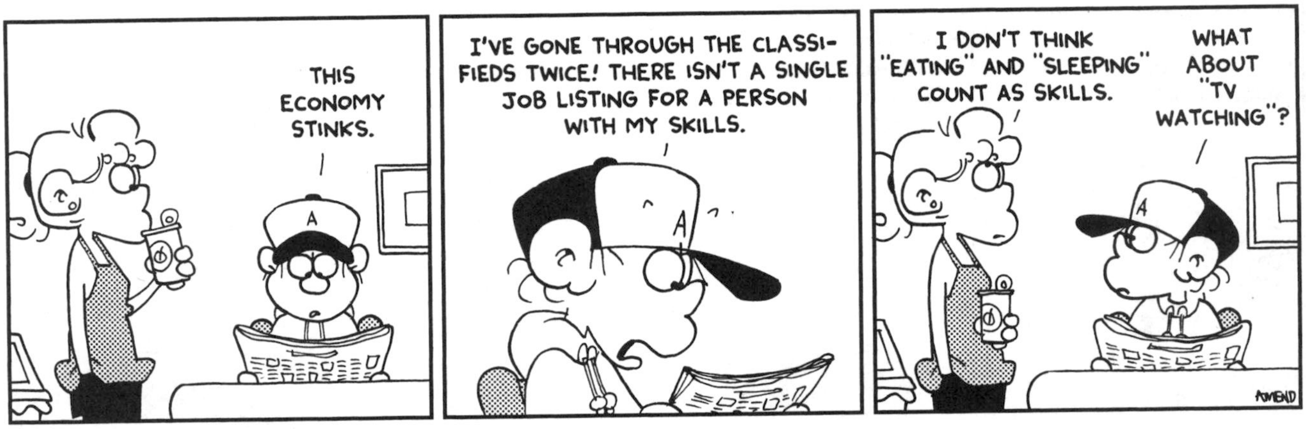
THIS ECONOMY STINKS.
I'VE GONE THROUGH THE CLASSIFIEDS TWICE! THERE ISN'T A SINGLE JOB LISTING FOR A PERSON WITH MY SKILLS.
I DON'T THINK "EATING" AND "SLEEPING" COUNT AS SKILLS.
WHAT ABOUT "TV WATCHING"?

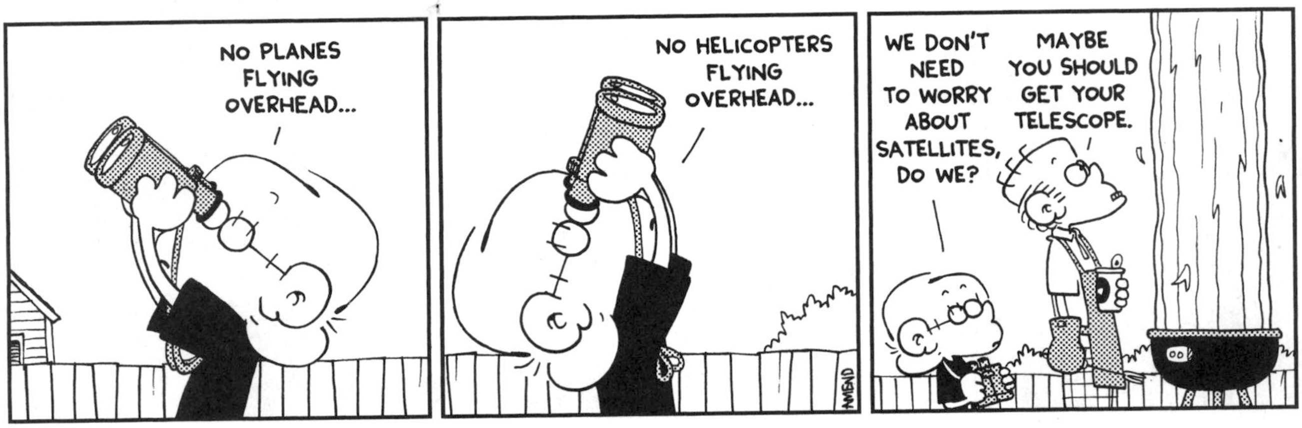
NO PLANES FLYING OVERHEAD...
NO HELICOPTERS FLYING OVERHEAD...
WE DON'T NEED TO WORRY ABOUT SATELLITES, DO WE?
MAYBE YOU SHOULD GET YOUR TELESCOPE.

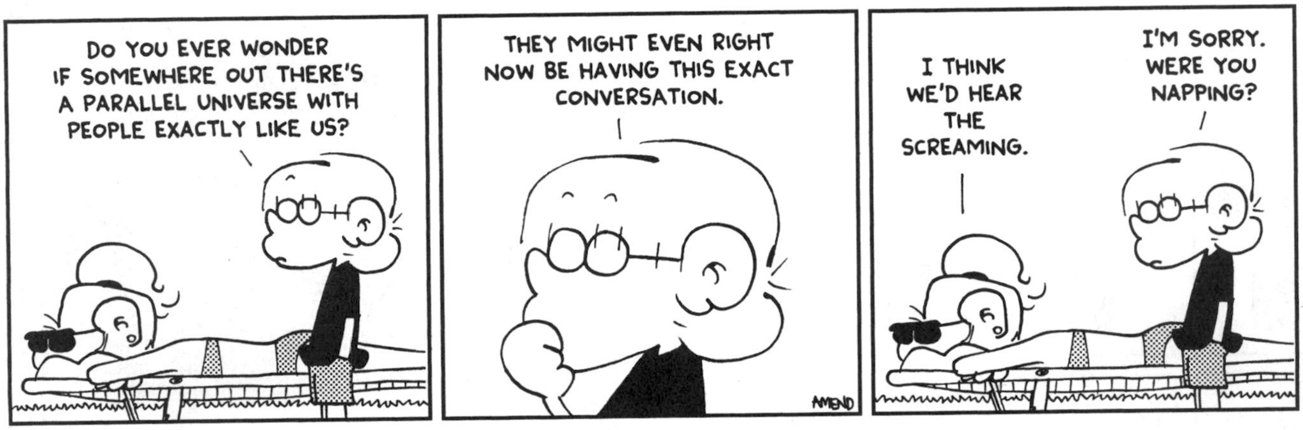
DO YOU EVER WONDER IF SOMEWHERE OUT THERE'S A PARALLEL UNIVERSE WITH PEOPLE EXACTLY LIKE US?
THEY MIGHT EVEN RIGHT NOW BE HAVING THIS EXACT CONVERSATION.
I THINK WE'D HEAR THE SCREAMING.
I'M SORRY. WERE YOU NAPPING?

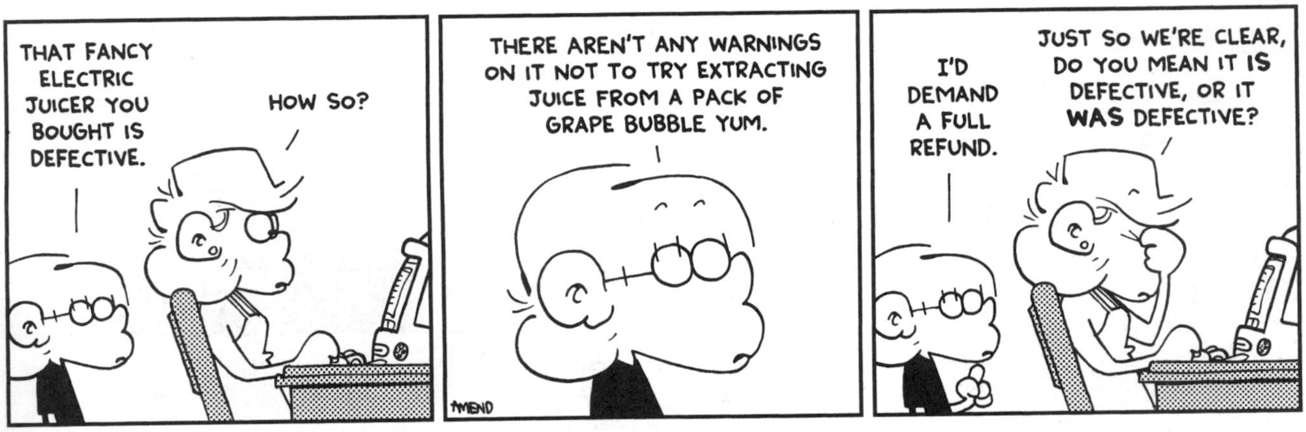
THAT FANCY ELECTRIC JUICER YOU BOUGHT IS DEFECTIVE.
HOW SO?
THERE AREN'T ANY WARNINGS ON IT NOT TO TRY EXTRACTING JUICE FROM A PACK OF GRAPE BUBBLE YUM.
I'D DEMAND A FULL REFUND.
JUST SO WE'RE CLEAR, DO YOU MEAN IT IS DEFECTIVE, OR IT WAS DEFECTIVE?

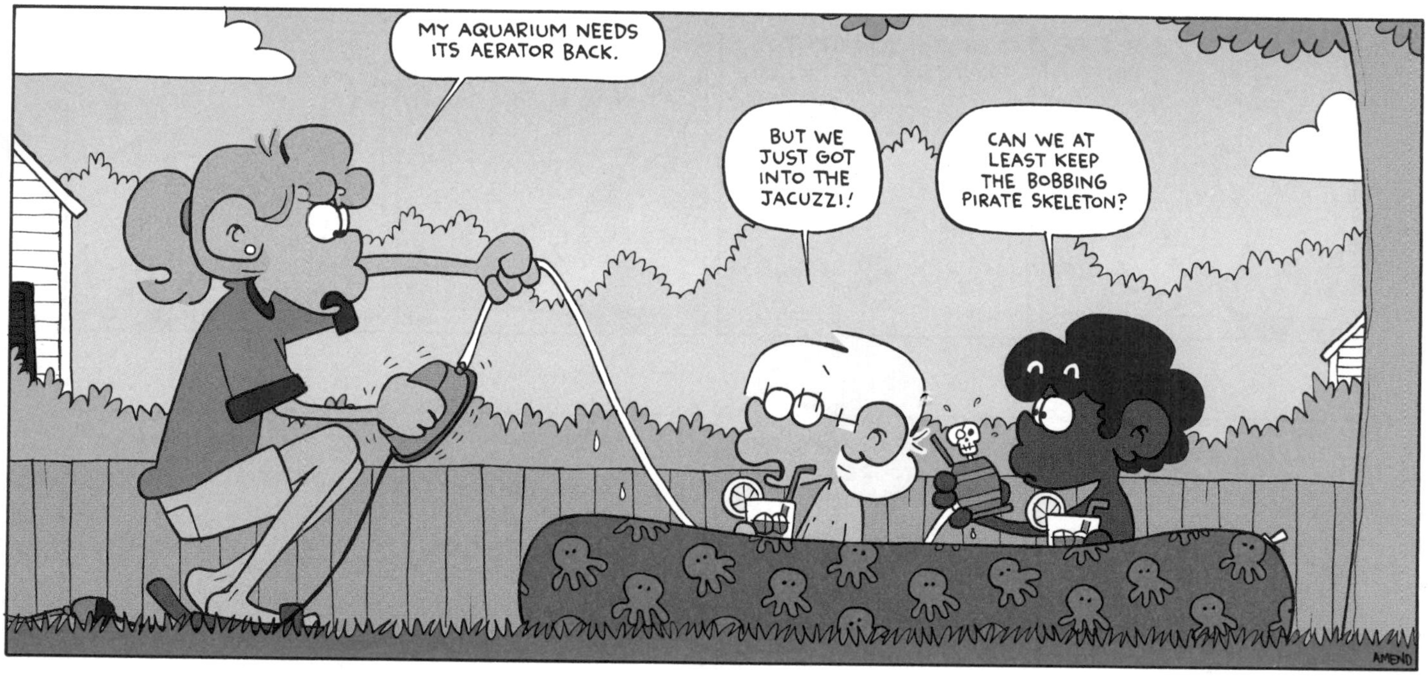
MY AQUARIUM NEEDS ITS AERATOR BACK.
BUT WE JUST GOT INTO THE JACUZZI!
CAN WE AT LEAST KEEP THE BOBBING PIRATE SKELETON?
AMEND

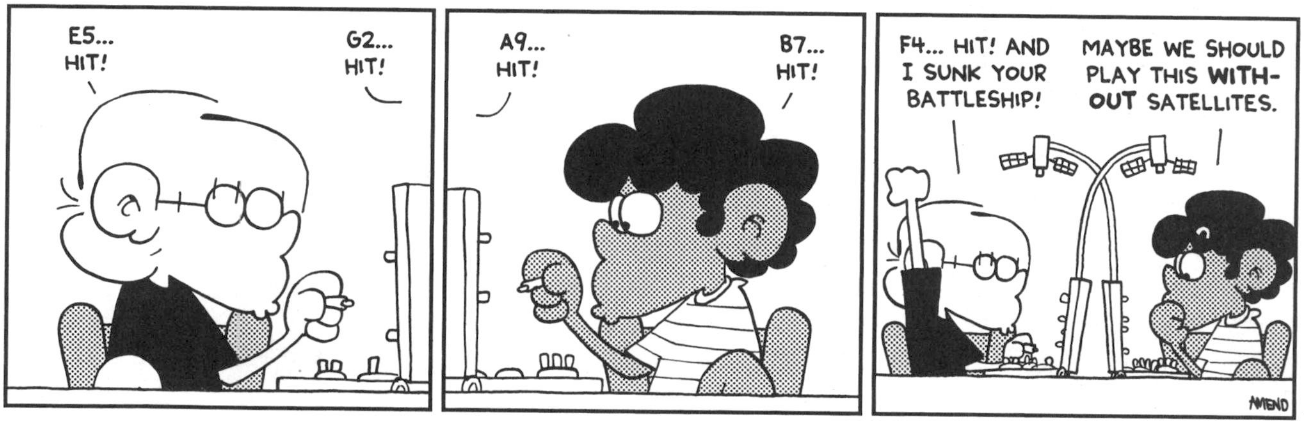
E5... HIT!
G2... HIT!
A9... HIT!
B7... HIT!
F4... HIT! AND I SUNK YOUR BATTLESHIP!
MAYBE WE SHOULD PLAY THIS **WITH-OUT** SATELLITES.
AMEND

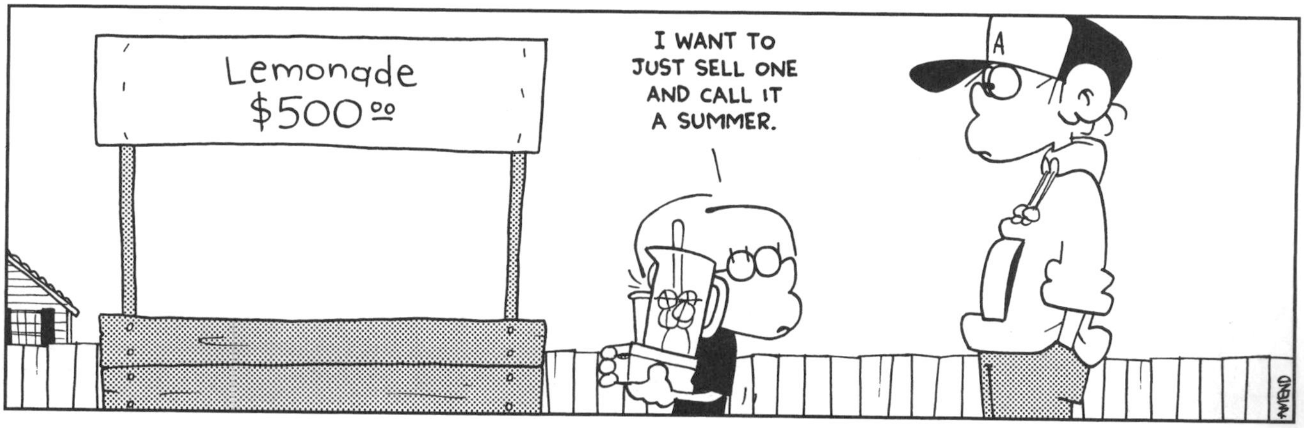
Lemonade $500⁰⁰
I WANT TO JUST SELL ONE AND CALL IT A SUMMER.
A
AMEND

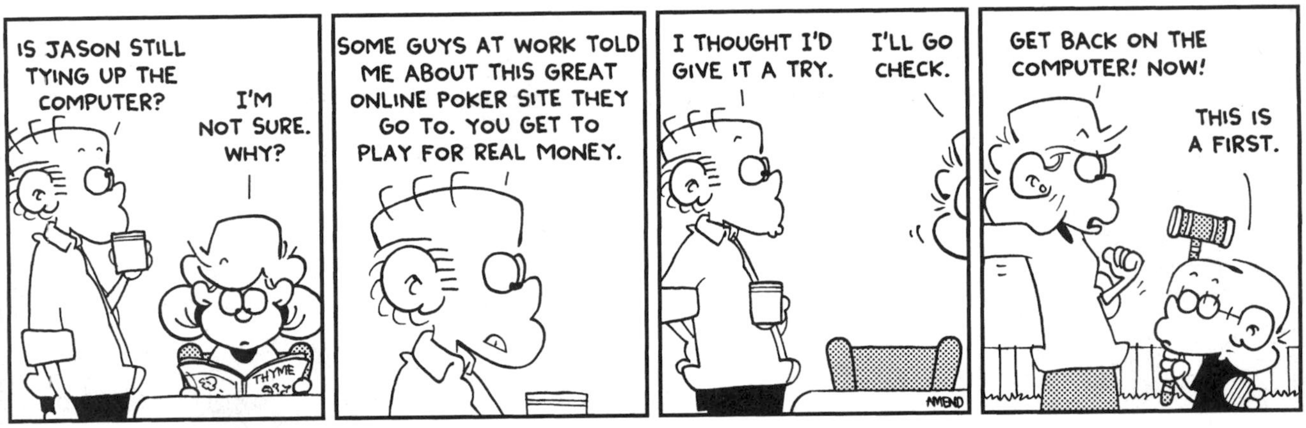
IS JASON STILL TYING UP THE COMPUTER?
I'M NOT SURE. WHY?
SOME GUYS AT WORK TOLD ME ABOUT THIS GREAT ONLINE POKER SITE THEY GO TO. YOU GET TO PLAY FOR REAL MONEY.
I THOUGHT I'D GIVE IT A TRY.
I'LL GO CHECK.
GET BACK ON THE COMPUTER! NOW!
THIS IS A FIRST.
THYME

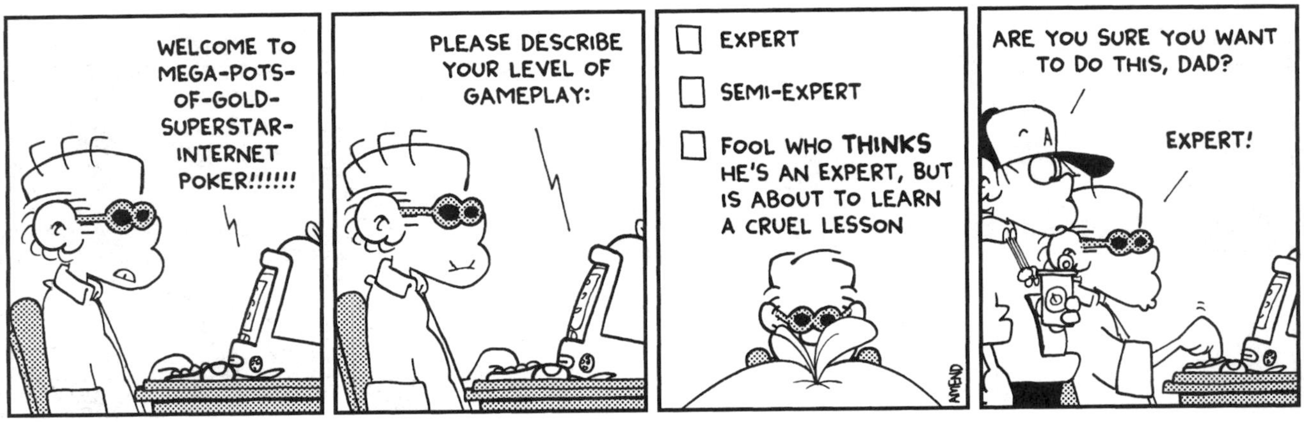
WELCOME TO MEGA-POTS-OF-GOLD-SUPERSTAR-INTERNET POKER!!!!!!
PLEASE DESCRIBE YOUR LEVEL OF GAMEPLAY:
EXPERT
SEMI-EXPERT
FOOL WHO **THINKS** HE'S AN EXPERT, BUT IS ABOUT TO LEARN A CRUEL LESSON
ARE YOU SURE YOU WANT TO DO THIS, DAD?
EXPERT!

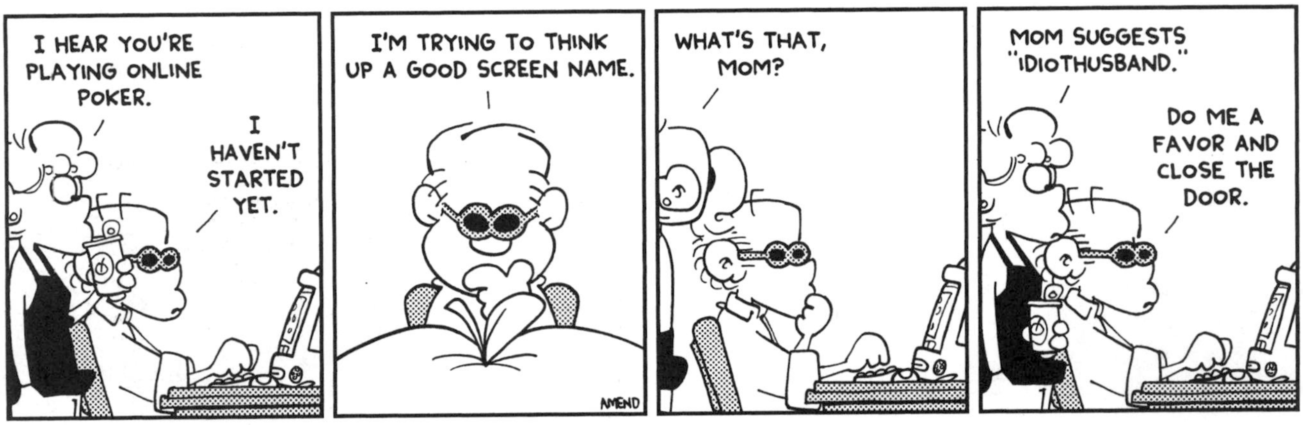
I HEAR YOU'RE PLAYING ONLINE POKER.
I HAVEN'T STARTED YET.
I'M TRYING TO THINK UP A GOOD SCREEN NAME.
WHAT'S THAT, MOM?
MOM SUGGESTS "IDIOTHUSBAND."
DO ME A FAVOR AND CLOSE THE DOOR.

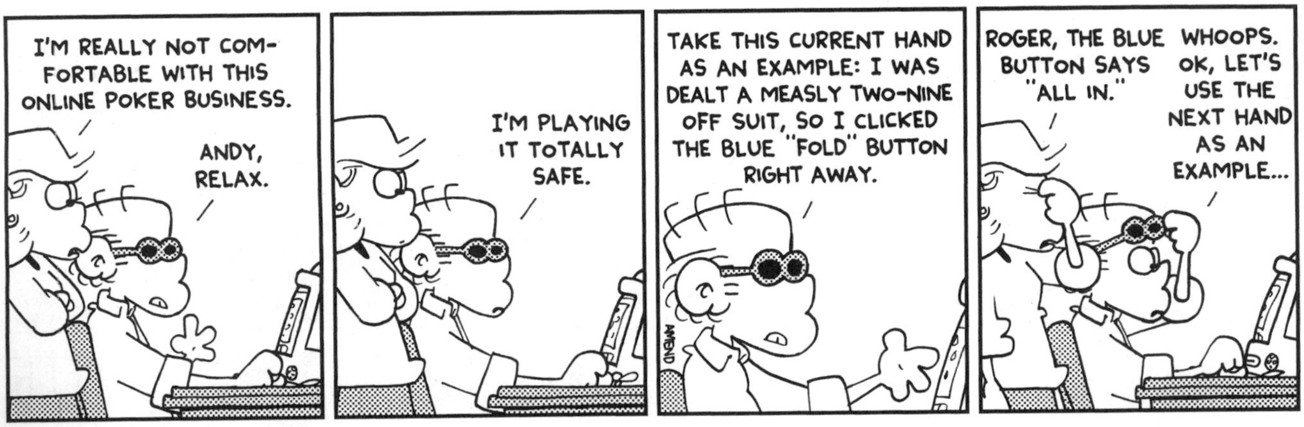
I'M REALLY NOT COMFORTABLE WITH THIS ONLINE POKER BUSINESS.
ANDY, RELAX.
I'M PLAYING IT TOTALLY SAFE.
TAKE THIS CURRENT HAND AS AN EXAMPLE: I WAS DEALT A MEASLY TWO-NINE OFF SUIT, SO I CLICKED THE BLUE "FOLD" BUTTON RIGHT AWAY.
ROGER, THE BLUE BUTTON SAYS "ALL IN."
WHOOPS. OK, LET'S USE THE NEXT HAND AS AN EXAMPLE...

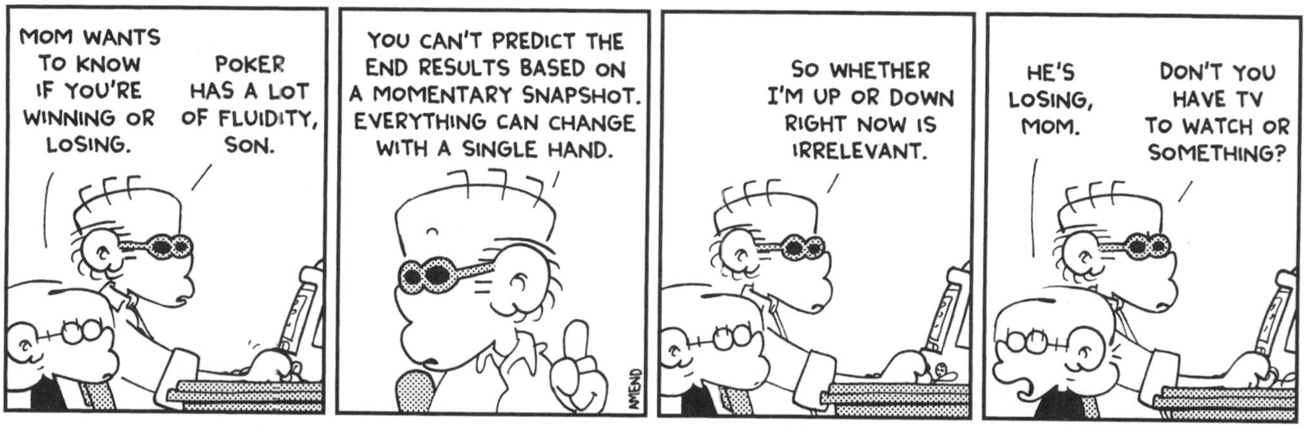
MOM WANTS TO KNOW IF YOU'RE WINNING OR LOSING.
POKER HAS A LOT OF FLUIDITY, SON.
YOU CAN'T PREDICT THE END RESULTS BASED ON A MOMENTARY SNAPSHOT. EVERYTHING CAN CHANGE WITH A SINGLE HAND.
AMEND
SO WHETHER I'M UP OR DOWN RIGHT NOW IS IRRELEVANT.
HE'S LOSING, MOM.
DON'T YOU HAVE TV TO WATCH OR SOMETHING?

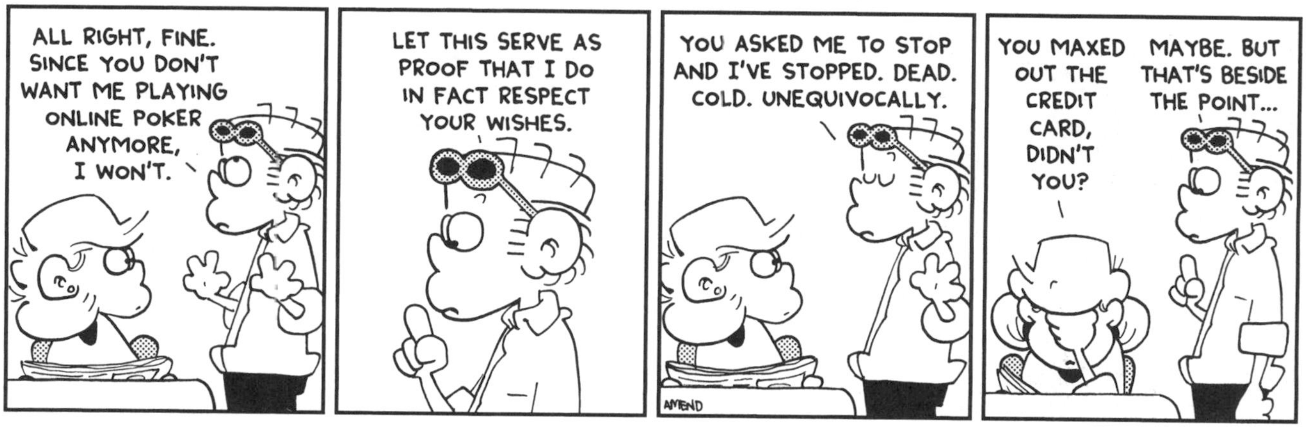
ALL RIGHT, FINE. SINCE YOU DON'T WANT ME PLAYING ONLINE POKER ANYMORE, I WON'T.
LET THIS SERVE AS PROOF THAT I DO IN FACT RESPECT YOUR WISHES.
YOU ASKED ME TO STOP AND I'VE STOPPED. DEAD. COLD. UNEQUIVOCALLY.
AMEND
YOU MAXED OUT THE CREDIT CARD, DIDN'T YOU?
MAYBE. BUT THAT'S BESIDE THE POINT...

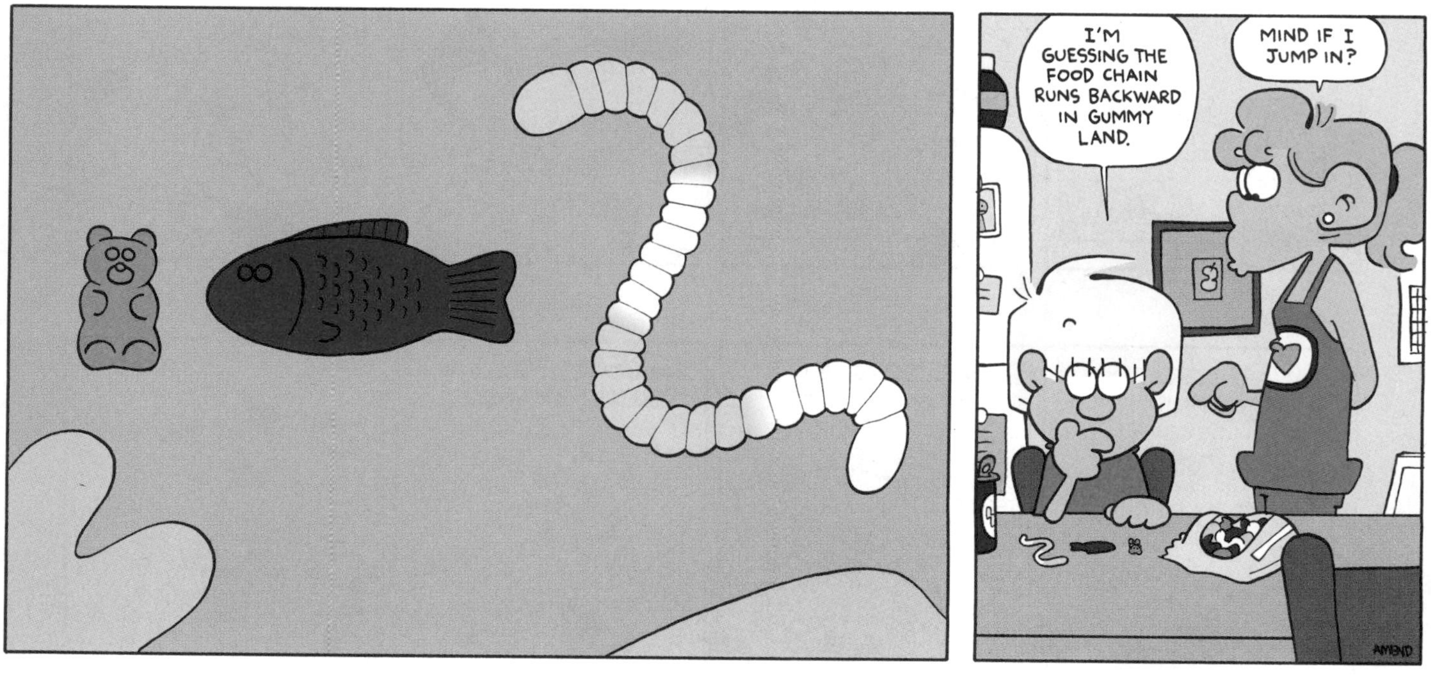
I'M GUESSING THE FOOD CHAIN RUNS BACKWARD IN GUMMY LAND.
MIND IF I JUMP IN?
AMEND

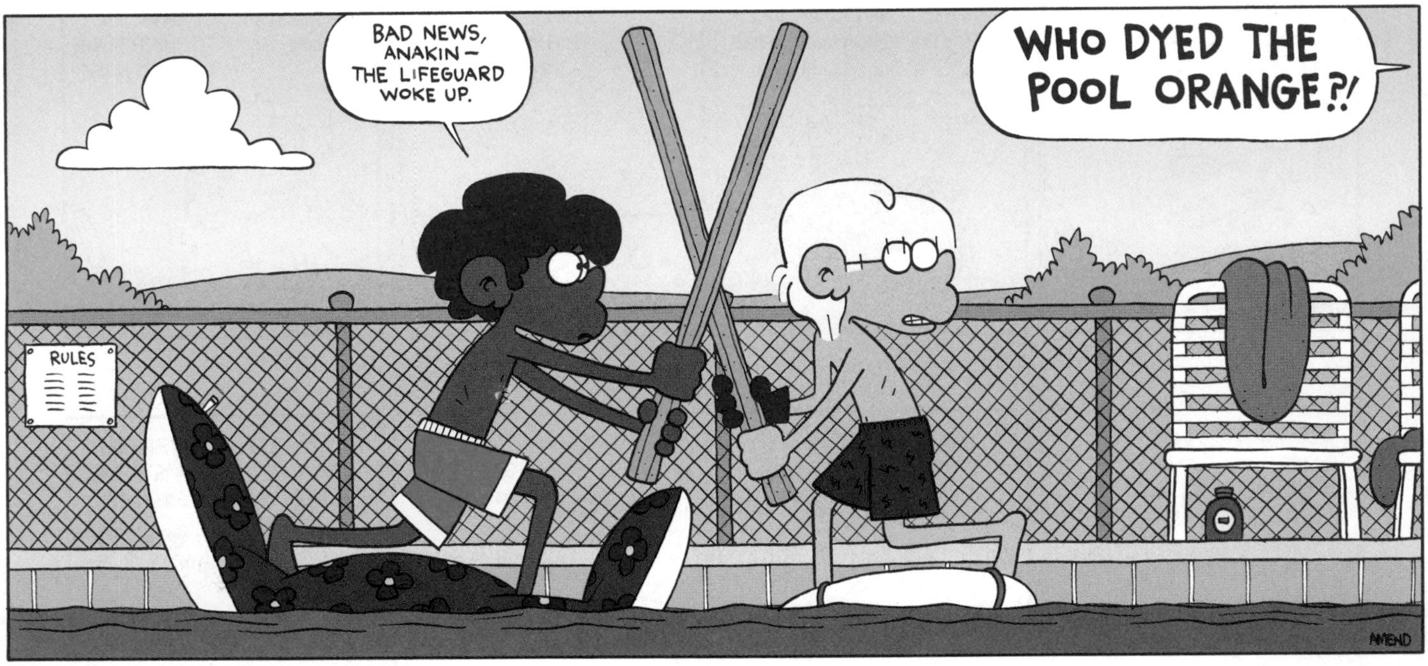
BAD NEWS, ANAKIN — THE LIFEGUARD WOKE UP.
WHO DYED THE POOL ORANGE?!
RULES
AMEND

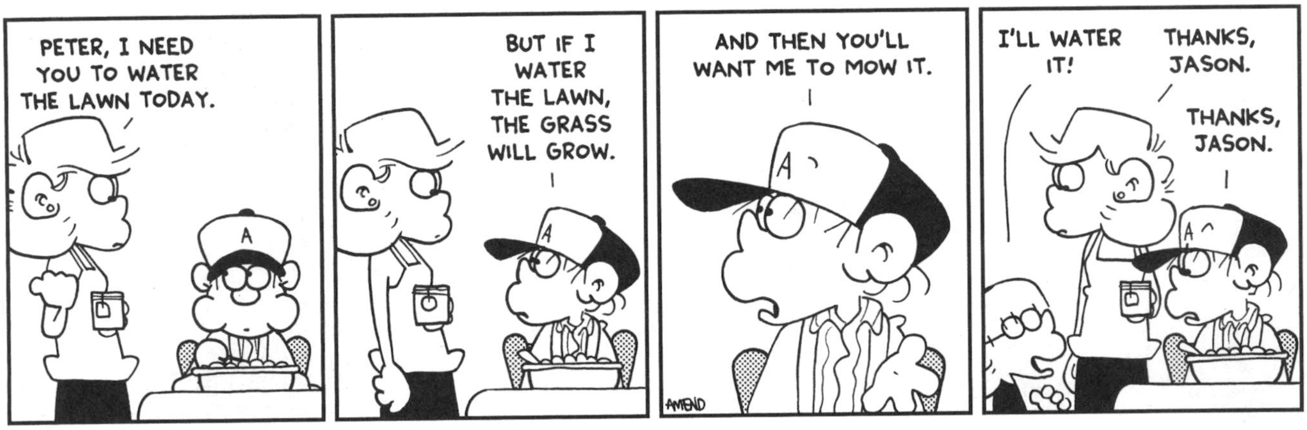
PETER, I NEED YOU TO WATER THE LAWN TODAY.
BUT IF I WATER THE LAWN, THE GRASS WILL GROW.
AND THEN YOU'LL WANT ME TO MOW IT.
AMEND
I'LL WATER IT!
THANKS, JASON.
THANKS, JASON.

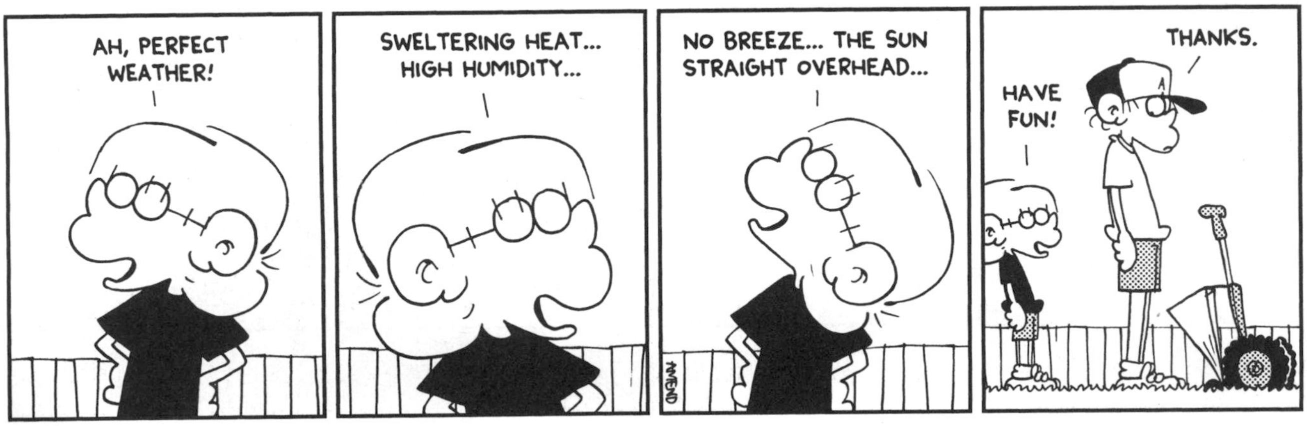
AH, PERFECT WEATHER!
SWELTERING HEAT... HIGH HUMIDITY...
NO BREEZE... THE SUN STRAIGHT OVERHEAD...
AMEND
HAVE FUN!
THANKS.

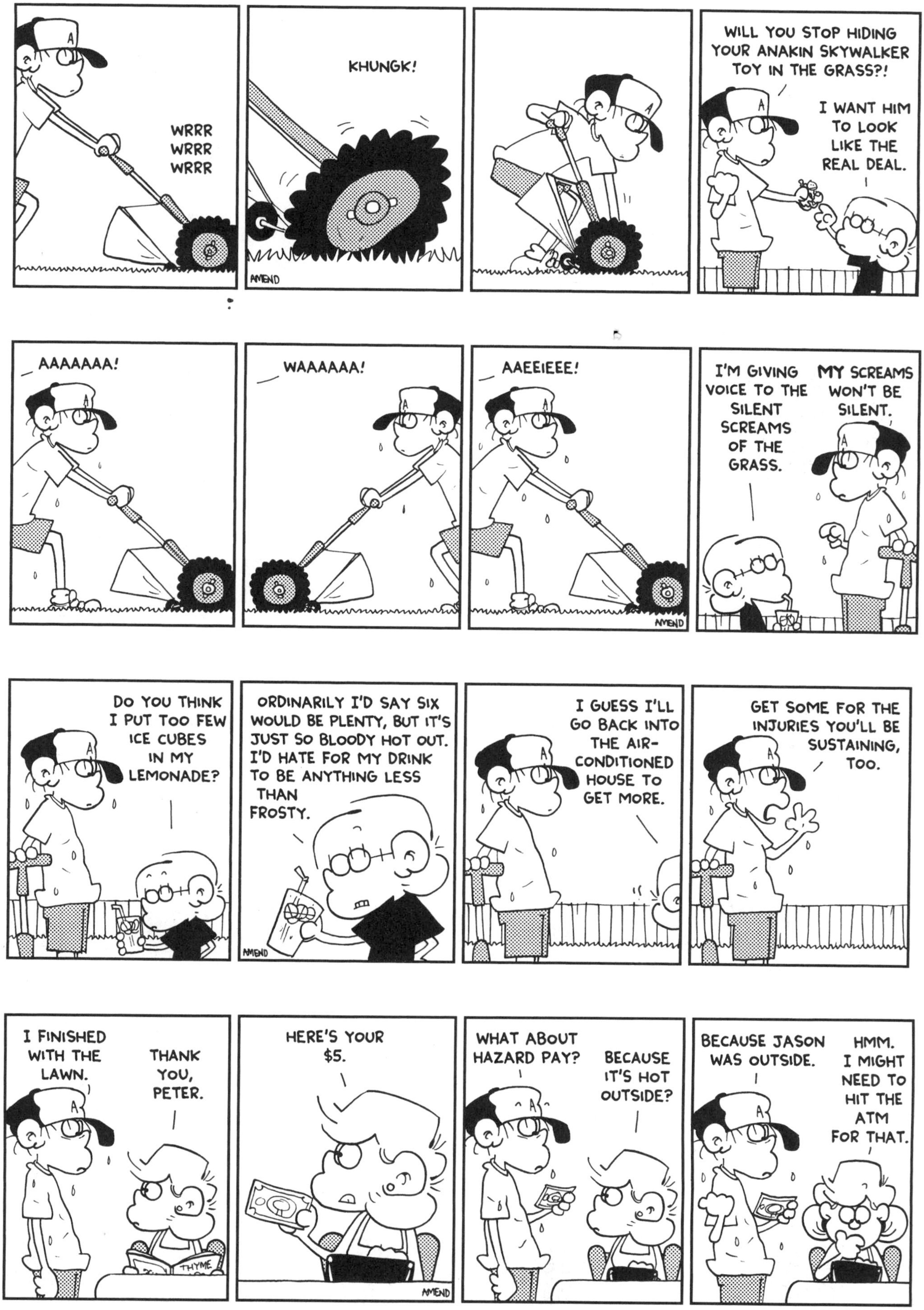
WRRR
WRRR
WRRR
KHUNGK!
AMEND
WILL YOU STOP HIDING YOUR ANAKIN SKYWALKER TOY IN THE GRASS?!
I WANT HIM TO LOOK LIKE THE REAL DEAL.
AAAAAAA!
WAAAAAA!
AAEEIEEE!
AMEND
I'M GIVING VOICE TO THE SILENT SCREAMS OF THE GRASS.
MY SCREAMS WON'T BE SILENT.
DO YOU THINK I PUT TOO FEW ICE CUBES IN MY LEMONADE?
ORDINARILY I'D SAY SIX WOULD BE PLENTY, BUT IT'S JUST SO BLOODY HOT OUT. I'D HATE FOR MY DRINK TO BE ANYTHING LESS THAN FROSTY.
AMEND
I GUESS I'LL GO BACK INTO THE AIR-CONDITIONED HOUSE TO GET MORE.
GET SOME FOR THE INJURIES YOU'LL BE SUSTAINING, TOO.
I FINISHED WITH THE LAWN.
THANK YOU, PETER.
THYME
HERE'S YOUR $5.
AMEND
WHAT ABOUT HAZARD PAY?
BECAUSE IT'S HOT OUTSIDE?
BECAUSE JASON WAS OUTSIDE.
HMM. I MIGHT NEED TO HIT THE ATM FOR THAT.

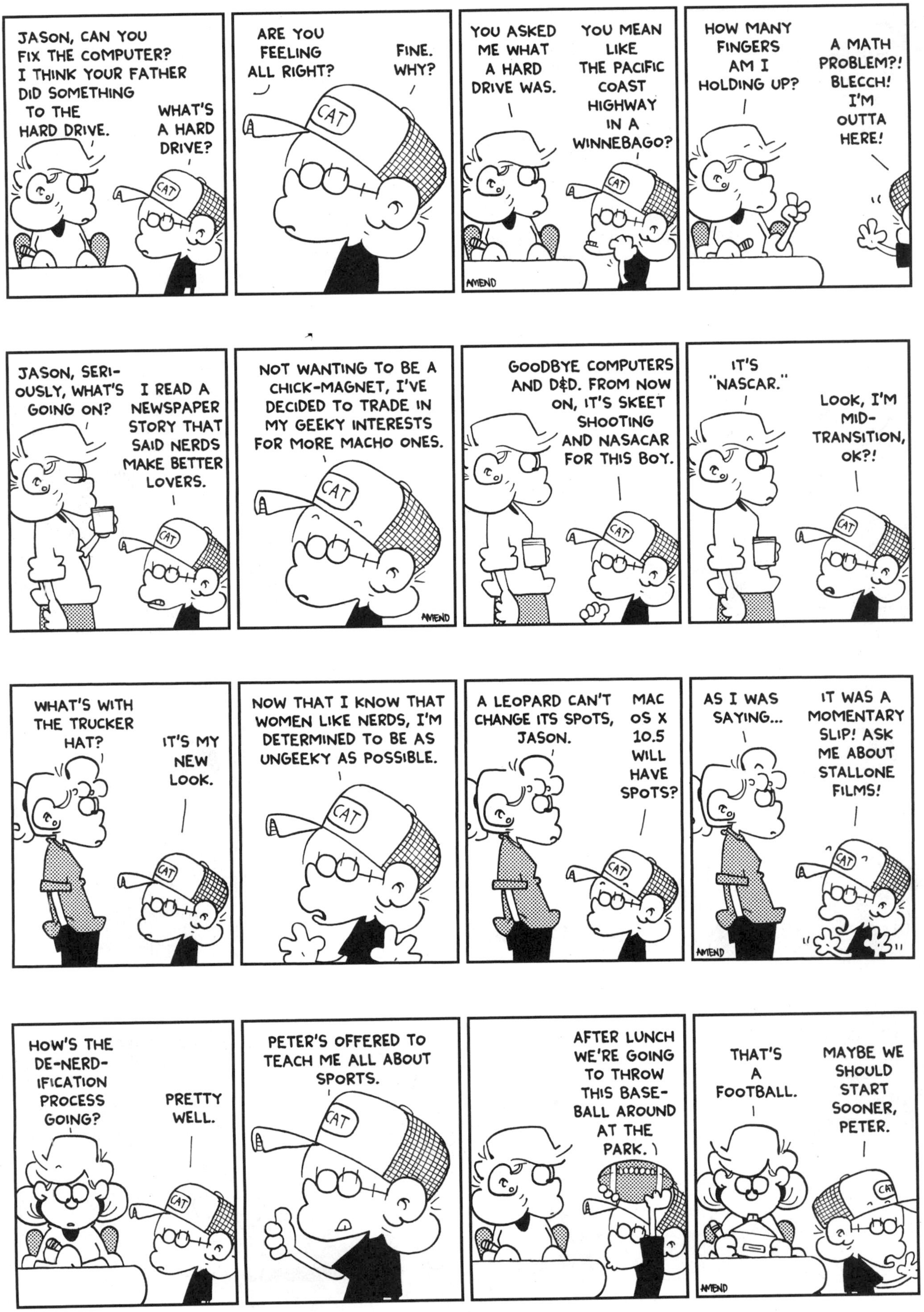
JASON, CAN YOU FIX THE COMPUTER? I THINK YOUR FATHER DID SOMETHING TO THE HARD DRIVE.
WHAT'S A HARD DRIVE?
ARE YOU FEELING ALL RIGHT?
FINE. WHY?
YOU ASKED ME WHAT A HARD DRIVE WAS.
YOU MEAN LIKE THE PACIFIC COAST HIGHWAY IN A WINNEBAGO?
HOW MANY FINGERS AM I HOLDING UP?
A MATH PROBLEM?! BLECCH! I'M OUTTA HERE!
AMEND
JASON, SERIOUSLY, WHAT'S GOING ON?
I READ A NEWSPAPER STORY THAT SAID NERDS MAKE BETTER LOVERS.
NOT WANTING TO BE A CHICK-MAGNET, I'VE DECIDED TO TRADE IN MY GEEKY INTERESTS FOR MORE MACHO ONES.
GOODBYE COMPUTERS AND D&D. FROM NOW ON, IT'S SKEET SHOOTING AND NASACAR FOR THIS BOY.
IT'S "NASCAR."
LOOK, I'M MID-TRANSITION, OK?!
AMEND
WHAT'S WITH THE TRUCKER HAT?
IT'S MY NEW LOOK.
NOW THAT I KNOW THAT WOMEN LIKE NERDS, I'M DETERMINED TO BE AS UNGEEKY AS POSSIBLE.
A LEOPARD CAN'T CHANGE ITS SPOTS, JASON.
MAC OS X 10.5 WILL HAVE SPOTS?
AS I WAS SAYING...
IT WAS A MOMENTARY SLIP! ASK ME ABOUT STALLONE FILMS!
AMEND
HOW'S THE DE-NERD-IFICATION PROCESS GOING?
PRETTY WELL.
PETER'S OFFERED TO TEACH ME ALL ABOUT SPORTS.
AFTER LUNCH WE'RE GOING TO THROW THIS BASEBALL AROUND AT THE PARK.
THAT'S A FOOTBALL.
MAYBE WE SHOULD START SOONER, PETER.
AMEND

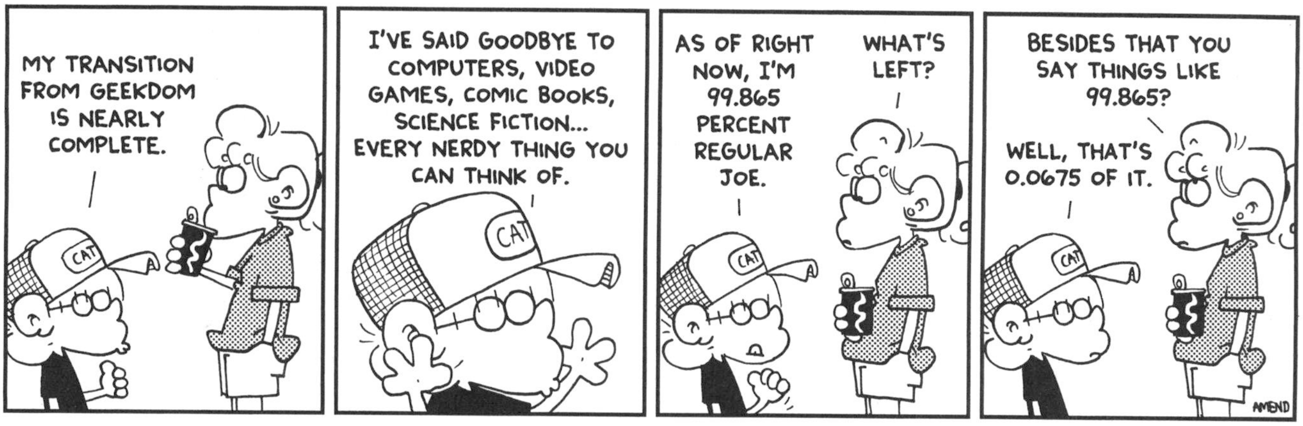
MY TRANSITION FROM GEEKDOM IS NEARLY COMPLETE.
I'VE SAID GOODBYE TO COMPUTERS, VIDEO GAMES, COMIC BOOKS, SCIENCE FICTION... EVERY NERDY THING YOU CAN THINK OF.
AS OF RIGHT NOW, I'M 99.865 PERCENT REGULAR JOE.
WHAT'S LEFT?
BESIDES THAT YOU SAY THINGS LIKE 99.865?
WELL, THAT'S 0.0675 OF IT.
AMEND

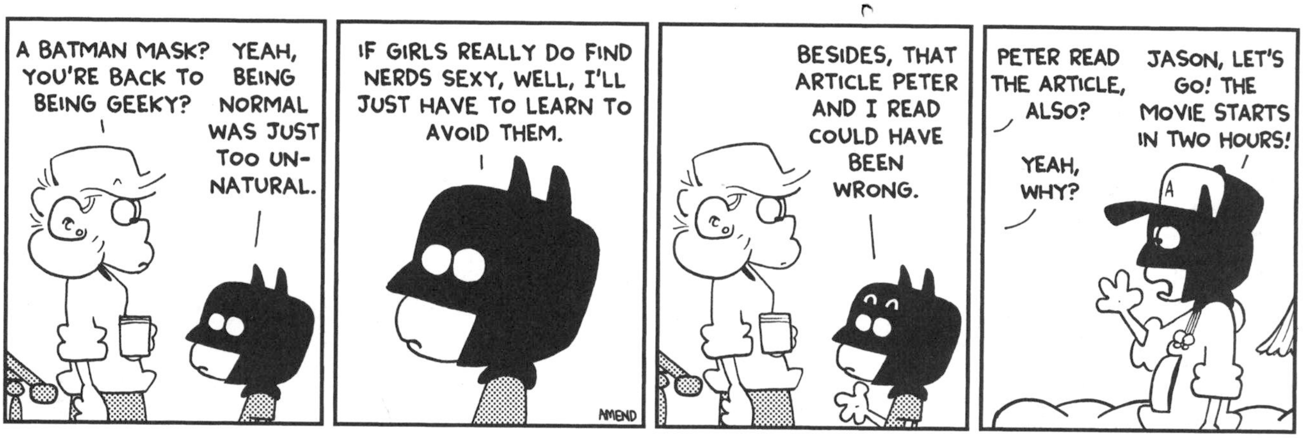
A BATMAN MASK? YOU'RE BACK TO BEING GEEKY?
YEAH, BEING NORMAL WAS JUST TOO UN-NATURAL.
IF GIRLS REALLY DO FIND NERDS SEXY, WELL, I'LL JUST HAVE TO LEARN TO AVOID THEM.
AMEND
BESIDES, THAT ARTICLE PETER AND I READ COULD HAVE BEEN WRONG.
PETER READ THE ARTICLE, ALSO?
YEAH, WHY?
JASON, LET'S GO! THE MOVIE STARTS IN TWO HOURS!

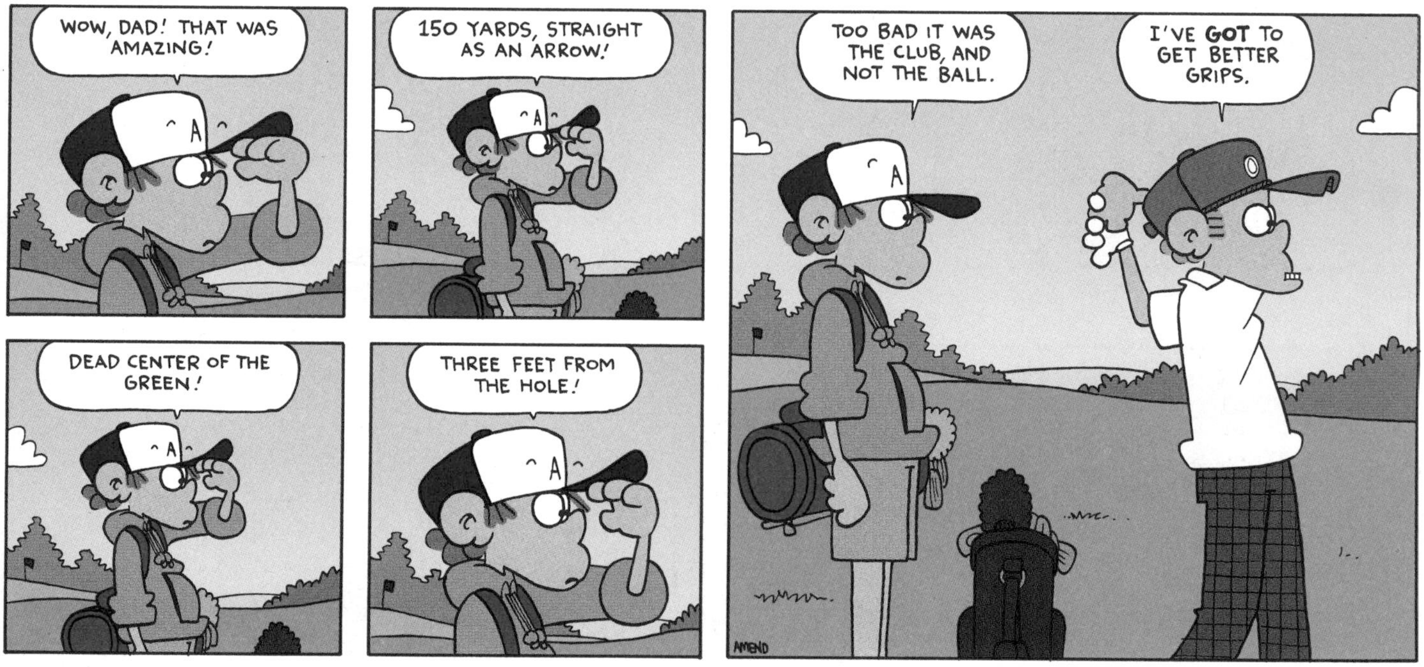
WOW, DAD! THAT WAS AMAZING!
150 YARDS, STRAIGHT AS AN ARROW!
DEAD CENTER OF THE GREEN!
THREE FEET FROM THE HOLE!
TOO BAD IT WAS THE CLUB, AND NOT THE BALL.
I'VE **GOT** TO GET BETTER GRIPS.
AMEND